1 MONTH OF
FREE
READING

at

www.ForgottenBooks.com

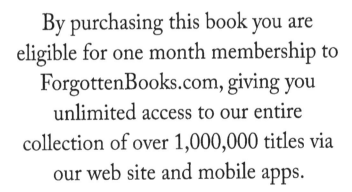

By purchasing this book you are eligible for one month membership to ForgottenBooks.com, giving you unlimited access to our entire collection of over 1,000,000 titles via our web site and mobile apps.

To claim your free month visit:

www.forgottenbooks.com/free713452

ISBN 978-0-266-64422-4
PIBN 10713452

This book is a reproduction of an important historical work. Forgotten Books uses
state-of-the-art technology to digitally reconstruct the work, preserving the original format
whilst repairing imperfections present in the aged copy. In rare cases, an imperfection in
the original, such as a blemish or missing page, may be replicated in our edition. We do,
however, repair the vast majority of imperfections successfully; any imperfections that
remain are intentionally left to preserve the state of such historical works.

DECISIONS

OF

THE DEPARTMENT OF THE INTERIOR

AND

GENERAL LAND OFFICE

IN

CASES RELATING TO THE PUBLIC LANDS

FROM JULY 1, 1889, TO DECEMBER 31, 1889.

VOLUME IX.

Edited by S. V. PROUDFIT.

WASHINGTON:

GOVERNMENT PRINTING OFFICE.

1890.

DEPARTMENT OF THE INTERIOR,
Washington, D. C.

This publication is held for sale by the Department at cost price, as follows:

Volume 1, from July, 1881, to June, 1883	$1. 05
Volume 2, from July, 1883, to June, 1884	1. 15
Volume 3, from July, 1884, to June, 1885	1. 07
Volume 4, from July, 1885, to June, 1886	1. 15
Volume 5, from July, 1886, to June, 1887	1. 05
Volume 6, from July, 1887, to June, 1888	1. 45
Volume 7, from July, 1888, to December, 1888	1. 10
Volume 8, from January, 1889, to June, 1889	1. 16
Volume 9, from July, 1889, to December, 1889	1. 15

Correspondence relating to the above publications, and all remittances (which must be by postal-note or money-order) should be addressed to the Secretary of the Interior, Washington, D. C.

II

TABLE OF CASES REPORTED.

TABLE OF CASES CITED.

TABLE OF OVERRULED AND MODIFIED CASES.

[From 1 to 9 L. D., inclusive.]

TABLE OF CIRCULARS AND INSTRUCTIONS.

TABLE OF CIRCULARS AND INSTRUCTIONS CITED AND CONSTRUED.

ACTS OF CONGRESS CITED AND CONSTRUED.

REVISED STATUTES CITED AND CONSTRUED.

RULES OF PRACTICE CITED AND CONSTRUED.

DECISIONS

THE PUBLIC LANDS.

PRE-EMPTION—FINAL PROOF—IMPROVEMENTS.

CHARLES L. HOFWALT.*

The pre-emption law does not specify the nature or extent of the improvements required thereunder, but only requires that they shall be such as will indicate the good faith of the entryman.

Secretary Noble to Acting Commissioner Stone, June 7, 1889.

I have considered the appeal of Charles L. Hofwalt from your office decision of March 31, 1888, rejecting his final proof for the NW. ¼ Sec. 24 T. 104 N., R. 55 W., Mitchell, Dakota.

The record shows that Hofwalt filed his declaratory statement for said tract February 23, 1882, alleging settlement on the 14th of that month. He gave notice of his intention to submit proof on the 2nd of September following, but the same was not made until one week thereafter owing to a protest filed by William Luy, which protest was withdrawn by said Luy before Hofwalt made final proof. On that day the land office accepted Hofwalt's proof as appears from the endorsement on the withdrawal of said protest. "The homestead claimant, Wm. Luy, having withdrawn his objections, the proof of Charles L. Hofwalt is this day allowed." On the same day to wit, April 9, 1883, Hofwalt paid $200, the price of said land and received a certificate therefor.

October 24, 1884, your office suspended Hofwalt's pre-emption cash entry on account of conflict with the homestead entry of William Luy, made February 27, 1882. It will be observed that Hofwalt filed his pre emption declaratory statement for said tract four days before Luy made homestead entry of the same, and that this suspension took place after Hofwalt's proof was accepted and after Luy's protest was withdrawn, without a hearing being had to determine the relative rights of the parties.

* Omitted from Vol. 8.

February 16, 1885, your predecessor, Commissioner McFarland, notified the local officers that as no appeal had been taken from the action of your office, holding for cancellation Luy's homestead entry of said tract, the same was that day canceled on the records and that Charles L. Hofwalt's pre-emption cash entry was approved for patent.

March 31, 1888, more than three years thereafter, your office rendered a decision, "Although the claimant resided continuously on the land for more than a year, and that the delay in making proof is held to be a continuance of the designated time for making the same, the small amount and value of improvements do not indicate good faith, therefore proof is rejected and the claimant required to re-advertise and make new proof."

From this decision claimant duly appealed to the Department.

The proof shows that Hofwalt was a single man and that his improvements consisted of a frame house eight by ten feet, a well and five acres of breaking—total value $45. His residence, from February 27, 1882 to April 9, 1883, the date of final proof, was continuous.

Although the improvements are somewhat meagre they are not inconsistent with good faith, which is the fundamental principle upon which the right of pre-emption rests. Pre-emption is a preference right of entry based upon settlement, inhabitancy and cultivation, and in the case at bar there is no question as to claimant's compliance with the law in the matter of settlement and residence. The pre-emption act does not specify the nature or extent of the improvements and only requires that they should be such as would indicate the good faith of the entryman.

In the case of William E. Young (14 C. L. O., 116) the Department held:

While the proof might have been fuller, it does not in its present form suggest to my mind any reason for concluding that the entry was not made in good faith, and it certainly meets the technical requirements of the law, which nowhere specifies the extent and value of the improvements to be made before a pre-emption cash entry can be allowed.

In the case of John E. Tyrl (3 L. D., 49) in which it appeared that the entryman cleared about one-half acre of the land, but cultivated no portion of it, nor raised any crop thereon, the Department held that clearing the land of timber for the purpose of planting it is cultivation within the meaning of section 2301 Revised Statutes.

More than six years have elapsed since the local officers accepted Hofwalt's final proof, and more than four years have transpired since Commissioner McFarland approved Hofwalt's pre-emption cash entry for patent, and I see no good reason now for re-opening the case and requiring new proof and publication, especially as the entryman seems to have acted in good faith and there is no adverse claimant.

The decision of your office is accordingly reversed.

TIMBER CULTURE—OSAGE ORANGE.

LEWIS v. CLARK.

The osage orange may be properly regarded as a timber tree when cultivated as such within the latitude where it attains its natural growth.

First Assistant Secretary Chandler to Acting Commissioner Stone, July 1, 1889.

I have considered the case of S. F. Lewis v. Alanson M. Clark upon the appeal of the former from your office decision of May 22, 1888, dismissing his contest against the timber culture entry of Clark upon the SE. ¼ of section 30, T. 17 S., R. 7 W., Salina land district, Kansas.

There appears to be no dispute about the facts in the case as to the defendant having a sufficient number of trees upon the tract to comply with the law, if the character of the tree planted by him is such as is recognized by the timber culture act.

It is admitted by the entryman that the only trees set out by him for the purpose of complying with the law are what are known as "osage orange." Hence, the only question involved in this controversy is, whether osage orange is a tree, the cultivation of which satisfies the demands of the law? It is contended by the defendant that it is. That in the locality of this tract and when cultivated as a tree, properly cared for and trimmed, it grows to be eight inches or more in diameter, with a body six or eight feet high, making excellent posts and firewood. While on the part of the plaintiff it is contended that osage orange is used for hedge purposes; that it is dwarfed in size, with limbs branching out near the ground, and that all the circulars and decisions of your office up to and after the date of the defendant's entry expressly excluded the osage orange as a tree to be recognized by the act.

There is force in the contention. Unquestionably in that locality the general use of the osage orange is for hedge purposes and it is likewise true that the rulings and decisions of your office up to the circular of February 1, 1882 (1 L D., 638), and perhaps to the letter of the Honorable Secretary of the Interior, of the date of July 6, 1887 (6 L. D., 119), did not recognize the osage orange as a tree to be planted and cultivated for the purpose of complying with the terms of the timber culture act. I believe there has never been a decision of the law department of the Secretary's Office passing upon the question, and it is here presented for the first time. Therefore the question arises, are the former circulars and decisions of your office correct?

This tree is sometimes called "*bodock*", corrupted from bois d'arc, and it is within the common experience of those living in Texas, Arkansas and Kansas, that when it is standing alone, it grows to be a tree of considerable proportions.

In speaking of this tree in Texas, Dr. Charles Mohr, (Vol. IX, Tenth Census of the U. S., p. 542) says:

The bois d'arc is common along the banks and water-courses in Eastern Texas, attaining a size large enough to be economically valuable. It is here, however, most probably adventitious from the region of the northwest, where it forms an almost uninterrupted belt of woods from four to ten miles wide, extending for a short distance south of the city of Dallas to the northern frontier of the State, entering the Indian Territory between Sherman and Paris. This tree attains a height of from forty-five to fifty feet, with a diameter of from one to two feet, and is of great value.

The American Encyclopedia (Vol. XII, p. 714), in speaking of the osage orange, says:

The tree is commonly from twenty to thirty feet high, but in the rich bottom lands of Texas and Arkansas it sometimes reaches sixty feet. . . . . The wood is of a fine yellow color, close grained, hard, strong and elastic; these qualities and its great durability make it one of the most valuable of our native woods. It is said by those where the tree is abundant that while the exposed wood may gradually waste away at the surface, from the action of the weather, a rotten or decayed stick is never seen.

In the report of the Kansas State Horticultural Society for the year 1881, ten pages are devoted to a discussion of the merits of this tree and therein it is said by V. T. Muson:

It possesses durability in a greater degree, probably than any other known wood. Posts set in the ground over fifty years ago are still firm and retain that metal like ring when struck common to very hard, sound timber. I drew out a stake which had been driven as a land mark four years previous and found the point and angles apparently as acute and sound as when hewn by the axe. Logs that have been buried in rich corroding soils from fifty to an hundred years or more, are yet firm and the wood is frequently worked up and used as posts, wagon felloes, etc. . . . . With culture in early growth in good soil and thinned to twelve or sixteen feet each way, trees ten years of age should average five inches in diameter and twenty-five feet in height, or enough to make two fence posts each.

And therein S. H. Nolan says:

It attains a size of two feet in diameter, depending upon its location and age. Its tendencies are towards the formation of a tree rather than a shrub, and it will always grow into a tree when sufficiently isolated to admit of such development. It is extensively used in the prairies of northern Texas and southern Arkansas for fence posts and is regarded as superior to all other woods for the purpose. For railroad ties there could be nothing better. There is nothing in our forests more hardy. I never knew of a tree being killed either by the rigors of winter or the heat of summer.

Professor J. B. Turner, of Illinois College, says:

As to durability, I have never known or heard of any timber equal to it. I have known it almost forty years and have never yet seen a piece of rotten heart-wood of the Osage that was not worm eaten at the start.

After speaking of its height, size and durability, W. H. Mann remarks:

For all purposes I consider the osage orange the most valuable timber the forester can plant, south of latitude 40. With a little care and protection, while young, it proves valuable up to latitude 45.

In a letter of the Commissioner of Forestry to Secretary Lamar of the date of May 3, 1886, the following language is used:

While the osage orange in the east and north is mainly planted for hedges, there can be no doubt, I think, that it is essentially a *tree* rather than a *shrub*. Evidence of this is close at hand by several trees of this species in Georgetown, one of which measures one foot ten inches, another one foot seven inches in diameter and about thirty feet in height. In Texas, Arkansas and Indian Territory, which may be considered the home of the osage orange, it grows to a height of from fifty to seventy-five feet with a diameter of from two to four feet, and furnishes one of the most valuable hard woods we possess in the union. It appears that below the 40*th degree* of north latitude at least, the osage orange may be safely considered as a tree dependent of course somewhat on its treatment when planted, etc.

I hope I have cited sufficient authority to show that south of the 40th degree of north latitude the osage orange may be very successfully grown as a valuable timber. Within this latitude, from an examination of the authorities without quoting them, I have reached the following conclusions:

1st.—That the osage orange may be grown to a tree of very considerable proportions.

2d.—That it is very hardy and tenacious of life, capable of withstanding the rigor of winter and the drouths of summer.

3d.—That it is not so liable to the attacks of borers or to be defoliated by worms as many other of our forest trees.

4th.—That it is of dense foliage, making splendid shade.

5th.—That as a timber it is exceedingly hard, close-grained, very strong and durable, making excellent posts, ties, spokes, hubs, felloes, plow-handles, harrows, firewood, etc., serving as a valuable factor for the farmer in subduing the western prairies.

One of the objects of the timber culture act, I take it, is to shade the ground so as to retard evaporation. The osage orange serves this purpose in a high degree.

The evidence in this case shows that the witnesses knew of osage orange trees in that locality eight inches in diameter, and that it "makes excellent firewood and posts." I am satisfied that it is a more profitable tree to cultivate on these prairies than the maple, box elder and other trees of a like character which have been accepted.

This opinion, however, is not written for the purpose of encouraging solely the growth of osage orange as a timber tree. It is a hearty feeder and impoverishes the soil to a greater extent than many other trees, therefore its extensive growth ought not to be encouraged. I am inclined, however, to hold in this case that it comes within the meaning of the act in the latitude of this tract in controversy, and that inasmuch as the entryman has apparently acted in good faith, having one hundred acres of the land under cultivation, he should be protected in his entry and this contest dismissed.

Your said office decision is therefore affirmed.

———

W. H. H. FINDLEY (ON REVIEW).

Motion for review of departmental decision rendered June 9, 1888 (6 L. D., 777), overruled by Secretary Noble, July 1, 1889.

GALLAHAN ET AL. v. SULLIVAN.

In determining whether a patent should issue under a desert land entry the Land Department is invested with the requisite jurisdiction to pass on the question of the entryman's right, based on a *bona fide* prior appropriation, to a sufficient quantity of water to effect a permanent reclamation of the land.

The sale of a water right confers upon the purchaser all the rights and privileges acquired by his vendor through a prior appropriation thereof.

The right to water by appropriation relates back to the beginning of work thereunder, when such work is prosecuted with reasonable diligence.

An adverse claim of right as against an alleged prior appropriation of water will not be recognized, where it appears that under such appropriation an actual and undisturbed possession has been maintained for a sufficient period to establish title by prescription.

After the allowance of a final entry, a charge against the same must be established by a clear preponderance of evidence to warrant forfeiture thereunder.

First Assistant Secretary Chandler to Acting Commissioner Stone, July 1, 1889.

Denis Sullivan, on December 27, 1879, made desert land entry for the S. ½ of the NW. ¼ and the N. ½ of the SW. ¼, Sec. 20, T. 4 S., R. 5 W., Helena land district, Montana, and, on May 14, 1883, made final proof and payment for said tract.

On August 2, 1884, William J. Gallahan, Albert W. Pillsbury and Christian Christianson addressed to H. J. Harrison, a special agent of the General Land Office, their sworn complaint against said entry, in which they charge non-compliance with the desert land act in the matter of irrigation, and that "Sullivan has no water right for this land."

On August 13, 1884, as appears from the decision herein, your office directed that a hearing be had to determine the truthfulness of the allegation, " that Sullivan had not such prior appropriation of the water as would entitle him to use it for reclaiming said land."

The hearing ordered was duly had before the local land officers May 13, 1885, the testimony, with the exception of one deposition taken by agreement, having all been previously taken before M. H. Lott, a notary public, of Madison county, Montana, and by him reduced to writing. On June 15, following, the local officers, after considering the evidence, found:

That at the date Mr. Sullivan made his desert entry, No. 268, December 27, 1879, all the water in Wisconsin creek had been appropriated, and that the water of this creek was the only source from which he could procure water to irrigate and reclaim the land embraced in his desert entry ; that he had not since that time procured by purchase or otherwise the necessary water to reclaim this land; and that he is not now, nor was he at the date of entry or making final proof, nor ever was, the owner of any water right with which he might irrigate and reclaim the land embraced in his said desert land entry,

and therefore they held that said entry should be canceled. On appeal from this finding and decision, your office, on January 30, 1888, found from the evidence, that one Philip E. Evans, about the year 1866 or 1867, constructed a ditch from Wisconsin creek, carrying from two hundred to two hundred and fifty inches of water; "that all the water in Wisconsin creek was appropriated before Evans constructed his said ditch, and that what water he used was by sufferance only, he never claiming an absolute right to any portion of the water;" and that Sullivan, about the year 1879, bought Evans's ranch or claim, and therewith all his interest in and to said water right. On this finding, your office affirmed the decision of the local officers, and held said entry for cancellation.

From this decision Sullivan prosecutes his present appeal and assigns as grounds therefor, in substance, that you erred in your finding of facts and in holding his entry for cancellation; and also "In holding, that the Land Department has power and jurisdiction under the law to try and determine, as affecting the validity of the entry of the appellant, any question as to the priority of water rights."

Where a party has filed his declaration of intention to reclaim a tract of desert land by conducting water on the same, the act for the sale of desert lands of March 3, 1877 (19 Stat., 377), makes the provision:

That the right to the use of water by the person so conducting the same on or to any tract of desert land of six hundred and forty acres shall depend upon *bona fide* prior appropriation; and such right shall not exceed the amount of water actually appropriated and necessarily used for the purpose of irrigation and reclamation; and all surplus water over and above such actual appropriation and use, together with the water of all lakes, rivers, and other sources of water supply upon the public lands, and not navigable, shall remain and be held free for the appropriation and use of the public for irrigation, mining, and manufacturing purposes, subject to existing rights.

The duty of passing upon a desert entryman's right to a patent, as in other cases, is devolved upon the Land Department, and in the discharge of this duty the Department must necessarily pass on the question of his right, secured by a *bona fide* prior appropriation, to a sufficient quantity of water to permanently reclaim the tract of land entered from its desert condition. The jurisdiction to hear and determine the question of this right is, from the nature of things, inherent in the Land Department. Therefore, in sustaining the local officers in overruling the claimant's motion to dismiss the contest, on the grounds of want of jurisdiction to try the question submitted to them by your order herein, there was no error committed.

The decision of your office recognizes the clearly established fact, that whatever right to water from Wisconsin creek Evans may have had in 1866 or 1867 had been transferred by him to Sullivan; and, consequently, that the finding by the local office that at the date of Sullivan's entry, December 27, 1879, all the water of said creek had been appropriated, was a finding of fact, irrelevant to the issue.

Your office found, as a matter of fact, that Evans, "about the year 1866 or 1867, constructed a ditch from Wisconsin Creek, carrying from two hundred to two hundred and fifty inches of water." A preponderance of the evidence shows, that said ditch was commenced in the fall of 1866 and completed in the spring of 1867, and that its capacity was then two hundred and fifty inches. It is further shown by a preponderance of the evidence, that during the years 1867, 1868, and 1869, Evans used water from said ditch in irrigating a portion of the claim which he sold to Sullivan, and that Sullivan, without formal notice or protest from prior appropriators, continued to use water from said ditch from and including the year 1870, up to the year 1879, at which time a notice was posted at the head of his ditch by Christianson, Pillsbury and two others, warning him not to use the water from said creek. No attention appears to have been paid to this notice, as Sullivan continued to use the water as he needed it. Nor were any legal steps taken at that time or since by any party, so far as shown by the evidence, to prevent Sullivan using water from Wisconsin creek.

Sullivan's ditch from said creek is about two miles long, and its construction by Evans was prosecuted from the time he commenced it, in 1866, with reasonable diligence. And where work of this kind is prosecuted with reasonable diligence, the appropriation of the water relates back to the beginning of the work. Kimball v. Gearhart, 12 Cal., 27; Irwin v. Strait et al., 18 Nev., 436; Woolman et al. v. Garringer et al., 1 Montana, 535, on page 544. Therefore such right as Sullivan has to water from Wisconsin Creek dates from the fall of 1866.

At that time the contestant, Pillsbury, owned a third interest in the Hunter Brothers' ditch, which he testifies was five feet wide and eighteen inches deep, and that said ditch appropriated water from Wisconsin creek in the spring of 1864 and was the first water right on said creek.

He further testifies, that he and Sacket & Fenn, who owned another one-third interest in the Hunter Brothers' ditch, gave Evans the privilege of taking water from Wisconsin Creek, "but he was not to interfere with our water rights." Two or three other parties also appear to have had ditches conveying water from said creek prior to the time the Evans ditch was constructed. The capacity of these ditches is not shown by the evidence, nor is the quantity of water flowing in said stream during the irrigating season so shown. Nor is it shown, that the two hundred and fifty inches of water diverted from said stream by Sullivan's ditch interfere with the water rights of the present owners of the Hunter Brothers' ditch. The water supply of said creek seems, from the evidence, to be sufficient to meet the present demand on it till July 1st of each year. After that time it usually becomes scarce, and is insufficient to satisfy the wants of all parties claiming rights thereto.

The contestants Christianson and Gallahan did not acquire any right to divert water from said creek prior to the time Evans commenced the construction of his ditch, nor till some time in the spring or summer of 1867. The evidence shows, that there has been a number of appropriations, or attempted appropriations, of the water of said creek since the

Evans appropriation. Among these are, the Gallahan and Bitney ditch (1867), with a capacity of two hundred and fifty inches; the Zigler ditch, now owned by contestant Christianson (1867), capacity not stated; two mining ditches (1876 and 1877), capacity not stated; and two irrigating ditches, about the latter date, each with a capacity of one hundred inches.

Evans, when he sold this ditch and water right, with other property, represented to Sullivan that he was the owner of it, and in this case he testifies that he appropriated the water from said creek—be thinks, about four hundred inches—in 1866; that he claimed all the water his ditch would carry, and that his right to the water was not held "by sufferance or permission of Albert W. Pillsbury, Sacket & Fenn, Bonaface Zigler and John Bitney, with the understanding that his ditch should have no water when they desired to use the water of said creek in their respective ditches," but that his right was absolute and was never questioned.

The testimony shows that Sullivan's right to water from Wisconsin creek has been disputed by certain parties since the time he made his desert entry, and that from the spring of 1867 up to the date of the hearing had herein, a period of eighteen years, he and his grantor have each year used water from said creek for irrigating purposes to the apparent inconvenience and injury, when water was scarce, of parties claiming a superior right, and yet his right to the use of water from said creek has never been legally called in question or assailed in the courts. This fact alone affords a strong presumption that Sullivan's use of the water claimed by him is of right and not by sufferance. No contract or agreement entered into by Sullivan or his grantor whereby their right to water from said creek was acknowledged to be by permission and at the sufferance of prior appropriators of the water of said creek is shown, and in the absence of such a contract or agreement, Sullivan's right to the amount of water originally appropriated (250 inches) can not, I apprehend, be now disturbed, as in such case he would hold that amount of water by prescriptive right, the statutory period of limitation for the recovery of real property in Montana being five years. Revised Statutes of Montana 1879, p. 45.

At all events, the evidence does not clearly show that Sullivan's right to two hundred and fifty inches of water from Wisconsin creek is held only by sufferance. And to warrant the forfeiture of his claim to the government on the issue joined herein, such fact should appear by a clear preponderance of the evidence, he having more than a year before the institution of this proceeding made satisfactory proof, and full payment for the described tract of land.

In addition to the water obtained from Wisconsin creek, the evidence shows that Sullivan is the owner of a ditch from Indian creek, which conveys from two hundred to three hundred inches of water; that water from the latter ditch is used on forty or fifty acres of his desert claim, and that it can be extended over the entire claim; that his right to water from Indian creek is in no manner disputed, and that two hundred and fifty inches of water is sufficient to properly irrigate said claim.

I am of the opinion that the decision of your office, holding said desert land entry for cancellation, is erroneous, and the same is accordingly reversed.

PRIVATE ENTRY—RESTORATION NOTICE.

RICHARD E. PAIRO.

An erroneous notation of record, showing a disposition of the land covered thereby, precludes the allowance of private cash entry for such land, until after restoration notice.

The general withdrawal of public land from private entry, directed by the act of March 2, 1889, is not applicable to public lands in the State of Missouri.

Secretary Noble to Acting Commissioner Stone, July 1, 1889.

This is an appeal by Richard E. Pairo from your office decision of June 26, 1888, sustaining the local office and rejecting his application dated May 7, 1888, to purchase at private entry (it having been offered in 1846), the E. ½ SW. ¼ Sec. 21, T. 31 N., R. 18 W., Springfield Missouri "on account of conflict with the uncanceled warrant location No. 42,619 by Martin McBride of date June 1, 1856."

The warrant location mentioned was erroneously posted upon the records of the office, it having in fact been made upon a like subdivision of township "33" in the range aforesaid.

Your office, however, held that any marks upon the tract books of the local office are "sufficient to preclude a private entry until restoration to market by public notice under 9th section circular of January 1, 1836." Opinions and Instructions, Vol. 2, p. 514.

The precise question that is presented by this appeal was fully considered and disposed of adversely to the appellant in the case of John C. Turpen (5 L. D., 25).

In that case the Department concurred in the opinion of July 14, 1837, by Attorney-General Butler (3 Op., 274), regarding the said 9th section of the circular of January 1, 1836, to the effect that when lands subject by law to private entry have been improperly withheld therefrom, if a considerable time has elapsed since the close of the sale, to allow them to be entered by any particular individual without a public notice that they are subject to private entry, would, in most cases, give such individual a preference over the rest of the community and not be a faithful execution of the law. This view was also adopted in the case of James Steel (6 L. D., 685).

Nor does the foregoing conflict with the case of McAndrews v. Chicago, Milwaukee & St. Paul Ry. Co. (5 L. D., 202), upon which counsel for the appellant relies. In the McAndrews case the Department considered the effect of inadvertent marking upon the records of the local office with reference to the grant which gave to the company certain land which, at the time its line of road was definitely located, had not been sold or reserved for any purpose whatever or to which the right of pre-emption or homestead settlement had not attached, and held that the erroneous notation of a warrant location upon the tract books did not work an exception to the grant mentioned.

The remaining authorities (Cole *v.* Markley, 2 L. D., 847 and Mining Co. *v.* Ish, Copps Mineral Lands, 365), are also without bearing upon the question presented.

The conclusion reached by your office that the tract named should not be sold at private entry until after public notice of at least thirty days, in accordance with the said circular of January, 1836, being in the line of the settled rulings of the Department, and no such notice having been given, the action of your office in sustaining the rejection of the appellant' said application is accordingly affirmed.

By the first section of the act approved March 2, 1889, entitled "An act to withdraw certain public lands from private entry and for other purposes" (Chapter 381), the public land in Missouri is excepted from the general withdrawal of public land from private entry. The case at bar is therefore not affected by the act referred to.

———

PRACTICE—ATTORNEY—APPEAL—SPECIFICATION OF ERRORS.

CAMPBELL *v.* VOTAW.

The authority of an attorney to appear in a case cannot be questioned by another, who in the service of papers in said case, relies solely upon notice to such attorney.

An appeal will not be dismissed for the want of a sufficient specification of errors, if, from the whole statement, the errors alleged can be fairly determined.

First Assistant Secretary Chandler to Acting Commissioner Stone, July 1, 1889.

On January 29, 1879, Moses Votaw made timber culture entry for the SE. ¼ of section 6, T. 5 S., R. 27 W., Kirwin land district, Kansas. Martin L. Campbell on June 13, 1885, filed his contest affidavit against such entry, charging that said Votaw "has failed to plant to timber, tree seeds or cuttings ten acres of said land the fifth and sixth years since said entry, and has also failed to cultivate said tract as required by law."

A hearing was had before the local officers at which both parties appeared in person and by attorneys. The local officers decided that the entries should be canceled.

Upon appeal your office reversed that decision and allowed the entry to stand subject to future compliance with the law.

From this decision the contestant appealed.

The attorney for the entryman filed a motion to dismiss said appeal— 1st. Because no specification of errors was filed therewith and 2nd., Because " the attorneys for the appellant failed to comply with Rule

82, or circular of March 19, 1887, C. L. O., No. 13–101, and 45 and Rule 101." Circulars referred to in this objection and in the authorities cited are published, the circular of July 31, 1885, in 4 L. D., 503, the circular of March 19, 1887, in 5 L. D., page 508. The circular of July 31, 1885, has reference to attorneys appearing for alleged fraudulent entrymen, the other to attorneys appearing before local officers. By Rule 101, only a party or attorney that has filed his appearance is entitled to a notice of the proceedings. The circulars and the rule have no applicability to the case. F. M. Heaton (5 L. D., 340). Beside, when appellee's attorneys served notice of the motion for dismissal upon McBride and Marsh, attorneys for appellant, and accepted the latter's acknowledgment of service and bring their acknowledgment of service into court as the only proof of service, they, appellee's attorneys, forego the right to question the authority of McBride and Marsh to appear as attorneys for the appellant.

The first objection of appellee's attorneys to the appeal presents a question of some difficulty. The specification of errors, if such it can be termed, filed with and forming a part of the appeal, reads as follows: " We maintain that the Hon. Commissioner erred: first as to the law, and second as to the facts. How the Hon. Commissioner can hold that 1,690 trees on a T. C. E. 6½ years old to be an honest effort to raise timber is more than plaintiff can see, and the testimony that no cultivating was done on said land during the year of 1884, these two pieces of testimony should of themselves cancel said entry." It is apparent, that this specification of errors is very inartistically drawn; according to Rule 88, of the Rules of Practice, the same should clearly and concisely designate the errors of which the appellant complains. It can hardly be asserted that the specification is clear and precise, yet from the whole statement I think it can be gathered what errors the appellant complains of; I feel, therefore, inclined to accept the document as a substantial compliance with the rule. Appellee's motion is overruled.

FRAUDULENT SURVEYS—ACT OF JUNE 3, 1878.

EMILY A. LAIRD ET AL.

The Commissioner of the General Land Office is warranted in withholding lands from entry, pending an examination of the survey in the field, when it appears that the original survey thereof is false and fraudulent.

As the act of June 3, 1878, provides only for the sale of surveyed lands, an entry thereunder should not be permitted, if it is found that the survey of the township, in which the land is situated, is false and fraudulent, and that a resurvey of such township will be required.

Secretary Noble to Acting Commissioner Stone, July 1, 1889.

I have considered the consolidated cases of Emily A. Laird, Nathan M. Mayfield and Harvey N. Denny, upon their appeals from your office decision of May 5, 1888, affirming that of the local officers, of Visalia, California, land district, who refused to sell to each of said parties land applied for by them under the act of June 3, 1878 (20 Stat., 89).

On April 5, 1888, the said parties presented applications to purchase land as follows: Laird for SW. ¼, Sec. 9; Mayfield for NE. ¼, Sec. 17 and Denny for NE. ¼, Sec. 8, all in T. 15 S., R. 29 E., M. D. M.

Their applications were all rejected by the local officers because all entries in said township had been stopped by order of the Commissioner of the General Land Office.

I find in the record the following telegram:

WASHINGTON, D. C., *Dec.* 2, 1885.

REGISTER & RECEIVER,
Visalia, California.

Allow no entries or filings on land in townships fifteen and sixteen, south, ranges twenty-nine, thirty and thirty-one east, M. D. M., until further orders.

(Signed) WM. A. J. SPARKS,
Commissioner.

I also find your office letter "E" of December 24, 1885, directed to the same local office, and after heading as follows:

Upon receipt hereof you will suspend all entries of and filings for, lands in the following described townships in your land district, viz:—

Townships 17 and 19 S., R. 14 East,
Townships 13, 15 and 16, S., Range 26 East,
Townships 15 and 16 S., Range 29 East,
Townships 13, 14, 15, 16, 17 and 18, S., Range 30, East,
Townships 15, 16 and 18, S., Range 31 East,
Townships 17 and 18, S., Range 32 East, all of Mt. Diabolo Meridian.
You will acknowledge receipt of this order.

Very respectfully,

(Signed) WM. A. J. SPARKS,
Commissioner.

No reason for withdrawing said lands from entry was assigned, but upon inquiry at the proper division of the General Land Office, I have learned that on December 1, 1885, Gabriel C. Wharton, an inspector of the General Land Office, reported to your predecessor that while inspecting the local office at Visalia his attention was called to the alleged fact that a number of persons had arrived at Visalia by train about 3 a. m., on or about October 1, 1885, who commenced to make timber land locations as soon as the office was open, and that after making their respective filings most of them had, on the same day, returned to their homes in San Francisco. The said inspector further says, "I could not learn that these parties had ever visited or examined the lands upon which they filed applications, nor was it believed by well informed persons that it was possible that more than one or two of those whose names were signed to these applications could have had any definite knowledge of the lands or townships. I feel quite confident that these men are what are called "dummies" and are engaged by some corporation or individuals to file these applications thus evading and violating the law." He further states that the deputy United States surveyors who had surveyed said township 15 and several other townships in that vicinity had made certificates and surveys which to him appeared to be fraudulent and that said townships contained large bodies of pine and redwood timber lands. He also said that for the purpose of preventing the consummation of the frauds initiated by said applications and by such fraudulent surveys, he recommended that all entries and filings in said townships should be stopped until the Land Department might be able to have such surveys examined in the field by a duly authorized agent of the government. He further said that in view of the fact that the said applications filed October 1, would ripen into entries within a few days upon the expiration of the time of publication of notice, he thought the suspension of said townships should be by telegram.

This was accordingly done, by the telegram and letter above given, and such suspension still continues.

Upon appeal of applicants herein from the ruling of the local officers your said decision of May 5, 1888, was made in which it is said,—

It was the intention of this office to order an examination of the surveys in said township at an early day, but owing to the exigencies of the service, and lack of funds applicable to the purpose, the proposed examination has not yet been made. The west and south boundaries of said township were surveyed by P. M. Norboe, D. S.; the north and east boundaries by J. R. Glover, D. S.; and the subdivisional survey by W. H. Norway and J. R. Glover, D. S. These are all under indictment in U. S. circuit court, 9th district, California, for fraud and conspiracy in United States public land surveys in California, and in view of the developments thus far made, and the facts ascertained through the instrumentality of a special agent of this office in regard to the action of said surveyors in the matter of obtaining contracts for surveys, and their method of executing the same, it is deemed inexpedient to restore the land in said township to entry in advance of an official examination of the surveys in the field. The suspension will be continued until the character of the surveys shall have been ascertained.

The said act of June 3, 1878, provides only for the sale of the "surveyed" public lands of the United States within the States and Territories mentioned and if an alleged survey in any township should prove false or fraudulent to such an extent as to require a resurvey, then the lands in such township could not be denominated surveyed lands within the meaning of the said act until such resurvey was completed.

By Sec. 449, Revised Statutes, the General Land Office is required to superintend the surveys of the public lands and Chapter 9, of the Revised Statutes, commencing with Sec. 2395, prescribes the manner in which surveys shall be made.

It appears from Land Office Report for 1886, page 238, that a special agent of the land department had examined alleged surveys made by P. M. Norboe, one of the U. S. deputy surveyors engaged upon the survey of the townships involved in the case at bar, and had reported that field notes returned by him were fictitious and unsupported by any actual survey. On page 285 of the same report it is stated upon the authority of a special agent that W. H. Norway had been engaged in making fraudulent surveys.

On page 249 of Land Office Report for 1887, it appears that J. R. Glover had been indicted for conspiracy in relation to surveys in California and for perjury in relation thereto, and was one of the partners of J. A. Benson, in alleged conspiracies to defraud the government by false and fraudulent surveys.

The information received by the Land Department in regard to surveys in California made by the said surveyors, a synopsis of which is given in Land Office Reports for 1886, 1887, and 1888, under the heading of " Surveys," is amply sufficient in my opinion to justify the belief that the surveys of the townships mentioned in your said office letter " E " of December 24, are false and fraudulent to such an extent as to render a resurvey necessary, and I think the action of your predecessor in withholding the lands therein from entry pending an examination in the field, was proper.

Your said decision is accordingly affirmed.

COAL LAND—POSSESSORY RIGHTS.

McDANIEL v. BELL.

A prior possessory right, set up to defeat a private cash entry of coal land, must rest upon actual and *bona fide* occupation of the land.

Secretary Noble to Acting Commissioner Stone, July 1, 1889.

This case involves the NE. ¼ of Sec. 18, T. 21 N., R. 116 W., Evanston, Wyoming. The township plat was filed in the local office on April 7, 1882. On April 25, 1882, Abner G. McDaniel, by his agent Jesse Bell, purchased said land at private cash entry at $20 per acre, agreeably to the provisions of section 2347 of the U. S. Revised Statutes.

On May 11, 1882, William Bell, alleging "actual possession continuously" since April, 1881, and an expenditure of four hundred dollars in "stripping, cutting, tunnelling, and shafting" upon the land, applied at the local office to file coal declaratory statement for the same, under section 2348 of the U. S. Revised Statutes. This application was rejected by reason of the cash entry of McDaniel.

Upon appeal by the applicant, Bell, your office, by letter of July 1, 1882, directed that said coal declaratory statement be received, and " that when Mr. Bell applies to enter the land in question, you will order a hearing to determine the date of his possession, whether continuous and uninterrupted, the character and value of his improvements, and such other questions as may seem . . . . . relevant and pertinent."

The said declaratory statement was, in pursuance of the foregoing, filed in the local office on July 11, 1882, and on October 28th following the applicant Bell gave notice of his intention to make proof at the local office on December 5th of the same year. On the day named, the parties appeared by counsel and by consent the hearing was continued until December 7, 1882, when both the entryman, McDaniel, and the applicant, Bell, appeared. Upon the testimony submitted, the local office rejected the application of Bell, and recommended that the cash entry of McDaniel be passed to patent. This action was (on appeal by the applicant) sustained by your office decision of January 21, 1888. Appeal by the applicant Bell brings the case here.

The greater part of the voluminous testimony was submitted with reference to the identity of the applicant's claim as located on unsurveyed land and the quarter section involved. But, for reasons which will hereafter appear, I have deemed it unnecessary to determine this question.

The applicant, through Jesse Bell (who, as stated, also acted for the cash entryman), as agent, in January, 1877, laid claim to one hundred and sixty acres as a coal claim in the district named. He subsequently relocated the same by the said agent, who filed the claim for record with the county clerk on April 18, 1881.

The applicant states, that the first improvement upon his claim was made by his agent Jesse Bell; that it consisted of "an approach, with the view of running a tunnel;" that he (applicant) sunk "a shaft, some six feet in diameter, to the depth of about five feet;" that the work by himself and said agent (Jesse Bell) was done in the spring of 1881, and would amount to $15 or $20; that the work, which represents the balance of a total expenditure of about $500 upon the land, was done, as applicant's agent, by one James D. Negus, who it appears was at that time the superintendent or manager of the Utah and Wyoming Railroad.

The evidence shows, that some five cuts or drifts were made upon an original association claim of one square mile, and which presumably included the land in dispute. These cuts or drifts, which appear to have been made by or under the direction of Negus, were five or six feet in width, six to twenty feet in length, and of an average depth of six feet, and two of them seem to have been on the land in question. The applicant, however, can not describe the work done by Negus. He states that he gave the latter possession, and does "not know the localities of all the work he has put on."

Negus states, that his agency began on June 16, 1881, about which time he put a force of men on the claim, "for the purpose of opening and developing coal mines thereon," and that said force worked from the date mentioned until the time of hearing.

The applicant further testified, that in June, 1881, an arrangement was made between himself and Negus by which "he (Negus) should continuously hold possession for me until such time as I could settle with the government for the land," and that "when the land came into market, he (Negus) would pay me so much for my interest there, if he chose to, and enter it himself, otherwise this agreement was null and void."

The applicant, in June 1881, received from Negus "a certain sum of money" to be applied on this agreement, if its terms were complied with. He states, that the arrangement between himself and Negus was canceled about December 5, or 6, 1882, at which time he paid Negus $500. This payment appears from the applicant's testimony to have been for the purpose of settling with Negus for the expenditure (almost entirely made by him) upon the land, and also of returning to him the amount paid as aforesaid, on account of the said agreement.

Both the local office and your office found, that the applicant Bell had failed to prove a *bona fide* occupation of the land. In this conclusion I fully concur.

The applicant Bell repaid, on December 5, or 6, 1882, to Negus the respective sums expended by the latter upon the land, and advanced or paid on account of the agreement upon them.

The hearing took place on December 7, 1882, but the applicant had previously given notice of his intention to make proof on the 5th instant. But admitting, although it is by no means clearly shown, that, as counsel contend, the agreement between the applicant and Negus was canceled when the former attempted to enter the land under section 2348 of the Revised Statutes, this record does not satisfy me that the applicant has acquired such rights as should prevail against the cash entry of McDaniel. Whatever may have been the condition of affairs between the applicant and Negus, when the former offered proof, it is clear that this arrangement was in full force on April 25, 1882, when the cash entry of McDaniel was made.

Section 2348 of the U. S. Revised Statutes provides that, "any person or association of persons severally qualified . . . . who have opened and improved or shall hereafter open and improve any coal mine or mines, upon the public lands, and shall be in *actual* possession of the same, shall be entitled to a preference right of entry," in accordance with the provisions of section 2347, *i. e.*, to make cash entry under certain conditions.

In his said declaratory statement, filed in accordance with the circular relating to the sale of coal lands, approved July 31, 1882 (1 L. D., 687), the applicant swears that he came into possession of this land April 18, 1881, and has ever since remained in actual possession. But, from June 1881 until December 1882, when the applicant offered proof, as aforesaid, the land was occupied, if at all, by Negus, in pursuance of the said agreement by terms of which he, Negus, could have entered the land upon the filing of the survey, without regard to the claim of the applicant.

It will, therefore, not do to hold, that at the date of McDaniel's entry the land was in the actual possession and subject to the rights of the applicant Bell. Section 2347 of the Revised Statutes, under which the McDaniel entry was made, provides for private cash entry upon "vacant coal lands of the United States, not otherwise appropriated or reserved by competent authority."

The problematical occupation of the land on April 25, 1882, by either the applicant or Negus, could not in my opinion at that time have worked such an appropriation of the same as to have precluded the cash entry of McDaniel. Said entry will, therefore, remain intact. The application of Bell to file as aforesaid is denied. The decision of your office is affirmed.

PRACTICE—AMENDMENT—SECOND CONTEST—ACT OF JUNE 15, 1880.

HAWKINS ET AL. *v.* LAMM.

The negligence of the local office in acting upon an application to contest an entry should not impair the right of the contestant.

The application of a second contestant may be received, but no action should be taken thereunder until the final disposition of the prior contest.

An affidavit of contest may not be amended after the intervention of an adverse right.

The initiation of a contest against the original entry suspends the right of purchase under section 2, act of June 15, 1880.

First Assistant Secretary Chandler to Acting Commissioner Stone, July 1, 1889.

I have considered the appeal of John W. Hawkins from your office decision of July 1, 1887, allowing the contest of Albert E. Trone in preference to that of said Hawkins against the homestead entry of Oscar F. Lamm, upon the SW. ¼ of Sec. 8, T. 12 S., R. 27 E., Gainesville, Florida.

The record shows, that Lamm made entry of above tract April 23, 1878, and that, on March 15, 1884, Trone initiated contest against the same, alleging that, although Lamm "made his affidavit before the clerk of the circuit court, he was not, neither was any member of his family, residing upon the land involved in the affidavit at the time said affidavit was sworn to by said Oscar F. Lamm before said clerk; that the present residence or post office address of said Lamm is to affiant unknown, and that after due diligence personal service can not be had on defendant."

March 19, 1884, the local officers wrote to William F. Forward, of Palatka, Florida, before whom Trone's affidavit of contest was verified, and who seems to have acted as Trone's attorney, advising that he (Trone) amend said affidavit so as to cover abandonment, and that by doing so action could be at once taken upon his contest without await- ing an order from your office. This letter is not found in the record, nor is there anything to show when Trone was apprised of its contents.

December 12, 1884, John W. Hawkins was allowed to contest Lamm's entry, and a hearing was ordered for September 25, 1885,

June 15, 1885, Trone filed an amended affidavit of contest, alleging " that the said Oscar Lamm has wholly abandoned said tract; that he has changed his residence therefrom for more than six months since making said entry and prior to the expiration of five years, and that said tract is not settled upon and cultivated by said party as required by law."

July 23, 1885, said Lamm purchased the tract in question under the act of June 15, 1880.

Under the rules of practice then in force, the local officers could not order a hearing in a contest alleging fraud at the inception of the entry, but the matter would have to be submitted to the General Land Office. As Trone's affidavit of contest alleged that, "the present residence or post-office address of said Lamm is to affiant unknown, and that after due diligence personal service can not be had on defendant," the local officers suggested, that Trone so amend his affidavit as to cover the ground of abandonment. It does not appear why Trone did not act in accordance with this suggestion, until after contest was initiated by Hawkins.

Trone's application to contest was not rejected, neither was it suspended. Had it been so, and had he failed to appeal from such rejection or suspension, he would have been concluded by his failure to do so. It was clearly the duty of the local officers to forward Trone's application to your office, and he should not suffer from their neglect. Hawkins's application to contest should have been received, and held in abeyance to await the final disposition of the prior contest of Trone. I am, therefore, of opinion that Trone's contest should be allowed in preference to that of Hawkins.

Inasmuch, however, as Trone slept upon his contest until a new right intervened by the initiation of Hawkins's contest, I am of opinion that the hearing on Trone's case should be limited to the allegations contained in his first affidavit of contest.

It also appears from the record, that on July 23, 1885, Lamm purchased the tract in question under the act of June 15, 1880. This was subsequent to the initiation of both contests and was improperly allowed while the same were pending. An application to purchase under the second section of said act, made after the initiation of a contest against the original entry, should be suspended until the final disposition of said contest. Freise v. Hobson, 4 L. D., 580; Lyons v. O'Shaughnessy, 5 ib., 606.

Lamm's cash entry will, therefore, remain suspended, pending the final determination of both contests.

The decision of your office is accordingly affirmed.

HOMESTEAD CONTEST—IRREGULAR ENTRY.

GRIFFIN *v.* SMITH.

The right of a homesteader to file a new preliminary affidavit, in lieu of one executed before a clerk of court without the pre-requisite residence, will not be defeated by the intervention of a contest charging such irregularity and setting up a claim of priority, if said priority is not established as alleged.

First Assistant Secretary Chandler to Acting Commissioner Stone, July 1, 1889.

I have before me the appeal of L. C. Griffin from your office decision of December 22, 1887, affirming the action of the local officers dismissing his (Griffin's) contest against Eli W. Smith's homestead entry, No. 9108, made August 3, 1880, for the SE. ¼, Sec. 6, T. 17 S., R. 23 E., Gainesville district, Florida.

The S. ½ of said SE. ¼ was embraced in Henry Lewis' homestead entry, No. 2921, which was canceled by letter of March 16, 1878; and the N. ½ of said SE. ¼ was embraced in Toby Nuff's homestead entry, No. 2521, which was canceled by letter of January 25, 1877.

Eli W. Smith having made the above mentioned homestead entry on August 3, 1880, L. C. Griffin, on March 17, 1881, filed a corroborated affidavit, to the following effect :—That he (Griffin) purchased the improvements of Lewis for $150, and was by said Lewis put into possession of his receiver's receipt, and of such improvements and the tract in question, in August, 1873; that during 1876 he (Griffin), with three witnesses, presented Lewis' receipt to the register, J. A. Lee, who thereupon " took possession of said receipt, saying to deponent that he would have the same canceled and of which said deponent would have notice and could homestead the same;" that he (Griffin) " continued to reside upon said land up to the present time (the date of said affidavit, February 26, 1881), and that he never had notice of the cancellation of the entry of Henry Lewis till in December, 1880, when he was informed it had been entered by Eli W. Smith ;" that he (Griffin) "laid out large sums of money, to wit, the sum of four hundred dollars in building and otherwise improving said land;" that " the said Eli W. Smith has never lived upon, settled or improved any portion of said land." Upon which grounds, Griffin prayed that Smith's entry should be canceled and he (Griffin) allowed to homestead the land.

Upon these allegations a notice addressed to E. W. Smith, and in which the charge is stated to be " *abandonment*," was issued by the local office, and a hearing held on May 13, 1881, at which Smith did not appear. Under date of October 13, 1882, the local officers united in a written decision in which they found, among other things, the following: " The records of this office show that the affidavit accompanying the application of E. W. Smith for the land in controversy was made before the clerk of the circuit court for the county in which the land sought is located. The testimony elicited shows conclusively that at the date of entry Smith was not resident upon the land applied for, but resided upon a tract of land belonging to the widow McGaha gan, about a mile distant from the land in dispute." The decision recommends the cancellation of Smith's entry.

On January 7, 1884, your office affirmed the said decision, and held Smith's entry for cancellation.

On July 16, 1884, your office, upon a sworn petition by Smith, alleging that he had never been served with notice of the contest, ordered a re-hearing, which was duly held, October 14, 1884, both parties appearing.

On April 28, 1885, the local officers rendered a joint decision holding (among other things) that "entryman (Smith) was not upon the tract embraced in his homestead at the time of making the affidavit before the clerk, but resided about two miles distant upon a place owned by Mrs. McGahagan; that he built a house upon the land in controversy, sometime during the month of October, 1880, and moved therein with his family" the decision does not say *when*—"and has continued to reside thereon from that time until the present;" in view of which fact the opinion concludes "that the allegations of *abandonment* upon the part of the contestant in this case, are not sustained by the evidence, and that this contest should, accordingly, be dismissed." On December 22, 1887, by the decision appealed from, your office affirmed this decision of the local officers.

There can be no question, either as to the priority of Griffin, or as to the fact that at the time when Smith made his entry he had not settled upon the tract, so that he had no right to make his affidavit before the circuit court clerk. It might be that, were this all, Smith's entry would have to be canceled, as the irregularity in question is one which cannot (it would seem) be cured in the face of an adverse claim other than that of a mere contestant with no interest but the "preference right" which success in the contest would give him (Brassfield v. Eshom, 8 L. D., 1, and cases cited).

Did Griffin's original connection with the land still continue, he could not now be treated as a mere contestant, whose intervention would not prevent Smith's curing the irregularity in his entry. For, though the local officers called his proceeding against Smith's entry, a contest "for abandonment," an examination of the affidavits shows that the facts substantially set up by Griffin are, his own priority of settlement, improvement, and attempt to enter, and, Smith's non-residence at the time when he improperly made his affidavit before the circuit court clerk, on a (false) allegation of residence. And both in the appeal to your office, and the appeal now pending here, Griffin relies upon both these grounds of objection to Smith's entry.

But, in the light of Griffin's own admissions at the second hearing, it seems impossible to consider him as still holding unimpaired his original relation to this land, in any such sense as would make his interest a bar to Smith's curing of the defect in his entry. From the testimony at the second hearing it very clearly appears that the "Henry Lewis" claim, which Griffin at one time held, embraced only the S. ½ of the tract in question; that since October, 1880, Smith has resided with his family on the said tract, his improvements, before February, 1881, having been on the N. ½ thereof (which Griffin says he "did not intend to contest for"); that during February, 1881, Griffin, having been told by Smith "that he (Smith) had the latest claim and thought he had the best right and would like to have his land," moved away from the S. ½ of the tract, to which he has never again returned, that he has since gone to live upon another tract, of which he "made a pre-emption entry September, 1883," and on which he was residing at the time of the hearing.

Under such circumstances I think it must be held that Griffin voluntarily abandoned the tract in dispute as far back as February, 1881, and that he could have succeeded in this proceeding only by establishing as against Smith some ground of contest other than his (Griffin's) own priority of right (since waived), and the irregularity in the making of Smith's entry. In other words, Griffin is now a mere contestant, with no interest save the contingent one of a preference right to enter, in the event of his succeeding. Accordingly, his intervention is of itself no bar to Smith's being allowed to cure the defect in his entry by filing a proper affidavit.

As a contestant, Griffin has failed to show that Smith's entry should be canceled, the evidence at the hearing proving, not that Smith had abandoned the claim, but, on the contrary, that he had made valuable improvements on it, and had resided thereon with his family since October, 1880.

Upon these grounds your decision is affirmed.

———

HOMESTEAD CONTEST—RESIDENCE—DURESS.

SWAIN v. CALL.

A homesteader who makes an entry with knowledge of an existing adverse settlement claim, asserted for a portion of the land, must establish residence on some part of the land covered by his entry in order to show due compliance with the law.

The adverse claim and occupancy of another, as to a part of the land covered by a homestead entry, will not excuse the homesteader from the maintenance of residence during the pendency of contest over the land in conflict.

Judicial proceedings, instituted by the homesteader to recover possession from an adverse claimant, do not excuse said homesteader from compliance with the law in the matter of residence.

The plea of duress will not be accepted as an excuse for failure to establish residence when a part of the land was, at date of entry and thereafter, free from all adverse claims.

In order to constitute duress, the threats alleged must be such as are calculated to operate on a person of ordinary firmness in such a manner as to inspire a just fear of the loss of life, or great bodily injury.

First Assistant Secretary Chandler to Acting Commissioner Stone, July 1, 1889.

I have considered the case of Robert Swain *v.* Wilkinson Call on appeal of the former from your office decision of May 3, 1886, dismissing his contest and sustaining the homestead entry of said Call for the W. ½ NE. ¼ and Lot 1, (E. ½ NW. ¼) Sec. 15, T. 10 S., R. 23 W., Gainesville, Florida, land district.

It appears from the record that about 1872, the contestant, a colored man, established his residence upon that part of the land in controversy, described as lot No. 1, and improved the same by building two cabins, and some outbuildings, and by clearing about nine or ten acres and planting thereon an orange grove, and has, with his family continuously resided on said lot for about thirteen years prior to the hearing before the local officers.

On October 11, 1879, said Swain filed a pre-emption declaratory statement for said lot 1, and received from the local officers a certificate stating that he might make proof and payment within thirty months.

On December 1, 1880, Wilkinson Call, then U. S. Senator from Florida, commenced a contest against Swain's filing, and on December 18, 1880, Call made homestead entry for said lot 1, and for W. ½ NE. ¼ of said Sec. 15.

Upon the evidence taken at the hearing of said contest your office decided in favor of Swain and held the entry of Call for cancellation, and upon appeal to this office Secretary Teller affirmed your decision, holding that Swain's failure to make final proof and payment within one year, the tract having been "offered land," was excused by reason of the statement upon his certificate that payment might be made within thirty months.

Afterwards Acting Secretary Joslyn on July 28, 1884, (3 L. D., 46), upon a motion to reconsider said decision, reversed the same, canceled the filing of Swain, and allowed Call's entry to stand. (In said cases spelled "Swaim").

On May 14, 1885, Swain initiated the contest in the case at bar, upon the ground that "the said Wilkinson Call has never since the date of his entry res.ded upon or cultivated or improved the land in any manner."

On May 21, 1885, D. M. Coffman, special agent of the Land Office, reported said entry of Call as fraudulent and your office held the same for cancellation and notified Call to appear and show cause why the same should not be canceled, but learning that Swain had commenced this contest said order was recalled.

The hearing of the contest at bar was closed November 24, 1885, and the local officers decided that Call had never resided upon or cultivated any part of the tract embraced in his homestead entry, but had since said entry, resided at Washington, D. C., and at Jacksonville and Mc-Meekin, Florida.

Your said office decision of May 3, 1886, reverses that of the local officers and allows Call's entry to stand subject to his future compliance
with the law.

At the hearing it was admitted of record by Call as follows: "Contestee desires to state that he has never resided upon the tract in question or cultivated any part thereof," and he added, " as I have never
been in possession of said tract since December 1, 1880, prior to date of
contest."

Call in his appeal to your office urges that he was prevented from establishing residence upon said homestead tract by reason of the refusal
of Swain to surrender to him the possession of said lot 1, which he says
was all of the entry he cared to have and he says: " I took the homestead for the purpose of getting the land embraced in the pre-emption
of Robert Swain.   That was the valuable portion of my homestead."

It appears that the portion of Call's homestead entry described as W.
½ NE. ¼, Sec. 15, was not embraced in Swain's filing, and that he never
made any claim to it whatever.

Your said decision appears to me to rest upon the following propositions:—

1st. That " the first contest was depending from December 1, 1880,
until July 28, 1884, and all action on the part of Call relating to the possession of the land occupied by Swain was legally suspended during the
pendency of said contest."

2nd. That Swain's occupancy of lot 1, after the termination of the contest gave Call no opportunity to establish residence on his homestead
and the short time (one day only) which elapsed from the ejectment of
Swain until he moved into the house again was not such reasonable
time to move in as Call should have had.

3rd. That although Call might without opposition have built upon W.
½ NE. ¼ at any time, he had a right to demand the entire quarter section,
and he had a right to demand the portion upon which the improvements
were located.

4th. That Call's abandonment was enforced by the conduct of Swain
in refusing to surrender the possession of lot 1, and he can not now be
heard to charge the former with an abandonment which " may have
been the result of his open defiance of the decree of a court of his own
State and the decision of the Secretary of the Interior."

If by the first of the above propositions, it is intended to hold that
an adverse claim and occupancy by another as to a part of the land
included in the homestead entry, releases the entryman during the
pendency of contest from compliance with the law in regard to residence
I can not concur in such conclusion.

In Byrne v. Dorward (5 L. D., 104), it is said:

There can be no doubt of the correctness of the position, that pending a final decision in a contest on whatever ground or charge, the entryman whose claim is attacked
should continue to comply with the law, and that, if he fail to do this he lays himself liable to attack in a subsequent contest should he successfully defend in the one

pending. To hold differently would be to condone laches and to open the door to a practice which would enable parties, under the guise of a contest, to hold lands indefinitely without complying with the requirements of law under which their entries were made.

While the case above cited was one in regard to compliance with law in a timber culture entry pending contest I see no reason why it should not be applicable in homestead entries, and the reasons given apply as well in the one as the other.

Swain had as much right to the possession of lot 1 during the first contest as Call had, to say the least of it, and the contest was commenced by Call eighteen days before he made entry so that he knew all about the possession and claim of Swain when he made entry, and if he chose to make entry pending contest, then he should have complied with the law by establishing residence upon some portion of the land entered.

The other propositions above enumerated may be summed up in this: Call was prevented from establishing residence upon lot 1, of his homestead by duress on the part of Swain, and on account of such duress he was not required to reside upon the part that was free from other claims.

In this again I can not concur. The evidence relied upon as showing duress upon the part of Swain is not by any means sufficient to sustain such finding. First because the W. $\frac{1}{2}$ NE. $\frac{1}{4}$ was always open for him to establish his residence thereon and he made no attempt to do so, and second, because to excuse failure to reside upon land by reason of duress, it must appear that the threats were such in character as were calculated to operate on a person of ordinary firmness in such a manner as to inspire a just fear of loss of life or great bodily injury. Dorgan v. Pitt, (6 L. D., 616).

The evidence must show such a state of facts as rendered the absence compulsory. (Plugert v. Empy, (2 L. D., 152).

The evidence in the case at bar which it might be claimed tends to establish such duress is substantially that after issuance of a writ of possession in an action of eviction against Swain, the sheriff took with him L. R. Walker to receive possession for Call, went to the house, called Swain out to the gate and after some conversation the subject of which does not appear, told him he was out of possession and went away leaving Swain and Walker together; that after the sheriff left, Swain said to Walker he had better go home instead of fooling around there as he was not going to give possession to any one; that the sheriff being informed of this sent his deputy and two or more assistants to execute the writ, that they arrived at the house in the absence of Swain, whose wife offered some resistance and was speedily overpowered and forcibly ejected from the premises, and the household effects were put over the fence into the road and Walker put in actual possession. He says that he went off to work and when he come back he found Swain had taken possession again, and the women folks told him he had better not come back around there.

He said he had married a daughter of Swain's wife and was not then living with her and was not on friendly terms with Swain, and that the said threats were directed solely against himself, and testifies to none against Call.

It does not appear from Call's own testimony that Swain had made any threats or demonstrations of violence or that he had any fear of bodily injury whatever. He seems to rely wholly upon his frequent demands for the possession of lot 1, his propositions to purchase the improvements made by Swain, and his actions of eviction brought against him. While he filed no argument upon his appeal to this office, his counsel in a brief filed upon the appeal from the decision of the local officers cites Hudson v. Docking (4 L. D., 501), as the "strongest decision imaginable." Said decision simply holds that evidence of actions for possession brought in the local courts are admissible upon the question of abandonment, but in Forbes v. Driscoll (3 L. D., 370, on review) it is held that bringing such suits will not excuse failure to comply with the law in regard to settlement.

It seems to me that Call in the case at bar like Forbes in the case last above cited, "chose to pursue a certain plan of action, in the consummation of which he failed to comply with the law."

I cannot find from the evidence that Call's failure to establish a residence upon the land included in his homestead entry, was through no fault of his own, indeed I think the evidence clearly establishes the opposite.

The decision of your office is accordingly reversed.

PLACER MINING CLAIM—KNOWN LODE.

RAILROAD LODE v. NOYES PLACER.

A vein or lode known to exist at date of application for placer patent, and not included in said application, must be excluded from the placer entry.

The formal location of a lode claim is not necessary to exclude it from a placer patent, the only requisites being that it was known to exist, and was not included in the placer application.

Secretary Noble to Acting Commissioner Stone, July 2, 1889.

I have considered the appeal of James Murray from your office decision of June 16, 1888, holding mineral entry No. 1594 Railroad Lode claim for cancellation to the extent of 7.18 acres, in conflict with mineral entry No. 1347, Noyes Placer claim, Summit Valley Mining district, Silver Bow County, Helena, Montana. Said entry was made February 12, 1886.

The record shows that on June 24, 1880, John Noyes and Elmira Noyes filed application for patent on their said placer claim embracing fractional lot 9 in NE. ¼ of SE. ¼ Sec. 13, T. 3 N., R. 8 W., embracing 28.44 acres.

Olivia Hopkins, claimant of the Marie Louise lode, filed during the period of publication, an adverse claim against Noyes' application for patent. Suit was instituted on September 2, 1882, and by virtue of a judgment rendered in favor of Hopkins the Marie Louise lode was excluded from this entry.

This exclusion reduced the area of the Noyes placer claim by 15.12 acres and cut lot 9 into two non-contiguous tracts, one tract retaining the lotting "9" and the other tract being designated as "14". This explains the discrepancy between the application and the entry, in the former the tract was designated as lot "9" and the acreage given as 28.44 acres, whereas in the latter the tract is stated as lots 9 and 14 and the acreage given as 13.32 acres.

February 7, 1883, protests were filed by the attorney for claimants of the Ella and Oneida No. 2 lodes, asking that a hearing be ordered. July 31, 1883, your office refused a hearing, but directed the register to receive applications for said lodes upon proof being made that they were known to exist prior to the date of the placer application. No application, however, appears to have been filed for said Ella and Oneida No. 2 lodes.

October 19, 1882, Stephen Bynum, claiming the Railroad lode, filed a protest which, however, was dismissed by your office on January 11, 1883, for the reason that it was not shown that said lode was known to exist at the date of filing said placer application.

May 2, 1887, Stephen and Frances W. Bynum conveyed all their interest in and to said Railroad lode to James A. Murray, who in August 1887, made application for a patent for said lode and who made entry of the same November 12th following.

June 16, 1888, your office rendered a decision as follows:

The Railroad Lode claim is based upon a location made October 29, 1881. As said Railroad Lode was not located until long subsequent to the filing of the placer application, and as it is not shown that it was known to exist at the date of said application, said entry No. 1594 is hereby held for cancellation to the extent of 7.18 acres, the area of the conflict with said mineral entry 1347.

From this decision Murray duly appealed to the Department.

Subsequently, and on September 27, 1888, the local officers transmitted a number of affidavits relating to mineral entry No. 1594 Railroad Lode claim.

L. S. Scott made affidavit that he is a miner by occupation and is familiar with the lode claim known as the Railroad Lode claim, located by Stephen Bynum; that he is also acquainted with the surrounding ground claimed by John Noyes as placer ground; that said lode existed prior to 1880, and that the same had been worked upon as a lode claim; that there were two shafts sunk upon said lode, from one of which he took ore and had the same assayed from which he got returns of $18 per ton; that said lode was what is termed among miners a well defined lode and was at least two feet wide, at a depth of fifteen or twenty feet from the surface; and that the shafts referred to were so near the traveled road that they were visible to all passers-by, "particularly to persons in search of such knowledge."

Michael A. Hickey, made affidavit that he was a miner by occupation and that he was "quite familiar with, and knew the ground well" that is known as the Railroad Lode located by Stephen Bynum, as he worked in its immediate vicinity in 1878, 1879 and 1880; that he saw men working upon said lode at different times during those years and knew it to be a well defined lode prior to 1880, as there were two or more shafts sunk upon the same, one at least to a depth of about twenty feet " where it shows a vein of ore about two feet between two granite walls," and that these shafts were so situated that all passers-by could readily see them as there was one on each side of a traveled road.

Max Lalande also made affidavit that he is well acquainted with the claim known as the Railroad Lode claim; that it is a bona fide lode claim since 1878 and that he himself worked upon said lode developing the same as a lode claim prior to 1880; that it is a well defined lode claim, and that prior to 1880 a shaft was sunk upon said claim to a depth of about twenty feet; that the claim was worked upon as a quartz lode prior to its location by Stephen Bynum as the Railroad Lode claim, when it was known as the Calumet Lode claim.

Attached to the last affidavit is a certified copy of said Calumet Lode claim, which was located in February 22, 1879, and recorded on March 10th following.

Besides on the plat, made by the United States deputy mineral surveyor, subsequent to the determination of the Marie Louise contest already referred to, and on which the present entry is based, the Railroad Lode claim is delineated. And the said surveyor in his field notes states that "the Railroad Lode, lot No. 330, survey No. 1201, conflicts with the south portion of these premises, but that no vein or lode in said Railroad Lode has been traced or shown to extend into this placer claim."

The foregoing is sufficient to indicate that the Railroad Lode claim existed at the date of the application and entry of the Noyes placer, and the facts also tend to show that it was then a "known lode."

Upon the facts above recited, Murray's attorney asked the Department " to direct a hearing to be had before the local officers, as to the single point, whether or not this Railroad Lode claim was known to exist at the time of the placer location."

It appears that the then claimant of the Railroad Lode claim failed to adverse Noyes application for patent during the period of publication. Neither did Noyes adverse Murray's application for patent for the Railroad Lode claim during the period of publication, nor has he since filed any protest against Murray's entry. John Noyes or Elmira Noyes does not appear in this case either in person or by attorney.

Section 2333 Revised Statutes provides :

Where a vein or lode is known to exist within the boundaries of a placer claim, an application for a patent for such placer claim, which does not include an application for the vein or lode claim shall be construed as a conclusive declaration that the claimant of the placer claim has no right of possession of the vein or lode claim; but when the existence of a vein or lode in a placer claim is not known, a patent for the placer claim shall convey all valuable mineral and other deposits within the boundaries thereof.

If, therefore, the Railroad Lode claim was known to exist at the date of Noyes' application for a patent for his placer claim, said lode claim would be excluded from the entry made by Noyes, as in his application for the same he made affidavit that "the land is purely placer mining ground, and that there are no known lodes or veins within the exterior boundaries of the same other than the Hesperus and Marie Louise lodes." If, on the contrary the existence of the Railroad Lode claim was not known at the date of Noyes' application for a patent for his placer claim, then a patent for the placer claim would convey all mineral deposits within the boundaries of the same. The lode claim, now known as the Railroad Lode claim, could have been known to exist at the date Noyes applied for a patent for the placer claim, although the same was not located until subsequent to said application. The formal location of the lode claim is not necessary to exclude it from a patent for the placer, the only requisite being that it be known to exist and that it be not included in the application for the placer.

For the foregoing reasons a hearing should be had to determine whether the vein or lode claimed by Murray was known to exist at the time Noyes made application for patent for his placer claim.

You will accordingly direct the local officers to order a hearing, after due notice to the parties in interest, at which Murray may prove, if he can, the allegations contained in his attorney's application for a hearing.

Without taking any action upon the appeal, the papers in the case are herewith returned to you for re-adjudication upon the testimony taken at the hearing.

————

HOMESTEAD ENTRY–APPLICATION TO ENTER.

HUGHEY v. DOUGHERTY.

A legal application to make homestead entry protects the right of the applicant from the intervention of any adverse claim until final action thereon.

An applicant for public land may at any time withdraw his pending application and thus abate his claim.

An application to enter made pending appeal from the rejection of a former application is in effect a waiver of the first application.

First Assistant Secretary Chandler to Acting Commissioner Stone, July 2, 1889.

October 27, 1887, Dominick A. Dougherty made application at the local office at St. Cloud, Minnesota, to enter the E. $\frac{1}{2}$ of the SW. $\frac{1}{4}$ and

the W. ½ of the SE. ¼ of section 9, T. 121 N., R. 30 W., under the home
stead law. Said application was rejected by the local officers for the
reason that said tracts of land had been selected and approved to the
St. Paul & Pacific (now St. Paul, Minneapolis & Manitoba) Railway
Company.

Dougherty appealed from said action and his appeal was transmitted
to your office October 27, 1887.

November 29, 1887, Dougherty filed an application in the form of an
affidavit to withdraw the aforesaid appeal, and his said affidavit was
transmitted to your office by the local officers upon the same day.

November 14, 1887, Dougherty made homestead entry—No. 13,947—
of the N. ½ of the SE. ¼ and the SW. ¼ of the SW. ¼ in section 5, T.
139 N., R. 31 W.

November 21, 1887, Daniel H. Hughey presented an affidavit of contest against said entry setting forth the facts in relation to the application made by Dougherty October 17, 1887, to enter lands in section 29,
T. 121 N., R. 30 W., its rejection by the local officers and the appeal
from their action taken by Dougherty. Hughey asked to be allowed
to prove said allegation and that the said homestead entry be canceled.
Upon said affidavit of contest the local officers under date of December 9, 1887, made the following endorsement:

The within application is hereby rejected for the reason that the ground of contest therein alleged is insufficient upon which to order a hearing.

Hughey appealed and March 20, 1888, your office rendered a decision
sustaining the action of the local office, in which it is stated that:

The allegations are not considered sufficient to warrant an investigation of said
entry, nor would they be, even if the appeal of Dougherty should be decided in his
favor, for the reason that he would not be required to enter the tract.

Hughey appealed from your said decision and alleges error in holding " Substantially that a person may have more than one homestead
entry, the application for each of which is pending at the same time;"
in holding "substantially that a person may have more than one homestead application pending at the same time, and so exclude all contests;
and "as a matter of law, in holding that Dougherty could, while having one application for a homestead entry pending, make another valid
homestead entry."

Counsel for Hughey contends that the effect of the commissioner's
ruling is to allow a person to apply for and withhold from entry any
number of tracts of land.

The argument is based upon a misconception of your office decision.
The record shows that Dougherty made but one homestead entry, the
one Hughey applied to contest. The ruling that "a legal application
to enter is, while pending, equivalent to actual entry so far as the applicant's rights are concerned"—Pfaff v. Williams, (4 L. D., 455)—was
made concerning land subject to entry and upon the right of an applicant possessing the necessary qualifications. It protects the applicant

whose application was improperly rejected from the intervention of any subsequent claim until his rights are finally passed upon, but it does not hold that he cannot withdraw his application or render himself disqualified to enter the land applied for. In the case of Mary J. Woolley *et al.* (5 L. D., 222), it was held that "an applicant for public land has the right at any time to withdraw his pending application and thus abate his claim."

The application made by Dougherty November 14, 1887, to enter the land involved herein was a waiver of his application to enter the tract applied for in October and the waiver was made in a more formal way by his affidavit withdrawing his appeal from the action of the local officers in rejecting the application first made by him. The appeal having been withdrawn the action of the local officers became final—and the claim, if any, that Dougherty initiated by said application was abated by his own act.

I see no reason for disturbing the conclusion reached by your office and your decision refusing to allow the contest is affirmed.

HOMESTEAD CONTEST—DEATH OF ENTRYMAN.

SWANSON *v.* WISELY'S HEIR.

The heirs of a deceased homesteader are not required to reside on the land in order to protect their rights under the entry.

A contest charging abandonment and failure to maintain residence must fail where the entryman died within less than six months after making entry, and prior to the establishment of residence, but the heirs thereafter cultivated and improved the land.

First Assistant Secretary Chandler to Acting Commissioner Stone, July 2, 1889.

March 7, 1883, George A. Wisely, made homestead entry of the E. ½ of the NE. ¼ and the E. ½ of the SE. ¼ of Section 20, T. 17 R., 16 W., Grand Island, Nebraska.

October 26, 1885, Charley Swanson filed an affidavit of contest against said entry charging that said entryman "has wholly abandoned said tract; that he has changed his residence therefrom for more than six months since making said entry; that said tract is not settled upon and cultivated by said party as required by law."

The case was continued by stipulation from December 28, 1885, to March 9, 1886, upon which day James L. Wisely, filed a motion asking to be made a party defendant in the case and in support thereof, filed an affidavit stating that George A. Wisely had died and that the affiant was his sole heir at law. The motion was granted and the case proceeded to trial May 24, 1886. Upon the testimony adduced at the hearing the local officers found in favor of the defendant and that the contest should be dismissed.   June 19, 1888, your office affirmed the action of the local officers and dismissed the contest.

Swanson appealed.

The entry was made March 7, 1883, and the testimony shows that the entryman died August 26, 1883, less than six months after the entry was made. It is not shown that he ever settled upon the land but the law allowed six months from the date of the entry in which to establish residence. The testimony fails to show that the tract was abandoned by the entryman's heir at law, on the contrary, it appears that as soon as he heard of the entryman's death, he commenced the erection of a sod house upon the tract and that he has broken and cultivated several acres of land and made arrangements for breaking more.   .

The heirs are not required to reside upon the land but only to cultivate it. Tauer v. The Heirs of Walter A. Mann (4 L. D., 433).

In the case of Stewart v. Jacobs (1 L. D., 636) the entry was made March 24, 1874, and the entryman died June 25, 1874, without having entered upon or cultivated the land. The contest initiated in November, 1877, was held not to be good in so far as it related to the failure of the entryman to establish residence upon the land prior to his death which occurred before six months had expired after entry; but was sustained on account of the failure of the heirs of Jacobs to keep up a continuous cultivation of the tract after the expiration of said six months.

This decision is directly in point and sustains the action of your office. See also Townsend's heirs v. Spellman (2 L. D., 77).

The decision appealed from is affirmed.

PRE-EMPTION—HOMESTEAD—TRANSMUTATION.

EDWARD YOUNG.

When a pre-emptor transmutes his claim into a homestead entry his rights, under such entry, relate back to the settlement and filing made under his pre-emption claim.

Failure of the local office to properly note of record the fact of transmutation cannot affect the rights of the entryman.

First Assistant Secretary Chandler to Acting Commissioner Stone, July 2, 1889.

I have considered the case of Edward Young on his appeal from your office decision of May 21, 1888, holding for cancellation his homestead entry for SW. ¼, SE. ¼, Sec. 4, T. 31, R. 99 W., Evanston, Wyoming, land district.

Your said letter assigned no reason for such cancellation but recites the fact that the said SW. ¼ SE. ¼ was included in the homestead entry of one Jonathan Pugh, dated August 2, 1884, leaving it to be inferred that it was for conflict with the said entry, which was prior in date.

With the appeal are filed certain *ex parte* affidavits to the effect that

Young settled upon a tract of land including the forty acres in controversy in 1871; that the plat of official survey of the township was not
filed until May or June, 1884; that within three months thereafter said
Young made application to file pre-emption declaratory statement but
said application was rejected by the local officers because said land was
embraced in the desert land entry of said Pugh; that prior to making
said application Young had instituted a contest against the desert land
entry of said Pugh so far as the same affected his right to said SW. ¼
SE. ¼ Sec. 4 and hearing was set for August 4, 1884; that on August
4, 1884 said Young appeared at the local office with his witnesses when
he learned that Pugh had relinquished his desert land entry, whereupon Young asked to make homestead entry for said SW. ¼ SE. ¼, Sec.
4, but the same was refused by the local officers upon the ground that
his application to file a pre emption declaratory statement which had
been rejected by them a few days before must now be taken up; and
the same being taken up and allowed by the local officers he filed declaratory statement No. 229, dated August 4, 1884, and alleging settlement October 20, 1871.   Said affidavits also state that on the same day,
viz., August 4, 1884, the said Pugh also made homestead entry for a
tract of land including the one in controversy, and this also appears to
be the date of Pugh's entry from an abstract of the record in the local
office certified to by the register, but upon examination of the original
papers on file in your office I find that said entry was dated August 2,
1884, as stated in your said decision.

However, it appears both from the abstract certified by the register
and from the original entry papers of the said Pugh that his entry so
far as said SW. ¼ SE. ¼ is concerned, was allowed subject to Young's
said declaratory statement No. 229.

It further appears from the affidavits filed with the appeal that on
December 31, 1886, Young presented at the local office his application
to transmute his said declaratory statement to a homestead entry, and
his application presented with the record shows plainly upon the face
thereof that the same was an application to transmute, but it is claimed
by appellant that the local officers made no entry upon their books that
the same was a transmuted pre-emption filing, and that because of their
erroneous omission to note said fact the same appeared to be in conflict
with Pugh's entry and was held for cancellation in your said office decision.

It very clearly appears that the homestead entry of said land made
by Young, June 20, 1887, was simply a transmutation of his pre-
emption filing, and whether Pugh's entry was made August 2, or August 4, 1884, it just as clearly appears that it was allowed subject to
the said filing, and the fact that the local officers failed to note upon
the record that the same was a transmutation, can in no wise affect the
rights of Young, which in transmuting relate back to his settlement
and pre emption filing.

And this ruling can in no wise be unjust to Pugh, because his entry was allowed subject to the said declaratory statement No. 229, of Young, without objection on his part so far as the record shows.

It would seem that your said decision should be reversed and that the entry of Pugh, in so far as the same affects the SW. ¼ SE. ¼, said Sec. 4, should be canceled and that of Young for said land be sustained; but inasmuch as said Pugh has not been made a party in this case, such order is made upon the condition that the local officers cause notice to be given to Pugh of this decision and that he shall for sixty days after such notice, have the right to ask for a hearing to determine the right of the respective parties to said land, and upon his making application within said time, by corroborated affidavits showing his superior right a day for hearing shall be fixed by the local officers and said hearing proceeded with in regular order.

Upon failure of said Pugh to make such request for rehearing, his entry shall be canceled, so far as the same affects said SW. ¼ SE. ¼, Sec. 4, and Young's entry therefor re-instated.

Your said decision is modified accordingly

RAILROAD GRANT—SETTLEMENT RIGHT.

JACOBS v. FLORIDA RY. & NAVIGATION CO.

Under the relinquishment executed by the company the rights of actual settlers within the limits of the grant, prior to March 16, 1881, are recognized and protected.

Where the fact of such settlement right is conceded, the burden of proof is with the company to show that the settler has by his subsequent acts waived the benefit of said relinquishment.

Secretary Noble to Acting Commissioner Stone, July 2, 1889.

The case of Agrippa Jacobs v. The Florida Railway and Navigation Company is before me on appeal by said company from the decision of your office, dated March 7, 1888. Said decision held for cancellation the selection, made by said company on May 24, 1884, of the NE. ¼ of Sec. 35, T. 15 S., R. 22 E., Gainesville land district, Florida, and allowed Jacobs to make a homestead entry for the same tract.

The land in controversy, as stated in said decision, is within the six miles primary limits of that portion of the grant of May 17, 1856, located between Waldo and Tampa, claimed by the Florida Railway and Navigation Company, as successors to the Atlantic, Gulf and West India Transit Company. On April 1, 1876, the last named company waived "all claim to so much of the land on each side of the road between Waldo and Tampa Bay . . . . . as may be found by the General Land Department, at Washington, to be occupied by settlers who may be entitled to equitable relief up to December 13, 1875." And on June 25, 1881, this waiver was extended so as to include "all bona fide settlers who made improvements prior to the 16th day of March, 1881." See Senate Ex. Document, No. 91, 1st Session, 48th Congress, on page 84.

In June, 1886, Jacobs applied to make homestead entry for the described tract of land. In a corroborated affidavit, made June 16, 1886, he states, among other things, that he moved on said land about October 1, 1872, built and furnished a house for himself and one for his daughter during the following winter, and has lived there continuously since; that he then (June, 1886,) had on the land "two respectable dwelling houses, three out-houses, several bearing orange trees, a number of small orange trees, ten acres of said land cleared, fenced and under cultivation, worth $500."

In pursuance of instructions from your office, a hearing in the case was duly had; the testimony being taken before Robert Bullock—who was duly authorized to take same—on March 4, 1887, at Ocala, Florida, and by him reduced to writing. On November 19, following, the register and receiver at Gainesville, after considering the evidence so taken, recommended "that this contest be dismissed and Jacobs' application for homestead entry rejected."

The railroad company—now designating itself by the name of the Peninsula R. R. Co.—introduced in evidence an instrument (partly written and partly printed), called a certificate of purchase, whereby it acknowledges, May 30, 1883, the receipt from Jacobs of $50.07 and three promissory notes, each for a like sum, dated May 30, 1883, and payable respectively in one, two and three years after date; the same being for the purchase of the west half of the tract in controversy. On the payment of said notes, the purchaser, his heirs or assigns, were to be entitled to a deed from the railroad company for said west half. Written on the back of this instrument is found the following, to wit:

($200.00.)

OCALA, *June* 7, 1883.

For and in consideration of the sum of two hundred dollars to me paid, I hereby assign to Mrs. Clemmie B. Burlingame and D. J. Carrol, of Marion Co., Florida, all my right, title and interest to and in the within certificate and the lands therein described.

his
AGRIPPA x JACOBS.
mark

In presence of
  R. L. ANDERSON,
  JAMES A. SCOTT.

All the improvements of Jacobs are shown to be on said west half of the tract in controversy, and the local officers found that the writing above copied, "is a valid instrument," and that it "should be accepted as an absolute waiver by Jacobs of whatever rights he may have acquired upon this land by virtue of his said settlement, and operates as a bar to his further claiming the same under the public land laws of the United States."

On appeal from said decision, your office seems to be of the opinion that Jacobs entered into no contract of purchase of said railroad, and that his signature to the supposed assignment, solemnly denied by him, has not been proven, though there is no distinct finding to that effect. Your office decision further holds as follows:

But the whole question as to whether Jacobs did or did not contract with the R. R. Co. in 1883 to purchase the land, and subsequently assigned said contract, is, it appears to me, immaterial in the consideration of this case. The sole question, so far as the company is concerned, is, was Jacobs an actual bona fide settler who made improvements prior to March 16, 1881. Any subsequent transactions by him would not affect the status of the land at that date, and a contract subsequently made, whereby he agreed to pay the company for the land, would not take away his right to enter the same under the homestead law, if he was an actual settler thereon. And if the making of such a contract would not affect his rights to enter as a settler, it follows that his relinquishment, or assignment, of his claim under said contract would not affect such right.

Said decision further finds Jacobs to be an actual settler, within the terms of the company's relinquishment, and entitled to enter said land, and, therefore, the company's selection of said tract was held for cancellation.

On appeal from this decision the company, by its attorney, assign the following errors therein, to wit:—

1. In holding that the entire question, relating to Jacobs' purchase of said land from the company and his subsequent sale thereof, is immaterial to the case. ·

2. In holding that the sole question, so far as the company is concerned, is whether Jacobs was an actual bona fide settler prior to March 16, 1881.

3. In holding that Jacobs was a settler in good faith on this land.

4. In holding Jacobs' application to enter for allowance.

5. In failing to deny Jacobs' application to enter.

6. In holding for cancellation the selection of the company.

The railroad company admits that its waivers, in favor of actual *bona fide* settlers, prior to March 16, 1881, are effectual to defeat the company, "provided the parties entitled to take the benefit of said waivers did themselves, *in propria persona*, follow up their claims and comply with the law in respect to them." But it insists that such settler by sale would deprive himself of all right to the land settled on. It further insists that Jacobs bought the eighty on which his improvements are from the company on May 30, 1883, and eight days thereafter, for a valuable consideration, assigned the same to one Burlingame; that having done so, neither he nor Burlingame have any right to said tract of land under or by virtue of said waivers, and that Jacobs can not repudiate his purchase and transfer, and is estopped thereby from afterwards asserting any claim to the land in dispute by virtue of his prior settlement and improvements.

The first question of any difficulty presented for determination herein is, whether the alleged purchase and transfer by Jacobs did in fact take place, because the evidence shows that prior thereto he was entitled to the benefit of said waivers by the railroad company.

The evidence clearly shows that Jacobs is a qualified homesteader;

that ten years prior to the time of the alleged purchase and transfer he settled on the land in dispute, and has since continuously resided thereon; that his improvements consist of two dwelling houses—one occupied by himself and one by his daughter and son in-law—three out-houses, about eight acres of land fenced, cleared and cultivated, a number of orange trees, some of which were grown from seed planted since his settlement and are now in bearing; that his said improvements are worth from $250 to $500, and that he is a very poor man; that he intended to secure title to the home thus established at least ten years prior to the date of the hearing had herein, and that the probable cause of his not having sooner applied to make homestead entry was poverty and lack of information of his rights and of how to proceed in order to secure them.

The burden of proving the alleged purchase and transfer is on the railroad company, and the evidence produced does not satisfactorily establish the alleged facts. That Jacobs, with full knowledge of said waivers by the railroad in favor of actual settlers, prior to March 16, 1881, should pay or agree to pay $200 for one half of a tract of land, which at the time he had a right, as against said railroad, to enter under the homestead laws, seems not only highly improbable, but almost incredible. To gain credence such a fact should be shown by the clearest and most satisfactory testimony. And, if the purchase was made by Jacobs in ignorance of the fact that the government would allow him to enter the land, I apprehend that he would be entitled to repudiate the supposed contract on the ground of want of consideration, or on the ground of fraud.

The only documentary evidence which I find in the record tending to show the alleged purchase and transfer is the aforesaid certificate of purchase and the written endorsement thereon. No one testifies that Jacobs, or any authorized agent of his, ever applied to purchase said tract of land, or any part of it, from said company. Jacobs swears positively that no such application was ever made; that he never paid any sum of money, or signed any promissory notes payable to the railroad company, for this land, and that said company never called on him to pay any such notes. He further testified on this point, that S. S. Burlingame came out to his house and told him that the land belonged to the railroad, and that he (Burlingame) was going to buy it from the railroad and that he would give him (Jacobs) ten acres, but that he made no agreement whatever with Burlingame, or any one else, about the land.

S. S. Burlingame testifies that he paid the railroad company fifty dollars in cash and Jacobs' three notes; that Jacobs is an ignorant man, and that he (Burlingame) supposes that a title from the railroad company for this land would not be good, unless it came through Jacobs.

It appears that one of the supposed assignees in the instrument copied

above is the wife of S. S. Burlingame, and the inference, from the
evidence in the case, is that he is the party who made, not only the
payments to the railroad company for this land, but all the negotiations
in relation to the purchase of the same. As to the alleged assignment
by Jacobs, he testifies that it was written by Tom Rickards—who it
appears was at that time an agent of said railroad company—that he
paid Jacobs no money, but gave him a written agreement that when
he (Burlingame) got his deed from said company, he would deed him
(Jacobs) ten acres of the land. He failed to testify, however, that he
was ever in any manner authorized by Jacobs to act for him in relation
to the alleged purchase.

R. L. Anderson testifies that his signature and James A. Scott's
signature to said instrument are genuine, but that he had no recollec-
tion of any of the circumstances connected with such signing, no recol-
lection of seeing Agrippa Jacobs at that time, could not say that he
recognized him at the time he (Anderson) was testifying, and, in short,
that he did not recollect anything whatever about the transaction.
Neither James A. Scott, the other witness to said instrument, S. S.
Burlingame, evidently the active manager in this matter, Clemmie B.
Burlingame, nor D. J. Carrol, the alleged transferees, nor in short any
one, testifies that Jacobs in fact attached his signature to the alleged
asignment or transfer. On the other hand, Jacobs swears positively
that he did not sign said instrument, or authorize any one to sign it for
him, and that his signature thereto is fraudulent.

I find nothing in the facts detailed, and the circumstances surrounding this case, to warrant me in rejecting Jacobs' positive testimony in
relation to the alleged purchase and transfer. His testimony being
taken as true, my finding is that the alleged purchase and transfer
were in fact never made, or authorized to be made, by Agrippa Jacobs.
This finding makes it unnecessary for me to discuss appellant's first
and second assignments of error.

For the reasons above given, the decision of your office is affirmed.

SETTLEMENT ON UNSURVEYED LAND.

McWEENEY v. GREENE.

An act of settlement upon unsurveyed land must be of such a character, and so open
and notorious, as to be notice to the public generally of the extent of the claim.

Secretary Noble to Acting Commissioner Stone, July 2, 1889.

I have considered the case of Patrick McWeeney v. Charles W. Greene,
upon the appeal of Mary McWeeney, widow of the former, from your
office decision of October 11, 1887.

The land involved is the E. ½ of the NW. ¼ of section 35, T. 154 N.,
R. 64 W., Devil's Lake land district, Dakota.

Greene filed his pre-emption declaratory statement September 29,

1883, for the E. ½ of the SW. ¼ of section 26, and the E. ½ of NW. ¼ of section 35, town and range aforesaid, alleging settlement thereon April 28, 1883.

Patrick McWeeney filed October 5, 1883, his pre-emption declaratory statement for the NW. ¼ of the said section 35, alleging settlement April 1, 1883.

It also appears that Sioux half-breed scrip was located October 11, 1883, by Tracy B. Bangs, as attorney, for Scott Campbell, on the S. ½ of the NW. ¼ and N. ½ of SW. ¼ of said section 35. John Farrington represented the purchasers from the scrip claimants, as trustee.

The town plat was filed in the local office September 29, 1883.

On November 10, 1883, Greene gave notice by publication of his intention to offer final proof in support of his claim and cited said Farrington and Patrick McWeeney to appear at the local office January 3, 1884, and show cause why his entry should not be allowed.

On January 3, 1884, said Farrington and Patrick McWeeney appeared by attorney and filed protests against allowing Greene's entry on the ground, substantially, of prior right. McWeeney's attorney set forth under oath, that his client was then confined in jail under an indictment for murder and asked for time to present his witnesses in support of his claim, whereupon hearing was set for February 4, 1884. On the day appointed all parties were represented and trial had.

From the evidence adduced the register held that McWeeney and Greene should be allowed to make joint entry for the tract in dispute, while the receiver was of the opinion that Greene should be allowed to perfect his entry to his said claim. As to Farrington's claim the local officers united in the decision that in the evidence nothing was disclosed to sustain his protest.

McWeeney and Greene, each for himself appealed to your office. Farrington did not appeal.

Your office considering the evidence, sustained the decision of the said receiver and held the filing of McWeeney for the lands in conflict for cancellation. The scrip location you allowed to stand subject to the right of Greene to the SE. ¼ of the NW. ¼ of said section 35.

Patrick McWeeney having died December, 1885, his widow, Mary McWeeney, appealed from you said office decision, to this department.

The evidence is voluminous and exceedingly contradictory. It appears, however, clearly established that one R. W. Hurlbut in February, 1883, made claim to the land covered by the filing of Greene. He built a house on the E. ½ of the NW. ¼ of the land in dispute. On April 28, 1883, he sold out his interest to the said lands for the sum of twelve hundred dollars, to Greene, describing his said interest as " all my right, title and interest acquired as squatter." Hurlbut pointed out the corners of the said land to Greene, at the time, and the latter took possession of the claim, marked out the corners, commenced his improvements and resided thereon continuously.

McWeeney claims that his "shack" which is shown to be situated on the W. ½ of the NW. ¼, was built in March, 1883, "by his friends;" that he broke fifteen acres in June and built an addition to his house in October, 1883. He asserts that he established his residence on the land April 1, of the same year, and that the same was continuous till October, 1883, when he was arrested and confined in jail. In these statements he is corroborated by his witnesses, who, it should be said, were mostly in the employ of a company interested in the laying out of town sites in the vicinity of the land in dispute. Of this company one P. M. Creel was a member at the time of the trial and previously.

Greene and several of his witnesses, on the other hand, testify that McWeeney never resided on the land previous to July, 1883. Greene swears that the first intimation he had that the tract was claimed by another was about August, 1883, when hauling hay from his claim; he was then notified that McWeeney claimed the tract. It is not shown that notice was brought home to Greene at any time prior thereto.

McWeeney claims, that when he settled on the land, it was his intention to take up the entire NW. ¼, and that he set up stakes at each of the four corners. He said "I had quarter posts stuck up about my claim determined by lines run from township lines run by Lieutenant Creel," meaning the said P. M. Creel.

Creel testifies that in surveying the lands in question and surrounding claims he would stick laths marked with the name of the claimants and the respective corners in the ground at the various corners. He continues—"I don't remember when I stuck the laths on McWeeney's claim, it was some time in the late fall or early winter of 1882. I was with him at the time when the claim was marked. The stakes were stuck in snow and in the ground also. There was snow on the ground. I did not renew the stakes."

Greene testifies that there were not stakes, mounds, or marks of any kind whatever, to indicate that the E. ½ of the NW. ¼ of said section was claimed by another, at the date of his purchase, and when he took possession of his claim. In this statement he is supported by several witnesses.

In your office decision it is stated:

Upon a full consideration of all the facts and circumstances in this case I am led to the conclusion that on the day Greene entered upon made settlement and took possession of the tract in question, April 28, 1883, there was no evidence or indication whatever that the land was claimed by a third party; that said Greene made settlement thereon in good faith and without knowledge of any adverse claim thereto, and that he has ever since fully complied with the pre-emption law, therefore, his is the paramount right. Declaratory statement No. 94, filed by McWeeney is hereby held for cancellation to the extent of the conflict named.

In this conclusion I concur. The finding upon the facts is fully authorized by the evidence. I am convinced that when Greene established his claim to the E. ½ of the said NW. ¼, Sec. 35, settled upon it, built his house and made other improvements thereon, there were no marks on this land indicating that McWeeney's claim included the said eighty acres, or any part of it, nor had Greene otherwise notice that McWeeney's settlement covered the land in question, until August, 1883. An act of settlement upon unsurveyed land must be of such a character and so open and notorious, as to be notice to the public generally of the extent of the claim. Little v. Durant, 3. L. D., 74.

As to the land in conflict, therefore, I must conclude Greene to have been the prior settler.

Your said office decision is affirmed.

PRE-EMPTION ENTRY—SECOND FILING.

PARIS MEADOWS ET AL.

Settlement and filing confer an inchoate right in the land covered thereby which will be protected as against the claims of others who have not an equal or superior right; but until there has been due compliance with the law, payment of the purchase price, and receipt given therefor by the proper officer, there is no vested right acquired under the pre-emption law.

The office of a declaratory statement is to give notice that the settler intends to purchase the land described therein, and such notice, during the statutory period, protects the claim as against subsequent settlers.

A declaratory statement filed with the receiver during the temporary absence of the register, and duly made of record, has the effect of notice as intended by the law, and exhausts the right of filing as provided thereunder.

The right to make a second filing will be recognized where, through no fault or neg-* lect of the pre-emptor, consummation of title was not practicable under the first.

The case of Christian F. Ebinger cited and distinguished.

Secretary Noble to Acting Commissioner Stone, July 2, 1889.

On the 11th of October, 1887, this Department, having under consideration a motion filed in behalf of Paris Meadows for review of departmental decision, dated January 22, 1887, adverse to him, in the matter of his application to make pre-emption filing for the SW. ¼ of SW. ¼ of Sec. 4, the N. ½ of NW. ¼, and the SE. ¼ of NW. ¼ of Sec. 9, T. 6 S., R. 89 W., Glenwood Springs, Colorado, revoked said decision of January 22, 1887, and directed the allowance of the application to file for the tract above described. To this, one John L. Noonan objects, and moves a reconsideration and revocation for reasons which will be made to appear in the succeeding pages of this decision.

The following statement, giving an outline of the history of the case, seems necessary in this connection.

July 14, 1885, Meadows applied to file as a pre-emption claimant for the tract in question. His application was denied by the receiver, on the ground that he had previously exercised his pre-emption right by his declaratory statement, No. 476, filed March 15, 1875, for a tract in Sec. 18, T. 13 S., R. 74 W., Fair Play series, in the same State (Colorado). The reasons assigned by him for not making entry under that filing were that the tract filed for required irrigation ; that he tried in vain to get water on it for the purposes of irrigation, and finding himself unable under these circumstances to support his family on the land he, in July, 1875, abandoned the same. October 3, 1882, he made settlement upon the tract now in question, and has made improvements thereon to the value of $1,000. This was followed by his application, presented at the local office July 14, 1885, as already stated, to file pre-emption declaratory statement for the tract. On August 6th following, Noonan filed a statement, making certain allegations of bad faith against Meadows, in relation to the tract filed upon by him in 1875.

Your office, without entering into a consideration of Noonan's charges, proceeded, under date of September 4, 1885, to dispose of the case by approving the action below rejecting the application of Meadows to file for the tract which he now claims. Said action was based on the inhibition of law which restricted a pre-emption claimant to one filing (Sec. 2261, R. S.).

In reaching the conclusion above indicated, your office, speaking of the first filing of Meadows, which he afterwards abandoned by reason of the character of the land, held it to be the duty of the settler before placing a claim of record to inform himself as to the suitability of the land claimed for the purpose desired, and that his failure to do so can not operate to re-instate him in his pre-emption privilege.

From your said office decision Meadows appealed to the Department, which on January 22, 1887, affirmed the action of your office.

Meadows then moved for review; hence the decision of October 11, 1887, referred to in the opening sentence hereof, a review and revocation of which Noonan now asks.

One of the grounds upon which Meadows urged a review and revocation of departmental decision of January 22, 1887, was that his first filing, viz: that made in 1875, was void, it having been filed with the receiver and not with the register, as the law directs, and that, therefore, not having exhausted his right to make a pre-emption filing, he is qualified and entitled to make the filing which he applied in 1885 to make for the land in question.

The decision of the Department, dated October 11, 1887, revoking its previous decision of January 22, 1887, and directing the allowance of Meadows' application to file, was ruled on the proposition of law presented as above indicated. Said decision held that the filing made by Meadows in 1875 was void, because presented to and accepted by the receiver, instead of the register, of the local land office, and that it was therefore no bar to his (Meadows') second filing.

Now comes Noonan, the intervenor, and asks a reconsideration of said departmental decision of October 11, 1887, and urges that, if the holding of the Department that Meadows' first filing was void for the reason stated was correct, then also is his second application to file void *ab initio*, and incapable of being vitalized and ratified, for the reason that it, like his first application, was presented to and acted upon by the receiver and not the register; that it having been so presented and acted upon, the Department was in error in directing the allowance of the filing "as of the date of its presentation," and it is now too late for him to file, citing Sec. 2264 of the Revised Statutes.

Also that, under the rule laid down in the departmental decision of October 1887, sought to be reviewed, the tender of the declaratory statement to and its rejection by the receiver, when it should have been tendered to and acted upon by the register, furnishes no sufficient basis for the appeal by Meadows, because until the application had been properly presented, viz: to the register, and had been acted upon by that officer, there was no adjudication from which an appeal would lie.

To this, it is replied that, waiving the technical objection that Noonan has not such an interest in the issue being tried as to warrant his recognition as an intervenor, there is a difference between the filing made by Meadows in 1875 and that which he sought to make in 1885, in this, that the first was made with and was accepted by the receiver in the absence of the register, while the second, though presented to and rejected by the receiver, was afterwards acted upon by the register, who joined with the receiver, in a letter transmitting to your office the appeal of Meadows from the rejection of his filing by the receiver.

The contention is, that the action of the receiver in the first case was void, because in the absence of the register he performed an official act belonging exclusively to the register to perform, while in the second case the irregularity, similar in character, was cured by the subsequent action of the register, whose action in signing the letter transmitting the appeal was tantamount to the rejection by him of the application.

The above recital as to the points of contention is made simply as a part of the history of the case, and not because there is necessity for here discussing or passing upon the distinction sought to be drawn.

Recurring to the departmental decision of October 11, 1887, a review of which is asked, I am of the opinion that while the judgment rendered therein, allowing the application of Meadows to file, may have been correct, the reason on which said judgment was based is wrong. The reason assigned by said decision for allowing the filing of Meadows for the tract in question was that the filing made by him in 1875 was absolutely void because presented to and accepted by the receiver in the absence of the register.

A pre-emption declaratory statement is an unsworn statement by a settler on a tract of public land subject to pre-emption, that he has settled and improved said tract, and that he, by said statement, declares his intention to claim said tract as a pre-emption right under Sec. 2259 of the Revised Statutes of the United States. Under the terms of Sec. 2264 of the Revised Statutes he is to file this statement " with the register of the proper district," or as 2265 Revised Statutes puts it, he is

" to *make known* his claim in writing to the register of the proper land office."

Occupation and improvement of the public lands, with a view to pre-emption, do not confer a vested right in the land so occupied, nor does such right become complete under the pre-emption law until the law has been complied with and the purchase money has been paid, and the receipt of the proper land officer given to the purchaser; but, in these cases, settlement and filing confer an inchoate right, which will be protected against the claim of other persons who have not an equal or superior right. Rinehart *v.* Willamette Valley and Cascade Mountain Wagon Road Company (5 L. D., 650); Frisbie *v.* Whitney (9 Wall., 187); Yosemite Valley case (15 Wall., 77).

What then is the office of the declaratory statement? It is a notice given by the settler of his intention to purchase the land described therein, and such notice protects for a limited time his claim against subsequent settlers, by being duly filed in the proper local land office, where it is to be noted on the proper record. Any one thereafter seeking to claim the land is not prohibited from putting a claim of record, but he is notified that he does so subject to the claim of the pre-emption declarant, whose intention has thus been announced.

With this understanding of the purpose and effect of a declaratory statement, it becomes evident that the filing made by Meadows in 1875 in the local office at Fairplay in the temporary absence of the register, was such filing as met the object and purpose of the law, that is, it had the effect of notice as intended by the law.

I do not see how it could have done otherwise. A local land office is an office occupied by two officers. It is the office of the register and also of the receiver. Must any paper, to be properly filed in the office, be handed to the register or the receiver in person, according as it may be for the action of the one or the other? I think not. If the question were answered affirmatively, it would be necessary for an applicant in every case to have identified the officer with whom he might wish to file a paper before he could feel assured that such paper was properly filed. I can not think that the law contemplated any such proceeding. On the other hand, I have no doubt that, when a paper is presented to and received by the register, receiver, or an authorized clerk, and is duly made of record as a declaratory statement, and placed on the proper files, it is then within the meaning of the law filed not only in the office, but with the officer to whom the law directs it, provided the two offices of register and receiver are then filled. To hold otherwise would tend to unsettle titles and give rise to interminable litigation, imposing upon parties, who have in the utmost good faith attempted to fulfill every requirement of the law, great trouble and expense, followed by the loss of claims and homes, which on every principle of right and justice they had reason to think secure. (See Walker *v.* Sewell, 2 L. D., 613.)

It can not be assumed that both the register and the receiver are actually present in their office during every hour of every business day. Temporary absences are necessary for various reasons, but because one or the other of these officers is thus absent, it can not be said that the business of the office must thereby be entirely suspended until his return, or that any paper presented for filing to either may not be received, and that when received and placed on the records it has not been filed where the law contemplated it should be.

In the case of Potter v. United States (107 U. S., 126), the facts showed that not only clerical or ministerial functions but quasi judicial duties as well were for a time performed by a clerk who acted for both the register and receiver, both of these officers being absent.

The facts as stated in that case do not show that said clerk had any direct or expressed authority so far as the receiver was concerned, yet the court held that the securities of said receiver were bound for the monies received during said absence and not properly accounted for.

Had Meadows's filing, made in 1875, been attacked because presented to the receiver at the common office of both the register and receiver, there being no vacancy in either office, I have no doubt the land department would have sustained his said filing.

This case is to be distinguished from that of Christian F. Ebinger (1 L. D., 150), in which it was said that, " the duties of registers and receivers are distinct, and neither can discharge those of the other in the absence of express authority therefor, but the action of each is necessary in their (his) appropriate sphere, to the administration of the office." That case was one in which there was a vacancy in the office of receiver by reason of death.

The rule shut off action by one officer for the other in case of a *vacancy* in either office, but does not apply in its literal sense to a case where both offices are filled.

In such case, where one, as a matter of fact, performs a mere clerical or ministerial act belonging to the other, the law will regard and treat such act as performed by the proper officer through the other acting in his behalf.

This, on the theory that where two constructions can be placed upon an official act, one that it is valid and legal, the other that it is invalid and illegal, that will be preferred which gives it validity, which will preserve rather than destroy, thus following the maxim *"ut res magis valeat quam pereat."*

In the case of Clewell and Marsh (2 L. D., 320), in which Marsh had visited the receiver at his residence some distance from his office and presented an application to enter a particular tract under the homestead law, at the same time tendering the fees, the receiver accepted said application and fees, and the entry was allowed. It will be observed, first, that said application was presented to and accepted by the receiver, while the homestead law (Sec. 2290 R. S.) provides for its presentation to the register; and, second, it was so presented and accepted at a place other than the local office. The Department, while criticising the action of the receiver for taking the application and fees at a place other than that designated for the transaction of official business, raised no objection, because the receiver rather than the register accepted said application, and decided that the entry should be permitted to stand.

If an entry, made under such circumstances, could stand, surely the filing of Meadows made in 1875 in the local office would not be disturbed merely because it was presented to the receiver rather than to the register.

This view of the case has been dwelt upon at some length because, as I am informed, it involves a question of vital importance to many settlers and claimants of public lands.

Finding that the first filing made by Meadows was not ineffective as held in departmental decision of October 11, 1887, it next becomes necessary to inquire and determine whether, on the reasons given and the facts disclosed, his abandonment of his claim under said first filing was justifiable or excusable, and whether therefore his right to make a second filing as asked can properly be recognized.

His showing by his own affidavit corroborated by those of others, is in substance, that the land originally settled upon and filed for by him in 1875 and afterwards abandoned, was at the time of his settlement and filing well supplied with water from springs which then furnished sufficient for domestic use and for irrigating purposes; that said springs in 1875 dried up, and water could no longer be had; that in consequence the land which had theretofore been good agricultural, hay and grazing land, became arid and unfit for agriculture, and such has been its condition ever since; that by reason of said changes, which it was not possible for him to foresee nor guard against, he could not continue his residence there, nor meet the requirements of the pre-emption law as to inhabitancy and cultivation, and consequently through no fault of his he would have been unable to make the proof required upon final entry.

If this showing is in accord with the actual facts, I am of the opinion that Meadows should not be held to have exhausted his pre-emption right by his filing made in 1875, and that he should be allowed a second filing, on the ground that he had used due diligence; that the failure of his first claim was through no laches or fault of his, but was due to causes not growing out of his acts, but which were beyond his control and which rendered the consummation of title in him impracticable.

But the record discloses two applications to intervene in the case by parties, who, as required by rule 102 of Rules of Practice, under oath assert an interest in portions of the tract covered by the filing made by Meadows in 1885. One of these, John L. Noonan, states, in an affidavit filed in this Department September 29, 1887, that he made pre-emption filing May 26, 1885, for a tract embracing one half of the land now claimed by Meadows, to wit: the E. ½ of NW. ¼ of said section 9; and the other, M. E. Morrow, avers, in an affidavit filed April 13, 1888, that he made a filing on May 26, 1885, which embraces forty acres of the tract covered by the filing of Meadows, viz: the NW. ¼ of NW. ¼ of said section 9. It thus appears that Noonan has been in the case as intervenor since 1887, and has constantly been opposing the allowance of Meadows' application to file, and that Morrow has since the departmental decision, now under consideration on review, filed his petition to be allowed to intervene and show that Meadows is not entitled under the pre-emption law to the land covered by his filing of 1885. Affidavits have been filed directly in conflict with those filed by Meadows. They set out, that the land covered by the Meadows filing in 1875 did not and has not become arid, as alleged by him; that he (Meadows) himself resided upon and cultivated said land up to 1882 or '83, and raised grass thereon; that said land has all the time been arable and has all the time had good springs upon it; that by reason of said springs it has been specially valuable as a watering place for cattle; that Meadows sold the improvements thereon and abandoned the claim voluntarily and not from necessity because of the failure of water.

With said affidavit is what appears to be a certificate made by N. R. Pendrey, register of the land office at Leadville, Colorado, setting out the facts that certain settlement claims were filed in 1884 and 1885 for the land covered by Meadows' filing of 1875, and abandoned by him; that one of these claims, a homestead embracing one forty of the old Meadows claim, has been commuted to cash, paid for, and final certificate issued. This would seem to indicate that the land covered by the old filing of Meadows is not arid as he claims it is, or that if for a time arid, it has again become arable.

On these flat contradictions in statements made *ex parte*, I find it impossible to satisfactorily determine the true facts in the case as to the character of the land for which Meadows filed in 1875, and as to the cause of his abandonment of the claim so filed for.

I therefore deem it essential that a hearing be ordered with notice to parties in interest with a view, if possible, of rendering certain what is now extremely uncertain from the record as it exists.

You will direct that a hearing be ordered as indicated, and upon the testimony taken thereat the register and receiver will render their opinion subject to appeal as in other cases. The departmental decision of October 11, 1887 is modified accordingly.

MINING COMPANY—PROOF OF INCORPORATION.

ALTA MILL SITE.   (ON REVIEW.)

Proof furnished by a mining company under a patented entry, and of record in the
General Land Office, showing due compliance with local requirements in the matter of filing its articles of incorporation, may be accepted in proof of such filing
in a subsequent application made by said company.

Secretary Noble to Acting Commissioner Stone, July 2, 1889.

I have considered your office letter of June 8, 1889, referring to the
case of the Alta Mill Site, decided by this Department on appeal February 9, 1889 (8 L. D., 195).

In said decision the Lester Mining Co., was required within sixty
days to furnish proof that articles of incorporation had been filed in the
office of the Secretary of the Territory, and in the office of the recorder
of the county in which said mill site is situated, as required by the local
laws.

With your said office letter of June 8, 1889, you enclose a letter from
the attorney for said company calling attention to the fact that the
proof above specified was on file in your office in the case of the Alta
Lode (patented) and asking that said proof might be accepted as a sufficient compliance with the terms of said departmental decision in that
particular.

And you say, "In view of his statement—borne out by the record in
the case to which he refers, viz., M. E. No. 153, (patented) the Alta
Lode claim—I recommend that the evidence as to the incorporation of
the company claimant already on file in this office, and passed as satisfactory in the case of mineral entry, No. 153, referred to, be accepted
as sufficient for this case."

When the said mill site case was before my predecessor on appeal,
the fact that proof of filing said articles of incorporation in accordance
with the local laws had been shown in connection with the application
of said company for patent for the Alta Lode claim, did not appear in
the record, but it now appearing that such proof is already on file in
your office, I can see no objections to the same being considered in the
mill site case.

The said departmental decision of February 9, 1889, is modified accordingly.

STATUTE—DESERT LAND—REPAYMENT.

ANNIE KNAGGS.

Statutes are repealed by express provisions of a subsequent law, or by necessary implication, and in the latter case there must be such a positive repugnancy between the provisions of the old and new law that they cannot stand together, or be consistently reconciled.

The act of March 3, 1853, fixing the price of public land within railroad limits at two dollars and fifty cents an acre, was not repealed by the desert land act which fixed the price of desert lands at one dollar and twenty five cents per acre.

The right to repayment cannot be recognized in the absence of express statutory authority.

Repayment can not be allowed for the excess over one dollar and twenty five cents per acre paid on a desert entry within railroads limits, though the land was held at single minimum at the date of the initial entry.

Secretary Noble to Acting Commissioner Stone, July 2, 1889.

I have considered the appeal of Annie Knaggs from your office decision of January 28, 1888, declining to recommend the repayment of the purchase money over-paid on Cheyenne, Wyoming final desert land certificate No. 796.

The record shows that Annie Knaggs made desert land entry No. 2803, October 31, 1885, upon lots 1 and 2 and N. $\frac{1}{2}$ of SW. $\frac{1}{4}$ Sec. 14, T. 14 N., R. 67 W. Cheyenne, Wyoming. This tract contains 148.40 acres. At the date of the entry she made a payment of twenty-five cents per acre for said land receiving a duplicate certificate therefor, and the balance of $1. per acre was to be paid when she submitted final proof.

October 7, 1887, Knaggs submitted final proof on said entry, and tendered the local officers the sum of $148.40, being the balance due on said entry at the rate of $1.25 per acre. The receiver declined to accept proof and payment as tendered, in view of a telegram received from your predecessor and which was as follows:—"On final desert entries within railroad limits, where parties paid twenty-five cents per acre, on original entries, collect two dollars and twenty-five cents per acre, so that the total payment will be two dollars and fifty cents per acre."

Knaggs' entry being upon land within railroad limits, the receiver refused to accept final proof unless upon payment of $333.90, being the balance due at the rate of $2.50 per acre. The applicant, therefore, paid under compulsion an excess of $185.50, which she did under protest, as appears from her own affidavit and a letter of the local officers dated March 1, 1888.

November 11, 1887, Annie Knaggs made application for the repayment of the amount over-paid on her final desert land certificate, and on January 28, 1888, your office denied her application.

From this action Knaggs duly appealed to the Department.

In your said decision you state, "that by reason of the claimant hav-

ing made her original entry prior to the issuance of said circular, she
was entitled to pay one dollar per acre when she made final proof.
Although the claimant has over-paid $112.50, it is not in the power of
this office to refund the amount, as the law governing the return of
purchase money does not provide for repayment in a case of this character."

Section 2357 of the Revised Statutes (act of March 3, 1853, 10 Stat.,
244), provides:

The price at which the public lands are offered for sale shall be one dollar and
twenty-five cents an acre; and at every public sale the highest bidder, who makes
payment as provided in the preceding section shall be the purchaser; but no land
shall be sold, either at public or private sale for a less price than one dollar and
twenty-five cents an acre; and all the public lands which are hereafter offered at
public sale according to law and remain unsold at the close of such sales, shall be
subject to be sold at private sale by entry at the land office at one dollar and twenty-
five cents an acre, to be paid at the time of making such entry: *Provided*, That the
price to be paid for alternate reserved lands, along the line of railroads within the
limits granted by any act of Congress, shall be two dollars and fifty cents per acre.

It will be observed that in the above section no distinction is made
as to the class or character of public lands subject to double minimum
price within railroad limits.

The act of March 3, 1877, provides for the sale of desert lands in certain States and Territories (amongst others in the Territory of Wyoming, in which the land in question is situated) to qualified persons upon
their paying twenty-five cents an acre when making entry and a balance of one dollar an acre when submitting final proof.

The act of March 3, 1853, fixing the price of public lands within railroad limits at two dollar and fifty cents an acre, was not repealed by
the act of March 3, 1877, fixing the price of desert lands at one dollar
and twenty-five cents an acre. Congress in the latter act did not refer
to desert lands within the limits of a railroad grant.

Statutes are repealed by express provisions of a subsequent law, or
by necessary implication, and in the latter case there must be such a
positive repugnancy between the provisions of the old and new law
that they can not stand together, or be consistently reconciled. Repeals by implication are not favored in law, and are never allowed but
in cases where inconsistency and repugnancy are plain and unavoidable, and it is a question of construction whether or not an act profess-
ing to repeal, or interfere with the provisions of a former law operates
as a total, or partial, or temporary repeal; and if there are two acts
seemingly repugnant, if there is no clause of repeal in the latter, they
shall, if possible, have such construction that the latter may not be a
repeal of the former by implication. (Potter's Dwarris, 154, and citations.)

Besides, the Department construes the desert land law as fixing the
price of desert land within railroad limits at two dollars and fifty cents
an acre.

Nor does this price seem to be excessive or unjust to the entryman, as the privilege of purchasing an entire section instead of a quarter section, and of having three years within which to pay for the land instead of one year, would seem to compensate for the trouble and expense of conducting water upon the tract for the purpose of reclaiming the same. Neither can Knaggs complain of any want of equity in this matter, as she has only paid the government price for the land.

In Opinions of Attorneys General, Vol. 4, p. 229, it is said:

In reference to cases of error arising out of miscalculations of the amounts to be paid, I have had more difficulty. Money thus paid is never properly in the treasury of the United States. It is paid and received by mutual mistake; and as long as it remains in the hands of the receiving officer, I can perceive no good reason why, upon the discovery of the error, he should not be authorized to correct it. After it has found its way into the treasury, however, like all other money, it should be withdrawn in strict fulfillment of the requirements of the law, which the administrative power of the executive department of the government can not control.

Ibid., 253, it was said:

It will not do for the Department to refund money which has erroneously found its way there, simply on the ground that it is just that it should be repaid, for the reason that it would require the Department to disregard a most wholesome and salutary restraint, upon the due and strict observance of which the most important interests depend.

The power of repayment by the Secretary of the Interior is limited and defined by statutes. The present legislation upon the subject is as follows:

Section 2362 of the Revised Statutes provides, for repayment in cases where a tract of land "has been erroneously sold by the United States and can not be confirmed." The act of June 16, 1880 (21 Stat., 287) provides, that repayment may be made of fees and commissions and excess payments upon the locations of claims under section 2306, where "said claims were after such location found to be fraudulent and void, and the entries or locations made thereon canceled," or where entries are "canceled for conflict, or where from any cause the entry has been erroneously allowed and can not be confirmed," or where double minimum price has been paid for lands afterwards found not to be within the limits of a railroad grant, the excess $1.25 per acre may be returned.

It is clear that appellant's application is not authorized by any of the above provisions, and therefore must be refused.

Your decision is accordingly affirmed.

MORRIS v. SAWIN.

Abandonment should not be presumed from temporary absences where the settler's family remains on the land during such periods of absence.

Children, whether legitimate or otherwise, that remain with the parent, and under his care and protection, are members of his "family."

First Assistant Secretary Chandler to Acting Commissioner Stone, July 2, 1889.

In the case of Lewis Morris v. Sanford M. Sawin, involving the SW. ¼ of section 3, T. 20 S., R. 27 E., Gainesville, Florida, I have considered the appeal of the former from your office decision of April 13, 1888, adverse to him.

Sawin made homestead entry of said tract May.13, 1882, and published notice of his intention to make final proof under section 2301, Revised Statutes, May 13, 1884. Upon the said date proof was duly submitted and it was met by an affidavit of protest filed by J. Heron Foster, and A. Myrtle Foster, charging that Sawin had not made the entry for his own exclusive use and benefit; that he had agreed to deed, after final entry, to Mrs. Foster, the west one-eighth of said land and had also agreed to deed to Mrs. Foster, as trustee for her two boys, about sixty acres of said land being about thirty acres to each; and that the entryman had not established and maintained residence upon the said land as required by the homestead law.

April 2, 1884, Lewis Morris made before a notary public in Putnam county (the land in contest is in Orange county) an affidavit of contest against said entry, charging that the entryman had changed his residence from said land for more than six months since making said entry; and further "deponent says that he has information to the effect and believes that said Sanford M. Sawin did not enter said land wholly on his own behalf and for his own use and benefit."

Said affidavit is corroborated by J. Heron Foster and A. Myrtle Foster.

A hearing was duly had and both parties were present and testified. After considering the testimony the local officers found that the allegations of the contestant were not sustained by the evidence and they recommended that the contest be dismissed and that final or commutation entry of the homestead may be made. Upon appeal, your office by letter dated April 13, 1888, affirmed the action of the local office and held that neither charge had been sustained. From your said decision Morris appealed.

The principal witnesses in support of the contest are Mr. and Mrs. Foster. The latter was married to Sawin in 1864 and became the mother of two sons by him. It was subsequently ascertained that, at the date of said marriage, Sawin's first wife, from whom he had not been divorced and whom he supposed to be dead, was living. He, however, continued to live with the woman called Mrs. Foster and recognized her as his wife. Together they removed from New York to Kansas, made what they termed a contract of divorce and Mrs. Foster went away and lived with Foster taking her children with her, and Sawin again married. In 1881 Foster and the woman called herein Mrs. Foster came to Florida and in response to a letter from the latter Sawin came to Florida. Foster relinquished in favor of Sawin his preference right to enter the land in contest which he had obtained by securing the cancellation of the entry of one Polk therefor. Sawin built a house upon the tract and made entry thereof. His house was about five or six rods from the house of Foster and was occupied by Sawin's two sons. At this time, it is alleged, Sawin made the agreement to convey, after final entry, a portion of the land to Mrs. Foster for her own use and another portion as trustee for her two sons.

Sawin who in Kansas had been a "magnetician" or doctor, soon after his arrival in Florida in his capacity as local preacher united Mr. and Mrs. Foster in marriage, and appeared in a new character as "architect and carpenter" and was also said to be a photographer. The two Fosters seem to have maintained friendly relations with Sawin until about the time he advertised his intention to make proof and from the sundering of such relations, to whatever cause due, the contest no doubt resulted.

Mr. and Mrs. Foster swear positively to the agreement Sawin made to convey portions of the land after the acquisition of title and Sawin swears with equal positiveness that no such agreement was entered into. Under such circumstances in the absence of satisfactory proof of the agreement, I agree with the local and your office, that the charge has not been sustained.

In reference to the charge of abandonment I do not find it proven that Sawin abandoned the tract. He obtained employment as a carpenter and builder at Mt. Dora, three miles from the tract. While so engaged he slept over his shop and returned nearly every Sunday to the homestead. He claims that his absence was due to poverty and the necessity for earning money with which to improve the claim. The testimony shows that he had on the tract at the date of the trial, improvements of the value of $1,500. While Sawin stayed in Mt. Dora his two sons lived on the tract and kept up the cultivation of the land. These sons were, it is alleged, illegitimate, but whether such was their legal status or not, it appears that they adhered to their father, considered him their protector and worked under his direction. On his side he acknowledged them as his sons, gave them fatherly care and counsel and from time to time supplied them with the necessities of life. Both sons lived on the tract until one died; the other continued to reside thereon and was living there at the date of the trial. Under such circumstances, they should be considered as part of Sawin's family and their continuous presence a circumstance indicating the absence of any intent upon his part to abandon the tract. I, therefore, see no sufficient reason for disturbing the conclusion reached by the local office and by your office and the same so far as it relates to the contest is affirmed.

Your office seems not to have passed upon the sufficiency of the proof and no opinion on that point is expressed herein.

PRACTICE—APPLICATION TO CONTEST.

JOHN W. NICHOLSON.

An application to contest an entry, received through the mail and placed of record before office hours, and prior to the opening of the office for business, takes precedence over an application presented on the opening of the office.

First Assistant Secretary Chandler to Acting Commissioner Stone, July 3, 1889.

The appeal of John W. Nicholson from your office decision of February 17, 1888, brings up for determination the question whether the affidavit of contest filed by him or the one filed by William A. Wren, against the homestead entry of David S. Tubbs, for the NW. ¼ of section 2, T. 28 S., R. 35 W., Garden City, Kansas, should be awarded the precedence.

The facts are as follows:

Both affidavits were filed in the local office September 23, 1887; that of Wren was received through the mail having been inclosed in an envelope to which was affixed a special delivery stamp and put in the post-office at Garden City. It was delivered at the local office at Garden City at 8:14 a. m. and was placed of record. Exactly at 9 o'clock of the same day the affidavit of Nicholson was presented at the counter of the register's office. The register held the contest of Nicholson to be subject to the prior contest of Wren. The receiver filed a dissenting opinion holding that the contest of Nicholson should have precedence. Upon appeal your office by letter of February 17, 1888, affirmed the action of the register, whereupon Nicholson appealed.

It appears from the record that Wren and his corroborating witnesses swore to the affidavit of contest September 23. This must have been done at a very early hour as the letter containing said affidavit, was placed in the Garden City post-office in time to be delivered at the local office at 8:14 a. m. From the opinion of the receiver, it appears that both the attorneys for Wren and Nicholson have offices in the building in which the local office is situated; that one waited until the local office was opened, for the transaction of business and immediately presented the affidavit of contest, while the other went to the post-office and forwarded the affidavit of his client by special delivery so that the same would reach the local office before the latter was opened. The receiver states that the practice of giving precedence to papers received through the mail by special delivery over those presented at the office had grown into an abuse. "We have had," he says, "cases in which actual contestants have waited at the door of this office all night to be the first at 9 o'clock the next morning and have only met with utter failure, because an attorney with an office in this very building has employed the mails." The receiver is of opinion that the practice "is certainly not justice," that there is a difference in cases of mail matter from another office, and that "to give attorneys, residing in this city an opportunity to use the mail and fight for priority through the mail, when they can reach this office openly and equally through the doors of this office, is positively to give a premium for their trickery and cunning." "Further," he continues, "in case of letters received by special delivery the postmaster and his clerks are the persons who have it in their power to give priority of filing contest papers and not the register and receiver of this office."

It is not alleged that Wren had knowledge of Nicholson's intention to contest the homestead entry of Tubbs, and had recourse to the mail in order to forestall him. So far as the record shows each party acted in good faith and in ignorance of the other's intention.

The ruling in the case of Sayer *et al. v.* The Hoosac Consolidated Gold and Silver Mining Company (6 C. L. O., 73), cited with approval in the case of Sears *v.* Almy (6 L. D., 1), is, in brief, that while the local officers are not expected or required to transact business out of office hours, yet there is no law of the United States prohibiting them from doing such business, and in case they do, their acts are valid.

The application of Wren to contest, having been received by the register and placed of record before Nicholson presented his application, must, under the ruling cited, be held to have the precedence.

The decision appealed from is, therefore, affirmed.

PRACTICE—REVIEW—PRE-EMPTION PROOF.

CAMPBELL *v.* RICKER.

Where there is conflicting evidence, or where the circumstances are such that fair minds may reasonably draw different conclusions, a review will not be granted.

It is not enough to allege that the weight of evidence does not sustain the judgment; it must be shown that the conclusion is against the palpable preponderance of the evidence.

A pre-emptor who offers final proof in the presence of a valid adverse claim, and fails to show compliance with the law, must submit to an order of cancellation.

Secretary Noble to Acting Commissioner Stone, July 3, 1889.

I have considered the motion for review, filed by the attorney of Enos M. Ricker, asking a review and revocation of departmental decision,

dated September 1, 1888, in the case of Douglas R. Campbell *v.* said
Ricker, affirming the decision of your office, dated January 24, 1887, rejecting his final proof and holding for cancellation his pre-emption declaratory statement, No. 5278, filed in the St. Cloud, Minnesota, land
office, on June 25, 1885, for lots 6, 7 and 8, of Sec. 4, T. 141 N., R. 35 W.

The applicant alleges that said decision is erroneous—

(1) In finding from the testimony that Ricker was only making the tract an occasional and temporary habitation. (2) In holding that the evidence of residence
upon, and improvement of, the land is insufficient. (3) In reciting as a material finding that "the indications are, that he was moved to file upon the land by a conviction
of his own, and that of his father and associates, that it would be a good thing to
secure." (4) In holding, by necessary implication, that a pre-emption claimant is
precluded, by law, from settling upon and perfecting title to land, which, in his
judgment, may prove to be valuable. (5) In not holding that the presumption of
good faith accompanied his act in the premises, and that the burden of proof is upon
contestant, and (6) In not holding that the weight of evidence failed to sustain the
contest.

The record shows that Ricker filed as above stated ; that said Campbell made homestead entry, No. 13,152, of the same land, on July 27,
1885; that, upon the offer of Ricker to make final proof, Campbell
having protested, a hearing was had, testimony was submitted and decision of the local office was rendered, recommending the acceptance of
Ricker's final proof, and the cancellation of Campbell's said entry;
that a rehearing was ordered by your office, on October 13, 1886, "to
determine when Ricker began an actual residence upon the land, and
when and for what period he has been absent therefrom, with a view
to test his bona fides in the matter;" that said rehearing was had on
November 17, 1886, and from the evidence submitted, the local officers
found that Ricker had failed to show due residence upon said land, and
they recommended that his filing be canceled; that your office affirmed
the findings of the local officers, and, on appeal, the Department concurring in the conclusion of your office, made a formal affirmation of
said decision.

The rules of this Department state, that motions for review or reconsideration "will be allowed in accordance with legal principles, applicable to motions for new trials at law." (Rule No. 76, 4 L. D., 46.)

The legal principles, applicable to the granting of new trials at law,
are presumably known to counsel, and need not here be repeated. It
may be observed, however, that where there is conflicting evidence, or
where the circumstances are such that fair minds may reasonably draw
different conclusions, a review will not be granted. Richards *v.* Davis
(1 L. D., 111); Long *v.* Knotts (5 L. D., 150); Neilson *v.* Shaw (5 L. D.,
387); Seitz *v.* Wallace (6 L. D., 299); Mary Campbell (8 L. D., 331);
Creswell Mining Co. *v.* Johnson (ibid., 440).

The first two allegations of error refer to the several findings upon
the weight of the evidence as to the sufficiency of the residence of
Ricker upon said land, and as there was conflicting evidence it is not
shown that the decisions were erroneous.

The third allegation of error is equally without foundation. It is true that the local officers and your office mention that "the indications are that he was moved to file upon the land by a conviction of his own, and that of his father and associates, that it would be a good thing to secure," but this was not given as a reason for the cancellation of the filing. The statement follows the express finding of the local officers, which was quoted in the decision of your office, that "He has, so far as we have been able to gather, no connection with parties desiring to secure this land for the value of the timber thereon." If, therefore, Ricker failed to comply with the requirements of the law, as to residence, then, having offered his final proof in the presence of an adverse claim not shown to be illegal, his filing must necessarily be canceled. Wade v. Meier (6 L. D., 308); Hults v. Leppin (7 L. D., 483).

The record also fails to sustain the fourth and fifth allegations of error. It nowhere appears, either directly or by implication, in my judgment, that the final proof of Ricker was rejected because he settled upon land that might "prove to be valuable." Nor is it stated that the "burden of proof" was not upon the contestant.

It will be observed that the final certificate has not been issued for said land, and although the local officers at the first hearing decided in favor of Ricker, yet, at the second hearing, the decision was adverse to him, and that decision has been affirmed by your office and the Department.

The sixth specification of error, if true, would furnish no ground for review. It is not enough to allege that "the weight of evidence failed to sustain the contest," it must be shown that the conclusion is against the "palpable preponderance of the evidence." Mary Campbell, *supra.* This is not shown in the case at bar, and a careful examination and consideration of the whole record fails to disclose sufficient reasons for disturbing said departmental decision.

The motion is therefore denied.

COMMUTATION—FINAL PROOF—RESIDENCE.

MONTGOMERY *v.* CURL.

Though the submission of final proof during the pendency of proceedings on appeal
    is irregular, such proof may be considered on final disposition of the adverse claim.
Where the good faith of the settler is otherwise sufficiently established, temporary
    absences during any period of the inhabitancy, for the purpose of earning a living,
    not inconsistent with an honest intention to comply with the law, may be ac-
    counted constructive residence.

First Assistant Secretary Chandler to Acting Commissioner Stone, July
5, 1889.

I have considered the case of W. E. Montgomery *v.* Bertie Curl, on appeal of the latter from your office decision of March 27, 1888, holding for cancellation her homestead entry for E. ½, NE. ¼ and E. ½, SE. ¼, Sec. 2, T. 2 S., R. 20 W., Kirwin, Kansas, land district.

It appears from the evidence that the claimant had been partly raised in the family of her husband Mr. Weeks, and that she had on the removal of his family to Kansas, remained in Iowa teaching school and that some months prior to her entry she had written to him that she had saved a little money and would like to get a homestead for herself and asked him to find one for her that when her school closed she might come out and do what might be necessary to secure her a homestead. Weeks ascertained that the party who then claimed the land in controversy would sell his relinquishment and so informed her; she then came on, purchased said relinquishment for $130 and on February 2, 1885, made homestead entry therefor. Immediately after she caused the house hereinafter described to be erected and as soon as finished established her residence therein.

She claims that she was so nearly destitute of means after paying the $130 for the relinquishment that she was compelled to do something to earn money for her support and to pay for her improvements and that in three days after commencing to reside in the house on her land she commenced to work as a clerk or saleswoman in the store of Weeks.

On August 31, she gave notice by publication of her intention to make final proof on October 19, 1885, but protest being filed by Montgomery, September 29, and affidavit of contest being filed by him October 5, the final proof was not presented.

Upon a hearing before the local office, the register and receiver decided in favor of the entry and recommended that the contest be dismissed.

Your office upon appeal reversed that of the local officers and held that from the evidence it was manifest " that claimant never changed her residence from her home in Long Island, and that she is seeking title to said land under a mere pretense of compliance with law."

It appears from the evidence taken at the hearing that immediately after entry, claimant caused to be erected on said land a frame house twelve by fourteen feet, with shingle roof and board floor, which being completed about the last of March, she established her residence therein with stove, bed, and other furniture. She remained there two days and nights at this time and then went to work in the store of Mr. Weeks at the town of Long Island about two miles distant in which she was employed as a clerk.

From this time until June 21, 1885, she continued to work in the store returning to her house on the land one or more times each week, usually remaining over one or two nights at each time, and during the spring she had some ten or twelve acres of the land broken and planted to crops.

On June 21, the claimant was married to Martin Weeks, the merchant in whose store she was employed, but prior to said marriage it was agreed that she should still maintain her residence upon her homestead and that he should remove his residence to her house on said land as soon as he could arrange matters to do so. Accordingly, immediately after the marriage he removed part of his household effects to the land and during the month of July, they both stayed on the land several nights, and were there several times in the day time, besides, but as she was still assisting him in the store, they stayed most of the time in town. In August they both stayed upon the land about as in July, but in September they only stayed two nights on the land, this fact being explained by them as being on account of the removal of the store building from the old town to the new and the doors being sprung so that they could not be shut requiring his presence, while she stayed to help cook for the hands who were at work in the removal and subsequent repairing of the building. ·

The house was lathed and plastered in October and while this was being done claimant remained in town with the family of her brother-in-law, Pillsbury.

It seems to me that it is clear that the claimant established actual residence upon said land after the completion of her house in March, 1885, and that the evidence fails to show an abandonment for six months at any time, nor in fact can I conclude from the evidence that there has been any intention to abandon the land upon her part. The expenditure of $130, by her in the purchase of the relinquishment of former claimant, the erection of a house much better than the ordinary claim shanty, the cultivation of the land, causing a fire break to be plowed and burned around the whole claim, causing a well to be dug and preparation to plaster the house, before notice of contest, all tend to show the opposite of any intent to abandon.

It is true her absences were frequent but it seems to me they were of the character spoken of in Israel Martel (6 L. D., 566) that " where the good faith of the settler is otherwise sufficiently established, temporary absences during any period of the settlement for the purpose of earning a living, not inconsistent with an honest intention to comply with the law, will be accounted constructive residence."

I cannot, therefore, concur in the conclusion of your said decision, " that claimant never changed her residence from her home in Long Island and that she is seeking title to said land under a mere pretence of compliance with the law."

I find with the record final commutation proof of claimant submitted May 16, 1887, and certificate of final payment to the local officers upon such proof.

This action of the local officers was irregular being in violation of rule 53, of practice, which provides that,—

The local officers will thereafter (after appeal) take no further action affecting the disposal of the land in contest until instructed by the Commissioner.

It was held in Marcus J. De Wolf (7 L. D., 175) that cash entries of this character are not void, although improperly allowed by the local office and my decision being in favor of the entryman you may consider said proof if in other respects regular.

Your said office decision is accordingly reversed.

————

FEES ON PRE-EMPTION FINAL PROOF—REPAYMENT.

FRANK W. HULL.

The local officers are not authorized to collect fees for reducing to writing the testimony in pre-emption final proof unless such service is actually performed by them.

There is no statutory authority for the repayment of final proof fees improperly collected and paid into the Treasury.

Secretary Noble to Acting Commissioner Stone, July 6, 1889.

By letter " M " of November 8, 1888, your office transmitted the appeal of Frank W. Hull from your decision, dated October 17, 1888, sustaining the action of the register and receiver at Pueblo, Colorado, in collecting fees for the reduction to writing of the testimony, the work having been performed by a person not in government employ.

Hull gave notice of intention to submit pre-emption proof " before the United States office, at Pueblo, Colorado, on September 13, 1888."

The subsequent proceedings are described by claimant as follows:

He presented himself and witnesses at the local office on the 13th day of September, 188 I, and a clerk was furnished to whom he paid the sum of $4.00 for taking the evidence. He was also charged and made to pay $6.15, being 22½ cents per hundred words written. The $4.00 was a private fee to the clerk who was not an employe of the government. The $6.15 went into the hands of the receiver and has been credited to the United States government for fees in reducing testimony to writing.

Claimant appealed from the action of the local officers in collecting said fee of $6.15.

The local officers in transmitting the case, say:

Pursuant to your letter " A " of January 17, 1888, this office is in the habit of allowing settlers to employ a private clerk to write final proofs but the regular government fee at rate of 22½ cents per hundred words has invariably been collected and accounted for.

The proof appears on its face to have been regularly taken before the local officers.

Your said letter of January 17, 1888, referred to, to the local officers at Pueblo, is as follows:

In my letter of November 4, 1887, to Inspector Hobbs in answer to one through him from the Lamar office, as to the manner of taking final proof, the following was communicated:

" If however, the register and receiver can make any arrangement by which proofs can be written out in their presence and under their supervision and direction by persons, (other than land agents or attorneys for claimants) who are not to be paid by the government, I shall make no objection provided the proofs are properly scrutinized and examined by the local officers before acceptance, and if no abuse or cause of complaint should result from this procedure. The fee provided by law for reducing testimony to writing must be charged in all cases where proofs are taken at the local office."

The government fee referred to in above communication must be collected and accounted for as other fees under act of Congress approved March 3, 1887. The same instructions will apply to your office.

Said act of March 3, 1887, provided:

And hereafter all fees collected by registers and receivers from any source whatever which would increase their salaries beyond three thousand dollars each a year, shall be covered into the Treasury, except only so much as may be necessary to pay the actual cost of clerical services employed exclusively in contested cases; and they shall make report quarterly under oath, of all expenditures for such clerical services with vouchers therefor. (24 Stat., 526).

This was a re-enactment of the provision of the act of August 4, 1886.

Your office, as stated, affirmed the action of the local officers on the ground that it was "in accordance with the decision of this (your) office, 'M', September 15, 1888, in similar cases at the Denver Colorado office. See Copps L. O., Vol. 15, page 145."

Your said letter "M" of September 15, 1888, is as follows:

The following rules should be observed in making final proofs in pre-emption cases:

1. When proofs are made before registers and receivers the testimony must be reduced to writing by them or some one in their employ.

2. The legal fees chargeable therefor will be collected, reported and accounted for to the United States.

3. Testimony must not be reduced to writing by claimant, his attorney, nor by any one in his employ.

As this letter had not been written at the date of the making of proof in this case, the local officers presumably acted under your said instructions of January 17, 1888.

The law on this subject is as follows:—

Section 2237 R. S., allows an annual salary of $500 to every register and receiver.

Section 2238. Registers and receivers in addition to their salaries shall be allowed each the following fees and commissions, namely:

*　　*　　*　　*　　*　　*　　*

Tenth. Registers and receivers are allowed jointly at the rate of fifteen cents per hundred words for testimony *reduced by them to writing* for claimants, in establishing pre-emption and homestead rights.

*　　*　　*　　*　　*　　*

Twelfth. Registers and receivers in California . . . Colorado, . . . are each entitled to collect and receive fifty per centum on the fees and commissions provided for in the first, third, and tenth subdivisions of this section.

Section 2240. The compensation of registers and receivers including salary, fees, and commissions, shall in no case exceed in the aggregate three thousand dollars a year, each.

Subsequently the act of March 3, 1883, (22 Stat., 484) provided:

That the fees allowed registers and receivers for testimony reduced by them to writing for claimants in establishing pre-emption and homestead rights and mineral entries, and in contested cases shall not be considered or taken into account in determining the maximum of compensation of said officers.

Thus the law stood until the enactment of said provision in the act of August 4, 1886, re-enacted in the law of 1887, *supra*.

Substantially the same question presented here was passed upon in the case of Caldwell *v.* Smith (3 L. D., 125) after the passage of the law of 1883. The facts in that case were that,

though the proofs were made before the local officers, the testimony which went to make up such proofs was as a matter of fact prepared and written by claimants or their attorneys. . . . . . The register and receiver at Grand Forks claim that they and similar officers, are legally entitled under the act of March 3, 1883, to fees for all testimony examined by and sworn to before them, whether said testimony has been actually reduced to writing by them or their employees or not.

After a very full consideration of the question in all its phases, it was held (syllabus,) that:

Fees may be collected by the local officers for testimony actually reduced to writing by them or their clerks, but not for that reduced to writing by claimants or attorneys, and examined by them.

On the authority of that case and in view of the plain letter of the law I am of opinion that the local officers were not authorized to collect said fee in this case, inasmuch as the testimony was not "reduced by *them* to writing." They have acted, however, in entire good faith in the matter and were actuated by your said instructions of January 17, 1888, *supra*. They were obliged by the pressure of work, and the limited force at their command to refuse to do the actual work of reducing such testimony to writing. If your instructions still require that such proofs made in towns where local offices are situated must be reduced to writing under the direct supervision of registers and receivers, it might be that local officers would find their only justification in rejecting those proofs reduced to writing by outsiders.

Appellant herein asks for repayment.

The fee received by the local officers has been covered into the Treasury, and was receipted for by the Assistant Treasurer on September 27, 1888. In said case of Caldwell *v.* Smith, *supra*, wherein repayment was directed this element did not enter. "The money . . . . having in due course of business been turned into the Treasury, cannot be withdrawn without authority of law." Elijah M. Dunphy, decided January 22, 1889, (8 L. D. 102). "After it has found its way into the Treasury, however, like all other money, it should be withdrawn in strict fulfillment of the requirements of law, which the administrative power of the executive department of the government cannot control." (4 Op. Atty. Gen'l. 229). "It will not do to say that the department may refund simply because it is just that the money should be repaid or that it is in the hands of the government by mistake or without consideration. The case . . . . . may evince the propriety of some general legislative provision by which the Secretary of the Treasury may be clothed with authority to grant relief in like cases, but it can afford no warrant for the disregard by the Department of a most wholesome and salutary restraint upon the due and strict observance of which, the most important interests depend." (ibid., 253). The statutes of the United States fail to make provision for repayment in a case such as is here presented. Joseph Brown (5 L. D., 316). Repayment is accordingly denied.

Said decision is modified accordingly.

HOMESTEAD AND PRE-EMPTION—CONCURRENT CLAIMS.

MYERS v. McPHERSON.

A person cannot at the same time legally maintain one claim under the pre-emption law and another under the homestead law, for both laws require residence, and one cannot maintain two residences at one and the same time.

A homestead entry, made while the entryman has a pending claim of record under the pre-emption law for another tract, is not necessarily void, for the entryman may have in fact abandoned his pre-emption claim. The inhibition is against one person prosecuting two settlement claims at the same time.

Secretary Noble to Acting Commissioner Stone, July 9, 1889.

On the 20th of December last this Department having before it the appeal of W. M. McPherson in the case of S. A. Myers against said McPherson as administrator of the estate of Thomas McGarvey, deceased, affirmed your office decision of July 10, 1886.

The land involved was the SW ¼ of NW ¼, the SE ¼ of NW ¼ and lot 4 of Sec. 5, and lots 11 and 12 of Sec. 6 T. 21 N., R. 22 E., Hailey, Idaho.

McGarvey had filed pre-emption declaratory statement for said land February 8, 1882, alleging settlement January 25, same year. September 22, 1884, Myers made homestead entry for the same tract. February 2, 1885, McGarvey died.

June 12, 1885, McPherson as administrator of the estate of McGarvey, offered final pre-emption proof. Myers objected to the acceptance of said proof and a hearing was ordered and had.

Upon the evidence taken thereat, the local officers on September 8, 1885, rendered their joint opinion in which they found that McGarvey had by quit-claim deed transferred to Myers all his right, title and interest in and to the land herein described, and the improvements thereon, thereby forfeiting his right to make proof and secure title to the land as a pre-emptor. They therefore refused to approve the final proof submitted by McPherson as administrator of the estate of said McGarvey, deceased.

Your office by its decision of July 10, 1886 concurring in the finding of the local officers, rejected the proof offered by McPherson and held the filing of McGarvey for cancellation. That, as already stated, was the decision affirmed by this Department under date of December 20, 1888.

The 5th specification, ... presents a matter which does not appear to have been considered by your office, nor was it brought to the attention of the Department when the decision on the appeal was rendered. It is averred in the argument on the motion for review that the records of your office show that on January 21, 1882, Socrates A. Myers filed pre-emption declaratory statement No. 309 for the S ¼ of NE ¼ Sec. 5, the SW ¼ of NW ¼ and NW ¼ of SW ¼ Sec. 4 T. 21 R. 22, alleging settlement November 1, 1881, and that on June 9, 1885, he made cash entry, and received final certificate No. 93, for said land. An inspection of the records of your office verifies this statement, and presents a new phase so far as the claim of Myers under his homestead entry of the tract in question is concerned. He made said homestead entry September 22, 1884. At that date he was claiming the tract covered by his pre-emption filing, which was land adjoining his homestead claim on the east. He did not abandon this to make the homestead entry and settlement, but continued to claim it, and, as above stated, made final pre-emption proof, paid for the land and received final certificate June 9, 1885, nearly nine months after making his homestead entry. He was thus prosecuting two claims—a pre-emption and a homestead claim—at the same time, and continued so to do until his pre-emption claim was apparently consummated by final proof, payment for the land and the issuance of final certificate.

It is well settled that a person cannot at the same time legally maintain one claim under the pre-emption law and another under the homestead law, since both laws require residence, and one cannot maintain two residences at one and the same time. On the face of the record, therefore, it would appear that the homestead entry of Myers was illegal when made. Allen v. Curtius (7 L. D., 444); Murphy v. Deshane (6 L. D., 831); Krichbaum v. Perry (5 L. D., 403), and cases cited.

A homestead entry made while the entryman has a pending claim of record under the pre-emption law for another tract, is not necessarily void, for the party making it may in fact have abandoned his claim under his pre-emption filing, in which case he could proceed to consummate his homestead claim. Benj. P. Knaus (8 L. D., 96). The inhibition is against one person prosecuting two settlement claims at the same time. Though, as already indicated the records on their face show that Myers was at the same time asserting and prosecuting a pre-emption and homestead claim, the question as to his right so to do was not raised at the hearing, and he has not been heard on this point.

Since the motion to reconsider the former decision of the Department, and award the land to the administrator of McGarvey must be denied for the reasons given herein, to wit, that McGarvey had prior to his death disqualified himself as a pre-emptor by the sale of his claim,— the claim of Myers becomes one against which there appears no adverse claim, and as between him and the United States he may be heard to show cause why his homestead entry should not be canceled.

The motion for review, filed in behalf of W. M. McPherson, admin-istrator, is accordingly denied and you will direct that a hearing be or-dered citing the homestead claimant S. A. Myers to appear and show cause why his entry should not be canceled for illegality. Should he fail to appear the entry will be canceled. Should he appear and make his showing the evidence offered will be considered and passed upon by the local officers subject to appeal as in other cases.

PRACTICE—APPEAL—REVIEW.

MAISON v. CENTRAL PAC. R. R. CO.

Failure to appeal precludes the consideration on review of questions that should have been presented by way of appeal.

A motion for review should be accompanied by an affidavit showing that it is made in good faith and not for the purpose of delay.

Secretary Noble to Acting Commissioner Stone, July 9, 1889.

John Maison filed a motion for review of departmental decision ren-dered August 13, 1888, in the case of said Maison v. Central Pacific R. R. Co.

Maison applied April 17, 1883, to file soldiers' homestead declaratory statement for the NW. ¼ of Sec. 5, T. 2 S., R. 2 W., San Francisco, Cal-ifornia land district, and thereupon a hearing was had to determine whether said tract was excepted from the grant to the Central Pacific R. R. Co. As a result of that hearing the local officers decided that the west half of said tract was excepted from said grant by the settlement claim of one Joshua H. Proctor, but that the east half was not ex-cepted.

Both parties appealed from that decision to your office where the same was affirmed. The railroad company alone appealed from your office decision to this Department where, on August 13, 1888, said decision was affirmed.

It is thus seen that the only question before this Department was as to the respective claims of these parties to the W. ½ of said NW. ¼ of Sec. 5, T. 2 S., R. 2 W., and that question was decided in favor of Maison the pres-ent applicant for review. He does not allege that there is any error in said departmental decision upon the question there presented, but asks an adjudication on his claim to the east half of said tract of land. In other words, he seeks to accomplish by means of this motion what could properly be done only by way of an appeal. He states that his attor-ney took no appeal from your office decision "because I was unable to pay him up." This statement of the facts in the case shows clearly that the relief sought by Maison can not be secured through a motion for review, and that said motion must be refused. I have thought best to pass upon the merits of this motion, although it is informal in that it is not accompanied by the affidavit prescribed by rule 78 of Rules of Practice, and although the proof of service of notice of the filing is not satisfactory.

Said motion is denied.

PRACTICE—APPLICATION TO CONTEST.

GAGE v. LEMIEUX (ON REVIEW).

It is within the authority and discretion of the Commissioner of the General Land Office to refuse an application to contest an entry, when the validity of said entry is under investigation by said office.

Secretary Noble to Acting Commissioner Stone, July 9, 1889.

The plaintiff in the case of Frank W Gage *v.* Timothy W. Lemieux has filed a motion for review of departmental decision of February 5, 1889 (8 L. D., 139) affirming the decision of your office of October 13, 1887, refusing to accept Gage's application to contest Lemieux's pre-emption cash entry of lots 1, 2, 3, and 4 of Sec. 14, and lots 3 and 4 of Sec. 13, T. 62 N., R. 14 W., Duluth Minnesota land district. This motion is made upon the following grounds:—

1st. Error of law apparent upon the face of the record in that said decision holds that in the absence of an application by him to enter the lands a party applying to contest a pre-emption cash entry sustains no injury by the refusal of the Commissioner of the General Land Office to permit said application to contest to go to a hearing.

2nd. Error in law in affirming the decision of the Commissioner of the General Land Office that the report of a special agent is in the nature of a contest, and that he—the Commissioner—had the right to act upon it in preference to a subsequent application to contest if deemed advisable.

3rd. Error in not finding and holding that under and in accordance with the settled practice and administration of the law by the Department an application to contest an entry is entitled to precedence and preference over the report of a special agent upon which, at the time of filing and presenting the application to contest, no action whatever by the General Land office had been had.

4th. Error in affirming the action of the Commissioner of the General Land Office in this case.

The second and third grounds specified present virtually the same question *i. e.*, as to the authority of your office to refuse an application to contest an entry, the validity of which entry is at the time of such application being investigated in your office. This is too the real and only question in the case.

In the case of Joseph A. Bullen (8 L. D., 301), this same question was presented to and passed upon by this Department. It was there held that such application should not be allowed. This ruling was followed in the cases of George F. Stearns (8 L. D., 573), and United States *v.* Scott Rhea (8 L. D., 578).

After a careful consideration of the question I perceive no reason for establishing a rule different from that laid down in these cases. To allow an application under such circumstances would be to give to the contestant the advantage of the facts disclosed by the efforts of the agents of the government and not by his own diligence. This disposition of this question is decisive of the case and renders unnecessary a consideration of the other questions presented by the motion for review.

With this motion for review Gage filed a number of affidavits and exhibits to show that on November 8, 1887, Sioux half-breed scrip was located on the land in question by James A. Boggs as attorney in fact for Augusta Brown; that on the same day said Brown by her said attorney in fact conveyed the land to Timothy W. Lemieux, and that Lemieux on the same day conveyed undivided interests therein to said Boggs and various other parties. These facts do not affect the disposition of the motion for review, but may properly be taken into consideration by your office in passing upon the validity of said scrip location.

For the reasons herein set forth the motion for review is denied.

ABANDONED MILITARY RESERVATION—FORT LYON.

THOMAS J. YEATES.

The right to acquire lands within the former limits of Fort Lyon reservation, under the pre-emption, homestead, or timber culture law, is confined to persons who had made filings or entries therefor prior to the passage of the act of July 5, 1884.

Lands within said reservation that had not been entered or settled upon, prior to the date of said act, are subject to disposal only in accordance with the terms of said act.

The statutory limitation of February 14, 1853, as to the amount of land that may be withdrawn for a military reservation is applicable only within the territorial limits of Oregon.

Secretary Noble to Acting Commissioner Stone, July 9, 1889.

Thomas J. Yeates has appealed from your office decision of September 9, 1887, rejecting his application [of July 13, 1887,] to make timber culture entry of the S. ½ of the NE. ¼ and lots 1 and 2, of Sec. 4, T. 23 S., R. 47 W., Lamar land district, Colorado.

By executive order of August 8, 1863, a certain described tract in Colorado (in townships 22 and 23 S., ranges 47, 48 and 49 W., embracing about thirty-eight thousand acres), was reserved for military purposes, and thereupon became known as the " Fort Lyon Military Reservation." Its use for military purposes being afterward abandoned, the land embraced therein was surveyed in 1874, and treated as public land thereafter until your office, by letter of March 24, 1882, directed the local officers at Pueblo, Colorado, to reject all filings and entries offered, and to suspend action upon those already made, within the limits of said abandoned Fort Lyon reservation.

From the action of the local officers Yeates appealed to your office, which sustained the local office; thereupon Yeates appeals to the Department—claiming:

(1) The act of July 5, 1884 (23 Stat., 103), "for the disposal of abandoned and useless military reservations," contains a proviso permitting the making of such an entry as that which Yeates applied to make.

(2) That the executive order of August 8, 1863, which reserved said land for military purposes, having withdrawn more than six hundred and forty acres, contrary to the provisions of Sec. 9 of the act of February 14, 1853 (10 Stat., 158) the same is void, and cannot debar settlers from appropriating said lands under the general land laws.

The act referred to contains the following proviso relative to lands within the old Fort Lyon reservation, to wit:

That all patents heretofore issued, and approved State selections covering any lands within the old Fort Lyon military reservation, in the State of Colorado, declared by executive order of August 8, 1863, are hereby confirmed; and the rights of all entrymen and settlers on said reservation to acquire title under the homestead, pre-emption, or timber culture laws are hereby recognized and affirmed to the extent that they would have attached had public lands been settled upon or entered: and *such portions of said reservation as shall not have been entered or settled upon as aforesaid shall be disposed of by the Secretary of the Interior under the provisions of this act,* including lands that may be abandoned by settlers or entrymen.

From the language of the foregoing proviso it is apparent that the right to acquire lands within said reservation under the pre emption, homestead, or timber-culture laws is confined solely to persons who had made filing or entry under such laws (within the limits of said reservation) prior to the passage of said act; and that all lands that had not been entered or settled upon prior to the date of said act are subject to disposal only in accordance with the provisions of said act.

As to the second ground of error alleged, it is sufficient to direct attention to the decision of this Department in the case of Fort Ellis (6 L. D., 46), holding that "the statutory limitations of February 14, 1853, as to the amount of land that may be withdrawn for a military reservation is applicable only within the territorial limits of Oregon. (See syllabus.)

PRACTICE—NOTICE OF CONTEST.

BURKHOLDER *v.* CANFIELD.

The issuance of a new notice of contest, in the absence of an affidavit showing due diligence and inability to serve the prior notice, may be irregular, but will not defeat service thereunder.

First Assistant Secretary Chandler to Acting Commissioner Stone, July 9, 1889.

On July 3, 1880, Lorenzo B. Canfield filed soldier's declaratory statement, alleging settlement the same day upon N½ NW¼, N¼ NE¼ Sec. 30,

T. 6 N., R. 12 W., Bloomington, Nebraska, and on May 26, 1883, he made homestead entry for the tract named.

On September 10, 1885, Noah Burkholder filed an affidavit of contest against said entry alleging that Canfield had "never resided upon the land, but made occasional visits thereto since entry."

On October 26, 1885, the day finally fixed for hearing on said contest at the local office, the claimant (Canfield) by his attorney appeared specially and moved to quash the proof of service of notice for the reason that the original notice had not been returned; that the affidavit of service did not show when the service was made, and that the original notice was returned and a new notice issued without the " necessary affidavit as required by the rules of practice."

This motion was overruled by the local office, and an exception taken by the claimant.

The record contains a copy of the notice dated September 14, 1885. The register's certificate of even date endorsed on said copy, shows that the time of hearing had been changed to October 26, 1885, the date mentioned. The service of notice is shown by the affidavit of S. J. Burkholder dated October 26, 1885, and also endorsed on the copy referred to. Said affidavit states that he personally served a copy of the notice of contest upon the claimant at his residence on September 21, 1885.

The contestant (Burkholder) by affidavit dated the said day of hearing avers that "he inadvertently left the original notice of contest . . . . at his home."

The affidavit provided for by rule twelve of practice to which the claimant undoubtedly refers in his motion to quash, was not so far as the record discloses filed by the claimant. The record, however, shows that the notice of contest was served more than thirty days before the hearing, and that the absence of the original notice was satisfactorily explained. Rule twelve of practice permits the issue of a new notice of hearing when service cannot be had in time for the hearing named in the prior notice, and provides for an affidavit "showing due diligence and inability to serve the notice in time." The issue of the new notice in the absence of such affidavit, while possibly irregular, cannot be permitted to avoid the return as the manifest purpose of the affidavit mentioned is simply to satisfy the local officers that a new notice could properly be issued in the premises.

The motion to quash was properly denied.

* * * * *

PRACTICE—NOTICE TO SUCCESSFUL CONTESTANT.

GEORGE PREMO.

Notice of the preference right of entry given to the attorney of the successful contestant is notice to such contestant, and he is accordingly bound thereby.

An entry may be allowed subject to the preferred right of a successful contestant, and if said contestant fails to exercise his right within thirty days after notice of cancellation such entry will be held good as against the contestant.

First Assistant Secretary Chandler to Acting Commissioner Stone, July 9, 1889.

In the matter of the application of George Premo to make pre-emption filing on the SE¼ of Sec. 17, T. 115 N., R. 54 W., Watertown land district, Dakota, appealed from your decision of October 8, 1887, the record discloses the following facts:

Premo contested a former homestead entry on said tract, and, October 25, 1886, procured its cancellation.

December 16, following, L. D. Deming, who was Premo's attorney in said contest, was notified of said cancellation by the register of the office in which the land is situated.

January 11, 1887, one Patrick Conner entered said tract under the homestead laws.

Premo—as appears from his affidavit—received personally no notice of said cancellation, till February 21, 1887. March 7th following he settled upon said tract, and the day after applied to make pre-emption filing. His application was rejected by the local officers, on the ground that his preference right to enter or file expired January 16, 1887, and because said tract had been entered as aforesaid by Conner.

On appeal from this decision, your office sustains the action of the local officers, and in doing so says:

The rules of practice provide that notice to the attorney is deemed notice to the party in interest. Premo's right to file is held to have been concluded by the failure to submit his application in time and before an adverse claim attached.

This ruling is sustained by the decision of the Department in the case of Thomas Howard (3 L. D., 409), and on full consideration of the question involved no sufficient reason has been discovered for reversing the decision of your office herein, and changing the practice of the Department in cases of this kind. If appellant is not personally to blame for not having received notice of said cancellation in due time, the case presented is one of great hardship, but one which the Department can not remedy. If appellant has sustained injury because of the negligence of his attorney in this matter, reparation must be sought from him.

At the time Conner's entry was made, it was properly allowed, subject to Premo's preference right to enter within the time allowed by statute (Shanley v. Moran, 1 L. D., 162), and Premo having failed to exercise his preference right within thirty days from the time notice of said cancellation was received by his attorney, Conner's entry will remain intact.

The decision of your office, rejecting Premo's application to make preemption filing, is accordingly affirmed.

RAILROAD GRANT—TRANSFER—FINAL PROOF.

ATLANTIC AND PACIFIC R. R. CO. *v.* SANCHEZ.

A decision against one claiming as the grantee of a railroad company will not affect rights of the company, in the absence of notice to it or proof of the alleged transfer.

Where the company asserts a right under its grant it is entitled to special notice on offer to make final proof.

Secretary Noble to Acting Commissioner Stone, July 9, 1889.

The Atlantic and Pacific Railroad Company has appealed from the decision of your office of March 2, 1888, rendered in the case of C. W. Kennedy *v.* Jose Sanchez, of which decision said company was duly notified by your office, and also notified that it would be allowed sixty days to appeal therefrom.

November 17, 1882, Jose Sanchez entered the N.½ NE.¼, the NE.¼ NW.¼, and the SE.¼ NE.¼, all in Sec. 29, T. 13 N., R. 13 W., Santa Fe land district, New Mexico, alleging settlement thereon in 1870.

The described land is within the limits of the congressional land grant to said railroad company, and the line of its road, as appears from said decision, was definitely located March 12, 1872.

January 25, 1883, C. W. Kennedy instituted a contest against said entry, alleging, among other things, that he was owner of the land under a contract of purchase from the Atlantic and Pacific Railroad Company. In March following, a hearing was had in the case, before the register and receiver of the local land office, which resulted in a decision adverse to said contestant, and from which he has not appealed.

No notice of this hearing was given to said railroad company, nor was its appearance entered in said proceeding.

Your office decision finds, "that Mr. Kennedy was a tie contractor of the company, and instituted this contest as the grantee of the company," and holds that these facts show sufficient notice to the company of said contest proceedings.

It is not shown in proof that said Kennedy is appellant's "grantee." In his contest affidavit, he claims the described land "under a contract of purchase" from said company, and the alleged contract even is not introduced in evidence. I am clearly of the opinion that the above stated ruling of your office is erroneous, and that any right appellant may have to the land entered by Sanchez is in no manner affected by said decision.

Since the Atlantic and Pacific Railroad Company has appeared in this case as a claimant for the described land, you are directed to specially notify said company, when Sanchez gives notice of his intention to make final proof. See Southern Pacific R. R. Co. r. Reed, 4 L. D., 256.

The decision of your office is modified accordingly.

———

RAILROAD GRANT—ACT OF JUNE 22, 1874.

FLORIDA RY. AND NAVIGATION CO. r. WILLIAMS.

A selection of indemnity under the act of June 22, 1874, involves an absolute and un. conditional relinquishment of the basis. and the company can not subsequently set up any claim therefor.

Secretary Noble to Acting Commissioner Stone, July 9, 1889.

On July 28, 1883, Isaac Williams entered, under the homestead law, the NE. ¼ of the NE. ¼ of Sec. 33, and the NW. ¼ of the NW. ¼ of Sec. 34, T. 14 S., R. 22 E., Gainesville land district, Florida.

In pursuance of notice duly given, Williams, on September 3, 1887, made final proof in support of his claim before Robert Bullock, clerk of the circuit court at Ocala, Florida, and said proof being found satisfactory to the local land officers, Williams, on October 14 following, commuted his homestead entry to a cash entry, paying for said tract two dollars and a half per acre, and receiving from the register a certificate, which on presentation to the Commissioner of the General Land Office entitles him, *prima facie*, to a patent for the described tract of land.

On March 5, 1888, your office approved said final proof and held said cash entry for confirmation. Upon being notified of this action, the Florida Railway and Navigation Company appealed from said decision.

Said company claims title to the NE. ¼ of the NE. ¼ of said Sec. 33, by virtue of the grant of May 17, 1856 (11 Stat. 15), to the State of Florida to aid in the construction of certain railroads in said State.

The described tract of land is within the primary limits of said grant, and appellant claims that the title of the Florida Railway and Navigation Company, as the successor of the Florida Railroad Company, attached to said tract upon the filing by the latter company of its map of definite location, December 14, 1860; citing Van Wyck v. Knevals (106 U. S., 360), and Atlantic, Gulf & West India Transit R. R. Co. (2 L. D., 561).

And appellant, by its attorney, insists that your office erred:

1. In recognizing that said Williams could acquire any right by his entry of July 28, 1883; and

2. In failing to hold the entry of Williams for cancellation.

It appears that, on April 2, 1876, the company under which appellant claims title—then called the Atlantic, Gulf and West India Transit Company—waived "all claim to so much of the land on each side of the road between Waldo and Tampa Bay (on the line of which road the land in controversy is situated) as may be found by the General Land Department at Washington to be occupied by settlers who may be entitled to equitable relief up to December 13, 1875." And on June 25, 1881, this waiver was extended so as to include "all *bona fide* settlers who made improvements prior to the 16th day of March, 1881." In making this relinquishment the company reserved "the right to select, under the act of June 22, 1874, equal quantities of other land in lieu of tracts embraced in such entries as may be relieved thereby." Atlantic, Gulf & West India Transit R. R. Co. (*supra*), on pages 564 and 565.

The said act of June 22, 1874, provides:

That in the adjustment of all railroad land grants, whether made directly to any railroad company, or to any State for railroad purposes, if any of the lands granted be found in the possession of an actual settler, whose entry or filing has been allowed under the pre-emption or homestead laws of the United States subsequent to the time at which, by the decision of the land office, the right of said road was declared to have attached to such lands, the grantees, upon a proper relinquishment of the lands so entered, or filed for, shall be entitled to select an equal quantity of other lands in lieu thereof from any of the public lands not mineral and within the limits of the grant not otherwise appropriated at the date of selection, to which they shall receive title the same as though originally granted. (18 Stat., 194.)

The records of your office show—as appears from your said office decision—that one Sampson Patterson, on March 3, 1875, made homestead entry for the land in controversy; that the Atlantic, Gulf and West India Transit Company, on March 29, 1882, applied to select the NW. ¼ of the SE. ¼ of Sec. 8, T. 13 S., R. 23 E., under the act of June 22, 1874, in lieu of the tract entered as stated by Patterson; and that said selection is now pending before your office.

Your office holds, "that by such application to select the company lost all claim to the land in question."

Nearly a year after said selection of lieu land was made by said company, to wit, on March 9, 1883, Patterson's entry was canceled, and appellant, in argument, insists that, "It is immaterial that a settler may have been on these lands at the date of the waiver of the company, as said settler thereafter abandoned the same, and the waivers of the company were only in favor of that individual settler, and if he did not take advantage of it, no one else could, and the title of the land therefore remained in the company." Citing Florida Ry. and Navigation Co. *v.* Miller, 3 L. D., 324.

The case cited is distinguished from the present one in that in the case cited no selection of lieu land is shown. In this particular there is a material difference in the two cases. The act under which the company made said selection provides, among other things, that grantees of railroad land grants are only entitled to make such selections "upon a proper relinquishment" of the land entered or filed for. A proper relinquishment implies an absolute relinquishment of all right, title and claim whatsoever to the land constituting the basis for the selection. The selection made by the Atlantic, Gulf and West India Transit Company, in March, 1882, of a tract of land in lieu of the tract in controversy was, in my opinion, an absolute relinquishment of all rightful claim to the latter tract.

In the belief that the land in controversy was public land, the officers of the government having charge of such matters permitted Williams, on July 28, 1883, to enter the same as his homestead. After residing thereon for more than four years with his family, he made proof showing full compliance with the requirements of the homestead law, paid for the land and received his final certificate of purchase, entitling him, *prima facie*, to a patent for said land. The land entered—one half of which is in controversy—together with the improvements thereon, is now worth from $800 to $1,000 and Williams, prior to making proof, had cultivated from fourteen to thirty acres of the same each season for four years. To now refuse him a patent and deprive him of his home would be an act of palpable injustice.

In holding that said company by its selection of a tract of land in lieu of the tract in controversy lost all claim to the latter tract, and in recognizing that Williams has acquired a valid right to the same, no error is perceived; and your said decision is therefore affirmed.

———

RAILROAD LANDS—INDEMNITY SELECTION.

DINWIDDIE *v.* FLORIDA RY. & NAVIGATION CO.

The right of purchase accorded by the act of January 13, 1881, must be exercised within three months after the withdrawn lands are restored to the public domain.

Lands included within pending selections were not restored to the public domain by the revocation of the indemnity withdrawal.

Secretary Noble to Acting Commissioner Stone, July 9, 1889.

The case of Oscar Dinwiddie *v.* The Florida Railway and Navigation Company is before me on appeal by Dinwiddie from the decision of your office, dated March 17, 1888, rejecting his application to purchase under the act of January 13, 1881, (21 Stat., 315,) the SE. ¼ NW. ¼ and NE. ¼ SW. ¼ Sec. 15, T. 29 S., R. 23 E., Gainesville land district, Florida.

It appears from your decision that the described tract of land is within the indemnity limits of the grant of May 17, 1856 (11 Stat., 15), to the State of Florida to aid in the construction of certain railroads in said State; that the aforesaid company claim the benefit of said grant and of a withdrawal made by this Department March 16, 1881, in favor of the Atlantic, Gulf and West India Transit Company; that said withdrawal was revoked by the Department on August 15, 1887 (6 L. D., 92); that prior to said revocation, to wit, on April 5, 1887, the Florida Railway and Navigation Company applied to select the land in controversy, which application was rejected by the local office; that an appeal was taken by the company from said action, and that afterwards, to wit, on November 10, 1887, said selection was admitted by the local land office.

Your office held that said application and selection held said tract in reservation, and consequently that "it is not restored railroad land within the meaning of the act of January 13, 1881 (21 Stat., 315)." This holding appellant assigns as error.

Said application to purchase was made January 9, 1888, nearly five months after said revocation. The act under which appellant asks to be permitted to purchase provides, that his right to do so shall be exercised within three months after the withdrawn land shall be restored to the public domain; therefore, if said revocation of the withdrawal restored the tract in question to the public domain, his right to purchase would be questionable.

No error, however, is found in your decision holding that said tract was not restored to the public domain by said revocation, the same having been, prior thereto, selected by said railroad company.

The decision of your office rejecting said application to purchase is accordingly affirmed.

PRACTICE—NOTICE—ACT OF JUNE 15, 1880.

WATSON v. MORGAN ET AL.

The question of notice is jurisdictional and may be raised at any time, and when raised the Department is bound to take cognizance thereof.

In the absence of legal notice to the defendant the local office is without jurisdiction.

Service of notice by publication is not warranted in the absence of an order therefor based on showing of due diligence and inability to secure personal service.

In the service of notice by publication sending a copy by registered letter and posting are essentials without which notice is incomplete.

Rights acquired by a purchase under section 2, act of June 15, 1880, that became vested prior to the decision in Freise v. Hobson are not affected by the change of ruling announced therein.

First Assistant Secretary Chandler to Acting Commissioner Stone, July 9, 1889.

I have considered the appeal of D. M. Tiffany, transferee of William H. Morgan, from your office decision of January 13, 1888, holding for cancellation the homestead entry of said William H. Morgan, No. 2,009, upon the NW. ¼, Sec. 18, T. 102 N., R. 59 W., P. M., Springfield, now Mitchell, Dakota.

The record shows that Morgan made homestead entry of above tract

June 20, 1879, and that on October 19, 1880, George Watson initiated contest against the same, alleging that he (Morgan) "has wholly abandoned said tract and changed his residence therefrom for more than six months since making said entry and next prior to the date herein; that said tract is not settled upon and cultivated by said party as required by law."

Upon the foregoing affidavit, notice was served upon Morgan by publication, and the hearing was set down for the 18th of December following. This notice was signed by the local officers, and dated October 18, 1880, one day before the affidavit of contest was verified.

It may be well to observe in this connection, that it does not appear from any affidavit of contestant or of any one else that personal service could not be made upon Morgan; nor is it alleged, either in the affidavit of contest, or in any other affidavit filed herein, that due diligence was exercised to make personal service upon Morgan, or that he was not a resident of the Territory. Neither does it appear that the local officers ever made an order authorizing service of the notice by publication. The allegation, therefore, in your office decision that "upon due proof of inability to make personal service upon claimant notice was given by publication," is not sustained by the record. No such proof is found among the papers filed herein. The affidavit of contest is the ordinary one, and it does not appear that the slightest effort was ever made to make personal service of the notice of contest upon Morgan.

On the day set for hearing contestant and his witnesses appeared. The defendant, however, did not appear at the hearing, either in person or by attorney.

Upon the testimony submitted the local officers, on March 10, 1881, found, "that the above named claimant has failed to comply with the requirements of the homestead law, and so therefore adjudge said homestead entry forfeited to the United States."

Notice of this decision and of the time allowed for an appeal therefrom was served by publication for five consecutive weeks. No appeal was, however, taken from said decision.

March 1, 1882, Morgan made application to purchase said land under the act of June 15, 1880, and on the 29th of that month your office allowed his application. Accordingly, on May 3, 1882, Morgan made cash entry of the tract in question. On the 29th of that month, he, in consideration of the sum of five hundred dollars, conveyed said land to D. M. Tiffany, the present appellant.

Your office dismissed Watson's contest on November 14, 1882. January 22, 1885, your predecessor called upon the local officers for report as to whether Watson had been duly notified of said decision of November 14, 1882.

On February 3, 1885, the register reported that there was no evidence that notice had been served on Watson, and that he had on that day notified him of said decision and of his right of appeal.

March 2, 1885, Watson filed an appeal, with notice to Morgan. The latter filed a motion to dismiss said appeal, upon the ground that Watson failed to appeal from the decision of March 29, 1882, allowing Morgan's application to purchase, and that he also failed to appeal from the decision of November 14, 1882, dismissing his contest. He, at the same time, filed a number of affidavits, setting forth that Watson was notified of the decision dismissing his contest, and that he admitted he received notice thereof, and that he said he would not appeal.

Watson filed counter affidavits, and on September 25, 1886, the case having been forwarded to the Department, a hearing was ordered " to determine whether Watson had notice of the decision adverse to him."

A hearing was accordingly had, at which both parties appeared in person and by their attorneys.

December 15, 1886, the register found that "no attempt is made by Morgan to show that personal service of notice of said decision was made upon Watson, or that notice was sent him by registered letter." The receiver endorsed the above decision as follows: " I concur with the opinion of the register as a means of arriving at a solution of the question at issue, but in so doing desire to state that the testimony before me throws no additional light upon the subject."

From this decision Morgan duly appealed, and on January 13, 1888, your office rendered a decision : " No appeal was taken from your decision of March 10, 1881, adjudging his entry forfeited ; therefore said decision has become final as to the facts. No reason for disturbing said decision appearing, the same is affirmed, and homestead entry No. 2,009 is hereby held for cancellation." From this decision Morgan appealed to the Department.

Your said decision is therefore based upon the validity of the decision rendered by the local officers.

Morgan, in support of his motion to dismiss Watson's appeal, submitted the affidavit of William Letcher, who was register of the land office at Mitchell, Dakota, at the time Watson's contest was dismissed. In this affidavit Letcher states, that on receipt of your letter of November 14, 1882, or very soon thereafter, he notified George Watson of the dismissal of his said contest and of his right of appeal, " by sending him a written notice directed to him at Mitchell, Dakota, that being his post-office address." The Rules of Practice did not then require that notice should be sent by registered letter. Neither was personal service necessary.

Morgan also submitted the affidavit of George S. Bidwell, who acted as his (Morgan's) attorney in making cash entry of the tract in question. In this affidavit Bidwell states that soon after the receipt of your office letter of November 14, 1882, he asked the said Letcher to notify Watson of your dismissal of his contest, and that he (Letcher) replied that he had notified Watson by sending him a written notice to Mitchell, Dakota, his post-office address. He also stated that in 1883, he remarked to Watson that he did not appeal from the decision dismissing his contest, and that Watson replied " there was no use of appealing, that Tiffany had the land." He further stated that about the same time he had a conversation with Watson's attorney, and that the latter said, " he ought to have appealed the Watson case; that it was too late now, but if he had, Watson would have got the land."

At the hearing Bidwell reiterated the statements already referred to. Watson and his attorney, however, denied that notice of the dismissal of the contest was ever served upon either of them, and further denied the conversation mentioned by Bidwell. These were the only witnesses who testified at the hearing as to " whether Watson had notice of the decisions adverse to him."

Moreover, Watson's attorney resided in Mitchell, where the local office is located. Watson lived within one half mile of the tract in dispute. He called every month upon his attorney in reference to this contest; was in Mitchell two or three times a week, and was informed by O. T. Letcher, chief clerk of the land office, that Morgan was allowed to purchase under the act of June 15, 1880, and that he should appeal.

Morgan's purchase was made in conformity with the action of your office of March 29, 1882. According to the rulings and decisions of the Department then in force, a homestead claimant, whose entry was being contested, could, under the act of June 15, 1880, purchase the tract entered, and thus prevent any right of the contestant from attaching. Gohrman v. Ford, 8 C. L. O., 6; Whitney v. Maxwell, 10 id., 104; Bykerk v. Oldemeyer, 2 L. D., 51; Simpson v. Foley, 4 L. D., 21.

As already stated, Morgan purchased the tract in accordance with the decisions of the Department then in force, and Tiffany, relying upon these rulings and believing that Morgan's title to the land was valid, .. purchased the tract from Morgan. It is not denied that the action of your predecessor in allowing Morgan's cash entry under the rule laid down in the cases above cited was legal. Neither is it contended that his action in dismissing Watson's contest was not correct under the rule above referred to. Had Watson been duly notified of the dismissal of his contest, an appeal therefrom would have been of no avail under the laws then governing such cases. A failure to thus notify him would be the fault of the trusted officers of the government, and their mistakes or omissions should not operate to defeat Morgan's rights or those of his grantee, who had purchased in good faith and for a valuable consideration. Lytle v. Arkansas, 9 How. 154.

In the case of Hollants v. Sullivan, decided on August 31, 1886 (5 L. D., 115) the Department held:

Under the rulings and decisions of the Department, in force at that time, Sullivan had a right at any time pending the contest to purchase under the provisions of section two of the act of June 15, 1880, and thus, as against the contestant, as well as against the rest of the world, could secure title to the tract in question. This interpretation has recently been changed in the case of Freise v. Hobson (4 L. D., 580), but such change does not affect rights which were acquired and which, as in this case, became vested under previous rulings and decisions.

At the time of Morgan's purchase, Watson's contest may be regarded as still pending, the decision of the local officers not being final, except as to the facts in the case, and the Commissioner having the authority to reverse or modify that decision, even though there was a failure to appeal from the same.

Rule 10 of Practice then in force provides: "Personal service shall be made in all cases when possible, if the party to be served is a resident in the State or Territory in which the land is situated, and shall consist in the delivery of a copy of the notice to each person to be served."

Rule 12 of Practice then in force provides: "Notice may be given by publication alone only when it is shown by affidavit of the contestant, and by such other evidence as the register and receiver may require, that personal service can not be made." (2 C. L. L., 194.)

There is no affidavit of contestant that personal service could not be had upon Morgan, or that due diligence had been exercised to so serve him, or that Morgan was not a resident of the Territory. Neither does it appear that an order had been made by the local officers, directing service of notice by publication.

In the case of Ryan v. Stadler (2 L. D., 50), the Department held that the affidavit upon which publication is authorized must show diligence in the matter of attempting to procure personal service, and that an allegation to the effect that the whereabouts of the defendant is unknown did not warrant publication of notice.

The same doctrine is held in the case of Hewlett v. Darby, 9 C. L. O., 230; England v. Libby, 11 id., 2; Sweeten v. Stevenson, 3 L. D., 249; Jackson v. McKeever, Ibid., 516; Thorpe et al. v. McWilliams, Ibid., 341; Winans v. Mills et al., 4 L. D., 254; Shinnes v. Bates, 4 L. D., 424; Bone v. Dickerson's heirs, 8 L. D., 452, and Stayton v. Carroll, 7 L. D., 198.

In the latter case it was said: "It has been repeatedly held by this Department, that jurisdiction is acquired by the due service of notice upon the claimant, and if there has been no legal notice to the claimant, then there is no authority in the local office to adjudicate his rights."

From the foregoing, it is apparent that the publication of notice in this case was irregular and not sufficient to confer jurisdiction upon the local office to hear and determine the issues presented by the contestant.

Rule 14 of the Rules of Practice, in force at the time this contest was initiated, provided:

Where notice is given by publication, a copy of the notice shall be mailed by registered letter to the last known address of each person to be notified, and a like copy shall be posted in a conspicuous place on the land during the period of publication, for at least two weeks prior to the day set for hearing.

There is nothing in the record to show that either of these requirements has been complied with. There is no affidavit or certificate, showing that a copy of the notice of contest was posted upon the land, neither is there any receipt or other evidence that a copy of said notice was mailed by registered letter to Morgan's last known address.

The appeal filed by D. M. Tiffany, transferee of William H. Morgan, attacks the legality of the contest proceedings, and alleges that legal notice was not given. Hence, it is proper to inquire whether the rules and regulations of the Department in this respect have been complied with.

In the case of Kelly *v.* Grameng (5 L. D., 611), it is held that "notice by publication includes the posting of notice upon the land in contest, and if such posting is omitted, the notice is incomplete."

In the case of Parker *v.* Castle (4 L. D., 84), it is held that the sending of a copy by registered letter and the posting of a copy on the land are essential parts of a notice by publication.

In the case of Kelly *v.* Grameng (*supra*), it was held that, if such posting is omitted, the notice is incomplete, and jurisdiction is not acquired. It was further held in that case, that the record must show affirmatively all matters of notice requisite to confer jurisdiction.

For the foregoing reasons the land office was without jurisdiction to decide the case on the testimony submitted, it not appearing from the record that due and legal notice had been given. The decision, therefore, of the local officers was invalid, and could not deprive the entryman of any rights he might have in the tract in question.

Nor can it be claimed that Morgan waived any rights by reason of his failure to raise the question of the jurisdiction of the local officers sooner. As already stated, he did not appear at the hearing, and it was only last October that his attorney, after an examination of the record in your office, first discovered the character of Watson's affidavit of contest, and the facts connected therewith, and already referred to. Moreover, this question being a jurisdictional one, could be raised at any time, and, when raised, the Department is bound to take cognizance of it.

Apart from the legal aspect of the case, the equities are also on the side of Morgan and his transferee. He purchased the tract in question on May 3, 1882, more than seven years ago. This purchase was in compliance with the instructions of your office and in accordance with the rules and regulations of the Department then in force. Tiffany had every reason to believe that Morgan's purchase was legal and that the transfer to him was equally valid. Tiffany has resided upon the land for the past seven years and has no doubt valuable improvements thereon. Watson's only outlay was the expense incident to the contest, and if he had not actual or constructive notice, he had at least actual knowledge of the decisions of your office in favor of Morgan.

For the foregoing reasons, I am of the opinion that the cash entry of William H. Morgan should remain intact, and that the contest of George Watson should be dismissed.

The decision of your office is accordingly reversed.

PRACTICE—REVIEW—PRE-EMPTION FINAL PROOF.

HOFFMAN v. HINDMAN.

A review will not be granted on the general allegation that the decision is not supported by the evidence.

A pre-emptor who submits final proof in the presence of an adverse claim is not precluded from making supplemental proof where the adverse claim fails for want of good faith.

Secretary Noble to Acting Commissioner Stone, July 9, 1889.

I have considered the motion for review filed by the attorney of Thomas E. Hoffman, asking a revocation of the decision of the Department in the case of said Hoffman v. Oscar R. Hindman, rendered August 2, 1888 (unreported), canceling Hoffman's pre-emption declaratory statement No. 6073, filed in the La Grande land office, Oregon, on September 25, 1884, for the N. $\frac{1}{2}$ of the NW. $\frac{1}{4}$ and SW. $\frac{1}{4}$ of the NW. $\frac{1}{4}$ of Sec. 3, T. 11 S., R. 42 E., and the SW. $\frac{1}{4}$ of the SW. $\frac{1}{4}$ of Sec. 34, T. 10 S., same range.

Said departmental decision canceled said filing, because it was made for another person, and said Hindman was permitted to make supplemental proof showing compliance with the pre-emption law, within sixty days from due notice thereof.

The record shows that two hearings have been had in the case. At the first hearing the local officers decided in favor of Hoffman, but your office dismissed the proceeding, because neither party had advertised to make final proof. Subsequently, Hindman offered his final proof, and upon the protest of Hoffman, a hearing was held at which both parties were present and submitted a large amount of contradictory testimony. From the evidence offered before them, the local officers found that Hindman was the prior settler, that his final proof should be accepted and final certificate should issue for the land.

On appeal, your office reversed the decision of the local officers, and decided that Hoffman " was the prior legal settler," and that the land should be awarded to him subject to his future compliance with law. Both filings were allowed to stand. On appeal the Department, after reciting the evidence at some length relative to the priority of settlement, and without expressly ruling thereon, considered the question whether Hoffman had acted in good faith in the premises. The facts relative to the ownership of the improvements upon said land and the status of the tract, as shown by the filings and a desert entry, were set out at length, and, from the evidence it was found that Hoffman filed his declaratory statement in the interest of one Low, and that he had not acted in good faith. His filing was therefore directed to be canceled.

The errors assigned in said motion are:

(1) In finding that Hindman was the prior settler.

(2) In finding that " there is a particle of testimony showing that one Low had anything to do with Hoffman's entry."

(3) In finding that Hoffman's filing was not made in good faith.

(4) In holding that, because Hoffman elected to make proof in the presence of an adverse claim, he must abide the result, and in not applying the same rule to Hindman.

(5) In holding that Hoffman's filing is invalid.

(6) In holding that the question was simply between Hindman and the government.

(7) In not ordering a rehearing of the case in order to bring out the facts more clearly.

In support of said motion was filed the affidavit of Hoffman, corroborated by two witnesses, alleging that he is still on the land, and that he has never sold or contracted to sell said land to Leonard Low, or to any other person whatever. This denial of Hoffman is but a repetition of his statement at the trial, and is, at best, but cumulative. It, therefore, furnishes no good basis for a revocation of said decision. Besides, the Department did not pass upon the question which would have been the prior settler, provided both parties had acted in good faith, but, having found that Hoffman was only the agent of another and not acting for himself, it necessarily followed that Hindman, if a settler at all, was the prior legal settler.

The assertion of counsel, in the second assignment of error, that there was not a particle of testimony showing that Low had anything to do with Hoffman's filing, is not sustained by the record.

Counsel has not filed a brief pointing out specifically wherein the statement in said departmental decision of the evidence relative to Hoffman's filing is incorrect.

It is not enough for counsel to make sweeping assertions that there is no evidence warranting a conclusion arrived at in the decision sought to be revoked. He must go further and state what the evidence is upon the question, and show that the finding of the Department is against the "palpable preponderance" of the evidence. Such showing Hoffman has not made, and the 1st, 2d, 3d and 5th assignments of error are not well taken. Nor can the contention of counsel, as set forth in the 4th and 6th assignments of error, be maintained.

Having shown that the filing of Hoffman was invalid, then the case is simply between the government and the entryman. If one of two claimants has acted in good faith and shown compliance with the requirements of the law, and his entry would be sustained but for the prior applicant who seeks to make final proof in support of his claim and he fails, then in such a case the one seeking to make proof must submit to a cancellation of his claim. But this ruling has no application to a case where it is shown that one of the claimants has not acted in good faith. This, every applicant must show before he can acquire title to any portion of the public domain. Dayton v. Hause et al. (4 L. D., 263).

In the case at bar, no sufficient showing is made for disturbing said departmental decision, and the motion is accordingly overruled.

MINING CLAIM—TOWNSITE—PATENT.

THOMAS J. LANEY.

Under a mineral application for land partly included within a prior townsite patent the claim must be restricted to the land not in conflict.

The proof in such a case must show the discovery of mineral within the limits of the new survey and the requisite expenditure on the claim as thus defined.

In the absence of an allegation or offer to prove that the land in conflict was of known mineral character prior to the issuance of the townsite patent, the record will not justify proceedings against said patent, or adverse to rights claimed thereunder; but on due showing a hearing may be ordered to determine whether suit to vacate the patent should be advised.

The issuance of patent terminates the jurisdiction of the Department over the land covered thereby, and such patent can be invalidated by judicial proceedings only.

A subsequent discovery of mineral can not affect the title as it passed at the time of sale.

First Assistant Secretary Chandler to Acting Commissioner Stone, July 9,
1889.

I have considered the appeal of Thomas J. Laney from the decision of your office, dated June 29, 1887, requiring that an amended survey be made of his Centennial No. 2 Lode and Mill-site claim, Central City Colorado, and additional evidence furnished relative to the discovery of mineral and the value of the improvements made upon or for the benefit of said claim.

The record shows that on June 4, 1885, said Laney made mineral entry, No. 2864, for the Centennial No. 2 Lode and Mill-site claim, lots 2168 A and B; that the lode claim embraces fifteen hundred linear feet and about eleven hundred and twenty-five feet of the same is embraced in the town-site of Georgetown, which was entered at the local land office on January 7, 1874, and patented April 15, 1875. The location upon which said mineral entry is based was made January 17, 1885. It embraces 1.16 acres and excludes the surface ground in conflict with the patent for said town-site.

Your office found that there was no evidence in the case showing that the vein or lode, for which patent is sought, was known to exist prior to the entry of the town-site nor that the land covered by said lot 2168 A, was known to be mineral at the date of said entry. Your office, therefore, held that the claimant could not obtain any rights, by virtue of said location, within the limits of said town-site, and that, before any patent could issue upon said entry, the survey thereof must be so amended as to include only that portion lying outside of the limits of said town-site, and that the claimant must duly show the discovery of mineral upon the ground embraced in the new survey and furnish due proof of the requisite amount of improvements upon or for the benefit of said claim.

The appellant insists that your office erred in said decision, in not allowing him to prove that said lode was known to exist prior to the issuance of patent to said town-site, and that his entry should be passed to patent because the town-site law contemplates a separate ownership of the surface and of the mineral deposits.

The contention of appellant can not be maintained for the reason (1) That there was no allegation made by the applicant that the lands embraced in said townsite were known to be mineral prior to entry and issuance of patent to the townsite, and there was no offer to make proof relative thereto prior to said decision of your office, and (2) That with the issuance of patent all jurisdiction over the land embraced therein ceased so long as the patent remained outstanding. United States *v.* Stone (2 Wall., 525); Moore *v.* Robbins (96 U. S., 530); United States *v.* Schurz (102 U. S., 378); Thorp Williams *et al.* (2 L. D., 114); Wisconsin Central R. R. Co. *v.* Stinka (4 L. D., 344); Garriques *v.* Atchison, Topeka and Santa Fe R. R. Co. (6 L. D., 543). The townsite patent upon its face purports to convey the legal title to the land covered thereby, and any attempt to invalidate it must be made in the proper forum. The legislation relative to townsite and mineral claims was fully considered by the United States Supreme Court in the case of Deffeback *v.* Hawke (115 U. S., 392) wherein the Court said:

It is plain from this brief statement of the legislation of Congress that no title from the United States to land known at the time of sale to be valuable for its minerals of gold, silver, cinnabar, or copper can be obtained under the pre-emption or homestead laws or the townsite laws, or in any other way than as prescribed by the laws specially authorizing the sale of such lands. . . . . We say "land known at the time to be *valuable* for its minerals" as there are vast tracts of public land in which minerals of different kinds are found, but not in such quantities as to justify expenditures in the effort to extract them. It is not to such lands that the term mineral in the sense of the statute is applicable. . . We also thus say lands *known at the time of their sale* to be valuable in order to avoid any possible conclusion against the validity of titles which may be issued for other kinds of land, in which, years afterwards, rich deposits of mineral may be discovered. It is quite possible that lands settled upon as suitable only for agricultural purposes entered by the settler and patented by the government under the pre-emption laws, may be found, years after the patent has been issued, to contain valuable minerals. Indeed, this has often happened. We therefore use the term 'known to be valuable at the time of sale,' to prevent any doubt being cast upon titles to land afterward found to be different in their character from what was supposed when the entry of them was made and the patent issued.

The case of Deffeback *v.* Hawke (*supra*) was quoted in the case of the Colorado Coal Company *v.* United States (123 U. S., 327), and the Court added:

A change in the condition occurring subsequently to the sale, whereby new discoveries are made, or by means whereof it may become profitable to work the veins as mines, can not affect the title as it passed at the time of sale. The question must be determined according to the facts in existence at the time of the sale.

Upon the record as presented, the conclusion of your office is unquestionably correct. If, however, a sufficient showing shall be made that the land was known to be valuable at the date of the townsite entry and issuance of patent thereon, proceedings should be instituted with a view to the recommendation that suit be duly instituted to declare the townsite patent inoperative as to the portion of land proven to have been known to be valuable for mineral at the time of the entry and issuance of patent. You will therefore advise said applicant that he will be allowed to apply for a hearing to prove the allegations made in his appeal "that this particular mine was known to exist prior to the entry of the townsite patent." Said application should be under oath, and corroborated by at least two witnesses, and should set out fully and specifically all of the facts upon which applicant relies to establish his said allegations. If said application be made within thirty days from notice hereof, your office will consider the same, and if deemed sufficient a hearing will be ordered in accordance with the rules of practice. In case no application for a hearing is made within the time required, the decision appealed from will be affirmed.

The decision of your office is modified accordingly.

PRE-EMPTION—SECOND FILING.

James B. Boone.

A second filing is permissible where the pre-emptor was, by armed violence, driven off the land covered by the first, and compelled to abandon the same.

First Assistant Secretary Chandler to Acting Commissioner Stone, July 10, 1889.

I have considered the case of James B. Boone, from your office decision of December 10, 1887, rejecting his application to make a pre-emption filing for NW. $\frac{1}{4}$, NE. $\frac{1}{4}$, S. $\frac{1}{2}$, NE. $\frac{1}{4}$ and NW. $\frac{1}{4}$, SE. $\frac{1}{4}$, Section 28, T. 30 S., R. 68 W., Pueblo, Colorado, land district.

Boone filed with his said application an affidavit stating substantially that he is a qualified pre-emptor as to age and citizenship and he is the head of a family. That in the year 1858 he filed upon one hundred and sixty acres of land in the then Territory of Nebraska, the description of said tract he has forgotten. That he was driven off his said land by border ruffians and desperadoes who then infested that country and there were no courts to give him protection. That to have remained upon said land would have endangered his life.

This affidavit is not corroborated but applicant says that on account of the great lapse of time and his change of residence he has not now knowledge of any person by whom he can corroborate the same.

The local officers in their letter transmitting his application state that the land applied for is vacant public land.

You say in your said office decision, after reciting the above facts as set forth in Boone's affidavit, " Under the restriction of Sec. 2261, Revised Statutes, limiting the settler to one legal filing, this application is denied."

While Sec. 2261, prohibits a second filing under the pre-emption law, the said section never contemplated that when a settler was driven off the land upon which he had filed by violence, or the public enemy, in a locality where for the time being the government was powerless to protect the settler, he should lose his pre-emption right.

It is a matter of history that at about the time stated in the affidavit a considerable portion of the Territory of Nebraska was terrorized by desperadoes and that for a time the civil authorities were powerless to maintain order.

An exception to the general rule has always been allowed in cases where the first filing failed through no fault of the pre-emptor. Hannah M. Brown, 4 L. D., 9.

Your said decision is accordingly reversed.

TIMBER CULTURE ENTRY—FINAL PROOF.

INSTRUCTIONS.

In computing the period of cultivation required in timber culture final proof, the rule should govern which was in force at the time the entry was made.

In entries made under the ruling that prevailed prior to the circular of June 27, 1887, the time allowed by the statute for the preparation of the land and planting of the trees may be computed as a part of the eight years of cultivation required by the statute; but under entries made after the change of ruling, as announced in said circular, the period of cultivation should be computed from the time when the full acreage of trees, seeds, or cuttings was planted.

The case of Henry Hooper, modified.

Secretary Noble to Acting Commissioner Stone, July 16, 1889.

In reply to yours of the 10th instant suggesting a change of rule in timber culture cases I herewith transmit to you a copy of an opinion of the First Assistant Secretary, which I have examined and approved, whereby it will appear to you that no change of the rule is necessary. The rule requires that the eight years of cultivation must be computed from the time the required acreage of trees, seeds or cuttings are planted. But if the entry was made under rulings of the Department in force when the application was made that ruling should be allowed to stand and control the case. Until a rule is changed it has all the force of law, and acts done under it while it is in force must be regarded as legal. It will thus appear that the hardships complained of by you are avoided by the construction of the rule formerly existing, or are rather to be attributed to the statute itself, over which this Department has no control. It is desirable to be liberal, as I have often instructed you, in all these matters pertaining to the Land Office; but this must not go to the extent of disobeying the statute.

Mr. SECRETARY : I have had occasion to give this timber-culture act some consideration, and, in order to properly express my views, it will be necessary to call your attention to some parts thereof.

The act is that of June 14, 1878, (20 Stat., 113) and that part thereof necessary for your consideration in section one, reads as follows :

That any person who is the head of a family, or who has arrived at the age of twenty-one years, and is a citizen of the United States, or who shall have filed his declaration of intention to become such, as required by the naturalization laws of the United States, *who shall plant, protect, and keep in healthy, growing condition for eight years* ten acres of timber, on any quarter section of any of the public lands of the United States, or five acres of any legal subdivision of eighty acres, or two and a half acres on any legal subdivision of forty acres or less, shall be entitled to a patent for the whole of said quarter section or of such legal subdivision of eighty or forty acres, or fractional subdivision of less than forty acres as the case may be, at the expiration of *said eight years* on making proof, etc.

Section two prescribes the form of the affidavit, the amount to be paid upon the filing of the affidavit, the number of acres to be broken and plowed the first, second and third years ; and then provides,

that no final certificate shall be given, or patent issued for the land so entered until the expiration of *eight years from the date of entry;* and if at the expiration of *such time, or at any time within five years thereafter,* the person making such entry, or, if he or she be dead, his or her heirs, or legal representatives, shall prove by two creditable witnesses that he, or she, or they have planted, and for *not less than eight years, have cultivated and protected such quantity* and character of trees as aforesaid, and not less than 2700 trees were planted on each acre ; and, at the time of making such proof, that there shall then be growing, at least, 675 living and thrifty trees to each acre, they shall receive a patent to such tract, etc.

In construing these provisions, the Department in the case of Benjamin F. Lake, 2 L. D., 309, held the preparation of land and planting of trees are acts of cultivation, and the time actually so employed should be computed as a part of the eight years required in the timber-culture cases, quoting from the circular of instructions issued by Commissioner MacFarland to registers and receivers, dated February 1, 1882, (1 L. D., 638), and holding that one half the trees must have actually been growing for five years, and the remaining half for four years to conform to the terms of the act ; and, that, on the theory that in the second section of the act it is provided that

the party making an entry of a quarter section under the provisions of this act, shall be required to break or plow, five acres covered thereby the first year, five acres the second year, and to cultivate to crop or otherwise the five acres broken, or plowed the first year ; the third year he or she, shall cultivate to crop, or otherwise, the five acres broken the second year, and to plant in timber, seeds, or cuttings, the five acres first broken or plowed ; and to cultivate and put in crop the remaining five acres ; and the fourth year to plant in timber, seeds, or cuttings, the remaining five acres.

This would within the eight years keep the first planting growing five years, and the second planting four years ; and in the case of Charles E. Patterson, (3 L. D. 260), this same rule and doctrine was followed, as it is likewise recognized in the case of Peter Christofferson (3 L. D., 329).

This rule was followed by the Department from that time up until Jun 27, 1887, when Commissioner Sparks, by circular of that date to regis ters and receivers, (6 L. D., 280), directed : " In computing the perioc of cultivation, the time runs from the date when the total number o trees, seeds, or cuttings, required by the act are planted."

Following this circular is the case of Henry Hooper, (6 L. D., 624), in which are reviewed all these decisions heretofore cited, and in constru- ing the act, the following conclusions are reached :

The eight years of cultivation required under the timber-culture law, must be computed from the time the required acreage of trees, seeds, or cuttings, *is planted ;* and this construction was followed and adopted in the case of Charles N. Smith, (7 L. D., 231,) and also in the case o John N. Lindback, decided July 1, 1889 (not reported).

I am fully satisfied that these later decisions which are complained of in this letter are the correct exposition of the law, for, the first sec- tion of the act requires the applicant to " plant, protect, and keep in a healthy, growing condition for eight years, ten acres of timber." Clearly, this language imports and requires this area to be growing dur- ing this period, as trees could not be kept in a healthy, growing condi- tion that were not planted, and in existence.

Turning to section two, this conclusion gains strength by the proviso " That he, or she, or they, have planted, and for not less than eight years, have cultivated and protected such quantity and character o trees as aforesaid." It cannot be disputed that " such quantity " refers to the ten acres mentioned in section one, which requires that ten acres be cultivated and protected for the full period of eight years ; and this is borne out by the further proviso that, if the entry is not completed at the expiration of eight years, that five years thereafter is given the applicant within which to complete the same, so that the entry-man really has thirteen years, if he chooses to avail himself thereof, within which to comply with the law. I have no doubt, if he plants the re- quired area the first year, that then the entry may be made within eight years thereafter, but I am fully satisfied that it was the intent and purpose of Congress to require the claimant to cultivate the trees for eight years, deeming that at the end of that period the young tim- ber would be able to protect itself without further cultivation. While all this is true, yet it seems to me that, inasmuch as the Department, from the time of the passage of the bill up to the circular of the date of June 27, 1887, erroneously construed the true spirit and intent o the act, and in pursuance thereof, numerous entries have been made under the law as thus promulgated, amounting to some twenty-five hundred or more, that such entries should be protected under the con- struction thus given the act, giving such construction all the force and effect of law. Were it not so, great wrong and inconvenience would result.

In this character of entries it has been repeatedly held that, if the entry is made under rulings of this Department in force when the application is made, it should be allowed to stand. Until a rule is changed, it has all the force of law, and acts done under it while it is in force, must be regarded as legal. James Spencer, (6 L. D., 217); Miner *v.* Marriott *et. al.* (2 L. D., 709); David B. Dole (3 L. D., 214); Henry W. Fuss (5 L. D., 167); Allen *v.* Cooley (5 L. D., 261); Kelly *v.* Halvorson (6 L. D., 225).

Believing that justice would be subserved by following the rule of the Department in force at the time these entries were made, I think the case of Henry Hooper, (6 L. D., 624), referred to should be so far modified as to hold that all entries made under the act, as construed from February 1, 1882, up to June 27, 1887, should pass to patent; and that all entries made after the announcement of that doctrine, should be governed and controlled by the principles therein enunciated. To do this, fully, fairly and equitably protects the interest of those who acted under the old regime, and only requires those who have made timber-culture entries since the law has been correctly stated, as I believe, to comply with its plain provisions, and fairly observe its spirit and intent.

Very respectfully submitted.

GEO. CHANDLER,
First Assistant Secretary.

CONFLICTING SETTLEMENT RIGHTS-SANTEE SIOUX RESERVATION.

ROTHWELL *v.* CROCKETT.

Lands within the Santee Sioux reservation, remaining unallotted to and unselected by the Indians on April 15, 1885, were on that day restored to the public domain by virtue of the previous executive order.

The purpose of that part of the order which provided that said land should be " subject to settlement and entry on May 15, 1885," was to fix a time when claims to said land could be made of record, and the rights of claimants determined.

Conceding that such land was not subject to settlement prior to May 15, 1885, as between claimants therefor, priority of settlement, alleged previous to that date, may be considered.

First Assistant Secretary Chandler to Acting Commissioner Stone, July 16, 1889.

The S. E¼ Sec. 25, T. 31 N., R. 4 W., Niobrara, Nebraska, having formerly been a part of the Niobrara or Santee Sioux Indian Reservation, was restored to the public domain by executive order dated February 9, 1885. This order provided that all the lands within said reservation in the State of Nebraska " remaining unallotted to and unselected by the Indians . . . . . on the 15th day of April, 1885, except such as are occupied for agency school and missionary purposes be, and the same are hereby restored to the public domain from and after that date, and made subject to settlement and entry on and after May 15, 1885."

On May 20, 1885, the local office agreeably to your office instructions (3 L. D., 534), received the simultaneous applications of Charles Crockett, Samuel J. Rothwell and Generous L. Wilson to make homestead entry for the tract named.

Thereupon a hearing to determine the right of entry among the parties was after continuance commenced at the local office on June 15, and proceeded with until June 20, 1885, when it was closed.

The local officers rendered separate opinion upon the testimony produced. The register found that the said applications of the three parties named "should be considered as simultaneous, allowing each to continue his settlement and improvements and either bid for preference right of entry, settle among themselves which one should hold the tract, or by complying with the requirements of the homestead law be allowed o make proof separately and hold an undivided interest therein."

The receiver found "that the application of Crockett should be allowed and the application of Wilson and Rothwell be refused."

Crockett appealed from the decision of the register and Rothwell from that of the receiver. No appeal was taken by Wilson.

On February 14, 1888, your office found that Crockett had the superior right, and that his application should be allowed. From this decision Rothwell appeals.

It appears from the testimony that Crockett settled on the land April 15, 1885, built a frame house about twelve by twelve feet, and continued to live thereon; that a part of his family (wife and five children) joined him on the 5th, another part on the 26th of May, and the remainder on June 6, 1885; that on May 15, 1885, his improvements comprising his house and some five acres of breaking were worth about $130, and that at the time of the hearing he had from twenty-two to twenty-five acres broken and three or four cultivated.

It further appears that Rothwell,—although he claims to have been on the land April 15, 1885 and turned over two or three spades of earth —first made a settlement thereon at midnight between the 14th and 15th of May 1885, about which time, with his brother and two others he went on the tract and dug a hole for a well, one spade deep and three feet across, and laid a foundation of sod twelve by fourteen, feet; that on the 17th of the same month he began building a frame house which he finished on the morning of the following day; that he broke some six acres, planted two or three in corn, and set out some trees; and that his improvements are valued at $100.

Rothwell, who is a single man of twenty-seven years, claims to have placed a bed, stove, table etc., in his said house, and to have lived therein until about June 14, 1885, when it was blown down, and about which time he came to the hearing. Some of the evidence, however, tends to show that he used said house as a stable, and he admits that he put a sick horse in it one night during the latter part of May.

Wilson also went on the land at midnight between May 14th and 15th, and performed some acts of settlement but which (in the absence of appeal) have not been considered.

Rothwell claims that he was deterred from settling on the land until the midnight mentioned by information obtained from the register, the Indian agent, and letters of your office to persons in the neighborhood, to the effect that he could secure no preference right by going on the land before May 15, 1885. The record contains a copy of such a letter from your office dated April 2, 1885.

Rothwell intimates that he was also deterred from settling on the land by fear of personal violence, but the evidence fails to sustain the allegation of duress.

Crockett states that he was induced by the executive order to settle on the land April 15, 1885, and that he did so with the knowledge and consent of the Indian agent.

With regard to the information given by the local officers and the Indian agent concerning lands within the said reservation, there is some confusion in the record before me. But this is not material. The land in question having been on April 15, 1885, unallotted to and unselected by the Indians, it became by the executive order mentioned, restored to the public domain on that day.

The obvious purpose of that part of the said executive order wherein land so restored was stated to be " subject to settlement and entry," on May 15, 1885, was to fix a time when claims to such land could be made of record and the rights of claimants determined.

Crockett, who has maintained a residence on the land, made his settlement thereon after it had been so restored and before the settlement of Rothwell. The rights of Crockett are therefore, I think the better. It is contended that Crockett could acquire no rights by his occupancy of the land prior to May 15, 1885, by reason of executive order referred to. Conceding that by said order the land was reserved from settlement until May 15, 1885, then the case at bar is clearly within the rule laid down in Geer *v.* Farrington (4 L. D. 410), in accordance with which the case was properly decided by your office. In that case the Department held that while a settler upon segregated land could acquire no rights against the government, yet as between himself and another claimant priority of settlement would be considered. This ruling is also sustained in Tarr *v.* Burnham (6 L. D., 709).

It may be possible that Rothwell's settlement was delayed by reason of information obtained from the local office, and by the letters of your office. But however unfortunate this may have been for Rothwell the manifest rights of Crockett cannot be thereby affected.

Your decision is therefore affirmed.

CONTEST—PREFERENCE RIGHT—APPLICATION.

PETERSON *v.* WARD.

A preferred right of entry can not be secured through a contest against a pre-emption filing.

A legal application to make homestead entry is, while pending, equivalent to actual entry, so far as the applicant's rights are concerned, and withdraws the land embraced therein from any other disposition, until final action thereon.

First Assistant Secretary Chandler to Acting Commissioner Stone, July 17, 1889.

I have considered the case of Peter Peterson *v.* Geo. H. Ward, on appeal of Myron E. Hardendorf from your office decision of April 11, 1888, holding for cancellation his homestead entry for NW. ¼, Sec. 35, T. 1 S., R. 29 W., Oberlin, Kansas, land district.

Said Peterson filed his declaratory statement for said tract April 22, 1885, and subsequently published notice that he would make proof thereon November 22, 1887

On October 15, 1887, however, the said Ward filed protest against the acceptance of Peterson's proof and on the same day made application to make homestead entry for said land. There was filed by him at the same time an application to contest Peterson's filing.

On November 16, 1887, Peterson's relinquishment was placed on file and on the same day the local officers permitted said Myron E. Hardendorf to make homestead entry for said tract but marked his papers "Entered subject to the preference right of Geo. H. Ward."

On November 17, Ward appeared and made homestead entry for said tract. The local officers so far as the record shows, neither accepted nor rejected Ward's application to enter filed October 15, but on November 17, his entry was made upon a new set of papers of that date.

On November 29, Geo. H. Ward, by his attorney filed in the local office a motion or petition asking the said officers to cancel the entry of the said Hardendorf, and after hearing thereon on December 5, 1887, they overruled said motion for the reason that in their opinion they had no authority to cancel an entry of record except upon relinquishment or acting under instructions of the Commissioner of the General Land Office directing such cancellation. No evidence was offered or taken at such hearing.

From such decison of the local office appeal was taken by Ward and your office in the decision now under consideration held the decision of the local officers to be correct.

In said decision your predecessor says *inter alia*—

Ward made application to enter the tract in question October 15, 1887, and followed it up by making an entry thereof November 17, 1887. The records do not show that any action was taken by you on the application of October 15; therefore, I conclude that said application was pending November 17, and so far as Ward's rights are concerned was a withdrawal of said land from other disposition until such time as it was finally disposed of; see Pfaff v. Williams et al, (4 L. D., 455).

In view of the foregoing the application of Ward to enter said tract is considered the first in point of time, and being so, his entry will be allowed to stand and that of Hardendorf canceled.

The application to contest filed by Ward does not seem from the record to have been allowed by the local officers and no day was set for hearing or notice given, but if such proceedings had been had or commenced, Ward could have acquired no preference right thereby for a contest against a pre-emption filing is not recognized by this Department. (Field v. Black, 2 L. D., 581.)

The local officers seem to have fallen into error by failing to recognize the principle last above stated and their decision that Ward had a preference right of entry by reason of his application to contest was erroneous. Ward's right was based upon the application to enter filed October 15, 1887, for a legal application to enter is, while pending, equivalent to actual entry, so far as the applicant's rights are concerned, and withdraws the land embraced therein from any other disposition, until final action thereon. Pfaff v. Williams, et al., (4 L. D., 455).

Hardendorf made his entry subject to whatever rights Ward had, and the mere fact that the local officers called the same a preference right, instead of basing it on his application to enter, cannot now make Hardendorf's claim superior to that of Ward.

Your said decision is accordingly affirmed.

PRACTICE—APPEAL—MOTION FOR REVIEW.

DAYTON v. DAYTON.

An appeal will not lie from a letter of the General Land Office promulgating a departmental decision.

A petition for re-review will not be granted unless it presents facts, or points of law, not previously discussed or involved in the case.

It is not a good ground for such a petition that the oral argument on review was heard by the same official that rendered the decision in the first instance.

Secretary Noble to Acting Commissioner Stone, July 17, 1889.

With letter of June 20, 1889 you transmitted motions by James R. Dayton and Lyman C. Dayton for a review and reconsideration of the decision of February 25, 1889 in the case of Dayton v. Dayton (8 L. D., 248). . The decision sought to be reviewed was rendered upon motions by each of these parties for review of departmental decision of October 1, 1887, in the case of Dayton v. Dayton (6 L. D., 164).

Lyman C. Dayton sets forth that he filed a motion for review of the decision of Acting Secretary Muldrow rendered October 1, 1887, and applied for an oral argument; that said argument was heard by said acting secretary and "That the appellant considers that his rights have been prejudiced by reason of the said review and reconsideration of the decision of October 1, 1887, being heard and determined by the same official of the land department who rendered the same in the first instance." This objection is without force even if the facts sustained it. The records, however, show that the motion for review was considered and the decision refusing the same was signed by Secretary Vilas. The other reasons set forth in the motion now being considered are exactly the same as were presented in the motion for review.

The motion by James R. Dayton is based upon the ground that the question of good faith on his part had not been raised until the decision of October 1, 1887, and that he had not been afforded an opportunity to present testimony showing his good faith. He filed with his motion the affidavits of three parties in support of the claim that he was all the time acting in this matter in entire good faith. This question was presented when the original motion for review was before the Department, and was then fully considered. The affidavits do not present such new facts as would justify a change of the decision then rendered.

In the case of Neff v. Cowhick (8 L. D., 111), it was held that motions for re-review should not be allowed but that " if the defeated party is able to present any suggestions of fact or points of law not previously discussed or involved in the case, it may be done by petition which shall contain all the facts and arguments." The papers now under consideration even if they are to be considered as such petitions as are contemplated by the ruling cited, do not present any suggestion of fact or point of law not previously fully considered and determined in the decision refusing the motion for review. The said motions or petitions are therefore each denied.

By letter of May 6, 1889, your office also transmitted an appeal by Lyman C. Dayton from your office letter of March 8, 1889, promulgating departmental decision of February 25, 1889, and directing the local officers, " to notify the parties in interest that sixty days are allowed after due service of notice in which to present the claim of the City of Aberdeen under the townsite laws, and no entries will be allowed until such time as the right of said city may be determined," and also a motion by the City of Aberdeen to dismiss said appeal. This motion is made upon the ground that said action of your office " was not a decision in the case but was solely ministerial as carrying into effect the decision and order of the Secretary of the Interior of February 25, 1889, and for this reason no appeal can lie."

It is plain that said letter of your office to the local officers was simply for the purpose of carrying out the directions of the Department, and was in no sense a decision from which an appeal would lie.

The motion to dismiss is allowed, and said appeal is hereby dismissed.

TIMBER CULTURE CONTEST–"DEVOID OF TIMBER."

MORROW *v.* LAWLER.

The departmental construction of the timber culture act, prevailing at the time when an entry is allowed thereunder, must govern in determining whether such entry is for land of the character contemplated by said act.

First Assistant Secretary Chandler to Acting Commissioner Stone, July 17, 1889.

I have before me the appeal of John D. Lawler from your decision of March 23, 1888, holding for cancellation his (said Lawler's) timber culture entry, No. 1847, Springfield series, made August 19, 1879, and covering the NE. ¼, Sec. 22, T. 104 N., R. 71 W., Mitchell district, Dakota.

December 30, 1885, Charles C. Morrow initiated a contest against said entry on the ground that the section in question was not, at the date of entry, naturally devoid of timber; and on the further ground that the entryman was in default, the breaking and cultivating not having been properly done, and there not being ten acres of trees (other than those spontaneously upon the land) growing on the tract at the date of contest.

On March 9, 1886, pursuant to a notice duly issued, the contestant appeared with his counsel before J. A. Strube, a notary public at Chamberlain, Dakota, who had been appointed commissioner to take testimony, and the claimant appeared by his attorneys, J. T. Stearns and W. A. Porter. On this occasion nineteen witnesses (including the contestant himself) were examined on the part of the contestant and cross-examined by the attorneys for the claimant.

On May 12, 1886, the claimant, through his attorneys, submitted the testimony of eight witnesses (including J. T. Stearns, his agent and attorney), at the local office at Mitchell.

Pursuant to your office order of August 17, 1886, a further hearing was had in the case on September 13, 1886, before John T. Williams as commissioner; at which hearing the contestant appeared in person and by attorney, and examined eight witnesses. The contestee's attorney was present, but protested against this additional testimony, substantially on the grounds that the evidence offered was not properly rebuttal testimony, and that the commissioner, not having heard the evidence in chief, was not competent to take testimony offered as in rebuttal. I find it unnecessary to pass upon the objection, inasmuch as my conclusion as to the facts does not rest upon the testimony objected to.

The entry having been made August 19, 1879, the construction of the law *then prevailing*, as to what land is "devoid of timber" within the meaning of the act, must be taken to be that indicated by the decision in Linden *v.* Gray (3 C. L. O., 181), made January 4, 1877; which construction seems to have remained substantially in force until after the date of Lawler's entry. See Nicholas Noel, 6 C. L. O., 112, decided September 12, 1879, followed by your office in B. F. Griffin, 6 C. L.O., 154, on December 18, 1879. The case of Blenkner v. Sloggy (2 L. D., 267), the earliest departmental decision relied on by the entryman's counsel, was not made until July 18, 1883. What, then, is the rule in Linden v. Gray, which is thus pointed out as the one which must govern this case ? The following passage from the opinion shows:

> At the tiial two witnesses testified that there were six hundred and eighteen trees on the section that measured over five inches in circumference six inches from the ground; that some of them were upwards of one foot in diameter, and that the six hundred and eighteen trees would average ten inches in circumference. Also that there were over a thousand smaller trees growing upon the section, mostly oak and elm. If such is the fact, I think your decision holding that the land was subject to timber-culture entry is erroneous . . . . It cannot, I think, be reasonably considered that a section of land upon which the number of forest trees above specified are growing, is naturally devoid of timber or that it is of the class of land subject to entry under the provisions of the (timber culture) act.

The testimony in this case, confused and contradictory as it is, very decidedly, in my opinion, establishes a state of facts, as to the spontaneous growth of timber upon the section, very much stronger against the entry here in question than that which in the leading case referred to was held to be clearly fatal.

D. W. Spalding, who "located" Lawler's entry, and who, as one who had specially examined the tract at about the time that the entry was made was introduced as a witness on behalf of Lawler, was asked whether there were not, at the date of hearing, "growing in all the gulches native timber, cedar, elm, ash, cottonwood, over thirty thousand trees ranging from two to twenty inches in diameter and from ten to forty feet in height?" His answer was: "I haven't counted them, but I shouldn't think there was that many there of that size. I don't think there was one-third of that number that size : there might be a fourth or more although I never counted them." This and similar admissions by Lawler's own witnesses seem to me very largely to corroborate at least the general purport of the testimony of Morrow's eighteen witnesses in chief, to the effect that there were from six to eight or ten acres of native timber growing upon the section, embracing several hundreds of standing trees of considerable size, and quite a number of stumps, (the presence of which is significant as implying that to some extent at least the tract had been actually resorted to for a supply of timber).

Taking all the testimony together, I cannot doubt that, at least according to the rule above shown to have been the one prevailing at the date of Lawler's entry, the tract covered thereby was not so far "devoid of timber" as to be properly open to entry under the timber-culture law.

Upon this ground I affirm the decision appealed from. I do this without passing upon the question of the alleged default of Lawler in respect to breaking, cultivation, etc.; it being doubtful, in my opinion, whether the entryman has been satisfactorily shown to have incurred forfeiture upon that ground.

•

——

RELINQUISHMENT—ACT OF JUNE 15, 1880.

GEORGE T. JONES.

A transferee, holding under the purchase of a final certificate, will be protected as against the subsequent relinquishment of the entryman.

A cash entry under the act of June 15, 1880, allowed on the affidavit of the entryman's attorney, will not be disturbed, where, after transfer of the land, the entryman refuses to make the personal affidavit required by the regulations.

Secretary Noble to Acting Commissioner Stone, July 17, 1889.

I have before me the appeal of George T. Jones from your office decision of May 12, 1888, affirming the action of the local officers rejecting his (said appellant's) application to make homestead entry, of the NE. ¼, Sec. 17, T. 2, R. 24 W., Kirwin land district, Kansas.

From the record before me the following facts appear:—

January 9, 1880, one Joseph J. Sperry made homestead entry No. 13781 for the tract above described.

May 12, 1884, Sperry's duly appointed attorney, John R. Horn, made cash entry No. 3434, under the second section of the act of June 15, 1880 (21 Stat., 237), for said land.

On the 14th day of May, 1884, said Sperry sold the tract in question, for a consideration of $300, to William E. Crutcher, to whom he executed a formal deed, and delivered the cash certificate issued by the local office.

April 18, 1885, your office suspended the said cash entry "for the reason that the affidavit required in such cases was made by the (claimant's) attorney, instead of the claimant himself," and Sperry was therefore required to furnish a personal affidavit.

December 14, 1885, Sperry, who had declined to make the personal affidavit called for by your office, executed a relinquishment of his entry before the register.

December 14, 1885, cotemporaneously with the execution of said relinquishment of Sperry's entry—Jones, the appellant here, made application to enter the land under the homestead law. This application the local officers rejected on account of the existing cash entry of Sperry (No. 3434). From such rejection Jones appealed.

June 22, 1886, the local officers transmitted an affidavit by Wm. E. Crutcher, setting up the above-recited facts as to his purchase of Sperry's interest in the entry, and Sperry's refusal to perfect his proof, and petitioning that, in view of those facts, the proofs already filed in the case be accepted and a patent issued thereupon.

By said decision of May 12, 1888, your predecessor, Commissioner Stockslager, held that this petition should be granted, and approved the action of the local officers rejecting Sperry's relinquishment and Jones's application. From the decision so made said Jones appeals.

The case made by the facts set up in this record, is substantially this: The cash entryman, Sperry, after having sold all his interest in his entry, for a valuable consideration, to Wm. E. Crutcher, declines to perfect his proof by filing the usual personal affidavit, and undertakes to defraud the purchaser from him by "relinquishing" the entry which is no longer his, and thus giving Jones, the appellant here, an opportunity to become the "first applicant" for the tract. A wrong of this character cannot be done with the conscious aid of this Department. Such cases as those of Falconer v. Hunt (6 L. D., 512), Addison W. Hastie (8 L. D., 619), and Daniel R. McIntosh (8 L. D., 641), show it to be an already established rule, that the seller of a final certificate will not be allowed to take advantage of an irregularity in his proof, to ignore rights which he himself has conferred and dispose again of property already once assigned.

In the present case, in the absence of the personal affidavit which Sperry declines to make, the best attainable evidence in support of the entry seems to be that already filed by Horn, Sperry's attorney in fact. On this account, and because, after full notice of Crutcher's allegations, Jones has omitted to file any sworn contradiction of any of the essential facts in Crutcher's case, I see no reason why anything further should be required by the Department as a pre-requisite to the issue of patent upon the cash entry already made.

Your said office decision is accordingly affirmed.

OSAGE LANDS—AMENDED FILING—REVIEW.
GRIGSBY v. SMITH.

The only qualification and condition required to authorize an entry of Osage Indian trust and diminished reserve lands is, that the claimant must be an actual settler on the land at the date of entry and have the qualifications of a pre-emptor.

The purchaser of such land after having complied with the law and received his final certificate, may lawfully remove from said land, or sell and convey it absolutely.

The right to amend a filing, and the proof thereunder, to correspond with the actual settlement of the claimant will be recognized in case of an honest mistake.

The subsequent settlement of another, upon land included within an application for such amendment, is subject to the applicant's right.

The right of amendment will not be defeated by the failure of the local officers to make a proper record of the application therefor.

A strong preponderance of evidence against the decision will justify review.

Secretary Noble to Acting Commissioner Stone, July 17, 1889.

In the case of James W. Grigsby v. Toney Smith the attorney for Grigsby has filed a motion for review of departmental decision of November 20, 1888, affirming the decision of your office of March 17, 1887.

Grigsby on October 30, 1884, filed Osage declaratory statement for lots 1, 2, 3, 4, 5, 6, 7 and 8, Sec. 1, T. 30 S., R. 12 W., Larned, Kansas, land district, alleging settlement August 1, 1884, and made final proof in support thereof January 31, 1885, before the clerk of the district court of Barber county. This proof was approved by the Larned officers, and receipt for the first payment issued February 4, 1885. Grigsby afterwards discovered that a mistake had been made in his filing and final proof papers and that the land upon which he had actually settled and intended to file for was described as lots 1, 2, 3 and 4 in Sec. 1 T. 31 S., R. 10 W. He thereupon made an application sworn to May 21, 1885 to amend his filing and final proof papers to make them describe said last named land. This application was, he says, immediately forwarded to the Larned land office. This last named land being in the Wichita land district, he went to said office and informed the local officers of his application, and in accordance with instructions given by them prepared another application to amend, dated July 25, 1885, and forwarded the same to said Wichita land office. There is nothing to show when these papers were filed in the respective offices, but both applications were forwarded to your office September 24, 1885, by the Larned office. The attorney for Grigsby states in an affidavit dated October 23, 1888, that he sent the application of July 25, 1885, to the Wichita office from whence it was returned to him in a few days with the statement that the proper place to file it was in the Larned office. This application was considered in your office and in letter of April 8, 1886, to the local officers it was said, "It appears satisfactorily that a mistake was made in attempting to describe the land claimed, and that Grigsby's improvements lie upon the tracts to which he now applies to amend. You will accordingly allow applicant to re-advertise and make new proof for the tract covered by his actual settlement and cultivation."

Smith, on October 5, 1885, filed declaratory statement for lots 1 and 2, Sec. 1, T. 31 S., R. 10 W., alleging settlement September 5th, and afterwards gave notice that he would on March 6, 1886, submit final proof thereunder. Against the acceptance of this proof Grigsby filed a protest setting up his prior claims. A hearing was had on said protest May 20, 1886. Grigsby, who had in accordance with the instructions in your office letter of April 8, 1886, made publication of his intention to submit new proof on June 17, 1886, was allowed to make such proof. The local officers, after considering the testimony adduced at the hearing, and the final proofs of the respective parties, decided that Grigsby had not acted in good faith, and that he ought not to be allowed to enter any of the land covered by his amended filing. That decision was affirmed in your office. Upon appeal to this Department, your office decision was affirmed, it being said "after a careful review of the testimony I agree with you that Grigsby was not an actual settler in good faith upon the land in dispute, and this conclusion rests largely on the fact that the local officers with the witnesses before them and taking part in the cross-examination, so found."

There is no dispute as to the material facts in this case, but it is claimed that those facts do not justify the conclusion reached in the various decisions. These facts are substantially set forth in the decision of the local officers as follows :

Plaintiff settled upon the lots 1, 2, 3 and 4 Sec. 1 T. 31 S., R. 10 W., on August 1, 1884, and together with his family resided upon the land until March 1, 1885, at which time he moved off and has not since resided upon the land. He made final proof of his residence upon and cultivation of the land February 1, 1895. At the time he made his proof he had resided continuously on the land for a period of six months, and had upon the land a house, stable and chicken-coop, and had broken 12 acres of land. When he moved away from the land he also removed the buildings and placed them upon another tract of land he now lives upon.

Smith with his family settled upon lots 1 and 2, September 5, 1885, and has resided upon the same continuously since that time. He also built a house, dug a well, put up a stable, put out some forest trees and cultivated the land which had been broken by Grigsby. At the time Grigsby made his final proof he was a qualified pre-emptor and we find the same in regard to Smith. The parties have each acted in good faith in that they both complied with the law while residing upon the land.

In speaking of Grigsby's claim, after reciting the facts as above set forth it is said—

His action in moving off the land and destroying the improvements thereon by removing the same is something we ought to consider. We do not think he intended to make that his home or that his improvements were made in good faith, but that the residence upon and improvements made by Grigsby we think were simply done that he might enter the land.

It may be noted here that it is shown by the evidence in addition to the facts thus set forth that Grigsby in the spring of 1885 sowed millet on said land, which however, did not make a crop sufficient to justify him in harvesting it and that he went to the land in the fall of that year for the purpose of sowing wheat, but was prevented from so doing by Smith.

The land involved here being a part of the Osage Indian trust and diminished reserve lands, the rights of claimants thereto must be considered and determined under the laws relating to the disposition of those lands and the rulings of this Department under those laws. The provisions of the act of May 28, 1880 (21 Stat. 143) providing for the sale of these lands were considered and very fully discussed in the case of United States v. Woodbury et al. (5 L. D., 303). The conclusion there reached by the Department was "that under the act of May 28, 1880, the only qualification and condition required to authorize an entry upon the Osage Indian trust and diminished reserve lands is, that the claimant must be an actual settler on the land at the date of the entry, and must have the qualifications of a pre-emptor." This theory was again announced in the circular of April 26, 1887 (5 L. D., 581), and has been since that time recognized by this Department as the proper rule in such cases.

The United States circuit court for the district of Kansas in considering this question said—

All that is required of the applicant is that he shall have the qualifications of a pre-emptor; that he shall be an actual settler, and that he shall make payment. As the government held these lands under a trust to convert them into cash its primary object was, of course, to realize as soon and as much as possible, and not, as in respect to public lands generally, to have them occupied and improved ; so it might properly ignore the questions of improvement or length of occupation,

and cited approvingly the case of United States *v.* Woodbury *et al.*, *supra.* United States *v.* Edwards *et al.* (33 Federal Reporter, 104).

The local officers find that Grigsby was an actual settler upon the land at the date of his entry, and that he was a qualified pre-emptor. They further find that he acted in good faith in that he complied with the law while residing upon the land. This finding seems to bring Grigsby clearly within the requirements of the law governing such cases. The local officers apparently so regarded this case because they say—" We think that had Grigsby continued his occupation of the land no adverse right could attach." The law, however, does not require that he should continue to occupy the land nor that he should hold the title thereto. After having shown a compliance with the law, and having received his final certificate he had a right not only to remove therefrom but to sell and convey it absolutely. Myers *v.* Croft (13 Wall, 291); Fritz Schenrock (7 L. D., 368).

This Department also holds that if a pre-emptor had in fact complied with the pre-emption law up to the time of making final proof, a sale subsequently made, though prior to the issuance of final certificate would not of necessity defeat his right to a patent.

Magalia Gold Mining Co. *v.* Ferguson (6 L. D., 218); Orr *v.* Breach (7 L. D., 292); Charles Lehman (8 L. D., 486).

The conclusion by the local officers that Grigsby had not acted in good faith, is apparently based solely upon the fact that he some time after the submission and approval of his final proof took up his residence somewhere else and removed his buildings from this land. This action on Grigsby's part was not a violation of any law or of any regulation of this Department. It was the exercise on his part of a right recognized by the courts and this Department provided he had complied with the law up to the date of his final proof. This the local officers found he had done because they say—" he complied with the law while residing upon the land," which takes him to a date considerably later than the date of his final proof. The conclusion that Grigsby acted in bad faith is not justified by the facts in the case as found by them, and the decision based upon that conclusion cannot be sustained. The fact that it was subsequently discovered that a mistake had been made in both his filing and final proof papers in the description of the land, does not affect his rights. As soon as this mistake was discovered and before any one else had asserted a claim to the land, Grigsby applied to have the mistake corrected and his application was, and properly so, allowed.

It is true that Smith claims to have written to the local officers at Wichita as to the status of this land and to have been informed by them that there was no claim of record for it. This information was received however, after he had settled on the land and hence his settlement was not induced by such information. The statements of Grigsby and his attorney as to the steps he took to give notice of his application to amend are not contradicted or denied. These statements show that Grigsby took due precaution to give notice of his application, and he should not be held responsible for the neglect of the local officers to make a proper record of that application.

Rule 76 of Rules of Practice, provides that—

Motions for re-hearings before registers and receivers or for review or reconsideration of the decisions of the Commissioner or Secretary, will be allowed in accordance with legal principles applicable to motions for new trials at law, after due notice to the opposing party.

In Hilliard on New Trials, 2nd Edition, Chapter 14 Sec. 1, it is said— "A verdict may be set aside as being *against evidence* or *against the weight of evidence*. More especially a verdict ' entirely without evidence to support it.' Or having nothing to support it and being therefore capricious. Or a verdict decidedly and strongly against the weight of evidence" etc. After discussing the question of granting new trials because the verdict was against the evidence it is said in Sec. 21 same chapter:

The rule, however, is more frequently stated in the qualified form, as we have already remarked, in general terms that a verdict will not be set aside as against the mere *preponderance* of testimony Or unless clearly against evidence or the palpable preponderance of evidence. More especially in case of a large body of evidence on both sides contradictory in its character.

And in Sec. 21 a.—

But it is held in numerous cases and perhaps the weight of authority is now to the effect that *strong preponderance* of evidence against the verdict will justify a new trial.

Testing the case now under consideration by the rules thus laid down it is clear that it is one in which the motion for review should be allowed.

Where there are concurring decisions of the local officers, of your office, and of this Department, that departmental decision will not be disturbed on a motion for review unless it is clearly wrong and substantial justice has not been done thereby. If it be shown, however, that the decision is clearly and decidedly against the weight of evidence, and that substantial justice has not been done, this Department should not hesitate to correct the error. This case comes clearly within this latter rule, and the said departmental decision of November 20, 1888, is therefore hereby set aside, the decision of your office of March 17, 1887, is reversed and it is directed that Grigsby's final proof be approved and that he be allowed to perfect his title to the land included in his amended filing.

REPAYMENT—FRAUDULENT ENTRY.

EDMUND F. MORCOM.

Repayment cannot be allowed in case of an entry allowed on false testimony.

Secretary Noble to Acting Commissioner Stone, July 18, 1889.

In the matter of the application of Edmund F. Morcom for repayment of the purchase money paid by him on his commuted homestead entry No. 26,492, before me on appeal from the decision of your office dated May 11, 1888, denying said application, the record shows the following material facts bearing on the question to be determined.

March 4, 1884, Morcom made homestead entry for the E. ½ of SE. ¼, and the SW. ¼ of SE. ¼ Sec. 23 T. 101 R. 48, Mitchell land district Dakota.

November 28, 1884, he made commutation homestead proof before the clerk of the district court of Minnehaha county Dakota. In making proof he testified, among other things, that he moved a house on the described tract of land March 4, 1884, and established actual residence thereon the same day. In answer to the usual question as to periods of absence since settlement he made the following statement,—" I have been engaged as insurance solicitor and in the insurance business in the vicinity, and have been absent part of the time attending to this; but it was only a few days at a time. I was making this my constant home." His two witnesses testified to substantially the same facts.

November 29, 1884, John Robinson filed in the local land office his duly corroborated affidavit of contest against Morcom's entry wherein he charged that Morcom had never resided on said tract since the date of his entry. Robinson also filed an application to enter said tract as a homestead.

January 22, 1885, Morcom's homestead entry No. 26,492 was commuted to cash entry No. 13,547.

January 30 and 31, 1885, a hearing was had in the contest case, initiated as above stated, of John Robinson *v.* Edmund F. Morcom. This hearing was had before the clerk of the district court of Minnehaha county, Dakota, each of the parties being present in person and by attornies.

The testimony taken at this hearing shows clearly and beyond a reasonable doubt that Morcom did not, at any time between the date of his original entry and the date of his proof, establish a residence on the described tract of land, or make it his home, and that the testimony given by him and his witness, as above stated, was untrue in substance and absolutely false.

His entry was held for cancellation by the local office on March 18, 1885. This decision was affirmed by your office February 3, 1886 and by the Department Jan. 7, 1888.

Morcom applies for repayment under the provisions of Sec. 2 act of June 16, 1880. (21 Stat. 287). The described tract of land was, at the time Morcom made his homestead entry properly subject to such entry, and his proof on its face showed a compliance with law.

By departmental regulation it is provided that "if a tract of land were subject to entry, and the proof shows a compliance with law, and the entry should be canceled because the proofs were shown to be false, it could not be held that the entry was 'erroneously allowed,' and in such case repayment would not be authorized." (General Circular of January 1, 1889—pages 66–67).

The facts in this case show not merely a failure on the part of the entryman to comply with the law, but that he procured the allowance of his entry by means of false testimony, and therefore his application for repayment must be denied.

For the reason above given the decision of your office is affirmed.

ABANDONED MILITARY RESERVATION—FORT LYON.

FRANK BOUSLOG.

Settlement and entry are not authorized on lands embraced within the limits of an abandoned military reservation after such lands have been placed under the control of the Secretary of the Interior as provided in section one, act of July 5, 1884.

Section nine, act of February 14, 1853, limiting the area of military reservations to six hundred and forty acres is not applicable outside the territorial boundaries of Oregon.

Secretary Noble to Acting Commissioner Stone, July 18, 1889.

I have considered the appeal of Frank Bouslog from the decision of your office of September 9, 1887, affirming the action of the local officers in denying his application to make homestead entry on the S. ½ of the SW. ¼ of Sec. 22, and lots 3 and 4 of the NW. ¼ of Sec. 27, T. 22 S., R. 47 W., Lamar district, Colorado. (I note that said decision by mistake designates Bouslog's application as one to make timber culture instead of homestead entry.)

The application to enter was made July 18, 1887, and was denied because the land is within the limits of the Old Fort Lyon military reservation. The appellant contends, that the land, although within said limits, was subject to entry at the date of his application, by virtue of the special proviso in reference to said Old Fort Lyon reservation, in the second section of the act of July 5, 1884, entitled "An Act to provide for the disposal of abandoned and useless military reservations." (23 Stat., 103).

The first section of said act is as follows:

That whenever, in the opinion of the President of the United States, the lands, or any portion of them, included within the limits of any military reservation heretofore or hereafter declared, have become or shall become useless for military purposes, he shall cause the same or so much thereof as he may designate, to be placed under the control of the Secretary of the Interior for disposition as hereinafter provided, and shall cause to be filed with the Secretary of the Interior a notice thereof.

The second section authorizes the disposition by the Secretary of the Interior of said lands so placed under his control, by sale thereof after survey and subdivision, with a general proviso protecting actual settlers prior to January 1, 1884, or prior to the location of such reservation, and also, with said special proviso in reference to the Old Fort Lyon reservation, relied on by appellant, which is as follows:

That all patents heretofore issued, and approved state selections, covering lands within the old Fort Lyon Military Reservation, in the State of Colorado, declared by executive order of August 8, 1863, are hereby confirmed; and the rights of all entrymen and settlers on said reservation to acquire title under the homestead, pre-emption, or timber-culture laws, are hereby recognized and affirmed to the extent they would have attached had public lands been settled upon or entered; and such portions of said reservation as shall not have been entered or settled upon as aforesaid, shall be disposed of by the Secretary of the Interior under the provisions of this act, including lands that may be abandoned by settlers or entrymen.

The appellant's application was made about three years after the approval of said act, but it is contended by his counsel, that the operation of said special proviso above quoted, is not limited to entrymen and settlers prior to the passage of the act, but that the lands embraced in said Old Fort Lyon reservation not already entered or settled upon at date of the act, were thereby rendered subject to future entry and settlement, at least, up to the time they were placed by the President under the control of the Secretary of the Interior, and "that it is only such portions of the reservation as may not be entered or settled upon at the time the same may be turned over by the President to the Secretary of the Interior for disposal, that are subject to any action of the Secretary."

It is unnecessary in this case to consider and determine the question, whether or not said special proviso applies to and protects only entries and settlements made prior to or in existence at the date of the act. It seems to be conceded by counsel for appellant, and it is, at any rate, clear, that entries and settlements on said lands are not authorized by said proviso after said lands have been, pursuant to section one of the act, turned over by the President to the Secretary of the Interior for disposal as provided by section two of the act. After such executive action, the lands of said reservation are only subject to disposition according to the provisions of said section two. The order of the President, by authority of said act, placing said lands under the control of the Secretary of the Interior, was issued July 22, 1884, nearly three years before the date (July 18, 1887,) of appellant's application to enter. (Land Office Report of 1886, p. 251.)

Appellant's counsel also insists, that your office erred in said decision, "in not allowing said entry, for the reason that said Old Fort Lyon military reservation in the State of Colorado exceeded six hundred and forty acres." In support of this proposition, he cites section nine of the act of February 14, 1853 (10 Stat., 158), and the case of Fort Boise Hay Reservation (6 L. D., 16). The said act of 1853 limited reservations for forts to "an amount not exceeding six hundred and forty acres at any one point or place," but it was amendatory of an act approved September 27, 1850 (9 Stat., 496), and the latter act applied only to the Territory of Oregon as then constituted. "The same is true of the amendatory act." (Fort Ellis, 6 L. D., 46.) The Fort Lyon reservation is south of the forty-second degree of north latitude, and not within the boundaries of the Territory of Oregon (9 Stat., 323), and hence does not come within the purview of said act limiting reservations to six hundred and forty acres to each fort. The land involved in the Fort Boise hay reservation case, *supra*, was within the area covered by the Territory of Oregon. Said case is, therefore, no authority for the position contended for in the present case.

The decision of your office is affirmed.

SCHOOL INDEMNITY—ACT OF MARCH 1, 1877—CERTIFICATION.

HENDY ET AL. *v.* COMPTON ET AL.

A mere applicant for the right of purchase from the State is not entitled to purchase under section 2, act of March 1, 1877, as a "purchaser from the State for a valuable consideration."

An innocent purchaser from the State is protected under section 2 of said act, whether the purchase was made before or after the passage of said act.

Official notice to the State of the invalidity and cancellation of a selection is such notice to one applying to purchase thereunder from the State as to preclude him from pleading the status of an innocent purchaser.

One applying to purchase from the State is put upon inquiry as to the validity of the State's title by the constructive notice which follows from the possession and cultivation of the land by another.

The holder of a certificate of purchase from the State, not yet entitled to patent, can not claim the protection extended to a purchaser for a valuable consideration without notice.

A selection, resting upon a basis already exhausted by a prior approved selection, is not confirmed by section 2 of said act.

By selection, approval, and certification the title to school land is passed to the State as fully as though transferred by patent; and the Department is thereafter without authority to set aside such certification and cancel the selection.

An invalid selection, approved and certified, can only be canceled on the judgment of a court competent to try the question of title.

Secretary Noble to Acting Commissioner Stone, July 18, 1889.

I have considered the appeal of Charles M. Compton from your office decision of October 13, 1886, awarding to George Hendy the right to purchase, under the provisions of the act of March 1, 1877 (19 Stat., 267) relating to indemnity school selections in the State of California, the NE. ¼ of Sec. 23, T. 17 N., R. 17 W., M. D. M., San Francisco, California, and holding for cancellation the pre-emption cash entry of said Charles M. Compton for the same tract.

October 13, 1869, the State of California made indemnity school land selection (R & R No. 2384) for the N. ½ of Sec. 23, T. 17 N., R. 17 W., M. D. M., in lieu of the E. ½ of Sec. 16, T. 9 S., R. 2 E., M. D. M., which selection was approved on the following dates—viz: The NW. ¼ on July 21, 1870, per list No. 16, and the NE. ¼ on July 1, 1871, per list No. 22; the latter being approved upon the basis of the NE. ¼ of Sec. 16, T. 9 S., R. 2 E., as aforesaid.

Subsequently it was found that the State had, upon the last mentioned basis, made a prior selection covering the NE. ¼ of Sec. 1, T. 6 N., R. 1 W., M. D. M., on June 23, 1869, and that the same had been approved and certified to the State.

Your office accordingly advised the State surveyor general of the fact of said duplicate selections and requested him to notify the vendee of the State under the selection, R & R No. 2384 (that being the later selection), that he would be required to perfect his title to the NE ¼ of Sec. 23, T. 17 N., R. 17 W., (the land involved in this appeal) under the provisions of the act of March 1, 1877 (19 Stat., 267), and that upon failure to do so the land would be disposed of in the manner provided by law.

In reply a telegram was received from the State surveyor general, stating that the land embraced in said selection had not been sold by the State, and requesting that the selection be canceled. Thereupon your office on June 30, 1883, canceled said selection (R. & R No. 2384) as to the NE. ¼ of Sec. 23, T. 17 N., R. 17 W., under the provisions of the second section of the act of March 1, 1877.

July 10, 1883, Horace A. Pine filed an application to enter this tract as timber land under the act of June 3, 1878.

July 22, 1883, Charles M. Compton filed pre-emption declaratory statement for said tract, alleging settlement June 1, 1883, and on December 12, 1883, made final proof and entry, paid for the land, and received final certificate No. 9677 therefor.

September 20, 1883, William Heser filed with the register a formal protest against the allowance of the entry of Compton and also against the cancellation of the State selection. Said protest was accompanied by duly certified copies of papers showing that applications had been made to the State for the purchase of said tract by four different persons, including himself, and that by reason of said conflicting applications upon demand of the applicants, the State surveyor general had, on July 14, 1879, certified the cause to the district court for the twenty-second judicial district of the State, for determination of the right of purchase.

The matter was pending for several years, and was not decided until June 26, 1885.

The superior court of Sonoma county, to which it had been transferred, then rendered judgment whereby it was decreed that George Hendy was entitled to purchase the said N. ½ of Sec. 23, T. 17 N., R. 17 W., from the State as per his application, filed October 14, 1876, and that neither the plaintiff in the case (J. J. Perkins) nor any of the other defendants (one of whom was Heser) was entitled to purchase said land.

Hendy and not Heser therefore appears as plaintiff in the case against Pine, the timber land claimant, and Compton the pre-emption claimant.

The first question to be determined is whether Hendy had the right to purchase the land under the act of March 1, 1877.

The second section of said act reads as follows:

That where indemnity school selections have been made and certified to said State, and said selection shall fail by reason of the land in lieu of which they are taken not being included within such final survey of a Mexican grant, or are otherwise defective or invalid, the same are hereby confirmed, and the sixteenth or thirty-sixth section in lieu of which the selection was made shall, upon being excluded from such final survey, be disposed of as other public lands of the United States: *Provided*, That if there be no such sixteenth or thirty-sixth section, and the land certified therefor shall be held by an innocent purchaser for a valuable consideration, such purchaser shall be allowed to prove such facts before the proper land office, and shall be allowed to purchase the same at one dollar and twenty-five cents per acre, not to exceed three hundred and twenty acres to any one person: *Provided*, That if such person shall neglect or refuse, after knowledge of such facts, to furnish such proof and make payment for such land, it shall be subject to the general land laws of the United States.

Upon a careful consideration of the law above quoted I am unable to conclude that Hendy's case comes within its provisions. The evident purpose of Congress in enacting that law was to enable persons who had in good faith purchased of the State without notice of any defect in its title, to protect themselves to the extent of three hundred and twenty acres by purchasing from the United States the same land at one dollar and twenty-five cents per acre. The provision of the act is that the land certified " shall be held by an innocent purchaser for a valuable consideration."

Hendy, at the date of the act, had not purchased from the State. He had filed his application October 14, 1876, to purchase, but he did not purchase until July 31, 1885, which was after the decree of the State court in his favor as against the other applicants to purchase. He then paid the State $89.95, being twenty per cent of the purchase money plus interest on the balance up to January 1, 1886, for three hundred and twenty acres described as follows: The N. ½ of Sec. 23, T. 17 N., R. 17 W., M. D. M., for which he received a certificate from the register of the State land office, dated August 19, 1885.

He did not apply to purchase from the United States under the provisions of section two of the act of 1877 (the land in controversy being the NE. ¼ of said Sec. 23) until May 7, 1886, but he explains his delay by the statement that not until a few days prior to that date did he discover that the title of the State to the land was defective; that he was never notified by the State, or from any source whatever, of said defect, or to appear and make proof of his right under the act of 1877.

In the meantime, other claims had attached to the land, to wit, that of Pine by his application filed July 10, 1883, to enter it as timber land, and that of Compton by his pre-emption cash entry made December 12, 1883, the last named being now here as appellant objecting to your decision awarding the land to Hendy.

The ground upon which Hendy rests his claim and upon which your said decision is based is that his right under his purchase from the State in July, 1885, related back to the date of his application to purchase, filed in October, 1876, so as to cut off intervening claims or rights and bring him within the purview of the act of 1877 so as to entitle him to its benefits. This position, in my judgment, is not well founded and can not be sustained under the law.

The proviso in the second section of the act of 1877 was for the relief of innocent purchasers from the State for valuable consideration. Neither the language nor the purpose of the act bring Hendy within its provisions. To term a mere applicant to purchase a purchaser would be to pervert the plain language of the act, and to extend its provisions beyond its manifest purpose which, as already indicated herein, is to protect and secure those who, as innocent purchasers, have expended money in purchasing from the State land which had been wrongly certified to it. Your decision seems to hold that a vendee of the State in order to bring himself within the provisions of section two of the act of 1877 must have been a purchaser from the State prior to the passage of said act of 1877, for it is argued in your said decision that though the actual purchase by Hendy from the State was not until after the date of the act, yet since he had filed his application to purchase prior to the act his rights under his purchase related back so as to entitle him to the right to purchase from the United States under the act of 1877.

I do not think this position is tenable. To so hold would be, in my judgment, to defeat in part the object of the law which is remedial and should be liberally construed.

Its object is to protect innocent purchasers and a purchaser after as well as before the passage of the act of 1877 may be an innocent purchaser. He would be such if at the date of his purchase the certification to the State was regular on its face and its validity had never been questioned by any one or from any source. In such case he would be without notice either actual or constructive of any defect and would be entitled to protection under the act should it be found at any time after his purchase that the title which he got from the State was defective or invalid for any of the reasons mentioned in section two of said act.

But Hendy, as shown by the facts herein recited, has not brought himself within the provisions of the act as above interpreted. Though

at the date of his application to purchase from the State its title had
not been questioned and had he purchased then he would have been in
the position of innocent purchaser, yet when he did actually purchase,
in 1886, the title of the State had been questioned. Your office had in
1883, notified the surveyor general of the State of its defect, and subsequently, upon information from that officer that the land embraced
in the invalid selection had not been sold, canceled said selection. The
effect of that cancellation and the question as to the jurisdiction of your
office to make it will be considered further on in this paper. This
much, it may here be said, was true of your office action as affecting the
rights of Hendy. It furnished notice by which he was bound that the
title of the State to the land was not unquestioned, and put him upon
inquiry as to what he was buying. The rule *caveat emptor* applied.
Personal notice to him was not necessary. The public records furnished the requisite notice to take him out of the category of innocent
purchaser.

In addition to the public records was the open, notorious occupancy
and possession of the tract by Compton, the pre-emptor, who after due
advertisement proved his inhabitancy and improvement without protest
from Hendy paid in full for the land, and received final certificate from
the United States. His possession and cultivation of the land were
constructive notice to Hendy, the applicant to purchase from the State
and was sufficient to put him upon inquiry. Landes *v.* Brant, 10 How.,
348; Hughes *v.* United States, 4 Wall., 232; Noyes *v.* Hall, 97 U. S., 34.

Moreover, he took the land on a certificate of purchase from the
State, and paid one-fifth of the purchase money. He would not be entitled to patent from the State until final payment has been made.
(Sec. 3519, Polit. Code, California.) The certificate of purchase could
be regarded as nothing more than a quit claim, if, indeed, it attained that dignity, or was anything more than an equitable title from
the State. But a purchaser by deed of quit claim, without covenant of
warranty, is not entitled to protection as a purchaser for valuable consideration without notice. Oliver *v.* Piatt, 3 How., 333; May *v.* Le
Claire, 11 Wall., 217; Villa *v.* Rodriguez, 12 Wall., 323; Dickerson *v.*
Colgrove, 100 U. S., 578; Baker *v.* Humphrey, 101 U. S., 494.

Under all the circumstances Hendy was bound to inquire as to the
validity of the title in his vendor. The judgment of the State courts
in his favor does not affect the above proposition. That judgment was
one involving a determination of the question as to which of several
litigants, all claiming the right to purchase from the State, had the superior right, and it was doubtless binding upon the State. Under it
Hendy was entitled to purchase whatever title the State had to the
land, but it is not binding upon the United States. The latter can dispose of the land only in accordance with the law which must be interpreted and administered by the Land Department, and not necessarily
in accordance with the judgment of a State court.

Having arrived at the conclusion that Hendy is not an innocent purchaser from the State, and therefore that he is not entitled to purchase
from the United States under the provisions of the second section of
the act of March 1, 1877, the next question which suggests itself is,
was the tract in question confirmed to the State by said section two of
the act? To properly construe the language of the section on this point
the object and purpose of the law makers must be kept in view.

That was, in general, to save the State or innocent purchasers under
it whole where defective or invalid indemnity school selections had
been made, so far as this could be done without injury to the United
States. Keeping this in mind the question suggested must be answered
in the negative.

The basis on which this selection rested had already been exhausted
by a prior approved selection on the same basis.

The supreme court in the case of Durand v. Martin, (120 U. S., 366,)
classified the cases to which the statute relates as follows:

1. Cases where the State was entitled to indemnity but the selection was defective
in form;

2. Cases where the original school selections were actually in place, and the State
was not entitled to indemnity on their account; and,

3. Cases where the State was not entitled to indemnity because there never had
been such a section sixteen or section thirty-six as was represented when the selection was made and the official certificate given.

As to the first of these classes, the certificate was simply confirmed because the
State was entitled to its indemnity, and nothing was needed to perfect the title but
a waiver by the United States of all irregularities in the time and manner of the selections.

As to the second, the selection was confirmed, and the United States took in lieu of
the selected land that which the State would have been entitled to but for the indemnity it had claimed and got. In its effect this was an exchange of lands between
the United States and the State.

And as to the third, in lieu of confirmation, *bona fide* purchasers from the State
were given the privilege of perfecting their titles by paying the United States for the
land at a specified price.

Under these circumstances, it was a matter of no moment to the United States
whether the original selection was invalid for one cause or another. If the State
claimed and got indemnity when it ought to have taken the original sections, the
United States took the school sections and relinquished their rights to the lands
which had been selected in lieu. And if the State had claimed and sold land to
which it had no right, and for which it could not give school land in return, an
equitable provision was made for the protection of the purchaser by which he could
keep the land, and the United States would get its value in money. In this way all
defective titles, under government certificates, would be made good without loss to
the United States.

To hold that the act of 1877 confirms in the State the title to the tract
in question under the selection made (it being a second selection on the
same basis) would be to give the State two tracts for one, thus causing
a loss to the United States of one of the tracts selected. In other
words, it would be to enlarge the school grant, which the supreme
court in the language above quoted from Durand v. Martin, in effect
says was not contemplated.

The Attorney General of the United States, in an opinion rendered July 12, 1878, with relation to school lands in California (16 Op., 69) in speaking of two or more selections made in lieu of the same sixteenth or thirty-sixth sections used the following language:

By the statute of July 23, 1866, in regard to school lands in California, it was pro. vided that the State of California could not receive under this act a greater quantity of land for school improvement purposes than she was entitled to by law, and although this provision is not repeated in the act which we are at present considering, (Act of March 1, 1877,) yet there is nothing in it from which it can fairly be inferred that when double selections are made they were to be ratified, or that the State was, by reason of any mistake in the making of duplicate selections, to obtain a greater quantity of land than had originally been allowed by law for school purposes.

The act of 1877 for the reasons above given does not operate to confirm to the State title to tract in question.

There being in Hendy no right of purchase under the act, and the title not being confirmed to the State, the question remains what action shall be taken relative to the selection, the approval and certification of which was not authorized by law ?

That it should be canceled seems clear, but has the Land Department the authority and jurisdiction to set aside the certification, or must that be done by the courts ?

The supreme court, in the case of Frasher v. O'Connor (115 U. S., 102), a case involving school land selections in the State of California, after stating that the lands then in question had been listed to the State by the Commissioner of the General Land Office and the Secretary of the Interior, said :—"The title of the State thus became as complete as though transferred by a patent of the United States."

In United States v. Stone (2 Wall., 525) the supreme court say :

A patent is the highest evidence of title and is conclusive as against the government and all claiming under junior patents or titles until it is set aside or annulled by some judicial tribunal.

See also Hughes v. United States (4 Wall., 232) ; Moore v. Robbins (96 U. S., 530); United States v. Schurz (102 U. S. 378).

I am aware that the Department has held that it has under the provisions of section two of the act of 1877 the authority in such cases as this, to cancel invalid selections after they have been approved and certified to the State.

Secretary Schurz in a letter to your office under date of November 22, 1880, construing the act of 1877, after a somewhat lengthy discussion of said act, concluded with the following language :

Hence where selections certified as aforesaid shall be found defective or invalid, and adjudged by you to fail for any of the reasons contemplated by the act of 1877, as herein construed, and not confirmed thereby, the State surveyor general should be duly notified of your decision in the premises, and advised that a certain time, say ninety days from date of notice, will be allowed within which any purchaser of the land from the State may appear to perfect his claim under the second section of the act, and that if no one claiming as such purchaser shall come forward and establish his right to enter the land within such time, the land from and after the expiration of such period will be subject to disposal under the general land laws of the United States.

November 11, 1884, Secretary Teller in a letter to your office relative to the adjustment of the school grant to the State of California, under the act of 1877, modified the order above quoted so as to deal first with the State and afterwards act upon the application of the vendee of the State to purchase. Said letter contained the following:

Hence, where selections certified as aforesaid shall be found defective or invalid, and adjudged by you to fail for any of the reasons contemplated by the act of 1877, as herein construed, and not confirmed thereby, the State surveyor general should be duly notified of your decision in the premises and advised that a certain time, say thirty days from date of notice, will be allowed within which the State may appeal from said decision; and if the State fail to appeal therefrom within the time, then the listing of such selections shall be canceled. After said cancellation, the purchaser from the State, if any there be, shall be allowed sixty days to make proof that at the date of said cancellation he was a *bona fide* purchaser from the State, and has not parted with his title except to the State, in order to recover the purchase money to perfect his title under the provisions of section two of the act of March 1, 1877. But if no one claiming as such purchaser shall come forward and establish his right to enter the land within such time, the land from and after the expiration of such period will be subject to disposal under the general land laws of the United States.

At the time the above orders were made the decision of the supreme court in the case of Frasher *v.* O'Connor (cited *supra*) which places lands certified in the same category as lands patented had not been rendered. Under that decision, rendered May 4, 1885, the rulings and orders of the Department above quoted can no longer be properly enforced unless there be found in the act of 1877 such special provision as clearly indicates the purpose of Congress to confer upon the executive department jurisdiction to cancel approved selections which the latter may have concluded were made and certified without authority of law, and to throw the lands covered thereby open to disposal under the public land laws as unencumbered public lands.

If such authority is conferred by Congress it is in section two of the act of 1877, which has been quoted herein. Upon a careful inspection and consideration of said section, I am unable to conclude that it contains any provision which, in the face of the supreme court's decisions herein referred to, can fairly be construed as vesting in this Department the authority on its own judgment to cancel a school selection which has been approved and certified to the State.

It follows, therefore, that the selection in question can be legally canceled only after the judgment of a court competent to try the question of title.

Having arrived at the conclusion that the approval and certification were erroneous and without authority of law, and that title to the land is not confirmed to the State, the next step necessary in order to protect the interests of the United States, is to invoke judicial action. To this end you will, at an early day, return the papers transmitted herewith, and with them such other papers or data as the files of your office may furnish and you deem appropriate, together with a copy of this decision, upon receipt of which this Department will request the Honorable Attorney General to cause suit to be instituted in the proper court with a view to having the title to the land in question declared in the United States. The pre-emption cash entry of Compton will remain of record but will stand suspended pending the proposed proceedings. Should the United States be successful in the suit, Compton, because of what he has done, should be preferred, and his said cash entry could ripen into a complete and perfect title.

GERARD SCRIP—EFFECT OF PATENT.

JOHN P. S. VOGHT.

The location of Gerard scrip is limited to "public lands," and can not be permitted for lands included within an existing patent.

The officers of the Land Department act within the general scope of their authority in issuing patents for lands that were prior thereto a part of the public domain, though in particular instances their action may be unwarranted.

The issuance of a patent for land which was a part of the public domain, or the fee to which was in the United States, *prima facie* passes the title, whether such patent is valid, or a void instrument without authority, and precludes the further exercise of departmental jurisdiction over the land until such patent is vacated by judicial action.

An applicant for land covered by an outstanding patent should initiate his claim thereto by proceedings looking toward the vacation of said patent.

Secretary Noble to Acting Commissioner Stone, July 19, 1888.

I have considered the appeal of John P. S. Voght from the decision of your office, dated December 6, 1887, affirming the action of the local officers rejecting his application to locate special certificate No. 2, subdivision No. 7, of William Gerard scrip (issued under the act of Congress approved February 10, 1855 (10 Stat., 849), on the SW. ¼ of the NE. ¼ of Sec. 2, T. 4 S., R. 68 W., Denver, Colorado.

The local office rejected said application for the reason that said tract was entered on November 4, 1872, by Joseph E. Bates, mayor of the city of Denver, in trust for said city, and patent was issued thereon November 15, 1873. Your office affirmed said decision for the reason that until said patent covering said tract was regularly set aside by a court of competent jurisdiction, the tract was not subject to any other appropriation.

The appellant insists that said patent is void as to the tract in question, for the reason that the act of Congress approved May 21, 1872 (17 Stat., 140) specifically designated the lands subject to be entered by the mayor of said city, and the tract in question was not included or described in the act, and hence, the patent is no bar to the location of said scrip.

Said act of May 21, 1872, *supra* provided—

That the mayor of the city of Denver, in Colorado Territory, be, and he is hereby, authorized to enter through the proper land office, at the minimum price per acre, the following lands belonging to the United States, to wit: The northwest quarter of the southwest quarter of section number one, and the southwest quarter of the southeast quarter and the north half of the southeast quarter of section number two, in township number four south, of range number sixty-eight west of the sixth principal meridian in the Territory of Colorado, being one hundred and sixty acres of land, lying adjacent to said city of Denver, to be held and used for a burial-place for said city and vicinity.

The act of February 10, 1855 (*supra*) provided for the location of said scrip upon " public lands." An inspection of the records of your office shows that one of the tracts designated in said act of 1872, namely the SW. ¼ of the SE. ¼ of said section 2 was located with warrant No. 67,094 by B. F. Woodward on October 4, 1866, and patent issued for the same April 17, 1867. See Record of Patents (Vol. 233 p. 421).

It also appears from the records of your office that the only public land in said NE. ¼ and SE. ¼ of said section 2, at the date of said act of 1872, was that subsequently entered in trust for said city of Denver. It must be remembered that said act of May 1872, allowed the mayor of Denver to enter one hundred and sixty acres of land " belonging to the United States," and, since the tract designated as the SW. ¼ of the SE. ¼ in said section did not belong to the United States, the mention of said tract in the description of the particular subdivisions allowed to be entered under the act, was clearly a mistake. But independently of the foregoing, in my judgment the jurisdiction of the Department has been exhausted by the issuance of patent for the tract in question, and it has no authority to allow the location of said scrip so long as the patent remains uncanceled.

In the case of Polk's Lessee *v.* Wendell (9 Cranch 87), Chief Justice Marshall said,

The laws for the sale of public lands provide many guards to secure the regularity of grants, to protect the incipient rights of individuals, and also to protect the State from impositions. Officers are appointed to superintend the business; rules are framed prescribing their duty. These rules are, in general, directory; and when all the proceedings are completed by a patent issued by the authority of the State, a compliance with these rules is presupposed. That every pre-requisite has been performed, is an inférence properly deducible, and which every man has a right to draw from the existence of the grant itself. It would, therefore, be extremely unreasonable to avoid a grant in any court for irregularities in the conduct of those appointed by the government to supervise the progressive course of a title from its commencement to its consummation in a patent. But there are some things so essential to the validity of a contract, that the great principles of justice and of law would be violated, did there not exist some tribunal to which an injured party might appeal, and in which the means by which an older title was acquired, might be examined. In general a court of equity appears to be a tribunal better adapted to this object than a court of law . . . . . In the general, then, a court of equity is the more eligible tribunal for these questions; and they ought to be excluded from a court of law. But there are cases in which a grant is absolutely void; as where the State has no title to the thing granted; or where the officer had no authority to issue the grant. In such cases, the validity of the grant is necessarily examinable at law.

In the same case (5 Wheaton 293), upon a second appeal, the court re-affirmed its former decision saying—

Two sentences will give the substance of that decision; they are expressed in the following words: "But there are cases in which a grant is absolutely void; as where the State has no title to the thing granted, or where the officer had no authority to issue the grant." In such cases, the validity of the grant is necessarily examinable at law.

The doctrine enunciated in said cases was subsequently re-affirmed in the case of Doe, *ex dem*, Patterson *v.* Winn and others (11 Wheaton 380). In the case of Brush *v.* Ware (15 Peters, 93), the supreme court quoted at length from the case of Polk's Lessee *v.* Wendell *et al.*, (*supra*) and in addition said—

A patent appropriates the land called for, and is conclusive against rights subsequently acquired. But where an equitable right, which originated before the date of the patent, whether by the first entry or otherwise is asserted, it may be examined.

See also Rice *v.* The Minnesota & Northwestern R. R. Co. (1 Black, 360); Minter *v.* Cromelin (18 How, 87); Reichart *v.* Felps (6 Wallace 160); Morton *v.* Nebraska (21 Wallace, 660).

In the case of the United States *v.* Stone (2 Wallace 252), the supreme court considered the validity of certain patents for lands issued under the provisions of certain treaties made with the Delaware Indians, to said Stone, the assignee of said Indians. In the report of the case (p. 528) it is stated—

The patents all recited the promises of the treaty of 1860 to grant lands to the chiefs, and went on to grant the particular tract 'in conformity with the provisions, as above recited, of the aforesaid treaty.' In 1862, the Secretary of the Interior decided that the patents had been issued without legal authority, and he declared them void and revoked. However to proceed rightly, the United States filed a bill in the federal court of Kansas, against the Indian Chiefs and Stone to have them judicially decreed null, and the instruments themselves delivered up for cancellation.

The court gave the decree prayed for, and, on appeal, the supreme court held (1st) That the land claimed by appellant never was within the tract alotted to the Delaware Indians in 1829, and surveyed in 1830; (2nd) That it is within the limits of a reservation legally made by the President for military purposes. Consequently, the patents issued to the appellant were without authority and void.

In the body of the opinion, Mr. Justice Grier, speaking for the court said—

A patent is the highest evidence of title, and is conclusive as against the government, and all claiming under junior patents or titles, until it is set aside or annulled by some judicial tribunal. In England, this was originally done by *scire facias*, but a bill in chancery is found a more convenient remedy. Nor is fraud in the patentee the only ground upon which a bill will be sustained. Patents are sometimes issued unadvisedly or by mistake, where the officer has no authority in law to grant them, or where another party has a higher equity and should have received the patent. In such cases, courts of law will pronounce them void. The patent is but evidence of a grant, and the officer who issues it acts ministerially and not judicially. If he issues a patent for land reserved from sale by law, such patent is void for want of authority. But one officer of the land office is not competent to cancel or annul the act of his predecessor. That is a judicial act, and requires the judgment of a court.

In the case of Moore *v.* Robbins (96 U. S. 530) involving the rights of contestants under the pre-emption laws, the supreme court (Mr. Justice Miller delivering the opinion), after speaking of a case "in which the officers of the Department have acted within the scope of their authority," and quoting from the Stone case (*supra*) said—

If an individual setting up claim to the land has been injured, he may, under circumstances presently to be considered, have his remedy against the party who has wrongfully obtained the title which should have gone to him. But in all this, there is no place for the further control of the Executive Department over the title. The functions of that Department necessarily cease when the title has passed from the government. And the title does so pass in every instance where, under the decision of the officer having authority in the matter, a conveyance, generally called a patent, has been signed by the president and sealed and delivered to and accepted by the grantee. It is a matter of course that, after this is done, neither the Secretary nor any other executive officer can entertain an appeal. He is absolutely without authority. If this were not so, the titles derived from the United States, instead of being the safe and assured evidence of ownership, which they are generally supposed to be, would be always subject to the fluctuating, and in many cases unreliable, action of the land office. No man could buy of the grantee with safety, because he could only convey subject to the right of the officer of the government to annul his title. If such a power exists, when does it cease? There is no statute of limitations against the government; and if this right to reconsider and annul a patent after it has once become perfect, exists in the Executive Department, it can be exercised at any time, however remote. It is needless to pursue the subject further. The existence of any such power in the Land Department is utterly inconsistent with the universal principle on which the right of private property is founded.

And the court held that the order of the Secretary of the Interior directing that the patent to Moore be recalled and another patent be issued to Bunn, was made without authority and was "utterly void."

In the case of the United States *v.* Schurz (102 U. S. p. 378), which arose upon an application for a mandamus directing Secretary Schurz to deliver to the applicant a certain patent alleged to have been duly executed, the court said—

It is argued with much plausibility that the relator was not entitled to the land by the laws of the United States, because it was not subject to homestead entry, and that the patent is, therefore, void, and the law will not require the Secretary to do a vain thing by delivering it, which may at the same time embarrass the rights of others in regard to the same land. We are not prepared to say that if the patent is absolutely void so that no right could possibly accrue to the plaintiff under it, the suggestion would not be a sound one. But the distinction between a void and a voidable instrument, though sometimes a very nice one, is still a well-recognized distinction on which valuable rights often depend. And the case before us is one to which we think it is clearly applicable. To the officers of the Land Department, among whom we include the Secretary of the Interior, is confided, as we have already said, the administration of the laws concerning the sale of the public domain. The land in the present case had been surveyed, and, under their control, the land in that district generally had been opened to pre-emption, homestead entry, and sale. The question whether any particular tract, belonging to the government was open to sale, pre-emption or homestead right is in every instance a question of law, as applied to the facts for the determination of those officers. Their decision of such question, and of conflicting claims to the same land by different parties is judicial in its character. It is clear that the right and the duty of deciding all such questions belong to those officers, and the statutes have provided for original and appellate hearings in that department before the successive officers of higher grade up to the Secretary. They have, therefore, jurisdiction of such cases and provision is made for the correction of errors in the exercise of that jurisdiction. When their decision of such a question is finally made and recorded in the shape of the patent, how can it be said that the instrument is absolutely void for such errors as these? If a patent should issue for land in the State of Massachusetts, where the government never had any, it would be absolutely void. If it should issue for land once owned by the government, but long before sold and conveyed by patent to another who held possession, it might be held void in a court of law on the production of the senior patent.

After mentioning the provisions of law for the issuance of patents, the court said—

But we are of opinion that when all that we have mentioned has been consciously and purposely done by each officer engaged in it, and where these officers have been acting in a matter within the scope of their duties, the legal title to the land passes to the grantee, and with it the right to the possession of the patent. No further authority to consider the patentee's case remains in the land office. No right to consider whether he ought in equity, or on new information to have the title or receive the patent. There remains the duty, simply ministerial, to deliver the patent to the owner. . . . On the other hand, when he obtains this possession, if there be any questionable reason why, as against the government, he should not have it, if it has been issued without authority of law, or by mistake of facts, of by fraud of the grantee—the United States can, by bill in chancery, have a decree annulling the patent, or possibly a writ of *scire facias*.   •

In the case of Bicknell v. Comstock (113 U. S. 150) the court speaking of the action of your office in ordering the return of a patent and cancelling the same without the consent and against the protest of those claiming under it said—

That this action was utterly nugatory and left the patent of 1869, to Bicknell in as full force as if no such attempt to destroy or nullify it had been made, is a necessary inference from the principles established by the court in the case of the United States v. Schurz (102 U. S., 378). That principle is, that when the patent has been executed by the President and recorded in the General Land Office, all power of the Executive Department over it has ceased. It is not necessary to decide whether this patent conveyed a valid title or not.

In the case of Moffat v. United States (112 U. S., 24) the supreme court affirmed the decree of the court below cancelling two patents purporting to be issued to certain persons, for land in Colorado, under the pre-emption laws, and decreed to be void the mesne conveyances purporting to pass the title from the alleged patentees to third parties. The court said—

The patents being issued to fictitious parties could not transfer the title, and no one could derive any right under a conveyance in the name of the supposed patentees. A patent to a fictitious person is, in legal effect. no more than a declaration that the government thereby conveys the property to no one. There is in such case, no room for the application of the doctrine that a subsequent *bona fide* purchaser is protected. . . . . To the application of this doctrine of a *bona fide* purchaser there must be a genuine instrument having a legal existence, as well as one appearing on its face to pass the title.

The court distinguished the case of Polks' Lessee v. Wendell (5 Wheaton, 293), holding that the language used in said case had reference to collateral attacks upon patents in cases where the irregularities were committed by officers in the exercise of their admitted jurisdiction, and had " no application to the acts of officers in fabricating documents in the names of persons not in existence."

In the case of the United States v. Minor (114 U. S. 233), the supreme court held that the United States had the same remedy in a court of equity to set aside and annul a patent for land, fraudulently procured, that an individual would have in regard to his own deed obtained under like circumstances. The same court in the Maxwell Land Grant case (121 U. S. 381) said—

We take the general doctrine to be, that when in a court of equity it is proposed to set aside, to annul, or to correct a written instrument for fraud or mistake in the execution of the instrument itself, the testimony on which this is done must be clear, unequivocal, and convincing, and that it cannot be done upon a bare preponderance of evidence which leaves the issue in doubt. If the proposition, as thus laid down in the cases cited, is sound in regard to the ordinary contracts of private individuals, how much more should it be observed where the attempt is to annul the grants the patents, and other solemn evidences of title emanating from the government of the United States under its official seal. In this class of cases, the respect due to a patent, the presumptions that all the preceding steps required by the law had been observed before its issue, the immense importance and necessity of the stability of titles dependent upon these official instruments demand that the effort to set them aside to annul them or to correct mistakes in them, should only be successful when the allegations on which this is attempted, are clearly stated and fully sustained by the proof.

See also Colorado Coal Company v. United States (123 U. S. 307); United States v. San Jacinto Tin Co. (125 U. S. 273).

On January 27, 1821, Mr. Attorney General Wirt (1 Op., 458) gave an opinion that where patents had improvidently issued to the New Madrid sufferers for lands to which at the time others had a right of pre-emption,—

The patents having issued from a mistake of the rights of the United States to the lands granted, are void; and if the parties who hold these patents will not, on this discovery voluntarily return them to the office to be canceled, they can be repealed by a *scire facias*, or bill on the chancery side of the court of the United States within whose jurisdiction the lands lie; which proceeding may be instituted by the United States in their own name, or the pre-emptioners may be authorized to use the name of the United States for this purpose.

On November 26, 1842, Mr. Attorney General Legare (4 Op., 120) advised your office in reply to the following questions:

(1) Whether the land office would be justified in issuing a patent on the pre-emption entry of Robert Johnson, reciting therein the issue and delivery, by mistake, of the patent to Giles Carter (which includes a portion of the land embraced by Johnson's pre-emption entry), leaving the question of title to be settled by them in their local courts upon the two patents so issued; or (2) Whether it will be necessary first, by *scire facias* or bill in chancery, to procure the vacation of the erroneous patent to Carter prior to issuing one to Johnson;

—that the proper mode of proceeding to vacate a land patent erroneously issued was by filing a bill in equity and that a second patent for same land should not issue until the first patent shall have been judicially avoided. In the same volume p. 559, Mr. Attorney General Clifford said—"On the first point I am of opinion that a second patent should not issue. This question has been repeatedly before this office, and it may now be considered the better opinion that a second patent for the same land should not issue so long as a prior patent remains unrevoked by the judicial tribunals." But Mr. Attorney General Toucey (5 Op., 7) subsequently was of the opinion that patents might properly issue to pre-emptors although other patents to ordinary purchasers for the same land had been issued and were outstanding, where the prior pre-emptors had complied with all the conditions of the law.

Mr. Solicitor General and Acting Attorney General Bristow, on June 20, 1871 (13 Op., 457) was of the opinion upon the authority of United States v. Stone (supra) that—

These patents could not be canceled or annulled by the mere act of the Department. That is a judicial act, and requires the intervention of a court. A second patent should not issue for the same land so long as the prior patent remains unrevoked by a judicial tribunal.

The decision of the Department upon the question at issue, like the opinions of the Attorneys General have not been altogether uniform. In the case of Beck et al v. The Central Pacific R. R. Co. (2 C. L. L., 954), my predecessor Mr. Secretary Schurz refused to allow filings or entries of lands within the limits of the Moquelemas grant, for which patents had been issued to said company until the patents had been set aside by some judicial tribunal, although the supreme court of the United States had decided in the case of Newhall v. Sanger, (92 U. S. 761), as stated by the Secretary " that the act of 1851 created a reservation of the lands within the exterior boundaries of the alleged private grant, and as the reservation existed at the date of the withdrawal for railroad purposes, the tract in question was not embraced in the grant to the company and the patent issued was therefore void."

In the case of Streeter v. Missouri, Kansas and Texas R. R. Company (id., 836), Mr. Secretary Schurz held that the confirmatory act of Congress approved April 21, 1876 (19 Stat., 35) required the issuance of second patents in certain cases and the question " whether a patent issued under such circumstances will be good, void or voidable," was not for the Department to decide " as that is a question which the courts alone have authority to determine."

In the case of Rancho Cuyama No. 2 (id., 1241) the Department held that a second patent should issue in that case and that the prior patents for the land were absolutely void and conveyed no title. Secretary Schurz said—" If the patents had been for lands constituting a part of the public domain, proceedings in court would be required to cancel them, although improvidently and fraudulently issued."

In the case of Willis F. Street (2 L. D. 116) Mr. Secretary Teller affirmed the decision of your office, " that as patent has issued upon this scrip location, its regularity can not now be questioned by your office." Street claimed in his appeal that said scrip was issued without authority of law, and that its location was void.

In the case of Baker v. The State of California (4 L. D. 137), Mr. Acting Secretary Jenks held that the erroneous certification of a tract in the place of land selected deprives the Department of further jurisdiction of the land.   The appellant, Baker claimed that the patent was erroneously issued because the State applied for another tract and " that the case comes under the list of patents being void upon their face and over which the Land Department has jurisdiction and can issue a second patent." But the Department held that " none of these objections are well founded."

In the case of the Wisconsin R. R. Co. v. Stinka (4 L. D. 344) Mr. Secretary Lamar refused to hold that said act of 1876 (*supra*) required the issuance of a second patent where it appeared that a patent had already issued for the land.   He said—

It is conceded on all hands that patent for the lands in controversy was issued to this railroad company on the 23rd of November, 1832.   As to the validity of said patent it is not our province to determine herein.   It is sufficient in the determination of this case that the patent was issued by the Land Department acting within the scope of its authority.

After citing and commenting upon some of the decisions of the courts and of the Department, the Secretary concludes :

If the patent to the railroad company is for any reason invalid, and the settler herein has been injured in any way, the courts are the proper tribunals to adjudicate the matter.

In the case of William H. McLarty (ibid., 498) the Department held that a patent, issued in contravention of the record is without authority and void, and will not be delivered by the Department.   The case of the United States v. Schurz (*supra*) was cited and distinguished, but no reference was made in the decision to any other cases in the courts or the Department.   But in the case of Pueblo of San Francisco (5 L. D. 483), Mr. Secretary Lamar in an exhaustive opinion upon the authority of Moore v. Robbins (*supra*), Johnson v. Towsley (13 Wall., 72) and Steel v. The Smelting Company (106 U. S., 450), held that there was no authority in the Department after the issuance of patent to control the land or the title thereto.   In the case of Garriques v. Atchison, Topeka and Santa Fe R. R. Co. (6 L. D. 543), Mr. Secretary Vilas held that " The certification of lands by the Land Department, acting within the scope of its authority, deprives the Department of all jurisdiction over them," and that

The question as to whether the lands were rightfully or wrongfully certified to the State is not one which the Department can now properly consider and pass upon. That is a question for the courts.

In the case of Wright et al v. The State of California (8 L. D. 24) *et al.*, the Department held (re-affirming Story v. Southern Pacific R. R. Co. 4 L. D. 396), that " an application to enter patented land confers no right upon the applicant, either in the courts or the Department, to question the validity of the patent by which title passed from the government."

Numerous other decisions of the courts and the Department might be cited relative to the status of lands covered by patents purporting to convey the title of the United States thereto. But enough cases, and more than enough, have been mentioned to show that the Department ought not to issue a second patent for lands that have been a part of the public domain, so long as the patent remains outstanding. If the lands upon which patents have issued were a part of the public domain, the officers of the Land Department unquestionably act within the general scope of their authority in issuing the patents, although in particular instances their action may have been unwarranted. They are by law charged with the supervision of all the various steps required for the acquisition of the title of the government. It, therefore, follows that when the patent has issued for land which was a part of the public domain, or the fee to which was in the United States, the patent whether it be considered valid or, as stated in Hughes *v.* United States (4 Wall 232) " a void instrument issued without authority, it *prima facie* passed the title," and, if the United States is under any obligation to issue patent to another for land upon which a patent has already issued, its plain duty is to seek to vacate and annul the prior patent.

If the government is dissatisfied with issuance of the patent it may take proper action in the courts to have it annulled. The proper course of procedure where parties desire to enter lands covered by an existing patent, is clearly pointed out by the supreme court in Steel *v.* Smelting Company (*supra*) wherein the court said—

So with a patent for land of the United States which is the result of the judgment upon the right of the patentee by that department of the government to which the alienation of the public lands is confided, the remedy of the agrieved party must be sought by him in a court of equity, if he possess such an equitable right to the premises as would give him the title if the patent were out of the way If he occupy with respect to the land no such position as this, he can only apply to the officers of the government to take measures in its name to vacate the patent or limit its operation. It cannot be vacated or limited in proceedings where it comes collaterally in question. It cannot be vacated or limited by the officers themselves; their power over the land is ended when the patent is issued and placed on the records of the Department. This can be accomplished only by regular judicial proceedings, taken in the name of the government for that special purpose.

In the case at bar, the applicant has no special equity that ought to be considered. His application to locate said scrip was made more than fourteen years after the land had been patented to said city. The land in question was public land at the date of the purchase, the government received the money in payment therefor, and up to the present time has not expressed any dissatisfaction on account thereof. The right of the applicant to locate said scrip is expressly limited to " public land," and I am satisfied, both upon principle and authority that the land applied for was not subject to such location ; that it was taken from the category of public lands when said entry was made and patent issued thereon, and that the decision of your office refusing said application was correct. It is accordingly affirmed.

RULES TO BE OBSERVED IN PASSING ON FINAL PROOFS.

DEPARTMENT OF THE INTERIOR,
GENERAL LAND OFFICE,
Washington, D. C., July 17, 1889.

Rules 1, 2, 3, and 4 of the circular of February 19, 1887, approved February 21, 1887,* are hereby modified to read as follows, viz:

1. Final proofs in all cases where the same are required by the general land laws or regulations of the Department, must be taken in accordance with the published notice; provided, however, that such testimony may be taken within ten days following the time advertised in cases where accident or unavoidable delays have prevented the applicant or his witnesses from making such proof on the day specified. Section 7 of the act of March 2, 1889 (25 Statutes, 854).

2. Where final proof or any part thereof has not been taken on the day advertised, or within ten days thereafter under the exception and as required in Rule 1, you will direct new advertisement to be made; and if no protest or objection is then filed, the proof theretofore submitted, if in compliance with the law in other respects, may be accepted.

3. If the testimony of either claimant or witness is taken at a different place than that advertised, you will require new advertisement for the proof to be taken at such place as you may deem advisable; and if no protest or objection is then filed, the proof theretofore submitted, if regular in all other respects may be accepted without further testimony.

4. When a witness not named in the advertisement is substituted for an advertised witness, unless two of the advertised witnesses testify, require new advertisement of the names of the witnesses who do testify at such time and place as you may direct; and if no protest or objection is then filed, the proof theretofore submitted, if satisfactory in all other respects, may be accepted.

5. Where final proof is taken before an officer not named in the advertisement, it may be accepted if otherwise sufficient, provided the proof is taken at the time and place designated in the printed notice, or within ten days thereafter under the exceptions provided in Rule 1; and provided further, that both the officer advertised to take such proof and the officer taking the same, shall officially certify that no protest was at any time filed before him against the claimant's entry.

6. The certification of the declaration to become a citizen of the United States, or other evidence necessary to establish citizenship, should be received only when made under the hand and seal of the clerk of the court in which such papers appear of record. But where it is shown that the judicial record has been lost or destroyed, the proof

---

* See 5 L. D., 426, and 8 L. D., 3.

of such citizenship may be established by the rules governing the introduction of secondary evidence.

7. When proof is made before the register or receiver and the final certificate does not bear the date of the proof, and the record contains no reason therefor, require of the register and receiver an explanation thereof; and if the delay was caused by a failure to tender the money or other consideration at the time of making the proof, require additional evidence to show that the claimant had not, at the date of the certificate, transferred the land, which evidence may consist of the claimant's affidavit taken before some office authorized to administer oaths.

8. When proof is made before any other officer than the register or receiver, allow a reasonable time for a prompt transmission of the papers to the district land office, and if any longer interval is shown between date of proof and date of certificate (if proof is otherwise sufficient and the record contains no reason for the delay), require of the register and receiver an explanation thereof; and if such delay was caused by the fault of the claimant, require the same additional evidence as prescribed under Rule 7.

9. Where final proof has been accepted by the local office prior to the promulgation of said circular of February 19, 1887, if in all other respects satisfactory, except that it was not taken as advertised, the cases may be submitted to the Board of Equitable Adjudication for its consideration.

Nothing herein shall be construed to affect proofs taken under and conforming to prior rules and regulations.

W. M. STONE,
Acting Commissioner.

Approved July 17, 1889:
    JOHN W. NOBLE,
        Secretary.

SWAMP LAND—ADJUSTMENT OF GRANT.

POWESHIEK COUNTY.

In determining the character of land claimed under the swamp grant the sworn testimony of competent witnesses should not be ignored on a superficial examination in the field made by a special agent.

The act of 1850 granted not only such lands as might strictly come under the description, "swamp lands," but also such as were so "wet" as to be rendered thereby unfit for cultivation.

Secretary Noble to Acting Commissioner Stone, July 19, 1889.

I have considered the case arising upon the appeal of the State of Iowa, from your office decision of November 16, 1886, in the matter of the claim of Poweshiek county, Iowa, for indemnity on account of certain alleged swamp and overflowed lands in said county.

By act of the legislature of the State of Iowa, passed January 13, 1853, all the rights of said State of Iowa in and to lands and indemnities for lands granted to said State under acts of September 28, 1850 (9 Stat., 519), as extended by act of March 2, 1855 (10 Stat., 634), and March 3, 1857 (11 Stat., 251), were granted to the respective counties in which said lands were situated.

The duly authorized agent of the State of Iowa filed in your office, in accordance with the rules and regulations laid down by your office in its circular of August 12, 1878 (5 C. L. O., 173), a list of lands selected and claimed by Poweshiek county, in said State.

Under instructions from your office, dated January 22, 1883, supplemented by further and more specific instructions of October 10, 1883, and September 5 and November 28, 1884, Robert L. Ream was sent to Iowa as special agent of the United States, to take testimony relative to the character of said lands in Poweshiek county. In due time said Ream made a report relative to said lands—embracing in all six hundred and eighty-five tracts, aggregating twenty-seven thousand and four hundred acres.

On June 15, 1886, your office instructed Special Agent Forrey to make an investigation of the lands in Poweshiek county which had previously, by Special Agent Ream's report, been shown to be swampy in character. On September 9, 1886, Agent Forrey reported upon three hundred and ninety-nine tracts, embracing 15,960 acres. Of the tracts examined he reported that three hundred and twenty-six were dry, that sixty-nine were swampy, and that the State agent waived claim to the remaining four.

Your office, on November 16, 1886, rendered a decision as follows:

The claim of the State of Iowa to indemnity under the acts of March 2, 1855, and March 3, 1857, on the following described lands in Poweshiek county, Iowa, is hereby held for rejection for the reason that evidence on file in this office shows that said lands are not of the character contemplated by the act of September 28, 1850.

Thereupon follows a list of two hundred and twenty-five tracts thus held for rejection. The tracts so rejected appear to be identical with the three hundred and twenty-six tracts reported by Agent Forrey to be dry—your office decision describing, sometimes by half-sections, and sometimes by entire-sections, tracts which Agent Forrey describes by quarter-sections.

While your office decision rejects the tracts in question "for the reason that evidence on file shows that said lands are not of the character contemplated by the act of September 28, 1850," it gives no indication of the nature of such evidence. The natural presumption is that the evidence referred to is that of the field-notes on file in your office, and the report of Special Agent Forrey.

The testimony taken before United States Agent Ream consisted of sworn statements of at least two disinterested witnesses in each case, properly taken in the manner prescribed by your office. The witnesses are in each case certified by the judge of the district court of the judicial district in which the county of Poweshiek is situated, to be persons with whom he is "personally acquainted, and who are citizens prominent in their respective counties for probity and good judgment." The majority of them were more than fifty years of age; five of them were between seventy and eighty years of age. In a considerable number of cases the witnesses had personally known the tract since before the passage of the act of September 28, 1850. In no case had a witness been well acquainted with the tract concerning which he testified for less than fourteen years.

The substance of the testimony is to the effect that Poweshiek county, especially along its streams, is a comparatively level region. The bed of its rivers and streams incline but slightly; hence their current is not rapid. As a natural consequence, after a heavy rain the streams become choked with surplus water, which overflows the adjacent land, from a few inches to several feet deep (according to the amount of rain-fall), remaining from a day to a week, until the stream gradually sinks to its ordinary level. The land subject to such overflow becomes thereby unfit for cultivation. The condition of such land is well set forth in the affidavit of John Sanders, regarding the SW. ¼ of the SW. ¼ of Sec. 23, T. 78 N., R. 15 W., — which your office rejects from the list of swamp and overflowed land claimed by the State:

That at one time I had a part of said forty-acre tract broken, and tried to cultivate it for several years, but failed at least four out of every five years to get a crop; that I finally tried to set it in timothy grass, with the hope of being able to use it for tame grass pasture, but this, too, failed; and the attempt to cultivate it was at last wholly abandoned as a futile and hopeless task; that the tract was then let go back to wild grass, in which condition it has ever since remained; . . . . . that it is very uncertain and practically worthless as hay or meadow land, on account of its liability to overflow and leave sand, dirt, weeds, and driftwood scattered promiscuously through the grass, just on the eve of hay-harvest, entirely ruining it for the purpose of feeding stock.

Special Agent Forrey, on the other hand, took no testimony, basing his report exclusively upon his own personal observation. It is in evidence from men who drove the team used by him that this observation was but partial and very superficial. Witness Carr makes affidavit:

During the six days . . . . . Mr. Forrey did not get out of his buggy only twice to examine land, and then he did not go out of the public highway . . . . . At one time in particular I remember that said Forrey made an examination of a tract that was one and a half miles from the buggy.

C.W. Boody makes affidavit that he drove team for Mr. Forrey while making a part of his examinations; that all of said examinations made by said Forrey while witness was driving team for him were made from the buggy, "Mr. Forrey saying in substance that he did not come out here to walk."

There is abundance of other testimony to the same effect.

But no amount of merely personal observation made at the time when Agent Forrey examined the land could determine its condition in 1850.

First, because ditching and draining had been carried on throughout this region for thirty-six years (intervening between the passage of the swamp land act and the date of Mr. Forrey's examination). Secondly, because Mr. Forrey made said examination at the dryest time of an exceptionally dry year. T. S. Appelgate makes affidavit that he had been a resident of the county since 1852:

That the year 1886 was an extremely dry year—more so than any other year since I came to this county—no rain having fallen for ninety days and more; that stock running in pasture had to be fed to keep them from want, on account of the pasture drying up.

There are numerous affidavits in the record to the same effect.

Certainly the sworn testimony of men of character and probity, who have been intimately acquainted with the land for from fifteen to forty years, ought not to be set aside upon the report of an examination like this, made under circumstances like these.

The field notes of survey of the tracts in controversy are rarely or never sufficiently full to afford satisfactory evidence as to whether a given tract does or does not come within the provisions of the swamp land act. Thus, the field notes of the first tract named in the list rejected by your office decision—the NW. ¼ of the SW. ¼ of Sec. 1, T. 78, R. 13—say simply, "creek bottom." In other cases the sole comment is "level creek bottom;" "level rich creek bottom;" "creek bottom, first-rate land;" "level creek bottom, second rate land," etc. Such statements contain nothing to indicate even inferentially that the land thus referred to may not be overflowed as hereinbefore described to an extent to render it so wet as to be "unfit for cultivation." Such a notation as is made in the field notes opposite the NW. ¼ of the NE. ¼ of Sec. 22, T. 79, R. 13, "level bottom, rather wet," would seem to corroborate Agent Beam's report rather than Agent Forrey's; yet your office rejects the tract as not granted by the swamp land act.

Section 3 of the act of September 28, 1850, provides:

That in making out a list and plats of the land aforesaid, all legal subdivisions the greater part of which is wet and unfit for cultivation shall be included in said lists and plats.

Taking this section in connection with the first section of the act, donating to the State "those swamp and overflowed lands made unfit thereby for cultivation," it is clear that the act intended to grant not solely such lands as might strictly come under the description, "swamp lands," but such as were so "wet" as to be rendered thereby unfit for cultivation. This is apparent when it is considered that the act of March 2, 1849, designated the lands contemplated by the grant as "swamp and overflowed," whereas the grant of September 28, 1850, enlarged the provisions of the grant by including therein "land the greater part of which is *wet* and unfit for cultivation."

In the case of Marrill *v.* Tobin (30 Fed. Rep., 738,) the United States circuit court for the Northern District of Iowa held that lands which by reason of swamp *or overflow* become unfit for cultivation, are within the purview of the act of Congress of 1850, granting certain swamp and overflowed lands to the State of Iowa. In that case it appeared that the land was low bottom land, liable to overflow sometimes once and sometimes oftener each year; "some years it was so completely overflowed that not even a crop of wild hay could be saved from it, and at no time since 1857 could the land, or any part of it be cultivated for the raising of any kind of grain, corn, or the like." Upon this state of facts the court held: "No other conclusion can possibly be reached under the evidence than that the land is 'overflowed,' within the meaning of the term as used in the act of 1850."

To the same effect is the decision of the court in the case of Keeran v. Griffith (31 Cal., 461), in which the court held that "if land is not susceptible of cultivation in grain or other staple productions, by reason of 'overflow,' it is 'swamp and overflowed.'" See also Thompson v. Thornton (50 Cal., 142).

Nothing hereinbefore said is to be understood as deciding the question of the character of the specific tracts now in controversy, or any of them. The case has not yet reached a stage where such decision by the Secretary is necessary or proper. Your office (by its decision of November 16, 1886, held for cancellation a large number of tracts in Poweshiek county, "for the reason that evidence on file shows that said lands are not of the character contemplated by the act of September 28, 1850." Such evidence, if reference be had to the report of Special Agent Forrey, is alleged to be partial, superficial, and unreliable; certainly it is wholly *ex parte*, and as such can not properly be made the basis of a decision. If to the field notes, they are entirely insufficient to show whether or not the tracts therein described are subject to overflow whereby they become so "wet" as to be unfit for cultivation. Besides, the State of Iowa elected not to abide by the field notes, but to select land by its own agents and report the same to the surveyor general, with proof as to the character thereof. Upon the testimony taken in due form and in strict accordance with the law and the regulations of your office and approved by the Department, your office has never passed. The papers in the case are herewith returned in order that you may do so. If you find the testimony so taken to be sufficient to satisfactorily show whether or not the lands in question, or any of them, by reason of being overflowed, are rendered so wet or swampy as to be unfit for cultivation, you will decide accordingly, unless the facts reported by said special agent Forrey are such as to cast serious doubt upon the correctness of said testimony. But if such doubts should arise, or if in the case of any tract or tracts the testimony should be found insufficient to enable you to arrive at a satisfactory conclusion as to the true character of the said lands, you will order another hearing with reference thereto.

Your office decision of November 16, 1886, is modified accordingly.

PRE-EMPTION DECLARATORY STATEMENT—HOMESTEAD.

McCRORY v. CASTEEN.

Tho pre-emptive right is not exhausted by a declaratory statement filed without the authority or knowledge of the pre-emptor.

The pre-emptive right is not defeated by making a homestead entry pending consummation of the pre-emption claim, where residence on, and improvement of said claim were maintained, and the said entry was subsequently relinquished.

First Assistant Secretary Chandler to Acting Commissioner Stone, July 20, 1889.

This case involves the pre-emption cash entry No. 248, of Charles O. Casteen, for the S ½ of SE ¼, Sec. 3 and N ¼ of NE ¼ Sec. 10, T. 32 S., R. 28 W., Garden City district, Kansas.

Casteen filed a declaratory statement for said land August 14, 1884, alleging settlement August 12, 1884, and March 18, 1885, made final proof and payment and received final certificate.

February 12, 1886, John K. McCrory filed an affidavit of contest against said entry, and hearing was ordered and set for November 15, 1886. On the voluminous and conflicting testimony adduced at the hearing, the local officers decided in favor of Casteen, and on appeal by McCrory from said decision, your office sustained the action of the local officers by the decision of February 15, 1889, from which McCrory now appeals to this Department.

As stated in your office decision, McCrory's contest raises two material questions :

First—Did the previous filing by Casteen, of a declaratory statement in the Wichita land office bring him within the inhibition of Sec. 2261, Revised Statutes?

Second—Did he (Casteen) comply with the requirements of the pre-emption law as to residence and improvements upon said land?

As to the first question, the proof shows conclusively that the said declaratory statement was filed by mistake by one H. O. Meigs, without the knowledge of Casteen, and contrary to his instructions to said Meigs, and that Casteen never in any manner ratified said filing. It was not, therefore, in fact or in law, a filing by Casteen, and his pre-emptive right was not exhausted thereby. Vesta F. Bonebrake (7 L. D., 503).

As to the second question, the proof also establishes that Casteen settled upon the land, August 12, 1884, and commenced actual residence about September 12, 1884, and maintained said residence to the exclusion of a home elsewhere until sometime after he made proof, March 18, 1885. His improvements, consisting of a frame dwelling house (well furnished), a sod barn with lumber roof, a corral and about 5½ acres of breaking, were valued at $175.00.

It is true, Casteen (believing he had the right to do so) made homestead entry of an adjoining tract, during the period he was consummating his pre-emption claim, but he did not abandon his residence on, or improvement of his pre-emption claim, and said homestead entry was subsequently canceled on relinquishment.

After careful examination of the entire record, I find no sufficient reason for disturbing the conclusion attained by both your office and the local officers, and the decision of your office is therefore affirmed.

PRACTICE—EVIDENCE—ATTORNEY.

WARE ET AL. v. JUDSON.

The local officers have no authority to exclude testimony that is offered, but should summarily put a stop to obviously irrelevant questioning.
Briefs containing scurrilous and impertinent matter will be stricken from the files.

Secretary Noble to Acting Commissioner Stone, July 20, 1889.

I have considered the appeal of Herbert H. Judson from your decision of April 11, 1888, holding for cancellation his mineral entry, No. 2486, upon the Miller Placer, Leadville land district, Colorado.

The survey was made December 26, 1884, and on January 17, 1885, Judson filed his application for patent. Notice of his intention was given by publication and by posting.

March 28, 1885, no adverse claim having been filed and no objection having been made, entry was allowed, the money paid for the land and final certificate issued.

February 10, 1887, your office directed the local officers, " because of allegations contained in certain protests against said entry, filed in this office by A. J. Ware, Hezekiah Storms, Otto Eckhardt, Henry Shuester and Thomas H. Clague, to cause a hearing to be held to determine what, if any, improvements have been placed on the Miller placer by the claimant or his grantors, their character, extent, location, value, and the time when placed on the claim, and also to receive testimony, if offered, touching the sufficiency of the publication in the Dillon Enterprise. "

Said hearing was commenced on September 20, 1887, at which the parties, their witnesses and counsel appeared. A number of days was spent in taking testimony, and, on November 28, following, the local officers rendered a joint opinion in favor of the applicant. April 11, 1888, your office rendered a decision, holding said entry for cancellation.

At the hearing much testimony was submitted, some of it conflicting, much of it irrelevant and inconclusive, and all of it so unsatisfactory that I am unable to come to an intelligent conclusion thereon.

The case is therefore remanded for a further hearing, when it is expected that proper testimony, bearing upon and confined to the issues involved, will be presented.

In excluding the testimony relating to the lease, the local officers acted in violation of rule 41 of the Rules of Practice, which plainly prohibited such exclusion.   But, whilst under this rule, they may not exclude testimony offered, it is their imperative duty under the last clause thereof, when the privileges accorded the parties are being abused, to "summarily put a stop to obviously irrelevant questioning."

You will also cause the brief of protestant's attorney, filed in the local office November 22, 1887, the brief of one of applicant's attorneys, filed in the local office on November 24, 1887, and the brief of another of the attorneys for applicant, filed in the local office on June 6, 1888, to be stricken from the files of your office and returned to them, as containing matter both scurrilous and impertinent.   When an attorney so far forgets the dignity of his profession, the courtesy which should characterize his conduct towards his associates, and the duty he owes the Department, as to print in his brief insulting epithets and vulgar vituperation, as has been done, especially in the last two briefs referred to, the respect due the officers of the law demands that such conduct should be severely rebuked.

You will, therefore, direct the local officers to fix a time for a further hearing of said case, after due notice to all parties.   The same will then be re-adjudicated upon the testimony submitted at such hearing, and Judson's entry, in the meantime, is to remain intact.

PRACTICE—NOTICE—FEE DEPOSIT—MORTGAGEE.

WILLIAM W. WATERHOUSE.

Hearings ordered on the report of special agents are required to be conducted in accordance with the rules of practice prescribed for contests so far as the same are applicable.

Publication of the notice once a week for four consecutive weeks is an essential in service by publication.

Failure to post a copy of the notice on the land is a fatal defect in service by publication.

A special appearance for the purpose of objecting to the service does not waive the errors in said service.

Participation of counsel in the examination of witnesses, after motion to dismiss is overruled, does not affect the force of his objections to the jurisdiction.

The receipt of notice by either a registered or unregistered letter amounts to personal service of the notice.

A requirement of the local officers that the claimant shall make a deposit, to pay for the cross-examination of witnesses introduced by the government, will be presumed to be a proper exercise of discretionary authority in the absence of any showing to the contrary.

A mortgagee cannot plead want of notice if it is not shown that the existence of the mortgage was made known to the local office in time for service of such notice.

Secretary Noble to Acting Commissioner Stone, July 20, 1889.

On July 25, 1883, William W. Waterhouse made homestead entry of Sec. 25, T. 130 N., R. 57 W., at the Fargo land office, Dakota, and on

July 1, 1884, he submitted commutation proof thereon, and received final certificate July 12, 1884. Subsequently, on report of a special agent that said entry was fraudulent and ought to be canceled, a hearing was ordered and had before the local officers on September 11, 1885. On the testimony then taken the entry was held for cancellation by your office on May 31, 1887; on appeal, this action was approved by my predecessor, Secretary Vilas, December 19, 1888. It is now asked that his decision be reviewed and reversed for errors therein, and that the cause be remanded for a further hearing.

With the motion for review are filed eleven specifications of error, which in substance, claim a reversal of said decision, because of the erroneous finding of bad faith on the part of the entryman; because no legal notice of said hearing was given to the entryman or his mortgagees; because application for continuance was denied; because counsel for defense was not permitted to cross-examine the witnesses; and because claimant has had no opportunity to present his case upon its merits. Any one of these allegations, if sustained, would be sufficient to secure a reversal of said decision.

The question of notice being jurisdictional in its character, will be first examined.

Hearings, ordered on the report of a special agent, being analogous in many respects to ordinary contests to secure the cancellation of entries, are required to be conducted in accordance with the rules of practice prescribed for contests, so far as the same are applicable. J. W. Hoffman, 5 L. D., 1; United States v. Copeland, ib., 171. In the present case, the special agent having made a sufficient showing of the non-residence of the entryman, an attempt was made to give "notice by publication," as prescribed in rules 13 and 14.

An inspection of the record shows, that the required notice was published only from July 17, to August 1, 1885, and consequently was not published "once a week for four successive weeks," as required by rule 13. Nor does it appear that notice was posted upon the land as required by rule 14. This defect is equally fatal. Kelly v. Grameng, 5 L. D., 611.

Nor were these errors waived by the appearance of counsel for defense at the hearing, since that appearance was special and for the purpose of moving dismissal of the proceedings, because of want of legal service. Nor did the subsequent participation of counsel in the examination of witnesses, after his motion to dismiss was overruled, in any way affect the force of his objection to the jurisdiction. Harkness v. Hyde, 98 U. S., 476; Milne v. Dowling, 4 L. D., 379.

These defects were not referred to in either your office decision, or in that of my predecessor, though presented on the face of the record, and specified as errors on appeal. In view of all this, it is plain that there was no legal "notice by publication." Parker v. Castle, 4 L. D., 84.

But, whilst this is so, the record also discloses that a registered letter, containing notice of the hearing, was mailed by the receiver on July 14, 1885, directed to said Waterhouse, at Oshkosh, Wisconsin, and that the receipt of said letter was acknowledged by him on the return card, on July 17, 1889, more than thirty days before the date fixed for the hearing.

Rule 15 of practice provides that:

Proof of personal service shall be the written acknowledgment of the person served, or the affidavit of the person who served the notice attached thereto, stating the time, place, and manner of service.

There is no denial of the receipt of the registered letter; and the receipt of notice by either a registered or unregistered letter has been held by the Department to amount to personal service. Crowston *v.* Seal, 5 L. D., 213, approved of in United States *v.* Richardson, ib., 254; New Orleans Canal and Banking Co. *v.* State of Louisiana, ib., 479, approved in Ida May Taylor's case, 6 L. D., 107.

It must therefore be held that the entryman had legal notice of the hearing, and his assignment of error in this respect is not sustained. Nor is there any force in the objection that the mortgagees were not notified of the hearing, inasmuch as it is not shown that the existence of said mortgage was made known to the local officers in time, so that such notice might have been given. If parties fail to notify the local officers of the acquisition of an interest in entered lands, after proof, and before patent, they can blame no one but themselves if notice is not given to them of proceedings involving said lands; it being out of all reason to require those officers to examine the records of the county offices to ascertain if any assignment of or incumbrance upon said land has been therein recorded, before notice shall be issued for contest or hearing. American Improvement Co., 5 L. D., 603; Cyrus H. Hill, ib., 276.

The assertion that application for a continuance was denied at the hearing need not be considered, inasmuch as there is nothing in the record to show that any such application was made, and consequently there was no improper denial thereof.

The fifth specification of error is the refusal to allow counsel to cross-examine the witnesses of the prosecution.

The record discloses that during the cross-examination of the first witness for the prosecution, the attorney for defense was notified, that, under the rules, he was "required to make a deposit for folio fees in his cross-examination of witnesses for the government and the direct examination of witnesses that he may produce. Attorney for claimant refuses so to do, and withdraws." This action was not commented on in either of the decisions in the case, though specified as error on appeal. It is necessary, therefore, to dispose of it now.

The right to be confronted with and cross-examine witnesses in a proceeding involving life, liberty, or property is one which all tribunals, charged with the administration of justice, guard most jealously, and an interference with its free and orderly exercise, within legitimate bounds, is not to be tolerated But it has been found necessary in order to promote and expedite the administration of justice that an abuse of this right should be guarded against. In this Department rules 41 and 56 undertake to do this. The last clause of rule 41 says: "Officers taking testimony will . . . . . summarily put a stop to obviously irrelevant questioning." Rule 56 provides that—

Where the officer taking testimony shall rule that a course of examination is irrelevant, and checks the same under Rule 41, he may, nevertheless, in his discretion, allow the same to proceed at the sole cost of the party making such examination.

Nothing is stated as to the reasons which actuated the officers in making such demand; nor can anything be very clearly gathered from the record in respect thereto. The cross-examination, as reported, whilst, perhaps, strictly speaking, somewhat loose and latitudinous, was not clearly illegal or beyond bounds.

No allegation, charge, or showing is made by the defense in relation to the matter, further than the naked statement in the motion for review that, "It was error . . . . . to refuse to allow" said cross-examination.

The rules do not require that the officers should place upon record the reasons which moved them to act in such cases. The power given to them was summary in character, and intended to aid in the orderly administration of justice in matters pending before them, sitting as a statutory tribunal of limited jurisdiction, and without the power even to preserve order in its sessions, or to punish for contempt, as is the case with almost every other known tribunal charged with administration of justice.

It must be conceded that the officers are clothed with ample power to make such demand, in their discretion, upon the happening of a contingency. Because no statement to that effect is in the record, shall we assume that none such arose, and, as a corollary, that these officers unwisely, improperly and wantonly exercised this summary power to defeat justice; and this, too, in the absence of any allegation to that effect by those questioning the legality of the act? In the absence of any statement or showing that they acted within the line of their duty, shall we assume that they acted without that line of duty?

On the contrary, the power given having been exercised, everything is presumed to be rightly and duly performed until the contrary is shown; the presumption *omnia rite esse acta* being clearly applicable. Broom's Legal Maxims, 944; Bank of the United States *v.* Dandridge, 12 Wheat., 69.

As the assignment of error only goes to the denial of a right to further cross-examine the witness, without making a deposit to cover the cost of reducing the cross-examination to writing, for the reasons given said assignment is not sustained.

The conclusion arrived at that the entryman had personal notice of the hearing is an answer to the charge that he has had no opportunity to present his case upon its merits. He has had his day in court, and that he did not avail of his opportunity is his own fault. If sickness of himself or witnesses prevented him from properly presenting his case, he could have easily obtained a continuance on that ground, as his counsel was then present. But, instead of seeking an opportunity to present a meritorious defense, the effort was to make a technical one, on the ground of want of notice and want of authority in the land officers to cancel an entry for any cause after certificate had issued and before patent.

On the evidence in the case, it is clear to my mind that claimant never established residence, in good faith, upon the land in question. Therefore the motion for reconsideration and reversal of the former decision is overruled.

____

PRACTICE—NOTICE—EVIDENCE—DEPOSITIONS.

LEIMBACH v. LANE.

The entryman's address, as appearing in the application to enter, may be properly accepted by the local office as the post office address of the claimant, in transmitting a copy of the notice of contest by registered mail.

Under an order appointing a commissioner to take the testimony of certain witnesses, named in the application for such order, said commissioner is not authorized to take the testimony of witnesses not thus specified therein.

First Assistant Secretary Chandler to Acting Commissioner Stone, July 20, 1889.

I have considered the appeal of Hester A. Lane, from your office decision of April 20, 1888, holding for cancellation her homestead entry for the NE. ¼ of Section 12, T. 30, R. 46 W., Valentine, Nebraska.

The entry was made May 14, 1885, and December 19, 1885, William Leimbach filed affidavit of contest charging abandonment and failure to establish residence. Upon the affidavit of the contestant that personal service could not be had upon the claimant, notice by publication was ordered. Notice of the complaint, citing the claimant and the contestant to appear at the local office March 18, 1886, and furnish testimony concerning said charge was published for four consecutive weeks, in the "Hay Springs Alert," a weekly newspaper published in the county in which the land in contest is situated. The first publication was on January 27, and the last on February 18, 1886. December 19, 1885, the contestant made affidavit that "he is unable to secure the services of John Leimbach and L. W. Johnson his witnesses both of Hay Springs Nebraska, for the reason that said witnesses live over one hundred miles from the land office and that said witnesses are material. Contestant, therefore asks the Hon. Register to commission R. T. Milford, a notary public, at Hay Springs, Nebraska, to take deposition of witnesses."

March 1, 1886, the register using the printed form, appointed said R. T. Milford a commissioner "to take the testimony of witnesses in the contest case of William Leimbach v. Hester A. Lane." The testimony was taken before said commissioner March 13, 1886. The claimant was represented by counsel who objected to the testimony of several witnesses for the reason that they had not been named in the affidavit asking for the appointment of the commissioner. The local officers considered the testimony, held that the charges made by the contestant were sustained and recommended the cancellation of the entry. Lane appealed and alleged that her counsel had made special appearance and moved to dismiss the contest for failure of proper service of notice, and that the local officers erred in rejecting said motion and that they also erred in not striking out the testimony of witnesses D. A. Post and Belle Leimbach. In deciding the case, April 20, 1888, your office found that the rules had been complied with and jurisdiction acquired; and held that upon the merits of the case the evidence sustained the finding of the local office. You, therefore, held the entry for cancellation.

The claimant appeals from your said decision alleging generally error therein.

The chief assignment of error is that proper service of notice was not made upon the defendant and that consequently jurisdiction was not acquired.

I find that a notice of the contest was published for four weeks in a newspaper published near the land, such publication having been ordered upon the affidavit of the contestant that he had used due diligence to ascertain the whereabouts of the claimant and that personal service could not be made; that a copy of said notice was posted upon a conspicuous place upon the land for the requisite period, and that the register mailed January 19, 1886, a registered letter containing a copy of said notice addressed to Mrs. Harriet A. Lane, Bordeaux, Nebraska. It is stated in the brief filed by counsel that the defendant only learned of the contest four days before the trial and therefore did not have time to prepare for it. In an affidavit filed with the appeal, the claimant deposes that when she made homestead application she gave her post office address as Hazel Green, Iowa, that neither Bordeaux, Nebraska, the placed named in the homestead application and to which the register sent registered letter, containing notice of the contest, nor Valentine, Nebraska, to which the contestant sent the notice, had ever been her post office address. She further deposes that if she had received proper notice of the contest and had been allowed the usual time she could and would have made a sufficient defense, and that since making said entry her residence has been continuous and that she has never been absent from said land over thirty days at any one time with the exception of six months next after making her entry; that she has made valuable improvements and that such absences as have occurred were due to sickness. She prays that if the contest is not dismissed that the case be returned for a new hearing.

In answer to these allegations I find that the homestead application begins,— " I Mrs. Hester A. Lane, of Bordeaux, Nebr. do hereby apply to enter " etc., and that in an affidavit of the same date setting forth that she is a deserted wife the claimant described herself as "I, Hester A. Lane, of Bordeaux, Nebr." etc. Under these circumstances the register was justified in sending the registered letter containing the notice to Bordeaux, Nebraska.

In deciding the case the local officers and your office considered the testimony of certain witnesses not named in the affidavit upon which the order appointing a commissioner was based, notwithstanding the objection interposed by counsel for defendant at the time. I think it a fair inference from the language of Rule 24, that when an application is made for the appointment of a commissioner to take the testimony of certain material witnesses who are named in said application, that the commissioner should not take, and should not be authorized to take, the testimony of witnesses not named therein I, therefore, sustain the objection made by defendant's counsel to the testimony of witnesses Post and Belle Leimbach. This leaves for consideration the testimony of Johnson who is the only witness having competent knowledge of the tract. His testimony is strongly against the defendant but is of a negative character and is not conclusive.

Inasmuch as the testimony is not wholly satisfactory, does not bring out all the facts and leaves a doubt whether the claimant did not establish residence before the contest was brought, and upon consideration of the sworn allegation of the claimant as to the post office address given by her when she made homestead application,—an allegation attacking the sufficiency of the notice,—I modify your decision to the extent of suspending your order holding the entry for cancellation, and grant her request for a new hearing to be had in accordance with the rules and regulations of your office.

DESERT LAND ENTRY–FINAL PROOF–NON-IRRIGABLE LAND.

W. R. WILLIAMS.

In establishing the fact of reclamation the testimony on final proof should show explicitly the character of the water supply and the means provided for its distribution, giving full information as to the number and length of all ditches on each legal sub-division.

In the absence of an adverse claim, a desert entry, made in good faith will not be canceled though it includes non-irrigable land.

Secretary Noble to Acting Commissioner Stone, July 20, 1889.

I have considered the appeal of W. R. Williams from your office decision of August 22, 1887, holding for cancellation his desert land entry for the NW. ¼, SE. ¼, and the SW. ¼, section 33, T. 20 N., R. 68 W., Cheyenne, Wyoming land district.

Claimant made desert land entry for said land May 1, 1883, and on April 19, 1886, he presented final proof and received final certificate.

On May 3, 1887, your office called upon claimant to furnish evidence as to the number, location and dimensions of his lateral ditches.

Upon this, claimant wrote your office stating that since making final proof a railroad has been built across the land destroying part of his original ditch and obliterating his lateral ditches and he has been compelled to dig a new main ditch and uses the railroad grade for one side thereof, and that he now distributes water upon the opposite side of said railroad by flumes or chutes.

Your office upon the receipt of said letter held his entry for cancellation for want of further evidence in regard to lateral ditches.

It appears from the evidence taken on final proof, that claimant had conveyed water upon each forty acres of said tract and in 1885 had raised a crop of hay, potatoes and beans, thereon, by means of irrigation; that twenty acres of the tract were sown to timothy and irrigated and that the portion of it cut, yielded ten tons of hay, part of said twenty acres being used for pasturage.

It also appears, that the water is taken from Chugwater Creek, a mile and a half above the land by a main ditch, thirty inches wide, at the bottom, carrying eighteen inches of water in depth, and that from this ditch the water was carried upon each subdivision of the land by small lateral ditches tapping the main ditch at intervals, and that one and a quarter inches of water per acre were distributed upon said land continuously from May 1, to August 1, 1885, but he says he cannot now prove the exact location of the lateral ditches at the time of final proof, as his employes who made the same have left the locality and their whereabouts are now to him unknown.

While the testimony in this case is to the effect that the water was equally distributed over about one hundred and sixty acres of said land completely saturating the soil and that with such irrigation, would produce hay, oats, barley, beans, potatoes, and such other crops as can be grown in that region, and that by means of lateral ditches the water was carried and distributed over each sub-division of said land, yet it was ruled by the Department in the case of Charles H. Schick (5 L. D., 151) that "the source and volume of water supply, the carrying capacity of the ditches and the number and length of all ditches on each legal subdivision should be specifically shown." This seems to be a reasonable requirement and I see no reason why it should not be complied with in this case. See also George Ramsey (5 L. D., 120).

The reasons given by claimant why he cannot prove the exact location of his lateral ditches at the time of final proof, to wit: because his employes who made them have left the locality and their whereabouts is now unknown, furnishes no excuse for refusing to show the locality and carrying capacity of the ditches by which the land is now irrigated.

It appears that the original lateral ditches which existed in 1885 were destroyed or obliterated by the construction of a railroad since that time and that claimant has constructed other lateral ditches since. If he can not now show the number and location of the original lateral ditches he may, by his own affidavit, corroborated by two witnesses show the number, size, and location of the new ones, and this should be required of him.

The proof shows that about thirty acres of the NW¼, SW¼, of said Sec. 33, were not irrigated, being high and rocky and it being impossible to carry water thereon; the land was so barren that it would have been useless. The other ten acres of said forty, however, were thoroughly irrigated being crossed close to the bluff by the main ditch. About ten acres of the SE¼, SW¼, of said section also were not irrigated being also too high and rocky. All the rest of the land the proof shows to have been reclaimed and brought under irrigation.

This feature of the case does not seem to have been considered by you, but the land upon which water was not brought was not susceptible of irrigation and was but a small part of the whole entry.

In David Gilchrist (8 L. D., 48) about one-third of one quarter section was not susceptible of irrigation, yet in view of the valuable improvements placed upon the land both before and after final proof, which it was held tended strongly to show good faith, and the further fact that there was no adverse claim, the entry was sustained, and I think the same views equally applicable in the case at the bar, upon this branch of the case.

Upon furnishing affidavits as above set out, patent may issue, otherwise the entry will remain canceled.

Your said decision is modified accordingly.

———

SCHOOL INDEMNITY–SETTLEMENT RIGHTS–RESIDENCE.

STATE OF CALIFORNIA v. SEVOY.

The State acquires no right to land as school indemnity prior to the selection thereof.

Until the filing of a declaratory statement, a change of settlement does not affect the rights of a settler or impeach his *bona fides.*

The sale of improvements by one holding under a mere possessory claim, while not conferring any right under the settlement laws, is not in violation thereof.

A pending application to amend a filing protects the pre-emptor as against intervening claims, and if granted relates back to the date when it was made.

Though land may be chiefly valuable for the timber thereon, it may be taken under the pre-emption law, if the good faith of the claimant is clearly shown.

Voting in a different precinct from that in which the land is situated does not raise a conclusive presumption against a claim of residence thereon.

Actual continuous residence for six months immediately preceding final proof is not required of the pre-emptor if his good faith is otherwise shown.

Secretary Noble to Acting Commissioner Stone, July 20, 1889.

This case involves the question of priority of right to lot 7, N. ½ of SE. ¼ and the SE. ¼ of SE. ¼ of Sec. 30, T. 18 N., R. 1 E., Humboldt meridian, California, Sevoy claiming a preference right of entry under the pre-emption law, and the State claiming under indemnity school selection, per list No. 50, as amended and filed December 12, 1884.

The township plat was filed April 14, 1884, and on May 13th thereafter, Sevoy filed his pre-emption declaratory statement for the entire SE. ¼ of said section alleging settlement June 15, 1882.

Subsequently Sevoy filed an application to amend his declaratory statement so as to exclude therefrom the SW. ¼ of said SE. ¼ and to include in lieu thereof lot 7, alleging that a mistake had been made in including in his declaratory statement the entire SE. ¼ of said Sec. 30, and that his most valuable improvements, including his residence, were upon said lot 7.

This application was forwarded to your office by the local officers by letter of July 1, 1884.

In passing upon this application, your office by letter "G" dated February 12, 1885, said :

It appears satisfactorily that a mistake was made in attempting to describe the land claimed, and that his improvements lie upon lot 7, of Sec. 30, and N. ¼ of SE. ¼ and SE. ¼ of SE. ¼, said section, township, and range, which latter tract he supposed he had embraced in said filing.

Under the circumstances the claimant will be allowed to amend his filing so as to embrace the tract covered by his actual settlement and cultivation, subject to any prior valid adverse claim.

On December 12, 1884, the State made selection of said tract, as per list No. 50, amending list 39. By decision of the Department of May 21, 1888, it was held that the State's claim to the land dated from the amended selection, filed December 12, 1884.

Three questions are presented for consideration in this cause · First, Does the evidence show that Sevoy had a *bona fide* right of pre-emption to the tract in controversy existing at the date of the State's selection, December 12, 1884. Second, Had he a right to change or amend his filing, and was such amendment made prior to the date when the State's selection attached, and Third : Has he complied with the pre-emption law as to inhabitancy, cultivation and improvement of said tract, and is the land of the character subject to entry under the settlement laws ?

It appears from the testimony that in 1877 or 1878, Sevoy went upon said section 30 with his uncle John Brady, while it was unsurveyed, each intending to take a claim under the settlement laws ; Brady built a cabin upon what proved by subsequent survey to be the NW. ¼ of the SE. ¼ of said section, and Sevoy built a cabin on what was subsequently shown by survey to be the NE. ¼ of said SE. ¼. In 1880 Brady left the claim and Sevoy took possession of his cabin occupying it at times until 1882, when he sold the Brady claim to W. H. Otto. Otto subsequently sold to Trimble who afterwards lived upon and occupied the Brady claim up to May 1884, when he sold to Frank Frames.

When the land was settled upon it was not known where the lines of survey would run, nor is it shown what land each intended to claim.

Sevoy did not occupy his cabin after he took possession of Brady's claim, but in 1883, he built another house and made improvements on lot 7. At that time Frames had a cabin on lot 7, and testified that he intended to claim the land as a pre-emptor. He never filed a declaratory statement for the tract nor took any steps to secure it under the settlement laws, but purchased it, and also the SE. ¼ from the State and sold the entire tract to Hume, the present claimant under the State.

It is contended by counsel for the State that the sale by Sevoy of the Brady claim was an abandonment of all right and claim to the SE. ¼ of said section, and that Trimble, the assignee of Otto, took possession of the tract and remained there until May 1884, after Sevoy's filing, and years after his alleged settlement in 1882. But neither Otto, Trimble nor Frames claimed the land under the settlement laws, and Frames only claimed as a purchaser under the State. As the State could acquire no title to the land until after selection, and no valid selection having been made of this tract until December 12, 1884, the pretended conveyance by the State could not affect the rights of any pre-emptor who may have filed for the land prior to an approved selection, nor could the settlement of the State's grantees prior to such selection add any force or validity whatever to claims of the State or her grantees.

It is further argued by the State that the conduct of Sevoy, in ranging over the entire section, covering various portions thereof with fictitious claims, and the sale of the Brady claim, impeaches his *bona fides* and shows that he went upon the land not with the intention of purchasing it as a *bona fide* pre-emptor, but for the purpose of speculation.

I do not see how such conduct can in any manner affect his claim to the tract so far as it involves the question of priority between him and the State, and that is the material question in this case. The land was not surveyed at the date of his settlement, and he had the right to change his settlement from one tract to another until filing, provided it did not interfere with the rights or claims of other settlers. Until the filing of a declaratory statement a change of settlement does not affect the rights of a settler or impeach his *bona fides*.

Nor do I see how the sale of the Brady claim can in any way affect his qualification. All that he could sell were the improvements of Brady, and the sale of such improvements could not give any claim to the land except such as might be asserted by a settler who went into possession under such sale and perfected a claim under the settlement laws. The sale of these improvement was not a contract or agreement prohibited by the pre-emption law.

As to the second point, it is shown by the record, that on May 13, 1884, Sevoy, filed declaratory statement for the entire SE. ¼ of said section, but on July 1st, thereafter, the register and receiver forwarded his application to amend so as to exclude part of said section and to embrace in lieu thereof lot 7 of said section. While it is true that this application was not acted upon until after the selection was made by the State, yet it being a pending application at the date of the State's selection, his right to the same related back to the date of his application. Hence it was not a change or amendment of his filing after the right of the State had attached, but an amendment made prior thereto, and, therefore, the right of the State had not intervened.

The remaining question to be determined is whether the land is of the character subject to pre-emption, and whether Sevoy has complied with the pre-emption laws as to inhabitancy, cultivation and improvement of the tract in controversy.

The evidence shows that a greater part of the land is covered with heavy red-wood timber, but it is also shown that part of the land is rich bottom land valuable for agricultural purposes, and that part of it has been cultivated by claimant. It is also shown that while the greater part of the land is chiefly valuable for its timber, yet it could be cleared so as to make the land valuable for pasturage. But although the land may be chiefly valuable for timber it will not defeat the right of a *bona fide* pre-emptor to take it under the settlement laws, if the *bona fides* of the pre-emptor are clearly shown. Porter *v.* Throop (6. L. D., 691) ; Wright *v.* Larson (7 L. D., 555).

Upon the question of residence and cultivation of the tract, the finding of the local officers, which is sustained by the testimony, is substantially as follows, to wit : That on February 12, 1884, Sevoy moved his family on the land and lived steadily on the tract until August, when he moved his wife to Crescent City, and placed her under the care of a physician, as she was about to be confined, but he left his two boys on the tract until October 12th. On March 4, 1885, he returned to the tract with his entire family, and has lived there continuously to date of contest (August 25, 1885.) "That he has a house built of split red-wood eighteen by thirty feet, having two rooms and veranda,— about three acres cleared and fenced and about one and one-third acres grubbed and cultivated in garden vegetables, and has raised some hay."

I find nothing in the record tending to impeach the testimony as to his residence upon his claim except the admission made by Sevoy, that in the fall of 1884 he voted in Crescent City, a different precinct from that in which the claim is located. While this is a circumstance that may be considered in determining the residence of the claimant at that time, it does not necessarily impeach the testimony that his only home was upon the tract in controversy, and considering all the evidence together I am inclined to believe that his voting in Crescent City, indicated an illegal act rather than a change of domicile. It was during the time his wife was sick in Crescent City, where he went on account of his wife's health, leaving two members of his family on the claim to which he returned as soon as his wife's health would permit, indicating that it was not his intention to change his domicile when he left the claim in August 1884.

The local officers found that Sevoy's residence was not continuous for six months immediately prior to date of final proof, but that he had shown a valid compliance with the pre-emption laws and should be allowed the land, subject to further and satisfactory proof, and your office affirmed said decision.

The actual continuous residence for six months immediately preceding final proof is not required where the good faith is otherwise shown, and the proof in this case being in all other respects satisfactory, Sevoy's entry should be approved for patent.

Your decision is to this extent modified.

HOMESTEAD ENTRY—SEGREGATION OF MINERAL LAND.

LANNON *v.* PINKSTON.

Where a homestead entry covers contiguous tracts, and a segregation of a part thereof is made necessary by a subsequent discovery of mineral, the entry will stand intact as to the agricultural tracts, though rendered non-contiguous by the segregation survey.

Secretary Noble to Acting Commissioner Stone, July 22, 1889.

By letter of April 11, 1889, you directed the attention of this Department to the decision of March 29, 1889, in the case of Michael Lannon *v.* Edward Pinkston [not reported], holding that a part of the land embraced in the latter's homestead entry is mineral in character, and that said entry should be canceled as to those tracts. After this finding, it was added:

Since, however, the cancellation of said entry as to the mineral tracts would leave the other tracts embraced thereby non-contiguous, the entryman will be required within thirty days from notice of this decision to notify the local officers what tract or tracts he elects to retain. Said entry will thereupon be canceled as to the tracts not so selected, and, if he should fail to make known his election within the time specified, the whole entry will be canceled.

It is said in your letter that the question as to the effect on a homestead entry of the segregation of a part of the land covered thereby because of the discovery of mineral subsequently to the date of his homestead entry was considered in the case of Sarah A. Mann, your office decision of July 12, 1881, holding:

As to the tracts not being contiguous, it will be noticed that as originally applied for they were contiguous, but that by subsequent mineral segregations the tract has been separated into two tracts, non-contiguous to each other. This state of facts being brought about after the entry was made, by a series of developments and surveys, necessary to a proper disposal of the public domain, and by no fault or failure to comply with the law on the part of the homestead claimant, I do not think that the law requiring the land to be contiguous is violated in allowing this entry.

It is also said, that this has been the uniform practice of your office since that time, and it is requested that authority be given to continue that practice and that Pinkston's claim may be adjudicated under the same ruling.

The act of May 20, 1862 (12 Stat., 392), now incorporated in section 2289 of the Revised Statutes, provides that "every person, who is the head of a family, etc., shall be entitled to enter one-quarter section or a less quantity of unappropriated public lands, etc., to be located in a body, in conformity to the legal subdivisions of the public lands, and after the same have been surveyed." That the tracts of land embraced in a homestead entry should be contiguous has been the uniform ruling of this Department. Hugh Miller, 5 L. D., 683; O. P. Masterson, 7 L. D., 172.

Section 2330 of the Revised Statutes provides that:

Legal subdivisions of forty acres may be subdivided into ten-acre tracts; and two or more persons or associations of persons, having contiguous claims of any size, although such claims may be less than ten acres each, may make joint entry thereof; . . . . . and nothing in this section contained shall defeat or impair any *bona fide* pre-emption or homestead claim upon agricultural lands, or authorize the sale of the improvements of any *bona fide* settler to any purchaser.

The wording of this section seems to justify the practice of your office to allow the claim to go to patent as it stands after the segregation of that portion of the land found to be mineral in character, and such practice is certainly equitable and just. Paragraph 102 of the circular of October 31, 1881, recognizes the correctness of such a practice, when it says, speaking of surveys to set apart the mineral from the agricultural land in a forty-acre tract: "The survey in such case may be executed in such manner as will segregate the portion of the land actually containing the mine, and used as surface-ground for the convenient working thereof, from the remainder of the tract, which remainder will be patented to the agriculturist to whom the same may have been awarded." Paragraph 109 of the same circular says that, if a ten-acre tract should be found to be mineral, "that fact will be no bar to the execution of the settler's legal right to the remaining non-mineral portion of his claim, if contiguous." The addition of this proviso "if contiguous" would at first seem to make this paragraph antagonistic to the practice of your office. If, however, this paragraph is read with the two preceding it, it will be seen that the claims referred to are those which have not yet proceeded to entry, and that, therefore, all that can be said is, that it prohibits the *entry* of tracts settled upon and afterwards rendered non-contiguous, by the segregation of mineral lands.

I am of the opinion that the practice of your office in such cases is not prohibited by nor inconsistent with the statute, but that it is a just rule and should be continued. Governed by this rule, Pinkston's entry should be allowed to remain intact as to all the land covered thereby, except as to that portion found to be more valuable for mineral than for agricultural purposes, and the departmental decision of March 29, 1889, is to that extent modified.

SECOND HOMESTEAD ENTRY—ACT OF MARCH 2, 1889.

ROBERT R. BRATTON.

A second homestead entry for the same tract may be accorded under the act of March 2, 1889, where the first was illegal, when made, by reason of the entryman having previously filed a soldier's declaratory statement for another tract.

First Assistant Secretary Chandler to Acting Commissioner Stone, July 22, 1889.

On December 22, 1884, Robert R. Bratton made homestead entry No. 609, for the W. ½, NE. ¼, and NE. ¼, NE. ¼, of section 11, and NW. ¼, NW. ¼, of section 12, T. 159 N., R. 70 W., Devil's Lake land district, Dakota.

Under date of January 14, 1888, Bratton informed your office by letter:

In the spring of 1884, I filed a soldiers' declaratory statement on one hundred and sixty acres of land intending to file a homestead on same but lost my team of oxen and was compelled to sell my right to the aforesaid claim in order to buy another team.

He states that he has lived on the land covered by his entry, together with his family for two years and made valuable improvements thereon. He enquires of your office, whether he could legally make his final proof for his said entry.

Your office thereupon, by decision of March 2, 1888, held said entry, No. 609, for cancellation, on account of illegality Bratton having previously, as shown by his own admissions, exhausted his right under the homestead law. The entryman appealed to this Department.

His entry, at the time it was made, was as the law then stood illegal, and your decision is correct; but the act of Congress, approved March 2, 1889 (25 Stat., 854), entitled, "An act to withdraw certain public lands from private entry, and for other purposes," provides:

That any person who has not heretofore perfected title to a tract of land of which he has made entry under the homestead law, may make homestead entry of not exceeding one quarter section of public land, subject to such entry, such previous filing or entry to the contrary notwithstanding.

If the claimant has not heretofore perfected title under the homestead law, he may enter the land under the provisions of this act, and to this end he should be notified that his entry on the land heretofore made is canceled, and that the application to re-enter the land, in accordance with said act and the regulations thereunder, should be made to the local office, and that he may be protected in his improvements upon said land, so far as it lies in the power of the Department, no other disposition should be made of the land for sixty days, of which he should have notice.

HOMESTEAD ENTRY—RESIDENCE.

ALFRED M. SMITH.

After a *bona fide* residence is established, temporary absences, caused by the ill health of the settler, do not interrupt the continuity of his residence.

The cultivation of crops, from year to year, are an indication of good faith on the part of claimant.

Secretary Noble to Acting Commissioner Stone, July 22, 1889.

By letter of September 14, 1886, your office rejected the final proof made by Alfred M. Smith on his homestead entry for the NE. ¼, Sec. 35, T. 125, R. 60, Aberdeen, Dakota, and held for cancellation his original entry and final certificate.

Smith appealed.

The cancellation was based on the ground "of claimant's failure to maintain residence upon the land."

The entry was made November 18, 1882, and final proof in accordance with published notice, submitted February 17, 1886. Said decision concedes that claimant is entitled to credit for one year, nine months and one day on account of service in the army, which added to the period of his residence on the land, as claimed, makes five years, the time required to perfect title. (Sec. 2305, R. S.)

In the proof claimant states that he is forty years of age, unmarried, native born, and that his post office address is Groton, Brown Co., Dakota; that he had on the land a house twelve by sixteen feet, a well twenty-two feet deep, with good water, and thirty-five acres broken and cultivated, valued in all at from two hundred and fifty to three hundred dollars; that he has made the tract his "home most of the time since making residence thereon. Absent at intervals." He says he has been "absent for two to six weeks at a time during summers of 1884 and 1885, on account of sickness, and was absent during winters for same reason." In answer to the question, "for how many seasons have you raised crops thereon?" he says, "Crops 1883, 1884, 1885." One witness says that claimant "resided on land the greater part of seasons March to November, though absent at intervals. Absent during winters." The other says he "resided on land a very large part of the warmer part of the year, but not much during winters. Was absent at different periods during summer seasons, on account of sickness, and almost all winter seasons." In an affidavit submitted with the proof claimant avers that during the year 1883 he was prostrated several times by dangerous epileptic fits "and has grown constantly worse," and requires the constant and immediate care of his brothers and mother, and treatment by physicians; that during the years 1884 and 1885 and up to the present time he had not been able to make said land his permanent home, but had stayed there as much of the time and as often as his health would allow, and has had no other home of his own; that during said years he "worked and caused to be worked the land, and had continued to improve said land by breaking and cultivating to crop each year." He further states that his sickness and physical disability "result from paralysis resulting from sunstroke sustained while a soldier in the late civil war."

A certificate of one physician states that claimant has suffered from "epilepsiform convulsions" for the past twenty years, "and that his life is in danger any moment when left alone."

Another physician certifies as follows:

On examination I found him an invalid, the right side partially paralyzed, and suffering with very severe cramps of the stomach. I treated him during the fall of 1882 and spring of 1883, but without any benefit except to allay the cramps for the time only. Since the spring of 1883 I have seen Mr. Smith occasionally, and know him to be getting very much of an invalid. At present Mr. Smith is an invalid not able to do any labor and suffers from severe cramps and spasms; during past five days some ten or twelve convulsions, some of them lasting for nearly an hour. He requires an attendant not being safe alone or without one.

Upon this state of facts the local officers issued final certificate to claimant. This circumstance is entitled to considerable weight. Those officers saw him and personally took his testimony and that of his witnesses. They all swore that claimant had established residence on the land and the local officers believed that statement. Furthermore, no one appeared to contradict it, though public notice of the proof had been given. Your office does not claim that Smith failed to *establish* residence, but that he did not continue to "maintain" it. It is not denied by any one that he established residence; on the contrary the local officers decided that point in his favor, on the unimpeached testimony of three witnesses.

Residence on land and presence thereon are not synonymous or convertible phrases. Actual presence on the land is necessary in the first instance in order to acquire residence as the entryman must go on the land for that purpose; but continuous presence thereafter is not essential to the continuity of residence once acquired. Residence having been established, subsequent absence *animo revertendi* and for a purpose which the law recognizes as a sufficient excuse for such absence, does not indicate an intent to abandon, and without such intent, the legal continuity of the residence is not broken, as, in such cases, the act and intent must concur." Patrick Manning, (7 L. D., 144).

In Martha M. Olson it was said by my predecessor, Secretary Lamar, "The absence of Mrs. Olson from the land caused by sickness and poverty and confinement in the asylum, is excusable, and such periods may be properly estimated as a part of the required five years residence." (6 L. D., 311). See also Evan L. Morgan, (5 L. D., 215). In Anderson v. Anderson, (5 L. D., 6), it was said:

While it is true that residence under the homestead law must be continuous and personal, it is also true that residence once established can be changed only when the *act* and *intention* of the settler unite to effect such a change.

Inasmuch as it seems to be conceded that claimant established residence on the tract, and there is no proof that he changed his residence, and as his absences are excusable in law, I conclude that his residence continued on said tract to the date of final proof. There is no dispute but the crops were raised and gathered. These were excellent representatives.

Said decision is accordingly reversed.

———

TIMBER CULTURE CONTEST—EVIDENCE—CULTIVATION.

BELL v. BOLLES.

The contestant is not entitled to a judgment of cancellation unless he shows a substantial non-compliance with law in a matter distinctly charged in the contest affidavit.

Though the government is indirectly a party to a timber culture contest, it will not, of its own motion, cancel an entry if bad faith is not clearly shown.

The entryman's non-compliance with law can not be taken advantage of, in proceedings instituted before the termination of the year in which such non-compliance is alleged to have occurred.

While the law requires that the trees planted should be kept in a healthy growing condition, it does not necessarily require that the trees planted one year shall be, in all cases, cultivated the following year.

Secretary Noble to Acting Commissioner Stone, July 23, 1889.

March 20, 1878 George Bolles made timber-culture entry for the SE¼ Sec. 12 T. 107 N., R. 50 W., Mitchell land district Dakota.

March 8, 1883, William F. Bell filed in the local land office his affidavit of contest against said entry wherein he makes the following charges, to wit, "George Bolles has failed to cultivate the first five acres of trees, and has failed to set out the second five acres of trees, or to cultivate the second five acres."

A hearing in the case was duly had before a notary public, and on June 26, 1883 the local land officers found that Bell had failed to sustain the allegations of his contest affidavit, and that his contest should be dismissed. On appeal your office, May 14, 1885, reversed this decision and held Bolles' entry for cancellation. On motion for a review of said decision it was adhered to by the decision of your office of September 24, 1885.

The case comes before me on appeal by Bolles. The testimony taken at the hearing shows a full compliance with the timber-culture law on the part of Bolles for the first three years after his entry was made. Early in the third year—May 1880—he planted two and a half acres of said tract to cottonwood trees, and later (October) two and a half acres to ash tree seeds. No exception can be taken to the manner in which this first five acres of trees were planted, nor to the condition of the ground for the reception of the plants and seeds. In the fall of 1880, Bolles also buried a barrel of butternuts that they might sprout in the following spring and be ready for transplanting. W. N. Severance was employed to set out these sprouts where trees were missing, and he afterwards spent a half day in transplanting them.

The fourth year of the entry, ending March 20, 1882, was rather wet during the spring and summer, (1881) and the trees planted the year before were not cultivated, though Bolles employed Severance to cultivate them that year. Severance testifies that he was hired to cultivate the trees in 1881, but did not because it was too wet, and that he went there several times to cultivate them but couldn't. It is in evidence, however, that though the ground at the time of hearing was grown up to grass and weeds, yet the trees grown from the planting of 1880 were then in a thrifty growing condition, and were from two and three, all the way up to eight and ten feet in height. In the spring of 1881 five acres of said tract, which had been cultivated the season before, were sown to wheat, and in November of that year these five acres were planted to tree seeds—ash.

Your office finds that this planting was not properly done; that the seeds failed to germinate, and that Bolles failed to replant the following year. And your office decision held that this failure to replant was fatal to his entry.

The contest affidavit did not charge a failure to *properly plant* the second five acres to trees, or a failure to replant the same, but a failure " to set out the second five acres to trees, or to cultivate the second five acres." The point on which your office decided the case was, therefore, not in issue between the immediate parties to the contest. It is true the government is indirectly a party in a case of this kind, but the government will not of its own motion cancel an entry and forfeit an entryman's claim unless bad faith on his part is clearly shown, and bad faith on the part of Bolles has not been satisfactorily shown in this case. The tree seeds planted in November 1881, failed to germinate and the Department concurs in the opinion expressed by your office that "they were not properly planted." The ground had not been plowed since early in the spring and was at the time of planting frozen. This planting it seems to me, shows carelessness or lack of judgment, but it cannot be fairly said, when considered in connection with all the evidence, that it shows bad faith. Bad faith on the part of the entryman not being shown his entry should not be canceled unless the contestant has shown a substantial non-compliance with the timber-culture law in a matter distinctly charged in his contest affidavit.

The contest herein was instituted March 8, 1883, and the fifth year of the entry terminated March 20, 1883. The contest having been instituted before the termination of the fifth year after entry all evidence of failure to cultivate during said fifth year is irrelevant to the issue joined between the parties directly interested, because no mere non-compliance with law can be taken advantage of by a contestant in proceedings instituted before the termination of the year in which such non-compliance is charged to have occurred. Reynolds v. Pettit (7 L. D., 452) and cases cited.

The timber-culture law requires that the trees planted shall be protected and kept in a healthy growing condition, but this does not necessarily require that trees set out or planted one year shall be cultivated the following year. Doubtless such cultivation would generally conduce to the healthy growing condition of young trees, but under some circumstances it might be injurious, and it is not shown in this case that the five acres of trees set out and planted in 1880 would have been benefited by cultivation during the rather wet season of 1881, even though such cultivation were practicable. Severance, who was hired to cultivate the trees that year, testifies that it was not practicable to do so, and the testimony shows that such trees as were standing at the time of the hearing were then in a healthy growing condition. Therefore the fact that Bolles failed to cultivate the first five acres during the year 1881, does not show a non compliance with law. This disposes of the contestant's first allegation, and his second allegation as to Bolles failure to plant the second five acres is disproved. Of course no trees of this planting could possibly be cultivated before the termination of the fourth year of the entry.

Appellant having failed to support by proof a single material allegation of his contest affidavit, and the evidence when fairly weighed having failed to satisfy me that Bolles has acted in bad faith, said contest is dismissed, and the decision of your office holding Bolles' entry for cancellation is reversed.

HOMESTEAD ENTRY—COMMUTATION—RESIDENCE.

PETER WEBER (ON REVIEW).

The right of commutation depends upon prior compliance with the homestead law, up to the date of commutation.

If, on proof submitted under section 2291, R. S., an entryman is not entitled to patent, because of his failure to comply with the homestead law, he is also by such failure debarred from the exercise of the right of commutation.

After residence is actually acquired, the continuity thereof is not interrupted by absences caused by the poverty of claimant.

Secretary Noble to Acting Commissioner Stone, July 23, 1889.

In the case of Peter Weber, involving his homestead entry on the SE. ¼ of Sec. 11, T. 101 N., R. 55 W., Mitchell district, Dakota Territory, motion is made for review and revocation of the departmental decision therein of December 4, 1888 (7 L. D., 476).

The entry was made June 10, 1879, and final proof March 19, 1886. From this proof it appeared, that the claimant, a single man, established actual residence on the land, April 30, 1880, at which time he built a sod house, twelve by fourteen feet, with door and window and shingle roof, and furnished it with bed, bedding, table, stove, chairs and dishes; that subsequently (in 1884), he built a second house, which was sixteen by twenty-two feet, framed, with shingle roof and one door and four windows, and that at the date of proof he had a well of water and fifty-five acres of breaking and had raised crops for six consecutive seasons. His improvements at the time he offered proof were shown to be of the value of $355.00. As to his residence, it appears from his own testimony and that of his final proof witnesses, that he lived upon the land, except "during the winters of 1880–1, 1882–3, and 1884," and from December 31, 1885, to March 18, 1886, his longest absence being from November 15, 1880, to April 1, 1881, about four months and a half, and that during these absences, he was at work with his father on an adjoining section " to gain means to live, and improve his claim."

This proof was approved by the local officers and final certificate, No. 6295, was issued March 23, 1886.

February 15, 1887, your office rejected said proof and held the claimant's original entry and final certificate for cancellation, on the ground that he had not "maintained continuous residence upon his claim as required by the homestead laws." The claimant thereupon appealed to this Department and accompanied his appeal with an affidavit, that since the date of his final proof (March 19, 1886), he had continued to reside on said tract and had made the following improvements in addition to those mentioned in his proof: a frame, shingle roof barn, thirty by thirty-two feet, of the value of $300.00; six acres of breaking, valued at $18.00; a fenced cattle yard, ten by ten rods, valued at $20.00; and a well sixteen feet deep, valued at $20.00. In said affidavit he further states, that he had not alienated any part of said tract, but had used it for a farm and home for himself and family (having married since making proof).

In said departmental decision of December 4, 1888, now sought to be reviewed, it is said:

The proof does not show to my satisfaction, that the residence of the entryman during the whole period claimed was on the tract involved to the exclusion of one elsewhere. There is, however, no adverse claim and no testimony controverting his statements. His residence after proof was made, as stated in his affidavit (affidavit accompanying appeal referred to, *supra*), and the valuable improvements made by him may be taken into consideration as showing that the entry was not made in bad faith, but with the intention of securing the tract for a home. The statements of the entryman, however, are not corroborated. Under these circumstances, while the entry can not be passed to patent upon the proof submitted, and while new proof can not be made within the statutory period, I will so modify your decision as to give the entryman the opportunity within ninety days after the receipt of notice hereof to commute his entry in accordance with the provisions of section 2301, Rev. Stat.

It is well settled by the decisions of this Department, that the right of commutation depends upon prior compliance with the homestead law up to date of commutation. (Samuel H. Vandivoort, 7 L. D., 86; Frank

W. Hewit, 8 L. D., 566.) If, therefore, the claimant in this case was not entitled to patent because of his failure to comply with the homestead law, he was, it would seem, by such failure also debarred from the exercise of the right of commutation.

I am of the opinion, however, that the local officers were justified in accepting the claimant's final proof and issuing final certificate to him thereon. Having established residence, his subsequent absences, unless, in the light of all the facts disclosed by the proof, they indicated an intent to abandon that residence, did not in law break the continuity thereof. The absences in this case were for the purpose of " gaining means to live, and improve his claim," and being for that purpose were excusable and no evidence of an intent to abandon. The value of his improvements, $355.00, and their character, and the fact that in 1884, the fifth year after entry, he built a new and more commodious dwelling, tend strongly to show, that he intended the claim as his permanent home to the exclusion of one elsewhere.

Moreover, as is said in said departmental decision in the extract therefrom *supra*, " His residence after proof was made, as stated in his affidavit, and the valuable improvements made by him, may be taken into consideration as showing that the entry was not made in bad faith, but with the intention of securing the tract for a home." It is stated in said departmental decision that, " The statements of the entryman " as to residence and improvements since making proof are not corroborated." On examining the affidavit, however, in which said statements occur, I find, that it is corroborated, as of their own personal knowledge, by two witnesses, Oscar Amonson and Robert O. Haugen, whom the judge of probate of the county (McCook) certifies to be reputable citizens and entitled to credit.

It further appears from an affidavit accompanying the motion for review and corroborated by four witnesses, that the claimant was still at the date thereof, February 12, 1889, living on the claim with his wife and family, and that he had never ceased to live thereon since making proof.

These affidavits showing residence and improvements subsequent to the date of the proof, are referred to, as shedding light upon the character of the claimant's residence prior to that date, and as confirmatory of the action of the local officers in accepting the proof as originally offered.

The motion for review and revocation of said departmental decision must be granted, and it is directed, that said entry and final certificate be re-instated and said proof accepted, and that said entry be passed to patent.

HOMESTEAD CONTEST—DEFAULT CURED PRIOR TO NOTICE..

HALL v. FOX.

A contest must fail if the default charged is, in good faith, cured prior to the service of notice. This ruling is predicated upon the theory that the claimant's action is not induced by the filing of the affidavit of contest.

The case of Burkholder v. Skagen, overruled.

First Assistant Secretary Chandler to Acting Commissioner Stone, July 23, 1889.

I have considered the appeal of F. G. Fox, from the decision of your office of May 20, 1888, holding for cancellation his homestead entry for the NW. ¼ of section 10, T. 3 S., R. 26 W., Oberlin land district, Kansas.

October 1, 1884, F. G. Fox made homestead entry of said tract and June 27, 1885, A. G. Hall, filed an affidavit of contest against said entry charging that "said F. G. Fox has wholly abandoned said tract; that he has changed his residence therefrom, for more than six months since making said entry; that said tract is not settled upon and cultivated by said party as required by law."

On June 27, 1885, notice was issued citing the defendant to appear at the local office August 7, to answer the charge. August 7, the defendant appeared by his attorney and moved to dismiss the contest because notice of it had not been served upon him. In support of the motion he filed his affidavit positively stating that notice of the contest had not been served upon him. Upon this point F. O. Salisbury made affidavit written upon the back of the notice, "that he served notice of the pendency of the within contest on the defendant F. G. Fox by delivering him a true copy of the within notice personally at Clayton, Norton county, Kansas, on the 2nd day of July, 1885, between the hours of 1 p. m., and 4 p. m." The motion was overruled by the local officers and the hearing began August 8, both parties being present and represented by attorneys. Three witnesses were called by the plaintiff and six by the defendant.

Upon the testimony the local officers sustained the contest and recommended the cancellation of the entry.

The evidence showed (they said) that he (Fox) established his residence on the land on the 26th or 27th day of June, 1885. He states that he established his residence on the land on the 26th day of June, 1885. The entry being made October 1, 1884, if he established residence on the land on the 26th day of June, 1885, there was a period of nearly eight months that elapsed between the date of his entry and the date of his establishing a residence thereon, nor does there seem to be any excuse for his not establishing residence there sooner.

Fox appealed, and March 20, 1888, you affirmed the action of the local officers and held the entry for cancellation. From your said decision Fox took the appeal now before me.

It appears that the contest was not initiated until June 27, 1885, and

that previously thereto, viz : on June 26, 1885, the entryman established
his residence upon the land in contest, and thereby cured his laches, if
any there were, in that respect.

In the case of Stayton *v.* Carroll (7 L. D., 198), the entryman cured
his laches before he was served with notice of the contest. It was held
that jurisdiction is acquired by due service of notice upon the claimant
and that :

The entryman had cured his laches prior to the service of notice of contest and
hence the allegations of the contestant, that the claimant had abandoned his homestead claim or failed to establish his residence thereon, were not true at the time of
service of notice.

The entry was, therefore, sustained and the contest dismissed.

So, too, in the case of St. John *v.* Raff, (8 L. D. 552), it is held : "A
timber-culture contest must fail if the default charged is made good before service of notice."

All this, however, is dependent on the good faith of the entryman in
curing his laches.

If it were made to appear that an affidavit of contest was filed, and
the entryman, learning thereof, was moved thereby to go upon the land
before the service of notice upon him to save himself, quite a different
rule might be applied, as I take it, the Department will not favor sharp
practice of that character.

All these decisions are predicated upon the theory that the entryman
goes upon the land prior to service of notice of contest upon him, and
that he is not induced to do so by the filing of the affidavit of contest.

In the case of Burkholder *v.* Skagen (4 L. D., 166), the entry was
made June 17, 1881, and August 11, 1882, notice issued upon the
affidavit of Burkholder charging abandonment ; and personal service
was had upon Skagen June 23, 1883. At the trial it was shown that
Skagen went upon the land in March 1883, built a house, dug a well,
broke five acres and " has been on the land nearly all the time since
March 1883." Upon the facts as given it was held that abandonment
had been proven, and the entry was canceled without any reference to
the fact that the claimant had cured his default before he was served
with notice of the contest. The authorities cited do not support the
ruling made in the case, and as it is in direct conflict with the decision
in the case of Stayton *v.* Carroll and St. John *v.* Raff, *supra,* it is hereby
over-ruled.

Your decision is reversed.

RAILROAD GRANT—ACT OF APRIL 21, 1876.

McCLURE *v.* NORTHERN PAC. R. R. CO.

Filings and entries made in good faith by actual settlers, are the only class of claims
confirmed and made valid by the act of April 21, 1876.

When the map of general route was filed the withdrawal thereunder became at once
effective, and reserved from general disposal the odd numbered sections embraced
therein.

A cash entry of such land made after the map of general route was filed, but before
notice of withdrawal, is illegal and does not except the land from the grant.

Secretary Noble to Acting Commissioner Stone, July 24, 1889.

. About December 26, 1887, George L. McClure made application to
enter, under the homestead law, the NW ¼ Sec. 11, T. 13 N., R. 1 W.,
Vancouver land district Washington Territory, and his application, at
the date above given was rejected by the local office on the ground that
if allowed it would "conflict with the grant for the Northern Pacific R.
R. Co."

On appeal the action of the local office was sustained by your office
decision of February 27, 1888, from which McClure has appealed to the
Department.

The described tract is within the granted limits of the grant of July
2, 1864 (13 Stat., 365), to the Northern Pacific Railroad Company as
shown by its map of general route and definite location of its road.

Said map of general route was filed in your office August 13, 1870,
but notice thereof was not received at the local land office till October
19, following.

In the mean time, to wit, on September 12, 1870, one Rodger S. Green,
located or entered said tract with agricultural college scrip. The company's map of definite location was filed September 13, 1873, and this
entry, as appears from the decision appealed, was canceled June 29,
1877, because made after the filing of said map of general route in your
office.

In the case under consideration your office held that the filing of said
map, August 13, 1870, operated as a withdrawal of the tract in controversy from market from the date of said filing, and that the fact
that notice of such withdrawal had not reached the local office until
after Green's entry was made, did not make such entry legal. When
the case was before your office on appeal McClure insisted that the
Green location served to except said tract from the Company's grant,
and in support of this position the case of Jacobs *v.* Northern Pacific
R. R. Co., (6 L. D., 223) was cited.

It was properly held in the decision appealed that the case cited was
not in point; that Jacobs was an actual settler, and that therefore his
claim—initiated after the map of general rule was filed, and before
notice of such filing had reached the local office—was sufficient, under

the act of April 21, 1876 (19 Stat., 35), to except the land covered thereby from the operation of the railroad grant. Filings and entries made in good faith by actual settlers are the only class of claims confirmed and made valid by said act, and it is not shown that Green was an actual settler on the land which he located.

McClure's attorney insists that—

There could be no difference whether said Green made settlement on this tract of land under his cash entry, or if he had made settlement under a pre-emption or homestead entry. The title to said tract of land had vested in said Green by virtue of his said cash entry, and the United States by its own act had divested itself of title thereto.

Title to public land does not vest simply on the allowance of an entry by the local land officers, nor until such entry has been approved by the Commissioner of the General Land Office and a patent has issued, and it does not appear, as stated above that "said Green made settlement on this tract of land under his cash entry." As his entry was canceled after the passage of the act of April 21, 1876, the presumption is that he was not an actual settler in good faith on said tract.

The argument in behalf of McClure is based on the false assumption that the land in controversy was not withdrawn from sale, or other general modes of disposal by the government, until notice of withdrawal was received at the local land office. The land in controversy was withdrawn from such general disposal from the instant said company's map of general route was filed in your office. Being so withdrawn Green's location and entry, though made without actual notice of such withdrawal, was nevertheless illegal.

The decision of your office rejecting said application is affirmed.

RAILROAD GRANT—HOMESTEAD ENTRY.

REYNOLDS v. NORTHERN PAC. R. R. CO.

The existence of a homestead entry at date of withdrawal on general route does not except the land covered thereby from the grant, if such tract is vacant public land at date of definite location.

Secretary Noble to Acting Commissioner Stone, July 24, 1889.

December 15, 1885, William A. Reynolds made application to enter, under the homestead law, the S. ½ of NW. ¼ and the N. ½ of SW. ¼, Sec. 19, T. 13 N., R. 3 W., Olympia land district, Washington Territory.

This tract of land is within the granted limits of the Northern Pacific Railroad Company's grant, and its maps of general route and definite location of the line of its road opposite said tract were filed, respectively August 13, 1870, and September 13, 1873. From June 1, 1869, until October 4, 1870, said tract was included in the homestead entry of one James R. Johnson, which entry, at the latter date, was canceled.

The local officers, on the authority of the decision of your office in the case of Gentner v. Northern Pacific Railroad Company, held that Reynolds's application should be allowed. On appeal by said company, your office reversed this decision, because the case on which it was based had been reversed by the Department. See Centner v. Northern Pacific Railroad Company, 5 L. D., 311. From this decision of your office Reynolds appealed.

Appellant contends that Johnson's entry—being a valid subsisting entry at the time the company's map of general route was filed, August 13, 1870—excepted said tract from the company's grant, and he cites the case of Holmes v. Northern Pacific Railroad Company, 5 L. D., 333 as sustaining his position. The case cited is not in point. In that case .there was not only a valid subsisting entry at the time of the withdrawal on map of general route, but Holmes's homestead entry was made long before the company's map of definite location was filed, and he was then still in possession, and the Department found that the tract thus occupied by Holmes was not "free from pre-emption or other claims or rights." In this case, at date of definite location, there was no hostile claim whatever in existence to the tract in controversy. At the time the line of said company's road opposite this tract was definitely fixed, September 13, 1873, it was vacant public land, to which the United States had full title, and the right of the company then attached under its grant. Said tract was not, therefore, subject to homestead entry on December 15, 1885.

The decision of your office, rejecting Reynolds's said application, is affirmed.

SCHOOL LAND—ACT OF MAY 20, 1826.

STATE OF LOUISIANA. (ON REVIEW.)

The act of May 20, 1826, authorizes selections on account of school sections in place, but lost to the State by reason of being included within confirmed private claims.

Secretary Noble to Acting Commissioner Stone, July 24, 1889.

In the departmental decision of January 25, 1889, in the case of the State of Louisiana (8 L. D., 126), involving a list of school indemnity selections made by that State under the act of May 20, 1826 (4 Stat., 179), it is held that certain of those selections "marked as based upon section sixteen in place, but covered by a private grant," can not be allowed, and the ground for so holding is stated in said decision to be, that "from the passage of the law" (Act of May 20, 1826,) "it has been construed that it was not contemplated in said act to permit selections on account of sections sixteen in place, but covered by private grants." The case is now before this Department on motion for review of said decision as to said point.

So much of said act of May 20, 1826, as is material to the present inquiry, is as follows:

That to make provision for the support of schools, in all townships or fractional townships, for which no land has heretofore been appropriated for that use in those States in which section number sixteen, or other land equivalent thereto, is by law directed to be reserved for the support of schools, in each township, there shall be reserved and appropriated for the use of schools in each entire township or fractional township, for which no land has been heretofore appropriated or granted for that purpose, the following quantities of land, to wit:

By circular from the General Land Office, issued October 5, 1826, a few months after the passage of said act, addressed to the local officers at St. Helena and other points in Louisiana, they were directed, notwithstanding "Congress had omitted to make a *special* provision" in said act "in those cases where section sixteen had been covered by confirmed claims or donations," to select and reserve lands under said act in lieu of section sixteen in such cases. (Public Lands, Laws, Instructions and Opinions, p. 420.) By paragraph 10 of the circular of August 30, 1832, however, the local officers were informed, that—"The Secretary of the Treasury directs, that you bear in mind that no selections are contemplated to be made in those cases where section sixteen is entirely or partially interfered with by private confirmed claims or donations." (Ib., p. 466.) A third circular bearing on this point was issued, May 17, 1844, to the local officers, as follows:

Should there exist in your land district any instances where the sixteenth section usually set apart for school purposes, is interfered with in any township or fractional township, either wholly or partially, by private confirmed claims or donations, you are to regard such township or fractional township as entitled to a selection, for the use of schools of other lands in the district, under the provisions of the act of Congress approved May 20, 1826, entitled "an act to appropriate lands for the support of schools in certain townships and fractional townships," the Secretary of the Treasury having recently rescinded the tenth paragraph of the instructions contained in the printed circular of August 30, 1832, in relation to school lands under the act aforesaid, which is adverse to the decision now given. 1 Lester, 492.

In view of the first and last of the above circulars, the statement in said departmental decision of January 25, 1889, that "from the passage of the law (act of May 20, 1826) it has been construed that it was not contemplated in said act to permit selections on account of sections sixteen in place, but covered by private grants," would seem to be erroneous.

The act itself does not make specific provision for any particular class or classes of cases but is general in its terms, providing for the reservation and appropriation of lands for the use of schools "in all townships or fractional townships" in those States covered by the act, "for which no land has heretofore been appropriated for that use." The case of a township or fractional township in which section sixteen in place has been "interfered with" or lost to the State for school purposes, by reason of a private confirmed claim, existing at the date of the school land grant, is, in my opinion, a case where "no land has been" (before the act of May 20, 1826,) "appropriated for that use," and falls within the scope and reason of the law, though not expressly mentioned therein.

The said selections made on account of sections sixteen in place, but lost to the State for school purposes, by reason of confirmed private claims, must, therefore, be allowed, and the said departmental decision of January 25, 1889, is modified accordingly.

PRIVATE ENTRY—RAILROAD GRANT—TRANSFEREE.

BULLARD v. FLORIDA RY. AND NAVIGATION CO.

A private cash entry of land previously withdrawn, as within the primary limits of a railroad grant, though made in good faith is invalid and must be canceled.

A purchaser of land, prior to the issuance of patent therefor, takes no greater right than exists in the entryman.

Secretary Noble to Acting Commissioner Stone, July 25, 1889.

I have considered the case of G. F. Bullard v. The Florida Railway and Navigation Company, on appeal by the former from the decision of your office, dated January 13, 1888, holding for cancellation his private cash entry, No. 1364, of the N. ¼ of the SE. ¼ of Sec. 27, T. 10 S., R. 23 E., made February 21, 1881, at the Gainesville land office, in the State of Florida.

Your office held said entry for cancellation, because the land in question was not subject to entry, being within the six miles, or granted, limits of the grant to the State of Florida by act Congress, approved May 17, 1856 (11 Stat., 15). The withdrawal for the benefit of said grant was made on September 6, 1856.

The appellant insists that the NE. ¼ of the SE. ¼ of said section 27 is outside of the granted limits of said grant; that "It is a little more than six miles and ten chains from said road and to the west boundary of said land;" that he made said entry in good faith, and soon afterwards sold the land to one W. L. Pennington, who bought the same in good faith, and to whom he gave a warranty deed; that said Pennington has made valuable improvements on said land.

An inspection of the records of your office shows that the land in question is within the six mile limits of said grant, and has been withdrawn for many years prior to the allowance of said entry. The entry was therefore improperly allowed.

The plea of good faith and that valuable improvements have been made by the transferee can not be sustained. Parties purchasing prior to the issuance of patent stand in no better position than their vendors. Chauncey Carpenter (7 L. D., 236); Custer v. Smith (8 L. D., 269).

That the transferee has made valuable improvements upon the tract is his own misfortune, and the Department is without power to aid him. It may be a hardship, but "hard cases make bad law." Goist v. Bottum (5 L. D., 647).

A careful examination of the whole record discloses no sufficient reason for disturbing said decision of your office, and it is accordingly affirmed.

PRE-EMPTION ENTRY—REPAYMENT.

JOHN CARSON.

When a false oath is made by a pre-emptor, as to the matters required in section 2262 R. S., forfeiture of the purchase money follows as a statutory result; and repayment can not be allowed.

Secretary Noble to Acting Commissioner Stone, July 25, 1889.

I have considered the case of John Carson on his appeal from your office decision of June 11, 1888, rejecting his application for repayment of the purchase money paid by him in his pre-emption cash entry for SW. ¼, SW. ¼, Sec. 28, and NW. ¼. NW. ¼, Sec. 33, T. 26 S., R. 54 W., Pueblo, Colorado, land district.

On April 26, 1888, the local office transmitted to the land department Carson's relinquishment for said land together with his application to make homestead entry therefor, and a request for repayment.

On June 7, 1888, your office replied directing the cancellation of his cash entry and the acceptance of the homestead application, and by letter of June 11, 1888, your office rejected his application for repayment, basing said decision upon Sec. 2262, Revised Statutes.

It appears from the record that Carson filed his declaratory statement November 24, 1882, and on March 11, 1885, he made final proof and payment for said land.

In making the affidavit required of pre-emption claimants under section 2262, Revised Statutes, he swore that he was not the owner of three hundred and twenty acres of land in any State or Territory of the United States, but in his application for repayment, he admits that he was at the time, the owner of more than that amount of land in Colorado. As an excuse he says he was ignorant of the law, that he did not read said affidavit before signing, and that he was not asked whether he was the owner of other land or not.

In reply to this you say in your said decision of June 11, 1888, that— "It was the duty of the claimant to read the affidavit carefully before signing the same. The claimant cannot plead ignorance of the law in making his entry."

Section 2262 of the Revised Statutes, provides that before any person is allowed to make an entry under the pre-emption law he shall make oath before the register and receiver, which oath among other things recited therein, shall state " that he is not the owner of three hundred and twenty acres of land in any State or Territory; . . . . . and if any person taking such oath swears falsely in the premises, he shall forfeit the money which he may have paid for such land and all right and title to the same."

In John Longnecker (1 L. D., 535) where the entryman had removed from land of his own in the same State to reside upon his pre-emption claim, it was held that his failure to disclose the fact of his having so removed from his own land to the register and receiver, and stating categorically in his final proof that he had not removed from his own land etc., brought the case within the forfeiture clause of Sec. 2262, aforesaid.

It has frequently been held by this department that repayment cannot be made except in cases expressly provided for by statute. Joseph Brown (5 L. D., 316); Sarah D. Smith (7 L. D., 295). In Charles F. Coffin (6 L. D., 298), where the claimant had made affidavit that the land was devoid of timber, and applied to have his entry canceled without prejudice for the reason that he had learned that there were ten acres of native timber growing thereon, his application was refused for the reason that it was his duty to know the condition of the land before making affidavit, and he could not be allowed to take advantage of his own negligence. See also Falk Steinhardt, 7 L. D., 10.

Claimant in the case at bar in appeal cites Howard W. Lang (3 L. D., 518), in support of his claim, but it will be observed that Lang had removed from a homestead claim of his own to reside upon the pre-emption claim and while this is within the inhibition of Sec. 2260, it is not one of the things to which he is required by Sec. 2262 to make oath and while such removal would render his title to the land entered void or at least voidable, forfeiture of the purchase money need not follow necessarily, but when a false oath is made in regard to matters required in Sec. 2262, forfeiture follows as the statutory result.

The affidavit of the entryman in the case at bar was a false oath within the meaning of said section 2262, and your said decision is accordingly affirmed.

TIMBER CULTURE CONTEST—APPLICATION TO ENTER.

ROSENBERG v. HALE'S HEIRS.

An application to enter, filed with a timber culture contest, entitles the heirs of a deceased contestant to the right of entry, on the successful termination of the contest.

Pending final action upon an application to enter, filed with a timber culture contest, the entry of another should not be allowed for the land embraced therein.

A contest as to the validity of an entry cannot be entertained while the right to make said entry is pending on appeal.

No arbitrary rule can be followed in determining whether land is of the character contemplated by the timber culture act.

First Assistant Secretary Chandler to Acting Commissioner Stone, July 25, 1889.

On March 15, 1877, one James Edgar made timber culture entry for the SE. ¼, section 30, T. 1 S., R. 15 E., Kirwin land district, Kansas. This entry was canceled by letter "C" of your office dated March 18,

1886, upon the contest of R. B. Hale, who filed, as is stated by your office, with his contest affidavit an application to enter said tract under the timber culture act. On March 26, 1886, the local officers notified Hale's attorney, S. H. Bradley of the cancellation. On April 5, 1886, one W. T. Branch made timber culture entry for the said tract and on April 22, Ellen B. Hale, widow of the said R. B. Hale, made application to be allowed to enter the land under the timber culture act. Her application was rejected by the local office because of the entry of Branch. Ellen B. Hale appealed to your office May 22, 1886. Pending her appeal on June 8, 1886, W. T. Branch filed the relinquishment of his entry and on the same day Frederick Rosenberg filed his pre emption declaratory statement for the tract, alleging settlement that day. Also pending Mrs. Hale's appeal Rosenberg on April 2, 1887, submitted his final proof; the same was accepted by the local officers and final certificate issued the same day.

In support of her appeal, Ellen B. Hale forwards to your office her corroborated affidavit, bearing date March, 1887, in it she states among other matters, that she is the widow of R. B. Hale, who bought the improvements on the land in question from the heirs of James Edgar; that owing to the refusal of one of the heirs to join in a relinquishment of Edgar's entry, R. B. Hale instituted a contest against the entry, which resulted in its cancellation; that after the hearing of said contest and the cancellation of said entry, the said R. B. Hale died, leaving surviving him his said widow and six children, the oldest of the age of thirteen years, the youngest three years old; that within thirty days from the date of notice of said cancellation she, the affiant, as widow of said R. B. Hale, and heir-at-law made application to enter the said land under the timber culture law.

Your office, considering the case upon Mrs. Hale's appeal, on June 29, 1887, decided—

It was error to allow Branch's entry because the timber culture application of the contestant Hale, filed with his contest and returned to your office March 18, 1886, was, so far as his rights were concerned, equivalent to actual entry, and until disposed of, was a bar to any other entry. Pfaff v. Williams, et al., 4 L. D., 455. The right thus acquired by the contestant descended to his heirs and carried with it the right to perfect it after the cancellation of Edgar's entry, as heirs in the same manner that he might have perfected it, if he had lived. When on April 22, 1886, appellant applied to enter the tract she did so claiming under her husband. It appears that her application as originally filled out described her as the "widow of R. B. Hale, dec'd" and that the words "R. B. Hale, dec'd" were erased before it was presented, in accordance with the advice of her counsel Bradley. She should have applied in the name of all the heirs (Sharrar vs. Teachman, 5 L. D., 422), and at the same time have filed affidavit showing that her husband had never perfected a timber culture entry. Her omission to do so should not, under the peculiar circumstances of the case, deprive the contestant's heirs of their right to the tract. I return appellant's timber culture application, which, treating it as a substitute for a renewal of that originally filed by contestant, you will place upon record, after proper amendment, and the filing of supplementary affidavit showing that contestant never perfected a timber culture entry. Rosenberg's declaratory statement will be allowed to stand subject to the rights of R. B. Hale's heirs.

In conformity with the above decision Ellen B. Hale, on August 10, 1887, amended her application and filed the supplementary affidavit required by your office.

On October 21, 1887, the local officers forwarded to you Rosenberg's appeal from your said office decision of June 29, 1887. The appeal bears date October 8, 1887. The register of the said land office also transmitted to you the admission of service of notice of your said decision of June 29, by S. H. Bradley attorney for Rosenberg, bearing date August 8, 1887.

In your office letter of July 3, 1888, you say in reference to such appeal—

Said appeal not having been filed within the time required by rule 86, of Rules of Practice, further action therein will be suspended for twenty days from service of notice hereof, to enable Rosenberg to apply to the Hon. Secretary for an order in accordance with rules 83 and 84, of Practice.

In conformity with the above direction, McBride, Rosenberg's attorney, within the said period, filed an application to this Department for an order directing the Commissioner to certify the proceedings in the said case to this Department and to suspend further action until the Secretary shall pass upon the same.

Attached to such application are the affidavits of Rosenberg, his attorneys, and the certificate of H. A. Yonge, register of the land office, all of which documents tend to show that an appeal in the said matter was filed on behalf of Rosenberg September 5, 1887, and was forwarded to "the Department," October 21, the same year.

An appeal of Rosenberg from said decision, filed July, 1888, accompanies the said papers. The grounds of appeal are—

1st. That the said Ellen B. Hale, widow of R. B. Hale, deceased, was not entitled to the preference right to said land.

2nd. That the decision of the Hon. Commissioner was not in accordance with law and equity.

3rd. That the preference right in a contest is a personal right and not transferable.

Proof of service of copies of the said application and of the said appeal upon the opposite party is also attached.

No objection to the said application having been interposed on behalf of the heirs of R. B. Hale, and it appearing from said affidavits and certificates, that an appeal was filed by Rosenberg's attorney, within the time required by the rules, I shall consider the case upon the appeal attached to the said application.

Your said office decision of June 29, 1887, is based upon the fact, that R. B. Hale, when he instituted his said contest against the entry of Edgar, accompanied the same with an application to make timber culture entry for the land and that when he, Hale, was successful in his said contest, his said application was, so far as his rights were concerned, an appropriation of the tract and in point of law of the same force as an actual entry; it withdrew the land from any other disposi-

tion until final action had been taken thereon. In support of this principle you refer to the case of Pfaff *v.* Williams *et al,* 4 L. D., 455. The
right that Hale had thus acquired by his said application upon his
death descended to his heirs. In the case of Tobias Beckner, 6 L. D.,
134, it is said—" The broad underlying principle that controls the question is—that when a person initiates any right it will not escheat and
revert to the government but inure to those on whom the law and
natural justice cast a man's property and the fruits of his labor after
his death." I also refer to the case of Townsend's heirs *v.* Spellman, 2
L. D., 77. There Secretary Teller held that Townsend's application to
enter (under the homestead law) was equivalent to actual entry in respect to his rights and that having died without perfecting the entry,
his heirs were entitled to perfect the entry he initiated.

It is obvious therefore that upon the cancellation of Edgar's entry,
R. B. Hale's application to enter the land under the timber culture act,
became of full force and he, or in case of his death, his heirs, could
perfect the entry by him initiated. It was, therefore, error to allow the
respective entries of Branch and Rosenberg and the latter's entry being
still of record must give way to the rights of the Hale heirs and must
be canceled.

So far the law seems clear, but there is another difficulty in the case.

On November 11, 1887, after Rosenberg had made cash entry for the
land and after he had according to his and his attorney's sworn statements, appealed from your said decision of June 29, 1887, and before
you had suspended action on said appeal by your office letter of July
3, 1888, he instituted a contest against the timber culture entry made
on the said land in behalf of the said heirs of R. B. Hale, deceased, by
his widow, charging—

That the land embraced in said section 30, is not composed exclusively of prairie
land or naturally devoid of timber; that there are more than three hundred and
ninety-three growing trees on said south-east quarter; that there are about five
hundred trees growing on the rest of the section; that said trees are forest trees and
were not planted on said land; that said trees in diameter are from one twelfth inch
to one foot; and there are a large number of stumps that trees had been cut down
from.

Hearing was appointed for February 6, 1888. Both parties appeared
on that day. On behalf of the claimant it was moved that the contest
be dismissed for the reason "that the allegations of the said contest
are insufficient to constitute a cause of action." This motion was
granted by the local officers and contest dismissed. Rosenberg appealed to your office.

By your office decision of May 12, 1888, you affirmed the action of
the local officers. You say:

Your action in the matter is based on the precedent found in the decision of the
Hon. Acting Secretary of the Interior, rendered October 11, 1887, in the case of James
Spencer, 6 L. D., page 217. A consideration of the allegations in the present case
in connection with the decision referred to and the facts appearing satisfies me that
the case was properly dismissed and I, therefore, affirm your decision.

From this decision Rosenberg appealed, and the case is before me for consideration.

I have fully considered this part of the case and have come to the conclusion that Rosenberg's contest was prematurely brought, for when the same was instituted the Hale heirs had no entry on the land. While, therefore, the contest should not be entertained, the charges set forth in Rosenberg's contest affidavit seem to require an investigation. In the affidavit it is alleged that there are about nine hundred trees growing on the section of which the tract in question is a part and that there are in said section a large number of stumps of trees. In the recent case of James Hair, 8 L. D., 467, decided May 6, 1889, it was held that the phrase "devoid of timber" should be construed as meaning land practically so and in determining whether lands fall within such description, no arbitary rule can be formulated for the government of every case.

Controlled by this decision, it seems to me, that the charge in Rosenberg's contest affidavit presents sufficient ground for an investigation. I am, therefore, of the opinion that upon such charge a hearing should be had before the local officers with the view of ascertaining the fact, whether the land is legally subject to a timber culture entry. Of the hearing both parties should be notified.

The entry of the Hale heirs should therefore, not be finally allowed until this question has been judicially determined on the said hearing, in the affirmative.

Until then no other disposition should be made of the land.

In case it should be found that the land is not properly subject to the entry of the Hale heirs, and their said application for this reason should be finally disposed of, then Rosenberg's cash entry may be re-instated.

Your said office decisions of June 29, 1887, and of May 12, 1888, are accordingly modified.

PRACTICE—APPEAL—REVIEW.

SAPP v. ANDERSON.

The Commissioner of the General Land Office has no jurisdiction over a case after an appeal from his decision therein.

After appeal from the Commissioner's decision, a motion for the review of said decision can not be entertained.

In the absence of specifications of error an appeal will be dismissed.

First Assistant Secretary Chandler to Acting Commissioner Stone, July 25, 1889.

On December 7, 1888, your office decided the case of Jasper S. Sapp v. Mahlon L. Anderson, the latter of whom had, on January 21, 1885, filed Osage declaratory statement for the SE. $\frac{1}{4}$ of Sec. 8, T. 27, R. 11, Larned land district, Kansas On December 21, 1888, J. Thomas Turner, Esq., as attorney for Sapp, appealed, in his appeal saying that "points of exception and brief will be filed in due course, in acco: dance with official rules and regulations." February 18th Turner applied to your office for a review of said decision. This your office denied (April 9, 1889); an l from this decision Turner appealed (April 15, 1889). And now comes said Anderson by Wm. T. S. Curtis, his attorney, and moves to dismiss Turner's appeals.

"It is well settled that the filing of an appeal from the decision of your office places the case to which it relates beyond your jurisdiction." (Rudolph Wurlitzer, 6 L. D., 315; John M. Walker, 5 L. D., 504.) Consequently the motion for review found nothing in your office upon which to operate. The only thing remaining to be considered is the appeal (of December 21, 1888), to the Department. More than seven months have now elapsed, and no specifications of error have yet been filed in the Department, nor served on Anderson or his attorney. The appeal is therefore dismissed; and the papers in the case are herewith returned.

PRIVATE CLAIM—ACT OF JUNE 2, 1858.

WILLIAM GOFORTH. (ON REVIEW.)

The classification of a private claim will not bring it within the confirmatory provisions of the act of May 11, 1820, if it is in fact not subject thereto.

Secretary Noble to Acting Commissioner Stone, July 24, 1889.

The attorneys for the legal representative of William Goforth have filed a motion for review of departmental decision of January 17, 1889 (8 L. D. 80), affirming your office decision of October 22, 1887, refusing to authenticate and issue under the provisions of Sec. 3 of the act of June 2, 1858 (11 Stat. 294) certificates of location on account of a private land claim of said William Goforth.

This motion is made upon the ground that the authority upon which said decision is based was misunderstood and misapplied. The authority cited in said decision and upon which it really rests is the decision of the United States supreme court in the case of Blanc v. Lafayette et al., (11 How., 104) which involved the claim of one Louis Liotaud which is found in the same report, class and species as is the one here under consideration.

It is contended that by a reference to the decision on the Liotand claim in the supreme court of Louisiana it will be seen that s id claim "was not founded on an order of survey at all, and that the report of the register and receiver that it was so founded was erroneous; and by the decision of the supreme court of the United States referred to, it will be seen that for that reason alone it held it had been mistakenly placed in the first class of claims and hence was not confirmed by the act of 1820."

And further, " It not being proved or even alleged that the claims of Goforth etc., were erroneously placed in the first class, in other words that the recitals of the commissioners as to their origin and nature were erroneous, it must be presumed they were founded on orders of survey as reported and being recommended for confirmation, as the court say the Liotaud claim was, were therefore confirmed by the act of 1820."

The commissioners reported that the Liotaud claim was based "on an order of survey dated in the year 1802," while the Goforth claim they say was based "on an order of survey issued by the proper officer." The supreme court in discussing the Liotaud claim said—

The record does not contain a copy of the order of survey in favor of Liotaud mentioned by the register and receiver, dated, as they say in the year 1802. Nor is there in it either of those documentary papers, uniformly given by the intendants-general of Spain when grants of land were made. We have not before us either a grant or order of survey in favor of Liotaud. Nothing to make the claim an inchoate right upon which a title could be enlarged in favor of Liotaud. Indeed, we do not know anything from the record about it and all that we do know of the claim is the memorandum of the register and receiver already recited. That discloses that the order of survey mentioned had been given after the cession of Louisiana by his majesty to the republic of France   Register Harper and Receiver Lawrence say in their report that Liotaud's claim is founded on an order of survey dated in the year 1802. Apart from the consideration that the order for a survey is dated after the time when Spain had parted with her political sovereignty to grant land in Louisiana there is no proof of anything having been subsequently done by Liotaud or by any official of Spain to give to Liotaud even an inchoate equity to the land.

Every statement thus made with the exception of those as to the date of the order of survey is as true of the Goforth claim as of the Liotaud claim. Can it be said then that this authority was misapplied when it was made to govern in the decision of the case under consideration ? Surely not. It seems to be claimed by the attorneys for this applicant that the supreme court in the case of Lecompte v. The United States (11 How., 115), used language construing the decision in Blanc v. Lafayette in such a way as to render it favorable to their client's case. The part of that decision referred to is not fully set forth in their motion and is as follows :

And in the case of Blanc v. Lafayette (11 How., 104), decided during the present term, the person from whom the appellant deduced his title had upon a petition to the Spanish intendant obtained an order to the surveyor-general to lay off the land. No report was alleged or proved to have been returned by the surveyor-general upon the petition ; and although this claim was favorably reported upon by the commissioners, and although it was insisted upon as having been confirmed by the act of Congress of 1814 confirming a particular class of French and Spanish grants, concessions warrants of survey, having a special and definite location, yet as this order to survey had not been executed, and as the claim was not sustained by certain and definite boundaries nor by proof of certain and full possession, the supreme court of Louisiana decided, notwithstanding a recommendation by the commissioners and the act of Congress of 1814 that there being no survey and no definite location or description by possession such as would create a specific right or title under the Spanish authorities, the recommendation of the commissioners and the act of Congress did not cure these radical defects, nor confirm a title so wholly undefined, and deduced from so defective on origin.

The language here used does not in anywise change the decision in Blanc *v.* Lafayette or render it less apt of application to the case under consideration.

It is not claimed that the decision in Blanc *v.* Lafayette has been overruled or modified except in so far as the Lecompte case affects it. It is claimed, however, in the brief filed when this case was here on appeal that the ruling of this Department was different from that announced by the supreme court, and that the construction given by the Department had become a rule of property and should not now be disturbed. A careful examination of the cases cited will, however, show that each of them differed in some material respect from the one at bar, and that the exact question now under consideration was not passed upon in any of them.

After a careful consideration of this motion for review, I find no reason for disturbing the decision complained of and said motion is therefore denied.

PRACTICE—NOTICE BY PUBLICATION—APPEAL.

NEEL *v.* HERRICK.

An order for the publication of notice should not be made, if the affidavit therefor does not show what effort has been made to secure personal service.

The Department does not acquire jurisdiction over the appellee where the notice is not addressed to him in his true name, and it does not appear that he received the same.

First Assistant Secretary Chandler to Acting Commissioner Stone, July 25, 1889.

On October 20, 1884, Jerome D. Herrick, jr., made timber culture entry No. 1622 for the SE. ¼, section 2, T. 4 N., R. 34 W., McCook land district, Nebraska. It appears that he made his affidavit for the entry before John R. King, clerk of the district court, Dundy county, Nebraska, such county not being part of the said land district. His application was, however, accepted by the local officers and the entry allowed.

In a contest affidavit, that has on its face no venue, date or name of land office, James Neel charges "that he is well acquainted with the tract of land embraced in the timber culture entry of "James" D. Herrick, jr., No. 1622, made October 22, 1884, upon the SE. ¼ of Sec. 2, town 4 north, range 38 W., (no land district is named) and knows the present condition of the same; also that the said "James" Herrick did not come in the land district in which the land is situated to make the above entry." The corroborating affidavit bears date March 5, 1886.

The affidavit was filed in the local office of said district March 6, 1886. Hearing was first set for May 8, afterwards continued to May 24, of the same year. The claimant was not served with notice personally; an attempt was made to obtain service upon James D.

Herrick, jr., by publication, although no proper foundation was laid for it according to Rule 11, of the Rules of practice, for in his affidavit required by such rule, the contestant fails to state what effort he had made to get personal service. In the notice as published the claimant is described as " James " D. Herrick, jr.

The entryman did not appear at the hearing nor in the proceedings had for the taking of the testimony. The case was proceeded with, *ex parte*, against " James D. Herrick, jr." The local officers, deciding the case, were of the opinion that the said entry should be canceled, because from the testimony presented it appeared that " entryman who made said T. C. No. 1622, did not come within the land district in which the land is located to make his said affidavit."

Pending these proceedings, on April 21, 1886, the entryman by his proper name of Jerome D. Herrick, jr., makes his verified application " to be allowed to re-enter the land or that the entry remain intact by virtue of the amended application herein and affiant's good faith." As grounds for being allowed this privilege he deposes, among other matters, that in making his said affidavit for his said entry before John R. King, county clerk of Dundy county, he acted upon the latter's advice; that at the time he made the affidavit, he believed, assured by King's advice, that the law would allow him to make the said affidavit before such officer; that since the entry he had broken on the land five acres as required by law and had paid for the survey of the land the sum of twenty-five dollars; that he has acted throughout in perfect good faith.

Attached to this application is his amended application for the entry of the land under the timber culture act bearing date the same day, April 21, 1886, also his affidavit for such entry, bearing equal date, made before the receiver of the said local office.

On June 19, 1886, Jerome D. Herrick, jr., appeared specially in the case " for the sole and only object to object to the jurisdiction of the register and receiver herein over the person of the defendant herein," alleging as his reason, " that the entry herein was made by one Jerome D. Herrick, jr., and not by one James D. Herrick, as the allegations made in the affidavit of contest and made upon the returns of service and all papers in said case." He asks that the case be dismissed.

Your office considering the records and proceeedings in the case by your decision of May 12, 1888, reversed the action of the local officers and dismissed the contest. You further determined to allow the entry-man to file a supplemental timber culture affidavit, subscribed and sworn to by him before an officer authorized to administer an oath in the said land district.

The contestant appealed from your said office decision ; notice thereof was attempted to be served upon the entryman by registered letter. From the affidavit of contestant's attorney attached to the appeal, it appears that he on July 13, 1888, mailed to " James " D. Herrick at

Lincoln, Nebraska, which he believed was his, "James" D. Herrick's, last known post office address, by registered letter a copy of the notice of appeal and specification of errors. The attached post office receipt also shows that the letter enclosing the notice was addressed to "James" D. Herrick. It is not shown that the letter came to the hands of Jerome D. Herrick and he has not appeared in the case.

This attempted service of the notice of appeal is not in compliance with Rules 93 and 94 of the Rules of Practice. The name of the opposite party was in fact Jerome D. Herrick, jr., and the letters should have been addressed to the party by that name. By the want of proper service of the notice upon the entryman, this department has not obtained jurisdiction over the entryman, and the appeal must, therefore, be dismissed.

It may, however, be proper to add, that, as shown by the records herein set forth, the local officers had not gained jurisdiction over the person of the entryman when they heard the case and rendered judgment against him, and it does not appear that the claimant ever waived this defect.

Your office transmitted with the papers supplemental timber culture application for the entry of the said land by Jerome D. Herrick, also his supplemental timber culture affidavit sworn to before the register of the said land office; both bearing date July 25, 1888, were made in pursuance of the permission granted by your office in your said decision; the same are returned to your office with the papers in the case, for appropriate action.

———

PRACTICE—APPEAL—CERTIORARI.

REED v. CASNER.

Failure to appeal in time can not be excused on the ground that notice of the decision was not received by the losing party, if in fact his attorney received such notice.

An application for certiorari will not be granted if substantial justice has been done, though the record may show the proceedings to have been defective and informal.

An application for certiorari should set forth specifically the grounds on which it is made, and the facts relied upon in support of the application.

Secretary Noble to Acting Commissioner Stone, July 25, 1889.

In the case of Cornelius Reed, contestant, v. Nicholas Casner, contestee, involving the latter's homestead entry, No. 22,398, on the W. ½ of NW. ¼, SE. ¼ of NW ¼ Sec. 23, and NE. ¼ of NE. ¼, Sec. 22, T. 11, R. 8, Salina district, Kansas, the local officers, on the hearing thereof, June 23, 1886, decided in favor of the contestant and recommended the cancellation of said entry. Your office, by decision of October 23, 1888, affirmed the action of the local officers, and, having been advised by the local officers "that due notice had been served on the parties and that no appeal had been taken from" your said decision of October 23, 1888, your office by letter of January 25, 1889, canceled said entry and closed the case. Subsequently an appeal by the claimant from said decision of October 23, 1888, was transmitted to your office by the local officers, which your office by letter of May 2, 1889, disallowed, for the reason that it appeared from the records that no appeal had been taken from said decision within sixty days from the date, November 10, 1888, of service of notice thereof, as required by Rules of Practice 86 and 88, and the case had accordingly been closed.

The claimant now applies, under Rules of Practice 83 and 84, "for an order directing the Commissioner to certify the proceedings" in the case to this Department. In paragraph eight of said application, it is alleged that " he " (claimant) " had received no notice of the Commissioner's decision of October 23, 1888, and of his right of appeal therefrom," and hence that the cancellation of the entry, January 25, 1889, was erroneous. It is to be noted, in the first place, that the application is not sworn to by the claimant, but by his attorney, David W. Scott, who filed the same. It is true, the affidavit of the claimant's son, to the effect that claimant had not received notice accompanies the application, but the affidavit of the claimant himself, who alone presumably could have positive knowledge on the subject, is not filed. In the next place, if it were satisfactorily shown, that the claimant in fact had not received notice, this would not be sufficient, if he was represented by attorney. By Rule of Practice 105, it is provided, that "All notices will be served upon the attorneys of record," and by Rule 106, that " notice to the attorney will be deemed notice to the party in interest."

It appears from paragraph one of said application, that one D. C. Lockwood was the " local attorney " for the claimant at that time, and it is alleged, not that he was not served with or did not accept service of notice, but that "There is no evidence" of acceptance of service by him. This would seem to be a negative pregnant—the negation of the existence of evidence of the fact, implying an affirmation of the fact itself. If he was not served or did not accept service, why not so aver? Again, in paragraph five of the application, it is set forth, that in an affidavit made by said D. C. Lockwood he " distinctly states that he never authorized any one else to take his place as local attorney for the petitioner" (claimant) " or to accept notice for him of any proceedings had in the cause at bar." There is no affidavit by him, however, denying that he himself was served with, or accepted service of, notice. If such was not the case, this would seem to be an unaccountable omission.

Without further considering the statements of the application bearing on this point, it is sufficient to say, that there is no direct averment in the application, and it does not positively appear therefrom that the attorney of the claimant was not served with, or did not accept service of, notice.

If, however, it clearly appeared, that there was no due and legal notice to the claimant or his attorney, it is further to be considered, that "certiorari is not a writ of right; but whether it shall issue lies in the judicial discretion of the tribunal to which the petition is addressed, and the writ will not be granted if substantial justice has been done, though the record may show the proceedings to have been defective and informal." Dobbs Placer Mine, 1 L. D., 565. It devolved, therefore, on the claimant to show in his application that "substantial justice" was not done him in said decision of October 23, 1888. On this point, he alleges simply that said decision is "against the weight of evidence brought out on the trial and not upheld by law." Rule 84 of Practice requires, that applications for certiorari "shall fully and specifically set forth the grounds upon which the application is made," and in Hilliard on New Trials (p. 696, Sec. 32), the general rule of pleading is laid down as applicable to petitions for certiorari, that they "should state facts, and not the opinions or conclusions of the petitioner." (The Dobbs Placer Mine, *supra*.) The above averment, giving only the opinion or conclusion of the claimant, as to the correctness of said decision in law and on the merits, without the statement of any fact or facts in support of such opinion or conclusion, is wholly insufficient, under said Rule of Practice, as well as the rule of pleading referred to.

The decision of October 23, 1888, sets forth substantive facts as being disclosed by the testimony taken on the hearing, and which, if true and unexplained, justified the finding of your office and the local officers against the claimant. Among those alleged facts are the following:—

The crops taken from said land consisted chiefly of rye and were "volunteer" in their character, having sprung from a crop sown in 1880 by some one other than claimant. His family consisted, beside himself, of his wife and a son about seventeen years of age. About one half mile from the land in contest was a timber culture entry made by an elder son, whose death had occurred quite a while prior to this contest, and whose estate was being settled by his mother as administratrix. On this timber culture entry, located in Sec. 14, the mother and son resided—here, also, as the neighbors understood it, was the home of the claimant—when they wanted to see him, they went there to find him. His meals were for the most part taken there, and from the testimony of his own witnesses, notably that of his wife, he frequently slept there. It is also clearly proven, that he filled the office of overseer of roads, in the district in which Sec. 14 is situated, while the land in controversy is in another road district. The uncontradicted testimony of Wm. Griffin, "that while looking for a house for his son-in-law, he was informed by claimant, that the house on the land in contest was unoccupied," throws light on the question of residence. There can be no question that claimant frequently slept on the land in contest, but the testimony for claimant is not strong enough to overthrow the legal presumption that his home was where that of his family was, viz: on Sec. 14, nor is it strong enough to show that he had established his home on the land in controversy to the exclusion of one elsewhere.

The claimant's application should negative the facts set forth in said decision or state facts explanatory thereof, and also set up the facts developed on the hearing, which, he claims, show his compliance with the law.

The application is denied.

RAILROAD GRANT—SETTLEMENT CLAIM—CITIZENSHIP.

Southern Pacific R. R. Co. v. Brown.

A pre-emption claim, existing when the line of road is designated, excepts the land included therein from the operation of the grant; and on the subsequent abandonment of such claim the land reverts to the public domain, and is subject to appropriation by the first legal applicant.

While voting is not conclusive evidence of citizenship, it raises a *prima facie* presumption thereof, which is sufficient in the absence of proof to the contrary.

Secretary Noble to Acting Commissioner Stone, July 26, 1889.

This case involves the fractional NW. ¼, Sec. 7, T. 3 S. R. 7 W., San Bernardino meridian, Los Angeles district, California. Said land lies within the twenty mile primary limits of the grant of March 3, 1871 (16 Stat., 579, Sec. 23), to the Southern Pacific R. R. Co., branch line, as shown by said company's map of designated route, filed in your office, "April 3, 1871, in accordance with which lands were ordered withdrawn by letter of April 21, 1871, which was received at the local office May 10, ensuing."

November 7, 1884, Harry G. Brown made application to file a pre-emption declaratory statement for said land, which was rejected by the local officers, because "the tract applied for" was "within the limits of" said withdrawal. Brown's application was accompanied by his affidavit, setting forth, that "from about 1868 to about 1876" and at the date of said withdrawal, the land "was in the actual possession (of) and claimed by George Woods, who occupied and claimed the same as a pre-emption settler under the United States laws," and who "was at that time a duly qualified pre-emption settler on said land," and "that the Southern Pacific Railroad Company had no right or interest in or to said land." The application and affidavit having been transmitted to your office, a hearing was ordered by your office letter of November 20, 1884, which was had, December 22, 1885. Upon the testimony submitted at said hearing, the local officers found, substantially, that the matters of fact set forth in Brown's affidavit were proven, and on appeal by the railroad company your office, by decision of June 2, 1888, found the decision of the local officers "to be sustained by the evidence," and held "that by reason of the occupancy of the land by Wood at the date when the railroad grant took effect (April 3, 1871), said land was excepted from the operation of said grant." From this decision the company now appeals to this Department.

I have examined the testimony and it clearly appears therefrom, that Wood made settlement on the land in 1868 or 1869, at which time he dug a well and built a house, sixteen by eighteen or eighteen by twenty feet, which he furnished with bed, stove, etc., and was occupying and claiming as a home in 1871, at the date when said withdrawal took effect. His improvements were valued at from $100 to $150. He was a single man, and his actual occupancy of the land subsequent to 1872 was not continuous, but he cultivated and gathered crops thereon, and continued to claim it as a home. The township plat of survey was not filed in the local office until September 18, 1876, and within three months thereafter, on December 15, 1876, he filed a pre-emption declaratory statement for the land, alleging settlement thereon, September, 1868.

The company's grant (act of July 27, 1866, sections 18 and 3), embraced only lands to which the United States had "full title, not reserved, sold, granted, or otherwise appropriated, and free from pre-emption or other claims or rights at the time the line of said road is designated by a plat thereof, filed in the office of the commissioner of the general land office."

Wood having filed, as above stated, his declaratory statement within three months after the township plat of survey had been filed in the local office, preserved and duly asserted his claim as a pre-emption settler (Rev. Stat., 2266) and under the facts showing his *bona fide* residence on the land at the date, April 3, 1871, when the company's line of road was "designated by" the filing of the plat thereof in your office, he must be held to have had a "pre-emption claim" at that time, which excepted the land from the operation of the grant.

The claim of Wood having been subsequently abandoned, the land was not thereby rendered subject to the grant, but became public land, open to appropriation by the first legal applicant. (Northern Pacific R. R. Co. *v.* Johnson, 7 L. D., 357, and cases cited therein.) Such appears to have been its status when the application of Harry G. Brown to file a declaratory statement therefor was made, and said application, if in itself sufficient, should have been allowed.

It is insisted by the counsel for the company, that there was no competent or sufficient evidence of Wood's citizenship adduced at the hearing. It is not contended, and there is no evidence, that he was not in fact a native born citizen. The only testimony on this point, besides hearsay as to statements by his brothers that he was born in Illinois, was that he had exercised the right of a citizen by voting before and since the year 1871. While this is not conclusive evidence of citizenship, yet it raises a *prima facie* presumption thereof, sufficient (particularly, in the absence of a charge to the contrary) until overthrown by testimony in rebuttal. As was said by this Department in the case of William Heley (6 L. D., 631), "the offer and acceptance of a vote raises a strong presumption that it is legal and that the person voting is a citizen.

The decision of your office allowing David G. Brown, as administrator of said Harry G. Brown (whose death has been suggested) to file the necessary papers to complete said pre-emption claim, is affirmed.

PRE-EMPTION—FINAL PROOF—RESIDENCE.

SMITH v. BREARLY.

The pre emption right is a preference right of purchase, acquired by settlement, residence, and filing.

Published notice of intention to submit final proof and make pre-emption cash entry, so far reserves the land covered thereby, as to prevent its being properly entered by another pending final action thereon.

A *bona fide* pre-emption claim is not defeated by the mistaken location of the settler's house outside of the boundary line of his claim.

A charge of bad faith against a claimant finds corroboration in his unexplained failure to testify in support of his claim.

Residence is neither acquired nor maintained without inhabitancy of the land, either actual or constructive, and that to the exclusion of a home elsewhere.

First Assistant Secretary Chandler to Acting Commissioner Stone, July 26, 1889.

I have considered the appeal of Martha A. Brearly, from your decision of March 22, 1886, rejecting her final proof and holding for cancellation her pre-emption filing for the W½ of NE¼, SE¼ of NW¼ and NE¼ of SW¼, Sec. 14, T. 106 N., R. 68 W., Mitchell, Dakota.

The record shows that Brearly filed her declaratory statement for said tract on March 9, 1883, alleging settlement on the first day of the same month. Harrison Taylor made homestead entry of the same tract on May 22, 1883, and George A. Smith, the present protestant, instituted contest against the same, but on what particular date does not appear from the record.

May 28, 1885, your office canceled Taylor's entry, and on June 26, 1885, Smith made homestead entry of the same tract.

The action of the local officers in allowing Smith's entry was erroneous, as Mrs. Brearly had already published notice of her intention to submit final proof and make pre-emption cash entry of the tract in question. Her doing so reserved the land covered by such application so far as to prevent its being properly entered by another, pending the consideration of said application. L. J. Capps (8 L. D., 406); Henry A. Frederick (8 L. D., 412).

Mrs. Brearly gave due notice of her intention to submit final proof on September 25, 1884, and protest having been filed by Smith against the acceptance of such proof, a hearing was had to determine the truth of the allegations contained in said protest.

This hearing was commenced on October 11, 1884, and continued for several days. A large amount of testimony was taken, much of which is very conflicting. Independently, however, of the testimony submitted by protestant, the facts testified to by claimant's own witnesses satisfy me that Mrs. Brearly has not complied with the provisions of the pre emption law.

It appears that about March 1, 1883, W. H. Brearly, claimant's son, and one Thomas Gibson constructed a small dug-out or shanty either upon the tract in question or within about one hundred yards of it. Considerable testimony was submitted as to the exact location of this structure, but this question may be eliminated from the consideration of this case, as protestant admits that "they believed they put said shanty on Mrs. Brearly's claim."

A *bona fide* pre-emption claim should not be rejected because the claimant's house was by mistake beyond the lines of survey bounding his land.

Arnold *v.* Langley (1 L. D., 439); Opinions of Attorneys General (vol. 3, p. 312); Phylorman Higgins (2 C. L. L., 406).

The testimony shows that this shanty was partly a dugout constructed on the side of a bluff, with sod walls about four feet high at the highest point. The sides and front were partly open and it had neither a window nor a boarded floor. The roof consisted of rough unmatched, unbattened boards covered with some hay or rushes. It would not keep out the rain and the shanty was entirely unfitted for human habitation. It was certainly not a proper shelter, much less a suitable residence for claimant who was then sixty-two years old and in a feeble, sickly condition.

It does not appear that it was provided with the necessary furniture and cooking utensils, and the place was in no way suited for a dwelling in a climate like Dakota, and especially during the months of March, April, and May.

It is claimed that Mrs. Brearly slept in this shanty on March 7, 1883, and also slept there one night in each of the following months of April, May and June. This structure together with a well six feet deep by three feet wide constituted Mrs. Brearly's first settlement upon the tract.

Another and somewhat better shanty was erected in July following at a short distance from the first one. John Brearly, another of claimant's sons, alleges that he at the same time broke three acres of the tract.

It is claimed that this breaking was sown to wheat that year, and that about an equal quantity was broken the year after.

Wm. H. Brearly had a tree claim on the land adjoining the one in question. He resided near Mt. Vernon, some fifty miles from his tree claim, which he visited occasionally. He testified, that his mother (claimant) spent about fifteen weeks on the tract between July and November 1883. In this he is not corroborated; on the contrary James Affleck, one of claimant's witnesses, a near neighbor and intimate friend of Mrs. Brearly's computed the length of this stay at about seven weeks.

On the other hand witnesses for protestant, who resided in the immediate vicinity of the tract, who saw the shanty almost daily and who appear to have no interest in the result of this controversy, testified explicitly that claimant did not remain upon the tract during the time testified to by W. H. Brearly; that she only stayed there a few days at a time; that there were then no signs of human habitation around the shanty, and that she could not have occupied it for any considerable length of time without their knowledge.

It is claimed that Mrs. Brearly left the tract about November 22, 1883, and returned about March 20, 1884. Medical testimony was submitted showing that she was in feeble health during this time and could not have remained upon the land. On her return she found the roof of her shanty gone. Her son covered it with a wagon box and canvas, and it is claimed that she slept in the shanty two nights in March 1884, and one or two nights during each of the following months of April, May and June. In July or August ensuing, another roof was put upon the shanty, and some of claimant's witnesses allege that from that time until final proof she (claimant) generally slept upon the land. This, however, is vigorously denied by protestant and his witnesses. Mrs. Brearly, however visited her family at least a few times during this interval.

Claimant attended the hearing, and was about to testify, but was withdrawn by her counsel after being sworn. The reasons assigned for so doing are not satisfactory, and her not testifying would, under the circumstances, tend to support the theory that the filing was made for the benefit of another, and that a *bona fide* compliance with the law was not shown.

April 4, 1885, the local officers rendered the following decision :—" In view of the sickness and poverty of the claimant, she is entitled to the benefit of the liberal doctrine laid down in Sandell *v.* Davenport and Engen *v.* Sustad. Her proof should be accepted and the homestead entry canceled."

The homestead entry above referred to must have been that of Harrison Taylor, which was not canceled by your office until May 28, 1885. It could not have referred to Smith's entry as that was not made until June 26th following.

From this action Smith duly appealed, and on March 26, 1886, your office rendered a decision rejecting claimant's proof and holding her filing for cancellation. You at the same time decided that Smith's homestead entry "may remain subject to compliance with law." An appeal by claimant from this decison brings the case before the Department.

The pre-emption right is a preference right of purchase acquired by settlement, residence and filing.

The Department requires, in evidence of the genuineness of settlement, that six months of actual residence shall be passed before proof and payment. It appears by a very large preponderance of the evidence that claimant has not complied with this requirement. Whilst she may have remained upon the land a few nights during each of the months claimed in 1883, and whilst her visits during the months of July, August and September of 1884, may have been more protracted than those of March, April, May and June of the same year, it does not appear that she has shown due compliance with the law in the matter of residence or inhabitancy.

Residence is an essential requirement of the homestead law, and is neither acquired nor maintained without inhabitancy of the land, either actual or constructive, and that to the exclusion of a home elsewhere. West v. Owen, (8 L. D., 576); Spalding v. Colfer, (8 L. D., 615).

Residence can not be acquired or maintained by going upon or visiting the land, solely for the purpose of complying with the letter of the law, no matter how honestly the claimant may believe such visits all that the law requires. Mary Campbell (8 L. D., 331).

I am satisfied from the evidence in the case that from the date of entry to the submission of final proof, claimant maintained her residence with her family at Mt. Vernon, and that she occasionally visited the tract for the purpose of maintaining a colorable compliance with law. Her improvements were of the most meagre character, and confirm this conviction.

From the foregoing reasons I affirm your decision.

ALABAMA LANDS—ACTS OF JUNE 15, 1880, AND MARCH 3, 1883.

JOHN C. HENLEY.

Land returned as valuable for coal prior to the act of March 3, 1883, is not subject to purchase under the act of June 15, 1880, until after public offering, though the original entry was made prior to the passage of the former act.

A cash entry allowed under the act of 1880, of land previously reported as valuable for coal, should be suspended until after public offering, and treated as an application to enter in the event that the land is not sold at such offering.

The protection given by the act of 1883, to a *bona fide* entry, previously made, does not extend beyond the relinquishment of such entry.

The right of purchase under the act of 1880, until exercised, does not preclude other disposition of the land by Congress.

Secretary Noble to Acting Commissioner Stone, July 27, 1889.

On September 12, 1870, John C. Henley, made homestead entry for N. ½ SE. ¼ Sec. 20, T. 16 S., R. 2 W., Montgomery, Alabama. This entry was canceled by relinquishment on April 5, 1871.

On January 17, 1887, Henley purchased said land under act of June 15, 1880 (21 Stat., 237). Henley's cash entry was held for cancellation by your office decision of June 6, 1888, for the reason that by the act of March 3, 1883, (22 Stat., 487) the land could not be entered until offered at public sale, it having been in 1879 reported as containing coal.

From this decision Henley appeals.

It is now settled that land returned as valuable for coal prior to the passage of the act of March 3, 1883, is not subject to homestead entry until after public offering.   Alice Jordan (7 L. D., 461).

Counsel, however, insist that Henley acquired by his homestead entry (made in September 1870, and canceled in April following) a right to purchase the land agreeably to the act of June 15, 1880, without regard to the provisions of the act of March 3, 1883.

Section 2 of the act of June 15, 1880, *supra*, enables " persons who have heretofore under any of the homestead laws entered lands properly subject to such entry " to " entitle themselves to said lands by paying the government price therefor."

The act of March 3, 1883, *supra*, entitled an act to exclude the public lands in Alabama from the operation of the laws relating to mineral lands, provides that all public lands in said State shall be disposed of " only as agricultural lands," and that when such land has " been reported . . . . as containing coal and iron " the same " shall first be offered at public sale."

In the matter of the application of the State of Alabama to select coal land as school indemnity (6 L. D. 493) the legislation concerning the disposition of such land was carefully considered.   In the case cited it was shown (Id., 501), that prior to act of March 1883, Congress had recognized two classes of lands within the State of Alabama,—agricultural and mineral, and that it proposed by the act mentioned " as to that State to disestablish the distinction and regard them all as agricultural lands."   But to prevent the disposal of "lands which had been previously dealt with as mineral lands under the mineral law system . . . . as homesteads, etc., or at a nominal price," Congress required to be first offered at public sale all lands which " have heretofore been reported " to the General Land Office as containing coal and iron   In this connection it was held that "the only meaning that can attach to the clause is that before this class of lands shall become subject to homestead right or private purchase, it shall be offered at public sale."   But it is contended that the act of March 3, 1883, did not repeal the act of June 15, 1880, but expressly excepted all lands embraced in former entries to which inchoate rights had been attached.   This contention, in my opinion, is without force.

The second proviso of the act of March 1883, provided that, land in Alabama subject to a *bona fide* homestead entry heretofore made, shall be patented without reference to act of May 10, 1872 " upon the application of persons who have in other respects complied with the homestead law."   The act of May 1872 (17 Stat., 91) provided for the disposal of " all valuable mineral deposits in lands belonging to the United States, both surveyed and unsurveyed."

Lands valuable for coal being, therefore, within the purview of the act just mentioned, the manifest intent of the said second proviso was to protect the entries previously made of such persons who rendered a substantial compliance with the homestead law.

The protection given by the act of March 1883 to such *bona fide* entry did not, however, extend beyond its relinquishment. David J. Davis (7 L. D., 560).

This case is not controlled by the ruling in the cases of the Northern Pacific R. R. Co. *v.* Burt (3 L. D., 490) and Northern Pac. *v.* McLean (5 L. D., 529), for the reason that Congress had ample power to make any disposition of the land prior to the exercise of the privilege of purchasing under the act of June 15, 1880, and the act of March 3, 1883, having made such disposition of the land in controversy as would be inconsistent with the right of purchase under the act of June 15, 1880, the former act must control—not because it operated as a repeal of the act of June 15, 1880, but because it prohibits these lands from being disposed of until after public offering.

But while Henley's cash entry, for reasons stated, can not at this time be passed to patent, I do not concur in your conclusion that the same should be canceled. In the Davis case *supra*, it was held that a homestead entry allowed in contravention of the terms of the act of March 1883, under which valuable improvements were made may be suspended, pending public offering of the land, and treated as an application to enter in event that the land is not sold at such offering.

Henley's payment having been accepted by the local office, and there being no suggestion of fraud, I can see no reason why the rule laid down in the Davis case should not obtain in the case at bar.

The cash entry of Henley will, in accordance with the rulings mentioned, be suspended pending the offering of the land at public sale.

The decision appealed from is modified accordingly.

TIMBER CULTURE CONTEST—BREAKING.

PURMORT *v.* ZERFING.

A timber culture entry will not be canceled for failure to break the requisite number of acres, where the entryman honestly supposed that he had complied with the law, and made good the deficiency as soon as practicable after its discovery.

First Assistant Secretary Chandler to Acting Commissioner Stone, July 31, 1889.

I have considered the case of Wales E. Purmort *v.* John Zerfing on appeal by the latter from your office decision of May 9, 1888, holding for cancellation his timber culture entry for the SW. ¼ of the SE. ¼, the S. ½ of the SW. ¼ and the NW. ¼ of the SW. ¼ of Sec. 22, T. 7 N., R. 1 E., B. H. M., Deadwood Dakota land district.

Zerfing made timber culture entry for said tract June 2, 1884. On March 31, 1886, Purmort filed affidavit of contest against said entry, alleging " that the said John Zerfing has, up to the present time plowed but two and one-half (2½) acres and has failed to comply with the law and said neglect still continues," and filed therewith his application to make timber culture entry for said land. Notice of this contest was served on Zerfing April 5, 1886. A hearing was duly had at which both parties appeared and submitted testimony. The local officers decided in favor of the contestant, and this decision was, on appeal to your office, affirmed.

The testimony for the contestant shows that at the date of the service of notice of this contest only a little more than two and one-half acres of ground had been broken.

The testimony for the entryman shows that he hired one Scoble to break five acres of ground on the land included in this entry, and that upon the statement of Scoble that such breaking was done, he paid the price agreed upon therefor.

Scoble testifies that in May 1885, he went to this land and plowed what he thought was five acres; that he was engaged at the work four days and received payment for plowing five acres at the rate of four dollars per acre; that before he commenced plowing he measured by stepping what he calculated to be a little more than five acres, marked it with stakes and plowed the tract thus staked out.

The entryman testifies that he relied upon the statements of Scoble and paid him for breaking five acres of the land. He was informed in January 1886, that the piece broken did not amount to five acres and that this was the first information he had of the deficiency. After this he went to the land and measured the breaking, finding it to be a little over two and one-half acres. He also claims that as early in the spring as he could, he hired a man to do more breaking, and at the date of the hearing ten acres had been broken.

There is nothing in this testimony indicating that entryman acted in bad faith in this m tter. He honestly supposed the law had been complied with, and the man he hired to do the work was apparently honest in his belief that he had broken the full amount which he had contracted for, and for which he was afterwards p id. And again, the entryman claims, and it is not denied by the contestant, that this deficiency in the breaking was supplied as soon after its discovery as the weather would permit.

The case is, in its material facts very similar to that of Vargason v. McClellan (6 L. D., 829), in which case the contest was dismissed and the entry allowed to stand. And inasmuch as the entryman, at the date of contest had three years yet to set out the required area of trees and grow them eight years in compliance with the law, I do not find here any such wilfull or inexcusable failure as demands the cancellation of Zerfing's entry, and the decision appealed from is, therefore, reversed and the contest dismissed.

TIMBER CULTURE CONTEST—"DEVOID OF TIMBER."

HONNOLD v. CUSHING.

The section in which a timber culture entry is made must be "devoid of timber," within the meaning of the statute, as well as the land actually embraced within the entry.

An extra-judicial opinion of the Commissioner of the General Land Office, as to the legality of an entry, expressed upon an *ex parte* and partial statement of the facts, will not preclude cancellation of the entry, under contest proceedings, if the land is in fact not subject to such appropriation.

First Assistant Secretary Chandler to Acting Commissioner Stone, July 31, 1889.

I have considered the case of William C. Honnold v. Edmund Cushing, upon the appeal of the former from your office decision of May 14, 1888, dismissing his contest against the timber culture entry of Cushing for the NE. ¼ Sec. 26, T. 6 N. R. 26 W., McCook land district, Nebraska.

Cushing made his timber culture entry No. 106 for the said land October 12, 1883; on January 2, 1886, Honnold instituted contest against the said entry, charging in his affidavit, "that tree culture entry No. 106 was illegal in its inception from the fact that said section twenty-six is not naturally devoid of timber and that there is now growing on said section twenty-six, more than twelve acres of natural timber, and more than six thousand seven hundred and fifty trees, many of the trees being more than two feet in diameter."

Hearing on the issue presented by the affidavit was had March 10, 1886; both parties were present and represented by their respective attorneys. The local officers decided the case against the entryman and were of the opinion that his entry should be canceled. Cushing appealed. Your office reversed the action of the local officers and dismissed the contest. Honnold thereupon appealed, and the case is before this Department for consideration. The testimony adduced by both parties shows that, though no natural trees are growing on the particular quarter section covered by the entry, there are a large number of trees growing on the west half of said section twenty-six. The spirit and the letter of the act both preclude the idea that Congress intended to permit a timber culture entry upon a *section* of land when there is a natural growth of trees thereon. In making the affidavit the entryman swears "that the *section* of land specified in my said application is composed exclusively of prairie lands or other lands devoid of timber." In this case a small stream passes through a rather wide strip of bottom land situated on the west half of the south west quarter and the south west quarter of the north west quarter of the section; the bottom land is bordered by high bluffs. The growth of trees on the said section is confined to this bottom land and its immediate vicinity. The trees are elm, ash, box elder and some hackberry. In some places they grow but scattering, while in others they are dense, fully covering the ground.

Francis M. Rathborn, a witness on behalf of the contestant, whose veracity is not impugned by any thing that appears in the testimony, testifies that he was, for five years county surveyor of Frontier county; that he, by actual measurement found the bottom land had an extent of thirty-two acres, and that on at least sixteen acres of it trees are growing. He says that the bottom land varies in width from three chains to ten.

Geo. P. Hughes, a witness for the claimant, and who visited the land only once, expresses his belief that the bottom land would average twenty-eight rods wide through the section.

Anthony Grigat, another of claimant's witnesses, says that the bottom land is from one to three rods wide, but that gulches branch out from it one to ten rods wide.

Francis Cushing a brother of claimant says that "to the best of his knowledge" the bottom land is eight rods wide; the claimant himself testifies to its width of from "one or two rods to ten rods."

Frank Griffith, who lived on the part of said section covered with this growth of trees for more than four years from 1878 to 1882, deposes that the bottom land is from six to sixteen rods wide; while he occupied the land, the timber thereon "was assessed to him as ten acres." By all the witnesses it is admitted that on this bottom land, between the bluffs, which rise at places to the height of from one hundred to one hundred and twenty feet, many trees are growing.

From this evidence I have drawn the conclusion, that at any rate, more than ten acres are covered with a growth of trees, in some parts thinly, in other parts more densely.

Regarding the number of trees growing there and their sizes, the testimony differs. The contestant and one Chas. L. Case swear, that they made on February 20, 1886, an actual count of all trees more than ten feet high; they kept tally of their count, and the tally sheet of Case was produced at the trial. Honnold found the number to be six thousand eight hundred, besides a few near the creek, which he omitted to count. Case's tally sheet shows six thousand seven hundred and fifty trees; he says he left some uncounted. Rathborn thinks that one hundred of the trees are of two feet or more in diameter. Honnold himself estimates the number of trees of such size at seventy. The testimony on the part of the contestant also shows that judging from the stumps still on the land, a great deal of timber has been cut and taken off. Rathborn estimates the number of stumps at from eight hundred to one thousand. Honnold says, they number not less than six hundred. Griffith states that when he moved on the land (he moved on the land March 1878) "the timber had been considerably cut off, but the young timber was young and thrifty. I cut some wood and hauled to Cambridge." He also cut down trees, using them for building a log house;

some he used for wagon tongues, ax-handles and the like mechanical purposes. He also says that trees were cut down and made into fence rails.

The statements of the claimant and three of his witnesses show, that they made an actual count of the trees on February 3, 1886, leaving out those that were less than four inches in diameter. They counted, each one, the same number, two thousand two hundred and forty-seven trees; they say that twenty-one of these were of two feet or more in diameter; they do not mention the number of stumps on the land.

Perhaps the conflict in the testimony of the witnesses may be accounted for by the difference in the count; the one party including therein all trees higher than ten feet, the other leaving uncounted all those of less than four inches in diameter.

Regarding the quality of the timber the witnesses for contestant pronounce the trees to be fit for farm and domestic uses, but not good for "sawing purposes," while claimant's witnesses say, that the larger trees are scrubby, rotten at heart and not fit for anything except fuel, and that of this they would make but a poor quality. The testimony of Griffith who actually used part of the trees for domestic and mechanical purposes, seems to give weight to the opinion of contestant's witnesses. The young trees are admitted to be sound and healthy.

Claimant says, he thinks that when he made his entry the trees on the land of more than four inches in diameter numbered about twelve hundred. He accounts for the rapid growth of the trees during the last three years by the plentiful fall of rain and snow during two seasons; and the partial protection of the land by a fence against the inroads of cattle. Is not this a strong argument against himself; does not this statement prove that trees grow naturally on this bottom land? and that the latter, if the trees there growing are not injured or destroyed will soon be covered by a dense forest?

This is the evidence in the case material to the issue; from it I am constrained to conclude, that the land is not legally subject to a timber culture entry, even under the most liberal construction of the timber act; to adjudge this section to be " devoid of timber " would be, I think a mis-interpretation of the clear and precise text of the act, and a construction against its spirit and design.

It seems, however, proper to refer to other testimony adduced by claimant, evidently for the purpose of proving his good faith in the matter of his entry. Claimant testifies that when he made his entry he had not discovered that trees were growing on the western portion of said section; that a few days after entry, when he gained knowledge of the growth of the trees he inquired of the local officers by letter " if the claim which he entered on the 12th instant was legally issued, or whether or not there was trees growing on the same section, how many natural, if any." The register replied—" I have no doubt your claim is all right, I do not think you can find a section in that part of the country with enough trees to render a timber claim invalid." Claimant further shows that, not fully satisfied regarding the legality of his entry he wrote to the Secretary of the Interior concerning the same. He gives further in evidence a letter of the Commissioner Hon. N. C. McFarland, addressed to the local officers, bearing date January 21, 1884, from which it appears that Edmund Cushing, for the purpose of being informed regarding the legality of his entry, transmited his duly corroborated affidavit showing " that there are in a gully on the west side of said section five hundred elm and soft wood trees from four inches to one and one-half foot in diameter, and that said trees are of a scrubby character." The Hon. Commissioner goes on to state " There is no indication on either the official plat or field notes on file in the office of the existence of any timber on section 26, 6, 26 W., and as it appears that the trees are confined to the borders of a small stream, I am of opinion that the entry was properly allowed, and is in accordance with the decision of the Hon. Secretary of the Interior in the case of Blenkner v. Sloggy."

Claimant further deposes that these letters confirmed his belief that his entry would never be canceled and that by reasons of these letters he continued to fence and cultivate the said entry, he adds, in good faith.

This testimony was received subject to the objections of contestant, who claimed the same to be immaterial.

I am of the opinion, that this testimony cannot be considered in determining the case between the parties. The question to be solved is—whether section twenty-six was at the time of entry exclusively prairie lands, or other lands devoid of timber; if not, then the entry was illegal by the terms of the statute, and the good faith of the entryman can not change the result. There is a particular objection to the admission as evidence of the Hon. Commissioner's letter. It is a reply to entry. man's inquiry; upon the facts as he stated them in his affidavit the opinion expressed in the letter, is based. The affidavit is not in evidence, it can not be known, therefore, whether the allegations set out therein were true. The indications are, judging from the reference made in the letter to the affidavit, that the latter did not state the real facts in the case, even according to claimant's individual testimony given at the trial. At any rate, the contestant is not bound by the opinion expressed in the letter; he can not be defeated upon ex parte affidavits, nor is the extra-judicial opinion of the Hon. Commissioner binding upon him.

Leaving then claimant's good faith out of the question and deciding the case upon the testimony material to the issue in the case, I conclude that the land in controversy is not subject to a timber culture entry, because the section of which it is a part is not devoid of timber.

It follows that claimant's entry must be canceled.

Your said office decision is accordingly reversed.

KAMANSKI v. RIGGS.

A "deserted wife" is qualified, as the "head of a family" to make a homestead entry.

The offer, on the part of the husband, of trivial sums nominally for the support of the family, and the refusal of such money, on the part of the wife, do not necessarily disprove the fact of desertion.

First Assistant Secretary Chandler to Acting Commissioner Stone, July 31, 1889.

The records of your office show the SW ¼ Sec. 24, T. 28 N. R. 8 E., Niobrara, Nebraska to have been embraced in the homestead entry of William A. Riggs, made April 3, 1883, and canceled by relinquishment April 7, 1885.

On June 13, 1885, Adaline Riggs made homestead entry for the tract named.

On or about December 5, 1885, Charles Kamanski initiated contest against the entry last referred to, alleging that "Adaline Riggs is the lawful wife of William A. Riggs, and he is a non-resident of the State, and contributes to the support of said wife, and that he has used his homestead right."

A hearing upon said contest was had at the local office on February 10 and 11, 1886. The claimant Riggs objected to the proof of service of notice in that it did not state place of service. The local officers allowed the contestant to amend the return, whereupon the claimant objected to the amended return for the reason that it was not signed by the contestant who "is supposed to have sworn to the said return."

The amended return is endorsed on the notice of contest. It is signed and sworn to by the contestant before the register, and dated February 10th, the day of hearing. The objection to said return was properly "held to be insufficient."

Upon the testimony submitted at the said hearing, the local officers rendered separate opinions. The receiver found the claimant (Riggs) to be a deserted wife, and that her entry should remain intact. The register found that the fact of her desertion had not been shown, and recommended the cancellation of the entry.

The contestant (Kamanski) appealed from the ruling of the receiver, and the claimant (Riggs) from that of the register.

On June 7, 1888, your office dismissed the contest subject to the right of appeal. From this action the contestant appeals here.

It appears from the evidence that the claimant, who with her husband, William A. Riggs had lived on the land, left the same about March 26, 1885, and for several months with her four children lived about among the neighbors, returning about the fall to the land; that her said departure was caused by her husband's brutal treatment and improper conduct with another woman, who by her husband's direction the claimant had invited from Illinois, and who had for more than three months been a member of his household; that Riggs, who had been bound over to answer the charge of assault preferred by his wife, and who with the other woman had been by the justice of the peace committed on the charge of adultery preferred by one Davis, but released by reason of a defect in the "mittimus," left the country about April 9, 1885, and did not return; that from the time of claimant's said departure in March 1885 until the date of hearing, her said husband did not contribute to her support, and that herself and children, during the period mentioned were supported chiefly through the benevolence of friends in the neighborhood.

The contestant who lived some eighteen miles from the land testified that he had known the claimant for two months and that the allegations upon which his contest was based were made upon information chiefly obtained from James M. McKeand and Irwin S. Swetland, the witnesses to his affidavit, and who testified in his behalf. The witness McKeand (the constable charged with the delivery of Riggs to the sheriff) stated that Hannah D. Kibbee, who, as shown by the records of your office filed declaratory statement for the land on April 7, 1885, the date of Riggs' relinquishment, was his mother-in-law, and also that he (witness) procured the relinquishment of Riggs. This witness also avers by affidavit that he lived on the land since April 9, 1885.

In support of the allegation that Riggs continued to support the claimant, the contestant produced a letter apparently signed by Riggs dated August 28, 1885, addressed to one Campbell, the step-father of the witness McKeand. The place from whence this letter was written does not appear, nor does the envelope bear any evidence of transmission by mail. The said letter purports to have enclosed two dollars for the support of the claimant and children. The man Campbell seems to have sent, together with two dollars to the claimant the said letter and also one of same date from Riggs to her. The claimant returned the amount with a note dated September 17, 1885, to the effect that she did not consider herself the wife of Riggs.

The witness McKeand in this connection states that Riggs sent him ten dollars for the claimant, but which he, (witness) did not deliver, believing that it would not be accepted.

I fully concur in the conclusion reached by your office. While the claimant left the place where she had lived with her husband before the latter left the country, the evidence shows that she was driven away by personal violence inflicted by the latter to say nothing of his misconduct. The evidence also repels the idea that the claimant's entry was for the benefit of her husband, who had exhausted his right. The trifling remittances referred to, if ever made by Riggs, indicate an attempt to make out a case for the contestant, rather than an effort to support the claimant and children.

It is not very probable that a man who is base and depraved enough to consort with an adulteress, and for her beat his wife and neglect his children, still continuing in the unholy alliance with his paramour, is imbued with those finer sentiments of the human heart which should entwine around the family of his youth, and in a substantial way contribute to the comfort of those whom he has left for the "wages of sin." On the contrary, it is the common experience of mankind in such cases, that his substance would go to adorn and contribute to the comforts and gratify the wishes of the siren who has turned him from the path of honor and virtue.

As I view the facts and circumstances surrounding this case, it would be merciless and unjust that this woman, who, in virtuous indignation, conscious of her injury and suffering; tortured by the shameful conduct of one who should love and cherish her; her soul embittered and her affections dried up by the libidinous conduct of her husband; deserted and abandoned by him as she is for the unlawful embrace of another, while refusing his proffered cankerous two dollars, should still be held to be supported and maintained by him.

Undoubtedly she is the head of this family, and should be protected as such.

The fact that in her homestead affidavit, evidently written for her by another, the claimant is described as "a widow and the head of a family" does not necessarily imply an intent by her to deceive, or constitute in itself a sufficient warrant for the cancellation of her entry.

The evidence not only shows the claimant to have been on June 13, 1885, when she made her entry, a deserted wife and consequently a qualified homesteader,—Glaze v. Bogardus, (2 L. D, 311); Porter v. Maxfield, (5 L. D., 42), but tends strongly to impeach the integrity of the contest.

The decision appealed from is affirmed.

PRACTICE—NOTICE OF APPEAL.

BAIRD'S HEIRS v. PAGE.

An appeal from the Commissioner's decision will not be entertained in the absence of notice to the opposite party.

Secretary Noble to Acting Commissioner Stone, August 1, 1889.

On October 3, 1888, your office transmitted to this Department the papers in the case of S. M. Baird's heirs v. Richard Page, involving the E. ½ of the SW. ¼ and lots 3 and 4, Sec. 18, T. 9 N., R. 3 E, Santa Fe, New Mexico, on appeal by the attorney for the plaintiffs, from the decision of your office, dated March 26, 1887, adverse to them.

It appears from an endorsement on the appeal that the same was filed in the local office June 1, 1887. On the 22d of that month it was transmitted to your office by the register. No proof of service accompanied the appeal, and on July 11, 1887, your office returned the same for such proof, as required by the Rules of Practice.

By letters "G", dated, respectively, January 4, 1888, and July 31, 1888, your office called upon the local officers to report what action had been taken in the matter of requiring service of the appeal; and on August 4, 1888, they reported that notice had been twice given by letter to the attorney for Baird's heirs, residing at Albuquerque, New Mexico, of the defect in the appeal, and that he was required to furnish proof of service thereof, but he had failed to give any attention thereto; that the distance from the local office to Albuquerque is "only a few hours run, with a daily mail service each way," and that Judge Trimble, the attorney for Baird's heirs, is a prominent lawyer living there.

In the meantime, namely, on July 5, 1887, Page filed a motion to dismiss the appeal, on the ground of insufficient specification of errors complained of, and because no copy of the same had been served on him, as required by the Rules of Practice. A copy of this motion was served on L. S. Trimble, attorney for Baird's heirs, July 2, 1887.

The Rules of Practice (86 and 93) require that notice of appeal, with specification of errors, must be served on the appellee, or his counsel, within sixty days from the service of notice of the decision from which an appeal is proposed to be taken. Provision is also made for proof of service of the appeal (Rules 94 to 96.)

There being nothing to show that notice of the appeal herein was ever served on the appellee, Page, or his counsel, or that such notice was ever, in any way, properly given to him, or that he has, in any manner, waived service of such notice, the appeal is fatally defective, and must for that reason be dismissed, which is accordingly done.

TIMBER CULTURE—FINAL PROOF—DEPARTMENTAL REGULATIONS.

MARY R. LEONARD.

A departmental construction of a statute, until revoked or overruled, has all the force and effect of law, and acts performed thereunder are entitled to protection.

Final proof should be adjudicated under the regulations in force at the time when it is submitted.

Timber culture proof showing the period of cultivation required by existing regulations, and accepted in accordance therewith by the local office, should not be adjudicated under later regulations that call for a longer period of cultivation.

Under the circular of December 15, 1885, final proof made before the local officers, and accepted by them, is not fatally defective for the want of a written cross-examination, if otherwise explicit and satisfactory.

Secretary Noble to Acting Commissioner Stone, August 1, 1889.

This is a motion for review of the departmental decision of September 29, 1888, in the case of Mary R. Leonard, involving her final proof on timber culture entry, No. 648, for the NW. ¼ of Sec. 30, T. 135, R.. 45, Fergus Falls district, Minnesota.

The entry was made June 13, 1878, and proof was offered June 20, 1886, and accepted by the local officers and final certificate and receipt issued. Your office, however, rejected the proof, by letter of April 5, 1887, and the departmental decision now sought to be reviewed affirmed your office decision, " for the reason that said proof fails to show the cultivation of ten acres of trees for the full period of eight years," citing as authority the case of Henry Hooper, 6 L. D., 624.

Under the circular of February 1, 1882 (1 L. D., 638), and the decisions of this Department (Benj. F. Lake, 2 L. D., 309; Charles E. Patterson, 3 L. D., 260; Peter Christofferson, ib., 329), in force at the date, June 20, 1886, when the proof was offered and accepted, it was held that "The preparation of the land and the planting of trees are acts of cultivation, and the time authorized to be so employed is to be computed as part of the eight years of cultivation required by the statute." Under this construction of the law, the proof was sufficient and properly accepted by the local officers.

Subsequently, by paragraph 22 of the circular of July 12, 1887 (6 L. D., 280) and said case of Henry Hooper, a different construction was adopted, namely, that "In computing the period of cultivation, the time runs from the date when the total number of trees, seeds, or cuttings required by the act, are planted." Under the latter, which, it is not denied by the counsel for the petitioner, is the correct construction of the law, the proof was insufficient. It is contended, that inasmuch as the proof was in accordance with the law as construed when it was offered and accepted, that the subsequent change of construction should not be held to operate retroactively so as to invalidate it

In the case of Miner v. Mariott et al. (2 L. D., 709), it is said by this Department, that though "a construction is clearly erroneous, such fact does not render illegal any acts which have been performed in accordance with and pursuant to that construction or interpretation." In the case of Henry W. Fuss (5 L. D., 167), Secretary Lamar says: "I think a reasonable construction of the act" (Desert Land) "as a whole . . . . warrants the rule against assignment, but being . . . . a question which has been involved in some doubt, as would appear from the fact that the rule has been changed, the regulation of your office which recognized the right of assignment had, until revoked or overruled, the force and effect of law," citing Miner v. Marriott, supra ; Robb's Lessee v. Irwin, 15 Ohio, 703 ; Ohio Life & Trust Co. v. Debolt, 16 How., 432 ; Gelpcke v. City of Dubuque, 1 Wall., 206.

Justice Miller, in his dissenting opinion in Gelpcke v. City of Dubuque, supra, states "the doctrine to be" in case of a change of ruling by a court, "not that the law is changed, but that it was always the same as expounded by the later decision, and that the former decision was not, and never had been, the law, and is overruled for that very

reason." This may be theoretically true, but in its practical administration, the law must be held to be what for the time being it is construed to be by the tribunals lawfully constituted for that purpose.
This course is not only dictated by the necessity of the case, but is in
accordance with reason and justice. To give a retroactive effect to a
change of construction by a court or other tribunal, so as to render illegal acts which have been performed with trouble and expense in accordance with and on the faith of the former construction would seem
to be as " unjust as to hold that rights acquired under a statute may
be lost by its repeal," and as objectionable as the enactment by legislative bodies of retrospective laws, which " are generally unjust and to
a certain extent forbidden by that article in the constitution of the
United States which prohibits the passage of *ex post facto* laws or laws
impairing contracts." (Bouvier's Dic., Title " Retrospective "). All
that can be required of the citizen by any just government, is, that he
conform to the law as at the time expounded by its courts or other
tribunals invested by it with such authority. I am of the opinion that
the position contended for by the counsel for the motion must in this
case be sustained.

It is to be noted, that the present case is distinguishable from the
Hooper case (cited in said departmental decision), in that the proof was
accepted by the local officers and final certificate and receipt issued in
the present case, whereas in the Hooper case the proof was *rejected*, and
stress is laid upon this point of distinction in the decision in the latter
case, wherein it is said, " inasmuch as his proof was *rejected* by the local officers, he can have suffered no injury rightfully attributable to
that ruling, except the inconvenience of his attempt to sustain his
proof."

As stated at the outset, your office, by letter of April 5, 1887, rejected
the proof. Said rejection, however, was not upon the ground set forth
in the departmental decision under consideration and which has been
discussed above, but because the proof was " not accompanied with the
cross examination as required by circular of December 15, 1885, and
September 23, 1886." (4 L. D., 297, and 5 L. D., 178). The proof in
this case was made, June 20, 1886, after the issuance of the first of said
circulars, but some time before the second. It is to be considered,
therefore, with reference to said first circular. (Lovia A. Short, 8 L.
D., 512). Said circular, as stated in the preamble or first paragraph
thereof, was made necessary by " The large number of defective, irregular, and insufficient proofs presented in public land cases, and the
looseness with which attesting officers, particularly others than registers and receivers," had " exercised their functions." Section three
provides, that " officers taking affidavits and proofs must test the accuracy and reliability of the statements of applicants and claimants and
the credibility and means of information of witnesses by a thorough cross

examination," which " will be reduced to writing and the costs thereof included in the costs of writing out the proofs." Section seven provides, that " proofs must in all cases be made to the satisfaction of registers and receivers," and " proofs that are not satisfactory must be rejected." By section eight, it is directed that "registers and receivers must thoroughly scrutinize all proofs taken before officers other than themselves," and that " they will not accept proofs so taken that are defective and insufficient."

It will be observed, that section three, by which cross-examination is required, is not addressed specifically to registers and receivers, but to " officers taking affidavits and proofs," and a consideration of the other sections above cited leads to the conclusion, that the requirement of cross examination was mainly (at least) intended to apply to cases of " proofs taken before officers other than " the local officers, whose " looseness " in the discharge of their " functions," it is stated in the preamble, was one of the leading abuses which necessitated the circular. The local officers are specifically charged to " scrutinize all proofs taken before officers other than themselves," to see that proofs so taken are sufficient and to reject in cases of insufficiency, but there is no express direction, that the proof be rejected when unaccompanied by the required cross-examination. The second circular, however (that of September 23, 1886), expressly requires, that " claimants and witnesses must be cross-examined in all cases of final proof"—that is, in cases of such proof taken before the local officers, as well as when taken before other officers—and the local officers " are instructed to reject all proofs not accompanied with the required cross-examination." The fact, that this second circular was deemed necessary, which makes the rule requiring cross-examination promulgated in the first circular applicable to " all cases of final proof," lends force to the conclusion, that the rule as laid down in the first circular was intended to apply mainly to cases of proofs taken before officers other than the local officers, and the instruction to the local officers in the second circular to reject proofs unaccompanied by the required cross-examination, would imply that such rejection was not obligatory under the first.

The proof in this case was made, as above stated, while the circular of December 15, 1885, alone was in force; it was made before the register himself, was found by him to be " sufficient " and accepted, and final receipt and certificate issued. It was, moreover, full and explicit, showing compliance with the law as then expounded by this Department, and there is nothing in the case indicative of bad faith in the claimant. Under this state of facts (Elizabeth B. Herrin, 6 L. D., 787; Lovia A. Short, 8 L. D., 512), and what would seem to be the reasonable construction of the circular of December 15, 1885, and without considering whether the default of the officers charged therewith in failing to perform the duty of cross-examination should be visited on a claimant without fault in the matter, I am of the opinion, that the proof in this case should be re-instated, and, there being no other legal objection in the way, that the entry should be passed to patent, and it is so directed.

The motion for review is granted, and said departmental decision is revoked.

TIMBER CULTURE CONTEST—ACT OF MAY 14, 1880.

DAYTON v. HAUSE ET AL.   (ON REVIEW.)

The application to enter, filed by a timber culture contestant, confers no right if it is abandoned prior to the termination of the contest.

A contestant secures no preference right under the act of May 14, 1880, unless the cancellation of the entry is caused by the contest.

Secretary Noble to Acting Commissioner Stone, August 1, 1889.

Lyman C. Dayton has filed a motion for review of the decision of December 19, 1888 (7 L. D., 542), in the case of Lyman C. Dayton v. Joseph F. Hause and James R. Dayton, involving the right to the NE. ¼ of Sec. 23, T. 123 N., R. 64 W., Aberdeen, Dakota, land district.

As grounds for said motion he alleges, that the decision was in error in the following particulars :

1. In holding impliedly of the decision rendered that the contest of this applicant against the Hause entry of the said land was legally dismissed on November 1, 1881 ;

2. In holding impliedly of the decision rendered that this applicant lost any rights by failure to improve and cultivate the land prior to the making of any entry therefor by him or the awarding to him of a preference right of entry ;

3. In holding impliedly of the decision rendered that his exercise of his timber-culture right elsewhere, subsequently to his contest against the Hause entry, deprives him of any right that he otherwise would have had by virtue of said contest ;

4. In not granting the petition of this applicant made during the pendency of his appeal from the decision of the Commissioner of the General Land Office for a stay of action until the question of his right under the homestead entry of the SE. ¼ of Sec. 14, T. 123, R. 64, had been determined ;

5. In holding that by reason of the aforesaid homestead and timber culture entry he was estopped from laying any claim to this land under his contest, because—

a. A contestant having a preferred right of entry under the act of May 14, 1880, may enter the contested tract, either under the homestead, timber-culture, or pre-emption law ; and

b. He may exercise that preferred right by the personal use of assignable scrip, such as Valentine or Porterfield.

6. In not awarding to this applicant a preferred right of entry of the land pursuant to the provisions of the act of May 14, 1880; and

7. In giving any consideration at this time to the question of whether this applicant may lawfully exercise the right conferred by said act.

For a history of this case reference is made to departmental decisions of November 28, 1885 (4 L. D., 263), and December 19, 1888 (7 L. D., 542). Lyman C. Dayton first claimed that he filed with his contest against Hause's entry an application to make timber culture entry for this land, and that he thereby became entitled to it. Whether or not he filed such an application is immaterial, for by afterwards making timber culture entry for other lands be abandoned his application for such an entry for this land. He now makes claim to a preference righ of entry for said land under the act of May 14, 1880.

If the cancellation of Hause's entry was not caused by L. C. Dayton's contest, then he secured no preference right of entry. The local officers dismissed his contest November 1, 1881, because not sustained by the evidence. The regularity of this proceeding was one of the matters directed to be inquired into at the hearing ordered by this Department, November 28, 1885. The local officers found that this contest was dismissed November 1, 1881, and that Dayton had due notice of that action. This finding was approved by your office and by this Department, and is sustained by the evidence. No good reason is now offered for a different conclusion.

It being thus determined that Lyman O. Dayton abandoned his timber culture application, if he ever made it, and that he did not procure the cancellation of Hause's entry, his claim to said land is by these determinations definitely concluded, and it is unnecessary to consider the other questions presented by said motion for review. This motion is therefore denied.

PRACTICE—HYPOTHETICAL CASE.

NEIL A. HILL.

The right of a person to make an entry will not be considered in the absence of an application to enter a specific tract.

Secretary Noble to Acting Commissioner Stone, August 1, 1889.

I have before me the appeal of Neil A. Hill from your office decision of June 14, 1888, denying his petition "to have restored to him his right to purchase one hundred and sixty acres of land under the act of June 3, 1878." (20 Stats., 89).

The petition in question is not an actual, present, application to make entry of a particular tract (under the act mentioned), but, on the contrary, amounts only to a request that the Department announce, in advance, whether such an application, if one should hereafter be made, would be granted. The paper does not even state that an actual application is contemplated, or mention or describe any tract of land other than the one which Hill now declares that he does not want.

Such a petition presents only that "hypothetical" sort of question which this Department makes it a rule to decline to answer (Fremont D. Graham, 4 L. D., 310; W. H. Miller, 7 L. D., 254).

For this reason your said office decision is hereby affirmed.

JOSEPH W. JONES.

The right to make soldiers' additional homestead entry is not assignable.

A soldier's additional homestead entry, based upon a certificate of right obtained by false statements, will not justify the allowance of an application to purchase the land covered thereby under section 2, act of June 15, 1880.

A transferee, holding in good faith under such a location, may be given a preferred right to secure title in his own name, under the homestead laws, if he has not previously exhausted his rights thereunder.

Secretary Noble to Acting Commissioner Stone, August 1, 1889.

I have considered the appeal of Joseph W. Jones, from your office decision of December 30, 1886, holding for cancellation soldiers' additional homestead entry, final certificate No. 22, made in the name of Archbell Callaway, for the SE. ¼ of the NW. ¼, the SW. ¼ of the NE. ¼ and the NW. ¼ of the SE. ¼ of Sec. 14, T. 43 N., R. 10 W., M. D. M., Shasta, California, land district.

Final certificate was issued for this entry May 13, 1879. By letter of October 7, 1884, your office notified the local officers that said entry was illegal "for the reason that the party Archibald Callaway exhausted his rights under the homestead laws by making an additional entry at Wausau, Wis., February 2, 1875", and that sixty days would be allowed the parties "within which to show cause why said entry should not be canceled, or to file in your office an application accompanied by the government price of the lands and the proofs specified on pages 16 and 17 of circular of this office dated March 1, 1884, to purchase the lands under the act of June 15, 1880."

On February 14, 1885, John Mullan, as attorney for Jones, filed in your office a petition asking that said decision "be not put into execution but that the same may be suspended and its execution be stayed until I can lay before you hereafter and fully all the facts in regard thereto and to show you the equities if not the legal rights of said Jones in these premises." The record now before me does not show what disposition was made of this petition.

No further papers seem to have been filed in or steps taken by your office in the case until December 30, 1886, when the case seems to have been further considered and in letter of that date after reciting the letter of October 7, 1884, it is said, "in reference thereto I have to state that as the above additional homestead entry is illegal there is no authority of law to permit the assignee to purchase the land under the act of June 15, 1880, hence the above letter of my predecessor is revoked as to that portion and the entry is this day held for cancellation subject to usual right of appeal."

Jones filed an appeal from that decision, filing therewith his affidavit claiming to set forth all the facts which statement is in substance as follows : Relying upon the certificate of the Commissioner of the General Land Office he purchased Callaway's soldiers' additional homestead right paying therefor the sum of $390, and made entry thereunder for the SE. ¼ of the NW. ¼, the SW. ¼ cf the NE. ¼ and the NW. ¼ of the SE. ¼ of Sec. 14, T. 43 N., R. 10 W., M. D. M. At the time of making said entry he had possession of and occupied said land and had thereon improvements consisting of a comfortable four-room dwelling house which cost $500, a frame barn one hundred and sixty feet by fifty-six feet which cost $1000, a granary eighteen feet by twenty feet, which cost $200, a small orchard, which cost $50, a frame milk house, which cost $200 and five hundred rods of eight rail fence which cost $500 all of the value $2250. Since making said entry he had caused to be placed on the land additional improvements consisting of a two-story ten-room frame house which cost $1250, a one-story milk house, double walls filled in with mortar which cost $500, an addition to the barn to stable sixty cows and eight horses cost $200, a smoke house, cost $50, one hundred and eighty rods of. rail fence, cost $180, and one hundred and forty-two rods of board fence, cost $142. He has been in peaceful possession of said land ever since the date of the said entry and has constantly used it for agricultural, dairy and grazing purposes, having about one hundred acres cultivated in grass and grain.

That there is appurtenant to and used with and upon this land an irrigating ditch about three miles long which cost $500.   It is further stated in said affidavit

Deponent further says that upon first receiving notice of the decision of the Hon. Commissioner of the General Land Office of October 7th, 1884, to wit, sometime in or about the month of January, A. D. 1883, and within sixty days thereafter, he trans-. mitted to the register and receiver of the United States Land Office at Shasta, California, the sum of $131, for the purchase of said lands at the government price pursuant to and under the act of June 15, 1880, and said decision of the Hon. Commissioner of the General Land Office. That said money was received by the receiver of said United States Land Office, to wit, A. Debrosky, and was by him had and held up to and until the day of the expiration of his term of office and the incoming of his successor William H. Bickford. That upon retiring from his said office said receiver returned said money to deponent.   That deponent has been ready and willing and anxious at all times since the receipt of notice of such decision by the Hon. Commissioner of the General Land Office, to perfect his right and claim to said land by purchase thereof at the government price or otherwise and is now desirous of perfecting the same.

This affidavit which is not corroborated, was executed December 1, 1886, but was not filed in the local office until March 31, 1887.

After this appeal was taken and on December 17, 1887, Jones filed in the local office a formal application to purchase this land under the act of June 15, 1880, which application was refused by the local officers " for the reason that the validity of the soldiers' additional homestead entry of Archibald Callaway is now pending on appeal before the Secretary of the Interior."   Jones appealed from this decision and at his request the papers have been transmitted to this department by your office.

An examination of the records and files of your office shows that one "Archable Calaway" of Vernon county, Wisconsin, on October 7, 1863, made homestead entry for the NW. ¼ of the NW. ¼ of Sec. 30, T. 13 N., R. 1 W., La Crosse, Wisconsin, land district, containing 47.98 acres and adjoining the SW. ¼ of the NW. ¼ of Sec. 30, T. 13 N., R. 1 W., and the NE. ¼ of the NE. ¼ of Sec. 25, T. 13 N., R. 2 W., upon which said adjoining land the entryman was then residing. This application and the papers connected therewith were signed by said Calaway by mark. In June, 1870, Calaway made final proof in support of said entry, and these papers are all signed by him by his mark.

On February 2, 1873, "Archabel Calaway" of Vernon county, Wisconsin, made soldiers' additional homestead entry for the S. ½ of the NW. ¼ of Sec. 34, T. 26, R. 2 W., as additional to his " original homestead on the NW. ¼, NW. ¼, Sec. 34, adjoining SW. ¼, NW. ¼, Sec. 30, T. 13, R. 1 West ", at the land office at Wausau Wisconsin, basing it upon entry 1211. The right to make this entry is based upon service in Company K, 43rd Regiment, Wisconsin Infantry Volunteers, from August 30, 1864, to June 24, 1865. Final certificate 585 issued on this entry February 2, 1875. The papers in this entry purport to have been signed by Calaway by his own hand.

By instrument dated and acknowledged February 15, 1878, "Archabell Callaway" made D. H. Talbot, of Sioux City, Iowa, his attorney, to obtain the approval of his claim to additional land under section 2306, Revised Statutes, to receive the certificate of such right and to locate land thereunder. The blanks left in said instrument for the description of the original homestead entry on which this application was to be based have never been filled in. By a writing on the back of this power of attorney, acknowledged May 17, 1878, D. II. Talbot, attempted to substitute and appoint some one in his stead to perform the duties imposed upon him by said power. The name of said substitute has, however, never been written into this appointment. On April 30, 1878, your office issued a certificate of Callaway's right to an additional entry not exceeding 112.02 acres, basing it upon his original entry No. 1211, La Crosse, Wisconsin, dated October 7, 1883. The proof upon which this certificate issued consisted of the affidavit of Callaway corroborated by two witnesses. This proof sets up that the applicant is the same person who made homestead entry 1211, at La Crosse, Wisconsin, October 7, 1863, for NW. ¼ of the NW. ¼., Sec. 30, T. 13, R. 1 W., that he enlisted under the name of Archabel Calaway on August 31, 1864, in Company K., 43rd Regiment Wisconsin Infantry Volunteers, and was discharged " on or about the last of June, 1863 and that I have not heretofore received my right to additional land by any previous application or entry, or by sale, transfer or power of attorney, but that the same remains in me unimpaired." This proof purports to have been sworn to by the applicant Callaway August 15, 1878, and by the two witnesses February 15, 1878, before G. I. Thomas, notary public.

On May 13, 1879, there was filed in the land office at Shasta, California, as certified by the register by " Archabell Callaway by his attorney in fact," the name of said attorney in fact not being given, an application—

To enter the SE. ¼ of NW. ¼ and SW. ¼ of NE. ¼ and NW. ¼ of SE. ¼ of Sec. 14, of T. 43 N., of range 10 W., containing one hundred and twenty acres as additional to my original homestead on the   of section   of township   of range   containing acres, which I entered 18   per homestead No.   per final certificate No. dated   .

In all these papers from the power of attorney down to the application to enter, wherever the name of Callaway purports to have been signed it is written in a clear legible hand, entirely dissimilar from the signatures in the former entries.

These are the papers upon which is based the entry by virtue of which the appellant here seeks to purchase the land in question under the provisions of the act of June 15, 1880.

Jones claims that he made the entry at the Shasta office for himself, having purchased the right of Callaway for an additional homestead. That these additional rights and the certificates thereof are non-assignable has been the well settled ruling of this department for a long time. But even if this right were transferable the transferee could not claim anything thereunder, to which the original holder would not have been entitled. The original claimant, Callaway had not, at the time he applied for a certificate of additional homestead right any such right, he having exhausted all rights given him by section 2306 of the Revised Statutes by the entry made at the Wausau, Wisconsin, land office, February 2, 1875. The certificate was obtained by the false statements under oath of the applicant therefor, and his corroborating witnesses that he had not received his " right to additional land by any previous application or entry " etc.

An entry based upon a certificate obtained in this manner will not justify the allowance of an application to purchase the land covered thereby under the second section of the act of June 15, 1880.   J. S. Cone (7 L. D., 94).

For the reasons herein set forth the application to purchase under the act of June 15, 1880, must be denied and the decision holding for cancellation the soldiers' additional homestead entry is affirmed.

By letter of July 17, 1889, the attorney for Jones forwarded to this department an affidavit executed by Jones July 9, 1889, in which he says " that he has never had the benefit of the homestead laws of the United States; that he is now seventy-eight years of age and is at present, and for a period of two and a half years last past has been constantly and continuously occupying and living on said land and has valuable improvements thereon." These statements being true there is no reason why Jones may not make an entry for said land in his own name and right and thus obtain title thereto. You will direct the local officers to notify Jones that he will be allowed ninety days from notice of this decision within which to make application for said land under the homestead or pre-emption law; and you will also direct them not to take any steps looking to the disposal of said land to any other person within that period.

———

RAILROAD LANDS–ACT OF MARCH 8, 1887.

WRIGHT v. COBLE.

The right of purchase accorded by section 4, act of March 3, 1887, to the *bona fide* purchaser from a railroad company, extends only to cases where the land has been erroneously certified or patented to the company.

The existence of a settlement right, acquired after December 1, 1882, defeats the right of a purchaser from the railroad company.

Secretary Noble to Acting Commissioner Stone, August 1, 1889.

I have considered the appeal of Charles H. Wright from the decision of your office, dated June 22, 1888, rejecting his application to purchase the NW. ¼ of Sec. 27, T. 1 N., R. 8 W., S. B. M., Los Angeles, California, under the provisions of the act of March 3, 1887 (24 Stat., 556).

The record shows that the land is within the primary limits of the grant by act of Congress, approved March 3, 1871 (16 Stat., 573), to the Southern Pacific Railroad Company (branch line), and was listed by said company on December 6, 1884 (per list No. 18).

The claim of the company was rejected by the decision of the Department on January 11, 1888 (6 L. D., 680), and said Coble was allowed to make homestead entry of the land, which he did on February 17, 1888, according to said decision of your office.

On June 4, 1888, the register transmitted said application to purchase, which was filed on May 26th same year.

Wright alleges that he and one Hughes purchased said land from said company on December 10, 1884, while residing on adjoining land, and agreed to pay the sum of two dollars and fifty cents per acre; that they paid a part of the purchase price, to wit, $102.40, and contracted, in writing, with said company to pay the balance with interest at the rate of seven per cent on December 10, 1889; that about the same time they purchased the improvements of a settler or squatter for the sum of fifty dollars; that, on December 3, 1885, said Wright bought out the interest of said Hughes for the sum of $120.00, who duly assigned to said Wright his interest; that the applicant has since paid the annual interest, amounting to $22.40, and has improved said land by developing a spring and bringing water on to his adjoining land, upon which there was no water; that except for the water upon the land, it would be of little value, being mountainous; that said land was entered on February 17, 1888, by said Coble under the homestead laws (No. 3876); that said land was selected by said company on December 6, 1884, per list No. 18, and was claimed by said company as inuring to them under said grant, when they contracted to convey the land to the applicant and said Hughes as aforesaid; that said Wright is a *bona fide* purchaser of said land from said company, and claims the right of purchase under the fourth section of said act of 1887; that at the time said Coble settled on said land and applied to make homestead entry thereof, he was told by the applicant that he claimed the land.

Your office rejected said application, for the reason that the section under which he claims "has reference solely to lands which have been erroneously certified or patented to a railroad company," and is not applicable to the case at bar, because the land in question has not been *certified* or *patented* to said company. Your office also held that the application could not be allowed under the fifth section of said act, for the reason that by the express terms of the proviso it is stated:

That this section shall not apply to lands settled upon subsequent to the first day of December, 1882, by persons claiming to enter the same under the settlement laws of the United States, as to which lands the same as aforesaid shall be entitled to prove up and enter as in other like cases.

The decision appealed from is in harmony with the rulings of this Department.

On November 22, 1887, the Department formulated instructions (having previously taken the advice of the Honorable Attorney General . . . 6 L. D., 272–6), which state that:

As to the lands which have been erroneously certified or patented to the company (being the lands referred to in the second section), the fourth section of the act provides for the disposal of such of those lands as may have been sold by the company to citizens of the United States or persons who have declared their intention, etc.

It is quite evident, therefore, that the second and fourth sections refer to lands the title to which has passed by certification or patent, and not, as contended by the appellant, to lands which had been listed, but not certified, or patented, to the grantee. With reference to the fifth section of said act, said circular states—

Under the last proviso of said section, however, if a settlement was made on said lands subsequent to December 1, 1882, by persons claiming the same under the settlement laws of the United States, it will defeat the right of the purchaser, whether said purchase was made prior to or subsequent to December 1, 1882, and the settler will be allowed to prove up for said lands as in other like cases.

This provision in said circular was quoted with approval by Mr. Secretary Vilas in the case of Roeschlaub *v.* Union Pacific Ry. Co. *et al.* (6 L. D., 750). See also Samuel L. Campbell (8 L. D., 27); circular of February 13, 1889 (idem., 350–1).

It is not denied that the land in question was settled upon by the homestead settler subsequently to December 1, 1882. Since the land has not been certified or patented, it follows that the application was properly rejected.

The decision of your office is accordingly affirmed.

MINING CLAIM—MILL SITE—SECTION 2337, R. S.

IRON KING MINE AND MILL SITE.

The appropriation of land as a mill site is not warranted unless the land is used or occupied for mining or milling purposes.

The appropriation and use of the water, on land claimed as a mill site, is not the use or occupation of the land contemplated by the statute.

Secretary Noble to Acting Commissioner Stone, August 1, 1889.

I have considered the appeal of Charles Siedler from your office de-cision of November 21, 1887, holding for cancellation as to the tract claimed as a mill site, mineral entry No. 205 for the Iron King Mine and Mill Site made December 6, 1884, in Las Cruces, New Mexico land dis-trict.

After considering the application for patent your office directed the local officers that among other defects there was no evidence "that the tract claimed as a mill site is either 'used or occupied' for either 'min-ing or milling purposes' as required by Sec. 2337 Revised Statutes."

In response to this the local officers forwarded a non-mineral affidavit executed by two witnesses to which was added the statement, "that said claim is now and has been in constant use and occupation by ap-plicant as a mill site, and for milling purposes." The evidence was still found insufficient and by letter of April 9, 1887, the applicant was re-quired to present other evidence. There was afterwards filed the joint affidavit of two parties in which it is said:

That said Iron King mill site has been in constant use and occupation by applicant and his grantors for milling purposes since the date of its location. . . . . . The improvements of said mill site consist of a dam on Middle Percha creek with a crib-bing on each side to keep embankment in place; a water box with screen; a pipe line extended thence to smelter reservoir as will more fully appear by reference to diagram and survey hereto attached.

Your office held this evidence still unsatisfactory, and directed the cancellation of said entry as to the mill site. It is contended that the use shown is sufficient to entitle the applicant to patent under Sec. 2337 of the Revised Statutes.

This case is very similar to that of Charles Lennig (5 L. D., 190) cited in the decision appealed from. In that case the land sought to be ac-quired as a mill site contained springs which afforded a supply of water. This water was conveyed in pipes a distance of some two miles, and used in running a smelter. The Department held—

These facts show plainly that the land is not used or occupied for the purpose for which it was located, or for any purpose in connection with mining or milling. The use of the *water* is, in my judgment, not a use of the *land.*

The above case was cited approvingly in the case of Cyprus Mill Site (6 L. D., 706)—Two Sisters Lode and Mill Site (7 L. D., 557).

It is not shown what distance the water is carried in pipes, but it is beyond the boundaries of the land claimed as a mill site.

The decision appealed from is in accord with the ruling of this Department, and is therefore affirmed. You will draw attention to Sec. 2339.

DESERT LAND ENTRY—COMPACTNESS.

J. H. CHRISTENSEN.

A desert entry is not compact, within the meaning of the statute, that covers a narrow strip of land lying along and upon both sides of a stream.

The requirement of compactness is statutory, hence an entry, in obvious violation thereof, is not protected by the fact that it was made prior to the issuance of departmental instructions as to said requirement.

On the adjustment of an entry to conform with said requirement, due regard should be given to the situation of the land and its relation to other lands at the time the entry was made.

The case of Joseph Shineberger overruled.

Secretary Noble to Acting Commissioner Stone, August 1, 1889.

I have before me the appeal of Julius H. Christensen from your decision of November 27, 1886, requiring him to "adjust his (desert land) entry, No. 399, so that it shall be in a compact form."

The said entry was made January 12, 1880, and covers the SW. ¼, SW. ¼, of Sec. 13, SE. ¼, SE. ¼, of Sec. 14; and N. ½, NE. ¼, SW. ¼, NE. ¼, and N. ½, SW. ¼ of Sec. 23, T. 19 S., R. 1 E., Salt Lake City district, Utah. Final proof was made February 17, 1883, and final certificate issued the same day.

The entry as made is obnoxious to the following regulation upon the subject (General Circular of March 1, 1884, p. 35):

The requirement of compactness will be held to be complied with on surveyed lands when a section, or part thereof, is described by legal subdivisions as nearly in the form of a technical section as the situation of the land and its relation to other lands will admit, although parts of two or more sections may be taken to make up the quantity or equivalent of one section. But entries running along the margin or including both sides of streams, or being continuous merely in the sense of lying in a line so as to form a narrow strip, or in any other way showing a gross departure from all reasonable requirements of compactness, will not be admitted.

The entry runs along on both sides of a stream, the forties composing it forming a narrow strip over a mile and a half in one direction, while the greatest width, at right angles to the first named line is less than three-eighths of a mile.

Though the original promulgation of departmental instructions as to the requirement of "compactness," seems to have been made September 3, 1880 (7 C. L. O., 138), after the making of the entry here in question, yet, as the requirement itself was made by the desert land act (19 Stat., 377), and as such an entry as the one above described clearly disregards the obvious meaning of the language of the statute, I see no reason why the entryman should not be required to amend his entry so as to make it a proper one under the law.

The circular instructions of September 3, 1880 (*ubi supra*) expressly provided as follows :

Entries heretofore made, whether by legal subdivisions on surveyed lands, or of an irregular form on unsurveyed lands, running along the margins or including both sides of streams, and not being compact in any true sense, will be suspended by this office, and the parties will be called upon to amend their entries so as to conform to the law ; failing to do which, after proper notice, such entries will be held for cancellation.

That the rule here laid down is enforceable (according to its terms) in cases of entries made before September 3, 1880, was distinctly held in the case of Joseph Himmelsbach (7 L. D., 247). In that ruling I concur, and, in so far as the decision in the case of Joseph Shineberger (8 L. D., 231), is inconsistent with the position thus announced, I am constrained to overrule it.

For the foregoing reasons the decision appealed from is hereby affirmed, with the modification that the adjustment required shall (in the language of the above-mentioned instructions) have regard to "the situation of the land and its relation to other lands" at the time the entry was made.

––––

ALABAMA LANDS—ACT OF MARCH 8, 1883.

JEFFERSON D. MASKE.

Land reported as valuable for coal prior to the act of March 3, 1883, is not subject to homestead entry until after public offering.

A commuted homestead entry, made in good faith, for land so reported and prior to such offering, may be suspended, pending public offering of the land, and confirmed thereafter, if the land is not sold when offered.

Or, if the entryman so elects, the entry may be canceled, with the right to repayment, and without prejudice to his right to make homestead entry elsewhere.

Secretary Noble to Acting Commissioner Stone, August 1, 1889.

On May 20, 1887, Jefferson D. Maske made commutation cash entry based upon his homestead entry of February 6, 1884, for the W. $\frac{1}{4}$ NE. $\frac{1}{4}$ N. $\frac{1}{2}$ SE. $\frac{1}{4}$ Sec. 28, T. 18 S. R. 2 W., Montgomery Alabama.

The claimant's proof made March 9, 1887, before the clerk of the court at Birmingham shows that he settled on his claim in June 1884, that with the exception of five months in 1885, with his wife and two children he lived thereon continuously ; that his improvements, valued at $155 consist of a log house with two rooms, a crib, four or five acres cleared and fenced, and that he cultivated one acre for one season.

The records of your office showing the NE. $\frac{1}{4}$ SE. $\frac{1}{4}$ of said section 28 to have been, in 1879 reported as coal land and that the same had not been offered at public sale in accordance with the act of March 3, 1883 (22 Stat., 487) the said cash entry in so far as it related to the "forty" mentioned was held for cancellation by your office decision of July 17, 1888, from which the claimant appeals.

The act of 1883, provides for the disposition of all public lands in Alabama (whether mineral or otherwise) only as agricultural lands, but required in its first proviso "that all lands which have been heretofore reported to the General Land Office as containing coal and iron shall first be offered at public sale."

By its second proviso the said act permits bona fide homestead entries "of lands within said State heretofore made" to proceed to patent without reference to the character of the land in cases where the entrymen have complied with the homestead law.

The "forty" involved was returned as "valuable coal" before the approval of the act of 1883, and it has not subsequently been offered at public sale.

Both the original and cash entries heretofore mentioned were made subsequently to the passage of the act of 1883. It was, therefore, error in the local officers to have permitted the said forty to be included therein.

But as the forty in question may not find a purchaser upon being offered, and the claimant seems to have acted in good faith with regard to his entire claim, his original and cash entries, so far as they relate to the said forty will be suspended, pending the offering of the same at public sale. Should the same not be sold upon such offer, both of his said entries will be confirmed. But, if the claimant should so elect, he will now be permitted either to relinquish the said forty, or to have both his original and cash entries canceled without prejudice to his right to make homestead entry elsewhere. Should the claimant elect to relinquish the said forty, then a proper proportion of the amount heretofore paid by him will be repaid, and, in the event that he elects to have his said entries canceled, as aforesaid, then the whole of the said amount so paid by him will be returned.

The decision appealed from is modified accordingly.

DESERT LAND ENTRY—NON-IRRIGABLE LAND.

ANDREW LESLIE.

The non-irrigable character of the greater part of a forty acre tract will not defeat a desert entry therefor, if all the land susceptible of irrigation is reclaimed in good faith, and the remainder is valueless from its hilly and rocky character.

First Assistant Secretary Chandler to Acting Commissioner Stone, August 1, 1889.

I have considered the case of Andrew Leslie on his appeal from your office decision of August 21, 1888, holding for cancellation desert land entry No. 1336 for NE. ¼, SE. ¼ Sec. 12, T. 14 S., R. 2 E., Salt Lake City land district, Utah.

It appears from the records that said entry was made May 22, 1885, by Andrew F. Leslie, son of claimant, who having died March 13, 1887, without other heirs, the claimant as heir-at-law proceeded to make final proof.

Your said decision pronounces his final proof unsatisfactory for the reason that not more than about one-third of the tract entered has been reclaimed by having water conducted upon it.

In the testimony presented upon final proof it was stated by claimant and each of his witnesses that there were two irrigating ditches cross-ing the land, one being eight feet by four and the other two feet by four feet, but in affidavits filed with his appeal to this office, they cor-rect such statement as error, and now state that said ditches average one and a half feet by two and a half feet in size.

It appears from the final proof and supplemental affidavits filed that the tract entered consists of forty acres, a little less than half of which is susceptible of irrigation, the remainder being high and rocky so that water can not be brought thereon, and even if watered most of it is too rocky and barren to produce anything.

Claimant's son after making his entry proceeded to bring water from a spring at the base of the mountains, and besides the two ditches above mentioned lateral ditches were made by plowing furrows from the main ditches and by said ditches the water was distributed over that part of the land susceptible of irrigation.

Rye, wheat and potatoes in paying quantities were raised upon the irrigated land.

Accompanying the final proof is a plat of the said NE. $\frac{1}{4}$, SE. $\frac{1}{4}$, with explanatory notes from which it appears that about the east half of the forty acres is high and rocky and also about four acres off the west side, and that there are three or four rocky mounds or points within the cultivated land upon which water can not be brought, and that some-thing over two acres of the land which might otherwise be brought under cultivation is occupied by a county road, so that the land ac-tually reclaimed is little if any over fifteen acres.

The evidence also shows that in addition to constructing the main and lateral ditches, the entryman was compelled to remove from the land now in cultivation many tons of loose stones.

It is claimed that no more than forty acres were entered for the rea-son that said forty were not contiguous to any other public land which had any reclaimable surface.

It must be conceded that under the evidence all the land upon said tract which is susceptible of irrigation has been fully reclaimed and that the remaining portion is so hilly and rocky as to be absolutely worth-less to the government or any one else, and the sole question to be de-cided is whether in an entry of a tract consisting of forty acres only, the reclamation of fifteen or sixteen acres, that amount being all of the entry which is susceptible of irrigation, is sufficient under the law to entitle the claimant to patent.

It is provided in the desert land act (19 Stat., 377), that a person qualified under the law and having filed the declaration and made the preliminary payment required by law may—

At any time within the period of three years after filing said declaration, upon making satisfactory proof to the register and receiver of the reclamation of said tract of land in the manner aforesaid, and upon the payment to the receiver of the additional sum of one dollar per acre, ... a patent for the same shall be issued to him:

The intendment of the act is to provide for the reclamation of such lands as are in a desert condition by conveying and distributing sufficient water thereon to render them fruitful agricultural lands. Wallace v. Boyce (1 L. D., 26).

In letter of Secretary Teller to Commissioner McFarland of February 9, 1885 (3 L. D., 385), it is said:

I do not wish to be understood as holding that water must cover all the land; but it must be carried to a part whence it can be distributed over the land, except where high points and uneven surface make it practically impossible that it should be done.

In the case of Levi Wood, 5 L. D., 481, where it was shown that all the land included in the entry which was not too high and rocky to admit of irrigation had been reclaimed, and that said reclamation, out of the one hundred and twenty acres entered, included all of one forty acre tract, from twenty to twenty-five acres of another and about fifteen acres of the third, it was held that claimant's evident good faith in the premises and the fact that all but the hilly and rocky portions of the claim had been properly irrigated and reclaimed should be taken into consideration, and while the general rule was that the entire tract should be reclaimed, yet in view of the peculiar circumstances of that case the proof should be approved.

The same idea appears in Owen D. Downey, (6 L. D., 23) in these words:

It is not shown in the final proof that said thirty acres are not susceptible of irrigation, so as to bring the case within the rule laid down in the cases of George Ramsey (5 L. D., 120) and Levi Wood (id., 481); but it is alleged in the argument on appeal that such is the case. If as a matter of fact, these thirty acres are so high and rocky as to be practically not susceptible of irrigation, and thus absolutely worthless to the government or any one else, then the case becomes similar to the Levi Wood case (supra) and the entry should be allowed to proceed to patent, otherwise I would see no objection to claimant relinquishing the subdivision not irrigated and taking patent for that part of his entry in relation to which the law has been complied with.

In the case of Wm. H. Holland (6 L. D., 38) it was held that the greater part of a particular forty acre tract not being susceptible of irrigation could not be included in the entry but in the case of David Gilchrist (8 L. D., 48) it is said—

The case of Holland (supra) will not be considered as a precedent for holding that in no case can a patent issue upon an entry, where all of the land in each smallest legal subdivision, susceptible of irrigation has been reclaimed, although it may appear that the greater part of one of said tracts is not susceptible of reclamation.

In the Gilchrist case, supra, entry was allowed although one entire forty acre tract and part of one or two others, were too high and rocky for irrigation.

In the case at bar the evidence is conclusive that all of the tract which is susceptible of irrigation has been reclaimed in good faith and that the portion of said tract not irrigated is barren and worthless to the government or any one else, and I conclude that under the construction of the statute made in the cases cited above final entry should be allowed upon payment of the necessary price.

Your said decision is accordingly reversed.

———

SECOND HOMESTEAD ENTRY—WATER SUPPLY.

WILLIAM E. JONES.

A second homestead entry is permissible, where the first is made in good faith, but the land covered thereby is not inhabitable on account of the non-potable character of the water obtained thereon.

The applicant in such a case should show the character and condition of the land covered by his second application as well as that embraced in his first entry.

An application for lands not intended to be taken under the original entry is for the privilege of making a second entry, and not for the right of amendment.

Secretary Noble to Acting Commissioner Stone, August 2, 1889.

I have considered the appeal of William E. Jones from the decision of your office dated January 21, 1888, refusing to allow him to enter under the homestead laws the E. ½ of the NE. ¼ of Sec. 30 and the E. ½ of the SE. ¼ of Sec. 19 T. 35 N., R. 54 W. Chadron Nebraska. The record shows that said Jones on March 6, 1886, made homestead entry No. 5336 of the SW. ¼ of Sec. 20, T. 35, R. 51 W., and on June 15, 1887, filed his application to be allowed to amend his entry so as to cover the tracts above designated. With his application was filed the corroborated affidavit of the applicant, alleging that he lived on the land covered by his entry for more than one year; that he has expended in improving said land not less than $1,000; that he has dug four wells, 27, 17, 14, and 12 feet deep, in which there is a great flow of water; that the water is not fit for domestic use, and his stock will not drink it. The affiant further states that "the water is salty, alkali and of a greasy nature, and is of the kind as is found all through that section of the country in wells," and he asks that your office "may send a special agent to make an examination of the water and the facts as stated, and, if found correct, that he may be granted an amendment" to the tracts applied for, in order that he may secure a home from the public domain. Your office refused said application because "the government does not contract for the supply of water when a man makes a homestead entry, and before making such entry the settler should make such an examination in an alkaline region as will be satisfactory, both as regards soil and water supply." This application must be treated as a request to make a second homestead entry. Goist *v.* Bottum (5 L. D., 643). If the allegations in the affidavit of claimant be true, the good faith of the entryman would seem to be established, and in the absence of an adverse claim he ought to be permitted to make another entry for land upon which he can make a home and receive the full benefit of the homestead law. But your office states that "this is one of many cases in which a change of entry has been applied for on account of the settler failing to get good water by digging wells." And the claimant alleges that the water " is of the same kind as is found all through that section of the country in wells." If this statement be correct, it does not clearly appear that the claimant would be in any better condition to secure a home on the tracts applied for, than he is in now on the land upon which he has made valuable improvements. His appeal will therefore be dismissed without prejudice, and he will be allowed to submit further evidence before the local officers, within sixty days from notice hereof,·showing the condition of the land applied for. It is suggested, if practicable that a special agent of your office examine said lands with a view to ascertain definitely the condition of the land covered by said entry and also the land applied for. The local officers should transmit the supplementary proof submitted by the applicant with their opinion thereon, and your office will readjudicate the case.

The decision of your office is modified accordingly.

SCHOOL INDEMNITY—ACT OF MARCH 1, 1877.

STATE OF CALIFORNIA.

An indemnity school selection made and certified to the State, which fails by reason of the land in lieu of which it was taken not being included within the final survey of a Mexican grant, is confirmed by section two, act of March 1, 1877.
Such a selection is within the confirmatory provisions of said section though the final survey of the grant was prior to the passage of said act.

Secretary Noble to Acting Commissioner Stone, August 2, 1889.

I have before me the appeal of the State of California from your office decision of October 7, 1887, adhering on review, to the order of May 29, 1887, holding for cancellation school indemnity selection R. and R. 1148, covering the SE. ¼, NE. ¼, Sec. 35, T. 30 S., R. 12 E., M. D. M., San Francisco district, California.

The ground for the said decision is that the said selection failed because the basis—NW. ¼, NW. ¼, Sec. 36, T. 14 S., R. 1 W., S. B. M.,—proved to be available to the State under the grant, a final survey having (before March 1, 1877) excluded such NW. ¼, NW. ¼, Sec. 36, from the limits of the Rancho El Cajon, within which it was, until such survey, supposed to fall.

But the selection in question being an indemnity school selection which has been made and certified to the State, and which failed by reason of the land in lieu of which it was taken not being included within such final survey of a Mexican grant, the same was confirmed by section two of the act of March 1, 1877 (19 Stat., 267). The circumstance that the ascertainment of the fact of exclusion from the Mexican grant antedated the passing of the said confirmatory act, did not take the selection out of the operation of the latter. Mower v. Fletcher, 116 U. S., 380.

Your said decision is accordingly reversed.

——

PRACTICE—CONTEST—HOMESTEAD ENTRY—SECTION 2294, R. S.

O'CONNELL v. RANKIN (ON REVIEW).

Under rule 35 of practice the testimony in a contest may be taken before an officer designated by the register and receiver.

A homestead entry based upon a preliminary affidavit executed before a clerk of court, without the prerequisite residence on the land, is voidable, and said defect can not be cured, if, prior to the establishment of residence, the adverse right of a contestant intervenes.

A contest against a homestead entry may be properly entertained upon any charge affecting the legality of the claim; and the successful termination of such a contest will secure the preference right conferred by the act of May 14, 1880.

Secretary Noble to Acting Commissioner Stone, August 2, 1889.

This is a motion filed by John J. O'Connell, asking for a review of the departmental decision of August 21, 1888 (7 L. D., 245), in the case of John J. O'Connell v. Luther D. Rankin, involving the NE. ¼ of Sec. 34, T. 147 N., R. 69 W., Bismarck, Dakota.

Rankin, an unmarried man, purchased the improvements (house and twenty-two acres of breaking) from a prior claimant, who filed a relinquishment. On March 25, 1885, Rankin made homestead entry for the tract. On May 8, 1885, O'Connell initiated contest against the said entry. This contest was based upon the allegation that Rankin had failed to make settlement or improvements or to establish or maintain a residence upon the land, and that " the affidavit upon which said entry is based was made before a clerk of the court; that the same alleges residence upon and improvement of said land by said Rankin, and that the same to that extent is false and fraudulent."

The local officers ordered that testimony be taken before the county clerk on June 27, and fixed July 3, 1885, for the hearing at the local office. On the day last named, the claimant (Rankin), who did not appear before the county clerk, appeared specially by his attorney, and moved to dismiss the contest, on the ground of insufficient notice. On the same day this motion was allowed.

On July 11, 1885, the contestant (O'Connell) served notice upon the claimant that he would, on July 25, following, move to correct the record and make the same conform to the facts, and that at the same time he would ask for an order opening said cause and also for a rehearing. This motion was sustained on August 13, 1885, after a hearing at which both parties appeared. A rehearing was accordingly ordered.

Upon the testimony taken before the county clerk on September 16, 1885, the local officers found, that the claimant's homestead affidavit was made in violation of section 2294 of the U. S. Revised Statutes, and sustained the contest. On appeal by the claimant, this action was reversed by your office.

The ruling of your office was, on appeal by the contestant, reversed by the decision that I am now asked to reconsider.

The motion for review assigns error in not finding that the local officers erred in citing the claimant to appear before the county clerk, before he had an opportunity of being heard at the local office; in allowing the contest to be re-instated and the record amended; in not dismissing the contest on the ground that the affidavit failed to state sufficient facts to sustain the same; and in finding against the claimant upon the evidence.

Regarding the first assignment of error, it is only necessary to state that the hearing upon the contest was ordered and had in accordance with Rule 35 of Practice.

The said motion by the contestant, asking that the contest be re-instated and a rehearing ordered, was in effect a motion to reconsider. It was shown at the hearing of said motion to the satisfaction of the local office, that sufficient notice of the contest had been given, and that the contest had been erroneously dismissed. The said motion was therefore properly allowed.

Section 2290 of the U. S. Revised Statutes provides that the person seeking the benefit of the homestead law shall make an affidavit before the register of the land office in which he is about to make such entry, that he is twenty-one years of age, and that the application is made for his own exclusive benefit.

Section 2294 provides:

In any case in which the applicant for the benefit of the homestead, and whose family, or some member thereof, is residing on the land which he desires to enter, and upon which a *bona-fide* improvement and settlement have been made, is prevented, by reason of distance, bodily infirmity, or other good cause, from personal attendance at the district land-office, it may be lawful for him to make the affidavit required by law before the clerk of the court for the county in which the applicant is an actual resident, and to transmit the same, with the fee add commissions, to the register and receiver.

It appearing that neither the claimant nor any member of his family was a resident upon the land at the date of his affidavit, the Department properly held that he did not come within the purview of the said section 2294.

On January 2, 1889 (8 L. D., 1), the Department considered a motion to review its previous decision of May 26, 1888, in the case of Brassfield *v.* Eshom, 6 L. D., 722, and held that a homestead entry, wherein the preliminary affidavit was executed before a clerk, was voidable only, and the intervention of a contest will not defeat the right of an entryman to cure such defect, where he had prior to said contest established his residence on the land in good faith.

In the case at bar, however, the claimant had not prior to the initiation of the contest established his residence upon the land, nor had he even seen it. It was accordingly correctly held by the Department that the claimant's defective affidavit could not be cured by reason of the contestant's intervening rights.

The contention of counsel that the affidavit of contest is insufficient, in that it does not allege an abandonment of the land for more than six months, is without force.

Rule one of practice provides, that contests may be initiated by an "adverse party or other persons," for "any sufficient cause affecting the legality or validity of the claim," and the second section of the act of May 14, 1880 (21 Stat., 140), gives a preference right of entry to any person who has contested, paid the land office fees, and procured the cancellation of any pre emption, homestead, or timber culture entry.

The motion is denied.

PRACTICE-CONTEST—PROCEEDINGS BY THE GOVERNMENT.

DRURY *v.* SHETTERLY.

An application to contest an entry should not be allowed where the government in its own interest has already instituted proceedings against the entry.

No preferred rights are secured under a contest, filed during the pendency of government proceedings against the entry of record, if such entry is canceled as the result of said proceedings.

The rejection of an application to contest, necessarily carries with it the rejection of the accompanying application to enter.

First Assistant Secretary Chandler to Acting Commissioner Stone, August 3, 1889.

In the case of Morgan S. Drury *v.* Andrew J. Shetterly I have considered the appeal of the former from the decision of your office of February 4, 1888, allowing Shetterly to file declaratory statement for the NW. ¼ of section 35, T. 1 S., R. 24 W., Kirwin, Kansas, and permitting Drury's timber culture entry for the same land to remain intact subject to Shetterly's superior claim.

It appears that Charles W. Bradbury made pre-emption cash entry of said land November 18, 1885, which was held for cancellation by your office January 20, 1887, and that no action having been taken and an appeal taken from your said decision having been withdrawn, the entry of Bradbury was canceled by your office October 20, 1887.

July 15, 1887, Drury filed an affidavit of contest (endorsed $1 fee paid) against the entry of Bradbury, and at the same time applied to enter the land under the timber culture act. The contest affidavit is endorsed "filed July 15, 1887, and held subject to the action of Commissioner."

At this time the government had proceedings pending for the cancellation of this entry, and on account thereof this application should have been refused as "an application to contest an entry should not be allowed where the government in its own interest has already instituted proceedings against the entry." (Joseph A. Bullen, 8 L. D., 301; George F. Stearns, 8 L. D., 573; United States v. Scott Rhea, 8 L. D., 578.) But instead thereof the application was "held subject to action taken by your letter "P" of January 21, 1887." October 24, 1887, the entry of Bradbury was canceled on the records of the local office by proceedings instituted by the government as directed by your letter of October 20, 1887. Drury was notified of said cancellation and on November 22, 1887, appeared at the local office and made timber culture entry of said land. Prior thereto, however, viz., on October 26, 1887, Shetterly applied to file a declaratory statement for said land which was rejected by the local officers on the ground that Drury by virtue of his application and contest was allowed thirty days preference right to enter said land. From such action Shetterly appealed.

By letter of February 4, 1888, you found that Bradbury's entry was set aside as a result of proceedings on the part of your office and in no manner as a result of the affidavit filed by Drury and that he cannot be regarded as a contestant who is entitled to a preference right of entry; and that he could acquire no advantage by the filing of a timber culture application at a time when the land was not subject thereto.

The entry of Bradbury had been held for cancellation prior to the filing of Drury's application to contest and was canceled as a result of proceedings instituted by your office. Drury was not a successful contestant and as he did not procure the cancellation of Bradbury's entry he was not entitled to a preference right of entering said tract. Clymena A. Vail (6 L. D., 833).

The effect of this application made by Drury to enter the land at the time he filed the affidavit of contest must be considered. It is argued that it attached the moment the entry of Bradbury was canceled and gave Drury the superior right notwithstanding the fact that the record shows that Shetterly offered his declaratory statement October 26, 1887, alleging settlement prior thereto, and that Drury's entry was not placed of record until November 22, 1887. This argument is not tenable. In the case of James A. Beckett (7 L. D., 352) it was held that the rejection of the application to contest necessarily carried with it the rejection of the accompanying application to enter the tract.

As at the time Shetterly [Drury] filed upon the land the government was testing the validity of Bradbury's entry and the tract was subsequently made a part of the public domain, not on account of any act of Drury, but by the proceeding of the government, Drury should not be permitted to reap the benefit of the action thereof by his premature filing and application to enter.

Your decision is therefore affirmed.

RAILROAD GRANT—CONFLICTING SETTLEMENT—EVIDENCE.

CENTRAL PAC. R. R. Co. v. SHEPHERD.

In a hearing ordered to determine the status of land, alleged to be excepted from a railroad grant, the existence of a pre-emption right at the date when the grant took effect may be established by one witness.

In a contest between two claimants the matter in dispute must be decided upon the preponderance of the evidence, whether parol or record, or both parol and record.

The existence of a pre-emption claim, based upon settlement, occupancy, and improvement, at the date when the grant attaches, excepts the land covered thereby from the operation of the grant.

Land within the limits of a railroad grant, but excepted therefrom, is open to entry without restoration notice.

Secretary Noble to Acting Commissioner Stone, August 6, 1889.

The attorney for the Central Pacific R. R. Co., has filed a motion for review of departmental decision of March 11, 1889, in the case of said Company v. Nancy H. Shepherd, affirming the decision of your office of January 7, 1888, holding that the NW. ¼ of Sec. 9, T. 14 N., R. 7. E., M. D. M., Sacramento California land district was excepted from the grant to said company.

The land in question is within the limits of the grant of July 1, 1862 (12 Stat., 489) to said company. It was within the limits of the withdrawal ordered by letter of August 2, 1862, received at the local office September 2, 1862. The map of the definite location of the line of said road was filed March 26, 1864.

The plat of this township was filed in the local office May 21, 1868. On August 21, 1868, one John W. McNulty filed pre-emption declaratory statement for said land alleging settlement thereon February 10, 1861.

On August 3, 1887, Nancy H. Shepherd applied to file pre-emption declaratory statement for said land alleging that it was excepted from the operation of the grant to said company by the claim of McNulty. A hearing was had in which both Shepherd and the company were represented. Mrs. Shepherd introduced one witness. The company did not submit any testimony. The local officers decided that in cases of this kind the testimony of at least two witnesses was required, held Shepherd's allegations "not proven" and rejected her application. Your office reversed this decision—found from the testimony "that John McNulty, a bona fide settler, resided on the land continuously from 1859 until 1870, cultivating and improving the same—his improvements being worth $500 "—and decided that the land having been thus occupied when the grant became effective was excepted from the operation of that grant. This Department by the decision now sought to be reviewed affirmed that decision of your office.

By the act of July 1, 1862 (12 Stat., 489), there was granted to said company—

Every alternate section of public land designated by odd numbers, to the amount of five alternate sections on each side of said railroad or the line thereof, and within the limits of ten miles on each side of said road not sold, reserved or otherwise disposed of by the United States, and to which a pre emption or homestead claim may not have attached at the time the line of said road is definitely fixed.

By the act of July 2, 1864 (13 Stat., 356), section three from which the above quotation is made was amended by striking out the word " five " where it occurred in said section and inserting in lieu thereof the word " ten ", and by striking out the word " ten " and inserting in lieu thereof the word " twenty."

In support of the motion for review the following allegations of error are submitted :

1. That one witness is insufficient to establish a claim to land under the pre-emption law.

2. That mere occupancy of the land does not warrant the finding that it is excepted from the railroad company's grant.

3. That a claim to accept land from the railroad grant must be such as is recognized in the grant itself.

4. That this land was granted to the company and falls within none of the exceptions found in the grant.

The question presented by the first allegation was presented to your office where it was held that there was no rule requiring the testimony of two witnesses to be submitted in such cases, and this ruling was affirmed by this Department in the decision sought to be reviewed. This was a contest between two claimants, and the matters in dispute must be decided upon the preponderance of the evidence produced. This evidence may consist entirely of oral testimony or entirely of record evidence, or, as in this instance of both. There was no error in the decision on this point.

The second allegation is based upon an assumption not justified by the facts in this case. There was here more than mere occupancy. There was settlement, inhabitation, cultivation and improvement, followed by the record assertion of a pre-emption claim in the manner and within the time prescribed by law after the filing of the township plat. Since this objection is not pertinent to the case under consideration it is not necessary to discuss or determine the correctness of the abstract proposition laid down.

The third and fourth propositions may be considered to assert that it was error to hold that the claim of McNulty was such as was provided for in the grant to said company, as sufficient to except land from the operation of that grant. As was hereinbefore said, the applicant to file pre-emption declaratory statement for this land has shown that at the date the company's right attached to this land, if at all, said land was in the possession of one who had settled upon, inhabited, cultivated and improved said land, and who as soon as an opportunity afforded, gave notice of his claim by filing the prescribed declaratory statement. This constitutes such a pre-emption claim as is contemplated by the excepting clause of said granting act.

Odgers v. Central Pacific R. R. Co. (8 L. D., 520).

For the purposes of this case it may be conceded that the railroad company has a right to inquire into the validity of a claim alleged to except land from its grant, and even after such concession the case must be decided against it because it has offered nothing to disprove the *prima facie* valid claim existing at the date its right under the grant took effect.

It is argued that if it is held that this land did not go to the company under said grant, that it having been held out of market for over twenty years it is not subject to entry until restored after public notice, and being an isolated tract it must be brought into market under the provisions of Sec. 2364 of the Revised Statutes. If this land was excepted from the operation of the company's grant, it has not been reserved or held out of market, and therefore there is no force in, or foundation for this proposition.

For the reasons herein set forth the motion for review is denied.

ANDERSON ET AL. v. BYAM ET AL.

Motion for the review of the departmental decision rendered April 2, 1889, 8 L. D., 388, denied by Secretary Noble, August 6, 1889.

PRE-EMPTION—MARRIED WOMAN—EQUITABLE ADJUDICATION.

MARY E. FUNK.

The board of equitable adjudication may confirm a pre-emption entry, in the absence of an adverse claim, where a single woman, after settlement, filing, due inhabitancy and improvement, marries prior to final proof, but after published notice of intention to submit the same.

A homestead entry for the land covered by such a pre-emption claim, made after the pre-emptor's published notice of intention to submit final proof, is not such an adverse claim as will defeat equitable confirmation of the pre-emption entry.

First Assistant Secretary Chandler to Acting Commissioner Stone, August 6, 1889.

I am in receipt of your letter of March 9, 1886, transmitting the appeal of Mary E. Berger (now Funk) from your office decision of December 19, 1885, rejecting her application to make pre-emption cash entry of the SW. ¼ of Sec. 1, T. 108, R. 66, Mitchell district, Dakota.

The appellant filed declaratory statement for the tract described on January 22, alleging settlement January 21, 1884. On June 27, 1885, she published notice of her intention to make cash entry on August 8th ensuing. On the last-named date she made proof before H. M. Rice, judge and *ex-officio* clerk of the probate court of Jerauld county, Dakota. The proof showed that she had broken twenty-five acres (including ten acres of breaking purchased of a prior occupant); raised flax, wheat, oats, and corn; erected a frame house fourteen by twenty-four feet; a frame barn fourteen by thirty feet; dug a well; and made other improvements,—the whole amounting in value to four hundred and fifty dollars. She (being a widow) and her three children had resided continuously on the land. Her offer of final proof at the local office was met by the protest of David Davidson against the acceptance thereof, for the reason that he had made homestead entry of the tract, and that said claimant, Mary E. Berger, on or about the 12th day of July, 1885, was married to one Mr. Funk, as per the following notice, which appeared in the Wessington Springs Herald, Jerauld county, Dakota Territory:

Two made one. At the residence of the bride, on Sec. 1, T. 108, R. 66, Jerauld county, on Sunday, July 12, 1885, Mr. Frank Funk and Mrs. Berger. The friends of the contracting parties have been looking for such a surprise for some time. The groom has a tree claim, and the bride a hundred and sixty acre farm; so they now have a half-section and occupy but one house. This is the second wedding for Harmony Township. Who'll be the next? Come bachelors, wake up and do likewise; golden opportunities are passing forever.

Because of this marriage and in view of departmental decision in the case of Rosanna Kennedy (10 C. L. O., 152), Davidson asked that Mrs. Funk's proof be rejected.

Upon the filing of said objection and protest, the proof and purchase money tendered by Mrs. Funk was rejected by the register, "for the reason that it appears from the proof papers, and from admissions of the claimant, Mary E. Berger, that since making D. S. 22, SW. ¼ 1-108-66, she has been married to one Dennis Funk." No action thereon appears to have been taken by the receiver.

There can be no question that under the rulings of the Department in similar cases, this entry may be submitted to the board of equitable adjudication if there is no adverse claim. Lydia Steele (1 L. D., 460); Melissa J. Cunningham (8 L. D., 433).

The only question to be determined in the case is, whether Davidson's protest is such an adverse claim as will prevent its submission.

Mrs. Berger's declaratory statement was filed on the 22d of January, 1884, alleging settlement the preceding day. She maintained a continuous actual residence on the tract until her marriage. At the date (June 27, 1885) of her notice to make final proof she had resided thereon for over seventeen months, and in all other respects fully complied with the requirements of the pre-emption law. "Published notice of an application to make pre-emption cash entry so far reserves the land covered by such application as to prevent its being properly entered by another pending the consideration of said application." (See L. J. Capps, 8 L. D., 406; Henry A. Frederick, ib., 414; Smith v. Brearly, 9 L. D., 175.) Davidson's homestead entry, dated July 17, 1885, was therefore improperly received; and his objection filed in the local office, calling the attention of the government to an alleged disqualification which was already shown by the record and not denied by the applicant, would not in my opinion constitute such an "adverse claim" as would prevent the submission of Mrs. Berger's proof to the board of equitable adjudication. And since he does not rightfully occupy the position of an adverse claimant—since it does not appear that his rights have been in any way impaired or infringed upon—it is immaterial whether or not he was served with notice of her appeal.

Your office decision of December 19, 1885, is modified and I direct that the homestead entry of Davidson be canceled and that the entry of Mrs. Funk will be submitted to the board of equitable adjudication.

PRACTICE—PROCEEDINGS BY SPECIAL AGENT—APPEAL.

SAMUEL J. BOGART.

An entryman should not be called upon to defend a second time against the same charges, unless there is reason to believe that there was collusion between the parties at the hearing already had.

An appeal will not lie from a decision of the General Land Office ordering a hearing; nor will the Commissioner's discretion in such matter be disturbed unless there is a clear and satisfactory showing of an abuse thereunder.

Secretary Noble to Acting Commissioner Stone, August 6, 1889.

Samuel J. Bogart has filed his petition for a writ of *certiorari* in the matter of his pre-emption entry for the SW. ¼ of Sec. 21, T. 113, R. 59, Watertown Dakota Land District.

It seems that by your office letter of October 5, 1838, Bogart was called upon to show cause why his entry should not be canceled under a special agent's report, and that Bogart filed an appeal from that action by your office. By letter of June 8, 1889, your office refused to transmit said appeal to this office unless the entryman would admit the truth of said report.

In support of this application there is filed the affidavit of J. B. Kelly, the attorney for Bogart. In this affidavit it is set forth that Bogart made his final proof in 1883, which proof was approved by the local officers and final certificate was duly issued. Afterwards one A. S. Martin, initiated a contest against said entry alleging priority in himself and a failure on Bogart's part to comply with the requirements of law. A hearing was had upon this contest as a result of which the local officers decided in favor of the contestant, and upon appeal to your office that decision was reversed and the entry of Bogart sustained. It is alleged that the question of Bogart's compliance with the requirements of law was at that hearing thoroughly investigated, and it is contended that he should not in justice be again put to the trouble and expense of meeting and disproving these same charges. If the charges now made against Bogart's entry are the same that were in issue in the contest of Martin v. Bogart, the entryman should not be compelled to defend a second time against said charges, unless indeed there is good reason to believe there was collusion between said parties whereby the facts were not disclosed at the former hearing. The question of ordering a hearing is a matter resting in the discretion of the Commissioner and an appeal will not lie from a decision of your office ordering a hearing. "The Commissioner's discretion in such matters will not be disturbed unless there is a clear and satisfactory showing of an abuse of it."

Reeves v. Emblen (8 L. D., 444).

It cannot be determined from the papers now before me whether the charges now made are the same as those heretofore successfully defended against by Bogart, and I therefore direct that the papers in the matter of this special agent's report, and also the papers in Bogart's final proof and in the contest case of Martin v. Bogart be transmitted to the Department for consideration.

———

PRACTICE—NOTICE TO MINOR HEIRS—PUBLICATION.

BURGESS v. POPE'S HEIRS.

Service upon an alleged guardian will not confer jurisdiction over a minor, if the fact of guardianship is not established.

The showing required to authorize publication of notice must be made prior to the issuance of the order therefor.

First Assistant Secretary Chandler to Acting Commissioner Stone, August 6, 1889.

I have considered the case of Elmer Burgess v. the heirs of Calvin W. Pope, involving the SW. ¼ of section 1, T. 104 N., R. 68 W., Mitchell land district, Dakota.

Calvin W. Pope, made timber culture entry for the said land June 10, 1881; on August 18, 1885, Elmer Burgess filed his affidavit of contest against the said entry, charging failure on the part of the heirs of Calvin W. Pope, during the third and fourth years of the said entry to properly plant trees on ten acres of the said land or cultivate the same.

In his said affidavit, Burgess further deposes "that diligent search and inquiry has been made for the address of the adult heirs of said Calvin W. Pope, by this contestant and can not ascertain the same and that ordinary notice cannot be served upon them." He asks that notice be given to the said adult heirs (not naming them) by publication.

The local officers appointed October 6, 1885, for the day of hearing.

On this day the local officers "upon the affidavit of Fannie M. Pope, widow and one of the heirs of Calvin W. Pope, deceased" and upon con. testant's consent, ordered that the hearing be continued to October 19, 1885, and that the testimony be taken at that time, by J. B. Long, of Kimball, Brule county, Dakota, a notary public.

On October 19, 1885, the contestant appeared and filed proof of serv. ice of notice for the hearing upon the defendants as follows, the return of the sheriff of Brule county, Dakota, showing that two copies of the notice for the hearing were personally served upon Fannie M. Pope, "as widow of Calvin W. Pope, guardian of minor heirs of Calvin W. Pope, and administratrix of the heirs of.Calvin W. Pope ; " also proof of service of the notice upon the adult heirs of the deceased entryman. Registered letters, enclosing the contest notice were mailed at Kimball, Dakota, addressed respectively to James W. Pope, Samuel E. Pope, and Bertram J. Pope, Kimball, D. T., it being made to appear by the affidavit of contestant's attorney that "he has made due and diligent search for the residence of said claimants (not naming them) by making ҽnquiry at Kimball, D. T., near land in controversy and finds their last known address was Kimball, county of Brule, Territory of Dakota."

Fannie M. Pope appeared specially, as widow of the entryman and one of his heirs, to move a dismissal of the contest on the ground among others, that no notice of the contest had been served upon all the heirs of said Calvin W. Pope, deceased. Attached to such motion is her affidavit showing that the heirs of such deceased consist of herself as widow and thirteen children of entryman, three of whom, James J., Samuel E., and Bertram J., being of age, the others of ages ranging from three to seventeen years.

James W. Pope, Samuel E. Pope, and Bertram J..Pope also appeared by their attorney, at the opening of the hearing specially and "only for the purpose" of moving the dismissal of the contest as against them. selves, on the grounds: First, Want of legal service of notice of contest upon them ; Second, Insufficiency of affidavit of contestant's attor. ney to authorize mailing of copies of notice of hearing to their address at Kimball, T. D. ; Third, Failure of contestant to show in his affidavit for publication of notice such diligence on his part "as could entitle him to an order for publication of notice." Attached to this motion is the affidavit of Fannie M. Pope, showing among other matters, that Calvin W. Pope, who made entry for the said land moved to Brule county, D. T., spring 1881, with his family ; that he died April, 1882, leaving surviving him children as set out in her said other affidavit above re. ferred to ; that James W. Pope ever since December, 1884, resided at Mezamona, Wisconsin. Bertram J. Pope since November, 1884, at Oregon, Wisconsin, and Samuel E. Pope, since spring 1885, at Madison, Wisconsin.

The motions for dismissal were overruled by the local officers. The hearing proceeded and the testimony was taken by J. B. Long, notary public. The records fail to show that James W. Pope, Samuel E. Pope, or Bertram J. Pope, after dismissal of their motion appeared further in the case. Upon the testimony as submitted the local officers decided that "the contestant has sustained his charges and the entry should be canceled."

From this decision Fannie M. Pope appealed, stating as ground for her appeal among others:

1st. There was no legal service of notice upon the minor heirs of Calvin W. Pope.

2nd. There was no legal appearance in the case by the minor heirs of Calvin W. Pope.

3rd. There was no evidence that Fannie M. Pope, widow of Calvin W. Pope, was the administratrix of the estate of said Pope or was the guardian of the minor heirs.

Your office by your decision of March 31, 1888, set aside all the proceedings under the said contest, because the local officers had not acquired jurisdiction over the persons of the heirs of the entryman by legal service of notice. Leave was granted to the contestant to proceed with his contest "after due and proper notice upon the charges alleged."

From this decision Burgess appealed and the case is before this Department.

Your said office decision is correct. By the civil code of Dakota, page 76, Sec. 128, a guardian appointed by a court has power over the person and property of the ward unless otherwise ordered. It was not shown in the evidence that Fannie M. Pope was the duly appointed guardian of the minor heirs of the entryman. The minor heirs were not served personally or otherwise with the notice of contest herein; they are, therefore, not in any manner before the court, and their rights cannot be determined in this proceeding.

Regarding the service of notice upon James W., Samuel E., and Bertram J. Pope, adult heirs of the deceased entryman, it appears that no proper foundation was laid to authorize service of notice upon them by publication. According to Rule 11, of the Rules of Practice, the party, making affidavit for a service of notice by publication is required to state "what effort has been made to get personal service." The general statement in the contest affidavit, before the issuance of the notice of the hearing " that diligent search and inquiry has been made for the address of the adult heirs of said Calvin W. Pope, by this contestant and cannot ascertain the same" is not a compliance with the rule. An affidavit of Burgess filed in the case after the hearing had commenced describing the ineffectual efforts he had made before and after the initiation of the contest to learn the respective residences of the adult heirs of the deceased entryman, fails to obviate the objection. The proof required by Rule 11, should be before the local officers, before service of notice by publication is resorted to. Allen v. Leet, 6 L. D., 669.

This defect is jurisdictional. When a service of notice by publication is substituted for a personal service, a strict compliance with Rule

11, is requisite to confer jurisdiction over the person of the defendant. Neither the minor nor the adult children of the deceased entryman have had their day in court; they are not legally bound by the proceedings had in the case; such proceedings must, therefore, be set aside.

Your said office decision is accordingly affirmed.

RAILROAD GRANT—SETTLEMENT CLAIM—ACT OF MARCH 3, 1887.

CHICAGO, ST. PAUL, MINNEAPOLIS & OMAHA RY. CO.

The existence of a pre-emption claim at date of definite location excepts the land covered thereby from the operation of the grant.

Failure of a pre-emptor to purchase within the statutory period does not necessarily forfeit his claim against the government, though subjecting the land to the entry of any "other purchaser."

A railroad company, claiming under its grant, is not entitled to plead the status of a "purchaser" as against a pre-emptor who fails to purchase within the statutory period.

Subsequent sales of land erroneously certified or patented to a railroad company, furnish the company no defense as against proceedings under the act of March 3, 1887.

A recognition of the company's claim by the widow of the pre-emptor will not estop the heirs of the pre-emptor, or the government, from asserting claim to the land.

Secretary Noble to Acting Commissioner Stone, August 6, 1889.

By letter of May 9, 1888, your predecessor transmitted to this Department certain papers relative to the claim of the Chicago, St. Paul, Minneapolis and Omaha Railway Company, successor of the La Crosse and Milwaukee Railroad Company, to the NW. ¼ of Sec. 7, T. 24 N., R. 4 W., La Crosse land district, Wisconsin, and recommended that proceedings be instituted in accordance with the provisions of the act of March 3, 1887 (24 Stat., 556), to secure the restoration of said tract to the United States.

The land in question lay within the six-mile, or primary, limits of the grant under the act of June 3, 1856 (11 Stat., 20), to the State of Wisconsin, to aid in the construction, among others, of a railroad from Madison, or Columbus, in said State, by way of Portage City, to St. Croix River or Lake, and thence to the west end of Lake Superior, and to Bayfield, as shown by the map of definite location of the line of said road filed by the La Crosse and Milwaukee Railroad Company, September 7, 1857; and the records of your office show that the same was certified to the State for the benefit of said road December 18, 1863.

The grant to the State by said act of 1856 was of "every alternate section of land, designated by odd numbers for six sections in width on each side of the roads, respectively," therein mentioned, not "sold, or otherwise appropriated" by the United States, or to which "the right of pre-emption" had not "attached," when "the lines or routes of said roads are definitely fixed."

By the act of May 5, 1864 (13 Stat., 66), which was amendatory and supplementary to that of 18˙6 (Wisconsin R. R. Farm, etc., Co., 5 L. D., 84), the grant of 1856, among other changes and modifications, was, as to that portion of the road then unconstructed, north westward from Tomah, enlarged to ten sections (odd numbered) in width on each side of the road, of lands not "sold, reserved, or otherwise disposed of" by the United States, or to which "the right of pre-emption or homestead" had not "attached," at the date "when the line or route of said road is definitely fixed." Under this act the line of the road from Tomah to St. Croix river was relocated, and the map showing such relocation was filed in your office June 9, 1865. The tract in question falls also within the ten mile limits of this latter location.

The records of your office show that on November 29, 1855, one Jacob Flake (Flick) filed his pre-emption declaratory statement for said tract of land, alleging settlement November 27, 1855. This filing has never been canceled, and still remains of record.

In an affidavit of Margaret A. Flick, dated December 14, 1887, and now on file in your office, it is stated, in effect, that she is the widow of Jacob Flick (the same person who filed for the tract, as stated, in 1855); that she with her husband, and their family of eight children, most of whom were born on the tract, resided thereon continuously from October, 1856, until her husband's death in September, 1867, and that she and her family have resided on said land ever since, and were still residing thereon at the date of the affidavit; that her husband broke five acres of the tract in 1856, and built a dwelling house thereon and moved himself and family into it; that he broke thirty acres more land the following summer, and, afterwards, sixty or seventy acres of the tract were broken and cultivated; that during the fall of 1857, her husband (the said Jacob Flick) went to the land office at La Crosse, Wisconsin, and offered to make final proof for the land, in accordance with the pre-emption laws, but the officers of the government at the land office would not allow him to make proof, stating, as a reason for their action, that the land belonged to the West Wisconsin Railroad Company, and that they could not, therefore, allow final proof to be made. And thereupon she asks that the claim of the railroad company be canceled, and that patent issue to her for the land, or she be allowed to make homestead entry therefor.

The affidavit of Mrs. Flick was corroborated, as to all the material statements thereof, by one J. L. Smith.

It also appears that under date of July 13, 1886, your office, acting upon information of the state of facts detailed in said affidavit, received in part through various letters from Mrs. Flick, in reference to her claim to the land, called upon the Chicago, St. Paul, Minneapolis and Omaha Railway Company, the then and present owners of the grant in question, to reconvey the land to the United States, in order that a clear and undisputed title might be given to the heirs of said Jacob Flick, apparently the rightful owners of the land.

No response was made by the company to this call, and, on March 21, 1888 (the said affidavit of Mrs. Flick having been filed in the meantime), your office gave notice to the company that it would be allowed thirty days within which to show cause, if any it could, why proceedings should not be instituted in accordance with the provisions of said act of March 3, 1887, to secure the restoration of the tract to the United States.

On April 20, 1888, the railroad company, through Messrs. Britton and Gray, attorneys, filed its answer to this rule to show cause.

The company makes no denial of the facts set forth in the affidavit of Mrs. Flick, in reference to the pre-emption claim of her husband, Jacob Flick, to the land, and the continuous residence of herself and family thereon, since his death in September, 1867, but alleges, as it were by way of avoidance, in effect, (1) that if such pre-emption claim ever existed, the same was forfeited by reason of failure on the part of Flick to make proof and payment within the time prescribed by law, and therefore, no right of pre-emption had attached to the tract, or existed, at the date when the road was definitely located under the act of 1856, such as to prevent the same from passing to the State by virtue of that act; (2) that if title to the land did not pass by the act of 1856, and proceedings thereunder, such title did pass to the State for the company under and by virtue of the act of 1864, and the proceedings had in pursuance thereof; (3) that the company had, on October 25, 1877, sold the north half of the tract in question to one Peter Beaver, for the price of $438, and had conveyed the same to him; and (4) that the company had, on the date last mentioned, sold the south half of the tract to said Margaret A. Flick, at the price of $439.36, and that sixty-five dollars of the purchase price had been paid by her to the company; and that such sale was evidenced by a written contract between the company and said Margaret A. Flick, bearing date aforesaid. Special attention is called by the company to the fifth clause of this written contract, by which it appears that Mrs. Flick agreed to thereafter hold the premises therein described as tenant at sufferance, of the company, until the same should be paid for in accordance with the price and terms stipulated. No payments have been made to the company by Mrs. Flick, under this contract, further than the sum of $65, aforesaid. She declines and refuses to make further payments, asserting a claim in herself to the land, and states that the company is threatening her with ejectment from the premises.

It is very apparent to my mind, from the records of your office, and the showing made by Mrs. Flick, which is in no material respect denied by the company, that at the date when the company's rights first attached under the grant of 1856, the land in question was covered by the pre-emption claim of Jacob Flick. He had settled thereon, had made his pre-emption filing, had built a dwelling house, and was living with his family in the same, and had been and was cultivating and improving the land, making the same his home. Clearly, under this state of facts, it can not be said that no "right of pre-emption" had "attached" to the land when the line or route of the company's road was "definitely fixed," which occurred when its map showing the location thereof was filed in your office, September 7, 1857. The fact that Flick did not make final proof and payment within twelve months from the date of his settlement (the tract being offered land when his filing was made) can not avail the company. A pre-emption filing for offered land is simply a protection to the *settler*, and insures the land to him as against the *sale* thereof to another during the period of twelve months after his settlement. The right of pre-emption rests in settlement, inhabitancy and improvements. If the pre-emptor should fail to purchase within the twelve months prescribed, his right or claim to the land, as against the government, is not necessarily forfeited, but the law merely refuses to longer protect him in his claim, by declaring that thereafter the land "shall be subject to the entry of any other purchaser." The Department is not precluded from accepting proof and payment after the twelve months have expired. Schetka *v.* Northern Pacific R. R. Company (5 L. D., 473), and authorities there cited.

A railroad company does not stand in the position of "any other purchaser," and in the case just cited it was held that the company "can not be heard to plead against a settler on public land under the pre-emption or homestead laws, that he has failed to perform his obligations to the government, if his claim has attached at the date of definite location." See also Allen *v.* Northern Pacific R. R. Company (6 L. D., 520); Central Pacific R. R. Co. *v.* Field (7 L. D , 406); Emmerson *v.* Central Pacific R. R. Co. (3 L. D., 271).

In view of the foregoing, I am clearly of the opinion that the land in question was excepted from the grant of 1856, and did not pass to the State or the railroad company thereunder; and that the same was, therefore, erroneously certified to the State for the company, December 18, 1863, as stated. This disposes of the first allegation of the company's answer.

The same reasoning applies also, with equal force, to the second point made by the company. The pre-emption claim of Jacob Flick was still in existence at the date of the passage of the act of 1864, and, also, when the relocation of the road was made thereunder, as shown by the map thereof filed June 9, 1865. He was still living on the land with his family, cultivating and improving the same. Moreover, he had applied at the local land office to be allowed to make his final proof and payment, which was denied him, as we have seen. I do not think, therefore, that any right or title to this land passed to the State, for the company, under the act of 1864.

As to the other matters alleged in answer to the rule to show cause, namely, the sales of parts of the tract to Beaver and Mrs. Flick, respectively, in October, 1877, it is sufficient to say that the fact of such sales can not avail to either create, or perfect, title in the company to lands that never passed to it under the grants in question. Subsequent sales of lands erroneously certified or patented to a railroad company, furnish no defense to the company under the act of March 3, 1887. Neither does the agreement made by Mrs. Flick, to the effect that she would hold the land purchased by her, as tenant at sufferance of the company, until paid for, admitting the same to have been voluntarily made, operate to estop the government, or the heirs of Jacob Flick, among whom were eight children, from asserting claim to the land.

Upon consideration of the whole matter, I am satisfied that the land in question was erroneously certified for the use and benefit of the company, and in accordance with the provisions of said act of March 3, 1887, you are hereby directed to demand from the company a relinquishment or reconveyance to the United States of such land; and after ninety days from the date of such demand, you will report to this Department the result thereof.

CONTEST—FRAUD AND COLLUSION.

PARRIS v. HUNT.

No rights can be acquired through a fraudulent or collusive contest, nor will the rights of others be defeated by such a contest.

First Assistant Secretary Chandler to Acting Commissioner Stone, August 8, 1889.

I have considered the case of Zimri Parris v. Nathan G. Hunt on appeal of the former from your office decision of April 13, 1888, dismissing his contest against the homestead entry of the latter for SW. ¼, Sec. 32, T. 101, N., R. 56 W., Mitchell, Dakota, land district.

It appears from the record that Hunt made entry July 12, 1880, and on February 13, 1883, said Parris filed affidavit of contest alleging abandonment for more than six months.

April 17, 1883, was fixed by the local office for hearing in said contest.

On February 23, 1883, one Chas. F. Rogers filed an affidavit of contest against said entry alleging abandonment and failure to reside upon said land for six months, and that Hunt had sold to said contestant all his right, title and interest in and to said land and had been paid $400, on account of such sale.

Filed with this contest affidavit is a special affidavit setting forth that the contest by Parris was fraudulent, collusive, and for speculative purposes.

Ex parte depositions in the contest of Parris v. Hunt were taken before J. B. Nation, a notary public, and also a business partner of said Parris, and on the day set for hearing Hunt made default. The local

officers, however, continued the case until October 9, 1883, for the purpose of giving Rogers an opportunity to establish fraud and collusion
in the Parris contest, and on September 12, 1883, they notified Parris
to appear on the day to which said cause was continued and show cause
why his contest should not be dismissed on account of such fraud and
collusion. Hearing however was postponed from time to time until
January 10, 1884, when it came on for hearing and both Hunt and
Rogers failed to appear and on motion of Parris, Rogers' contest was
dismissed but on the same day the local officers receiving a telegram
from Rogers who was *en route* but unavoidably delayed, they vacated
their former action and continued the case until the next day January
11, 1884, when all parties appeared and offered their testimony.

On September 26, 1884, the local officers decided that—

The evidence submitted sustains the charge that Parris' contest is in the interest of
Hunt. The relation of Hunt to Parris and to Nation and Paris, and the default of Hunt
in the Parris contest in the first instance, lead to the conclusion that the same was
instituted in a spirit of friendliness altogether unknown in cases of genuine contest.

From this decision Parris appealed but the local office by a mistaken
construction of a letter from your office ordered a hearing of the Rogers
contest. The said appeal of Parris also alleged as error the decision
of the local officers ordering a hearing in the Rogers contest. At such
hearing, however, all parties appeared and submitted testimony.

On March 26, 1885, the local officers decided the contest of Rogers v.
Hunt, in favor of Hunt for the reason that he had fully complied with
the law in regard to residence since March, 1883, and that before that
time he had a constructive residence upon the land from and after the
date of his entry. They say, however, in said decision—

The record in this case is rife with rascality, and Zimri Parris' attorney, is not only
a party to it, but is responsible for the loss of Rogers and the miserable trickery shown
by Hunt

In your said decision you do not pass upon the evidence submitted
in the Rogers v. Hunt contest, merely saying—

Under the circumstances, however, further proceedings in the case of Rogers v.
Hunt, will be stayed, until the final disposition of the appeal by Parris, which will be
considered now.

The evidence conclusively shows that on or about the 4th day of May,
1882, Hunt sold to Rogers his right and interest in the land in controversy and accepted from Rogers a span of mules, harness, and wagon,
and two notes of $65.50, each, secured by mortgage as the purchase
price of his relinquishment, total consideration five hundred and twenty-
five dollars; that Hunt took possession of the mules, harness, and wagon
and thereafter retained them as his own, and that he gave Rogers possession of his said homestead, Rogers moving his family into the shanty
thereon with the full consent of Hunt, and that Rogers had maintained
a continuous residence thereon. It further appears that on or about
the 6th day of May, 1882, Hunt and Rogers went to the office of the
contestant Zimri Parris or Nation and Parris, to have the necessary

papers drawn up to carry into effect their said agreement; that said Parris at their joint request prepared a written contract, a bill of sale of the mules, harness and wagon, a chattel mortgage securing the two notes, and a relinquishment of Hunt's interest which was signed by both Hunt and his wife.

It appears further that there was at the time of Rogers' purchase, a contest pending against said land and that as part of such contract it was agreed that Rogers should buy off the contestant and then Hunt would file his relinquishment but because of some disagreement in regard to the security for the payment of the two notes, Hunt refused to file a relinquishment and Rogers commenced a contest but this he subsequently dismissed. About the time of the trouble in regard to the security for the notes, Hunt employed Parris to look after his interests in the matter as he was apprehensive that Rogers was intending to evade payment of his notes and shortly after this employment Parris himself initiated contest against Hunt's entry and Hunt at the hearing made default although he resided within a few miles of the place where the evidence was taken.

There are many other circumstances shown in the evidence tending to prove collusion between Parris and Hunt in such contest or at least tending to prove that Parris' contest was in the interest of Hunt. His employment as attorney to look after Hunt's interest precludes the idea that he was acting adversely to him.

Your said decision is accordingly affirmed.

No rights could be acquired by such fraudulent contest; Van Ostrum v. Young (6 L. D., 25); nor could any rights be defeated thereby. Eddy v. England (6 L. D., 530).

While the hearing of the contest in Rogers v. Hunt may have been premature pending the appeal, yet as all parties were present and the testimony appears to be so full and conclusive as not to admit of a doubt upon the main question involved, it will not be necessary to remand the case for a re-hearing but your office may pass upon the evidence in such contest as the same is presented with the record in the case at bar.

RAILROAD GRANT—FORFEITURE—ACT OF MARCH 2, 1889.

ONTONAGON AND BRULE RIVER R. R. CO.

In the adjustment of the grant under the act of forfeiture the company is only entitled to lands for the portion of road constructed for the purpose of being used and maintained as a railroad.

Secretary Noble to Acting Commissioner Stone, August 8, 1889.

I am in receipt of your communication of the 2d instant, transmitting the report of Mr. Walter P. Jones, a clerk in the General Land Office, dated July 20th last, relative to the construction and condition of the Ontonagon and Brule River Railroad.

The act of March 2, 1889 (25 Stat., 1008), forfeited to the United States all lands opposite to and coterminous with the uncompleted portion of said road, and this report is made in accordance with the direction contained in your letter of the 31st of May last, detailing Mr. Jones to make an investigation of the twenty miles of the road which said company claims to have constructed prior to the passage of said act.

From said report it appears that, from the first to the twelfth mile inclusive, the road is in good order and repair, and in operation—one train each way being run over the same every week day. This is the only portion of the road that is being used by said company. He further reported that from the thirteenth to the seventeenth mile inclusive the road is in fair condition, considering that it was built eight years ago, but it has been in little use since that time. In places the ties showed signs of decay, and in others there was grass and weeds growing on the road bed, but not to any considerable extent; but that there were two or three gangs of men at work on this portion of the road at the time he was there. The eighteenth and nineteenth miles of the road he found to be in bad condition, grass and weeds a foot high growing between the rails in some places, many of the ties not being spiked to the rails (and no indications that they had ever been), and in some cases resting on the ground two or three inches below the rails. On the nineteenth mile there were places in which the ties were not spiked to the rails and the road bed had settled badly, so much so in one place that water had settled in the depression to an extent that covered the ties for a distance of about eight feet. The twentieth mile, as far as Adventure Creek, is in bad condition and there is no bridge across the creek; there is no track east of Adventure Creek. On the last fourth mile of the twenty mile section the trees had been cleared away for a width of about forty yards along the entire line, where the road was originally located. But this clearing is now covered with a thick growth of brush and young trees, which almost entirely obliterated the old road bed.

The company made no reply to the opportunity offered it to submit any evidence or statement as to the condition of said road, when called upon by Mr. Jones.

In view of all the facts set forth in said report, you recommend that the company be called upon to show cause why the grant of lands opposite to and coterminous with the last mile of the section in question should not be declared forfeited and the land restored to entry under said act of March 2, 1889, on the ground that for that mile the road never was constructed as contemplated in the act making the grant. From the facts set forth in said report, I am of opinion that this reason will apply as to the entire length of the last eight miles of said twenty mile section, because, although the road bed has been constructed and the rails laid, it would appear, judging from the facts reported by Mr. Jones, that at the time of the passage of the act of March 2, 1889, the last eight miles of said road had been practically abandoned, and only twelve miles of said twenty mile section was then and is now in operation.

I do not think it was the intention of Congress to authorize lands to be certified to this road along the full length of twenty miles, when only twelve miles of said section are in practical operation, and from the facts now before me, I would not feel justified in certifying to the company lands for this part of the road, until I have more satisfactory evidence that it has been completed, as contemplated by the act aforesaid, for the purpose of being used and maintained as a railroad.

You will therefore call upon the company to show cause, within sixty days, why the grant opposite to and coterminous with the last eight miles of said section should not be declared forfeited, and the land restored to entry under the act of March 2, 1889.

ACCOUNTS—CIRCULAR RELATING TO VOUCHERS.

DEPARTMENT OF THE INTERIOR,
GENERAL LAND OFFICE,
Washington, D. C., August 7, 1889.

To receivers of public moneys and surveyors general acting as disbursing agents:

GENTLEMEN: The following instructions relative to the preparation of vouchers transmited to this office in support of disbursements made by you are issued for your guidance.

Hereafter all vouchers forwarded to this office must be receipted, in accordance with the requirements herein, or they will be returned for correction, and your accounts suspended until legal vouchers are received.

1. The name of the payee as signed must correspond in spelling with that in the account.

2. Signatures by mark (x) must be witnessed by two persons who can write, giving their places of residence.

3. Receipts by executors, administrators, guardians, or other fiduciaries must be accompanied by certified copies, under seal, of letters testamentary, letters of administration, of guardianship, or other evidence of fiduciary character, as the case may be.

4. Payees must sign by their own hands; officials, officially with full title; firms, the usual firm signature by a member of the firm, not by a clerk or other person for the firm, and every signature must be written, not printed or stamped.

5. Evidence of authority to receipt for incorporated or unincorporated companies must accompany vouchers in the name of such companies or associations. Such evidence should be in the form of an extract from the by-laws or records of the company or association, having the

authority of the officer to receive and receipt for moneys for the company, and giving his name and date of his election or appointment, which extract must be verified by a certificate under seal signed by the president and secretary, or by one of these officers, and not less than two of the directors, which certificate must state that such authority remains unrevoked and unchanged. If the company has no seal the extract should be certified as correct by a competent officer under his seal.

6. In cases where an individual or a copartnership is doing business under a company title, the affidavit of the owner or of the members of the copartnership will be required, showing the fact of ownership and naming the person who is authorized to receive money and receipt for the owners.

☞The evidence of authority to receipt required in paragraph 5 may be dispensed with in the case of vouchers not exceeding in amount the sum of twenty-five dollars ($25), in the name of a corporation or company which necessarily employs a number of local agents in the transaction of its business, such as railroad, telegraph, steamboat, express, transfer, turnpike, hotel, newspaper, gas, and ice companies, when it is impracticable to obtain the signature of the secretary, treasurer, or other principal officer of such corporation or company.

You will please acknowledge the receipt of this circular by initial and date.

Very respectfully,

W. M. STONE,
Acting Commissioner.

Approved August 8, 1889:
JOHN W. NOBLE,
Secretary.

EQUITABLE ADJUDICATION—DESERT ENTRY.

JAMES H. TAYLOR.

The authority of the board of equitable adjudication is confined to entries so far complete in themselves, that when the defects on which they are submitted have been cured by its favorable action, they pass at once to patent.

An entry should not be submitted to the board before it has been perfected by payment of the purchase price and issuance of final certificate.

Acting Secretary Chandler to Acting Commissioner Stone, August 9, 1889.

The adjudication by you on the 20th ultimo of the fifty one suspended public land entries, submitted with letter of that day and embraced in abstract No. 7, was, on the 6th instant approved by the Acting Attorney General and Secretary of the Interior acting as a board, with the exception of the case No. 51, being the desert land entry of James H. Taylor.

The Taylor entry is remanded by the joint action of the Acting Attorney General and Secretary of the Interior, "that the purchase money due thereon may be paid, the final papers issued and the entry re-submitted under rule 29." This action is based on the view fully set forth in departmental letter of the 22nd ultimo submitting the abstract to the Attorney General.

I enclose herewith a copy of said letter for your information and guidance. In future you will submit to the board such suspended entries only, as are (in language of above letter), " so far complete in themselves, that when the defects on which they are submitted have been cured by its favorable action they pass at once to patent."

OPINION.

Secretary Noble to the Attorney General, July 22, 1889.

I have approved the adjudication by the Acting Commissioner of the General Land Office, on the 20th instant, of the suspended entries of Augusta A. Graham and fifty others (with the exception of that numbered 51 in the name of James H. Taylor) submitted, with abstract No. 7, for action by the board of equitable adjudication under sections 2450–2457 Revised Statutes, as amended by act of February 27, 1877.

I am of the opinion that the action of the Acting Commissioner in submitting the desert land entry of James H. Taylor is premature, as the entry has not been perfected by the completion of the payment of the purchase money required by the desert land act, and the final receipt and the final certificate have not issued.

In my view the province of the board of equitable adjudication is confined to entries so far complete in themselves, that, when the defects on which they are submitted have been cured by its favorable action they pass at once to patent.

The above case if perfected as to the omissions named before submission, would come under Rule 29, adopted May 12, 1888, by the board to meet precisely such a case as the one now under consideration. This rule provides for the confirmation of desert land entries where final proof and payment were not made within the statutory period, and contemplates the full payment of purchase money and issue of final papers before such entries can be properly submitted to the board.

In accordance with these views I have declined to embrace the Taylor entry in the certificate of approval that I have attached to the abstract, but have remanded it that the omission may be supplied and the case re-submitted under Rule 29.

I have the honor to submit the abstract herewith for such action as you may deem proper.

PRIVATE ENTRY–EQUITABLE ADJUDICATION.

EDWARD RILEY.

In the absence of an adverse claim, a private entry, made in good faith, of land withdrawn for railroad indemnity purposes may be submitted to the board of equitable adjudication.

First Assistant Secretary Chandler to Acting Commissioner Stone, August 8, 1889.

By decision, dated June 2, 1888, your office held for cancellation private cash entry No. 23, 218, made April 25, 1888, by Edward Riley, for the SW. ¼ of the NW. ¼ of Sec. 3, T. 9 N., R. 12 E., Grayling land district, Michigan. From this decision Riley has duly appealed.

Said tract, it appears, is within the indemnity limits of the grant made to the State of Michigan by the act of June 3, 1856 (11 Stat., 21), for the benefit of the Port Huron and Lake Michigan Railroad Company, and was withdrawn from market May 30, 1856.

Your said office decision states that said tract has not been restored to market, and holds that it is therefore not subject to private cash entry. Said decision further states, that the records of your office do not show any selection of the same by said railroad company, nor that any claim thereto has ever been asserted under the laws relating to public lands.

It may be safely inferred, therefore, that said tract, but for said withdrawal of May 30, 1856, would have been subject to entry and sale under the laws of the United States, at the time Riley's entry was allowed by the local land office.

Riley in his appeal makes oath, that he has occupied said tract as a home and family residence for thirteen years, and that his improvements thereon are now worth fourteen hundred dollars.

There being apparently no adverse claim to this tract of land, it seems to me that on the principles of equity and justice said entry should be passed to patent.

You will, therefore, please refer this case, under the appropriate rule, to the Board of Equitable Adjudication. The decision of your office is modified accordingly.

———

UNIVERSITY LANDS—IDAHO TERRITORY.

GEORGE HOGE ET AL.

Land selected for University purposes is not open to entry.

The Department has full control of University selections, until approved by the President, and may protect a subsequent entry, improperly allowed for land thus selected, by allowing another selection in lieu of the entered tract.

First Assistant Secretary Chandler to Acting Commissioner Stone, August 8, 1889.

I am in receipt of your communication of the 3d instant, transmitting for my consideration the entry papers of George Hoge, for lots 5 and 6, township 13 S., range 43 E., Blackfoot, Idaho, and of Thomas Van Vleck, for lot 1, of Sec. 7, and lot 7 of Sec. 6, same township, together with affidavits filed in response to the rule of your office to show cause why their entries should not be canceled for conflict with selections made for university purposes for said Territory, under the act of February 18, 1881 (21 Stat., 326), entitled, "An act to grant lands to Dakota, Montana, Arizona, Idaho and Wyoming for university purposes."

From the papers transmitted, it appears that the tracts in controversy were selected by the agent of this Department on June 26, 1882, for university purposes, for the Territory of Idaho, under the provisions of the act aforesaid, which requires that lands therein granted shall be immediately selected and withdrawn from sale, and located under the direction of the Secretary of the Interior, with the approval of the President of the United States, for the use and support of a university in said Territory, when it shall be admitted as a State into the Union.

These entries were made by the claimants, respectively, on August 4, 1886, and upon the entry papers the register indorsed: "Subject to university selections."

In response to your letter to show cause why their entries should not be canceled, they state that said selections had never been published, and that they considered the land covered thereby to be unappropriated public land at the date of their entries.

These cases are not similar to that of Fehlberg [Territory of Montana] (8 L. D., 55) referred to in your letter, for the reason that the local officers were not in that case notified of the selection of the tract for university purposes, and supposing that the tract was vacant, unappropriated public land, so informed Fehlberg by letter; and the latter, acting upon this information, improved the tract, made it his home in good faith, and arranged to make entry thereof. But in the cases of Hoge and Van Vleck, although they had notice that the tracts had been selected for university purposes, it appears that they acted in ignorance of the effect of such selection, on account of the action of the local office in allowing said entries to be made. The local officers should not have allowed these entries. They knew that the lands had been selected for university purposes, and therefore reserved from entry. As these claimants have made valuable improvements upon their claims, acting evidently upon the action of the local officers in allowing the entries, notwithstanding the selection for university purposes, and the Department having full control of university selections until they have been approved by the President, I can see no reason why these entrymen should not be protected, and their improvements saved to them, by directing that another selection be made by the Territory of Idaho, in lieu of the tracts entered by them respectively. You will therefore approve the entries of said Hoge and Van Vleck respectively for patent, and other selections will be made for the Territory of Idaho in lieu thereof.

You will instruct the local officers that in the future no entries shall be allowed of lands so selected.

DONATION—ORPHAN—ACT OF JULY 17, 1854.

JOHN NEWSOME.

Under section 5, act of July 17, 1854, orphans left within the Territory are entitled to a quarter section of land, if the parent, at the time of death was qualified to initiate a claim under the donation law.

Secretary Noble to Acting Commissioner Stone, August 8, 1889.

On August 11, 1877, the register and receiver of the Oregon City land office, Oregon, issued final donation certificate No. 4842, to the orphan children of John Havird, deceased, for lots 4, 5, 6, 7, 8, 9 and 10, of Sec. 23, T. 60 S., R. 2 W., containing 159.10 acres, the application on which said certificate was issued having been filed May 5, 1855.

There is nothing in the record to account for the lapse of time between the date of the application and the issue of certificate; nor to show when the certificate and accompanying papers were forwarded to your office. However, on January 13, 1888, your office held said certificate for cancellation, being of the opinion that the orphan children of John Havird had no just claim for land under the Oregon donation acts, because their father was not, at the time his death, "a resident of Oregon."

From this action John Newsome, claiming to be a party in interest, has appealed here.

The certificate in question was issued under section five, act of July 17, 1854 (10 Stat., 305), which provides:

That in any case where orphans have been, or may be, left in either of said Territories (Oregon or Washington), whose parents, or either of them, if living, would have been entitled to a donation under this act, or either of those of which it is amendatory, said orphans shall be entitled to a quarter section of land on due proof being made to the satisfaction of the surveyor-general, subject to the decision of the Secretary of the Interor.

The Oregon donation acts are three in number, the first being that of September 27, 1850 (9 Stat., 496), by section four of which was granted to—

Every white settler or occupant of the public lands . . . now residing in said Territory (Oregon), or who shall become a resident thereof, on or before December 1, 1850, and who shall have resided upon and cultivated the same for four consecutive years, and shall otherwise conform to the provisions of this act, the quantity of one half section or three hundred and twenty acres, etc.

By section five was granted "to all white male citizens . . . . emigrating to and settling in said Territory," between December 1, 1850, and December 1, 1853, one quarter section, or if married one half section of land, one half to the husband and one half to the wife in her own right, upon complying with the provisions of said act.

By section five, act of February 14, 1853 (10 Stat., 158), the provisions of the foregoing acts were extended and continued in force until December 1, 1855, and on July 17, 1854, was passed the act, section five of which is herein first quoted, and which makes provision for the orphan children of parents, who, "if living, would have been entitled to a donation," under any of the acts cited.

The donation acts have been repeatedly construed by the United States supreme and circuit courts and by this Department, and the citation of many decisions thereon may be found in Vol. 1, of the Land Laws, local and temporary. In these decisions it has been generally held that settlement and residence for the prescribed period were conditions precedent to the acquisition of any right, as against the United States, under said acts. See Hall *v.* Russell, 101 U. S., 503 ; Maynard *v.* Hill, 125 U. S., 191, and cases cited. If, then, we are to follow the language of section five of the act of 1854, Havird, if living, would not have been "entitled to a donation" under said acts, unless, being a "settler or occupant," he had resided upon and cultivated the land. For, says the supreme court, in the case last cited, p. 214:

> The settler does not become a grantee until such residence and cultivation have been had by the very terms of the act. Until then he has only a promise of title, what is sometimes vaguely called an inchoate interest.

Or, as is said on the next page "a right to remain upon the land, so as to enable him to comply with the conditions upon which the title was to pass to him."

On examination of the legislation in question, I can not think Congress intended that so strict a construction should be placed upon the section under which the present case is made; but that its intention was otherwise. In section four of the original act of 1850 was a provision that in case of death, after compliance with the prerequisites, but before the issue of patents, of married persons, intestate, their rights should pass to the survivor and children, or heirs. And section eight of the same act provided that in case of death before the expiration of the four years of required residence, the rights of the deceased should descend to his heirs at law, including his widow, if there was one. And section eight of the act of 1853, *supra*, provided that each widow, whose husband, if he had lived, would have been entitled "to a claim under the provisions of the act of" 1850, *supra*, shall have the same quantity of land as she would have received, but for said death; and in case of her death before the expiration of the four years of residence, her rights shall inure to her heirs.

· It is thus seen that Congress had made provision that, in the case of the death of the settler his interest should inure to his widow and children (1) in case of death after performance of the prerequisite conditions, but before issue of patent; (2) in case of death after settlement, but before compliance; (3) that a widow shall have the same rights she would have had if her husband had lived, and (4) in case of her death before compliance, her interests were to inure to her children. So that, provision was made for securing a donation claim to the widow or heirs of a qualified settler in the contingency of his death in almost every case, except where orphans were left, prior to the initiation by the parent of any claim under said laws. This class of cases, section five, act of 1854, was intended to cover.

In said section the concurrence of two conditions are required; the present qualification of the father, at the time of his death, to have made claim under said law; and the condition that the orphans must have been "left" within the territory. As personal settlement was prerequisite to any claim, the father must necessarily have been within the territory at the time of his death, to meet this requirement, and so must the children; for the death which would make them orphans, would not alone entitle them unless that death found them within the territory. In the case under consideration the testimony shows that the children accompanied their father and surviving parent on his long journey from Illinois to Oregon, and were with him at the time of his death. So that the inquiry is narrowed down to the single point as to whether the father died within the territory of Oregon.

The testimony in this case satisfied the local officers that Havird died in Oregon, and after a careful scrutiny thereof I am of the same opinion.

With the original application in this case, and under date of May 5, 1855, is filed the affidavit of Noah Watson, in which he states, " that in August, 1853, while on the road to Oregon, the said John Havird died, on Snake river." At the same time was made, before the register, an affidavit by Carey C. Havird, who states that John Havird, " died in August, 1853, while on his journey, at about one hundred miles this side of Fort Hall."

On March 6, 1875, a second affidavit was made by said Carey, who states therein that said John was his "reputed father," and that "he died in Oregon" on August 11, 1853. In the record is also an affidavit of Tryphenia Ann Symms, daughter of said John, who swears that she and her brothers and sisters came direct from Illinois to Oregon with her father in 1853, and that the latter " died on the 11th day of August, 1853, at the crossing of Snake river near Fort Boise, I. T."

Turning to the maps of Oregon and Idaho, it is seen that Snake river is the eastern boundary of the former and western boundary of the latter, until about its junction with the Boise river, at a point about forty miles due west from Fort Boise ; and that Fort Hall is over two hundred miles further east, it being situated in the south-eastern portion of Idaho and about fifty miles from its eastern boundary.

From this it seems that Carey Havird, when he spoke of the death of his " reputed father " having occurred about one hundred miles west of Fort Hall, was either confused as to distances, or must have had in his mind Fort Boise. Indeed in his second affidavit he is emphatic in the statement that his father "died in Oregon." If he died " one hundred miles this side (westward) of Fort Hall," it is not possible for him to have " died in Oregon," and the two affidavits are irreconcilable.

On consideration of all the testimony in the case, I am satisfied that

John Havird died in Oregon, at the crossing of Snake river, near Fort Boise, as stated in the affidavit of his daughter, Mrs. Symms. Being thus within the limits of Oregon at the time of his death, but for that death he could have then initiated a donation claim, and his children, being with him at the time of his death, were consequently, orphans "left" within said territory, and are entitled to a quarter-section of land, as provided in the act of 1854.

The judgment of your office is accordingly reversed.

RAILROAD GRANT—ACT OF JUNE 22, 1874.

NORTHERN PAC. R. R. CO. v. MUNSELL.

A relinquishment under the act of June 22, 1874, relieves the land included therein from all claim on the part of the railroad company.

The case of the Florida Railway and Navigation Co. v. Miller, overruled.

Secretary Noble to Acting Commissioner Stone August 8, 1889.

I have considered the appeal of the Northern Pacific Railroad Company from the decision of your office, dated June 11, 1888, rejecting the claim to the NW. ¼ of Sec. 3, T. 2 N., R. 3 E., W. M., Vancouver, Washington Territory.

The record shows that said land is within the granted limits of the withdrawal of August 13, 1870, on general route, and also within the primary limits of the grant, as shown by the map of definite location, filed in your office on September 22, 1882; that said company on May 4, 1876, executed its relinquishment of the land in question in favor of one Christopher Richard, a former claimant for the land, under the provisions of the act of June 22, 1874 (18 Stat., 194); that on October 17, 1887, said Munsell presented said relinquishment and was allowed to make homestead entry of said land.

The company insists that the allowance of said entry was erroneous, because the relinquishment being in favor of said Richard, if he failed to acquire title to the land, the same became subject to the claim of the company; that the company has not selected land in lieu of said tract under said act, and is therefore entitled to take the land covered by said entry.

Your office, however, held that the company waived its claim to said tract by the relinquishment thereof, and the land thereby became subject to disposal under the general land laws.

The decisions of the Department have not been altogether uniform upon the effect of a relinquishment executed by a railroad company under said act. In the case of the Peninsular Railroad Company v. Carlton and Steele (2 L. D., 531), Mr. Secretary Teller held, that lands which have once been relinquished under said act, can not be again claimed by the company. But in the case of the Florida Railway and Naviga-

tion Company *v.* Miller (3 L. D., 324), Mr. Acting Secretary Joslyn considered said act, and decided that:

> The sole object of this act (June 22, 1974), as is made fully obvious in the conclud-
> ing clause of the foregoing quotation, is to relieve entries and filings from conflict
> with railroad grants that would otherwise take the land so entered or filed for; and
> the effect of a relinquishment thereunder is merely to allow the settler an opportu-
> nity to show his compliance with the law under which his filing or entry was made.
> It can not therefore be held that a relinquishment, executed for such a purpose, could
> in any way affect the status of the land with respect to any one, except the railroad
> company, and the settler in whose name the original entry or filing stood.

No reference was made in said last named decision to the former ruling of the Department.

In the case of the Florida Railway and Navigation Company (4 L. D.,
148), Mr. Secretary Lamar cited with approval said case of Railroad
Co. *v.* Carlton & Steele (*supra*), but no reference was made to the decision in the Miller case (*supra*).

In the case of the Hastings and Dakota Railway Company (6 L. D.,
716), Mr. Secretary Vilas decided that:

> A relinquishment under the act of June 22, 1874, is made to the United States, and
> when accepted by the proper official of the government becomes at once operative,
> and the company is entitled to select lands in lieu of those relinquished, provided
> said lands were in such condition as to warrant a relinquishment, without regard to
> the ability, or intention of the settler to perfect his claim. The land by reason of
> such relinquishment is released from all claim of the company, and is subject to dis-
> posal under the general land laws.

No mention is made in said decision of the contrary doctrine announced by Acting Secretary Joslyn in the Miller case (*supra*), nor is
any case cited as authority for his ruling by Secretary Vilas.

In the case of the Florida Railway and Navigation Company *v.* Dicks
(7 L. D., 431), Mr. Secretary Vilas re-affirmed his ruling in the Hastings and Dakota Railway Company (*supra*), and held that the contention of the company upon the authority of the Miller case (*supra*) could
not be sustained. To the same effect is the ruling of the Department
in the case of the Southern Minnesota Railroad Company *et al.* (8 L. D.,
472.)

The case of the Florida Railway and Navigation Company *v.* Miller,
being in conflict with the repeated rulings of the Department, must be
and it is hereby expressly overruled.

The decision of your office is accordingly affirmed.

TIMBER CULTURE ENTRY—PRELIMINARY AFFIDAVIT.

SAMUEL B. MARTIN.

A timber culture entry based on preliminary papers falsely purporting to have been
properly executed, but in fact not sworn to before any officer, is illegal, and the
defect can not be cured by amendment.

Secretary Noble to Acting Commissioner Stone, August 8, 1889.

I have before me the appeal of Samuel B. Martin from your office decision of February 8, 1888, holding for cancellation his (said Martin's)

timber culture entry, of the NE. ¼, Sec. 25, T. 10 S., R. 45 W., Denver district, Colorado, "for illegality in the execution of the preliminary affidavits."

The entry in question was made June 26, 1886, upon papers purporting to be affidavits, in the usual forms, "sworn to and subscribed" by Samuel B. Martin before "R B. Presson, notary public," on the 22d day of June, 1886. In fact, however,—as Martin himself declares,—the papers in question were simply "signed" by him, at his home in Iowa, he never having "gone before any notary public to swear to them," or "visited the land filed on." Both the "preliminary" affidavit, and the "non-mineral" one, are expressly required to be made "before (an) officer authorized to administer oaths in the district where the land is situated;" and at least the "non-mineral" affidavit is clearly required to be made on personal knowledge, as in it the affiant expressly declares "that he is well acquainted with the character of said described land, and with each and every legal subdivision thereof, having frequently passed over the same," and states several other facts as being such "to his knowledge."

On January 25, 1887, your office held the entry for cancellation, but with permission to Martin to ask for a hearing in which to show cause why his entry should not be canceled.

Under date of May 16, 1887, Martin filed certain proposed new entry papers, together with a special affidavit in which he gives the following account of the matter:

In the fall of 1885 I resided at . . . Onawa . . . in the state of Iowa and there met one George W. Penn with whom I was well acquainted. In conversation with him he then told me that he had visited the eastern part of Arapahoe and El- bert counties in the state of Colorado . . . . . He at the same time advised me to locate on some of the land, and assured me that it could be done without my having to go out and visit the land, stating that he had been told by one R. B. Presson, who had located him, that land could be lawfully taken in that way, that almost daily, eastern parties were taking claims without visiting the land and that the visiting of the land in person by any party taking a claim was a mere matter of form and not an actual requirement of the law. Having every confidence in the business capacity and integrity of the said George W. Penn and being in ill health and with the hope that a change of climate would benefit my health, I requested the said Penn to se- cure for me a timber claim if it could be lawfully done as he had stated. In the month of April, 1886, said Penn returned to Colorado, and in the month of June or latter part of May of that year I received from said Penn some papers for my signa- ture; said Penn explaining to me in his letter accompanying them that they were to secure a filing on a timber claim he had selected for me as I had requested. These papers bore no seal or signature of any notary when received by me; I signed the papers and returned them to Penn and I think I received the timber culture receipt from said Penn in the month of July—the receipt bearing date 26th June, 1886. . . . . . . I signed the papers referred to in Onawa, Monona county, Iowa, and I did not go before any notary public to swear to them, nor had I visited the land filed on. I went out to Kingston in Arapahoe county, Colorado, in the month of June, 1886, and was there from about the 12th to the 19th of that month. Had I then known that there was any irregularity in filing in the manner hereinbefore set forth I could and would at that time have complied with the requirements of the

law. I took the said land in good faith intending to fully comply with all the requirements of the law and as a *bona fide* settler on government land. I have since that
time gone upon the land in person and can make intelligently the affidavits accompanying this affidavit. In the latter part of December, 1886, as nearly as I can recollect I stated to Frank D. Hobbs, inspector of the General Land Office, a history of
this case and substantially as herein set forth. . . . . I made my said filing in
ignorance of the fact that I was doing an illegal act and relying implicitly upon the
statements and assurances of said Penn in whom I had unbounded confidence.

On February 8, 1888, by the decision appealed from, your office held
that, notwithstanding the foregoing explanation, the illegality in the
entry " could not be cured by filing supplemental affidavits."

This decision I approve. It has been held, it is true, in such cases
as that of Griffith W. McMillan (8 L. D., 478), that the defect in the
execution of the preliminary affidavit may be cured by amendment
where good faith appears. But I can not see how it is possible to
find " good faith " in Martin's action as reported by himself in the
matter of the pretended affidavits. Only on the assumption of his being an illiterate and decidedly stupid person—an assumption which
the papers themselved sufficiently show to be unwarranted—could it
plausibly be contended that he innocently signed and mailed to Colorado the two printed blanks, each of which showed upon its face that
it must purport to have been "subscribed and sworn to" before a notary (a form of notary's certificate to this effect being printed immediately below the place at which he signed), while one of the two, the
" non-mineral " 'affidavit, expressly states that the person making it " is
well acquainted with the character of (the) land, and with each and
every subdivision thereof, having frequently passed over the same."
This statement was admittedly false, and Martin must of course have
known it to be false. He does not pretend that he supposed that the
papers were to be filed as unsworn declarations simply signed by him,
and without the filling in of the notary's certificate ; yet the only alter-
native is that he forwarded them with the idea that some notary should
falsely certify to their having been " subscribed and sworn to before "
him. Martin's statement is that Penn told him that Presson said " that
land could be lawfully taken in that way ; that almost daily, eastern
parties were taking claims without visiting the land, and that the visiting of the land in person by any party taking a claim was a mere
matter of form and not an actual requirement of the law." Read in
the light of all the circumstances, this seems to me to amount to this :
That on being told that " almost daily the precautions adopted by Congress were successfully nullified by the use of false certificates and declarations and pretended affidavits, he, Martin, undertook to obtain a
claim himself by fraudulently pretending to have "frequently passed
over" the land, and to have solemnly sworn to the two affidavits re
quired, within the jurisdiction contemplated by the statute. If he chose
to treat as " mere matter of form " the signing of false statements and
utilizing of false notarial certificates, and to assume that " the visiting

of the land in person," though it must be sworn to as a fact, is not an actual requirement of the law, but a merely apparent one, he did so at his own risk. If indeed such practices are of "almost daily" occurrence, it is high time that the government should show, in unambiguous fashion, that it is not safe to attempt to acquire title to public lands by merely pretended compliance with legal requirements, and the use of bogus affidavits which are neither true in fact nor really "sworn to" before the notary whose name is (criminally) used, or any other.

The decision of your office is affirmed.

___

PRIVATE CLAIM—ACT OF JULY 23, 1866.

CORNWALL v. BORACH ET AL.

The satisfaction by selection and patent of a Mexican grant of quantity, within larger out-boundaries, does not preclude the purchase, under section 7, act of July 23, 1866, of lands excluded from said grant on final survey.

The right of purchase under said section is assignable, and, in the absence of an adverse claim, extends to one who purchases and enters into possession of a tract of land, after final survey of a grant excluding said tract therefrom.

A settlement, made on land not subject thereto, does not constitute such a valid adverse claim as will defeat the right of purchase under said act.

Secretary Noble to Acting-Commissioner Stone, August 8, 1889.

I have before me the appeal of Bernard Borach from your office decision of October 21, 1886, in the cases, consolidated, of John Cornwall v. Bernard Borach, and Bernard McKenna v. Bernard Borach and William Seidell, refusing Borach's application to purchase under the seventh section of the act of July 23, 1866, lots 7, 8, 10, 11 and 14, being part of the SE. ¼ and part of the SW. ¼ of Sec. 34, according to supplemental survey, made for the purposes of said application, in T. 2 N., R. 3 W., M. D. M., San Francisco, California, land district, and holding intact Cornwall's homestead entry for the SE. ¼ of said Sec. 34.

The township plat was filed December 10, 1883. Cornwall made homestead entry for the SE. ¼ of said Sec. 34, December 13, 1883.

On January 7, 1884, Borach filed his application to purchase lots 7, 8, 10, 11 and 14 of above described supplemental survey, made for the purpose of such application, under the act of July 23, 1866 (14 Stat., 218), said application being in conflict with Cornwall's entry as to lots 7, 11 and 14.

On December 12, 1883, McKenna filed pre-emption declaratory statement for lot 1, Sec. 33, and lots 4 and 5 and the SE. ¼ of the SW. ¼ of said Sec. 34, alleging settlement September 6, 1883.

On December 10, 1883, Seidell made adjoining farm entry for lot 1, Sec. 33, and lots 4 and 5 of said Sec. 34.

A hearing was had before the local officers to determine the rights of the respective parties, Cornwall and McKenna having in the meantime advertised to offer final proof in support of their respective claims. The cases were, by agreement of all the parties, consolidated and heard together to save the expense of taking twice a large amount of testimony applicable to both cases. As a result of that hearing, which was begun September 10, 1884, and concluded January 21, 1885, the local officers, on July 24, 1885, decided that Borach was not entitled to purchase under the act of July 23, 1866, and that his application should be refused; that Cornwall should be allowed the land claimed by him under his homestead entry; that Seidell's entry should be held intact and that McKenna had not established a residence on the land covered by his filing, and that therefore his said filing should be canceled. From that decision Borach alone appealed.

Your office held that, by reason of McKenna's failure to appeal, the finding of the local officers as to his claim became final, and canceled his filing, approved the action of the local officers in holding Seidell's entry intact, rejected Borach's application to purchase and held Cornwall's entry intact, saying that in case said decision became final, his proofs would be examined and passed upon. From that decision Borach appealed.

The section of the act of July 23, 1866, under which Borach seeks to obtain title to this land provides:

That where persons in good faith and for a valuable consideration, have purchased lands of Mexican grantees, or assigns, which grants have been subsequently rejected, or where the lands have been excluded from the final survey of any Mexican grant, and have used, improved and continued in the actual possession of the same as according to the lines of their original purchase, and where no valid adverse right or title (except of the United States) exists, such purchasers may purchase the same, after having such lands surveyed under existing laws, at the minimum price established by law, upon first making proof of the facts, as required in this section, under regulations to be provided by the Commissioner of the General Land Office. (14 Stat., 218.)

In his application, filed January 7, 1884, Borach based his claim upon a purchase from the Mexican grantees or assigns of the Rancho El Sobrante. After considerable testimony had been taken in the case, he filed an amended application, basing his claim upon a purchase from the Mexican grantees or assigns of the Rancho El Sobrante, and also from the Mexican grantees or assigns of the Rancho El Pinole. At the hearing, however, testimony was taken and arguments made for and against his rights under said section, not only under the two grants above mentioned, but also under the grant of the Rancho La Boca de la Canada del Pinole, known also as the Rancho San Felipe.

This land, it seems, was at different times within the claimed boundaries of these several grants, but was upon final survey excluded from each of them. The final survey of the rancho El Pinole, approved April 12, 1866, excluded this land from that grant, the southern boundary thereof being by that survey located north of this tract. This land still remained within the claimed limits of the Rancho La Boca de la

Canada del Pinole, the north boundary of which was the south boundary of El Pinole, until excluded therefrom by final survey, approved January 4, 1869. It still remained within the claimed limits of El Sobrante until the final survey thereof, approved August 11, 1883, by which survey this tract was excluded from that grant.

The grants of El Pinole and La Boca de la Canada del Pinole were both grants of specified quantity, to be taken within certain larger exterior boundaries, and were both confirmed, surveyed and patented for the full amount of the grant. The grant of El Sobrante was for land lying between certain tracts named therein. A survey made under the order of your office included in said grant the tract now claimed by Borach. Upon appeal to this Department it was held that the grant was one by specific boundaries, and that it was limited by the boundaries of the five ranchos named in the decree of confirmation (1 L. D., 188). The survey made under the departmental decision excluded the tract in controversy from that grant.

Borach purchased the tract of land in controversy from Simon and Elias Blum, the deeds conveying the same bearing dates of May 4, and 6, 1881. The title of the Blums is traced back to the original grantees of the three grants above mentioned, as follows: Under the grant of the Rancho el Pinole the chain of title is:

1. Deed, dated January 11, 1858, from Martina Arelanes de Martinez, widow of the Mexican grantee, to Dolores Martinez de Higuera, who was daughter and heir of said Mexican grantee, conveying one half of the undivided one-eleventh part of said rancho, and also all her right, title and interest in and to a certain tract described by metes and bounds, said land being further identified by the following: "the intention being to include in these boundaries the one-eleventh part of the Pinole ranch, and being the portion now in the occupation and possession of said Dolores Martinez de Higuera."

2. Deed, dated March 15, 1864, from Pedro Higuera and his wife, Dolores Martinez de Higuera, to Simon Blum and Elias Blum, conveying one-eleventh part of said Pinole Rancho, and also all title in said rancho acquired by the grantors by virtue of the deed above mentioned, reserving, however, an undivided interest, amounting to four hundred acres.

3. Deeds from Simon and Elias Blum to Bernard Borach, conveying the land now claimed by Borach, describing the same by metes and bounds, dated May 4 and 6, 1881.

Under the grant of the Rancho La Boca de la Canada, the chain of title is:—

1. Deed, dated March 20, 1860, from Maria Manuela Valencia de Briones (the confirmee of said grant) to Encarnacion Briones de Vaca, conveying "four hundred acres of undivided land, situated, lying and being in the rancho known as the Rancho of San Felipe or Boca de la Canada del Pinole," etc.

2. Deed, dated October 31, 1867, from Teofila Baca and Encarnacion Briones de Baca, his wife, to Simon Blum and Elias Blum, conveying "the right, title and interest of the parties of the first part in and to four hundred acres of undivided land, situated, lying and being in the Rancho known as the Rancho of San Felipe or Boca de la Canada del Pinole," and described further as being the same land conveyed by the deed mentioned above.

3. Deed, dated March 20, 1860, from Maria Manuela Valencia de Briones to Simon Blum and Elias Blum, conveying all her right, title and interest in and to the Rancho Boca de la Canada del Pinole, or San Felipe, embracing and containing three square leagues of land, excepting and reserving four hundred acres.

4. Deeds from Simon and Elias Blum to Bernard Borach, conveying the land now claimed by Borach, describing the same by metes and bounds, dated May 4 and 6, 1881.

Under El Sobrante the title to an undivided interest is traced through a number of transfers from the original grantees to one John Strenzel, who, on May 2, 1878, conveyed to Gabriel Blum the undivided one-twentieth of the undivided three-two hundredths of said rancho, and on the same day Gabriel Blum conveyed to Simon Blum the tract here in dispute, describing it by metes and bounds.

In the matter of possession, it is shown that this particular tract was not in the actual possession or occupation of any one until about March 20, 1860, the date of the deed from Maria Manuel Valencia de Briones, the confirmee of the grant of La Boca de la Canada del Pinole to Encarnacion de Vaca, when Vaca or Baca, the husband of the grantee in said deed, took possession of a large tract of land, amounting in all to about four hundred acres, and including that here claimed by Borach. The land thus taken possession of by Vaca seems to have been recognized as belonging to him and the lines of his possession, although not perhaps designated by marks or monuments on the ground, yet seem to have been co-extensive with his purchase and to have been known and recognized in the neighborhood. His dwelling house was situated on the land embraced in the description contained in the deeds from Blum to Borach. He held possession of and occupied said land until October 31, 1867, the date of his deed to Simon and Elias Blum, at which time he delivered to his said grantees possession of the premises conveyed thereby. The Blums continued in the possession and occupation of the lands so conveyed, until the date of the deeds to Borach, May 4, and 6, 1881, at which time the latter took possession of the tract so conveyed, and through his tenants continued in the occupation thereof until the date of the hearing.

It thus appears that at the date of the passage of the act of July 23, 1866, the tract sought to be purchased by Borach was within the claimed limits of the Rancho La Boca de la Canada, and was also in the actual possession and occupation of the assign of the original grantee under said grant. Before the final survey of said grant, Blum, the grantor of the applicant herein, had purchased the land from the assign of the Mexican grantee for a valuable consideration, and had used, improved and continued in the possession thereof until the sale to the present applicant.

The evidence also shows that Borach, at the date of his purchase, which was for a valuable consideration, went into possession of the tract of land he now seeks title to, and had used, improved and continued in the actual possession thereof up to the date of the hearing. The applicant also filed his application within a reasonable time after the land was determined to be public land. Until August, 1883, this land was claimed as a part of the grant of El Sobrante and the question as to the validity of that claim was pending undetermined before this Department.

Cornwall settled on land adjoining this tract in 1871 and had continued to reside thereon until the date of the hearing. At the time of his settlement, the land was not public land, open to settlement, and hence he could acquire no valid claim to said land under the public land laws by virtue of that settlement. When the public survey was extended over this land it was discovered that the quarter-section upon which he had settled included a part of the land occupied by Borach. This claim of Cornwall's does not constitute such a valid adverse claim as would under the statute operate to defeat Borach's right to purchase.

I am of opinion that Borach, as purchaser under the grant of the Rancho La Boca de la Canada del Pinole, has brought himself within the provisions of the statute, and it is therefore unnecessary to discuss his rights under the other grants mentioned.

It was formerly held that "where a Mexican grant is of quantity within larger exterior boundaries, and the claimant has selected and had patented to him the quantity granted and confirmed, he will not be allowed to purchase under the 7th section of the act of July 23, 1866, any of the lands not selected within the exterior boundaries of the grant." Heirs of T. Wallace More (5 C. L. O., 67). This ruling was, however, changed in the case of Hill et al. v. Wilson et al. (11 C. L. O. 151). In the opinion, passing upon a motion for review in the latter case, it was said, after referring to the ruling in the More case: "But at the October, 1878, term of the supreme court, the ruling was overthrown by the decision in the case of Hosmer v. Wallace (97 U. S., 575)." The ruling allowing the purchase under such grants was adhered to and the motion for review denied. Hill et al. v. Wilson et al. (11 C. L. O., 204).

The question as to whether a party, who purchases and enters into the possession of a tract of land after the final survey of the grant excluding the land, can be permitted to purchase under the seventh section of the act of July 23, 1866, was considered and decided in the affirmative in the case of Welch v. Molino et al. (7 L. D., 210).

For the reasons herein given and under the authority of the decisions above cited, your said office decision is reversed, and the application of Borach is allowed.

The homestead entry of Cornwall will be canceled as to that portion of the land covered thereby and included in Borach's application to purchase. The proof heretofore offered by Cornwall has not been considered and passed upon in your office, and it is therefore returned to your office for proper disposition.

RAILROAD GRANT—ACTS OF JUNE 22, 1874, AND APRIL 21, 1876.

MJOEN v. ST. PAUL, MINNEAPOLIS & MANITOBA RY. CO.

Rights that attach by definite location are absolute until a forfeiture has been declared.

The company did not accept the conditions imposed by the act of June 22, 1874, hence said act did not become operative as against the company, or confer any rights upon settlers prior thereto.

In the absence of an entry, made under the permission of the Land Department, the protection accorded by section 3, act of April 21, 1876, is not applicable.

Secretary Noble to Acting Commissioner Stone, August 8, 1889.

I am in receipt of your report of July 31st last upon the application of Iver H. Mjoen, asking that the St. Paul, Minneapolis and Manitoba Railway Company (St. Vincent Extension) be required to relinquish and reconvey to the United States the E. ½ of the NW. ¼, the SW. ¼ of the NE. ¼, and lot 1, in Sec. 25, T. 148 N., R. 49 W., 5th P. M., Crookston, Minnesota, under the provisions of the act of March 3, 1887, alleging that he settled upon the land November 15, 1873, as a qualified pre-emptor, and that it was his intention to claim and did claim the right to enter the same under the pre-emption laws then; that he has resided upon the land with his family continuously from date of settlement, and that he has improvements thereon exceeding in value the sum of $1800.

He claims that the selection, certification and patenting of said lands to the railway company was illegal and erroneous, upon the ground that the line of railway opposite the land had not been completed at the date of selection and certificate of the governor, and that the period prescribed by the statute for the completion of the line expired December 3, 1873. He bases his claim upon the act of June 22, 1874 (18 Stat., 203). Said act is as follows:

That the provisions of the act of Congress approved March third, eighteen hundred and seventy three, entitled "An act for the extension of time to the St. Paul and Pacific Railroad Company for the completion of its roads," be, and the same are hereby revived and extended until the third day of March, A. D. eighteen hundred and seventy-six, and no longer upon the following conditions: That all rights of actual settlers, and their grantees who have heretofore in good faith entered upon and actually resided on any of said lands prior to the passage of this act, or who otherwise have legal rights in any of such lands shall be saved and secured to such settlers or such other persons in all respects the same as if said lands had never been granted to aid in the construction of the said lines of railroad.

Sec. 2. That the company taking the benefit of this act shall before acquiring any rights under it, by a certificate made and signed by the president and a majority at least of the directors, and sealed with the corporate seal, accept the conditions contained in this act, and file such acceptance in the Department of the Interior for record and preservation.

It appears from your report that the map of definite location of the road opposite the land in question was accepted December 19, 1871. The tracts were selected November 28, 1873, certified April 30, 1874, and patented January 14, 1875, and such action was taken upon the certificate of the governor, made November 22, 1873, that that portion of the railway opposite this land had been completed.

It is asserted by the applicant that the selection was made prior to the completion of the road, but he does not allege that the road was not completed at date of certification, which was prior to the date of the act.

The first question to be determined in this case is, whether the act of June 22, 1874, declared a forfeiture of lands within the limits of any uncompleted portion of said road in favor of settlers and their grantees, residing on said lands prior to the passage of said act.

In the case of Kemper v. St. Paul and Pacific Railroad Company (2 Copp's L. L., 805), Secretary Chandler held that as the company did not accept the conditions of the act, it therefore never became operative against the company, and conferred no rights upon the settlers. The theory upon which this decision is based is evidently this, that if the company had accepted the terms and conditions of the act, the grant as to the uncompleted portion would not be subject to forfeiture until March 3, 1876, but that if the company failed to accept the terms and conditions of the act, the grant was then subject to forfeiture at any time, and if Congress failed to forfeit the grant, it would be protected under the doctrine laid down by the supreme court in Schulenberg v. Harriman (21 Wall., 44), and the rights of the company as against settlers upon the land prior to the passage of the act of June 22, 1874, would be the same as if said act had not been passed.

It does not appear that the railway company accepted the terms and conditions of the act, and for this reason I am of the opinion that the ruling of Secretary Chandler, in the case above referred to, is decisive of the question now presented for consideration.

The right of the road under this grant attached to the land in question absolutely, upon the filing of map of definite location, December 19, 1871, and must so continue until a forfeiture has been declared.

No forfeiture having been declared, the settlement of Mjoen, made November 15, 1873, did not affect the right of the company. Nor is he protected by the third section of the act of April 21, 1876, because no entry had been allowed by the Land Department of said land. Nor do

I see how the act of the Legislature of Minnesota, approved March 1, 1877 (Laws of Minnesota, 257), has any bearing upon the question. That act forfeited the rights of the road opposite the uncompleted portion of the road at the date of the act, and there is no pretence that the road opposite this tract was not completed at that time.

For the reasons above stated, I concur in the d cision of your office, that he is not entitled to relief under the act of March 3, 1887. I therefore deny the prayer of the petitioner.

DESERT ENTRY COMPACTNESS.

FREDERICK A. BACON.

The existence of prio adjacent entries, and the topography of the country, must be taken into consideration in determining the question of compactness.

Secretary Noble to Acting Commissioner Stone, August 9, 1889.

I have considered the case arising upon the appeal of Frederick A. Bacon from your office decision of October 26, 1885, suspending his desert land entry, No. 2183, for the NE. ¼ of the SW. ¼, the S. ½ of the SE. ¼, and the SW. ¼ of Sec. 21, the E. ½ of the NE. ¼, the NW. ¼, and the N. ½ of the SW. ¼, of Sec. 28, T. 49, R. 62, Cheyenne land district, Wyoming Territory.

Said entry was suspended by your office for lack of compactness.

The principal limitations imposed by the desert land act are (1) as to quantity, and (2) as to shape. As to the quantity, only six hundred and forty acres are permitted to be entered by one person; this is to prevent such lands from being monopolized for a few to the exclusion of others who might desire to obtain possession on the same terms. As to shape, the entry must be compact; this to prevent the earlier comers from selecting the most eligible lands to the disadvantage of those who might follow—as by entering a narrow strip along a stream, thereby excluding others from access thereto. Not only the letter of the statute, but these primary purposes thereof, should be kept in view in the administration of the desert land act.

The entry in question in this case would appear at first glance to be far from compact. But a careful examination discloses the fact that this is a peculiar and exceptional case. It does not in any respect violate any purpose of the law. It is within the limitation as to quantity, since it contains but six hundred acres. As to shape it is simply as nearly compact as it possibly can be under the circumstances. The departure from compactness results from the fact that, prior to Bacon's application, one Carey had made pre-emption filing of a tract on the south, and one Thorpe had made timber culture entry of a tract on the north. Nor can this irregularity of shape now be cured in any way. Not by omitting the five eastern forties and taking land on the west of the present entry in lieu thereof, for the claimant swears, and the plats and field notes of your office show, that a mountain spur rises at this point, to such an elevation that it can not be irrigated by waters from the stream flowing through the tract entered, which have their source in the immediate vicinity. For the same reason no change can be made to extend the entry in the opposite direction. Inasmuch, therefore, as the entry conforms fully to the spirit of the law, and to the letter thereof as closely as possible in view of the prior entries of Carey and Thorpe, and of the topography of the surrounding country—being, as directed by circular instructions of March 1, 1884, (p. 35,) "as nearly in the form of a technical section as the situation of the land in its relations to other lands will admit," and not "lying in a line so as to form a narrow strip," or " running along the margin of a stream "—I reverse your decision, and direct that the entry be allowed.

<hr>

PRACTICE—APPEAL—RULE 102 OF PRACTICE.

EMMERT *v.* JORDAN.

An appeal, taken in the name of the "heirs" of the entryman, is defective in the absence of proof showing the death of the entryman, the names of the heirs, and the parties taking said appeal.

First Assistant Secretary Chandler to Acting Commissioner Stone, August 10, 1889.

On February 25, 1880, Hugh Jordan made timber culture entry for the NE. ¼ of section 14 T. 99 N., R. 40 W., Des Moines land district, Iowa.

On December 10, 1885, Harris L. Emmert filed his contest affidavit against the said entry, charging that Jordan "did not plant and cultivate the required number of trees, seeds or cuttings on said tract during the years 1882, 1883, 1884 and 1885 and that the number of trees required by law to be planted are not on said claim."

Hearing on contest was appointed for February 24, 1886, but changed by stipulation to April 15, 1886. The local officers found for the entryman. Contestant appealed. Your office by decision dated May 14, 1888, reversed the action of the local officers and held Jordan's entry for cancellation. From this decision " the heirs of Hugh Jordan " instituted an appeal.

The contestant now moves this Department for the dismissal of said appeal because " this contest was against Hugh Jordan, whose testimony was given on the record as a living witness, and no change of parties has been made of record, and no suggestion of the death of said Jordan has been made of record so far as contestant or his counsel are advised."

The record fails to show the death of the entryman. Before acting upon the appeal, of "the heirs of Hugh Jordan" due proof of the latter's death should be before this Department. The appellants styling themselves as aforesaid omitted to disclose on oath the nature of their interests. See Rule 102 of the Rules of Practice.

The appeal is therefore defective in this regard; but I am not inclined to dismiss said appeal at this time. The parties representing themselves as "the heirs of Hugh Jordan" will be required to file in this department within thirty days from notice hereof a statement under oath giving the names of the parties taking this appeal, within the same time they will be required to file satisfactory proof of the death of said Jordan, giving the date thereof, and giving also the names of all his heirs. If such proof shall be filed the appeal will be further considered, otherwise it must be dismissed.

RAILROAD GRANT—INDEMNITY WITHDRAWAL—SETTLEMENT RIGHT.

SOUTHERN PAC. R. R. CO. v. MEYER.

A filing for land included within a prior indemnity selection should not be recorded until final disposition of said selection.

A settlement right, acquired after revocation of an indemnity withdrawal, is superior to a subsequent selection under the grant.

Acting Secretary Chandler to Acting Commissioner Stone, August 10, 1889.

I have considered the appeal of the Southern Pacific Railroad Company from the decision of your office, dated May 26, 1888, holding for cancellation its selection of the SE.¼ of the SE. ¼ of Sec. 13, T. 6 N., R. 5 W., S. B. M., Los Angeles, California.

Said selection of said tracts was made on October 7, 1887, under the act of Congress, approved July 27, 1866 (14 Stat., 292).

On November 1, 1887, Charles Meyer filed his pre-emption declaratory statement (No. 4843) for said land, alleging settlement thereon September 6, 1887.

On February 10, 1888, the register gave notice by publication of the claimant's intention to make final proof before the register and receiver, at the local office, on March 16, same year.

On February 11, 1887, as appears by the affidavit of William E. Savage, the attorney of said company was served with a true copy of said notice of intention to make final proof. On the day fixed for making said final proof, the attorney for said company filed in the local office its protest against the application to make final proof, for the following reasons: (1) That the land is in an odd numbered section within the indemnity belt reserved for said company on March 22, 1867, under said act of Congress, upon the filing of the map of definite location in your office on January 3, 1867. (2) That said company has fully complied with the requirements of said act of Congress, and that said indemnity withdrawal is still in full force and effect, and that the order of the Secretary of the Interior, dated August 29, 1887 (6 L. D., 93), " was and is null and void and of no effect." (3) That said company on October 7, 1887, duly selected all of said section, and is legally entitled to the land in question, and, if said Meyer is permitted to make entry of said land, the company will be forced to contest the entry in the Department, and, if patent shall be issued thereon, also in the courts of the country. (4) That said tract is within the granted limits of the grant to the Atlantic and Pacific R. R. Company, and, consequently, it was not included within the order of revocation.

The final proof was made as advertised, and it shows that the pre-emptor settled as alleged, and that he has fully complied with the requirements of the pre-emption laws and the departmental regulations thereunder, relative to settlement, inhabitancy and improvements, the latter being valued at from five to eight hundred dollars.

The record shows that Meyer filed his declaratory statement on November 1st, instead of October 7th, as stated in said decision of your office. At that time the selection of the company was of record. The local officers ought not to have recorded said filing, until the selection had been disposed of. While this is true, yet since it clearly appears that Meyer's settlement was prior to said selection, that he offered to file for the land within the time required by law (R. S. 2265), and his filing was accepted by the local officers; also that the pre-emptor has fully complied with the requirements of the law as aforesaid, it is clearly within the power of the Department, and it is its duty to hold that the pre-emptor has the prior right, his settlement having been made prior to the selection. Lee v. Johnson (116 U. S., 48).

In the case of the Atlantic and Pacific Railroad Company (6 L. D., Op., p. 91), Mr. Secretary Lamar prescribed the procedure to be observed by the company and parties offering to file and enter lands within the indemnity limits of the withdrawal, which by said decision was revoked. The Secretary said:

As to the lands covered by unapproved selections, applications to make filings and entries thereon may be received, noted and held subject to the claim of the company, of which claim the applicant must be distinctly informed, and memoranda thereof entered upon his papers. Whenever such application to file or enter is presented, alleging upon sufficient *prima facie* showing that the land is, from any cause, not subject to the company's right of selection, notice thereof will be given to the proper representative of the company, which will be allowed thirty days after service of said notice within which to present objections to the allowance of such filing or entry . . . . . The order of revocation herein directed shall take effect immediately . . . . . it being the intention of this order, that as against actual settlement hereafter made, the orders of the Department withdrawing said lands shall no longer be an obstacle.

The main objection urged by the company in its protest is, that the order of revocation is a nullity, and that the land continued in a state of reservation for the benefit of said company.

It is not deemed necessary, or advisable, to review the action of the

Department in revoking the indemnity withdrawal. The order was made after due notice and careful consideration of the arguments presented by able counsel in behalf of the railroad companies, and no good reason has been offered to show that the order of revocation was not legally and duly issued. This being so, it necessarily follows that the settlement of Meyer was legal and his right must be held to be superior to the claim of the company. Northern Pacific R. R. Co. *v.* Waldon (7 L. D., 182); Central Pacific R. R. Co. *v.* Doll (8 L. D., 355).

The objection that the land is within the granted limits of the grant to the Atlantic and Pacific Railroad Company is without force, for that company has made no objection to the allowance of said final proof. It follows, therefore, that the decision of your office, holding for cancellation the selection of said land by said company, was correct. It is accordingly affirmed.

———

PRACTICE—INTERLOCUTORY ORDER—APPEAL.

HORN *v.* BURNETT.

Prior to final action in a case pending before the local office, it is within the discretion of the register and receiver to re-open said case for the submission of additional testimony.

An appeal will not lie from an interlocutory order of the local office.

Notice of an appeal from the local office should be duly served upon the appellee.

First Assistant Secretary Chandler to Acting Commissioner Stone, August 10, 1889.

I have considered the case of Charles Horn *v.* James Burnett, involving their respective claims to the SW. ¼ of section 14, T. 135, R. 55, Fargo land district, Dakota Territory.

It appears that James Burnett had made homestead entry for the said land; the entry was canceled in the local office August 18, 1884, by virtue of the decision of this Department dated August 6, 1884, in the case of Titus *v.* Burnett.

On August 21, 1884, Charles Horn made homestead entry for the said land; on October 6, the same year, James Burnett filed his pre-emption declaratory statement on the land, alleging settlement August 18, 1884, the date of the cancellation of his homestead entry.

Charles Horn, on June 11, 1885, made application to contest Burnett's pre-emption claim, which was refused by the local office. From this action Horn appealed; your office, September 16, 1885, sustained Horn's appeal and directed the local officers to proceed with the hearing for which he had applied.

The local officers appointed January 5, 1886, for the day of hearing, and Burnett was duly served with notice thereof. At the hearing on that day Horn appeared personally and was represented by his attorney. Burnett was not present, his attorney entered his appearance, then left the place of trial.

The testimony offered by Horn was taken and the case held over until 3 o'clock p. m., the same day, for the defendant or his attorney to appear. The defendant or his attorney not appearing within that time, the local officers entered of record that "the case is closed."

On February 25, 1886, Burnett's attorney on due notice to the opposite party moved the local officers for an order allowing "the defendant to introduce testimony in his own behalf." The motion was founded on affidavits of Burnett and the individual members of the firm of attorneys, employed by him in his defense. It appears from the affidavit of Burnett that he mistook the day set for the hearing supposing it to be January 6, instead of January 5; that he was not intentionally absent at the hearing; that he has read the testimony introduced in behalf of Horn; that (particularly referring to part of the said testimony) "he finds statements which are false and statements where part of the facts are concealed." He further stated that "at the date of the cancellation of said entry (August 18, 1884), and during the interim between said cancellation and the filing of Horn's said homestead entry, this tract was this defendant's only place of residence" and that he continued his residence on and cultivation of the said land "for the purpose of claiming said tract under the pre-emption clause."

From the affidavits of the said attorneys it appears among other matters, that the member of the firm who had this case in charge had neglected to note the case on their office docket, that he at time of hearing was away from home; that the other member of the firm was called upon by plaintiff's attorney on the morning of the day of hearing and told that Mr. Thompson, the absent member and he had agreed about the facts, and that this statement and the non-appearance of Burnett induced him to think his appearance in person at the trial unnecessary. The affidavits of plaintiff, his attorney and a Mr. Jones, filed in opposition to the motion deny the statements made by the said defendant's attorney regarding the conversation had in the morning of the day of trial. They say that the said attorney deliberately stayed away from the trial, because as he declared, the result of the case depended solely upon the fact whether Burnett had any improvements on the land and that he merely came to this hearing, had the appearance of his firm as the attorneys of defendant entered on the record, and informed plaintiff's attorney that he would not stay to cross-examine the witnesses.

Decision on this motion was rendered by the register of the said land office March 11, 1886, in form as follows: "the claimant's application is allowed, his default opened and a further hearing ordered. Such new hearing is set for April 15, 1886, etc."

The further hearing was continued "by stipulation" to June 15, 1886.

On April 6, 1886, Horn's appeal from said order was filed, no notice of this appeal seems to have been served upon the opposite party. On

April 16, 1886, Burnett filed a motion for the dismissal of the appeal to
be heard before the local officers April 27, 1886.   This notice so far as
the records show, was never presented.   On May 7, 1886, your office
upon the application of counsel for Horn, directed the local officers to
suspend proceedings and send up the record of the case.   The record
having been transmitted as required, your office, considering Horn's
appeal, on June 28, 1886, by a decision of that date, sustained his appeal and returning the testimony to the local officers required them to
render a decision thereon.

From this decision of your office Burnett appealed to this department, on the grounds :

1st. That register's order of March, 1886, was interlocutory and that no appeal from
it could lie.

2nd. That no notice of such appeal was served upon the defendant or his counsel.

3rd. That the proceedings, after the motion to re-open the case before the register
had been determined, were irregular and against the law and practice of all courts of
justice.

Before the institution of the said appeal the local officers, in accordance with the instruction of your office, determined the case upon the
merits, and on June 27, 1887, retransmitted the papers in the case, together with their joint decision in favor of plaintiff.   Burnett appealed.
Your office, by decision dated April 23, 1888, affirmed the action of the
local officers and held Burnett's declaratory statement for cancellation.
Burnett again instituted an appeal to this department and the whole
case is now before me for consideration.

Regarding your office decision of June 28, 1886, I am of the opinion
that the same is erroneous.   Burnett made his motion to be allowed to
introduce testimony for the defence at a time when the case was still
undecided by the local officers; they had rendered no decision and their
report was not forwarded to the General Land Office; the case was still
before them and it was resting in their discretion, whether to allow
more testimony to go in or not.   See rule 72 of the Rules of Practice.
I do not think that in this instance the discretional power of the local
officers was abused.   Besides the order granting to Burnett the privilege to put in his testimony was interlocutory, it was not a final action
or decision within the meaning of Rule 43, of the Rules of Practice.
See Jones v. Campbell et al. (7 L. D., 404).

Another reason why your said office decision should be set aside is
that notice of Horn's appeal from the action of the register was not
served upon the appellee as is required by Rule 46, of the Rules of Practice.   Burnett, I think, has not waived this objection by filing a motion
for the dismissal of such appeal, because he based his motion " upon
the rules and practice of the local office as well as those of the General
Land Office."   It seems, therefore, though it is not clearly expressed,
that this defect, in part at least, was the basis of Burnett's motion.

Again, it is the object of the Department to give parties who are interested in controversies of this character an opportunity to be fully

and fairly heard, untrammeled by technical rulings and construction, to the end that justice may be meted out upon full investigation of the facts.

In this case it is evident that the rulings of the register and receiver were in consonance with equitable principles and fair dealing, and should be encouraged so long as they do not lose sight of the law.

The conclusion of this Department therefore is that your said office decision of June 28, 1886, should be reversed and the papers transmitted to the local officers with the direction that they accord to Burnett the privilege of introducing testimony on the part of the defence in this case, that a day be set for the taking of such testimony, that due notice thereof be given to both parties, and that Horn may also introduce further testimony, direct and on rebuttal, if he so chooses.

This order necessarily sets aside all proceedings subsequent to Burnett's appeal from your office decision of June 28, 1886.

PRACTICE—CONTINUANCE—HOMESTEAD CONTEST.

SMITH v. JOHNSON.

A party will not be permitted to question the regularity of a continuance which was procured at his own instance.

The sufficiency of a charge, as laid in the affidavit of contest, will not be considered if the question was not raised before the submission of testimony.

In contest proceedings under Section 2297, R. S., it is not essential that "abandonment" for more than six months "immediately preceding" the contest should be specifically charged.

Proof that the homestead settler has actually changed his residence, or abandoned the land for more than six months "at any time," warrants an order of cancellation.

First Assistant Secretary Chandler to Acting Commissioner Stone, August 12, 1889.

The case of Marthin P. Smith v. John A. Johnson is before me on appeal by the latter from your office decision of June 18, 1888, holding for cancellation his homestead entry made May 22, 1883, for the NE. ¼ of Sec. 12, T. 145 N., R. 68 W., Bismarck, Dakota.

The record shows that on April 9, 1886, Smith initiated contest against the entry of Johnson, charging that the latter had " wholly abandoned" the land in question; that he had "changed his residence therefrom for more than six months since making entry," and that the land had not been " settled upon and cultivated . . . . . as required by law."

Upon this contest a hearing was ordered by the local officers, to take place before them on June 5, 1886, and it was provided that the testimony should be taken before one T. J. C. Wych, a notary public, at his office in Carrington, Dakota, on May 28, 1886. Notice was given accordingly, and on the day fixed for the taking of testimony both parties appeared before the notary, in person and by counsel. On that day the contestant submitted the whole of his testimony, but the claimant introduced part only of the evidence in his behalf; and thereupon, at the instance of the claimant, and by stipulation of the parties by their attorneys, made in writing, the further taking of the testimony was continued until June 15, 1886, to be resumed at ten o'clock on that day, at the same place and before the same notary; and it was further stipulated that the hearing before the local officers should take place on June 21, 1886, instead of the time originally fixed.

On the day thus agreed upon for the further taking of the testimony, the parties again appeared before the notary, and the claimant examined other witnesses in his behalf, both on that day and the following day, to which the case was again adjourned. No further testimony was introduced by the contestant and the case was thereupon closed.

The evidence was returned to the local office June 21, 1886, the date at which it was stipulated, as aforesaid, that the hearing at that office should take place, and on that date the parties again appeared, in person and by their attorneys. The local officers, upon consideration of the testimony, found that the land embraced in the entry in question had "never been occupied as the residence of the claimant, his evidence showing that eleven nights was the extent of his occupation at night in nearly three years," and recommended that said entry be canceled.

From this decision the claimant appealed. Various errors were alleged in the appeal, which amounted, in substance, to a contention by appellant, (1) that the local officers acted improperly and without jurisdiction, in considering the testimony in the case, when the same had not been returned to them by the referee (the notary) until after the day fixed in the original notice, for the hearing before them; (2) that the decision was against the law and the evidence in the case, on the merits, and (3) that the affidavit of contest, on its face, failed to state a cause of action.

On consideration of this appeal your office sustained the action below, as to the merits of the controversy, and held against the appellant on the technical points raised.

The appeal which brings the case here simply refers to and adopts the assignment of errors set forth in the original appeal from the finding of the local officers.

These alleged errors, as herein condensed in form, without alteration of substance, will be considered in the order in which they are above stated.

There is nothing, in my judgment, in the question of jurisdiction raised by the appellant. The stipulation under which the further taking of testimony was continued by the notary to a time beyond the date originally set for the hearing before the local officers was made, as appears from the record, at the instance of the claimant, and as a favor to him, in order to allow him time to secure further testimony in his behalf,

It was also accompanied by the further stipulation that the hearing before the local officers should be had on June 21, 1886, which, in effect, amounted to an agreement by the parties, that such hearing should be continued by the local officers from the date originally fixed, until the date named in the stipulation. In addition to this, it is stated by the contestant's attorney, in an affidavit dated August 24, 1886, and filed with contestant's reply to said original appeal, in which statement he is corroborated by the affidavit of the notary before whom the testimony was taken, that when said stipulation for a continuance was made, as stated, it was further agreed by the parties that the same should be sent to the land office at Bismarck, by the claimant's attorney, "in order that an order for continuance might be issued;" and there is no denial of the statements in these affidavits. Now, if it be conceded that this written stipulation of the parties was forwarded to the local officers, as agreed, and that, acting thereon, they continued the case in accordance therewith, then it can not be said that there was any irregularity in the proceedings before them, as touching the point now under consideration. There is nothing in the record, however, to show whether the stipulation was forwarded in accordance with said agreement, or not or whether a continuance of the case was ordered by the local officers in pursuance thereof; but the fact remains, nevertheless, that the contest was not dismissed by them on June 5, 1886, which it would have been their duty to do, in the absence of a return of the testimony, if no continuance were asked for by either party, and none ordered; but the same was allowed to remain on the docket until June 21, 1886, when it was taken up and considered in the presence of the parties and their attorneys, and without objection from any source, on the testimony then returned, the same as though it had been regularly continued to that day. I think it must be presumed, therefore, in the absence of any satisfactory or positive showing to the contrary, that the action of the local officers in the premises was in all respects regular.

It is stated in your office decision that the action of the notary in continuing the case beyond the day originally set for the hearing, "was decidedly irregular," and that because thereof, there had been "grave irregularities in the taking of the testimony." But whether this be so or not, in view of the special circumstances of this case, it is unnecessary now to consider, inasmuch as such irregularities, if any in fact existed, must be held to have been cured by the subsequent proceedings had in the case before the local officers, in the presence of the parties and their attorneys, and without objection being then raised.

Moreover, under the facts in this case, the claimant, in my judgment, would have been estopped from raising the question of such irregularities, even at that time, if he had attempted to do so. The continuance was had at his instance and for his sole benefit, to enable him to secure further testimony in behalf of his entry. By reason of the favor thus granted him, he did procure other witnesses, whose evidence was taken and filed in the record. If the action of the notary in the premises were irregular, it does not lie with the claimant to raise the question of such irregularity, nor can he do so with avail in this case. To hold otherwise would simply be allowing him to take advantage of his own wrong. This disposes of the first question presented.

*   *   *   *   *   *   *

Upon the last question presented by the appeal, namely, that the affidavit of contest fails to state a cause of action, it would be sufficient for the purposes of this decision to say that it is too late to raise the question for the first time, on appeal. If the affidavit be defective on its face, such defect should have been taken advantage of at the hearing, and before the testimony was introduced; and the question not having been raised at that time, such defect, if any in fact existed, must be considered, for obvious reasons, as having been waived.

But I do not think the objection well taken, even if it were raised in time. The affidavit of contest, after setting forth, the entry by the claimant, of the tract in question, and describing the same, further alleges, that the claimant "has wholly abandoned said tract; that he has changed his residence therefrom for more than six months since making said entry; that said tract is not settled upon and cultivated by said party as required by law." The objection now raised is that the affidavit should have charged abandonment for more than six months "immediately preceding" the commencement of the contest. This is not necessary. The affidavit is framed, as touching the charge of abandonment, in accordance with the provisions of section 2297 of the Revised Statutes, and is in this particular sufficiently specific. Under said section 2297, if it be shown that the homestead settler "has actually changed his residence, or abandoned the land for more than six months *at any time,*" it is provided that the land shall revert to the government. Construing this section, the Department has held that the settler, after having abandoned his claim, for more than six months, may, by re-establishing his residence thereon before the intervention of an adverse right, cure the default, so far as the government is concerned, and by subsequent compliance with the law carry his entry to patent. But when the abandonment " for more than six months at any time" after entry, is once proven, it thereafter rests with the claimant to show that he has cured the consequent default, by re-establishing his residence on the land, and subsequently complying with the law, and the burden of proof in this respect rests with him. If he fails to show this, the default is complete. It is not necessary, therefore, that the affidavit of contest should specifically charge abandonment for more than six months immediately preceding the filing thereof. It is sufficient if the charge be laid substantially in conformity with the provision of the statute, and such being the case with the affidavit in question, there is nothing in the objection raised against the same.

Moreover, the further allegation in the affidavit that the " tract is not

settled upon and cultivated . . . . . . as required by law," is a sufficient charge to have sustained the contest, even if the objection raised,
as to the charge of abandonment, were well taken.

In accordance with the views herein expressed, your office decision
holding claimant's entry for cancellation is affirmed.

DESERT ENTRY—FINAL PROOF.

INSTRUCTIONS.

Under desert entries made prior to the circular regulations of June 27, 1887, the final
proof will be held sufficient if in compliance with the regulations in force at the
time the initial entry was made.

*Acting Secretary Chandler to Acting Commissioner Stone, August 13,
1889.*

Upon a reconsideration of the question submitted by your communication of the 17th ultimo, inquiring whether persons who had made entry
under the desert land act prior to the issuance of the circular of June
27, 1887 (5 L. D., 708), but who have offered proof thereon since that
date, shall be required, in making such proof, to comply with the provisions of said circular, or whether their proof shall be deemed sufficient in case it complies with the regulations existing at the time
when the entries were made, I am of the opinion that said rule should
not be applied to such cases. It seems to me that to require the entryman to attend in person at the local office at the time of making final
proof would be to impose additional burdens that were not required by
the rules and regulations of the Department when said entry was made.
I therefore concur in your suggestion that all original entries made prior
to the issuance of said circular of June 27, 1887, should be adjudicated
according to the regulations then existing. The decision of July 23,
1889, is therefore hereby revoked.

REPAYMENT—PRE-EMPTION ENTRY.

PETER F. BINGHAM.

Where there is no concealment or attempt at fraud, and the local office holds the final
proof sufficient, repayment should be allowed, if the entry is subsequently canceled for the insufficiency of said proof.

*First Assistant Secretary Chandler to Acting Commissioner Stone, August
13, 1889.*

I have considered the case of Peter F. Bingham, on his appeal from
your office decision of July 11, 1888, rejecting his application for the
repayment of the purchase price paid by him in his pre-emption cash

entry for E. ½, NE. ¼, Sec. 6, T. 15 S., R. 49 W., Pueblo, Colorado, land district.

Bingham filed his declaratory statement April 13, 1883, alleging settlement April 2, 1883. He presented his final proof and was permitted to make cash entry of the said land June 20, 1884.

On October 26, 1886, your office having reached said entry for patent discovered that claimant had advertised to make proof before the local office on June 16, 1884, but that instead of so doing his papers showed that the testimony of witnesses had been taken April 30, 1884, before John W. Williams, a notary public, at a county distant from the local office.

For that reason and because the final proof was not sufficiently definite in regard to the continuity of his residence, his entry was by your office letter " G " of October 26, 1886, held for cancellation but he was allowed ninety days in which to file corroborated affidavit showing definitely the time he resided on the land during the six months immediately preceding final proof; and he was also required to make republication and posting of notice.

Bingham instead of attempting to make new proof, filed a relinquishment of his said entry, and made application for repayment of the purchase money.

By your office letter of July 21, 1887, the said entry was canceled upon said relinquishment, and it was stated that his application for repayment would be made the subject of another letter.

By your office letter " M " of July 11, 1888, Bingham's application for repayment was rejected, the reason assigned being as follows:

If Bingham had complied with the law under which he made his entry, the government could and would have confirm ed the same, but the laches were on his part and in such cases, the law does not provide for the return of the purchase money. The application is, therefore, denied.

Although claimant's witnesses on final proof were sworn by a notary public at a point distant from the local office, claimant himself made affidavit before the register, and he made not the slightest attempt at concealment of his conduct in regard to residence. In reply to the usual question in regard to the continuity of his residence he answered as follows:

I am a sheep-raiser, have one thousand lambs and thirty-seven hundred old head. Owing to my business, I have been unable to live all the time on the place, so that I have been off and on all the time since settlement. The place itself will not support my sheep more than three months at a time and I have had to take them elsewhere in order to keep them properly, and return again after the lapse of several months when the grass has had a chance to grow. That country is very barren and sandy and the food for stock is all the time at the most scarce. The grass is short and thin on the ground. The ground is unfit for cultivation. I am a *bona fide* settler, and am desirous of complying entirely with the law so far as it is possible so to do.

The claimant in his application for repayment states upon oath that as his residence for the six months next preceding his entry had not been continuous he could not make new proof of residence; that he then attempted to make continuous residence for six months upon the said land but was unable to remain there on account of sickness occasioned by drinking the water, which in that vicinity is unfit for use being strongly impregnated with alkali; that his brother who had a claim in the immediate vicinity lived thereon for about eighteen months when he died from disease caused by drinking said water, and that he is convinced that a longer stay on his claim would on said account have been at the sacrifice of his life or health, and that for this reason he left the land and relinquished the same to the United States.

There being no concealment or attempt at fraud and the testimony on final proof having been thought sufficient by the local officers repayment should be made. Oscar T. Roberts (8 L. D., 423), Saml. K. Paul (7 L. D., 474); Geo. J. Ruskrudge (id., 509).

Your said decision is accordingly reversed.

REPAYMENT—COMMUTED HOMESTEAD.

TRUMAN L. HODGE.

The fact that a homesteader was entitled to take the land under Section 2291, R. S., will not authorize repayment if he elects to make a commuted cash entry therefor.

Acting Secretary Chandler to Acting Commissioner Stone, August 13, 1889.

This is an application filed by Truman L. Hodge asking for repayment of two hundred dollars, alleged excess of payment made upon the SE. ¼ of the SE. ¼ of Sec. 6, T. 12 N., R. 5 W., Helena land district, Montana.

The facts are as follows: On May 27, 1879, Hodge filed pre-emption declaratory statement for the E. ½ of the SE. ¼ of said Sec. 6; and on the 12th of December, 1881, he transmuted said pre-emption claim into a homestead entry—at the same time embracing in said homestead entry the W. ½ of said SE. ¼, lying contiguous.

On December 17, 1885, after a residence of over six years on the E. ½ of said SE. ¼, Hodge offered final proof; but the local officers held that as he had not resided on the W. ½ of the tract for the full period prescribed by law, his offer to make final proof was premature. Hodge at that time wanted to be allowed credit for the whole time that he had lived on the E. ½, and take it under the homestead law, and to pay for the other half under the pre-emption law; but the local officers held that, although he had resided upon one part of the tract for the period required by law, yet it was not competent for him to make homestead entry of one part and pre-emption entry of another part, when both were embraced in his homestead claim. Having made arrangements to move into Helena to educate his children, Hodge preferred to pay for all the land rather than make further compliance with the homestead law by residing upon it longer.

While it appears from the record that the local officers were in error in not permitting Hodge to prove up under the homestead law for the entire tract, he having resided on the original claim for the full period required by law, yet he was fully advised by the local officers that he would be required to reside upon the entire tract for the period of five years, or to pay the full amount for the whole if he desired to commute; and having elected to pay for the tract, and the money having been covered into the Treasury, I can discover no authority of law for the repayment of the same. The tract being within the granted limits of the Northern Pacific Railroad Company, was double minimum land, and no excess of payment was made. If Hodge were entitled to anything, he would be entitled to the whole amount paid by him; but I know of no law that would authorize repayment in this case.

The act (21 Stats., 287) provides:

. In all cases where homestead or timber-culture or desert land entries or other entries of public lands have heretofore or shall hereafter be canceled for conflict, or where, from any cause, the entry has been erroneously allowed and cannot be confirmed, the Secretary of the Interior shall cause to be paid to the person who made such entry, or to his heirs or assigns, the fees and commissions, amount of purchase money, and excesses paid upon the same upon the surrender of the duplicate receipt and the execution of a proper relinquishment of all claims to said land, whenever such entry shall have been duly canceled by the Commissioner of the General Land Office, and in all cases where parties have paid double minimum price for land which has afterwards been found not to be within the limits of a railroad land grant, the excess of one dollar and twenty-five cents per acre shall in like manner be repaid to the purchaser thereof, or to his heirs or assigns.

In this case the entry was neither "canceled for conflict" nor "erroneously allowed." On the contrary, the entry was properly allowed, but in making the same, acting under the advice of the local officers, the entryman transmuted his entry and purchased the whole tract when he was under no legal obligation to do so. Acting upon this advice, he paid no more than he should have done, as the land was properly double minimum, it being within the limits of a railroad grant. Daniel O. Tilton, 8 L. D., 368; John Cameron, 7 L. D., 436; Annie Knaggs, 9 L. D., 49.

Your office decision of March 11, 1886, is affirmed.

PRE-EMPTION RIGHTS—TIMBER CULTURE ENTRY.

WALLER v. DAVIS.

Settlement and filing do not reserve land from appropriation under the timber culture law, but operate as notice to the timber culture applicant of the pre-emptor's claim to a preferred right of purchase.

The cases of Shadduck v. Horner, and Bender v. Voss, cited and distinguished.

Acting Secretary Chandler to Acting Commissioner Stone August 14, 1889.

In the case of Frank A. Waller, timber culture entryman, v. Noah N. Davis, pre-emption claimant, involving the SW. ¼ of section 30, township 119 north, range 62 West, Huron district, Dakota Territory, the latter files a motion for review of the departmental decision therein of September 15, 1888.

The motion is upon the ground that, inasmuch as it was found in said decision, that Davis had made improvements on the land and had settled thereon with his family, and "that Waller prior to and at the time he made his timber culture entry had full knowledge of the settlement and improvement of Davis," said entry of Waller should have been canceled, and it was error in said decision to allow said entry "to remain intact, subject to the right of Davis to make final proof showing full compliance with the law in all respects." In support of the motion the cases of Shadduck v. Horner, 2 C. L. O., 133; Bender v. Voss, 2 L. D., 269, and John A. Adamson, 3 L. D., 152, are cited.

In the case of Shadduck v. Horner, it is held that the doctrine laid down in Atherton v. Fowler (6 Otto, 513) is applicable to a contest between a pre-emption and a timber culture claimant. That doctrine is, that no right of pre-emption can be established by the forcible intrusion upon and expulsion of one, who had already settled on, improved and enclosed the tract. (Doty v. Moffatt, 3 L. D., 278; Brown v. Quinlan, 1 L. D., 424.) In Shadduck v. Horner reference is made to the Commissioner's decision for a full statement of the "circumstances connected with the case," and the facts making the doctrine in Atherton v. Fowler applicable are not set forth. It appears, however, that the pre-emption claimant Horner had been in possession several years, and had improvements on the land of the value of $3,000.00, at the date of Shadduck's timber culture entry, and referring to said entry Secretary Schurz says:

When all the circumstances of this case are taken into consideration, I can not think that the entry of Shadduck was made in good faith."

In the present case, while it is found, that Waller at the date of his entry knew of the settlement and improvement of Davis, it is also said that "he may not at that time have known of Davis' acts of settlement made prior to his" (Davis') "said filing." It is not intimated that Waller's entry was not in good faith and said entry was only an entry of record, unaccompanied by acts of forcible intrusion upon and expulsion of Davis. The case of Shadduck v. Horner is therefore distinguishable from the present case. The decision in the second case cited, that of Bender v. Voss, is expressly predicated upon the ground that the timber culture entry in that case "violated" the decision of this Department in Shadduck v. Horner, and said latter decision is stated to be "that timber culture entries 'should be made upon vacant, unimproved land, not upon cultivated land covered by the valuable improvements of another and in the possession of another.'" While that statement is made *arguendo* in Shadduck v. Horner, it is, as above shown, when taken by itself and disconnected from the context and facts in that case, broader than the doctrine warranted or intended to be laid down therein. The timber culture entry of Bender in Bender *v.* Voss was not found to be in bad faith, it was simply an entry of record without (so far as the decision discloses) any element of a naked forcible trespass, as in Atherton *v.* Fowler. The prior entry of Voss was, moreover, a homestead entry, which segregated the land, and Bender's entry was subject to cancellation for that reason.

It thus appears that the timber culture entry was correctly disposed of, but not upon the ground which in fact authorized such disposition.

The correct rule in such cases is, in my opinion, indicated in the following extract from the decision in John A. Adamson, *supra*, the last case cited by the counsel for the motion:

If there is a prior claim of record to the land applied for of a nature not to be a bar to an entry, and a timber culture entry is made of that land, the entryman takes his risk of final adjudication. . . . . If he makes entry of a tract of land upon which some other person is living and has improvements, although not having a claim of record, the fact of such occupation and improvement is notice, and the entry is made at the same risk as in case of a claim of record.

The pre-emption filing of Davis was of record at the date of Waller's entry, but such filing was "of a nature not to be a bar to an entry." Land covered by a pre-emption filing is still "public land," open to settlement or entry, subject only to the preferred right of pre-emption. (Field *v.* Black, 2 L. D., 581.) The timber culture law authorizes entry thereunder to be made on "any of the public lands of the United States," and the filing of Davis was no bar to such entry on the part of Waller (ib., p. 582). The settlement and improvements of Davis were also no bar to such entry of record, but were sufficient to protect him from a "forcible intrusion." (Doty *v.* Moffatt, Brown *v.* Quinlan, and Atherton *v.* Fowler, *supra*). Davis's prior filing of record and his settlement and improvements were both notice to Waller of Davis's pre-emption claim, and Waller's entry was subject to Davis's preferred right of pre-emption, and, as is said above in the case of John A. Adamson, was "at the risk of a final adjudication" establishing Davis's pre-emption claim. It follows, that there is no error as alleged in said departmental decision, and the motion for review is denied.

PRACTICE—APPEAL—SPECIFICATIONS OF ERROR.

GROOM *v.* MISSOURI, KANSAS AND TEXAS RY. CO.

An appeal will be dismissed if notice thereof, and a copy of the specifications of error, are not duly served upon the opposite party.

First Assistant Secretary Chandler to Acting Commissioner Stone, August 15, 1889.

I have considered the case of Linzy D. Groom *v.* The Missouri Kansas and Texas Ry. Co., on appeal of the former from your office decision of April 28, 1888, rejecting his application to enter the SE. ¼, Sec. 21, T. 33 S., R. 12 E., Independence, Kansas, land district.

In your said decision you say that the land in controversy is situated

In the indemnity limits of the grant to the Missouri Kansas and Texas R. R. Co., and there appearing no adverse claims to any of the tracts, the company was allowed to select the same April 14, 1873, and they were certified to the State of Kansas for the company's benefit October 16, 1873.

The government having parted with its title this office is without authority to accept applications to enter these lands.

Your action is approved and the applications are rejected.

Groom's application to make homestead entry was made September 8, 1887, and this being rejected by the local officers appeal was taken the same day and your office by the decision complained of, affirmed that of the local officers.

The record before me does not give the date when applicant was notified of your adverse decision but his appeal was filed in this office October 4, 1888.

It is alleged in appeal that the land in controversy is included in a tract now in litigation in the United States court at Topeka, Kansas; that is not within the twenty mile indemnity limits of the grant to said railroad company; that said land was erroneously deeded said railroad company; that applicant has not exhausted his homestead right and has been in peaceable possession of said land for more than two years and has made improvements thereon with a view to making the same his home; that the auditor of the State land office at Topeka, has certified that said land was never certified to the Missouri Kansas and Texas Ry. Co., or any other corporation or individual according to law and is still a part of the public domain; that title to said land remains in the United States because no selection and approval of the same to said company has been made according to law; that said land was included in a list erroneously patented to the Missouri Kansas and Texas Ry. Co., but that it comes within the lands contemplated in an act of March 1, 1881, providing that no title should pass in certain cases, wherein it had not been intended to include such lands in the grant; that in a circular of the Interior Department dated September 6, 1887, all the indemnity lands held by the Missouri Kansas and Texas Ry. Co., were restored to the public domain and opened for settlement under the homestead laws; and that by act of 1886 all unearned lands not patented on that date were declared forfeited and were made subject to homestead entry.

An inspection of the record discloses the fact that there is no proof whatever of compliance with rules 86 and 93 of practice.

Rule 86 provides that

Notice of an appeal from the Commissioner's decision must be filed in the General Land Office and served on the appellee or his counsel within sixty days from the date of the service of notice of such decision.

Rule 93 requires that—

A copy of the notice of appeal, specification of errors, and all arguments of either party, shall be served on the opposite party within the time allowed for filing the same.

No briefs or arguments have been filed by either party.

One of the appellants specification of error is that the title to said land is involved in a suit now pending in the United States circuit court at Topeka, in a case wherein the United States is plaintiff and the Missouri Kansas and Texas Ry. Co., is defendant. If this is true all the material matters alleged in this appeal will doubtless be passed upon by the court in its final decision and it would hardly be proper for this Department by awarding claimant the right of entry to assume in advance that the decision of that court would be adverse to the said railroad company.

Appellant's entire disregard however, of the requirements of rules 86 and 93 of practice and the other rules growing out of them, is a sufficient ground for dismissing his appeal before this office.

In case of Ariel C. Harris (6 L. D., 122) this Department said—

It may be that in some cases the enforcement of these rules will work hardship. But it is better to have an uniform rule on the subject, even though hardship be done in exceptional cases, than to have no rule at all, or which is worse, to have a rule that is not enforced. Certainty in law is always to be aimed at. And though in particular cases clients may be injured through the laches of their attorneys, yet upon the whole I am convinced that the best interests of the Department will be subserved by relying upon fixed and well known rules.

The said appeal is accordingly dismissed.

PRE-EMPTION—RESIDENCE—FINAL PROOF.

GEORGE F. LUTZ.

Residence on land, and actual presence thereon are not convertible or synonymous terms; and, residence being once established, subsequent absences *animo revertendi* and for a lawful purpose not indicating an intent to abandon, do not break the continuity of such residence.

Irregularity in final proof, caused by the substitution of a witness, may be cured by new publication, giving the names of the witnesses whose testimony was accepted by the local office.

First Assistant Secretary Chandler to Acting Commissioner Stone, August 15, 1889.

By your office decision of February 14, 1888, the pre-emption cash entry of George F. Lutz for the S. E. ¼ of Sec. 12, T. 143 N., R. 66 W., was suspended, and he was required " to give new notice and to make new proof."

After due notice by publication Lutz made proof August 4, 1883, which was approved by the local officers, and, the land being double minimum, he made payment of $400 therefor, and thereupon final receipt and certificate were issued to him August 9, 1883.

About four years and a half thereafter your said office decision was rendered, suspending said entry and requiring new proof and notice upon the grounds that the proof was made " in part by a witness who was not named in the published notice, and did not show actual residence by the pre emptor."

It appears from the proof and a special affidavit filed by Lutz, that he made settlement January 1, 1883, by building a house on the claim, and from settlement to date of proof, August 4, 1883, while he was absent from the claim the greater part of the time, yet he was on it assisting in the improvements on an average of once a week, sometimes stopping two or three day, never being absent more than two weeks at any one time, and his absences were because of his employment as book-keeper in a lumber yard at Jamestown and he devoted all the time not so occupied to his claim, and said absences and employment were necessary to enable him to " secure funds to carry on the improvements he was making " on the claim ; that he had " invested all his earnings and all he possessed in said claim with the determination of creating a home for himself " and " only held the position in the lumber yard as a stepping stone to making his claim his permanent abode," and had no other home except his claim ; that in February, 1883, he bought a team and farming implements and broke fifty acres of the land, and his improvements, consisting of a house, barn, well and said breaking were of the value of $400.

In your office decision it is said " under the rules of this office a preemptor is required to show six months actual personal residence upon his claim prior to making proof." By " actual personal residence " is doubtless meant actual " presence " on the claim. It is well settled, however, that residence on land and actual presence thereon are not convertible or synonymous terms, and residence being once established subsequent absences *animo revertendi* and for a lawful purpose not indicating an extent to abandon, do not break the continuity of such residence. Patrick Manning (7 L. D., 144).

Moreover, the departmental requirement of six months actual residence before entry is for the purpose of securing " an assurance of good faith on the part of the claimant and where good faith is otherwise sufficiently established, the object of the rule is attained and a literal compliance therewith is not necessary." Edward J. Doyle (7 L. D., 3).

While Lutz's proof is deficient in not clearly showing the original establishment of residence, yet his good faith is apparent from the character and extent of his improvements and his investment in the claim of his earnings and other means to the extent of $800.00. He made a full disclosure of his absences in his proof and the special affidavit filed therewith before the local officers accepted payment for the land and issued final receipt and certificate. The proof in this case both as to residence and improvements is stronger than that in the case of James H. Marshall (3 L. D., 411), and the two cases are similar as to the facts and the principle involved. In the latter case Secretary Teller said:

I do not find any evidence of fraud in Marshall's proceedings. He was very frank in submitting the particulars as to residence and in mentioning his business at St. Paul, when he offered his final proof. If there was failure to satisfy the register and receiver of his good faith at that time, they should have held him to further residence before admitting the entry. But with the facts voluntarily stated by him, they accepted his proof. At the most it was merely deficient—not fraudulent. He took no advantage by concealment, and if error was committed it was error of the government. I cannot consent to pronounce a forfeiture against him.

The irregularity in the substitution of a witness not named in the published notice may be cured by new publication "giving the names of the witnesses whose testimony was accepted by the local officers." Sec. 4, circular July 17, 1889; Wenzel Paours (8 L. D., 475).

It is directed that such new publication be made, and, in the absence of protest, that the proof already made be accepted, and, there being no other legal objection, that the entry be passed to patent. The decision of your office is modified accordingly.

HOMESTEAD ENTRY—ADMINISTRATOR.

JOHN KAVANAUGH.

An administrator is not authorized under section 2291 of the Revised Statutes to consummate the inchoate claim of a deceased homesteader.

First Assistant Secretary Chandler to Acting Commissioner Stone, August 15, 1889.

James Curry, as administrator of the estate of John Kavanaugh, a deceased homestead entryman, appeals to this Department from the decision of your office of April 20, 1887, involving the SW. ¼, Sec. 34, T. 141 N., R. 63 W., Fargo district, Dakota Territory.

In said decision it is found that Kavanaugh "has acted in bad faith," his final proof is rejected and his entry (homestead) and final certificate are held for cancellation.

The present appeal, however, is subject to dismissal on another ground. It is taken by Curry, as administrator of the deceased entryman, and prayer is made, that the entry be permitted "to stand and the administrator allowed patent for the land." If the proof were sufficient and the entry should be permitted to stand, patent could not issue to the administrator. (Bone v. Dickerson's Heirs, 8 L. D., p. 455). As to the right of Curry, as administrator, to appeal, the only case in which the *statute* expressly clothes an administrator or executor with any authority in reference to the claim of a deceased homestead entryman is where both parents are dead leaving an infant child or children (Rev. Stat. 2292), and Kavanaugh died a single man without children. It has been decided by this Department, that an administrator is not authorized under section 2291 of the Revised Statutes to consummate the inchoate claim of a deceased homesteader (H. A. Gale, 6 L. D., 573). Section 2296 of the Revised Statutes provides that "No lands acquired under the provisions of" the homestead law "shall in any event be-

come liable to the satisfaction of any debt contracted prior to the issuing of the patent therefor." This language is broad enough to cover
all cases where patent has not issued, but conceding for argument's
sake, that, where proper proof has been made and nothing is wanting
to perfect the title, except issuance of patent, and there are no alienees,
heirs, devisees, or others authorized to take directly, the land would be
assets liable to the satisfaction of the claims of creditors of the decedent rather than revert to the government, and that under such circumstances an administrator would have the right under the general
law to intervene, by appeal to this Department, for the protection of
the creditors, still it is not shown in this case, either that there are no
alienees, heirs, devisees, or others authorized to take, or that there are
any creditors.

I am, therefore, of the opinion that there is no error in the conclusion
reached by your office in said decision.

CONTEST—PREFERENCE RIGHT—RELINQUISHMENT.

GILMORE v. SHRINER.

An application to file a declaratory statement, accompanied by a relinquishment, and
presented during the pendency of a contest, can only be received subject to the
right of the contestant.

The settlement of a third party, on land covered by an entry, will not defeat the
right of a successful contestant who has secured the cancellation of said entry.

The purchaser of a relinquishment acquires no title to the land covered thereby, and
his failure to present the same, until after initiation of contest by another, will
not impair or defeat the right of the successful contestant.

*First Assistant Secretary Chandler to Acting Commissioner Stone, August
15, 1889.*

On August 3, 1885, John H. Shriner made homestead entry for lots
1 and 2 and the E. ¼ NW. ¼ Sec. 18 T. 22 N., R. 19 W, Neligh, Nebraska.

On October 31, 1887, Robert Gilmore filed an affidavit of contest
against the said entry alleging abandonment. Notice of said contest
was served by publication. The local officers directed that testimony
be taken before the clerk of the court at Taylor on January 20, 1888,
and fixed January 30, following as the date of hearing at the local office.

The claimant (Shriner) made default.

At the time so fixed for taking testimony the contestant (Gilmore)
appeared and produced several witnesses. At the same time one
Aaron C. Johnson, who claimed the land under a relinquishment from
Shriner appeared and cross-examined the witnesses for the contestant.

On January 28, 1888, Johnson presented the relinquishment of
Shriner, dated June 10, 1887 and applied to file a declaratory statement
for the land. This declaratory statement is not with the record, but in

his accompanying affidavit he avers that he settled on the land in good faith on or about October 1, 1887; that at the date of contest he was in actual and notorious possession; that the contestant then knew that he (Johnson) had purchased Shriner's "rights," that he bought the latter's improvements in May 1887, and that he was prevented by illness from attending to his affairs until the "cool weather." The affiant asked that a hearing be ordered to determine the matters alleged.

The local officers found for contestant and recommended the cancellation of the entry. They also found that Johnson had no standing in the case, and denied his said application to intervene.

No appeal was taken by the claimant (Shriner). The applicant (Johnson) appealed from the denial of the application just referred to.

On March 31, 1888, your office canceled Shriner's entry "as of January 28, 1888 when the relinquishment was presented" and returned the declaratory statement of Johnson with instructions to "file and enter the same as of the same date, subject to the rights of contestant." Johnson again appeals.

It appears from the record that some cultivation was done on the land by or for Johnson during the summer and fall of 1887, and that he was on the tract when the testimony was taken, but neither the extent of his inhabitancy or the value of his improvements is shown by the evidence.

The contestant stated that in April 1887, he had heard of the claimant's relinquishment and that at the time of contest he (contestant) knew that Johnson claimed the land by virtue thereof.

The purchaser of a relinquishment can acquire no rights by virtue of his purchase. Wiley v. Raymond (6 L. D., 246).

When Johnson, pending the contest, presented the claimant's relinquishment, he was without legal interest in the land and a stranger to the record. His accompanying application to file for land could only be received subject to the pending contest. Mitchell v. Robinson (3 L. D., 546).

At the time when Johnson alleges the settlement, the land was covered by the homestead entry of Shriner, and conceding that Johnson was an actual settler on the tract prior to, and at the date of contest, he by virtue of such settlement could acquire no rights as against the successful contestant. Paulson v. Richardson (8 L. D., 597).

That the contestant initiated contest with knowledge of Johnson's claim is not material. Johnson's failure to present the relinquishment until the day fixed for taking testimony on the contest, can not be permitted to prevent the contestant from securing the preference right for which the statute provides. In Mitchell v. Robinson, *supra*, the Department said in this connection that the rights of vigilant contestants shall not thus be defeated by the execution and retention of relinquishments.

The decision appealed from is affirmed.

DESERT LAND–DOUBLE MINIMUM PRICE.

CYRUS WHEELER.

Prior to the act of March 2, 1889, desert lands within the granted limits of the Texas
Pacific railroad could not lawfully be sold at less than $2.50 per acre.

Acting Secretary Chandler to Acting Commissioner Stone, August 16, 1889.

I have considered the case of Cyrus Wheeler on his appeal from your office decision of September 1, 1888, which rejects his application to have refunded to him the sum of twenty-five cents per acre, alleged to have been wrongfully exacted from him by the local officers upon his desert land entry for section 32, T. 8 S., R. 22 W., Tuscon land district, Arizona Territory.

It appears from the record that said land is within the limits of the grant to the Texas Pacific Railroad Company, forfeited by the act of February 28, 1885 (23 Stats., 337).

Wheeler made application at the local office May 26, 1887, to make desert land entry for said land and paid to the person in charge of the local office twenty-five cents per acre.

By your office letter of May 3, 1887, the register of the local office was notified that his term of office had expired and that from and after the receipt of your said letter, he would have no authority to act as register, but until his successor should be appointed and qualified, he should remain in the office as a clerk, and as such he was directed to assume charge of books, papers, records etc., to give information when required and to bring up the accumulation of work then on hand, but to perform no act as register. The letter further stated that no entry of public land should be allowed until his successor should have entered upon his duties.

On May 23, 1887, the receiver of said office was allowed a leave of absence from which he returned June 24. Before leaving, however, said receiver designated and appointed a clerk to represent him during his absence. Wheeler's application and purchase money at the rate of twenty-five cents per acre were received by said clerk; the papers being numbered and filed by him and the money placed in the safe and intermingled with the other funds of the office.

On July 5, 1887, the new register began to discharge his duties and as the receiver had returned, the office was again opened for business. Considerable business had accumulated and they did not reach the said application of Wheeler until July 27, 1887; but in the mean time the circular of June 27, 1887, (5 L. D., 708) had been received at the local office about July 20, 1887, and the local officers believing said land to come within the provisions of section three thereof, notified Wheeler that said land was double minimum and an additional twenty-five cents per acre must be paid before entry would be allowed. Claimant finally made such payment under protest and appealed from the said decision of the local officers and also asks for repayment of said additional twenty-five cents per acre.

Upon said appeal your office decided adversely to claimant upon the ground that the value of said land was governed by said section three of said circular of June 27, 1887, and as " In this case the application was not granted when made and was not reached for examination, until July 27, 1887, after the promulgation of circular of June 27, 1887, hence no rights were vested, prior to the going into force of the circular aforesaid."

Appellant complains that your said decision is erroneous because; there is no authority of law authorizing sale of any land subject to entry as desert land under the act of March 3, 1877, at more than one dollar and twenty-five cents per acre; section three of the said circular of June 27, 1887, is unauthorized by law; but if authorized by law then the application at bar comes within the exception of section sixteen of said circular and to hold otherwise would be giving said circular a retroactive effect contrary to the terms of section sixteen thereof; that it was error to hold that claimant's rights did not attach until it became convenient for the register and receiver to take up his application and act upon it, his rights having attached when he presented his application and paid his money long prior to the promulgation of said circular; that at least his rights attached on July 5, 1887, when both register and receiver were present and said local office was opened for business, which was ten days before said circular was mailed from the General Land Office to said local office.

In a brief filed in the case counsel for appellant argue that while by section 2357 Revised Statutes, the alternate reserved sections lying within the limits of a railroad grant were raised to two dollars and fifty cents per acre the desert land act of March 3, 1877, was passed after said section 2357, and enacted that all land subject to entry thereunder should be sold at one dollar and twenty-five cents per acre, and as this is the last expression of the will of Congress it must prevail over the former, as an "old statute gives place to a new one."

Counsel contends that said proposition is not affected by the act of February 28, 1885, declaring a forfeiture of the land granted to the Texas Pacific Railroad Company, for the reason that the only price fixed by law for the sale of the even sections within the limits which were of such character as to be subject to entry under the desert land act, was the price of one dollar and twenty-five cents per acre, fixed by the desert land act itself, and the act of February 28, 1885, simply made the odd sections which were desert in character subject to sale at the same price as the even numbered sections of a desert character.

The act of Congress of February 28, 1885 (23 Stats., 337), which restored the lands granted to the Texas Pacific Railroad Company is as follows:

That all lands granted to the Texas Pacific Railroad Company under the act of Congress entitled, "An Act to incorporate the Texas Pacific Railroad Company and to aid in the construction of its road, and for other purposes," approved March 3, eighteen hundred and seventy-one, and acts amendatory thereto, be, and they are hereby, declared forfeited, and the whole of said lands restored to the public domain and made subject to disposal under the general laws of the United States, as though said grant had never been made: *Provided*, That the price of the lands so forfeited and restored shall be the same as heretofore fixed for the even sections within said grant.

In the case of the Texas Pacific grant (8 L. D., 530) it was held that by the terms of the act the even sections which had been raised to double minimum on the filing of the map of general route remained at that price, and the price of the odd numbered sections restored by the act were also fixed at the double minimum price.

In Daniel G. Tilton (8 L. D., 368), section 2357 of the Revised Statutes, and the desert land act of March 3, 1877 (19 Stat., 377), were held to be *in pari materia*, and that they did not conflict, the former regulating the price of desert lands reserved to the United States within the limits of a railroad grant, and the latter the price of other desert lands outside of such limits. See also Annie Knaggs (9 L. D., 49).

As the cases above cited sufficiently answer the questions actually at issue it will not be necessary to discuss the argument of counsel against the reasons assigned by your office for the decision appealed from. Under the law as construed in the above cases the sections within the granted limits of said railroad, whether odd or even, desert or otherwise, could not be sold for less than $2.50 per acre, prior to the act of March 2, 1889, and this would be true of the land in question had the circular of June 27, 1887, never been promulgated, and the lawful price of the land in controversy was $2.50 per acre at the time Wheeler's application was first presented.

Your said decision is accordingly affirmed.

FINAL PROOF PROCEEDINGS—PROTEST—HEARING.

HOOVER *v.* LAWTON.

In the absence of an order under rule 35 of practice, a protestant, in final proof proceedings, who appears as an adverse claimant, is under no obligation to submit his testimony at the time and place, and before the officer, designated for taking the final proof.

Where an adverse claimant enters protest against the submission of final proof, it is the duty of the local officers to order a hearing at such time and place, and before such officer as they in their discretion may determine.

First Assistant Secretary Chandler, to Acting Commissioner Stone, August 29, 1889.

I have considered the case of John T. Hoover *v.* Wm. J. Lawton, involving the SE. ¼ of Sec. 33, T. 101 N., R. 70 W. Mitchell land district, Dakota.

John T. Hoover filed his pre-emption declaratory statement for the

2816—VOL 9——18

land July 6, 1886, alleging settlement July 3, 1886; Wm. J. Lawton filed a like declaratory statement for the land July 14, 1886, alleging settlement July 5, of the same year.

Lawton after due notice and personal citation to Hoover, made his final proof May 6, 1887, at Chamberlain, Dakota, before W. C. Graybill, judge of probate court for Brule county; Hoover at the time appeared personally and entered his protest against the acceptance of the proof and for this purpose filed his own affidavit corroborated by the affidavits of two other persons. The statements in these affidavits, if true, establish the fact that Hoover made a *bona fide* pre-emption settlement upon the land and established his residence thereon, earlier in time than Lawton and that he, Hoover, was entitled to the land in preference to Lawton. Attached to the record of final proof is the statement of Judge Graybill, from which it appears that after Hoover had filed his protest and the affidavits in support of it, the claimant demanded to cross examine the said protestant and his two corroborating witnesses and "that J. T. Hoover declined to be cross examined and that said J. T. Hoover refused to furnish said witnesses," and that thereupon Lawton moved to strike from the files " the objections filed by John T. Hoover, and the affidavit made by himself," and the corroborating affidavits. Attached is also the affidavits of Lawton, corroborating the statement of the said judge, and his motion in writing for the dismissal of Hoover's protest.

It does not appear that Hoover was present when the motion was made or had notice of Lawton's said affidavit.

The record of the final proof having been submitted to the local officers together with an application of Hoover asking " that a hearing be had in said case and that the testimony be taken before A. J. Troth, a notary public, residing at Bijou Hills, Brule Co., Dakota, on May 9, 1887, they ordered and adjudged " that the protest and application of John T. Hoover for a new hearing on the proof submitted by William J. Lawton, be and is hereby dismissed."

From this decision Hoover appealed June 4, 1887. In support of his appeal he filed a number of affidavits showing, among other matters, that Hoover in the forenoon of May 6, in the office of the said judge at Chamberlain, Dakota, filed his said protest and affidavits accompanying the same, that thereupon until evening he was engaged in the office copying the proof of Lawton, that when he had left the office and had prepared his team to go home which was thirty miles distant— it was then 5.30 o'clock p. m.—he was sent for to come the judge's office. That he went there and was then for the first time informed that Lawton demanded to cross examine him and his witnesses, that his said witnesses had left Chamberlain and were on their way home, that he informed the judge of this fact, and told him " that I (Hoover) could not possibly get them back that night... but that I would get them there as soon as I could if they desired it; ....that I am perfectly willing to be cross examined and have my men who had made the corroborating affidavits cross examined at any time when he desired it but that I could not do it that night, for the reason that I could not get them there that night."

Attached to the said affidavit is the certificate of Judge Graybill; he certifies that Hoover on the day of the said final proof,

did not refuse to have his witnesses as well as himself cross examined as regards affidavits of protest against said proof filed that day, only as far as said day was concerned, that he could not get his witnesses there for a cross examination that day, as the time was between five and six p. m., but that he, Hoover, stated that he and his witnesses were willing to be cross examined at any future time or as soon as he could procure the attendance of said witnesses, that he, Hoover, stated that he could not possibly get his witnesses there for cross examination that night.

Numerous affidavits were filed in support of the appeal and in opposition thereto by the respective parties, all tending to show the superior right of the one party or the other to the said tract.

Your office considering the said appeal by your decision of April 16, 1888, dismissed the same.

On May 22, 1888, Hoover made a motion for a reconsideration of your said office decision on the ground that "said decision amounted to a denial of right to be heard on a question of priority of settlement, improvements and record of prior claim to the land in controversy." Attached to the motion is the affidavit of Judge Graybill wherein he, in substance deposes to the facts set out in his certificate herein before mentioned.

Your office by decision of July 13, 1888, denied the motion. Thereupon Hoover appealed from your said decision of April 16, 1888, to this Department.

Pending the appeal, Hoover filed his affidavit bearing date August 9, 1888; in it he asserts that "he was the first legal applicant for the land in question and . . . . that the filing of said Lawton was made in fraud and the final proof was consummated by perjury by said Lawton and his witnesses." His affidavit is very lengthy and particularizes many facts, which, if true, seem to substantiate his said general assertion. He again asks that a hearing may be ordered and that "a special agent of the General Land Office may be present at said hearing and investigate the perjury herein charged to the end that Lawton and his final proof witnesses may be dealt with according to law." In corroboration of his said affidavit, Hoover also filed other affidavits tending to show the truth of his said assertions.

Also pending the said appeal on February 23, 1889, Hoover made application to the local officers to issue notice for the making of his final proof on his said pre-emption filing. The register refused "the case involving this land being now before the Secretary" to issue the notice.

From this action Hoover, March 23, 1889, appealed.

These documents and papers comprise the record before this Department. The hearing for which Hoover prayed with such persistency should be granted to him. At the final proof proceedings he objected to the submission of Lawton's final proof as an adverse claimant; he was not obliged to submit his testimony then and there before the officer taking the final proof without an order under Rule 35, of the Rules of Practice; see Martensen v. McCaffrey, 7 L. D., 315. Hoover as adverse claimant is entitled to a hearing. The record fails to show that the local officers, in the exercise of their discretion had directed the time and place of a hearing before Judge Graybill. Hoover therefore would have been justified, if he had absolutely refused to submit himself and his corroborating witnesses to a cross examination before the judge at the time and place of the final proof proceedings of Lawton. When Hoover had entered his protest as claim ant to the land, it became the duty of the local officers to order a hearing at such time and place and before such officer as they in their discretion might determine.

Your office is, therefore, directed to instruct the local officers to order a hearing in this case, when the respective claims of the parties to this land may be fully investigated and their rights determined.

Your said office decisions of April 16, and July 13, 1888, are accordingly reversed.

This determination, it seems, obviates special proceedings upon Hoover's application of August 9, 1888, for the charges therein set forth may be legitimately inquired into at the hearing herein provided for. However, such application and Hoover's appeal of March 23, 1889, are returned to your office, together with the o ther papers in the case for appropriate action.

———

PRACTICE—NOTICE OF APPEAL—SPECIFICATIONS OF ERROR.

BUNDY v. FREMONT TOWNSITE.

An appeal will not be entertained, if notice thereof and a copy of the specifications of error are not served upon the opposite party within the prescribed period.

Acting Secretary Chandler to Acting Commissioner Stone, August 16, 1889.

This case purports to be a contest by Hiram Bundy against the townsite of Fremont, involving the NE. ¼ of Sec. 23 and the SE. ¼ of Sec. 14, T. 8 S., R. 25 W., situated in the Oberlin land district, Kansas.

The tracts in question are claimed for townsite purposes under sections 2387, 2388 and 2389 of the Revised Statutes, and a declaratory statement, covering the same, appears to have been filed with the register on February 24, 1881, under the provisions of said section 2388, by the probate judge of Graham county, wherein the tracts lie, setting forth the purpose of the inhabitants and occupants thereof to enter the same as a townsite. No entry, however, has as yet been made.

On October 27, 1886, the local officers ordered a hearing in the premises, upon the affidavit of said Bundy, purporting to be an affidavit of contest against the townsite claim, which appears to have been executed

- April 26, 1886 (it not being shown at what date the same was filed), charging, in effect, the abandonment of said townsite for more than six months since the initiation of the claim; that the land had not been settled upon and occupied for townsite purposes, as required by law; and that the same had not been surveyed and platted and plat filed in transfer record and with the register of deeds as the law requires.

The hearing was had as ordered, at which the contestant and townsite claimants appeared by counsel and offered testimony.

The local officers, upon consideration of the evidence, found for the contestant Bundy, and recommended that the townsite entry (filing) should be canceled.

On appeal from this finding your office, on March 29, 1888, reversed the same and dismissed the contest.

On October 9, 1888, the papers in the case were transmitted to this Department by your office, on the appeal of Bundy from said decision.

This latter appeal is without date, and was forwarded to your office in May, 1888, by one J. R. McCoun, of Millbrook, Kansas, as attorney for the contestant, without proof of service ; and on May 25, 1888, the same was returned to the local officers, in order that proof of service in accordance with the Rules of Practice might be furnished.

On September 3, 1888, the appeal was again forwarded to your office, from which it appears that the same was filed in the local office July 17, 1888, accompanied by proof that notice thereof, including "a copy of the specification of errors, and argument," was served on the attorney for the appellees, by registered letter, July 13, 1888 ; also by the acceptance in writing, without date, of service of such notice, by Stephen Van Wyck, probate judge of Graham county ; and by the affidavit of said J. R. McCoun, stating that on or about May 20, 1888, he served on one J. B. Smith, " who, on the 17th day of September, 1884, made oath before the county clerk of Graham county, Kansas, that he was the founder of the town of Fremont, in said county and State," a certain notice in writing, which appears on the reverse side of the same sheet of paper on which the affidavit is written, and is in the words and figures following, to wit:

HIRAM BUNDY
        v.   } Notice of appeal.
THE TOWNSITE OF FREMONT, KANSAS.

To J. B. SMITH.

You are hereby notified that the contestant herein has appealed from the Honorable Commissioner's decision in aforesaid contest, to the Honorable Secretary of the Interior, and that said appeal was forwarded to the said Commissioner of the General Land Office at Washington, D. C., by registered mail May 10th, 1888.

HIRAM BUNDY,
pr. J. R. McCOUN, atty.

The affidavit of McCoun further states that he served said notice by reading the same to Smith, and delivering to him a true copy thereof in Millbrook, Graham county, Kansas.

On August 9, 1888, the attorneys of the townsite occupants filed in the local office a motion to dismiss the appeal, for the reason, among others, that the same was not filed in accordance with the Rules of Practice, which motion was forwarded with the appeal.

It further appears that notice of your said office decision was given to the attorneys for contestant Bundy by the local officers through registered mail, on April 11, 1888, and that such notice was received by said attorneys the next day.

By rule 86, of the Rules of Practice, it is provided that "notice of an appeal from the Commissioner's decision must be filed in the General Land Office and served on the appellee or his counsel within sixty days from the date of the service of notice of such decision." By rule 87, ten days additional are allowed in cases wherein notice of the decision is given through the mails.

Rule 88 provides that "within the time allowed for giving notice of appeal the appellant shall also file in the General Land Office a specification of errors, which specification shall clearly and concisely designate the errors of which he complains." By rule 93, it is further provided that "a copy of the notice of appeal, specification of errors, and all arguments of either party, shall be served on the opposite party within the time allowed for filing the same."

It is very clear from the foregoing statement of facts that notice of the appeal herein, and the specification of errors complained of, were not served and filed within the time, and in the manner prescribed by the Rules of Practice.

Notice of the decision appealed from was given by registered mail, as we have seen, April 11, 1888, and notice of the appeal was not served as required until July 13, 1888, nearly a month after the full seventy days time allowed in such cases had elapsed. The notice which the attorney McCoun swears he served on one J. B. Smith, on or about May 20, 1888, was simply a notice that the contestant, Bundy, *had appealed* from the decision of your office to the Secretary of the Interior, and that such appeal was forwarded to the General Land Office, by registered mail, May 10, 1888. No specification of errors is given in the notice, nor did any accompany the same when served, nor was a copy of the appeal ever served on said Smith. Such notice was, therefore, wholly insufficient, even if it were shown that said Smith was the proper party upon whom to serve the notice of appeal. Under the rules of practice it is equally important that the specification of errors complained of shall be served on the opposite party, as that the notice of appeal shall be served, and the service of both must be within the time prescribed.

The appeal when first received at your office was within time, but being without proof of service was properly returned. It now appears that it had not only been forwarded without proof of service, but without the plainly required service having been made at all. This was wholly irregular, and nothing is alleged by way of excuse or explanation thereof. That which purports to be an appeal can in no sense be considered as such, unless accompanied by proof that service thereof has been made as required.

In view of the foregoing, there is nothing to do but to dismiss the appeal herein as having been improvidently awarded, and it is accordingly so ordered.

. FINAL PROOF PROCEEDINGS—PENDING CONTEST.

LAFFOON v. ARTIS.

During the pendency of contest proceedings, a claimant for land involved therein is not required to submit final proof; and the local officers should not allow such proof to be made until final determination of the contest.

Secretary Noble to Acting Commissioner Stone, July 20, 1889.

I have considered Drewry Laffoon's motion for review of departmental decision, dated September 26, 1888, in the case of said Laffoon v. Joseph Artis, involving the S. ½ of the NE. ¼ of Sec. 22, T. 34 S., R. 19 W., Osage Indian trust and diminished reserve land, Larned, Kansas.

The record shows that said Laffoon, on October 15, 1884, filed his Osage declaratory statement, No. 5,861, for the NE.¼ of said section, alleging settlement thereon October 1st of the same year; that said Artis filed his Osage declaratory statement, No. 7129, for the S. ½ of said NE. ¼, on January 14, 1885, alleging settlement thereon September 24, 1884; that, after due notice, Artis made his final proof before a notary public, and upon protest being filed by Laffoon, alleging a prior valid claim, a hearing was had before the local officers, who rendered their decision on June 2, 1886, and found that the testimony in the case was "conflicting in the extreme, so far as it relates to the earlier acts of settlement;" that Artis was in laches in not filing "within the period prescribed by Sec. 2265 R. S. U. S." and, also, in not making the final affidavit prescribed in pre-emption cases; that Laffoon was the first "legal settler;" that his improvements indicated that he has acted in good faith, and his absence from the land for about two months was excusable under the circumstances. The local officers, therefore, held that Laffoon had the better right to the land, and that the filing of Artis should be canceled.

On appeal, your office, on September 23, 1886, found (*inter alia*) that Laffoon did not establish and maintain "a bona fide residence upon the land in controversy to the exclusion of one elsewhere;" that a pre-emptor is required to show a continuous residence on the land sought to be entered for a period of at least six consecutive months preceding the time of making proof; that Artis appears to be a qualified pre-emptor, acting in good faith; and that he made a bona fide settlement prior to the intervention of a valid adverse claim. Your office, therefore, reversed the decision of the local office, awarded the land to Artis, rejected Laffoon's proof, which was made before the local officers on June 8, 1885, and held his filing for cancellation.

Said departmental decision reviewed the testimony at length, and found that the testimony in behalf of Laffoon showed that he, in company with others, camped upon said land from September 29, until October 7, 1884, during which time the claim was measured by them by stepping it off, and mounds were erected upon the corners from one to one and a half of a foot high, near which stakes were driven, upon which were placed the name of said Laffoon, and the proper description of the land, embraced in his said filing; that on October 7, 1884, Laffoon left, returning to the land on the 25th of the same month, and remaining until December 24, same year, when, having completed his house, he went back to his former home in Missouri, where he remained until the last of February or the first of March, 1885; that, on April 12, 1885, Laffoon went again to Missouri, and returned with his wife about May 10, same year, since which time he has lived on said land continuously; that the reason given by Laffoon for his absences, as aforesaid, was his business engagements and the inclement weather; that on March 1, 1885, he moved his furniture and cooking utensils into his house on said tract, prior to which time he had slept in his house, but had done no cooking therein; that his improvements—consisting of a house, ten by twelve feet, a well, also from eight to twelve acres under cultivation in corn, and five acres of pasture, fenced—all were worth $200.

Said departmental decision further found that the testimony of Artis showed that he went upon said land on September 24, 1884, and placed his name upon a stake driven into a mound, about a foot high, raised by him on the land, also a notice that he claimed a tract in said Sec. 22; that Artis then went to Coldwater, Kansas, returning to the land on October 11, 1884, when he made an excavation in the ground one foot deep, covering it with a roof; that he then went away and returned to the land on October 18, same year, built a box house, and established his home on the land on November 27, 1884; that from that time until the date of said hearing he has continuously resided upon the land, and that his improvements, consisting of a house fourteen by eighteen feet, a well, and six acres of breaking, were worth $200. The Department decided that both parties were actual settlers on their respective claims, and in this regard both had established their right to the lands embraced in their respective filings (citing Woodbury et al., 5 L. D., 303); that upon the evidence submitted Laffoon was the prior settler upon the land; that the settlement of Artis could not be held to be prior to October 11, 1884, and that, had Laffoon complied with the regulations of the Department of June 23, 1881, requiring proof and part payment to be made within six months from date of filing, he would have been entitled to the land in contest; that, on account of the laches of Laffoon in making his final proof, the land in conflict must be awarded to Artis

" upon his compliance with the further provisions of the law, provided nothing appears on the records of your office to hinder such entry," and Laffoon was allowed to enter the land covered by his filing not in contest upon similar conditions.

There are six specifications of error in said motion which may be briefly stated as follows: (1) Error in holding that Laffoon did not comply with the law and regulations of the Department in making his final proof, and (2) error in holding that Artis had a valid claim to the land in question.

Counsel for Laffoon insists that his client can not be held to be in laches in making his final proof, because he filed in the local office his notice of intention to make final proof within six months from the date of his filing, and that under the departmental decision, in the case of Ramage v. Maloney (1 L. D., 461), his final proof was made in time.

The case of Ramage v. Maloney was cited in the case of Steele v. Engleman (3 L. D., 92), and it was there held that the ruling did not apply where the adverse claim was initiated prior to the filing of the notice. Therefore, the right of Laffoon to the land in question must depend upon the date of his actual settlement, if made in good faith, and if that was prior to the settlement of Artis, as was found by the local officers and the Department, then Laffoon is entitled to the land. Besides, it is shown that Artis did not file within three months from date of settlement, and not until after the filing of his declaratory statement by Laffoon, and, hence, under the regulations then in force, he was in laches and his filing must be held subordinate to that of Laffoon.

While the contest was pending to determine the right of Artis to enter the land in conflict, Laffoon was under no obligation to make final proof. Indeed, the local officers should not have allowed him to make final proof until the final determination of said contest. Rule of Practice 53 (4 L. D., 43); Stroud v. De Wolf (idem., 394); Bailey v. Townsend (5 L. D., 176); Wade v. Sweeny (6 L. D., 234); Lewis Peterson (8 L. D., 121).

A careful examination of the whole record leads me to concur with the finding of the local officers, before whom the witnesses were examined, which was concurred in by the Department, that Laffoon was the first actual settler on the land covered by his filing. This being so, and Laffoon not being required to make final proof until the termination of the contest upon Artis's final proof, it necessarily follows that the land in conflict must be awarded to Laffoon.

Said departmental decision is accordingly modified. The prior right to the land in conflict is awarded to Laffoon, and he will be entitled to give new notice and make new proof within a reasonable time (say sixty days) from notice hereof. In case such proof is in all respects satisfactory, the land officers will accept the same and issue certificate for the land covered by Laffoon's filing, and the filing of Artis will be held for cancellation, so far as the same includes the land in controversy.

[Circular.]

DEPARTMENT OF THE INTERIOR,
GENERAL LAND OFFICE,
Washington, D. C., August 5, 1889.

REGISTERS AND RECEIVERS,
United States Land Offices.

GENTLEMEN: Information having reached this Department that parties are endeavoring to make filings on arid lands reserved for reservoirs, irrigating ditches, and canals, and for the purpose of controlling the waters of lakes and rivers and their tributaries in the arid regions, I am directed by Hon. Secretary of the Interior to call your special attention to the act of Congress approved October 2, 1888, U. S. Statutes at Large, vol. 25, page 526, as follows:

> For the purpose of investigating the extent to which the arid region of the United States can be redeemed by irrigation, and the segregation of the irrigable lands in such arid region, and for the selection of sites for reservoirs and other hydraulic works necessary for the storage and utilization of water for irrigation and the prevention of floods and overflows, and to make the necessary maps, including the pay of employés in field and in office, the cost of all instruments, apparatus, and materials, and all other necessary expenses connected therewith, the work to be performed by the Geological Survey, under the direction of the Secretary of the Interior, the sum of one hundred thousand dollars or so much thereof as may be necessary. And the Director of the Geological Survey, under the supervision of the Secretary of the Interior, shall make a report to Congress on the first Monday in December of each year, showing in detail how the said money has been expended, the amount used for actual survey and engineer work in the field in locating sites for reservoirs, and an itemized account of the expenditures under this appropriation. And all the lands which may hereafter be designated or selected by such United States surveys for sites for reservoirs, ditches, or canals for irrigation purposes and all the lands made susceptible of irrigation by such reservoirs, ditches, or canals are from this time henceforth hereby reserved from sale as the property of the United States, and shall not be subject after the passage of this act to entry, settlement, or occupation until further provided by law: *Provided,* that the President at any time in his discretion, by proclamation, may open any portion or all of the lands reserved by this provision to settlement under the homestead laws.

The object sought to be accomplished by the foregoing provision is unmistakable. The water sources and the arid lands that may be irrigated by the system of national irrigation are now reserved to be hereafter, when redeemed to agriculture, transferred to the people of the Territories in which they are situated for homesteads. The act of Congress and common justice require that they should be faithfully preserved for these declared purposes.

The statute provides that all lands which may hereafter be designated or selected by the Geological Survey as sites for reservoirs, ditches, or canals for irrigating purposes, and all lands made susceptible of irrigation by such reservoirs, ditches, or canals are since the passage of said act absolutely reserved from sale as property of the United States, and shall not be subject after the passage of the act to entry, settlement or occupation until further provided by law, or the President, by proclamation, may open said lands to settlement.

Neither individuals nor corporations have a right to make filings upon any lands thus reserved, nor can they be permitted to obtain control of the lakes and streams that are susceptible of uses for irrigating purposes.

You will, therefore, immediately cancel all filings made since October 2, 1888, on such sites for reservoirs, ditches, or canals for irrigating purposes, and all lands that may be susceptible of irrigation by such reservoirs, ditches, or canals, whether made by individuals or corporations, and you will hereafter receive no filings upon any such lands.

This order you will carry into effect without delay.

Respectfully,

W. M. STONE,
Acting Commissioner.

___

FINAL PROOF—ACT OF MARCH 2, 1889.

MARTIN GLEESON.

Under section 7, act of March 2, 1889, an entry may be passed to patent without submission to the board of equitable adjudication, where the final proof was not submitted on the day advertised, but was made within ten days of said date, and the delay was the result of accident or unavoidable cause.

Section 9 of Final Proof Rules cited and construed.

First Assistant Secretary Chandler to Acting Commissioner Stone, August 16, 1889.

I have considered the appeal of Martin Gleeson from the decision of your office, dated April 11, 1888, requiring him to give new notice and make new proof in support of his pre-emption cash entry, No. 4680, of the SE. ¼ of the NE. ¼ of Sec. 9, the S. ¼ of the NW. ¼ and the SW. ¼ of the NE. ¼ of Sec. 10, T. 10 N., R. 60 W., made May 26, 1881, at the Mitchell land office, in the Territory of Dakota.

The reason given for requiring new notice and new proof was that the notice fixed the time for making said proof on May 24, 1881, and it was not made until two days afterwards, namely : on May 26, same year.

The claimant submitted to the local officers, at the time he offered his final proof, his explanation under oath of the cause of the delay. He stated that he was disappointed in not receiving the money which had been promised him, on the day advertised, and it was on that account that he did not make the proof as advertised.

With his appeal, claimant has filed an additional affidavit, showing that he made arrangements to secure the money to pay for said land in ample time, prior to the date set for making said proof, and the reason he did not receive it in time was, because the mail was delayed by a washout on the railroad.

The final proof shows compliance with the requirements of the pre-emption law as to settlement, inhabitancy and improvement. The explanation made at the time was satisfactory to the local officers, and the entry appears to have been approved twice by the examiners of your office; first on May 24, 1882, and again on September 18, 1885.

The seventh section of the act of Congress approved March 2, 1889, (25 Stat., 854), places a legislative construction upon the act of March 3, 1879 (20 Stat., 472), and allows final proof to be made within ten days after the day advertised, where the applicant is prevented by " accident, or unavoidable delays."

Section nine of the final proof rules, dated July 17, 1889 (9 L. D., 123), reads:

Where final proof has been accepted by the local office, prior to the promulgation of said circular of February 19, 1887 (5 L. D., 426), if in all other respects satisfactory, except that it was not taken as advertised, the cases may be submitted to the Board of Equitable Adjudication for its consideration.

In the case of William F. Simrall (8 L. D., 581), the Department held that the provisions of said seventh section (*supra*) were retroactive, and that Simrall's entry upon final proof, made two days after the day advertised on account of an unavoidable delay, was "regularly made," and that the entry should be passed to patent. Simrall's proof was made in February, 1884, and if it is to be followed as a precedent hereafter, said rule will be so construed as not to require entries to be submitted to the Board of Equitable Adjudication, where the final proof was made prior to the promulgation of said circular of February 19, 1887, if said proof was made within ten days from the day advertised on account of accident and unavoidable delay, and it is in other respects satisfactory.

The decision of your office must be and it is hereby reversed and said entry will be passed to patent.

———

TIMBER CULTURE PROOF—DEPARTMENTAL REGULATIONS.

JOHN M. LINDBACK.

A proper construction of the timber-culture act requires that the period of cultivation should be computed from the time when the requisite acreage is planted.

A departmental construction of a statute, while in force, has all the effect of law, and acts done thereunder must be regarded as legal, and entitled to protection at the hands of the Department.

In timber-culture entries made prior to the regulations of June 27, 1887, the time occupied in the preparation of the soil and planting the trees may be computed, on final proof, as forming a part of the statutory period of cultivation.

There is no authority under the statute for a requirement that the proof should show that the trees have attained a specific height or size, after cultivation for the requisite period.

First Assistant Secretary Chandler to Acting Commissioner Stone, August 16, 1889.

On July 1, 1889, this Department rendered a decision in the case of John M. Lindback, who on October 24, 1877, made timber-culture entry of the E. ½ of the NE. ¼ and the E. ½ of the SE. ¼ of Sec. 29, T. 144, R. 45 W., Detroit land district, Minnesota.   Said Lindback made final proof July 17, 1886, said proof showing that in June, 1878, he broke five acres of land; in 1879 five acres more; in 1879 he seeded to oats the five acres broken in 1878; in 1880 he seeded to wheat the five acres broken in 1879; the year after seeding to oats or wheat he planted each tract respectively to cottonwood cuttings; and when proof was made (July 17, 1886, *supra*,) there were twelve hundred living trees growing upon each of the ten acres.   In said departmental decision of July 1, 1889, it was ruled "that the eight years of cultivation required under the timber-culture law must be computed from the time the required acreage of trees, seeds, or cuttings, are planted;" and that, as "it appears from the testimony of the entryman that no trees, seeds, or cuttings were planted on the land in controversy until 1880, consequently, when proof was made, no trees had been cultivated for eight years.   It follows, therefore, that the proof was prematurely submitted and must be rejected."

The above conclusion is the same as that which had been previously arrived at by the Department in the cases of Henry Hooper (6 L. D., 624), Charles N. Smith (7 L. D., 231), and others not reported.

On July 12, 1889, the departmental decision of July 1 in the Lindback case was recalled for further consideration.

I am fully satisfied that said decision in the Lindback case, and in the other cases just cited, contain a correct exposition of the law.

The first section of the timber-culture act (20 Stat., 113,) requires the applicant to "plant, protect, and keep in a healthy, growing condition for eight years, ten acres of timber."   Clearly, this language imports and requires this area *of trees* to be growing during this period; for trees could not be kept in a healthy, growing condition that were not planted and in existence.

This conclusion is strengthened by the language of section two, which contains the proviso—

That he, or she, or they, have planted, and for not less than eight years, have cultivated and protected such quantity and character of trees as aforesaid.

It can not be disputed that "such quantity" refers to the ten acres mentioned in section one, which requires that ten acres be cultivated and protected for the full period of eight years.   This is borne out by the further proviso that, if the entry is not completed at the expiration of eight years, five years thereafter is given the applicant within which to complete the same; so that the entryman really has thirteen years, if he chooses to avail himself thereof, within which to comply with the law.   I have no doubt, if he plants the required area the first year, that then the entry may be made within eight years thereafter; but I am fully satisfied that it was the intent and purpose of Congress to require the claimant to cultivate the trees for eight years, deeming that at the end of that period the young timber would be able to protect itself without further cultivation.

While all this is true, yet the Department, in its earlier construction of the law, held that the time occupied in the preparation of the ground and the planting of the trees might properly be computed as forming a part of the statutory period of cultivation. (See circular of February 1, 1882; case of Benjamin F. Lake, 2 L. D., 309; Charles E. Patterson, 3 L. D., 260; Peter Christofferson, 3 L. D., 329.)

This rule was followed by the Department from that time until June 27, 1887, when your office, by circular of that date to registers and receivers, directed (6 L. D., 280):

In computing the period of cultivation, the time runs from the date when the total number of trees, seeds, or cuttings, required by the act, are planted.

It has been repeatedly held by the Department, in cases similar to that now under consideration, that until a rule is changed, it has all the force of law, and acts done under it while it is in force, must be regarded as legal. James Spencer (6 L. D., 217); Miner v. Marriott et al. (2 L. D., 709); David B. Dole (3 L. D., 214); Henry W. Fuss (5 L. D., 167); Allen v. Cooley (5 L. D., 261); Kelly v. Halvorson (6 L. D., 225).

Inasmuch as Lindback's entry was made under the former construction of the law, his acts performed while that construction obtained are entitled to protection at the hands of the Department; and therefore, for the reasons herein given, and in accordance with departmental instructions issued to your office July 16, 1889 (9 L. D., 86), the decision of July 1, 1888, in the case of John M. Lindback, is hereby revoked. As the proof therein shows full compliance with law, as construed by the Department at the time when said entry was made, and as the requirement of your office, in its decision of October 19, 1886, that the proof should show that the trees, after the proper cultivation for the statutory period, have attained a specific height or size, is not justified by the timber-culture law, your said decision is reversed, Lindback's proof will be accepted, and patent will issue thereon.

CONTEST—DEATH OF CONTESTANT—HEARING.

MEYER v. MITCHELL.

The right of contest conferred by the act of May 14, 1880, is personal and ends with the death of the contestant.

Where the statutory life of an entry has expired, and final proof has not been made, it is within the discretion of the Commissioner to either allow a contest against the entry, or call upon the entryman to show cause why the entry should not be canceled for failure to submit proof.

First Assistant Secretary Chandler to Acting Commissioner Stone, August 17, 1889.

On May 11, 1882, Arthur P. Mitchell made desert land entry of the E. ½ of Sec. 14, T. 2 S., R. 23 E., Bozeman land district, Montana.

In March, 1883, Chester T. Walker applied to make homestead entry of a portion of the tract above described; and on learning at the land office that it was covered by Mitchell's desert land entry, he applied to contest the same on the ground that it was not desert land. A hearing was ordered and commenced May 11, 1885.

Both parties appeared, and some testimony was taken, when a further deposit of money to pay for reducing the testimony to writing was demanded; this was refused, and the hearing proceeded no further at that time.

Before any further action in the matter was taken both contestant and contestee died.

Shortly thereafter applications were made by James White, Carl Jansen, and William F. Meyer, to contest said entry; but all of said applications were rejected because of the prior and pending contest of Walker. White and Jansen have not appealed to the Department; hence the claim of Meyer is the only one before it for consideration.

Said Meyer was attorney for said Walker, deceased (the contestee) and administrator of his estate. In this capacity he thus, on May 12, 1885, notified the local officers:

Take notice that I hereby, with consent and approval of the probate judge of Yellowstone county, Montana Territory, relinquish the contest now pending in your office between Chester T. Walker, deceased, and A. P. Mitchell, also deceased, affecting desert land entry No. 94, of said Mitchell, and covering the E. ½ of Sec. 14, T. 2 S., R. 23 E., and I hereby withdraw and dismiss said contest.

Meyer's withdrawal of Walker's contest and his application to institute contest in his own name were by the local officers transmitted to your office for instructions. Your office, by letter of March 4, 1886, refused to recognize any authority on the part of Meyer, even with the consent and approval of the probate judge, to withdraw Walker's contest, and declined to order a hearing upon his application. By same letter you directed the local officers to proceed, under circular of August 28, 1880 (then operative), to notify the heirs of the contestee that the time within which he was by law required to reclaim said tract had expired, and that he would be allowed ninety days wherein to show cause why said entry should not be canceled.

From the refusal of your office to order a hearing upon his (Meyer's) application, Meyer appealed to the Department.

The Department has decided that the right of contest conferred by the act of May 14, 1880 (21 Stat., 140), is a personal one. (Morgan v. Doyle, 3 L. D., 5; Hurd v. Smith, 7 L. D., 491). Therefore when Meyer, as attorney for Walker and administrator of his estate, attempted to withdraw and dismiss said Walker's contest against Mitchell's entry, there was in existence no contest to be withdrawn and dismissed. The matter of ordering hearing is one within your discretion (Rule 81 of Practice). It is also discretionary with you, in a case of this kind (where the statutory life of an entry has expired), whether you will allow a contest, or call upon the entryman to show cause why his entry should not be canceled on account of failure to submit proof within the statutory period after the entry.

Your office decision rejecting Meyer's application to contest said entry is therefore affirmed.

————

TIMBER CULTURE ENTRY—DEVOID OF TIMBER.
ALLEN v. SMITH.

A natural growth of trees, recognized in the neighborhood as valuable for domestic or commercial purposes, excludes the section from the operation of the timber culture law.

First Assistant Secretary Chandler to Acting Commissioner Stone, August 17, 1889.

I have before me the appeal of John Mack Smith from your office decision of June 21, 1888, holding for cancellation, on the contest of Otto Allen, said Smith's timber culture entry, No. 2146, made August 19, 1881, for the SW. ¼, of Sec. 28, T. 155, R. 46, Crookston district, Minnesota.

Allen initiated contest on April 5, 1886, charging that the entry had been improperly made, the land not being " devoid of timber."

On May 26, 1886, a hearing was held, both parties appearing and submitting testimony.

On July 20, 1886, the local officers rendered a decision recommending the cancellation of the entry on the ground that—

It appears from the testimony submitted, that there are fifteen acres of timber of a natural growth, such as poplar, balm of Gilead, and birch growing upon the section, averaging two to eight inches in diameter and from ten to thirty-five feet in height and valuable for domestic purposes in the neighborhood. (That) this timber appears to have been standing and growing on the section at the time the entry was made, as to which fact there is no conflicting testimony : one of the defendant's witnesses testified that the timber in these groves averaged eight to ten feet in height eight years ago.

On June 21, 1888, by the decision now appealed from your office approved said finding of facts, and held the entry for cancellation.

As the opinion of your office stated, there is practically " no dispute as to the finding of facts ; but it is claimed that the trees are not of the kind to render (prove) the land devoid of timber."

The argument of the appellant is, that your said office decision—

Is based on the theory that the circular of October, 1880, included "poplar" timber as trees within the meaning of the timber culture act because said circular included cottonwood, which belongs to the *genus* poplar. Now it is a well known fact that at the date of this entry and for a long time thereafter through a line of unbroken decisions, cottonwood was the only tree of the genus poplar that was recognized by the land department as a forest tree within the meaning of the timber culture act, and from the very fact that the circular designated cottonwood, and not poplar, it seems to be quite evident that the cottonwood tree was the only one of that genus entitled to recognition.

Of the "line of unbroken decisions" referred to, not a single one is cited by the learned counsel, and neither circular nor precedent has been found by me, showing that, either at the date of this entry or at any other time, a tract containing "fifteen acres of poplar, balm of Gilead, and birch" was supposed by this Department as "land naturally devoid of timber" within the sense of the timber culture law. The mere absence of departmental rulings the other way does not prove that the construction which would save this entry was a construction "prevailing at the date when said entry was made." To recognize, as good for entries made with reference to it, a former construction affirmatively made by the Department, is a very different thing from assuming that no kind of tree can be held to be "timber" unless the Department had "recognized" it as such before the making of the entry particularly in question. The statute can hardly require to be hypothetically "construed," in advance, in order to become enforceable in its true sense in any case arising under it. On this particular point, moreover, it was expressly announced as long ago as February, 1882 (1 L. D , 642) that "the enumeration of species on page 27, of the general circular of October 1, 1880, is only intended as a general guide, and is not to be construed to exclude any trees falling within the foregoing characterization—" *i. e.,* "such as are recognized in the neighborhood as of value for timber, or for commercial purposes, or for firewood or domestic use."

The decision appealed from is affirmed.

————

TIMBER CULTURE CONTEST—GOOD FAITH.

LEWIS *v.* PERSONS.

An attempt to cure a default after the affidavit of contest is filed, but before notice is served, can not be accepted as evidence of good faith, if such action is induced by the impending contest.

First Assistant Secretary Chandler to Acting Commissioner Stone, August 19, 1889.

I have considered the case of Geo Lewis *v.* Wm. Persons. on appeal of the latter from your office decision of February 9, 1888, holding for cancellation his timber culture entry for the NE. ¼, SW. ¼, Sec. 1, T. 10 S., R. 1 E., Concordia, Kansas, land district.

Persons made entry June 28, 1880, and on May 5, 1885, Lewis filed affidavit of contest alleging failure to break and cultivate said land, or to plant with trees the required acreage on said tract up to the time of filing said contest affidavit.

The evidence taken at the hearing shows that Persons, about the time of his entry, purchased the relinquishment of the land in controversy from a former timber culture claimant; that there was at the time of claimant's entry about five acres of plowed land upon the tract; in corn-planting time in 1882, claimant put in some cottonwood slips among the corn, sticking one in each hill of corn, in something over an acre of ground and they received whatever cultivation was given to the corn, which does not appear to have been very much, as it was allowed to become very weedy, large patches of very tall thistles and other weeds were grown and most of the slips failed to grow. In 1883 the defendant says himself that he cultivated only about half of the land planted to slips and other witnesses testify that it was less than that and he says that in 1884 he planted about half an acre of cuttings and cultivated about half the acre theretofore set out in cuttings.

Both the planting and cultivation was under the evidence poorly done and but few of the trees or slips grew.

On the day the affidavit of contest was filed, however, claimant was in the office of contestant's attorney and was by him informed that the application for contest had been filed and within the next two or three days he plowed up the ground anew where the slips had been planted, harrowed and put it in a good condition, and planted slips and young trees on two and a half acres. When asked if the information in regard to a contest affidavit being filed was not the cause of his last planting he answered, "not altogether." The evidence shows that young trees and slips in that locality should be planted in March or early in April.

I am of the opinion that the entryman was not endeavoring in good faith to comply with the law. Although nearly five years had elapsed from the date of the entry he had planted but little over an acre of the ground to trees until after contest was initiated and although he attempted to cure his laches and did get two and a half acres planted before the date of service of notice upon him which was May 19, 1 do not think this comes within the rule of Seitz v. Wallace (6 L. D., 299), wherein it was held that entryman might show compliance with the law after the affidavit of contest was filed but before notice was served on him, because in the determination of such questions good faith is always an important if not a controlling element. St. John v. Raff (8 L. D., 552).

Your said decision is accordingly affirmed.

PRACTICE—APPEAL—HOMESTEAD—FINAL PROOF.

JOHN O. MOUNGER.

An appeal will not be entertained if it is not taken in time and fails to allege error in the decision below.

While the Department has no power to extend the time within which a homesteader is required to submit final proof, yet, in the absence of an adverse claim, an entry may be submitted to the board of equitable adjudication where such proof is made after the expiration of the statutory period.

First Assistant Secretary Chandler to Acting Commissioner Stone, August 19 1889.

On January 18, 1881, John O. Mounger made homestead entry for the N. ½ of the SW. ¼, Sec. 27, and the E. ½ of the SE. ¼, Sec. 28, T. 3 S., R. 21 W., Camden land district, Arkansas, and on August 26, 1887, after due notice, he made his final proof thereunder, before the county judge of Garland county, in said State.

The proof on being submitted to the local officers was rejected by them "for the reason that claimant failed to maintain five years actual and continuous residence on the land, but boarded, as he says, 'about two-thirds of the time,' and as his witnesses say, the 'greater part of the time,' with his step-father, Mr. Parker."

From this finding the claimant appealed.

On May 17, 1888, your office, upon consideration of said appeal, concurred in the action below and affirmed the same. Due notice of this decision was given by the local officers, May 22, 1888, through registered mail, and on August 24, following, they reported to your office the fact that such notice had been given, and that no appeal, or other action in the premises, had been taken by the claimant. Thereupon, on September 1, 1888, your office held the entry in question for cancellation, as "having expired by limitation of the statute."

Upon receipt of this latter decision the local officers duly notified the claimant thereof, whereupon, on September 24, 1888, he filed with them, for transmission to your office, an appeal from your said office decision of May 17, 1888, without any assignment of error therein, either specific or general, but asking "that he be allowed a reasonable and sufficient time to complete his five years residence" on the land, "because . . . . . . his final proof shows that he was prevented from living thereon by reason of the continued sickness of his aged mother." Upon this appeal the papers in the case were transmitted here for departmental action.

The claimant's proof shows that, at the date of the making thereof, he was a single man, forty-four years of age, and in all respects qualified to make homestead entry; that his improvements consist of a log house, fourteen by fifteen feet, with shed nine by fourteen feet, built in 1881; a box house eighteen by twenty-five feet, with two rooms, plank floor, and board roof, three doors and two windows, built in 1884; two cribs and stable; garden, orchard of fifty trees, and twenty-seven acres cultivated, valued in the aggregate at from $275 to $380, and that he has cultivated to crop from three to twenty-seven acres of the tract each season for seven seasons. Upon the question of his settlement and residence on the land, his proof shows that he settled in June, 1881, when he cleared three acres, built a dwelling house and stable, and moved a family on the land, with whom, he says, he stayed, having no family of his own. To the question, "Where has been your actual, personal residence during the whole time since the date of this filing or entry?", he answers, "On the land and at Mr. Parker's near by." To the question, "Has your residence on the land now claimed been actual or constructive, continuous or at intervals?", he answers, "Actual part of the time and constructive the rest. My mother, Mrs. Parker, being old and afflicted, lived near by, and requiring my attention frequently, I stayed there a great part of the time at night, but cultivated the land all the time and kept a family there with whom I boarded when not needed by my mother." He further says: "I have boarded at Mr. Parker's about two-thirds of the time on account of my mother; she would not consent for me to leave." Then, in answer to a subsequent answer in his proof, namely: "Did you and your family live in said house" (meaning the house on the land) "during all of each or any winter, since the date of your filing or entry?", he says: "I did not, but my tenant and family did." His final proof witnesses both state that he boarded a greater part of the time with his step-father, John Parker; that he was not residing on the tract at the date of his proof, but had cultivated part of the land, and had rented out a portion thereof, or had it cultivated, during the whole time.

The first question arising upon the record is, whether the same is properly before the Department on the appeal filed, and, if so, to what extent the same can be here reviewed. This appeal, in form, is an appeal from the decision of May 17, 1888, affirming the action of the local officers in rejecting the claimant's proof because of insufficiency in the matter of his residence. It is wholly insufficient, however, as an appeal from the decision named, and can not be considered as such, for two reasons: (1) it was not filed within the time prescribed by the Rules of Practice, and (2) it alleges no error in the decision complained of.

The decision of May, 1888, became final, as to the questions therein decided, upon the expiration of seventy days from the date of mailing the notice thereof to the claimant by the local officers, without appeal having been filed; and that decision is therefore no longer subject to review by this Department, but must be considered as a final adjudication of the question of the sufficiency of the claimant's proof.

The most that can be done, therefore, is to treat the appeal filed as an appeal from the subsequent action of your office in holding the entry in question for cancellation, and as bringing the record here for review in that respect only. This action of your office was had as a matter entirely independent of anything contained in, or passed upon by the former decision of May, 1888, and was not based upon any defect in the proof, but solely upon the fact that the entry had expired by statutory limitation. It has no connection, therefore, with the decision finally rejecting the proof on the grounds stated.

The only claim asserted by the entryman in his said appeal is, in effect, that his entry should be allowed to stand, and that he be allowed time to complete his five years residence, because his proof shows that he was prevented from living on the land by reason of the sickness of his aged mother. In answer to this it is sufficient to say that there is no authority in the Department to grant, as a matter of right, the additional time asked for. The Department has no power to extend the time within which a homestead entryman is *required by statute* to make proof, showing compliance with the law under his entry.

Inasmuch, however, as there is no adverse claim to the land, and bad faith on the part of the claimant is not made apparent, I am reluctant, under the circumstances, to direct the cancellation of his entry solely because it has expired by statutory limitation. Edward Fullmer, 8 L. D., 614.

If, within a reasonable time, and prior to the intervention of an adverse claim, the entryman submits new proof satisfactorily showing compliance with the law in all respects, the same may be referred to the Board of Equitable Adjudication for the action of that tribunal. Goran Sandberg, 7 L. D. 384. Your office decision of September 1, 1888, is modified accordingly.

INDIAN LANDS—UTE RESERVATION—ACT OF JULY 28, 1882.

JOSEPH YULE.

The purpose of section 3, act of July 28, 1882, was to confirm the entries, settlements, and locations, within the ten mile strip described therein, of those who had mistakenly entered said strip believing it to be public land, subject however to the payment of the price fixed by law for the benefit of the Indians.

A soldier's additional homestead entry, made within said strip, may be perfected through cash payment of the purchase price.

First Assistant Secretary Chandler to Acting Commissioner Stone, August 19, 1889.

I have considered the appeal of Joseph Yule from your office decision of December 30, 1886, holding for cancellation his soldiers' addtional homestead entry for SW. ¼, NW. ¼, and NW. ¼, SW. ¼, section 8, T. 49 N., R. 1 W., Gunnison, Colorado, land district, made June 22, 1878.

This land is a part of the Ute Indian reservation ceded to the United States by treaty and confirmed by the act of June 15, 1880 (21 Stat.,

199) and is a part of the ten mile strip referred to in section three, of the act of July 28, 1882 (22 Stat., 178).

The one hundred and seventh degree of longitude west from Greenwich was the eastern boundary of the Ute Indian reservation, but by reason of some mistake in the surveys as to its location, the public surveys encroached upon said reservation in the locality in which the land in controversy is situated, and many settlers had filed upon lands actually within the said reservation and were living thereon and the object of section three of the act of July 28, 1882, was for the relief of those who had by reason of such mistake made entries or settlements on said strip.

The Indian title to the land in controversy was extinguished by act of Congress of June 15, 1880, which provided in section three, that after an allotment of lands in severalty to the members of the Indian tribes named,—

All lands not so allotted, the title to which is, by the said agreement of the confederated bands of the Ute Indians, and this acceptance by the United States, released and conveyed to the United States, shall be held and deemed to be public lands of the United States, and subject to disposal under the laws providing for the disposal of the public lands, at the same price and on the same terms as other lands of like character, except as provided in this act: *Provided*, That none of said lands, whether mineral or otherwise, shall be liable to entry and settlement under the homestead law; but shall be subject to cash entry only in accordance with existing law.

To carry into effect said treaty, Congress passed the act of July 28, 1882, providing in section three, thereof,—

That all entries, settlements, or locations heretofore made under any law of the United States, by duly qualified persons, upon a strip of land extending northerly and southerly, not exceeding ten miles in width, within that part of the Ute Indian reservation in the State of Colorado, lately occupied by the Uncompahgre and White River Ute Indians, and bounded on the east by the one hundred and seventh meridian of longitude, west from Greenwich, shall legally date from the time they were respectively made; and the rights of said persons shall be in all respects the same as if the lands had been legally subject to their claims when the same were initiated: *Provided, however*, That if homestead entries have been made on said strip, the lands so entered shall be paid for in cash, after proof which would be satisfactory under the pre-emption laws: And *provided further*, That none of said lands shall be disposed of for any consideration other than cash, nor for a less price than one dollar and twenty-five cents per acre.

It appears from the evidence that the appellant entered the land in controversy under the law providing for additional homestead entries for soldiers, and under which they were not required to settle or reside upon the land, and that soon after making entry he sold his interest in said land. The tract so entered was within the ten mile strip referred to in section three, of the act of July 28, 1882, which provides that all entries, settlements, or locations made prior to the passage of the act upon said ten mile strip made by duly qualified persons shall date from the time they were respectively made; "and the rights of said persons shall be in all respects the same as if the lands had been legally subject to their claims when the same were initiated."

Your office held the entry for cancellation on the assumption that proof could not be made "which would be satisfactory under the pre-emption laws," inasmuch as settlement and inhabitancy are not required in soldiers' additional entries. Said act, however, requires such proof only in "homestead entries." This term evidently refers to homestead entries under which proof of settlement and inhabitancy must be shown. Otherwise it would follow that this statute meant to discriminate against soldiers' additional homestead entries, and add thereto a new requirement, viz: settlement and inhabitancy. There is nothing in the act to warrant such a construction. It was not intended to deprive any class of a privilege conferred by law, but on the contrary to con-firm the entries, settlement and locations of those who had mistakenly entered the strip believing it to be public land; subject all the time to the payment of the price fixed by law, for the benefit of the said In-dians.

The object of the law being to permit all who had entries, settlements and locations on said ten mile strip to secure title to the same by pay-ment of one dollar and twenty-five cents per acre, but in ordinary homestead entries, in order to prevent fraud the law requires such proof as "would be satisfactory under the pre-emption laws."

The entry in the case at bar being for soldiers' additional homestead did not require residence, and could only come within the general re-quirement, that the land be paid for. The entryman may be allowed to pay for said land at the legal rate, and upon his so doing patent may issue.

Your said decision is accordingly reversed.

***

PRACTICE—REVIEW—PETITION FOR SECOND REVIEW.

ANDERSON ET AL. v. BYAM ET AL.

It is the practice of the Department to dispose of motions for review as soon as a proper consideration thereof will admit; such motions taking precedence of appeals on the regular docket, unless for some good reason an exception is made in a par-ticular case.

Evidence merely cumulative in character, or tending to produce a conflict with that already submitted, can not be accepted as a proper basis for review.

A petition for a second review should be limited to the office of suggesting new facts or questions not before presented.

Acting Secretary Chandler to Acting Commissioner Stone, August 21, 1889.

On August 6, 1889, this Department denied the motion for review and reversal of its decision of April 2, 1889, in the case of George An-derson *et al. v.* Henry S. Byam *et al.*, 8 L. D., 388. On August 13, 1889, the attorneys for Anderson filed a petition asking that said last decis-ion be recalled and the case be re-examined on the motion for review. Accompanying this petition are twelve affidavits and an argument by counsel, who state they were unable to file the latter earlier, because of delay in the receipt of the affidavits, and because of the time thereafter consumed in preparing their brief; and furthermore because they understood that action upon the motion could not be had for some time to come.

In regard to these statements of counsel, implying as they do undue expedition in the disposition of said motion for review, it is to be remarked that it was filed on May 13, 1889, that all of the affidavits now filed were sworn to in California on or before that day, and, finally, that decision was not made until nearly three months after the motion was made, during which period, it is my opinion, ample time was afforded counsel to have received the affidavits from California, to have prepared and filed their argument in the matter. It has been the practice of this Department to dispose of motions for review at as early day as a proper consideration thereof will permit, such motions taking precedence of appeals on the regular docket, unless for some good reason an exception is made in a particular case. No exception appearing in regard to the motion in question, the same was duly disposed of when reached.

Notwithstanding the very full and careful consideration which this case has received, and its determination in accordance with approved rulings, as numerous and well settled as any known to the bench and bar, the counsel for Anderson again asks the officers to re-open the judgment, upon the ground that work had not been resumed, within the meaning of the statute, prior to the relocation; the very point upon which the case was decided against them three times. And in support of the application twelve affidavits are filed, tending to show that work was not being done on the claim at the time testified to, and was not of the character stated, or contemplated by law as sufficient. These affidavits if true would have the effect only to produce a conflict with some of the testimony already in the case, and would be cumulative as to other testimony therein, all of which had been considered.

There is no rule of law known to me by which such testimony can be properly made, under the circumstances, the basis for granting a new trial, in a court of law, and therefore no sufficient reason, under our rules, for reviewing and reversing a former decision. · Certainly, if this case is now to be re-opened on the arguments and affidavits filed, it is difficult to see when we could deny an application for a second review; a practice which this Department has set its face against, and in relation to which it is said, in the matter of the application for a second review, in the case of Bartch v. Kennedy, 4 L. D., 383:

If when this Department, on review, determines a cause, it is again to be called upon to entertain a second application for review, I see no reason why such application may not be continued indefinitely, whilst the rights of parties are left unsettled, and the officials of the Department continuously and hopelessly are employed in iterating and reiterating conclusions long since deliberately arrived at and formally asserted. There certainly must be some point in a case where litigation ends and the rights of parties become finally determined.

These remarks apply with force and appositeness to the present application.   In addition, in Neff *v.* Cowhick, 8 L. D. 111, it was said:

Hereafter let the rule be that no motion for a re-review shall be filed. If the defeated party is able to present any suggestions of fact or points of law not previously discussed or involved in the case, it may be done by petition, which shall contain all the facts and arguments. On the filing of such petition, if it appears important, the Secretary will make such order for recalling the case . . . . . and such direction for further hearing as may be necessary . . . . . Such petition should not re-argue points already twice passed upon, but should be limited to the office indicated of suggesting new facts or considerations not before presented.

Counsel have not complied with the rule herein prescribed, but have proceeded to re-argue the case upon the old issues, and have submitted additional affidavits in relation thereto.   This rule in the Cowhick case, so necessary to the proper and orderly dispatch of the public business must hereafter be enforced.

The prayer of the petitioner is denied, the petition dismissed, and the papers filed are herewith sent to you for record.

NATURALIZATION—MINOR—FINAL PROOF.

JAMES H. ROBERTSON ET AL.

The father's naturalization during the minority of the son inures to the benefit of the latter and makes him a citizen.

Though a settlement under the pre-emption law by a minor is invalid the defect is cured, if, in the absence of an adverse claim, he attains his majority prior to making entry.

An entry may be referred to the board of equitable adjudication, where the final proof was accepted by the local officers prior to the regulations of February 19, 1887, and is satifactory in all respects, save that it was not taken on the day advertised.

First Assistant Secretary Chandler to Acting Commissioner Stone, August 22, 1889.

On October 2, 1882, James H. Robertson filed his pre-emption declaratory statement for the NW. ¼, Sec. 6, T. 130 N., R. 62 W., Fargo land district, Dakota, alleging settlement April 20, 1882. Plat of survey was filed in land office September 4, 1882.

Notice was properly given and advertised for the making of claimant's proof before Wesley Moran, clerk of the district court, Ellendale, Dickey county, Dakota, on January 26, 1883; it was actually made on March 8, the same year, before the said officer. No satisfactory reason or excuse is given why it was made on the day appointed.

Robertson in his said proof, testified, that he was of the age of twenty-one years, a native born citizen, unmarried; the proof further shows, that he made his first settlement on the land April 20, 1882, by building a house and established his residence thereon the same day. He asserts his residence to have been continuous. His improvements consist of a house fourteen by fourteen feet, valued by him at fifty dollars, and twenty acres of breaking, one hundred dollars. Total value of improvements one hundred and fifty dollars. He raised on the land a crop of twenty bushels of potatoes. His witnesses corroborate claimant's testimony; they also state that claimant is a native born citizen. The house on the claim they value at one hundred dollars.

Your office by letter " G " of October 23, 1884, required the claimant to furnish an affidavit showing his exact age at the time of his settlement, also a non-mineral affidavit.

The non-mineral affidavit was duly transmitted, also Robertson's affidavit, bearing date February 18, 1885, from which it appears that he was born in Rockwood, Wellington county, Canada, on the tenth of October 1861, and that at the date of his settlement on the said land he was twenty years, six months and ten days of age.

On September 28, 1887, the local officers transmitted to your office another affidavit of Robertson bearing date November 29, 1884, showing that he was twenty-one years of age on the tenth day of October, 1881.

Your office by decision of February 20, 1888, rejected claimant's proof and held his entry for cancellation, because " proof was not made until six weeks after date advertised, and claimant was not a qualified preemptor at date of residence and settlement, being under twenty-one years of age, and not a citizen of the United States."

From this decision, Curtis and Burdette, July 12, 1888, " as attorneys for parties in interest," appealed to this Department and filed the affidavit of Merrick E. Vinton, showing that he as first Vice President of the Middlesex Banking Company on March 31, 1883, negotiated a loan of three hundred dollars to the claimant secured by a mortgage upon the said land, that the said loan was made in good faith and that the debt remains unsatisfied. Vinton asks leave to intervene in the case.

Subsequent to the said appeal, July 1, 1889, the said attorneys filed a duly authenticated copy of the order of the circuit court of the county of Adair, Missouri, admitting one George Robertson, on October 18, 1880, to become a citizen of the United States. They also filed the affidavit of one Charteole Robertson, showing that she is the mother of the said claimant and that George Robertson, his father " took out his final or full citizen's papers on the 18th day of October 1880, in the county of Adair and State of Missouri, in the circuit court of said county."

This evidence removes one objection of your office to Robertson's entry. His father's naturalization, before claimant attained the age of twenty-one years, made him a citizen. Revised Statutes, Sec. 2172. Regarding the further objection, that he, at the date of his settlement on the land, was under the age of twenty-one years, I am of the opinion that this illegality was cured by claimant's attaining his majority before he made his entry. See case of James F. Bright, 6 L. D., 602.

The remaining question is the irregularity in the making of the proof, it not having been taken as advertised. The rule that is to be adopted on this objection has been pointed out in subdivision 9, of the circular of the General Land Office, July 17, 1889 (9 L. D., 123). Since the proof as submitted was accepted by the local officers and since it further appears that such proof, in all other respects is satisfactory, the case will be submitted, in accordance with said circular to the board of equitable adjudication.

Your said office decision is accordingly modified.

HOMESTEAD CONTEST–EVIDENCE–PRACTICE–FINAL PROOF.

SCOTT *v.* KING.

A contest must fail if the entryman in good faith cures his default before notice of contest is served.

The fact of compliance with law after affidavit of contest is filed, and before legal notice thereof, goes to the weight, and not to the admissibility of the testimony.

Actual knowledge of an impending contest will not prejudice the claimant, if his subsequent compliance with law is in pursuance of a previous *bona fide* intent.

The burden of proof is upon the contestant to establish his charges by a preponderance of evidence.

On questions of fact the Department will not, in the case of conflicting evidence upon which fair minds might reasonably differ, disturb concurring decisions of the local and General Land Office.

Under rule 5 ¦ of practice, the pendency of a contest on appeal precludes the submission of final proof for land involved therein.

First Assistant Secretary Chandler to Acting Commissioner Stone, August 22, 1889.

In the case of Joseph Scott, contestant, *v.* Aden D. King, involving the latter's homestead entry, No. 2217, on the NE. ¼ of Sec. 8, T. 3 N., R. 31 W., McCook district, Nebraska, Scott appeals from the decision of your office of May 22, 1888, affirming the action of the local officers in dismissing his contest of said entry.

The entry was made, January 19, 1885, and it appears from the affidavit and notice of contest and endorsements thereon, that said affidavit was made and filed February 1, 1886, and said notice was issued March 1, and served March 3, of that year.

It is contended on the part of the contestant, that a claimant's default in failing to comply with the law can not be cured after the filing of the affidavit of contest, and hence that compliance with the law after February 1, the date of the filing of the affidavit in this case could not avail the claimant, and proof thereof was inadmissible. The claimant insists, that such default (if it exist) may be cured at any time prior to service of notice of contest—in this case, March 3, 1886. The latter position is in accordance with the decisions of this Department. (Stayton *v.* Carroll, 7 L. D., 198; Hunter *v.* Haynes, ib., 8; St. John *v.* Raff, 8 L.

D.,552.) Evidence, however, of compliance with the law after the filing of the affidavit and before the service of legal notice, should be considered with reference to the question whether the claimant *in fact* had or had not knowledge of the filing of the contest and in the former event, whether his subsequent compliance with law was because of such knowledge and with a view of defeating the contest, and with no previous intent to comply with the law in good faith, or was uninfluenced by such knowledge and *bona fide* in pursuance of an original purpose to fulfill the law. In the former case, the evidence would be entitled to little or no weight, and in the latter, to as much as if no affidavit had been filed. The fact of compliance with the law after affidavit and before legal notice merely goes to the weight and not the admissibility of the testimony, and, accordingly, it is held in St. John *v.* Raff, *supra*, that, in considering questions as to such evidence, " good faith is always an important if not a controlling element."

In the present case, the claimant had offered commutation proof, and the contestant had filed a protest against its allowance, alleging failure on the part of the claimant to comply with the law as to residence and cultivation, and of this protest the claimant had knowledge some time in January, 1886. The commutation proof was subsequently withdrawn by the claimant, and the affidavit of contest was filed, as above stated, February 1, 1886. This and other circumstances in the case go to show, that the claimant, if he had not actual knowledge of the filing of the affidavit of contest, at least had reason to believe, on February 14, 1886— two weeks after the filing of said affidavit, when he moved his wife to the house upon the claim—that his entry would be attacked. If knowledge of the filing of the affidavit, however, were positively shown, the claimant should not be prejudiced thereby, if his subsequent compliance with the law was in pursuance of an original *bona fide* intent.

A large amount of testimony was taken on the hearing—the contestant introducing beside himself four witnesses, one of whom was his father-in-law and another his brother-in-law, and the claimant seven witnesses besides himself, all of whom appear to have been disinterested. The testimony of the former was largely negative, while that of the latter was for the most part positive. It appears from the claimant's testimony, that he with his eldest son established residence upon the tract, May 25, 1885 (within five months from date of entry), and from that time on he had resided continuously thereon. His wife and younger children at that time were in Iowa, the claimant's old home, and when he brought them to Nebraska (in August or September, 1885), they lived temporarily in a house built by the claimant " on speculation " on a school section nearer Culbertson than the homestead tract, on account of the serious illness of an infant. This was done under the advice of the family physician, and as soon as the physician advised that it was safe to move the child to the claim, namely, on February 14, 1886, the wife and the balance of the family moved to the claim, where the claimant had been living since May 25, 1885. The claimant had paid

$436.00 for the relinquishment of a prior entry, and prior to June 1, 1885, and within six months from date of entry, he had built upon the tract a house, twelve by sixteen feet, broken forty-one acres and set out two thousand forest trees, and since that date, he built an addition to the house of the same size, broke twenty acres more, and had a well dug, one hundred and fifteen feet deep. All of his improvements cost $575.00, and the total amount expended by him for the claim, including amount paid for relinquishment, was $1,011.00. The material for the addition to the house was on the claim prior to February 1, 1886, date of affidavit of contest, and the contract for digging the well had been made before that time. It is stated by counsel for the contestant, that the claimant when asked on cross-examination, "What his object in making proof was, answered in substance, that he wanted to prove up in order to get back to town." I have carefully examined the claimant's testimony, both on direct and cross-examination, and find nothing to warrant this statement. On the contrary, he states distinctly, that his intention "is to make the tract a home," and that his object in buying the relinquishment and making the entry "was to procure the land for himself and family in compliance with the homestead law."

If the claimant's testimony be true, he was not in default even at the date of the filing of the affidavit of contest, but was then himself resid-ing upon the land (where he had been continuously since May 25, 1885), as a home, with the intent to bring his wife and younger children there as soon as it was safe to move his sick baby. The physician testifies that the baby could not have been safely moved and that he so advised. This, with the other facts in the case, rebuts the charge that claimant's real home was in his house on the school section. (It appears the claimant did not own the school section, but for a consideration had only obtained the use of it from the State.)

The burden of proof is upon the contestant to establish his charges by a preponderance of evidence, and bad faith can not be imputed to a claimant upon mere circumstances of suspicion—particularly, in the face of positive testimony to the contrary. Neff v. Cowlick, 6 L. D., 660.

The local officers found in favor of the claimant, and your office sus-tained their action. There is evidence to support your conclusions.

The evidence being conflicting in its character and upon "which fair minds might reasonably differ as to the conclusions that should be drawn" therefrom, and it having been passed upon by two tribunals as triers of the facts, and each concurring, I do not feel warranted in re-versing your action. Indeed, in view of the improvements of the claim-ant and his residence upon the tract, I think your decision is in keeping with the spirit of the homestead act and should be sustained.

The decision of your office is therefore affirmed. The proof made by the claimant pending the contest and after the local officers had for-warded the contest papers to your office, must be rejected, under Rule 53 of Practice and numerous decisions of this Department.

APPLICATION—SETTLEMENT RIGHTS—PRACTICE.

CHICHESTER v. ALLEN.

A change made in the description of the land included in an application to enter,
pending final action thereon, must be held subject to intervening settlement
rights.

Concurring decisions of the local and General Land Office on questions of fact are
generally accepted as conclusive by the Department, where the evidence is conflicting.

First Assistant Secretary Chandler to Acting Commissioner Stone, August
22, 1889.

I have considered the case of Geo. A. Chichester v. Joseph Allen on
appeal of the former from your office decision of June 13, 1888, holding
for cancellation his timber culture entry for E. ½, SW. ¼, SE. ¼, NW. ¼,
and lot 3, of Sec. 3, T. 20 N., R. 5 E., Helena, Montana, land district.

On March 6, 1885, Chichester made timber culture entry for said
land, and on April 10, 1885, Allen made homestead entry therefor,
alleging settlement January 30, 1885.

By direction of your office a hearing was had April 5, 1886, to determine the rights of the parties. After hearing the evidence the local
officers decided in favor of Allen and your office on appeal affirmed their
decision.

It appears from the evidence that Allen's first act of settlement on
the land was on January 30, 1885, and consisted in putting down the
foundation for a log house, and on February 21, he hauled logs upon
the land and built the walls up several feet high and finally completed
it and occupied it with his family on April 14, 1885.

It appears that after Allen had commenced his settlement he was
informed that Chichester had made application to make timber culture
entry for said land and he thereupon sent the witness Malone to see
Mortson, the notary public who made out the application for Chichester
and was informed by him that said application was for the land lying
immediately east of that in controversy. It appears from Mr. Chichester's own testimony that he first made out papers on January 31,
1885, for timber culture entry and sent them to the land office but they
were returned for more fees on account of part of the land being fractional and that a foundation was built on said land between the time
he first sent his papers and the date of the entry and when asked on
cross examination if his application to enter as sent to the local office
January 31, 1885, was not for entirely different land and not for that
covered by Allen's entry, and if he did not change the description when
they were sent back so as to make them include Allen's entry, he answered " my papers show the land I filed on," and although the question

was several times repeated he declined to answer directely or to make any other answer than the one above given.

The original application and affidavit of Chichester are with the record and I find on inspection that as originally made out by Mr. Mortson the application and affidavit both describe the land as W. ½ SE. ¼, and W. ½ NE. ¼, which would be the land lying immediately east of that entered by Allen, but a pen has been drawn through some of the words and some words interlined, so that it now reads E. ½, SW. ¼, and E. ½, NW. ¼, the section in both cases being 3, T. 20, N., R. 5 E., which is the same land now in controversy, the NE. ¼, NW. ¼, being fractional, is called lot 3. A certificate of Notary Morston is attached but it says only that on January 31, 1885, Chichester filed a timber culture claim on land in section 3, T. 20, R. 5, and does not aid us in coming to a conclusion.

One witness at the hearing swore that he saw Chichester looking for the corners of the land in dispute and that night heard him talking about filing on the land and freezing " old Allen out."

I am of the opinion that under the evidence it is shown that Chichester did change the description of the land described in his application at first, and that before making such change Allen's improvement amounted to such obvious settlement as to give notice and that he had actual notice of Allen's acts of settlement before he made entry for said land.

It is strenuously insisted by counsel for the appellant that Allen has not acted in good faith, with the honest intention to make a home of this tract; that at best he only desired it for a sheep camp.

Upon this question the presumption of the law is that he did act in good faith and this presumption stands until it is overcome by evidence, direct or circumstantial. Allen testifies to his bona fides and offers proof to support it. The evidence is conflicting upon this point. It is of that character, that fair minds might reach different conclusions and I am constrained to believe that at the date of the institution of the contest there is sufficient evidence to support the good faith of the entryman. Whether his subsequent acts will justify the conclusion depends altogether upon his residence and improvements upon the tract.

This hearing was had within a year after his entry. If he has not, within the lifetime thereof, by inhabitancy of and improvements upon the land, satisfied the spirit of the law and the rulings of the Department, the question of the honesty of his purpose can be determined at any time before final proof.

I do not feel at liberty, with two concurring decisions upon this evidence against the appellant, to disturb your conclusions.

It has repeatedly been held by this Department, that where the evidence is conflicting the joint opinion of the local officers is entitled to special consideration. Kelly v. Halverson, 6 L. D., 225; Austin v. Thomas, id., 310; Murfey v. Barrows, 4 L. D. 135.

Your concurring in the conclusious reached by them and as there is evidence upon which to support Allen's entry as having been made in good faith, the timber culture entry of Chichester will be canceled.

Your said decision is accordingly affirmed.

－－

TIMBER CULTURE CONTEST—GOOD FAITH.

LOCKHART v. HECKEL.

A timber culture entry should not be canceled where, through mistake, a small portion of the area in cultivation is outside of the boundary lines of the land entered.

First Assistant Secretary Chandler to Acting Commissioner Stone, August 22, 1889.

I have considered the case of J. W. Lockhart v. Peter Heckel, on appeal of the former from your office decision of June 7, 1888, dismissing his contest against the timber culture entry of said Heckel for NW. ¼, Sec. 19, T. 31, R. 10, Niobrara, Nebraska, land district.

Heckel made his entry May 10, 1879, and the contest was commenced June 27, 1886, upon the ground that the claimant had failed to break or plant to tree seeds or cuttings the ten acres required by law.

Upon the evidence taken at the hearing the local officers recommended the dismissal of the contest and your office by the decision complained of affirmed that of the local officers.

The entry is for one hundred and fifty and twenty-two hundredth acres and contestant's witnesses testify that there are 9.62 acres of trees ranging from about two feet to over thirteen feet high and in a fairly good condition, while two or three witnesses who counted the trees made the number 11,200, but the contestant and some of his witnesses claim that only 8.04 acres of the land cultivated to trees is upon the land entered by claimant while the remainder is on adjoining land. The owner of the adjoining land, however, says that claimant put the whole amount of the broken tract in trees and that he does not claim any of them. He does not know whether the trees extend over on his claim or not, as he has never been able to find the government corner at that point which would determine the question.

The claimant was confined to his bed by sickness at the time of the hearing and for some weeks before and did not appear. Several of the witnesses testified that there were ten acres of trees, but this much is clear that the entryman duly planted and cultivated between nine and a half and ten acres to timber and has now growing thereon over 11,200 trees in a thrifty condition ; that if any part of said land extends over the line of his claim it was done through mistake, and as no regular survey of the line by a county surveyor has been made, it does not fully appear that all the timber is not upon his own land.

Nothing appears tending to show the least bad faith on the part of the entryman. Even if three-fourths of an acre of claimant's trees are upon his neighbor's land, under the circumstances of this case, I think he is protected by the following authorities; Peck *v.* Taylor, 3 L. D., 372; Thompson *v.* Sankey, id., 365; Jackson *v.* Grable, 7 L. D., 365. Your said decision dismissing the contest is accordingly affirmed.

PRE-EMPTION–HOMESTEAD–TRANSMUTATION.

HUGH TAYLOR.

The right of transmutation, after the statutory life of the filing has expired, is not defeated by an intervening homestead entry, made during the pendency of final proof proceedings on the part of the pre-emptor, and with full knowledge of his existing *bona fide* relation to the land.

Acting Secretary Chandler to Acting Commissioner Stone, August 23, 1889.

I have before me the appeal of Hugh Taylor from your office decision of March 30, 1888, rejecting his application to transmute into a homestead entry his pre-emption declaratory statement, No. 395 (for the NW. ¼. Sec. 34, T. 32 S., R. 30 W., Garden City district, Kansas) and declining to order the hearing asked for by Taylor for the purpose of proving the facts upon which his said application was based.

Taylor's pre-emption filing was made August 30, 1884, but, as then made, it by mistake misdescribed the land, as being in township No. 33 S., instead of township 32 S., as the fact really was. This error was corrected by amendment authorized May 4, 1887.

Taylor's said application to transmute, bearing date March 6, 1888, and which is sworn to by him and corroborated under oath by seventeen other persons, contains the following allegations:

That about September 20, 1884, he established a residence upon the NW. qr. of Sec. 34, T. 32 S., range 30 west, with his family, consisting of a wife and two children, and has had a daily, personal, continuous residence on said tract with his family from that day up to this date; that about October, 1886, he made final proof for said (tract) and presented the same to the United States land office for their acceptance; that said proof was rejected on the ground that the declaratory statement (as first made out) embraced the NW., qr. of sec. 34, Tp. 33 s., range 30 west, instead of the NW. qr. of Sec. 34, T. 32 s., range 30 W., the tract for which he had made final proof; that he, this affiant, immediately proceeded to take steps to have said declaratory statement amended to embrace the tract which he intended entering; that the Commissioner, in his letter " G " of May 4, 1887, allowed said declaratory statement to be amended, and that he, this affiant, was of the opinion that his time began to count on the declaratory statement as amended at the time said declaratory statement was amended, August 17; that he, this affiant, is a poor man and since the date that said amendment was allowed has been unable to raise the money to tender on said proof which was made October 20, 1886; that he has made application to loan companies and has been unable to perfect a loan on said tract; that he has used every effort to raise the money, but failed in each and every instance; that it has been utterly impossible for him to make the payments required for said tract, on account of his extreme poverty; that he has upon said tract at this time improvements as follows: A sod house, ten by twenty feet, board floor, board roof, one door, two windows, plastered inside, and twenty acres broken and under cultivation; that during the year 1886 he raised about twenty acres of corn and millet on said tract; that during the year 1887 he planted the whole of said twenty acres, or about, which is under cultivation on said tract to corn, sorghum and millet, but failed to realize anything from said planting except about one wagon-load of sorghum cane; that about the first seven months in which he resided upon said tract, being unable to dig a well, he had to haul water for the use of himself and family a distance of nine miles; that he is still unable to dig a well and hauls the water for the use of himself and family a distance of two miles; that during the greater part of the summers of 1885, 1886, and 1887, he, this affiant, has been unable to work or do anything out of doors on account of attacks of pneumonia, inflammatory rheumatism and malarial fever; that on the 14th day of February, 1888, one Thomas B. Roberts made homestead entry No. 16395 for said tract; that at the time of making said entry, said Roberts knew of the adverse claim of this affiant and the circumstances connected therewith; that on account of his extreme poverty and disability, his failure to raise the money to make the payment as required, affiant here asks that his declaratory statement be transmuted into a homestead, and that . . . . inasmuch as Thomas B. Roberts has filed a homestead entry on the tract with the full knowledge of the adverse right of this affiant, a hearing be ordered in said cause for a full investigation of all the facts and that he, this affiant, be allowed to prove the allegations hereinbefore set forth.

By the decision appealed from, your office held as follows:

It is found that Taylor's filing expired May 20, 1887. The fact of its expiration would not preclude him from making pre-emption entry or transmuting his filing to a homestead entry, in the absence of any valid adverse claim. A homestead entry has, since the date of expiration, attached to the tract. Taylor is, therefore, debarred, by it, from the transmutation desired. The ordering of a hearing would in view hereof, avail him nothing, and his application is denied.

In this view I cannot concur. Taylor having on file an uncanceled pre-emption filing; he and his family having all along continued to make the tract their actual and only home and place of residence; he having, after due notice, offered final proof, and the proceedings upon such proof being in law still pending undetermined (notwithstanding his having been unable since making proof to make the required final payment); and, finally, Roberts the so-called "adverse" claimant, having had full knowledge of these facts when he undertook to make his entry of the tract, that entry was irregularly allowed (L. J. Capps, 8 L. D., 406) and is in law no bar to the transmutation asked for by Taylor. The privilege of transmutation granted by section 2289, of the Revised Statutes to one who "may have filed" a pre-emption claim, must, I think, be held to continue available accordingly, at least until the "pre-emption claim" has been legally extinguished by a final determination to that effect, though, of course, the transmutation must be made subject to the rights, if any, of either prior adverse claimants or successful contestants of the "pre-emption claim" itself. The statute itself does not attach to a failure to transmute before the expiration of the pre-emption period, any such penalty as instant and necessary forfeiture of the right of transmutation, for the benefit of any other applicant to make entry, who must be preferred in any event and wholly irrespective of the equities of the case. Such a mere subsequent applicant not having been made by the statute, a beneficiary who is to profit by the pre-emption claimant's failure to transmute in time, this Department is not bound, for the former's benefit, to declare finally forfeited the claim of one whose relations to the land have never been abandoned, but on the contrary began long prior to Roberts' application and have ever since continued to be even unusually close and meritorious and precisely such as alone the government's policy requires on the part of applicant for homesteads (see Eploy *v.* Trick, 8 L. D., 110; Gainer *v.* Paazig, id, 346).

For the reasons stated the decision appealed from is hereby reversed, and you are directed to order a hearing for the determination of the conflicting claims of Roberts and Taylor.

DESERT LAND ENTRY—COMPACTNESS.

THOMAS SWAN.

The requirement of compactness is statutory, and an entry in violation thereof is not protected by the fact that it was made prior to the issuance of departmental instructions as to said requirement.

In adjusting an entry to secure compactness thereof, due regard should be given to the situation of the land, and its relation to adjacent tracts at the time the initial entry was made.

Acting Secretary Chandler to Acting Commissioner Stone, August 23, 1889.

By letter of April 9, 1889, your office transmitted a motion by Thomas Swan for review of the decision of the Department dated January 22, 1889, requiring Swan to reform his desert land entry in respect to compactness and to furnish further proof as to the desert character of the land, and its actual reclamation.

On April 3, 1879, Swan made desert land entry for W. $\frac{1}{2}$, NW. $\frac{1}{4}$, Sec. 13, SE. $\frac{1}{4}$, NE. $\frac{1}{4}$, N. $\frac{1}{2}$, SE. $\frac{1}{4}$, and N. $\frac{1}{2}$, SW. $\frac{1}{4}$, Sec. 14,—NE. $\frac{1}{4}$, SE. $\frac{1}{4}$, and S. $\frac{1}{2}$, SE. $\frac{1}{4}$, Sec. 15, W. $\frac{1}{2}$, NE. $\frac{1}{4}$ and SE. $\frac{1}{4}$, Sec. 22, T. 25 N., R. 69 W., Cheyenne, Wyoming, and on June 21, 1882, by permission of your office amended the same so as to embrace the W. $\frac{1}{2}$, of NW. $\frac{1}{4}$, Sec. 13 SE. $\frac{1}{4}$, NE. $\frac{1}{4}$, N. $\frac{1}{2}$, SE. $\frac{1}{4}$, E. $\frac{1}{2}$, SW. $\frac{1}{4}$, Sec. 14, –NE. $\frac{1}{4}$, NW. $\frac{1}{4}$, S. $\frac{1}{2}$, NW. $\frac{1}{4}$, NW. $\frac{1}{4}$, SW. $\frac{1}{4}$, Sec. 23, and SW. $\frac{1}{4}$, NE. $\frac{1}{4}$, SE. $\frac{1}{4}$, Sec. 22, T. 23 N., R. 69 W.

On September 20, 1882, the claimant made final proof and payment for the land embraced in his amended entry.

Your office decision of July 8, 1886, found said entry to be non-compact within the meaning of Maren Christensen (4 L. D., 317), and directed the local officers to "call upon the entryman to adjust the boundaries of his entry according to the above decision."

From this action the claimant appeals here.

The claimant avers in his final proof that every legal subdivision had been irrigated ; that " water was conveyed on the land by one main ditch three miles long, six feet wide, two and a half or three feet deep on an average. It was distributed by smaller ditches one foot deep and eighteen inches wide. I do not know what the length of the smaller ditches is. They are different lengths."

The Department held that. " This entry can by no possibility be regarded as justly within the statutory requirement as to compactness of form," and said :

> Were it not for the fact that your office had allowed the amendment of this claim, and thus given apparent recognition of its character, no question could be entertained that it should be substantially and materially reformed, or canceled. In view of that fact, however, your decision is affirmed—with the modification that, upon further proofs showing satisfactorily the original desert character of the land, its actual reclamation from desert land to agricultural, and such reformation in respect to compactness as may most fairly meet the law and the necessities of the case, the allowance of the entry may be reconsidered to the extent that justice shall by the facts as presented demand. The entryman should be required to make this showing within ninety days after notice of the decision ; and it would be prudent to direct a special agent to make a careful examination of the facts and circumstances.

The motion urges that the entry was made " previously " to the issue of the circular of the Department as to compactness of such entries and consequently should not be affected by such circular. But in the case of Julius H. Christensen (9 L. D., 202), it was held that the requirement of compactness is statutory and an entry in violation thereof is not protected by the fact that it was made prior to the issuance of departmental instructions as to said requirement. This entry, as the one in that case, is in no sense compact. See also Joseph Himmelsbach (7 L. D., 247).

It is urged that the order for further proof as to the original character of the land and its actual reclamation should not be insisted on. No new facts on this point, however, are presented. In view of the character of the entry and the situation of this land with reference to a running stream, I do not feel justified in disturbing the order as made.

The motion is, accordingly, denied.

The adjustment required shall have regard to the situation of the land and its relation to other lands at the time the entry was made.

HOMESTEAD CONTEST—DECEASED ENTRYMAN.

ROHRBOUGH v. DIGGINS.

A contest against the entry of a deceased homesteader, wherein the said decedent is made the sole party defendant, is a nullity, and the rights of the real parties in interest are not affected thereby.

First Assistant Secretary Chandler to Acting Commissioner Stone, August 24, 1889.

I have before me what purports to be the appeal of " Chas. Diggins " from your office decision of April 20, 1888, holding for cancellation his homestead final certificate No. 2469, dated July 26, 1884, for lots 15, 16, and 17, and NE. ¼, SW. ¼, Sec. 5, T. 24 N., R. 13 W., San Francisco district, California.

The township plat having been filed on April 1, 1882, Charles H. Diggins made homestead entry No. 4840 of the tract in question on April 12, 1882.

On June 1, 1882, John S. Rohrbough was allowed to file pre-emption declaratory statement No. 16, 474, alleging settlement May 25, 1877.

On July 1, 1882, Diggins, after notice by publication, but without special notice to Rohrbough, offered final proof before the clerk of the superior court of Mendocino county. On this occasion Rohrbough's counsel was refused permission to be present, for the "the reason . . . that said Gillespie was not there by virtue of any reference from the land office for a contest and that there had been no notice of such contest or of the grounds of contest from the land office."

In view of Rohrbough's adverse claim, the local officers declined to issue final certificate on the final proof thus offered by Diggins, and ordered a hearing for November 15, 1882, to determine which of the claimants had the superior right.

On September 28, 1882, Rohrbough published notice of intention to make proof on the 15th of November, 1882.

On November 2, 1882, your office approved the local officers' action in ordering a hearing.

On November 8, 1882, notice of the hearing so ordered was (for the first time) personally served on Diggins.

On November 15, 1882, Rohrbough and his witnesses appeared and testified, pursuant to notice; but Diggins put in no appearance.

March 11, 1883, the local officers reported to your office, expressing the opinion that the proceedings should be treated as *ex parte*, notice not having been duly served on Diggins.

September 11, 1883, your office directed the local officers to issue final certificate to Diggins, if they found compliance with law on his part, Rohrbough to be allowed to "contest the entry upon duly corroborated affidavit filed at any time before the issuance of patent."

May 14, 1884, your office again called the attention of the local officers to the instructions so given under date of September 11, 1883.

July 26, 1884, the local officers issued to Diggins homestead final certificate No. 2469.

On August 12, 1884, a deed from Diggins to one Montague, conveying the land in question, and bearing date August 9, 1884, was recorded in the recorder's office in Mendocino county, California.

In the latter part of August, 1884, Diggins died.

October 25, 1884, "upon affidavit filed by Rohrbough and duly corroborated, alleging that the homesteader's settlement was in inception and continuance fraudulent, a hearing was ordered to ascertain all the facts in the case."

On the 4th of February, 1885, Montague, assignee of Diggins, executed and acknowledged a deed assigning the tract to Abijah Ackerly.

On October 16, 1885, on application of "attorney for Diggins" (really the attorney acting on behalf of Ackerly) the local officers set down the hearing so ordered for December 16, 1885.

November 2, 1885, by an order which purports to have been made on request of "one of the parties, to wit, Charles H. Diggins, (really, on request of the attorney representing Ackerly, the assignee), the local officers ordered that the testimony in the case be taken before the county clerk of Mendocino county, at the county seat, on Thursday, December 10, 1885.

On December 9, 1885, the above mentioned deed from Montague to Ackerly was recorded in Mendocino county. December 10–16, 1885, the taking of testimony before the county clerk was proceeded with.

Under date of December 20, 1886, the local officers rendered an opinion in writing, upon the testimony so taken, recommending the cancellation of Diggins' entry, and that Rohrbough be allowed to offer final proof.

Under date of January 13, 1887, an appeal (*purporting* to be the appeal of " the defendant, Charles H. Diggins,") was taken from the decision of the local officers.

Under date of April 20, 1888, your office rendered the decision already mentioned, affirming the action of the local officers. From this decision the present appeal is taken.

Charles H. Diggins having died in August, 1884, it was wholly irregular to initiate and carry on, thereafter, contest proceedings against him by name, and to which those succeeding to his interest were not made parties. The whole proceeding is a nullity, as it could not be carried on in the name of a dead man, and all acts in his name after death were without jurisdiction.

The controversy as to the tract in question must therefore be held to be still at the stage which it had reached when the void order for a hearing was made October 25, 1884. That is to say, the final certificate issued in the name of Diggins is still outstanding in the hands of the transferee thereof, subject to the right of Rohrbough to contest its validity in a proper proceeding for the purpose, to which the real parties in interest shall have been made parties in due form.

The decision appealed from is accordingly reversed.

HOMESTEAD ENTRY—ACT OF JUNE 15, 1880.

ANDAS *v.* WILLIAMS.

While the right of purchase conferred by section 2, act of June 15, 1880, is not defeated by a prior contract of sale, such right is lost by an actual sale or disposition of the land.

A naked power of attorney, executed by the entryman and authorizing a sale of the land, is not evidence of a sale thereof, and will not defeat a subsequent purchase under said act.

First Assistant Secretary Chandler to Acting Commissioner Stone, August 24, 1889.

By decision of your office of April 3, 1888, in the case of William H. Andas *v.* Charles Williams, involving the SW. ¼ of Sec. 28, T. 16 S., R. 27 W., Wa Keeney district, Kansas, the action of the local officers in rejecting the application of said Andas to make homestead entry of said land is sustained, and he now appeals therefrom.

The ground of the decision of the local officers is, that said land was at date of said application covered by the prior cash entry of said Charles Williams made under the second section of the act of June 15, 1880. It is alleged on appeal, that " at the time the cash entry was made, the land did not belong to Charles Williams," but " he had not only attempted to transfer, but had actually transferred by *bona fide* instrument in writing his right to said land to another . . . . ." and that therefore said cash entry was invalid and no bar to the application of Andas.

This allegation is based upon a power of attorney in regular form, duly executed and acknowledged by Williams and his wife about two months before the date of his cash entry, authorizing and empowering one D. H. Henkel, in their names, to sell said land, and "convey" the same by warranty deed " unto any person or persons whom he may choose . . . . as soon as the receiver's final receipt for said tract shall have been issued." This instrument was not recorded until about a month after the date of the cash entry, and it does not appear, that a sale or conveyance has ever been made thereunder. In itself it was simply a naked power or authority to Henkel to act as the agent or attorney in fact of Williams and his wife to sell and convey the land, and, such being its nature, it was revocable by them at pleasure, and did not have the force even of a binding agreement to sell, which might be enforced by a bill in equity (or other proper proceeding) for a specific performance, or be made the basis of an action for damages for breach of contract. It was not, therefore, evidence that Williams had, as alleged by Andas, " actually transferred by *bona fide* instrument in writing his rights to said lands to another."

It is held by this Department, that the right of purchase conferred by the second section of the act of June 15, 1880, is not defeated by a contract of sale made prior to purchase (George E. Sanford, 5 L. D., 535), but the right is lost where a party has sold or parted absolutely with his interest in the land prior to the time he seeks to assert such right, as in that event, there is " nothing to base the entry upon." (Warden *v.* Shumate, 8 L. D., 330, and cases cited therein.)

As seen above, it does not appear in this case, that there was even a binding agreement or contract to sell, much less an actual sale or " transfer." The decision of your office is affirmed.

————

SECOND HOMESTEAD ENTRY.—ACT OF MARCH 2, 1889.

ARTHUR P. TOOMBS.*   (ON REVIEW).

A homesteader whose entry is canceled, because made during the maintenance of a pre-emption claim for another tract, may, under section 2, act of March 2, 1889, in the absence of an adverse claim, make a new homestead entry for the land included in his original entry.

Acting Secretary Chandler to Acting Commissioner Stone, August 24, 1889.

This is a motion for review of departmental decision of August 16, 1888, in the case of Arthur P. Toombs (7 L. D., 215) affirming your office decisions of November 19, 1886, and January 31, 1887, which held for cancellation the homestead and commuted cash entries of said Toombs, embracing the SE. ¼ of Sec. 18, T. 31 S., R. 28 W., Garden City land district, Kansas, and rejected his application to have the cancellation of his said homestead entry made without prejudice to his making new entry for said tract.

It appears that on June 14, 1884, Toombs filed his pre-emption declaratory statement for lots 3 and 4, and the E. ½ of the SW. ¼ of said Sec. 18, and that on March 10, 1885, he made final proof and cash entry thereunder; that on August 9, 1884, while his pre-emption was yet pending and unperfected, he made homestead entry for the tract in question; that subsequently to making said homestead entry he learned that the same was illegal, because made while his pre-emption claim was pending, and he thereupon, on August 4, 1885, filed his application, stating under oath, corroborated by the affidavits of two witnesses, that before making his homestead entry as aforesaid, he diligently inquired as to the legality of an entry so made, and was informed that the local officers at Garden City had ruled in favor of allowing such entries; that acting upon the information thus obtained he made his said homestead entry before he had made proof and received final certificate under his pre-emption filing; and in view of these circumstances he asked to be allowed to make new entry for the same tract under the homestead law.

————

* A similar decision was rendered in the unreported case of Ernst H. Ebert, decided by the Department August 23, 1889.

Before this application was acted upon by your office, to wit, on November 16, 1885, Toombs made commutation proof under his homestead entry, upon which he received cash entry certificate as of same date.

Your said office decision of November 19, 1886, held said homestead and commutation entries for cancellation, as illegal, because the original homestead entry was made while Toombs was claiming other land under the pre-emption law.

Toombs thereupon filed another application, in which he conceded that the cancellation of his said entries by your office was correct, stating that the same was in accordance with his wishes, but asking for a further consideration of the matter of his former application to be allowed the privilege of a new entry, and insisting upon a recognition of his right to make a new homestead entry for the tract. This latter application was, upon consideration, rejected by your said office decision of January 31, 1887.

On appeal to this Department, the said decisions of your office were affirmed by the decision now complained of.

It will be observed from the foregoing that all Toombs desires is, that he be allowed to make a new homestead entry for the land in question. In his motion for review he simply insists that he is, of right, entitled to make such new entry under the facts above stated, and that the Department erred in not recognizing his right in this regard.

Since the rendition of said departmental decision, the Congress, by act of March 2, 1889 (25 Stat., 854), entitled "An act to withdraw certain public lands from private entry, and for other purposes," has expressly provided in section two of said act:

That any person who has not heretofore perfected title to a tract of land of which he has made entry under the homestead law, may make a homestead entry of not exceeding one-quarter section of public land subject to such entry, such previous filing or entry to the contrary notwithstanding.

Under the provisions of this act of Congress, I see no reason why Toombs may not be allowed to make homestead entry for the tract in question and thus obtain, in effect, all he seeks to accomplish by his motion for review. This he clearly has the right to do, I think, under the law as it now s'ands, there being no adverse claim to the land, and as he could accomplish nothing more, even if the decision complained of were reversed, it is unnecessary to consider the questions raised by his said motion.

You will therefore direct the local officers to notify Toombs that he will be allowed a reasonable time within which to make application to enter the tract, under the provisions of said act of March 2, 1889; which application, when made, will be considered and allowed unless objection not shown by the present record is found to exist.

TIMBER CULTURE CONTEST—PRIORITY OF RIGHT.

FOREMAN v. WOLFE ET AL.

A *bona fide* contestant will not be defeated in his right to proceed against an entry by a fraudulent intervening contest, based upon false statements as to personal knowledge of the land involved.

First Assistant Secretary Chandler to Acting Commissioner Stone, August 26, 1889.

I have before me the appeal of Absalom Foreman from your decision of February 9, 1887, affirming the action of the local officers at Garden City, Kansas, dismissing his (Foreman's) motion for the dismissal of Wolfe's contest against Hamilton's timber culture entry, No. 3392, made July 13, 1885, and covering the SE. ¼, Sec. 15, T. 21 S., R. 31 W., Garden City district.

July 14, 1886, Jacob C. Wolfe filed a contest against Hamilton's entry, which was received and numbered 2626 on the docket.

On the same day but at a later hour, Absalom Foreman presented contest papers against Hamilton's entry, and at the same time filed a motion to dismiss Wolfe's contest, upon the following grounds:

1st. That the contestant (Wolfe) was in Garden City, Kansas, during the whole of July 13, 1886, and up to 9 o'clock a. m., the following day, and could not therefore have made affidavit properly to the condition of said tract on July 14, 1886, prior at (to) that date.

2nd. That the corroborating witness for Jacob C. Wolfe, W. W. Keyser, was in Garden City, Kansas, on Tuesday afternoon, July 13th, 1886, and affiant believes that he did not examine said tract after the hour of 12 noon on July 13, 1886, and therefore could not make affidavit as to the condition of said tract on the morning of the 14th of July, 1886. For these reasons it is alleged that the purported affidavit is insufficient, and his said application should be rejected.

The affidavits of Wolfe and Keyser, against Hamilton's entry, set forth that they (Wolfe and Keyser) were "well acquainted with the tract" and "know the (then) present condition of the same," "from personal observation."

On November 9, 1886, the register ordered a "hearing on facts set forth in affidavit of Absalom Foreman," to which order Wolfe's counsel excepted.

On December 13th, 1886, Wolfe filed proof of service of his notice of contest on Hamilton, and also a motion to dismiss Foreman's motion to dismiss his (Wolfe's) contest. In support of this motion Wolfe filed an affidavit stating—

That since the initiation of the above-entitled cause, to wit, on the 19th day of September, 1886, he, accompanied by one witness visited the tract above described, for the purpose of knowing the condition of the same; that he on this said date made a very thorough and careful inspection of said tract, as did also his said witness, James D. Goldsby, and found the tract wild prairie sod, entirely unimproved, no part thereof having ever been plowed, broken, or stirred.

This motion by Wolfe, to dismiss Foreman's motion to dismiss Wolfe's contest, was "sustained" by the register, and Foreman's attorney excepted.

Thereupon (on December 13, 1886) Wolfe and his witness, Goldsby, were examined (Hamilton, the entryman, being in default) and the register and receiver united in deciding that Hamilton's entry " should be canceled."

By the decision appealed from, you affirmed the action of the local officers.

In the argument filed by them, Foreman's attorneys say :

The facts we are asking to show, and which we believe we are entitled to show in this case are, briefly, these: On the morning of July 14, 1886, before the United States land office opened for public business, Foreman, a qualified timber culture entryman came into the office of B. F. Stocks, at Garden City, and employed him to prepare and file a contest on said tract of land in question, bringing with him his corroborating witness, both having personally inspected said tract. Wolfe was told that said tract was contestable ; thereupon contest papers were prepared for him and a corroborating witness picked up, who had not inspected the land in question, and as a matter of fact neither Wolfe nor his witness personally knew anything of the condition of said tract on July 14 or July 13, 1886. His contest was offered with evident intent to surreptitiously use the information that a *bona fide* contestant had acquired by personal observation. The contestant Wolfe is a real estate speculator residing in Garden City. The appellant, Foreman, is a farmer residing on the NE. ¼ Sec. 22, T. 21, R. 21, adjoining the tract in question. His corroborating witness also resides adjoining said tract.

By making and filing the above-mentioned affidavit as to his examination of the land on September 19, Wolfe seems to admit that in his affidavit of contest he falsely swore to personal familiarity with the tract and its condition on July 14, and thereby himself suggests the probable truth of the charge that in making and filing that affidavit of contest he was guilty of an attempt fraudulently to forestall the genuine contestant, and even by the aid of false swearing to rob the latter of the rights which the true spirit and policy of the law would confer upon him as the meritorious agent in procuring the cancellation of an abandoned entry. Enough appears to put the Department upon inquiry; for, if the case be actually such as on the face of this record seems to be indicated, it is one calling for the application of the principle announced in the case of Johnson *v.* Johnson (4 L. D., 158), that, " while this Department can not take cognizance of a fraud affecting the title to public lands for which patent has issued, nevertheless, under no circumstances will it permit itself knowingly to be made an instrument to further the fraudulent designs of an individual who is seeking to acquire title to land to which he has no right."

A hearing will, therefore, be ordered, to ascertain the facts bearing upon the comparative rights of Foreman and Wolfe as contestants against Hamilton, and when the local office shall have determined the question of priority of right as between the contestants, they will allow the successful party to proceed under his contest without unnecessary delay.

The decision of your office is modified accordingly.

TRAVELER'S INSURANCE CO.

The action of the local officers in accepting pre-emption final proof and payment
does not preclude the Land Department from subsequently inquiring into the
good faith of the transaction, and cancelling the entry, if obtained through
fraud, or allowed in violation of law.

A purchaser of land, prior to the issuance of patent therefor, takes only the equity
of the entryman, charged with notice of the law, and the supervisory control
of the Commissioner over the action of the local officers.

A sale of land, after issuance of final certificate, does not entitle the purchaser to the
benefit of a patent, unless it shall appear that the entryman has complied with
the law, and is in his own right entitled to patent.

*First Assistant Secretary Chandler to the Commissioner of the General
Land Office, August 28, 1889.*

I have considered the appeal of the Traveler's Insurance Company,
of Hartford, as mortgagee, and Job D. Stark, as grantee, from the decision of your office, dated December 22, 1886, canceling the pre-emption cash entry, No. 6163, of John C. Hague, for the NE. ¼, Sec. 12, T.
133 N., R. 60 W., and pre-emption cash entry, No. 6164, of George
Hague, for the NW. ¼, Sec. 12, T. 133 N., R. 60 W., respectively, Fargo
land district, Dakota Territory.

It appears from the record that on June 3, 1882, John C. Hague filed
his declaratory statement No. 10386, and on the same day George
Hague filed his declaratory statement No. 10,387 for said described
tracts, respectively.

On March 6, 1883, they made final proof for their respective claims
before the judge of the probate court of La Moure county, Dakota, and
on the 21st of same month the local officers approved said proofs and
issued cash certificates thereon.

In their final proof each of said entrymen testified that he was over
the age of twenty-one years, unmarried, and a native born citizen of
the United States; that he settled on his respective tract, May 17,
1882, and established his actual residence on his claim later that month.
Each also testified that his improvements consisted of a house, stable
and well, also about twenty acres of breaking. Total value of improvements on each tract $400.

In July, 1884, special agent W. W. McIlvain reported that he had
made a personal examination of the tracts covered by the entries of
John C. and George Hague, and found thereon a sod barn twenty by
twenty-seven feet, erected about on the line of the two tracts, that there
was about one acre broken on each tract but was never cultivated; that
said entrymen never established an actual residence on the land, nor
ever built a habitable residence on the tracts covered by their entries.
That in March, 1884, they mortgaged their respective tracts for the sum

of five hundred dollars each, and soon after date of entry they sold and conveyed their interest in said land for the sum of nine hundred dollars each, and that Perley Smith who appears as a witness to Hague's final proof was not present when the proofs were made and what purports to be his testimony was signed in his name by his brother Harvey Smith, and that said proof is false and said entries fraudulent and made for speculation.

On September 11, 1884, your office directed that a hearing be ordered in each case.

In May, 1885, the register and receiver ordered a hearing and the same was set for August 4th, 1885.

On the day appointed for the hearing the government was represented by special agent W. W. McIlvain; the entrymen did not appear and their whereabouts was not known, but they were duly served with published notice of said hearing.

Job D. Stark, as grantee, and the Travelers' Insurance Company of Hartford, Conn., as mortgagee, appeared by their attorney, C. W. Davis, Esq., and moved to dismiss the hearing in each case upon the ground of want of jurisdiction etc. Said attorney also filed two *ex parte* affidavits of one Charles T. Clement, for the purpose of showing that said Clement on March 23, 1883, loaned five hundred dollars of the money of the Travelers' Insurance Company of Hartford, Connecticut, to John O. Hague and took as security therefor, a first mortgage on the northeast ¼ of Sec. 12, T. 133, in R. 60 W., and that on the 28th day of the same month, he loaned five hundred dollars of the money of said company to one George Hague and took as security therefor, a first mortgage on the north-west ¼, of Sec. 12, in T. 133, of R. 60 W., in La Moure Co., D. T. That said money was loaned to said parties in good faith and believing that they had fully complied with all the requirements of the law under which receiver's receipts had been issued to them. That if said entrymen had practised any fraud upon the government said Insurance Company was at the time of making said loan entirely ignorant thereof; that said loan is wholly unpaid and that said company depends wholly upon said tracts of land as their security for the payment thereof.

Said attorney also filed two *ex parte* affidavits executed by Job D. Stark in which it is alleged that he, (Stark) on May 29, 1883, purchased of said John O. and George Hague, said described tracts of land and paid to each of said entrymen the sum of nine hundred dollars as the price of their respective claims. That he was a purchaser in good faith and relied upon the validity of the receiver's receipts which had been issued to said entrymen prior to said transfer.

The local officers overruled the motion to dismiss the hearings in each case.

Charles A. Rhine (one of the advertised final proof witnesses) and the special agent testified on the part of the government but the attorney for the defence declined to cross examine either of them or to offer any testimony. On motion of the special agent, the hearings were adjourned to September 4th, on which day the testimony of William H. Doherty was taken and filed on the part of the government. No appearance being made on the part of the defendants, the cases were continued on the motion of the special agent to October 2d.

On the last adjourned day, the special agent appeared and stated that he had no other testimony to offer. The defendants' attorney appeared and filed exceptions to the testimony adduced on the part of the government.

On December 14, 1885, the local officers without passing on the merits of either case, transmitted the papers and record of the proceedings in the hearings to your office, and on December 22, 1886, your office affirmed the action of the register and receiver in overruling the motions and objections made by the attorney for the transferee and mortgagee and further decided that "The testimony offered by the government was full and clear showing the character and extent of the alleged fraud in each case," etc., and held the entries for cancellation.

From an examination of the proofs herein it appears that the entrymen were brothers, and that soon after filing for said land they constructed a sod barn about twenty by twenty seven feet supposed by them to have been on the line between the north-east and north-west quarter of Sec. 12, T. 133, R. 60. They also dug two well holes neither of them exceeded ten feet in depth, one of which was a slough well and had a little water in it in the spring of the year, the other was dry; they also broke not to exceed one and a half acres on each quarter section, but never backset or cultivated any portion of the same. In or about the month of January, 1883, they constructed a board shanty on the land, but it does not appear on which quarter section the same was built.

Charles A. Rhine, who resided within thirty or forty rods of the land in dispute and whose residence was in view of the improvements made by the entrymen testified on the hearing that John O. and George 'Hague built the shanty and described it as follows:

There was also a shanty or pen twelve by twelve feet in size, the boards were put on horizontally, the space between the boards were from eight to twelve inches in width. It had a few boards thrown on top for a roof, not covering to exceed one-half the space, without any door except a few boards nailed to the side of the house. There was but one window and that was tacked up also to the side of the house. There was no floor.

He also testified that the entrymen resided with one Dr. O. O. Skinner about two miles from the land until about the first of July, or about the time they commenced haying; that the only time they resided on the tracts in dispute was during about three weeks in July, 1882, while they were making hay and that they then lived in one end of the barn and kept their horses in the other end; that from August 1, 1882, up to the spring of 1883, they resided in Ransom county near Plymouth, D.

T., and at the date of final proof they were living at the house of Perley Smith.

Upon review of the record and proof in each case it is apparent that neither of the entrymen ever established an actual *bona fide* residence on the land entered by him; that the shanty hereinbefore described was not occupied by either of them at any time as a dwelling, nor was it ever made habitable or supplied by them or either of them with any household furniture or cooking utensils; that the final proof by said entrymen was false, and fraudulently made and that they failed to comply with the requirements of the pre-emption law in the matter of residence and cultivation of their respective tracts; that Perley Smith, whose name purports to be signed as a witness to the final proof herein, was not present nor was he sworn or examined as a witness, but that one Henry Smith, at the request and connivance of said entrymen personated said Perley Smith and signed his name to said proofs.

The points relied upon by counsel for the appellant before the register and receiver, urged upon the Commissioner, and counted upon here as reasons why these entries should stand, are:

1st: It is error for the Honorable Commissioner to assume jurisdiction of and enter tain proceedings in the General Land Office to determine the sufficiency of the residence, cultivation and improvements made by the above named entrymen in complying with the law under which their respective rights were made.

2d. It is error to declare a forfeiture of and cancel claimant's entries.

3d. It is error to deny the issue of patent on the above mentioned entries for the benefit of appellants as the mortgagee and grantee of the entrymen.

The effect of this contention is to hold that the register and receiver by section 2263 are constituted a judicial tribunal to pass upon the question of whether or not the entryman has complied with the requirements of the pre-emption law ; that it is exclusively within their province to determine the sufficiency of the entryman's qualifications as to residence and improvements, and when once determined by them, favorably to the pre-emptor and the duplicate receipt is issued to him for the tract and the money paid to the government therefor, that the sale is complete and the government is estopped from afterwards inquiring into the bona fides of the transaction, as between it and the entryman, even if a fraud was perpetrated upon it by the claimant, relative to residence and improvement, where the affidavit provided for in section 2262 is filed.   Second: That the mortgagee and grantee for these several tracts, having invested their money therein, relying upon the presumption that the claimants have complied with the law, coupled with the fact that the register and receiver had found the facts to support the presumption and issued duplicate receipts to the claimants as evidence thereof, the government ought now in equity, as between them and it, to be estopped from declaring a forfeiture and causing them to lose their money, some $2,800 or more, which they have invested in these lands as *bona fide* purchasers.   Third: That standing in the light of such purchasers for value of these tracts, the patent therefor should issue and inure to the benefit of the grantee.

Each of these propositions has frequen tly been before the courts, and this Department, and as often as presented has been decided adversely to the position assumed by counsel for the appellant.   Upon the first proposi:ion, as to supervisory power of the Commissio ner of the General Land Office over the action of the register and receiver, attention of counsel is invited to the case of Harkness v. Underhill (1 Black., 316), where it is held that "a fraudulent entry of public land allowed by "a register and receiver upon false proofs of settlement, occupancy "and housekeeping, may be set aside and vacated by the Commissioner "of the General Land Office." Also, case of Frisbie v. Whitney (9 Wallace, 187), where the supreme court, discussing this question, say:

When all these prerequisites (settlement, improvements, payments of entrance money, etc.) are complied with, and the claimant has paid the price for the land, he is entitled to a certificate of entry from the register and receiver; and after a reasonable time to enable the land officer to ascertain if there are supe rior claims, *and if in other respects the claimant has made out his case* he is entitled to receive a patent which for the *first time invests him with the legal title to the land.*

And in case of Steele v. Smelting Company (106 U. S., 447) in speaking of the Land Department, the court remarks : " Necessarily, therefore, it must consider and pass upon the qualifications of the applicant, the acts he has performed to secure title, etc.

So in the case of the United States v. Schurz (102 U. S., 378), Justice Miller, speaking for the court, says:

Under this provision, the sale of public lands wa s placed by the statute under the control of the Secretary of the Interior.   To aid him in the perform ance of this duty a bureau was created, at the head of which is the Commissioner of the General Land Office, with many subordinates.   To them as a special tribuna! Congress confided the execution of the laws which regulate the surveying, the selling and the general care of these lands.

In the case of Carroll v. Safford (3 Howard, 441), cited by counsel to support the first proposition, the court say:

But where there has been fraud or mistake, the patent may be withheld. . . . . The sale for taxes is made on the presumption that the purchase from the government has been *bona fide,* and, if not so made, the purchaser at the tax sale acquires no title

It is useless to multiply authorities on this question, for such is the general tenor of the doctrine of the courts whenever it has been directly presented to them, and such ruling has been followed in this Department. Smith v. Custer *et al.,* 8 L. D., 269.

None of these cases conflict with the doctrine that a duplicate receipt is equivalent to a patent when rightfully and lawfully obtained, and no decision of a supreme court of any State or the United States, that I am able to find, goes so far as to hold that the government may not protect itself against fraud in the entry at any time before patent issues. Such is the universal holding of such courts.

Upon the second proposition contended for by counsel, the rule of the law is, that there can be no such thing as a *bona fide* purchase of government lands prior to the issuing of patent.   That one who deals with such lands under such circumstances takes only the equity of the claimant; charged with notice of the law and the supervisory control of the Commissioner of the General Land Office over the rulings and decisions of the register and receiver; acts at his peril in his purchase; has applied to him the rule of *caveat emptor* in all its rigor, as it affects the rights of the entryman with reference to qualifications, and compliance with the pre-emption law as to residence and cultivation.   Standing, so to speak, in his shoes, having no greater rights or equities than the entryman from whom he purchased.

In passing upon this question, Justice Miller of the supreme court of the United States, in the case of Root *v.* Shields (1 Woolworth, 349), uses the following language:

It is further insisted on behalf of the defendants that they are *bona fide* purchasers, that they as such are entitled to the protection of the court.   I think it pretty clear that some at least of the defendants purchased and paid their money without any knowledge in fact of any defect in the title.   Yet they are not bona fide purchasers for a valuable consideration, without notice, in the sense in which the terms are employed in the courts of equity, and this for several reasons . . . .   They all purchased before issue of patent . . . . .   Until the issue of patent, the legal title remained in the United States . . . . .   and in order to establish himself in the character of a *bona fide* purchaser, so as to be entitled to the protection of chancery, a party must show that in his purchase and by the conveyance to him he acquired the legal title.

And this rule has been followed by the Department in its decisions. Margaret Kissack (2 C. L. L., 421); R. M. Chrisinger (4 L. D., 347); United States *v.* Johnson (5 L. D., 442); C. A. Kibling (7 L. D., 327).

Passing to the third point, if the conclusions heretofore reached are a sound exposition of the law, it follows as a natural consequence, that the patent can not issue for these tracts to these appellants.   Standing in the place of the entrymen, and the entry being in its inception fraudulent, no title passes by the entry.   Both the legal and equitable title is vested in the government.   While the rule is apparently harsh and inequitable, and may work great hardship to the appellants, yet they went into this venture with their eyes wide open, being bound to know what the law is as heretofore announced by the highest judicial tribunals in the land.   To ignore the law as thus laid down, opens the door to fraud; places the government in a position where it can not protect itself from unlawful practices; and at the mercy of those who, unmindful of their duties and obligations to it, in securing the public domain, seek to impose upon it by falsehood and perjury.

The effect of this decision is salutary in its character, encourages honesty and fair dealing with the government, requires the mortgagee and grantee of public lands, upon duplicate receipt, if they desire to be protected, to see to it that the entryman has honestly and fairly complied with the law in its substantial requirements.   When this is done, security surrounds their investments, otherwise their pathway towards a patent is precarious, their journey perilous, and ultimate defeat stares them in the face at every step.

For the reasons herein stated and in view of the decisions cited, your said decision is affirmed.

———

EFFECT OF PATENT—PRACTICE—RULE 53.

EASTLAKE LAND CO. v. BROWN.

Legal title does not pass by a patent that is inadvertently issued, and which is neither delivered to nor accepted by the party named as patentee ; and issuance of such a patent does not take the lands covered thereby out of the category of public lands.

The pendency of contest proceedings on appeal precludes the submission of final proof for the land involved therein.

First Assistant Secretary Chandler to the Commissioner of the General Land Office, August 29, 1889.

I have considered the appeal of the Eastlake Land Company *et al.* from the decision of your office dated April 7, 1888, adhering to a former decision sustaining the homestead entry No. 19,700 of Isaiah C. Brown for the SW.¼, Sec. 14, T. 17 S., R. 2 W., Montgomery land district, Alabama.

The record shows that on April 23, 1887, Isaiah C. Brown made homestead entry for said described tract, and on November 29, same year, the Eastlake Land Company *et al.* filed a petition protesting against the allowance of said entry, alleging therein that they are the owners and occupants of said tract.

That their titles . . . are derived through various means conveyances from one Thomas Horne, who made private cash entry . . . . covering said tract which said entry was patented . . . July 9, 1823 . . . That your petitioners and their grantors have been in peaceable . . . possession . . . . of said SW. ¼, ... until the present year when one Isaiah C. Brown, in fraud of petitioners' rights and for speculative purposes . . . did make homestead entry covering said land.

They further alleged that the said patent was never legally canceled, that taxes were levied and collected thereon and that their titles rested upon deeds from said Horne and from the sheriff of Jefferson county, Alabama.

On December 16, 1887, Brown filed an answer to said petition, and on December 19, 1887, your office decided in favor of Brown's homestead entry.

On February 4, 1888, the attorney for said petitioners requested a review of the case, and on April 7, same year, your office again decided in favor of Brown's entry.

On June 4, 1888, the Eastlake Land Company *et al.* appealed to this Department and the case is now before me.

The records in your office show that on October 12, 1821, Thomas

Horne made private cash entry No. 884 (Tuscaloosa series) for the same tract that is now in controversy, containing 161.10 acres, and paid therefor the sum of $201.38 and about one month thereafter he executed an affidavit of which the following is a copy, viz:

STATE OF ALABAMA, *Tuscaloosa County, ss.*

This day Thomas Horne appeared before me Hume R. Field, judge of the county court, of Tuscaloosa, and deposed upon the holy evangelists of Almighty God, that he came to the town of Tuscaloosa for the purpose of entering with the register of the land office a quarter section of land which was offered and not sold, and which is designated as follows: range 2 west township 17, section 17, southwest quarter; but that instead thereof he entered the southwest quarter section 14, in the same range and township ; that this mistake was produced by some person altering and changing the mark or figure from 17 to 14 at the corner.

Given under my hand and seal this 10th day of November, An. Dom., 1821.

his

(Signed) THOMAS X HORNE.

mark

HUME R. FIELD, [SEAL],

Judge of the county, Tuscaloosa.

The signature of the judge to said affidavit was duly authenticated by the certificate of the clerk of the county court for said county, and bears date November 10, 1821.

Horne filed said affidavit in the local land office, at the same time requesting that patent should not be issued to him for the tract then covered by said entry, but that he be permitted to change his said entry so as to cover the land intended by him.

The register and receiver transmitted Horne's application to your office accompanied by the following statement, viz:

LAND OFFICE TUSCALOOSA, 22 *Nov.* '21.

Enclosed you will receive the affidavit of Thomas Horne setting forth that he has made a mistake in entry of a certain half quarter section of land therein mentioned ; as it is conceived that we do not possess the power to remedy such cases, we have thought it proper to submit it to your department. The desire of Mr. Horne is to transfer the payment made on the tract entered to some other tract.

In reply your office informed the local officers as follows:

2ND OF JANUARY, 1822.

To the register and to the receiver of the Land Office, at Tuscaloosa.

SIRS: It appears from the affidavit of Thomas Horne, enclosed in your letter of the 22nd of November, last, that the mistake arose from the alteration of the surveyor's marks at the corner of the sections. Before a decision can be made in the case by the Secretary of the Treasury, agreeably to law, you will be pleased to give a decided opinion on its merits.

On March 19, 1822, the receiver addressed a letter to your office stating:

I am decidedly of the opinion that that mistake made by Thomas Horne and others in their entries of land, should be rectified, and the amount refunded or applied to the purchase of some other tract. Those men, I am creditably informed, are in extreme indigent circumstances and quite illiterate. I hope my opinion of their cases will meet with your concurrence.

On May 8, 1822, the Commissioner in a letter to the register at Tus-caloosa, stated—

I return the affidavits of Thomas Horne and agreeably to direction from the Secre-tary of the Treasury, have to advise you that the act of March 19, 1819, requires the register and receiver both to report their opinion on cases coming within its pro-visions with the testimony in relation thereto; the affidavit of the party as to changes of the mark or figure at the corner of the tract is to be corroborated by the testimony of some one or more disinterested persons. I would refer you to the act itself, and request that in future the cases which the register and yourself may have reported under it will be reported directly to the Secretary of the Treasury.

On April 18, 1823, the Secretary of the Treasury addressed a letter to the Commissioner of the General Land Office in which, among other things, he stated,

It also appears by the report of aforesaid and by other testimony, that Thomas Horne, entered by mistake the seventeenth instead of the fourteenth section in town-ship seventeen, range two, west. I do, therefore, authorize you by virtue of the power vested in me by the act of the 3rd of March, 1819, to direct the land officers at Tuscaloosa, to permit the said Isaiah Bagley and Thomas Horne to withdraw their entries made by them as above stated, and to apply the money paid thereon to the purchase of any other public lands in the said district or to the payment of lands al-ready purchased of the United States in the district of Tuscaloosa.

On April 23, 1823, a copy of the foregoing decision and order of the Secretary of the Treasury, was transmitted to the register and receiver at Tuscaloosa, with instructions and authority to permit the withdrawal of Horne's said entry, and to allow the payment made to be otherwise applied by Horne.

On July 9, 1823, a patent was issued to Thomas Horne for said tract by mistake, but was never delivered to or accepted by him; but on August 1, 1823, the $201.38 was refunded to him, and he thereupon gave to the receiver of said land office his receipt for said money and the patent which had been issued as aforesaid was then and there can-celed, and subsequently the receiver was credited by the treasurer of the United States for the money so refunded.

The appellants herein seem to rely upon the decision of the supreme court in the case of Bicknell v. Comstock, (113 U. S., 149,) and contend that the rule laid down in said cited case should be applied to, and gov-ern the case at bar, and that Brown's entry should therefore be can-celed, "On the ground of invalidity." I can not concur in this view as in the case cited, it was shown that Bicknell never asked to have his entry changed, but on the contrary both he and his grantees made valuable improvements on the tract entered by him; and in June, 1878, when your office ordered a return of Bicknell's patent and tore off the seals and erased the President's name from said patent and mutilated the record thereof, all such acts were done without the consent and against the protest of the grantees of said Bicknell.

The record in the case at bar sufficiently shows that Horne fully ac-quiesced in the cancellation of the patent which was inadvertently issued to him and there is not any evidence either record or parol to show that Horne ever laid claim to said tract after he applied to have said entry canceled or made any improvements thereon, nor is there any record evidence tending to show that Horne ever offered to sell or convey to any person or persons his interest in said tract of land from the date of entry up to the date of its cancellation nor since.

From abstracts of title filed in this case both by the appellants and appellee, it appears that one Moses Field as tax collector, conveyed to Daniel Eustis, by tax deed on March 22, 1852, the NE. ¼, SW. ¼, Sec. 14, T. 17, R. 2, because of "failure of Thomas Horne to pay taxes for the year 1851;" this is the only evidence that Horne's name was identified with said tract for a period of twenty-nine years; and in my opinion is not sufficient to overcome the former record in this case, which sufficiently shows that he had parted with his interest in the land when he accepted from the United States officers a return of the purchase price of said tract. McGuire *v.* Tyler, (8 Wall, 663); W. A. Simmons, (7 L. D., 283).

The question as to the time when a patent from the government becomes effective as a conveyance was considered by the United States circuit court in the case of Leroy *v.* Jamison (3 Sawyer, 369), and in the decision of that case it was said,—

In order, therefore, that the patent of the government, like the deed of a private person, may take effect as a conveyance, so as to bind the party to whom it is executed, and transfer the title to him, it is essential that it should be accepted.

After stating that a patent from the government is in a condition for acceptance by the grantor "when the last formalities required by law of the officers of the government are complied with," it is said : "Its acceptance by the grantee will then be conclusively presumed, unless immediately upon knowledge of its issue, his refusal to accept it is explicitly declared and such refusal is communicated to the land office."

In the case now under consideration the grantee refused to accept the patent and that refusal was communicated by him to the proper officers. The essential requirements of acceptance hence never attached to that patent and under the rule laid down in said case of Leroy *v.* Jamison, it never became effective to transfer title to Horne.

The appellants in their petition claim to derive title through a conveyance from Horne which they have failed to prove; they also claim title through a tax deed executed in 1852 by the tax collector in the name of Horne. In the case of Carroll *v.* Safford (3 How., 509), the United States supreme court held—

That every purchaser at a tax sale incurs the risk as to the validity of the title he purchases. He incurs the same risk after the emanation of the patent. . . . The sale for taxes is made on the presumption that the purchase from the government has been *bona fide*, and if not so made, the purchaser at the tax sale acquires no title and consequently no embarrassment can arise in the future disposition of the same land by the government.

While to subject land to taxation it makes no difference who holds the legal title when the government is once divested thereof, yet this rule is not applicable to this case for the reason that the legal title to this particular tract has never passed from the government. A patent does not pass the legal title until delivered and accepted. This patent never having been delivered to Horne, he never had any legal title to the tract in question, hence the plaintiff in this action acquired no interest in this tract by virtue of the tax deed upon which it bottoms its rights.

Upon review of the whole record herein, I am of the opinion that the tract in dispute was public land when Brown made his homestead entry thereon, as the United States could not be deprived of its title thereto by reason of any squatters' claim or claims under the said tax deed; or by any statute of limitation, (Drew *v.* Valentine, 18 Federal Rep., 712), and as there is no evidence in your office that application for entry was ever made for said tract since the cancellation of Horne's entry, until Brown made his entry, I affirm your said decision.

It appears from papers recently filed in this case that while the case was pending undetermined in your office that Brown offered commutation proof and payment for said tract which was accepted by the local officers, and final cash certificate No. 22,687 issued thereon. As this proceeding was contrary to the provisions of Rule 53, of Practice, which declares that " The local officers will thereafter take no further action affecting the disposal of the land in contest until instructed by the Commissioner," said proof and payment was erroneously received and can not be accepted, and the entryman should be notified to make new advertisement and new proof. Iddings *v.* Burns (on review, 8 L. D., 559).

———

INDIAN LANDS—ACT OF MAY 15, 1888.

OMAHA LANDS.

Declaration of forfeiture, and order for public sale under section three, act of May 15, 1888.

Acting Secretary Chandler to the Commissioner of the General Land Office, August 31, 1889.

I am in receipt of your communication of the 13th instant, enclosing copies of three lists of Omaha Indian lands, upon which default has been made either as to payment of interest, or by failure to prove up, or which have not heretofore been sold, transmitted by the register at Neligh, Nebraska, under the instructions of your office of July 28, 1888.

The third section of the act of May 15, 1888 (25 Stat., 150), extending the time of payment to purchasers of Omaha Indian lands, provides:

The Secretary of the Interior is hereby directed to declare forfeited all lands sold under said act upon which the purchaser shall be in default, under existing law, for sixty days after the passage of this act, in payment of any part of the purchase-

DECISIONS RELATING TO THE PUBLIC LANDS.

money, or in the payment of any interest on such purchase-money for the period of two years previous to the expiration of said sixty days. The Secretary of the Interior shall thereupon without delay cause all such land, together with all tracts of land embraced in said act not heretofore sold, to be sold by public auction, after due notice, to the highest bidder over and above the original appraisal thereof, upon the terms of payment authorized in said act.

The lands embraced in said lists are hereby declared forfeited, and you will therefore cause them to be advertised and sold in compliance with the directions contained in said statute.

TIMBER CULTURE CONTEST—SPECIFIC CHARGE.

MEYHOK v. LADEHOFF.

A charge that an entry was made with speculative intent is not established by evidence showing a contract of sale executed after three years compliance with law.

Failure to establish the specific charge, as laid in the affidavit of contest, leaves the issue in the case as between the entryman and the government.

First Assistant Secretary Chandler to the Commissioner of the General Land Office, August 30, 1889.

I have considered the case of Louise Meyhok v. William Ladehoff, involving timber culture entry made by the latter November 12, 1881, for the SW. ¼ of Sec. 35, T. 107, R. 64, Mitchell district, Dakota.

Contest affidavit was filed July 4, 1884, on allegation that the entry was made with speculative intent. Hearing was delayed on account of failure to give defendant proper notice, and for other reasons; but finally a hearing was had commencing December 3, 1884.

The testimony taken at the hearing showed that defendant had five nd three fourths acres of breaking done the first year after entry; that during the second year claimant's agent broke five and one fourth acres more, and allowed the contestant's father to cultivate the five and three fourths acres broken the first year—the latter to have the crop thus raised by him on condition that he would plow the land after the crop had been removed.

On April 12, 1884, the claimant—as appears by a copy of contract filed with the testimony—entered into an agreement with Charles Meyhok (the father of contestant), to the effect that in consideration of twenty dollars in cash, eighty dollars payable in fifteen days, and one hundred and fifty dollars in one year, he (claimant) would assign his interest in a certain timber culture claim to said Meyhok. The number of the claim was left blank in the contract, but it was stated to be in Jerauld county, Dakota Territory, and there is no question but it referred to the tract in controversy, (claimant not having his entry papers with him and having forgotten the number of his claim when he executed the contract). It was provided that in case of default in making any one of the payments the contract should be void.

The first (twenty dollar) payment was made. About May 1, 1884, Meyhok went upon the land, built a house and stable, and made other substantial improvements—establishing his residence upon the tract. He failed, however, to make any other payments on the tract; and defendant, after several fruitless interviews with Meyhok relative to settlement, proceeded (as the end of the third year of his entry was rapidly approaching) to resume actual possession of the tract, and to prepare the ground and plant trees—which work he completed before the third year expired.

The local officers decided in favor of contestant. Claimant appealed to your office; which (February 20, 1886,) affirmed the action of the local officers, saying (*inter alia*):

As the evidence shows that claimant stood ready to sell, and would undoubtedly have delivered his relinquishment to Meyhok if the latter had lived up to the agreement made, or to any other person who was willing to pay what he considered it worth, the entry is held to have been made with speculative intent, and held for purpose of sale.

The charge under investigation was that the entry *was made* with speculative intent. Proof that a contract of sale was entered into, three years after the making of the original entry, would not establish the charge of speculative entry. Many circumstances might have occurred, since the making of the entry, which would render it desirable to the entryman to sell his land, without the sale carrying with it any implication of bad faith *at the time of entry*. The fact that the entryman complied with the requirements of the law in all respects, during the period—nearly three years—before he made the contract to sell to Meyhok, and that, after Meyhok's refusal to carry out the contract, the entryman hastened to prepare the ground and plant trees, so that the work required by law to be done during the third year was completed before the end of that year, are inconsistent with the hypothesis that the entry was originally made for a speculative purpose. So the specific charge in this case has failed. And the Department has held that, in matters not specially charged in the affidavit of contest, the question is one solely between the entryman and the government. (Platt *v.* Vachon, 7 L. D. 408).

In this case there does not seem to be such a showing of bad faith on the part of Ladehoff as calls for cancellation of his entry. I therefore reverse your decision.

CONTEST—PREFERENCE RIGHT—SETTLEMENT—INNOCENT PUR-
CHASER.

BUNGER v. DAWES.

An entry of Kansas Indian trust land is subject to contest for non-compliance with law, or other sufficient cause, and the successful contestant of such an entry is entitled to the preference right accorded by the act of May 14, 1880.

A settlement right is not acquired through the purchase of a prior settler's improvements.

A purchaser of land, prior to the issuance of patent therefor, acquires no better title than his vendor possessed.

First Assistant Secretary Chandler to the Commissioner of the General Land Office, August 30, 1889.

I have considered the appeal of Squire Bunger from a portion of the decision of your office dated May 8, 1888, in the contest case of said Bunger *v.* Sidney Dawes, involving title to the N. ½, SW. ¼, and lot 6, of the NW. ¼, Sec. 27, T. 14 N., R. 10 E., Kansas trust and diminished reserve lands, Topeka land district, Kansas.

The records show that on February 12, 1883, said Dawes appeared with two witnesses before a justice of the peace in and for Wabaunsee county, Kansas, and made proof of settlement right to said described tract, "under the act of Congress of July 5, 1876," in which he testified that his age was twenty-six years, he was a single man, that there was no timber on said land, his post office address was "Chalk Mound," he had never before made an entry under said act and that no one except himself claimed the land as a settler thereon. That he first made settlement on the land in January, 1880 and established a residence thereon the same month; that since he first established his residence on the said land he had lived a part of the time with his father on an adjoining farm, that he resided on said described land up to the present time, "but not all the time, am single and had to earn money away to improve the land." That his improvements consisted of a house ten by fourteen feet, he broke and cultivated twelve acres and had raised corn, rye, turnips and millet thereon; that he commenced a cellar and valued his improvements at $250.

His proof was corroborated by Henry Dawes and Edward Dawes, father and brother of the entryman, respectively.

On June 11, 1884, he paid at the local office the third and final installment of the money due for said described tract, and received receiver's receipt, No. 4286, therefor, and on the same date the register issued final certificate No. 769, to said entryman for said land.

On January 20, 1885, Squire Bunger initiated a contest against said entry alleging among other things

That said tract is not settled upon and cultivated by said adverse claimant as required by law, and this the said affiant is ready to prove at such time and place as may be named by the register and receiver for a hearing in said case; and this affiant therefore asks to be allowed to prove said allegations and that this affiant may be allowed to enter said land according to the law relating thereto.

The local officers transmitted to your office the application to contest said entry and asked for instructions in the premises.

On March 25, 1885, your office ordered a hearing which was set for June 25, 1885, the testimony to be taken before R. M. Armstrong, clerk of the district court of Morris county, at his office in the city of Council Grove, Kansas.

On the date appointed the contestant and entryman appeared in person and with counsel and Andrew J. Skeen, as transferee also appeared in person and by attorney. The taking of testimony closed June 30, and the evidence was duly transmitted to the local officers, who upon examination thereof found that the entryman had not complied with the requirements of the law in the matter of settlement, and they recommended that his entry be canceled, "and that A. J. Skeen be allowed to make the entry under the law."

The contestant's attorney appealed from that portion of the decision recommending that Skeen be permitted to make entry for said land.

On May 8, 1888, your office decided that it was clearly proven that the settlement proof made by Dawes was false and fraudulent, and held his entry for cancellation, and also held that "The testimony proves that the contestant had no right to claim the land in contest, having never been in any sense a settler thereon," and directed that—" If this decision shall become final, A. J. Skeen, who, as an innocent purchaser after issue of final certificate appears to be the only person now asserting anything like a *bona fide* claim to the land in dispute, will then be allowed to prove up upon the land, under the act of July 5, 1876."

The contestant appealed from the said decision " so far as it gives the right to A. J. Skeen to enter said land instead of the contestant."

The record herein shows that seven witnesses were sworn and examined on behalf of the contestant and six persons (including the transferee), testified on behalf of the entryman; and that on or about July 6, 1885, the transferee filed with the local officers his own sworn statement, and asked that it be made a part of the record in this case and considered by them in deciding the contest, and is substantially as follows, viz:

That on June 19, 1884, he in good faith purchased by warranty deed from Sidney Dawes the land in question, and paid him therefor $750; that he also purchased from Henry Dawes, father of the entryman an adjoining tract, upon which he and his family have resided ever since February 25, 1885; that he has broken three acres on the land in contest and has now thirteen acres under cultivation on said tract; that the reason he resides on the adjoining land is because he has a good house and other improvements thereon, and asked that in case the entry of Sidney Dawes was found to be invalid, then, that he, (Skeen) be allowed the " prior right and privilege for the space of sixty days, of building a house on the land in . . . . . contest and of making it my residence and of giving me the prior right to enter said tract of land upon my complying with the act of Congress of July 5, 1876."

Both the local office and your office found that Dawes' settlement proof was false, and that his entry was fraudulently made, and the same was held for cancellation; and no appeal having been taken from that portion of said decision the same became final. So that the only question to be considered in the premises is, whether Skeen as transferee is a valid settler upon the land in contest, and entitled to a prior right of entry to the exclusion of Bunger who was a successful contestant for said tract.

The attorney for the transferee contends that the act of July 5, 1876, under which said entry was made contains no provision authorizing contests, or in cases of contest, giving the contestant any preference right of entry whatever; and that the act of May 14, 1880, has no application "to Osage lands or sales made under the act of 1876; as it expressly applies to pre-emption, homestead and timber culture entries, and nothing else."

Section 2 of the act of May 14, 1880, (21 Stat., 140) provides that—

In all cases where any person has contested, paid the land office fees, and procured the cancellation of any pre-emption, homestead, or timber culture entry, he shall be notified by the register of the land office of the district in which such land is situated of such cancellation, and shall be allowed thirty days from date of such notice to enter said lands.

In the case of Fraser v. Ringgold (3 L. D., 69), in construing said last cited section this Department used the following language:

It must be conceded that the act of (May 14) 1880 is a remedial statute, changing the policy of previous administrations, both as regards the rights of settlers to make immediate entry without awaiting formal cancellations by you, as well as giving them preference rights by way of inducements to contest fraudulent and abandoned claims and their right to regard settlement as a pre-emption in cases of homestead claim. It covers descriptively the leading cases of inchoate claims which depended upon good faith, both of inception and performance, for their ultimate validity and the securing of title. The word pre-emption is one of broad signification, and was in use under State laws and in other statutes before its incorporation into the United States land system. It is held, in general, that claims under the townsite laws are pre-emptions; so of the settlement statutes respecting certain Indian lands; and broadly, that where a special preference is given to a claimant, dependent or contingent upon the performance of conditions which any one of a qualified class may reasonably fulfill, by which he may hold to the exclusion of others, such preference is a pre-emption, and inures to the individual upon the inception of his claim.

The lands involved in this case are subject to disposal under the provisions of the act of July 5, 1876 (19 Stat., 74), as amended by the act of March 16, 1880 (21 Stat., 68).

These acts provide that said lands " shall be subject to entry . . . only by actual settlers." This provision brings the claims under which title to these lands may be acquired within the definition given in the case of Fraser v. Ringgold, *supra*, of the word pre-emption. I am of the opinion that an entry made for Kansas Indian trust lands is subject to contest before the issuance of patent; and that a successful contestant would be entitled to a preference right of entry under the act of May 14, 1880.

Rule 1 of Practice (4 L. D., 37), makes no exception of Indian trust and diminished reserve land claims, but declares that—

Contests may be initiated by an adverse party or other person against a party to any entry, filing or other claim under laws of Congress, relating to the public lands, for any sufficient cause affecting the legality or validity of the claim.

In the case of Buchanan v. Minton, this Department held that "similar regulations obtain in respect to settlement on the Osage Indian lands" as govern in Kansas Indian trust and diminished reserve lands, (2 L. D., 186); Frazer v. Ringgold *supra ;* and in the case of the United States v. Woodbury (5 L. D., 303), it was held that a "claimant" upon Osage Indian trust and diminished reserve lands . . . must be an actual settler on the land at the date of entry and must have the qualifications of a pre-emptor." This same principle was followed in the case of Chitwood v. Hickok (on review, 7 L. D., 277).

Neither the swamp land act of September 28, 1850 (9 Stat., 519); nor the desert land act of March 3, 1877 (19 Stat., 377), contain any provision relating to contests yet the Department acting within the scope of its authority, has very frequently allowed contests against such entries and granted a preference right of entry to the successful contestant. See the swamp land cases: Ringsdorf v. The State of Iowa, (4 L. D., 497), State of Oregon (5 L. D., 31); and the desert land cases: Jefferson v. Winters, (5 L. D., 694); Sears v. Almy, (6 L. D., 1). See also homestead contest case of Henry C. Tingley (8 L. D., 205), and Crumpler v. Swett (8 L. D., 584).

Skeen went on this land not as a settler upon public lands with the intention of initiating a claim under the public land laws, but as a purchaser of the land from another. Conceding, however, that he thereby initiated a claim it is admitted by him that this settlement was made February 25, 1885, subsequently to the initiation of Bunger's contest January 20, 1885. Skeen could not claim any rights by virtue of his vendor's settlement. Knight v. Haucke (2 L. D., 188). Skeen being a purchaser before patent acquired no better title or greater right to this land than his vendor possessed. R. M. Chrisinger, (4 L. D., 347); Smith v. Custer (8 L. D., 269); William R. Stone, (8 L. D., 525).

For the reasons herein stated that portion of your office decision holding Dawes' entry for cancellation is affirmed, and I reverse that portion which allows Skeen, as transferee, to make entry for the tract in dispute; and direct that the contestant (Squire Bunger) be permitted to file for said land in accordance with his preference right of entry.

Your decision is modified accordingly.

SCHOOL LANDS—OKLAHOMA.

SIDNEY CLARK ET AL.

There is no authority, except in Congress, to dispose of lands reserved for the use of public schools.

The Department has no authority to permit land reserved for the benefit of public schools to be used for cemetery purposes.

Acting Secretary Chandler to Sidney Clark and C. T. Scott, August 31, 1889.

I am in receipt of your communication of the 2d instant, requesting that instructions be issued to permit the people of Oklahoma Territory and the surrounding country to use the NW. ¼ of the SE. ¼ of Sec. 16, T. 12, R. 3 W., for cemetery purposes.

In reply thereto, I have to state that section thirteen of the act of March 2, 1889 (25 Stat., 1005), reserved sections sixteen and thirty-six of each township in said territory for the use and benefit of the public schools; and while such reservation does not amount to a grant, so as to withdraw from Congress the power of disposition over them, yet so long as it continues it has, for the purpose of the reservation, the same force and effect as a grant, and there is no power, except in Congress, to make other disposition of said sections.

This Department has no authority, therefore, to grant your request.

SECOND HOMESTEAD ENTRY—WATER SUPPLY.

CHARLES F. BABCOCK.

The inability of the entryman to secure water fit for domestic use on the land first entered, is a sufficient cause for the allowance of a second entry, if due diligence and good faith are made apparent.

Secretary Noble to the Commissioner of the General Land Office, September 5, 1889.

I have considered the appeal of Charles F. Babcock from your office decision, dated December 13, 1887, rejecting his application for amendment of his homestead entry, No. 4410, covering the SW. ¼ of Sec. 1, T. 34 N., R. 50 W., Valentine series, Chadron, Nebraska, so as to have it embrace, in lieu of the above described tract, the S. ½ of SW. ¼ of Sec. 20 and the N. ½ of NW. ¼ of Sec. 29, T. 30 N., R. 52 W., same land district.

It appears that Babcock made his entry, No. 4410, August 24, 1885, and that he filed in the local office his application to amend in September, 1887. Said application was promptly forwarded to your office for action, which was taken by the decision of December 13, 1887, now before me on appeal.

This is not, properly speaking, an application to amend, although so termed. It is rather an application to be allowed to make a second entry, after the cancellation upon the records of that already made. Said application is under oath corroborated by two affiants, and assigns as reason therefor, that the land covered by the existing entry is unfit for cultivation or inhabitancy through an agency which the applicant could not foresee or foreknow, viz: unhealthy water, which can be used by neither man nor beast.

The applicant further states, in his corroborated affidavit, that he and his family consisting of wife and one child have resided upon the tract since October, 1885; that during said time he has hauled water for domestic uses between seven and eight miles, except during a portion of each winter, when he has melted snow; that he has dug two wells, and has failed to get from either of them water that could be used; that other wells have been dug in the immediate vicinity, and "not one drop of water that a human being can use has been found;" that he has on said tract a house, sixteen by twenty feet, a barn, twenty by twenty feet, and has cultivated and sown to crop five acres in each of the two years he has resided on the tract, but that both crops have been total failures; that having in good faith persisted for two years, with expenditure of time and means, in trying to make for himself and family a home on said tract, and now finding that with all his effort the land is still unfit for habitation, he asks permission to abandon the same and put his entry on the tract already described herein.

Your office decision finds no sufficient reason for allowing the change of entry as asked, and rejects the application with the statement that "the United States government can not furnish water to the settler, and if he can not obtain it by digging wells, he must by cisterns." To this proposition appellant very forcibly replies, that the making of cisterns and keeping in them sufficient water to meet the needs of the household and of stock on the farm imply an amount of roof surface which the average settler is unable to provide, and even if this could be done, it would not cure the defect in the soil, which renders it impossible to produce crops therefrom.

The Department has frequently said that it is slow to act favorably upon applications to amend or change entries deliberately made in accordance with the intention of the applicant but there are exceptional cases in which change may be allowed, and this I think, on the showing made, is one of them.

The applicant seems to have acted in the best of faith, and to have done everything in his power to make for himself and family a home on the tract entered. The obstacles which he met were such as could not well be foreseen, and it may truly be said that what the homestead law contemplates—to wit, the establishment of a home on the tract entered—has been in this case defeated through no fault of the entryman. The two necessities of life—bread and water—can neither of them be gotten from the land covered by the existing entry, and, where, as in this case, ordinary caution and extraordinary diligence and persistence in trying to make the tract habitable have been excercised, it would be a great hardship, and in my judgment would be in conflict with the purpose and spirit of the homestead laws to deny on proper showing an application like that in question, so long as it does not affect the rights of others.

After a careful consideration of the case in all its aspects, I am of the opinion that appellant should be permitted under the circumstances to change his entry as proposed. Your office decision is accordingly reversed.

———

TIMBER AND STONE ACT—FINAL PROOF.

INSTRUCTIONS.

An application to purchase under the act of June 3, 1878, does not effect a segregation of the land covered thereby.

The publication of intention to purchase under said act prevents the land from being entered by another, pending consideration thereof; but until said application is finally allowed the applicant has no right to, or control over the land covered thereby:

The departmental regulation requiring the submission of proof within ninety days from date of the published notice may be waived, where the pressure of business in the local office requires such action.

Acting Secretary Chandler to the Commissioner of the General Land Office, August 22, 1889.

From your letter of the 19th instant, enclosing draft of a proposed letter to the local officers at Seattle, Washington Territory, it appears that certain irregularities in final proof proceedings under the timber and stone act of June 3, 1878 (20 Stat., 89), have occurred at said land office.

The third section of said act provides:

That upon the filing of said statement, as provided in the second section of this act, the register of the land office shall post a notice of such application, embracing a description of the land by legal subdivisions, in his office for a period of sixty days, and shall furnish the applicant a copy of the same for publication, at the expense of such applicant, in a newspaper published nearest the location of the premises, for a like period of time; and after the expiration of said sixty days, if no adverse claim shall have have been filed, the person desiring to purchase shall furnish to the register of the land office satisfactory evidence, etc.

On May 1, 1880, your office issued a circular under this act (2 C. L. L., 1458), wherein it was said:

It has come to the knowledge of this office that many persons have taken the preliminary steps above indicated up to the point of making proof and payment, but have failed in the last essential particular. In effect, they withdraw the land from market on your records by making the application, sworn statement and publication, and then denude the land of its timber, the tract becomes valueless, and entry is not made.

It is clear that proof and payment should be made within a reasonable time after the expiration of sixty days from date of first publication of the notice of application.

You are therefore instructed to notify each claimant under said act that he is required to make the necessary proof and payment within ninety days from date of his original application. Should the claimant fail to meet this requirement within the period named, you will write the word "canceled" on his application, giving date thereof, and noting the same on your records.

This requirement, that proof and payment should be made within ninety days from date of the application, was not carried into the general circulars of October 1, 1880, and March 1, 1884; but in the circular approved by the Department July 16, 1887 (6 L. D., 114), it was said:

The published notice required by the third section of the act must state the time and place when, and name the officer before whom, the party intends to offer proof, which must be after the expiration of the sixty days of publication, and before ninety days from the date of the published notice. Where proof is not made before the expiration of said ninety days, the register and receiver will cancel the filing upon their records and notify this office accordingly, as prescribed by instructions of May 1, 1880.

This requirement was carried into the general circular of January 1, 1889 (see page 40), and is now a subsisting regulation adopted by your office, and approved by the Department.

It appears, however, that at the Seattle office a large number of cases are suspended where the proof was made after the expiration of the said ninety days; and that some thirteen hundred applications are pending wherein the dates for making proof are set for periods in the future, the latest as far off as February 21, 1891; and that this condition of affairs arises from the inability of the local office, under the pressure of other business and the large number of these applications, to apply the ninety day rule.

You call attention to the fact that under existing regulations, the date of the notice, and the date of making proof are placed under the control of the register, and if the latter is fixed for a period more than ninety days after the former, the register is responsible therefor, and not the applicant.

Taking this view of the case, and finding no statutory inhibition against such course, you propose to waive the ninety day requirement so far as it affects pending proofs and applications at the Seattle office, and direct that in the future due care shall be taken to have the date of making proof fixed at a period as near to the date of the original application as the pressure of business will admit, but not necessarily within ninety days.

This course of procedure meets with the approval of the Department, and the inability of this local office to carry into execution the requirement under consideration suggests the advisability of revoking it outright.

The reason for the circular of May 1, 1880, is not sound. An application to purchase under the act of June 3, 1878, does not operate as a segregation of the land covered thereby. Smith *v.* Martin, 2 L. D., 333; Capprise *v.* White, 4 L. D., 176; Henry A. Frederick, 8 L. D., 414. It is true that, as ruled in the Frederick case, the publication of intention to purchase would prevent the land from being entered by another, pending consideration of such application, but until the final allowance of said application the applicant has no right to, or control over the land covered thereby.

Again, under the circulars issued prior to that of July 16, 1887, there was no requirement that the notice should specify the exact date when the proof would be made. The proof was to be made some time *after* the sixty days, and *before* the ninety days. Now, under present regulations, the notice must name the date when the proof will be made, and the day for such act must be selected by the register, who is limited in his choice to some day *after* the sixty days and *before* the ninety days. The impraticability of this requirement is well illustrated by the condition of business in the Seattle office.

Under these considerations, I have to request that you will please report to the Department upon the advisability of striking out the ninety day requirement from the regulations now in force; and that if this course seems advisable to you, that you will prepare and submit to the Department an appropriate amendment to said regulations, whereby it will be within the power and discretion of the local office to fix the date of making these proofs at such a time, after due publication of notice, as the business of such office may permit.

PRACTICE—REVIEW—PRE-EMPTION—MORTGAGE.

HALING *v.* EDDY.

Review will not lie for the consideration of a question not in issue when the original decision is rendered.

A pre-emptor who has, in good faith, complied with the law, may mortgage his claim to procure money for the purpose of making final proof and payment.

Secretary Noble to the Commissioner of the General Land Office, September 7, 1889.

By letter of February 6, 1889, your office transmitted a motion by Frank A. Haling for review of the decision of the Department dated October 25, 1888, in the case of said Haling against Osmer J. Eddy, affirming the action of your office sustaining the pre-emption cash entry of Eddy for the E. ½, NE. ¼ and E. ½, SE. ¼, Sec. 29, T. 117 N., R. 40 W., 5th P. M., Benson, Minnesota, and rejecting Haling's application to file soldiers' homestead declaratory statement for the same.

The motion complains that no allusion is made in said decision to the fact that "Eddy had sold and alienated the land prior to date of his cash entry."

This necessitates a recital of the facts. Eddy's cash entry is dated March 6, 1871, his declaratory statement alleging settlement December 20, 1867. The entry was canceled on April 2, 1875, for conflict with the Hastings and Dakota railway grant. After ineffectual efforts to secure from the railway company a relinquishment of the land in his favor, under the act of June 22, 1874 (18 Stat., 194), Eddy applied for repayment of the purchase money. On December 11, 1883, while this application was pending, Haling applied to file soldiers' homestead declaratory statement for the tract. The application to file was rejected by the local officers for conflict with the railway grant, and Haling appealed. On May 15, 1884, a relinquishment under said act, was executed in Eddy's favor by the company and by decision of your office of March 30, 1885, the relinquishment was accepted, the entry re-instated, and Haling's application rejected. In that decision the alleged sale of the land by Eddy prior to entry was fully considered. It was shown by affidavits satisfactory to your office that Eddy's final pre-emption proof was submitted before the local officers on "January 16, 1871," and not on March 6, 1871, as indicated by the jurat attached to the papers, " that it was a common practice of the land officers at that time to permit pre-emptors to make proof and pay for the land at a subsequent time, the proof papers being held, by the district officers in the meantime and dated at the time payment was made," and that this practice was followed in Eddy's case; that on January 16, 1871, the day proof was submitted, Eddy executed a deed for part of said land, (E. ½, SE. ¼), to one Ward, that the deed " was executed simply to secure the payment to Ward of money by him loaned to Eddy, and by him used in making payment for the land, and was never considered by either of the parties as an actual conveyance of the land described therein." Your office thereupon said :

  In view of these facts I am of opinion that Mr. Eddy has acted in good faith, and without intention of fraud or violation of law, that the deed referred to above and in former correspondence while on its face an actual conveyance, was merely intended to be a mortgage and has been considered as such by all parties in interest.

Haling filed motion for review of that decision but it was based on allegations that Eddy was a minor, and had not complied with the law as to residence. The finding as to the transfer was not urged as ground for review. From that time that question disappeared from the case. Haling's allegations in said motion were considered by your office sufficient basis for a hearing, which was ordered and held. The local officers decided in favor of Eddy, and your office affirmed their finding in letter of March 8, 1887, deciding both questions as to Eddy's minority and his compliance with law, in his favor. That decision was affirmed, without discussion by the Department in the one now under consideration.

The question as to the sale of the land by Eddy before entry having been disposed of by your decision of March 30, 1885, and no appeal being taken therefrom on the question urged in the motion for review, was not an issue when the case was here on appeal from the decision of your office of March 8, 1887, and could not be re-opened upon the same allegations on appeal from said last decision. The motion for review was confined to other questions, and the hearing ordered thereon was really a new proceeding on new issues. These issues were decided by your said letter of 1887, from which appeal was taken. There is no law that prohibits a pre-emptor who has complied with the law in good faith, from mortgaging his claim to procure money for the purpose of making final proof and payment. William H. Ray (6 L. D., 340). See also Mudgett v. Dubuque and Sioux City Railroad Company, (8 L. D., 243).

The motion for review is accordingly denied.

FINAL PROOF PROCEEDINGS—PROTEST—EQUITABLE ADJUDICATION.

CAROLINE BRUNER.

If no protest appears in the record it will be presumed that none was filed.

An entry may be referred to the board of equitable adjudication whe re the final proof prior to the regulations of February 19, 1887, was accepted by the local office, and is in all respects satisfactory except that it was not taken at the time and place advertised.

First Assistant Secretary Chandler to the Commissioner of the General Land Office, September 7, 1889.

I have considered the case arising upon the appeal of Caroline Bruner from your office decision of October 28, 1887, rejecting the final proof, made December 31, 1884, upon her homestead entry for the SE. ¼ of Sec. 28, T. 113, R. 78, Huron land district, Dakota.

The ground of rejection of said proof is that it " was not taken on the day and at the place named in the published notice." The circumstances are set forth in claimant's affidavit accompanying the appeal as follows:

That on the day advertised for the making of said final proof the said affiant with her witnesses started to go to Okobojo, where said proof was advertised to be made; that the weather was intensely cold, the temperature being thirty degrees below zero; the wind was blowing a gale, and it was also storming; and the snow being deep, the roads were almost impassable; but after a number of hours' time, and by an almost superhuman effort, they reached the town of Okobojo, where said proof was to be made, but found the said probate judge absent, and it was stated that he was at Clifton, a town distant from Okobojo a few miles; that affiant and her witnesses started to go to the said town of Clifton; that before reaching said place their conveyance broke down owing to the heavy roads, and they were overtaken by night, and it was only by accident that they found a house, in which they took shelter for the night, it being impossible to get to said town of Clifton; that the next day they proceeded to the said town of Clifton, when they found the said probate judge, M. J. McCann; that the said McCann informed them that he was not at Okobojo the previous day, as he thought from the intense cold and severe storm that it would be impossible to get there; he also informed said affiant that her said final proof could be taken on that day and at the said town of Clifton, owing to the circumstances, and that the same would be in every way legal and regular.; that she thereupon proceeded to make said final proof, at said time and place, one day after the day advertised; that no protest was filed to said proof; nor was there any one at Okobojo on the previous day to object to said proof, and at no time was any protest or objection ever filed or attempted to be filed against said proof; and affiant says that said final proof was accepted by the officers of the Huron land office, and receiver's receipt duly issued therefor.

As there is no protest in the record against the final proof, it will be presumed that none was filed (F. C. Robinson, 8 L. D., 202).

The proof made before the probate judge on December 31, 1884, was accepted by the register and receiver January 5, 1885.

This case comes under paragraph nine of departmental circular of July 17, 1889 (9 L. D., 123), which says:

Where final proof has been accepted by the local office prior to the promulgation of said circular of February 19, 1887, if in all other respects satisfactory, except that it was not taken as advertised, the case may be submitted to the board of equitable adjudication for consideration.

The proof in the case of Caroline Bruner will be submitted to the board of equitable adjudication, in accordance with the rule above quoted.

REVIEW—PROCEEDINGS ON REPORT OF SPECIAL AGENT—RESIDENCE— FINAL PROOF.

ALBERT H. CORNWELL.

It is not sufficient in a motion for review to allege generally that the decision is not in accordance with the law and evidence; the errors of law should be specified, and attention directed to the particular evidence relied upon to warrant a reversal of the decision.

In hearings ordered on the report of a special agent the burden of proof is upon the government.

To establish residence there must be, concurrent with the act of settlement, or going upon the land, an intent to make it a home to the unqualified exclusion of one elsewhere.

It is not within the power of the Department to extend the time within which a preemptor is required by statute to make final proof.

Secretary Noble to the Commissioner of the General Land Office, September 10, 1889.

This is a motion by Albert H. Cornwell for review and reconsideration of departmental decision of November 23, 1888, in the case of the United States *v.* said Cornwell, involving the NE. ¼ of Sec. 9, T. 113 N., R. 56 W., Watertown, Dakota.

The decision complained of is a formal affirmance, on appeal, of your office decision of June 22, 1887, holding the pre-emption cash entry of Cornwell, made November 12, 1884, for the tract in question, for cancellation.

The controversy arose upon the report of Special Agent E. G. Fahnestock, dated November 14, 1884, stating that he had made a personal examination of the tract, and had found thereon ten acres of breaking (afterwards stated by him to be twenty acres) and a shanty seven by nine feet, containing a cot, but no other articles of furniture, and some oats; that Cornwell had never lived on the land, but had, during the time covered by his final proof, lived in De Smet, where he carried on business; that he had endeavored to get a statement from claimant, but he refused to give it; and that his said entry was fraudulent.

The report was supported by a number of affidavits, and thereupon a hearing was ordered by your office. The hearing took place before the clerk of the district court, at De Smet, Dakota, July 8–10, 1885, at which the claimant appeared and submitted testimony in support of his entry, which was followed by the introduction of several witnesses for the government, whose examination was conducted by the special agent.

The finding of the local officers upon the testimony was in favor of the claimant. This finding was reversed by your said office decision of June 22, 1887, and the entry held for cancellation, because of non-compliance with the law in the matter of residence, with the result aforesaid, on appeal here.

The grounds alleged as a basis for the motion for review are, that the decision complained of, (1) is unjust to the claimant, (2) is not in accordance with the law and evidence, (3) does not show that the testimony in the record has been considered, and (4) does not embody any facts indicating that the exceptions taken by claimant's attorney at the trial, to the enforcement of the rule then in existence, which required claimant to submit testimony in support of his entry, before the witnesses for the government were called, and to the introduction of irrelevant testimony by the special agent, have been considered.

As to the second and third of these alleged grounds of error, it may be said that neither of them is well taken. It is not sufficient, in a motion for review, to allege merely that the decision sought to be revoked is not in accordance with the law and evidence. In such cases, the errors of law, if any are charged, should be specifically pointed out, and attention should also be specially directed to the particular evidence which is claimed to be sufficient to warrant a reconsideration and reversal of the decision. Otherwise a re-examination of the whole record would be made necessary in every case wherein the unsuccessful party might see fit to allege, in general terms, that the judgment against him was contrary to the law and evidence; a practice which if allowed to prevail would entail upon the Department a great amount of unnecessary labor and consequent loss of time.

Neither is the allegation that the decision does not show the testimony in the case to have been considered, in any sense, a sufficient ground for review. This allegation bears upon its face the impress of having been either recklessly made, or made without a proper understanding of the office and function of a motion for review. It is moreover fatally defective in that it utterly fails to point out or suggest any error in the decision complained of, and must, therefore, be dismissed as wholly insufficient.

The first and fourth alleged grounds of error, when considered together, amount to a contention that said departmental decision is unjust to the claimant, because, under the rule in existence at the date when the hearing ordered on the special agent's report was had, he was compelled to introduce evidence in support of his entry before the witnesses for the government were examined touching the charges made against the same, and that the burden of proof was thus improperly and unjustly thrown upon him.

In view of this contention, the evidence in the case has all been carefully re-examined, and in determining the question involved the burden of proof has been considered as resting with the government. By thus shifting the burden of proof from the claimant to the government, it is not seen that any injustice can result to the former by reason of his having been subjected at the trial to the rule of which he complains. This will, in effect, give him the substantial benefits of the rule of practice on this subject, announced in the case of George T. Burns, decided July 25, 1885 (4 L. D., 62), and which has since prevailed, namely, that in cases of hearings ordered on a special agent's report as to the character of an entry, the burden of proof is upon the government.

But even when thus examined and considered, the record in this case fails, in my judgment, to warrant a reversal of the decision complained of.

*   *   *   *   *   *   *

I do not think it can be reasonably claimed, ... that Cornwell ever established a *bona fide* residence on the land in question. To establish residence, there must be, concurrent with the act of settlement, or going upon the land, an intent to make it a home to the unqualified exclusion of a home elsewhere. Without such intent, residence can neither be established, nor maintained, in good faith, under the pre-emption or homestead laws. Mary Campbell (8 L. D., 331). Under the facts disclosed by the record, it is apparent to any mind that this claimant did not, at the date of his pretended settlement, or during the time of his alleged residence on the land in question, have the intention to make the same his home to the exclusion of a home elsewhere. On the contrary, the evidence is convincing that he at no time intended to make the land his home, or to even pretend to make it his home, after having made his final proof. This is shown by his exceedingly meagre improvements, a shanty seven by thirteen feet, scarcely habitable, with no furniture except "a stove, cot-bed, chairs, lamp and shelf;" by his never having taken a single meal on his claim; by his converting his shanty into a granary and storing his grain therein on the very day he started to the land office to make his proof; by his never having pretended to reside there after making final proof; and by his almost continuous absence from the land during the time of his alleged residence thereon. His shanty was moved to the claim by hired men; his breaking was done by a hired man, though by his own team, so that the sum total of his personal presence on his claim, so far as this record shows, was the one hundred nights, during which he says he "slept there." The entire summer, with the exception of these one hundred nights and the Sundays which he spent in De Smet, was spent working on his tree claim, seventeen miles distant from the land, where he says he personally cultivated ten acres of trees eight times; cultivated ten acres of corn, and harvested seventy-five acres of grain which he planted in the spring; and in cultivating five other tree claims and harvesting and stacking fifty acres of grain, near his pre-emption.

Reference is made by counsel to an affidavit of the special agent who reported upon the entry, subsequently filed in the record, stating in effect that he was mistaken as to the area broken on the claim, and that the same was twenty instead of ten acres; also that he was mistaken in stating that the claimant was engaged in business in De Smet, other than farming and manual labor.

The statements in this affidavit do not, however, materially affect the question involved. The record has been considered allowing the full twenty acres of breaking claimed, and in all respects, upon the testimony taken at the hearing, without regard to the report of the special agent.

Counsel further state that claimant has offered to return to the land, if his residence is deemed insufficient, and remain there the six months required by law; and is still willing to so return and make "further residence and improvements," if the privilege is granted him, though it would be a hardship upon him, as he would have to divide his family and have his wife and babe live on her homestead, while he resides by himself on the land in question.

In reply to this, it is sufficient to say that it is not within the power of this Department to extend the time within which a pre-emption claimant is required by statute to make his proof, showing compliance with the law under his claim. But it may be further said, that this claimant seems wholly to misconceive what is meant by residence on his claim, as required by the pre-emption law. If he were granted the privilege of doing that which he offers to do, namely, leave his family on his wife's claim, where they now reside, and go to his pre-emption claim, and stay there by himself for the period of six months, having the intention to return to his family as soon as the six months have elapsed, he would in no sense be a resident on his pre-emption during such period. There could be no intention in such case of making the place a home, and the proceeding would be an evasion of, instead of a compliance with the law. West v. Owen, 4 L. D., 412; Van Ostrum v. Young, 6 L. D., 25; Spalding v. Colfer, 8 L. D., 615.

A number of affidavits have been filed in the record pending this motion for review, in which it is stated generally, in effect, that claimant is still the owner of the land, and has continued to cultivate the same every season since making proof; that he is still residing with his wife on her homestead claim; and that his residence on his pre-emption for six months prior to the date of his proof was such as was generally understood by his neighbors and the settlers of that community to be a full and complete compliance with the law, by a single person.

These affidavits bear date in May, 1889, and it is not seen how they can be considered as a part of the record in the case, in determining this motion, especially in view of the prior intervening adverse claim, hereinafter mentioned. If it were only a question between the claimant and the government, the latter as a matter of grace might waive a strict compliance with the law, but the adverse rights of McMullin having attached to the tract in controversy, the government is not in a position to thus summarily dispose of his claim. The affidavits do not, however, materially affect the case, as they in no sense avoid the effect of claimant's own testimony given at the trial.

In view of all the foregoing, I see no good reason for disturbing the former judgment of the Department herein, and the motion to reconsider that judgment is denied.

It is proper to further state that on April 16, 1889, one William McMullin applied to make homestead entry for the tract in question. The application was rejected by the local officers, because of the pendency of this motion for review. An appeal was taken to your office, and the papers have been transmitted here. These papers are returned, with the other papers in the case, for appropriate action, in view of the foregoing.

ADJOINING FARM HOMESTEAD—SETTLEMENT RIGHTS.

McHarry v. Stewart.

A deed executed by a widow, purporting to convey a specific portion of a "probate homestead," does not, under the laws of California, if there are minors, convey such an estate in the land embraced therein as will sustain an adjoining farm entry.

An undivided interest in the original farm does not constitute such ownership thereof as will afford a legal basis for an adjoining farm entry.

Possession under an invalid adverse claim, of a part of the land included within a pre-emption filing, does not interfere with the constructive possession of the pre-emptor, or his right to the entire tract covered by the filing.

Secretary Noble to the Commissioner of the General Land Office, September 16, 1889.

This is an appeal by D. S. C. McHarry from the decision of your office of September 1, 1886, in the case of D. S. C. McHarry *v.* James Stewart, involving lots 2 and 3, Sec. 22, and lot 1, Sec. 27, T. 2 N., R. 3 W., San Bernardino meridian, San Francisco district, California.

Stewart made adjoining farm homestead entry, No. 5734, for said land, December 10, 1883, and McHarry filed pre-emption declaratory statement, No. 17,834, for a tract embracing said land and other lands, December 13, of said year, alleging settlement, January 19, 1878.

McHarry, after due notice by publication, offered proof in support of his pre-emption filing, May 9, 1884, at which time Stewart appeared as contestant, and a number of witnesses were examined and a large amount of testimony taken on both sides. The decision of the local officers was adverse to Stewart, on the ground, substantially, that he did not "own" the land, upon which as a basis he claimed the right to make said adjoining farm entry. On appeal by Stewart, your office (in the decision from which McHarry now appeals to this Department) reversed the decision of the local officers on said point and awarded the land to Stewart.

The land claimed by Stewart as a basis for his entry is, the SE. ¼ of SW. ¼ and a fraction in the SW. ¼ of the SE. ¼, of Sec. 22, in said T. 2 N., R. 3 W. (about *sixty* acres in quantity), and is a portion of a tract of one hundred and seventy-five (175) acres, which, as a part of the estate of James McClellan, deceased, had been, February 19, 1876, duly set apart by decree of the probate court of Contra Costa county, California (in which it was situated) as a "probate homestead" under the laws of California, for "the use of" the family of said decedent. The family consisted of the widow and two minor children, a girl and a boy, aged respectively at date of said decree (February 19, 1876), four and five years. The widow subsequently married Stewart, and he claims the ownership of said sixty acres, under a deed from her therefor, executed October 2, 1882.

There are two classes of homesteads provided for by the statutes of California: namely, homesteads selected and recorded during the lifetime of the decedent, and where this has not been done, homesteads selected and set apart by the judge or the court of probate, "for the use of" the surviving husband or wife and minor children, if there be any. The homestead now under consideration belongs to the latter class, known as "probate homesteads?"

Homesteads are to be set apart and the interests of the parties entitled thereto determined, in pursuance of the statutes in force at the time when the order is made. Sulzberger *v.* Sulzberger (50 Cal., 387). In this case the order was made, as stated above, February 19, 1876, and at that time the statutes in force on this subject were section 11,465 *et seq.*, Vol. 2, "Codes and Statutes of California" of 1876, and section 6,237 *et seq.*, Vol. 1, of said Codes and Statutes. Under these laws a material distinction is made between the two kinds of homesteads; it being provided by section 11,474 (Codes and Statutes) as to a homestead selected and recorded during the lifetime of the decedent, that if so selected from the community property, it vests, on the death of the husband or wife, absolutely in the survivor, but, if from the separate property of either husband or wife, it vests, on the death of the person from whose property selected, in his or her heirs, "subject to the power of the probate court to assign it for a limited period to the family of the decedent," while, in case of a " probate homestead," it is held, that under section 11,468 (ib.), a homestead set apart out of the separate estate of a deceased husband is the property of the surviving wife, if there are no minor children, and, if the decedent left a minor child or children, *one half "belongs to" the widow*, and the other half to the child, or children, in equal proportions.   Mawson *v*. Mawson (50 Cal., 539).

The land set apart in this case, it appears, was not acquired by McClellan after marriage, but was owned by him before marriage, and, this being the case, it was under the California statutes his separate property. (Secs. 5163 and 5164, Codes and Statutes).   There being minor children, one half of it was, according to Mawson *v*. Mawson, *supra*, the property of the widow, and the other half belonged to the children in equal proportions.   Until partition is made, however, the widow owns no portion of the land in severalty, but holds an undivided half interest in the entire tract as tenant in common with the children. (Secs. 5685, 5686 and 5683, Codes and Statutes).

Mrs. Stewart, in the deed under which Stewart claims, does not undertake to convey her undivided half interest in the entire homestead (175 acres), but said deed purports to be an absolute conveyance by numbers of a particular portion (about sixty acres) of the homestead tract.   This was doubtless done with a view of satisfying the requirement of the law, that the tract used as a basis for an adjoining farm entry should be "contiguous" to the land embraced in such entry.   At the date of the deed, the minor children were aged, respectively, ten and eleven years, and they have not yet attained their majority.   Without intending to intimate an opinion upon the question, which presents itself at the outset, whether under a conveyance by one tenant in common of a particular part (described by numbers) of the common estate, any—and if so, what—interest passes to the grantee as against infant co-tenants, during the existence of their disability of minority or until such conveyance is sanctioned by a legal proceeding, in which such co-tenants are properly represented and their interests protected (Washburn, Vol. 2, p. 261 and Vol. 1, p. 654; Hilliard, p. 593), I am of the opinion, that the deed in this case does not convey such an estate in the land embraced therein, as will sustain an adjoining farm entry, for the reason, in the first place, that the widow, where there are minor children, can not make a conveyance of her interest in a "probate homestead" under the laws of California, which can take effect and be enforced by the grantee as tenant in common of the minor children—at least, so long as the premises are impressed with the character of a homestead and are needed for the use of the family. As to homesteads selected during the life of the decedent, it is provided by section 6242 (Codes and Statutes), that they "can not be conveyed or incumbered, unless the instrument be executed and acknowledged by both husband and wife." In the case of Lies *v*. De Diablar (12 Cal., 328), a mortgage by the husband alone of the homestead was sought to be enforced after his death, on the ground that by adultery and abandonment the wife had forfeited her rights, and the homestead had been divested of its character as such, but the mortgage was held to be void, and the court say, "It is a mistake to suppose that this provision" (as to joint conveyance) "was solely for the benefit of the wife. It was as much for the benefit of the children." While there is no statutory inhibition of the conveyance by the widow of her interest in the "probate homestead," such conveyance is manifestly contrary to the policy of the law and tends directly to defeat its object. Section 11,465 (Codes & Statutes), the law in force when the homestead under consideration was set apart, provides, that, if no homestead has been selected and set apart during the life of the decedent, "the judge or court must select, designate, set-apart and cause to be recorded, a homestead for the use of the persons hereinbefore named." The "persons hereinbefore named" referred to are "the surviving husband or wife, and minor children of the decedent." In the order or decree setting apart the homestead in this case, the widow and minor children are named as constituting the family of the decedent, and, it decreed, that the land "be and the same is hereby set apart for the use of his family." In the case of Estate of Moore (57 Cal., 437), the court say, that the homestead right "is a right bestowed by the beneficence of the law of this State" (California) "for the benefit of the family," and,

The homestead when set apart is to be set apart for the benefit of the widow and children. Every minor has an interest, and has a right to be named in the decree. The property set apart is to be a home for them all, she, the widow, taking her place as the head of the family. It certainly could not be said that her deed conveying her interest as a successor would interfere with and defeat the purpose of the law in giving the family an abiding place.

While in that case the question involved was as to the power of the widow to sell the homestead right or right to have a homestead set apart, yet the reason assigned by the court, in the following quotation from the decision, for denying such right, applies with equal (if not greater) force to a sale of her interest in the homestead after it has been set apart:

If one of the parties entitled to apply—say the mother of minor children—could sell her right, and her grantee apply, such grantee would be entitled to the possession of the homestead as against the mother, and would have a joint interest with the children, to the exclusion of the mother; which would be repugnant to the very idea of a homestead. It being the object of the Legislature to provide for a homestead, *i. e.*, a place of home for the family, we cannot hold that the statute enacted for that purpose shall have the construction and effect of destroying the object in view.

In the case of Whittle *v.* Samuels (54 Ga., 648), cited in Thompson on Homestead Exemptions (Sec. 551), it is held that a widow to whom a homestead exemption has been set apart under the laws of Georgia can not sell the same, even with the approval of the ordinary and the consent of the executor. "There appears," says Mr. Thompson, "to be no statute in that State inhibiting such sale; but the rule is placed on the ground that it is contrary to the policy of the law to permit it to be done; that statutes permitting sale of the homestead should be strictly construed; that the minor children have rights . . . . . which are endangered by such alienation."

The interest in the homestead tract given by the statute (Sec. 11,468, Codes and Statues) to the surviving husband or widow, or such survivor and the minor children, covers the entire estate therein, and, while the laws of California do not prevent the widow from taking as heir an interest in the remainder of the husband's property, left after the homestead has been set apart, she can not (as held in your office decision) take an interest as heir in the land so set apart, because the homestead estate leaves nothing to which such interest may attach.

But, admitting that the deed of Mrs. Stewart conveys to Stewart an undivided interest in the land embraced therein, does such interest entitle him to make adjoining farm homestead entry? While the Acting Commissioner, in the case of Douglass Emmett (2 C. L. O., 181), and the Commissioner in the case of Thomas S. Wetherbee (1 L. D., 38), held without discussion, that an undivided interest in land will sustain such entry, the question seems never to have been passed upon by this Department. The statute (Sec. 2289 Rev. Stat.), authorizing adjoining farm entries, provides, that "every person *owning* and residing on land may, under the provisions of this section, enter other land lying *contiguous* to his land, which shall not, with the land so already owned and occupied, exceed in the aggregate one hundred and sixty acres." Statutes are to be read "according to the natural and most obvious import of the language used, without resorting to subtle and forced constructions for the purpose of either limiting or extending their operation." (Waller *v.* Harris, 20 Wend., 555; Sedg. on Construction of Stat., and Con. Law, 220). "The natural and most obvious import" of the word "owning" is *absolute* and not *qualified* ownership—"the right by which a thing belongs to some one in particular to the exclusion of all others." (Bouvier's Law Dic.; Sec. 679, Codes and Statutes of Cal.), and not a right shared with one or more persons, or restricted in its use, or limited or deferred as to time of enjoyment. There is nothing in the context or subject matter of the statute authorizing a departure from the ordinary meaning of the language employed. On the contrary, au adherence to this meaning would seem to be essential to the enforcement of the law, both in its letter and spirit. *Contiguity* of the original farm to that entered is an essential under the statute of an adjoining farm entry; if an undivided interest in land owned in common with others, be held to sustain such entry, it can not be known whether the portion of the common estate which will be allotted to the entrymen on partition will in fact adjoin the land entered. A tract of one hundred and twenty acres might be owned in common by twelve persons, each having an undivided interest of one-twelfth and all residing in one house or on one part of the tract, and, if an undivided interest is a sufficient basis for an adjoining farm entry, each of the twelve might (if a sufficient amount of land circumjacent to the tract held in common could be found unappropriated) make entry of one hundred and fifty acres (1800 in all), and, on partition of the tract held in common, the tract allotted might in no instance be contiguous to that entered by the allottee, and only one of them will have had actual residence on the tract constituting his original farm. A construction of the law, which is not only a departure from the natural import of its language, but leads to a violation of both its letter and spirit, is not to be indulged. In consonance with this view, the adjoining-farm-homestead entryman is required in his final affidavit, to make oath, that he is " the *sole bona fide* owner as an actual settler" of the land constituting his original farm. A party owning only an undivided interest in land is not the " sole owner" of any part thereof. I am of the opinion that an undivided interest in land will not sustain an adjoining farm entry, and, conceding that Stewart by the deed from his wife acquired such interest in the land which he claims as an original farm, his entry would still be invalid.

There is still another fatal objection to Stewart's entry. The statute requires *residence* on the orginal farm. The proof shows, that Stewart and his family, while making a show of residence on the tract claimed as an original farm, had in fact leased said farm to a tenant for a number of years, covering the period of his adjoining farm entry, and that they in fact resided several miles from said farm in the town of Martinez, where Stewart had an established permanent business and a residence connected with his place of business. The excuse set up by Stewart for such non-residence, namely, that it was because of danger of violence and injury at the hands of the McHarrys, is not sustained by the evidence. Mrs. Stewart hereof testifies, that she went to the farm and remained there for such short periods, whenever she felt inclined, and seems never to have been molested, and no attempt by the McHarrys to prevent Stewart or his family from residing on the origi nal farm at any time is shown.

It further appears that Stewart owned another and distinct tract of two hundred and ninety acres of land. While under the pre-emption law, the proprietorship " of three hundred and twenty acres of land in any State or Territory," disables a party from exercising the pre-emptive right, there is laid down in the homestead law no disability to make homestead entry on account of ownership of other lands, except that in making adjoining-farm-homestead entry, it is provided that the land already "owned and occupied" as an original farm, shall not with that entered as an adjoining farm "exceed in the aggregate one hundred and sixty acres."

The entry of Stewart being invalid, it remains to consider the pre-emption claim of McHarry. The proof shows, as found by the local officers, that McHarry settled an established residence on a portion of the tract covered by his filing outside of that portion in contest between him and Stewart, claiming possession of the entire tract under his filing, and that he has reasonably complied with the law as to residence, improvement and cultivation. The possession by Stewart of a part of the tract covered by McHarry's filing being under his (Stewart's) invalid adjoining farm entry, did not prevent McHarry's constructive possession and rights under his filing extending over the entire tract. The pre-emption filing of McHarry will, therefore, be allowed to remain intact, subject to his further compliance with the law, and the entry of Stewart will be canceled.

The decision of your office is reversed.

TIMBER CULTURE CONTEST—EXTENSION OF TIME.

GALBREATH v. MAGUIRE.

An extension of time granted under section 2, act of June 14, 1878, does not, during its existence, protect the entry from contest.

First Assistant Secretary Chandler to the Commissioner of the General Land Office, September 16, 1889.

I have considered the appeal of William Maguire from the decision of your office dated March 12, 1888, in the contest case of Adam Galbreath v. said Maguire, affirming the action of the local officers in holding for cancellation the latter's timber culture entry No. 441, upon the SW. ¼, Sec. 22, T. 25 S., R. 5 W., Wichita land district, Kansas.

The record shows that Maguire made timber culture entry for said described tract June 20, 1874, and on October 7, 1885, Galbreath initiated a contest against said entry in which he alleged that the entry-man—

Did not have any timber growing on land above described in the year 1883, that there were about one hundred and eighty trees growing on said land in the year 1882, that said trees were dug up and disposed of in the year 1882, that said William Maguire has not planted or caused to be planted on land above described any trees, seeds or cuttings since the year 1882. That there is not a tree of any kind growing on said land at this date; that said land is now and has been for the past three years . . . . . abandoned as a tree claim.

A hearing was ordered before the local officers and set for November 17th, and continued to December 8, 1885, at which time the contestant appeared by attorney and the entryman appeared in person and with counsel.

The entryman offered in evidence an affidavit of extension which was filed in the local office June 23, 1885, and contended that the same was a valid bar to the contest.

Witnesses were sworn and examined on behalf of both parties and the hearing closed December 10, 1885. On January 4, 1886, the local officers found in favor of the contestant, and recommended that the entry be canceled. They also reported that they were "of the opinion that said extension does not estop the plaintiff, as the extension was granted upon the supposition that defendant was acting in good faith when he procured it."

On February 12, 1886, the entryman appealed, and on March 12, 1888, your office sustained the action of the local officers and held the entry for cancellation.

On May 18, 1888, counsel for the entryman appealed to this Department and alleges the following grounds of error, viz:

1. In holding that at the time of the initiation of this contest no trees were growing on said land.

2. In holding that it is "affirmatively shown that the claimant has been grossly negligent in caring for his trees after planting."

3. In holding that "instead of cultivating his trees and protecting them" the claimant "has used the land for pasture."

4. In affirming the decision of the local officers and in holding the entry for cancellation.

5. In not finding and holding that the claimant having in June, 1885, applied for and obtained an extension of time of one year within which to repair any defects in the matter of trees, the claim was subject to contest in October of that year, nor until one year from the date of such extension of time had expired.

6. In not sustaining the entry and dismissing the contest.

From a careful examination of the testimony adduced at the hearing I am of the opinion that the allegations of the contestant have been fully sustained by a preponderance of evidence,—hence the only other question to be considered is that raised by appellant's counsel in his fifth ground of error, viz: Was the entry subject to contest during the period of one year from the date the extension was granted to the entryman?

The second section of the act of May 20, 1876 (17 Stat., 54) amendatory of the act of 1874, declared, that the planting of seeds, nuts and cuttings, when well and properly done, and the ground properly prepared and cultivated should be considered a compliance with the timber culture act, and that in case the seeds, nuts or cuttings planted should not germinate and grow, or should be destroyed by the depredations of the grasshoppers, or from other inevitable accident, the ground should be replanted, or the vacancies filled within one year from the first planting. Parties claiming the benefit of this provision were to prove by

two good and credible witnesses, that the ground was properly prepared and planted," and that the destruction of the seeds, nuts, or cuttings was caused by inevitable accident in such year.

The act of June 14, 1878 (20 Stat., 113) is also amendatory of the act
of March 13, 1874, and as to all entries made since the date of its approval, is a substitution for the prior act (circular March 1, 1884, page
29). Section 2 of said act of 1878 among other things declares,

Provided, however, that in case such trees, seeds, or cuttings, shall be destroyed by
grasshoppers or by extreme and unusual drouth, for any year or term of years, the time
for planting such trees, seeds or cuttings shall be, extended one year for every such
year that they are so destroyed; *Provided* further, That the person making such entry
shall, before he or she shall be entitled to such extension of time, file with the register and receiver of the proper land office an affidavit corroborated by two witnesses,
setting forth the destruction of such trees, and that in consequence of such destruction, he or she is compelled to ask an extension of time, in accordance with the provisions of this act.

The affidavit of extension made and filed by the entryman, which
his counsel claims was a bar to the present contest, is as follows:

STATE OF KANSAS, *Reno County, ss.*
Personally appeared before me . . . . William Maguire, who being by me
duly sworn . . . . says, that I am the same identical person who made T. C.
Entry, No. 441. . . . . That in the spring of 1876, I planted ten acres of cottonwood and box elder timber on said tract which grew very well. In the spring of
1877, I refilled the said ten acres with cottonwood where they had died out, also
planted them so they stood four feet apart each way. I cultivated said trees during
the summer of 1877, and 1878, in the fall of 1878 there was at least two-thirds of said
trees destroyed by drouth. In the spring of 1879, I replanted the said ten acres with
cottonwood four feet apart and cultivated during the summer of 1879. In the summer of 1880, I again lost at least two-thirds of my timber by extreme drouth. In the
spring of 1881, I had the said ten acres again replanted with cottonwood timber which
were killed in the winter of 1882 and 1883, by extreme cold weather to the extent of
nearly all the trees that I had. In the spring of 1883, I cultivated said land to crops,
not being able to get any timber out. In the spring of 1884, I again replanted said
ten acres of land to cottonwood timber, it being dry when they were planted there
were but few of cottonwoods started at all, and in the spring of 1885, I have planted
six acres of said land to maple seed. I now, therefore ask for an extension of time
in which to complete the planting and growing of my said timber culture entry as
provided by law.
    (Signed)   WILLIAM MAGUIRE.

Also personally appeared at the same time and place A. L. Dull and S. H. Dull,
who being by me duly sworn depose and say that they are well acquainted with the
tract of land embraced in the within affidavit of William Maguire, and also with the
said affidavit, and know of our own personal knowledge that which he sets forth in
his written affidavit to be true.
    (Signed)   A. L. DULL,
                                               S. H. DULL,
Sworn and subscribed to before me this 22nd day of June, 1885.
    (Signed)   J. B. BROWN,
                                                Notary Public.

A. L. Dull and S. H. Dull (father and son) were examined as witnesses on behalf of the entryman. They testified that he gave them
permission to remove the dead timber from the tract in dispute and

that they removed it all in the spring of 1883, to their home seven and one half miles distant, where they used it for fire-wood.

On cross examination they severally admitted that when they executed the affidavit of extension as corroborating witnesses they only intended to swear " that Mr. Maguire was a man of good standing and reliable, and had known him for eight or nine years."

From their testimony it is shown that they had no personal knowledge as to whether the entryman had properly prepared and planted the tract to tree seeds, trees, nuts or cuttings, or cultivated the same prior to the filing of said affidavit. I am therefore convinced that said affidavit was not made in good faith and that the same was false and fraudulent. But aside from such fact I am of the opinion that if it had been made in the best of good faith, and an extension had been allowed by the local officers, yet the entry would be never-the-less subject to contest at any time during the period of such extension, in accordance with the provisions of section 3 of the act of June 14, 1878 (*supra*) which declares—

That if at any time after the filing of said affidavit and prior to the issuing of patent for said land, the claimant shall fail to comply with any of the requirements of this act, then and in that event such land shall be subject to entry under the homestead laws, or by some other person under the provisions of this act. *Provided*, that the party making claim to said land, shall give at the time of filing his application, such notice to the original claimant as shall be prescribed by the rules established by the Commissioner of the General Land Office, and the rights of the parties shall be determined as in other cases.

The record herein shows that at the time of the initiation of this contest Galbreath made a homestead application for said described tract and that the required notice was duly served on the timber culture claimant.

Upon review of the whole testimony and the law governing this case, I am convinced that the contestant had a valid legal right to contest said entry prior to the expiration of one year after the affidavit of extension was filed in the local office, and that Maguire's timber culture entry was properly held for cancellation.

Your office decision of March 12, 1888, is, therefore affirmed.

———

OSAGE LAND—FINAL PROOF—ACT OF MAY 28, 1880.

HESSONG *v.* BURGAN.

A departmental regulation under a statute, not in conflict therewith, has the force and effect of law.

Independently of the express provisions in the act of May 28, 1880, the Secretary of the Interior was authorized, by virtue of the general powers of the Executive under the Constitution, to prescribe rules and regulations for the proper disposition of the Osage lands.

A settler under said act acquires no vested right as against the United States until he has made final proof, and paid, or tendered, the required purchase money.

Failure to submit final proof, and make payment within six months after Osage filing, renders the claim thereunder subject to any valid intervening right.

The case of Epley *v.* Trick overruled.

Secretary Noble to the Commissioner of the General Land Office, September
16, 1889.

I have considered the motion for review of departmental decision, rendered on September 13, 1888, in the case of William H. Hessong *v.* Helena Burgan, awarding the E. ¼ of the SE. ¼ the SW. ¼ of the SE. ¼ of sec. 30, and the NE.¼ of the NE. ¼ of sec. 31, T. 27 S., R. 21 W., Garden City, Kansas, land district, to the latter.

The land in question is a part of the Osage Indian trust and diminished reserve land, the disposition of which is provided for by act of Congress approved May 28, 1880, (21 Stat. 143). The record shows that said Hessong filed his Osage declaratory statement No. 699 for said land on December 2, 1884, alleging settlement thereon October 18th, same year. On January 8, 1885, Miss Burgan filed her Osage declaratory statement for said land, alleging settlement thereon October 15, 1884, and on May 9 1885, she offered her final proof, which was rejected by local land office on May 26, same year, for the reason that it did not show compliance with the requirements of the law as to residence, and also because the good faith of the claimant was not sufficiently shown. From said action of the local land officers an appeal was duly taken.

On July 21, 1885, Hessong submitted final proof, which was transmitted to the local office with said appeal. On November 14, 1885, your office directed that a hearing should be duly ordered " to determine the rights of the respective claimants by priority of settlement, and also to show in what manner each has complied with the requirements under the law." The hearing was duly had, and upon the testimony submitted the local officers decided in favor of Hessong.

On appeal your office, on February 8, 1887, affirmed the action of the local office, for the reason that Hessong was shown to be the prior actual settler, and had duly complied with the requirements of said act.

The Department on September 13, 1888, reversed the decision of your office and awarded the land to Miss Burgan.

The facts stated to be shown by the record and testimony according to the departmental decision sought to be reviewed and revoked are, that Miss Burgan was born in the city of London, England, on October 2, 1863; that she afterwards came to the United States, and on October 16, 1884, she duly declared her intention to become a citizen of the United States, and at the date of filing her said statement, she was a duly qualified pre-emptor; that it was clearly shown that her alleged settlement on October 15, 1884, was made by her father for her; that she did not go upon the land until October 22, 1884, when she commenced to occupy her house, which had been built for her by her father; that her residence on the land was continuous, with the exception that she was absent a few weeks at her father's house on an adjoining tract while taking care of her sick mother; that Hessong went upon the land on October 18, 1884, began the construction of a sod-house, and had some plowing done on the land; that Hessong was the first settler and complied with the requirements of the second section of said act as to settlement and improvement of said land; that under the provision of section five of said act, the Department, "on June 28, 1880," issued regulations requiring filings for Osage Indian trust and diminished reserve lands to be made within three months from date of settlement, and proof and first payment to be made within six months from date of filing, after due notice by publication, as in other pre-emption entries; that "Hessong defaulted in making final proof and payment within the time required," and as Miss Burgan had complied with the requirement of said act and the regulations thereunder, she had the better right to the land.

The decision of the Department further found, that :

It is clearly shown by the contest testimony, that the final proof offered by Hessong was false in its most material parts; i. e., his improvements were not worth more than $50 or $60, his residence on the tract was merely nominal, and it clearly appears that one of his final proof witnesses was an interested party, and was as much interested in the result of the contest as was Hessong, while it as fully appears that Miss Bergan's final proof was truthful in every respect, and that she honestly endeavored to comply with the requirements of the law.

For the reason herein stated, I must reverse your decision, and direct that Bergan be allowed to enter the tract covered by her filing.

Hessong filed a motion for review of this decision, alleging error, (1) in holding that Hessong had unconditionally forfeited his right to the land by failure to make his final proof and first payment within six months after filing his declaratory statement; (2) in holding that after having complied with the requirements of section two of the act of May 28, 1880, it was obligatory upon Hessong to establish any particular character of residence as to time, or to make any particular amount of improvements, in order to show good faith, or having failed to do either, he forfeited his right to enter ; (3) in holding that because one of his witnesses was interested, he forfeited his right to the land; (4) in holding that, even though Hessong has forfeited his right, Helena Bergan had a right to said land.

I have carefully considered said motion for review in the light of the argument of counsel for Hessong.

In Rogers v. Lukens (6 L. D., 111), decided by Acting Secretary Muldrow, September 2, 1887, this Department held that a departmental regulation in due conformity with statutory authority has all the force and effect of law, and that failure to submit final proof within six months after Osage filing, as required by the regulations of the Land Department, renders the claim thereunder subject to any valid intervening right. In Reed v. Buffington (7 L. D., 154), this case was followed by First Assistant Secretary Muldrow, August 8, 1888. In Elliot v. Ryan (7 L. D., 322), decided September 19, 1888, First Assistant Secretary Muldrow re-affirmed the doctrine of the two former cases, and in Baker *v.* Hurst (7 L. D., 457), First Assistant Secretary Muldrow carefully considered the question again, and on the authority of Rogers *v.* Lukens, Reed *v.* Buffington, and Elliot *v.* Ryan declared the same rule.

The decision of this Department in the case at bar was rendered September 13, 1888, by First Assistant Secretary Muldrow, on the authority of the foregoing cases, although they were not cited in the opinion. This had been the uniform construction of the law by this Department since the promulgation of the rules and regulations, on the 23d day of June, 1881, requiring that filing must be made within three months from date of settlement and proof, and payment of not less than one-fourth of the purchase price within six months from the date of filing.

On January 22, 1889, Secretary Vilas rendered a decision, in the case of Epley *v.* Trick (8 L. D., 110), in which he reversed specifically Rogers *v.* Lukens, Reed *v.* Buffington, Elliot *v.* Ryan, and Baker *v.* Hurst, holding that, "In the absence of express statutory provision to that effect, it cannot be held that failure to submit final proof within six months after Osage filing renders the claim thereunder subject to the adverse right of a subsequent settler." The ruling was based on the proposition that

The provision is so clearly a merely 'directory' one, that even if Congress had made it a part of the statute itself, a failure to regard it could not properly have been held to involve, as a consequence, the destruction of the settler's right to purchase under the act. Had so severe a sanction been deemed expedient, the requirement to be thereby enforced would have been followed by an express announcement that a failure to comply with such requirement would involve a forfeiture of the claim. There being no such express provision, the requirement is not to be treated as mandatory, but as directory merely.

As a merely directory provision, the regulation in question seems to me to be entirely proper and expedient, and one which might in a proper case be enforced after due notice to a settler that he must make proof and payment within a specified period or his entry will be canceled for disregard of the regulation.

The fifth section of the act of May 28, 1880 (21 Stat., 143), provides, *inter alia*, that the Secretary of the Interior shall make rules and regulations necessary to carry into effect the provisions of this act. As early as June 21, 1880, regulations were formulated by the Commissioner of the General Land Office, approved by Secretary Schurz, providing that claimants under section two of the act of May 28, 1880, should be required to file their claims, with proof of settlement and qualifications, and pay not less than one-fourth the purchase price within three months from the date of settlement. On July 9, 1880, these regulations were amended, by requiring that all settlers on Osage lands, claiming the right to perfect an entry for the same, will be required to give notice of their intention to offer final proof, as provided by the act of March 3, 1879. On June 23, 1881, the regulations were further amended requiring—

That in entries hereafter made under section two, the general principles of the preemption law in respect to filing and proof of settlement and notice of making proof will be required to be followed, and that filings must be made within three months from the date of settlement, and proof, and payment of not less than one-fourth of the purchase price within six months from the date of filing, with notice by publication, as required in other pre-emption cases, and that a residence of not less than six months should be required to be shown as evidence that the settlement is made in good faith.

By these regulations the practice in the local offices was regulated for nearly eight years, and the propriety of the regulations frequently endorsed by this Department. See Morgan v. Craig (10 C. L. O., 234); Abraham L. Burke (4 L. D., 340); United States v. Woodbury (5 L. D., 303). See also United States v. Atterbery (8 L. D., 173).

On the 26th of April, 1887 (5 L. D., 581), your office issued a circular to the local officers, with the approval of Acting Secretary Muldrow, stating that:

> The Osage Indian trust and diminished reserve lands are subject to sale to parties having the qualifications of pre-emptors on the public lands. Claimants are required to file a declaratory statement within three months from date of settlement, and to make proof and payment within six months from date of filing. The proof must be made after notice by publication, before the officers authorized to take proof in pre-emption cases, and must show that the claimant is a qualified pre-emptor and an actual settler on the land at the date of application to enter. Six months continuous residence next preceding date of proof is not an essential requirement, but it is essential that the settlement be shown to be actual and bona fide.

The circular then states the requirements relative to payment for the land entered and the provisions when default is made, the rule relative to taxation and the persons to whom patents must be issued, and concludes with the statement, that " By filing Osage declaratory statements, in accordance with the act of May 28, 1880, the right of pre-emption to such—or any other lands—is thereby exhausted."

The second section of the act, under which the applicants seek to purchase, provides :

> That all the said Indian lands remaining unsold and unappropriated, and not embraced in section one of this act, shall be subject to disposal to actual settlers only, having the qualifications of pre-emptors on the public lands. Such settlers shall make due application to the register, with proof of settlement and qualifications as aforesaid, and upon payment of not less than one-fourth the purchase price shall be permitted to enter not exceeding one-quarter section each, the balance to be paid in three equal instalments, with like penalties, liabilities and restriction as to default and forfeiture, as provided in section one of this act.

It must be observed, that the settler applying to enter said second section must " make due application to the register," etc. Now, who is to determine what shall constitute " due application ?" Unquestionably, the Secretary of the Interior, for, by the fifth section of said act, he is expressly directed to make all rules and regulations necessary to carry into effect the provisions of this act. Whether such a requirement was necessary to carry out the provisions of said act was determined by the Department, when said regulation was promulgated, and, if not in conflict with said act, it must be held, under the decisions of the courts and the departmental rulings, to have the force and effect of law.

In the case of Harkness *r.* Underhill (1 Black, 325), the United States supreme court, in considering the question whether an entry allowed by the local land officers could be set aside by the Commissioner, said : " All the officers administering the public lands were bound by the regulations published May 6, 1836 (2 Pub. Lands, Laws, Inst., and Ops., 92). These regulations prescribed the mode of proceeding to vacate a fraudulent occupant entry, and were pursued in the case before the court." Again, if we examine the provisions of the general pre-emption law, we find that by section 2265 of the U. S. Revised Statute—

Every claimant under the pre-emption law for land not yet proclaimed for sale is required to make known his claim in writing to the register of the proper land office within three months from time of the settlement; otherwise his claim shall be forfeited and the tract awarded to the next settler, in the order of time, on the same tract of land, who has given such notice and otherwise complied with the conditions of the law.

And by section 2267, claimants under said section are required to " make the proper proof and payment for the land within thirty months after the date prescribed therein, respectively, for filing their declaratory notices, has expired." Although no penalty is prescribed in the statute for failure to make proof and payment within the time required, yet it has been the uniform ruling of the Department, so far as I am advised, that the settler delays to make the proof and payment for the land at his peril, and a subsequent settler who makes proof within the required time has the better right to the land.

By the sixth paragraph of the circular, issued December 30, 1870 (1 C. L. L., 306), construing the act of Congress approved July 14, 1870 (16 Stat., 279), limiting the time within which payment must be made in pre-emption cases, the local land officers were directed to treat as " abandoned" all filings upon *unoffered* lands, " unless, within the period fixed by law, proof and payment shall have been made." But said act of 1870 did not attach any penalty for failure to make proof and payment within the required time fixed by law.

The Department, in the case of Powers *v.* Forbes (2 C. L. L., 563), considered the effect of a failure to make proof and payment for unoffered land in due time, and said :

The tract in question was " unoffered " land, not subject to private entry, and by section 2267, Revised Statutes, McMains was required to make proof and payment therefor within thirty-three months from the date of his settlement. He failed to do this, but permitted four and a half years (from July 1872-1877) to elapse without compliance with said requirement. This delay was not fatal to his claim, under the ruling in Johnson *v.* Towsley (13 Wall., 72), provided he had made such proof and payment prior to the attachment of a valid adverse claim; but his failure left the tract subject to Forbes' entry, after which he was an occupant only of the public lands, without any valid claim thereto, and had no more right to the tract than if he had never claimed any, because his continued occupancy was unauthorized by any law providing for the disposal of the public lands. . . . . . The reasoning of the court in Atherton *v.* Fowler applies equally well to cases under section 2267, Revised Statutes, as to those under section 2264, and I entertain no doubt that failure to make proof and payment under the former section should be followed by like results, where an adverse claim intervenes, as a failure under the latter section.

See also J. B. Raymond (2 L. D., 854); Davis *v.* Davidson (8 L. D., 417).

In the homestead law no penalty is fixed for a failure to make final proof within the statutory period (Sec. 2291 U. S. Revised Statutes), and the only provision in the law for forfeiture is found in section 2297, namely: that upon due proof of abandonment for more than six months, or change of residence, after filing the homestead affidavit, "the land so entered shall revert to the government." But, under the regulations prescribed by the Department, homestead entries may be canceled for other reasons than abandonment and change of residence, and the right of the Secretary of the Interior to cancel entries upon a proper showing, for causes other than those stated in the statute, seems to have been expressly decided by the supreme court of the United States.

In the case of Lee *v.* Johnson (116 U. S., 48), on appeal from the decision of the supreme court of Michigan, it was held by the court below, that the decision of this Department canceling Johnson's entry was not conclusive, because it was rendered not upon a point in issue between the contestants, namely, abandonment. But the United States supreme court reversed said decision, stating that—

The Secretary of the Interior came to the conclusion upon the evidence returned by the register, that Johnson must be considered not as a *bona fide* homestead claimant, acting in good faith, but as one seeking, by a seeming compliance with the forms of law, to obtain a tract of land for his son-in-law, who had previously exhausted his homestead privileges, observing that the element of good faith is the essential foundation of all valid claims under the homestead law. Under these circumstances, so far from having exceeded his jurisdiction in directing a cancellation of the entry, he was exercising only that just supervision which the law vests in him over all proceedings instituted to acquire portions of the public lands.

See also Buena Vista County *v.* Railroad Co. (112 U. S., 165.)

Therefore, independently of the express provision in the act of May 28, 1880, the Secretary of the Interior had the right to prescribe rules and regulations for the proper disposition of the Osage lands, by virtue of "the general powers of the Executive under the constitution." Opinion of Attorney General Butler, July 14, 1837 (3 Op., 275).

The settler under said Osage act can have no vested right as against the United States until he has made proof and paid or tendered the required purchase money. Frisbie *v.* Whitney (9 Wall., 187); Yosemite Valley case (15 Wall., 77); United States *v.* Johnson (5 L. D., 442); Custer *v.* Smith *et al.* (8 L. D., 269).

The regulations of the Department gave claimants due notice of what they were required to do, in order to secure the lands sought to be entered.

It is true, as stated in Epley *v.* Trick (*supra*), that the regulation of June 23, 1881, did not attach a penalty for failure to make due proof and payment. But neither do the general circulars of the Department, issued prior to January 1, 1889, declare a forfeiture for failure of preemptors to make proof and payment in due time. But the circular of January 1, 1889, states that, "a failure to make proof and payment as prescribed by law renders the land subject to appropriation by the first legal applicant, but in the absence of an adverse claim, proof and payment can be made after the expiration of the twelve or thirty-three months allowed. This statement, however, is in accord with the prior rulings of the Department, relative to a failure to make proof and payment within the required time.

While the statute fails to prescribe any definite procedure whereby the rights of contesting settlers shall be determined, I am of opinion, both upon principle and authority, that the Secretary of the Interior has full jurisdiction to determine that the prior right shall be in one who duly complies with the law and regulations thereunder, rather than in him who, although the first actual settler on the land, yet failed to comply with the requirement relative to the time of making proof and payment.

The rule laid down in Rogers v. Lukens, Reed v. Buffington, Elliott v. Ryan, and Baker v. Hurst, *supra*, is more consonant with reason and the decisions of the supreme court and the uniform practice of the Department, than the doctrine announced in Epley v. Trick, *supra*. Therefore the latter case must be and is hereby overruled. I find nothing in the case cited by counsel for Hessong, in his brief on the motion for review, conflicting with this conclusion.

As this Department found as a matter of fact in its original opinion herein that Miss Burgan's final proof was truthful in every respect and offered within the time required by the legal regulations of this Department, and that she honestly endeavored to comply with the requirements of the law, I am not disposed to revoke said departmental decision.

The disposition of the above questions, renders it unnecessary to discuss the other questions arising in the record.

The motion for review is denied.

PRACTICE—REVIEW-APPEAL—RES JUDICATA SWAMP GRANT.

STATE OF OREGON (ON REVIEW).

The rules of practice adopted by the Department should be followed, and exceptions to such course only allowed to prevent grievous wrong or correct palpable error.

A motion for review, except when based on newly discovered evidence, must be filed within thirty days from notice of the decision.

An appeal will not lie from an interlocutory order of the General Land Office.

An appeal from a decision of the General Land Office will not be entertained if not filed within the time designated in the rules of practice.

A selection under the swamp grant protects the interests of the State under said grant.

Secretary Noble to the Commissioner of the General Land Office, September 16, 1889.

Your office by letter dated April 27th ultimo, transmitted to this Department a motion for review of departmental decision, rendered December 27, 1888 (7 L. D., 572), revoking and setting aside approved swamp land list No. 5, Lakeview, Oregon.

The lands embraced in said list have been claimed by the State of Oregon under the swamp land grant made to her by the act of March 12, 1860 (12 Stat., 3), which extended to said State the provisions of the swamp land grant of September 28, 1850 (9 Stat., 519).

The motion for review is filed in behalf of the State and her grantees.

Said list No. 5, embracing in the neighborhood of 90,000 acres, was approved by this Department, September 16, 1882. Said approval was based upon a report of R. V. Ankeny, an agent of your office, who, in connection with an agent of the State, was authorized and directed to examine the lands claimed by the State, to make a list of such as were found to be swamp, and report the same under oath as to their character.

It having been reported, after the approval of said list 5, that the examination and report upon which said approval rested were false and fraudulent, and that the list embraced a large amount of lands in no sense such as contemplated by the swamp land grant, and no patents having issued, this Department, under date of January 20, 1887 (5 L. D., 374), issued a rule upon the governor, requiring the State to show cause why the "certificate and approval of list No. 5 should not be revoked and canceled, and why a re-examination of said lands should not be ordered."

Said order of January 20, 1887, set April 18, 1887, as the last day of the time given to show cause as above. The limit of time thus fixed for hearing was at the request of the State, or of parties claiming under the State, several times extended, but the case was finally heard by argument, oral and by brief, before the Department, and following that the decision of Secretary Vilas, dated December 27, 1888, and now before me for consideration, in connection with the motion for review, was rendered. In the meantime, Charles Shackleford, a special agent of the government, acting under the direction of your office, and by authority of the Department (5 L. D., 300 and 374), had made examination and investigation as to these lands, and his report was before the Secretary at the time of the hearing and decision as above. The Secretary considered the same in connection with the other evidence in the case, and found from the whole record that fraud had been committed in connection with the examination and report submitted by Ankeny, which fraudulent report subsequently became the basis on which the list was approved by Secretary Teller, in 1882, without knowledge of the fraud.

The decision, after a full review of the facts as shown by the record, rendered judgment as follows:

The certification of the list number five of the Lakeview district is accordingly revoked and canceled, and that list entirely set aside.

It concluded with the following order to the Commissioner:

You will prepare another list, in which you will include such lands only as by satisfactory evidence, drawn from all reports and information at hand, are unquestionably shown to be swamp or overflowed and unfit for cultivation. Such other lands included in list number five as are doubtful in character, according to the evidence now at hand, you will make a separate list of, and will detail two trustworthy agents to carefully and thoroughly examine, with a view to determining their true condition at the date of the granting act in 1860, and require reports exhibiting by an accurate plat and description the present condition of each subdivision and such evidence as may be taken in respect to any difference in condition at the date of the act. In making this examination, opportunity should be afforded to the State and her grantees to be represented, in accordance with the usage on that subject. Such lands in the list number five as are satisfactorily disclosed to be not swamp or overflowed nor unfit for cultivation, you will restore to the public domain, subject to any rights which have attached to them under the laws.

Pursuant to said decision and order, your office, on January 18, 1889, rejected the claim of the State to about 20,000 acres of the land, which had been embraced in said list as not swamp or overflowed, but hilly and mountainous, and desert, rather than swamp in character, and directed the restoration of the same to the public domain, subject to any rights which had attached under the public land laws.

Your office, also, under said order, prepared and submitted to the Department for approval as swamp a new list comprising about 12,000 acres of said lands, which list was approved February 26, 1889, and the lands were patented to the State March 27, 1889.

Further acting under said order, your office, considering the residue of said lands (about 58,000 acres) doubtful in character, according to the evidence at hand, placed them in a separate list, and on April 11th last detailed two special agents to examine and report upon the same.

The motion for review presents several assignments of error in the decision of Secretary Vilas as reasons why the review of said decision should be granted.

Upon inspection of said motion, I find that it was not made until April 9, 1889, and your office letter transmitting it to the Department states that it was filed on that day.

The departmental decision to which it relates was rendered December 27, 1888, and your said office letter of transmittal states that counsel for the State, resident in this city, were notified by office letter dated January 18, 1889.

It thus appears that eighty days intervened between date of notice of decision and that of filing motion for review. Not only this, but there had in the meantime been a change in the head of the Department. Secretary Vilas had resigned, and the motion was addressed to me as his successor.

Rule 77 of Practice requires that such motions, except when based upon newly discovered evidence, must be filed within thirty days from notice of decision. There is no allegation of newly discovered evidence in this case. Had the motion been filed in accordance with the rule, it would have been before the officer who rendered the original decision. As presented, it is not only out of time, but the matters decided are, under the rulings and decisions, not now subject to review by this Department.

It has been well settled, by a long line of opinions of Attorneys-General of the United States, that the final decision of a head of department is binding upon his successors in the same department, subject to certain well defined exceptions, such as palpable error of calculation, or where new facts are subsequently brought forward which show that the former decision was erroneous and would probably not have been made, if they had been known at the time of the decision. See 2 Opinion, 9 and 464; 4 id., 341; 5 id., 29 and 124; 9 id., 101, 301 and 387; 12 id., 358; 13 id., 33, 226, 387 and 456. See also United States v. Bank of Metropolis (15 Pet., 401). The same rule has been followed in this Department. See 2 C. L. O., 83; 3 L. D., 196; id., 595; 4 id., 482; 5 id., 483; 7 id., 146.

Finding the principle above enunciated supported by the opinions and decisions cited and by others not here cited, I must recognize its application to the case presented and deny the motion for review, on the ground that the matters sought to be reviewed are not properly before me for decision.

In the argument of counsel on the motion for review, allusion is made to appeals which have been filed from certain decisions and actions of your office in execution of the decision of Secretary Vilas herein referred to, the claim being that even if the motion be overruled and the decision as made permitted to stand, then certain errors, which they alleged were committed by your office in the execution of said decision, should be corrected as asked in said appeals.

The appeals referred to, as appears from the letter transmitting the motion for review and from statement of counsel, were filed in your office on the same day that said motion for review was filed, to wit, April 9, 1889. There were two of them, one from your office action restoring to the public domain 20,000 acres of the land which had been embraced in list No. 5, and the other from the action of your office in ordering further investigation as to all of the 58,000 acres found by your office to be doubtful as to their character on the evidence at hand. These appeals have not been forwarded to this Department, but with the motion for review counsel have filed what they state, and I have no doubt, are copies of said appeals.

Your office states that it has refused to transmit said appeals, because the first mentioned (that as to the 20,000 acres) was not filed in time under the rules, and the second (that as to the 58,000 acres), because it is an appeal from an interlocutory proceeding, from which an appeal does not lie. These reasons given by the Commissioner seem to me to be sound and must be sustained.

The rules of practice adopted by the Department, like those of a court, should be followed. Exceptions should be allowed only to prevent grievous wrong or correct palpable mistake. I do not see that under the decision of Secretary Vilas as executed any grievous wrong will be done the State of Oregon. The State has already received patent to about 12,000 acres of the lands formerly comprised in list No. 5. If the facts be as stated in Secretary Vilas' decision, that the 20,000 acres which your office has restored to the public domain are high, dry and mountainous, and that their certification was procured by fraud in the report of the agent, then it is certain that the State is not entitled to them as swamp, and consequently is not wronged by that action. On the other hand, the time for appeal having passed, it would be a wrong to settlers who may have gone on the lands to jeopardize their rights by re-opening out of time this branch of the case; and there are settlers now here seeking to oppose the motion for review. The contention of the State that it had no opportunity to be heard on this question does not seem to be borne out by the record, as the proceeding was under an order on the State to show cause why the certification should not be set aside and the lands re-examined. The State was heard orally and upon brief, and Secretary Vilas disposed of that question, saying " no denial is made of the allegation in said report, corroborated as it is, that upwards of 20,000 acres certified in said list are high and dry, located on hills and steep mountain sides, embracing arid deserts and rock ridges of great height," and ordered those lands restored to the public domain.

As to the 58,000 acres in regard to which further investigation is ordered, such order is, as stated by your office, interlocutory and not appealable. Moreover, such order does the State no grievous wrong, for, if the lands are shown to be swamp within the meaning of the grant, it will get them. All questions involved in the appeal from your office on the order for re-examination of the lands can be presented when the report is made.

Some slight inconvenience may result from the delay necessary for the investigation, but better that than passing to patent, under the swamp land grant, lands not of the character contemplated by the act.

The State having made selections of these lands is protected thereby should they be found to be swamp.

Counsel for the State argue very earnestly and ably that Secretary Lamar, in issuing an order on the State " to show cause why the certificate and approval of list No. 5 should not be revoked and canceled, and why a re-examination of said lands should not be ordered," and Secretary Vilas in setting aside said list and ordering further action in the matter, acted beyond their authority and jurisdiction. This contention is based on the theory that the title to the swamp lands vested in the State by virtue of the grant, and attached on certification, and that the executive department had no further control over the title. To use the language of counsel for the State:

> After full investigation, that list (No. 5) has been approved by the Secretary of the Interior, and the right of the State under the swamp land grant to these tracts had thus been certified and completed. The legal title as to those lands was thereby vested in the State, taking effect as from the date of the grant, March 12, 1860. The executive department was thereafter *functus officio*. It could proceed against that list only upon such a case of fraud or mistake as would authorize a court to set aside a patent, and even in that case its remedy would be restricted to a direct proceeding in the courts by the Attorney General in the name of the United States to vacate the legal title vested in the State by the certified list. (Brief, page 38.)

In the present status of the matter it is unnecessary to express an opinion on this proposition, further than to say that, if correct, then, this Department has no jurisdiction to entertain the motion and appeals of the State, and the whole question is remitted to the courts.

Upon careful consideration of the whole matter as presented, I must, for the reasons herein given, not only deny the motion for review, but must decline to consider the appeals.

LOCAL OFFICERS—VACANCY IN OFFICE.

GRAHAM *v.* CARPENTER.

A vacancy in the office of either the register or the receiver, disqualifies the remaining incumbent for the performance of the duties of his own office, during the period of such vacancy.

Secretary Noble to the Commissioner of the General Land Office, September 16, 1889.

On May 13, 1885, John B. Carpenter made homestead entry No. 15,669, on lot 1, Sec. 27, lot 3 and N. $\frac{1}{2}$ of lot 2, Sec. 22, T. 18 S., R. 35 E., Gainesville district, Florida.

June 27, 1887, more than two years after date of said entry, the appellant, J. M. Graham, Sr., presented for filing an affidavit of contest, alleging as ground of contest, that the entryman (said Carpenter) "had never resided upon said homestead or cultivated any part thereof." The register refused to receive and file said affidavit, "on account of vacancy in the office of receiver." The vacancy was occasioned, it appears, by the death of the incumbent, and was filled July 18, 1887. Two days thereafter, July 20, 1887, before 11 A. M. of that day, the entryman relinquished said entry and filed a pre-emption declaratory statement, No. 1966, for said tract, and subsequently, at 11 A. M., on the same day, the appellant renewed his application to contest by presenting the same affidavit for filing, and the register denied the application, on the ground "that the entry had been that day canceled by relinquishment."

On appeal, duly taken from said first rejection, your office sustained the action of the local officers, citing as authority the case of Christian F. Ebinger, 1 L. D., 150. From that decision the case has been brought here on appeal; and the question for determination is, can the register act when the office of receiver is vacant?

I do not know of any decision wherein the question has been fully discussed, nor of any circular of your office directly touching the subject, but I am advised that the practice has been to regard the offices as closed during such vacancy. As the question is one of importance as a matter of practice, apart from the interests of the litigants, to determine it accurately it becomes necessary to examine the history of legisla tion in relation to the office and functions of register and receiver, and ascertain how and under what circumstances they or either of them may act.

The office of register and receiver was provided for by act of May 10, 1800 (2 Stat., 73). Therein the sales of public lands were placed under the direction of the register, and the money, proceeds thereof, was made payable to the Treasurer of the United States, or the receiver of public moneys, for lands of the United States. The receiver, as well as the register, is required by this act to give bond in the sum of $10,000.

By act of April 20, 1818 (3 Stats., 466), the salaries of the register and receiver were changed but not their duties.

By act of March 3, 1819 (3 Stats., 526), the register and receiver could hear testimony relative to mistakes and report testimony, with their opinion thereon, to the Treasurer of the United States.

By act of May 24, 1824 (4 Stats., 31), the register and receiver, or either of them, might administer an oath.

By act of May 29, 1830 (4 Stats., 420), proof of settlement or improvements should be made to the satisfaction of the register and receiver.

By act of July 4, 1836 (5 Stats., 107), the receiver shall make monthly returns of money to the Treasurer of the United States.

By act of June 1, 1840 (5 Stats., 382), a pre-emptor shall make satisfactory proof of his or her residence before the register and receiver.

By act of September 4, 1841 (5 Stats., 453), it is required that proof shall be made to the satisfaction of the register and receiver.

By act of August 30, 1842 (5 Stats., 567), it is provided that there shall be a register and receiver appointed to superintend the sale of public lands, etc.

By act of May 20, 1862 (12 Stats., 392), it is provided (Sec. 2):

That the person applying for the benefit of this act shall make affidavit before said register and receiver.

By act of March 21, 1864 (13 Stats., 35), amending the homestead act, it is provided that an affidavit of a soldier or sailor taken before a commanding officer shall be as binding as if taken before "register and receiver," and therein it is further provided:

That in lieu of the fee allowed by the 12th section of the pre-emption act of fourth of September, 1841, the register and receiver shall be allowed *jointly* at the rate of fifteen cents per hundred words, etc.

By the act of March 3, 1873 (17 Stats., 605, timber culture act), the affidavit is required to be made before the register and receiver, and relative to the sale of saline lands (act of January 12, 1877, 19 Stats., 221), it is provided, "whenever it shall be made to appear to the register and receiver," etc., "it shall be the duty of said register and said receiver," etc.

These excerpts are taken from a few only of the acts to be found in the statutes at large, and could, if occasion required, be largely increased, as the same language almost is found in nearly every statute relating to the disposal of the public lands. But those given are sufficient to illustrate my view.

While these statutes prescribed the duties of the two offices, yet in none of them does it seem to be contemplated that the one shall act when there is a vacancy in the other. The office is one, while its body is dual. To have a vitalized office, capable of transacting business, both offices must in some manner be filled and represented. Such, in my judgment, is clearly contemplated by all these statutes providing for the office of register and receiver.

Now, turning to the rules provided by the General Land Office for the government of these officers in the transaction of public business, we find the same theory pervades them all, and that is, that the one cannot move without the other; that the office is a machine, so to speak, and cannot be run except with both wheels (register and receiver).

The circulars are addressed to the registers and receivers, are for their joint consideration and action, follow the statute in not permitting the register to receive public moneys for any purpose, and the rules all contemplate that both offices shall be filled in order to transact business.

Rule 2 provides:

In every case of application for a hearing an affidavit must be filed by the contestant with the register and receiver, etc.

Rule 4: Registers and receivers may order, etc

Rule 6: Applications for hearings under rule 5 must be transmitted by the register and receiver, etc.

Rule 7: At least thirty days notice shall be given of all hearings before the register and receiver, etc.

Rule 20: When party asking for continuance makes affidavit before register and receiver showing, etc.

Rule 24: He must file with the register and receivers, interrogatories, etc.

Rule 26: Commissions to take depositions shall be issued by register and receiver, etc.

Rule 27: The register and receiver may designate officer to take deposition.

Rule 34: All stipulations, etc., must be filed with the register and receiver.

Rule 35: In the discretion of the register and receiver testimony will be taken, etc.

4. On the day set for hearing at the local office, the register and receiver will examine testimony, etc.

Rule 36: Upon the trial of a cause, the register and receiver may in any case, etc.

Rule 37: The register and receiver will be careful to reach if possible the exact condition and status of the land, etc.

Rule 43: Appeals from final action and decisions of register and receiver lie in every case, etc.

Rule 47: No appeal from the action of the register and receiver will be received, etc.

Rule 51: Upon the termination of a contest, the register and receiver will render joint report, etc.

Rule 52: The register and receiver will promptly forward their report, etc.

Rule 53: Registers and receivers will apportion the cost of contest, etc.

Rule 59: The costs of contest chargeable by the register and receiver, etc.

Rule 63: Preliminary costs will be collected by the register and receiver.

Rule 64: The register and receiver will require proper provision to be made, etc.

Rule 65: The register and receiver will append to their report, etc.

Rule 66: 1. The register and receiver will endorse upon every rejected application, etc.

Rule 68: The register and receiver will promptly forward the appeal to the General Land Office, etc. .

Rule 74: In cases pending on appeal from decision of the register and receiver, etc.

Rule 76: Motion for re-hearing before registers and receivers, etc.

Rule 87: When notice of decision is given through the mails by register and receiver, etc.

It will thus be observed, that each of the rules to which attention is called contemplates a joint action on the part of the register and receiver. That neither can act independently of the other. Hence, I take it, that where death invades the office and removes either of the officers, that the machinery thereof at that moment stops, and can not be put in motion again until the office is filled. Any act by the survivor during the vacancy, unless he is acting *de facto*, is an absolute nullity. I have no doubt that one person may fill both offices, that is, be a *de jure* officer in one case and a *de facto* in another, by order of the Department, but independently of such order, he can not fill the functions or perform the duties of his own office during the vacancy occasioned by the death of his associate. Dean Richmond Lode (1 L. D., 545).

In the case of Christian F. Ebinger (1 L. D., 150), it is held that the duties of register and receiver are distinct, and neither can discharge those of the other in the absence of express authority therefor, but the action of each is necessary within his appropriate sphere to the administration of the office.

Following this rule to its legitimate conclusion, it very clearly appears that upon a vacancy in the office of either of these officers, who constitute the tribunal for the transaction of business, the tribunal itself ceases to perform any of the functions over which it is given jurisdiction by statute. In fact, so far as the performance of its public duties is concerned, it is as though it did not exist.

Indeed, this Ebinger case may be regarded as an authority in the present instance. There an application to file a timber culture entry was rejected, because the office of receiver had become vacant by reason of the death of the late incumbent. On appeal here, this rejection was approved, because " Ebinger acquired no right by presentation of his application during the vacancy in the office of the receiver."

The question in the Ebinger case and the one at bar is to be distinguished from that considered by the Department in the case of Walker v. Sewall (2 L. D., 613), and in the Paris Meadows case (9 L. D., 41); and by the supreme court in Potter v. United States (107 U. S., 126), and in Lytle v. Arkansas, in 9 How., 319. In none of which cases was there a vacancy in the office of either the register or receiver. The question in the two cases before the supreme court was as to the necessity for concurrent as well as joint action by the two officers; and that tribunal said such concurrence was not required. In the two cases before the Department the question was as to whether applications could be received and made of record in the land office by one officer during the absence of the other. It was held that such filings were valid, on the theory, as was said in the Meadows' case, that there being no vacancy in either office, " the law will regard and treat such act as performed by the proper officer, through the other acting in his behalf."

All of the cases cited incline to sustain the conclusion herein arrived at by me. In that of Lytle v. Arkansas, *supra*, the court, whilst saying that, " the register and receiver were constituted by the act a tribunal to determine the rights of those who claimed pre-emption under it," held that the requirements of the law had been complied with, by the presence of one officer at the taking of the proof, if " the right was sanctioned by both." To the same effect is the decision in the Potter case, *supra*. Whilst concurrent action is not required, says the court, the action of both officers, though at different times, is demanded. " If both are satisfied, that is all the law requires." In the Paris Meadows case, *supra*, the language is more pointed, where it is said :

When a paper is presented to and received by the register, receiver, or an authorized clerk . . . . . and placed on the proper files, it is then, within the meaning of the law, filed not only in the office, but with the officer to whom the law directs it, provided the two offices of register and receiver be then filled.

Congress seems also to have considered that a vacancy in either office would necessarily suspend the entire operations of the particular district office during the existence of the vacancy; and provision was made to protect settlers, under the pre emption law, the only settlement law then known, during such period. See section 6, act 1843, 5 Stat., 620, now embodied in section 2270 R. S., which provides:

Whenever the vacancy of the office either of register or receiver, or of both, renders it impossible for the claimant to comply with any requisition of the pre-emption

laws within the appointed time, such vacancy shall not operate to the detriment of
the party claiming, in respect to any matter essential to the establishment of his
claim; but such requisition must be complied with within the same period after the
disability is removed as would have been allowed had such disability not existed.

After a full consideration of the case and the law applicable thereto,
as I read it, I affirm your judgment.

RAILROAD GRANT—INDEMNITY; PRACTICE—APPEAL.

IOWA RAILROAD LAND COMPANY

Lands lying within the indemnity-limits of the old line east of Cedar Rapids may be
selected in lieu of lands lost in place west of said city, if found necessary in
order to make up the full amount of six sections per mile, to which the company is
entitled for road actually constructed from Cedar Rapids to the Missouri River.

The validity of an indemnity selection cannot be determined if the basis of such selection is not designated.

The specific points of exception to the decision or ruling complained of should be set
forth briefly and clearly in the appeal.

*Secretary Noble to the Commissioner of the General Land Office, Septem-
ber 16, 1889.*

This is an appeal by the Iowa Railroad Land Company, successor in
interest to the Cedar Rapids and Missouri River Railroad Company,
from the decision of your office, dated February 15, 1888, holding for
cancellation the selection by the last named company on December 21,
1877, of W. ½, of the SE. ¼, Sec. 25, T. 85 N., R. 3 E., Des Moines land
district, Iowa.

The tract in question lay within the fifteen mile limits of the grant
of May 15, 1856 (11 Stat., 91), to the State of Iowa to aid in the construction of a railroad "from Lyons City" (on the Mississippi River) "to
a point of intersection with the main line of the Iowa Central Air
Line Railroad, near Maquoketa, thence on said main line, running as
near as practicable to the forty-second parallel across the State, to
the Missouri River." By this grant there was given to the State of Iowa,
as soon as the road is completed, "every alternate section of land designated by odd numbers for six sections in width on each side" of the
road, and provision was made for the selection of other lands, as indemnity, for those lost in place, in alternate sections or parts of sections,
designated by odd numbers, within fifteen miles of the line of said
road.

The State of Iowa, by an act of its legislature, dated July 14, 1856,
conferred the grant for this road upon the Iowa Central Air Line Railroad Company. The company immediately surveyed and located the
line of the road under the grant, from Lyons City, through the town
of Cedar Rapids, to a point on the Missouri River, near the town of
Onawa in Monona county, and the map of this survey and location was

accepted by the State of Iowa, and your office (the same having been filed in your office October 13, 1856), as the definite line of said road, and as governing the location of the land grant for the same.

But the road failed of construction by the company named, and thereupon the State resumed control of the grant, and on the 26th of March, 1860, by another act of its legislature, conferred the same upon the Cedar Rapids and Missouri River Railroad Company, with conditions similar in all material respects to those of the act which conferred the grant, in the first instance, upon the Iowa Central Air Line Company. Meanwhile, however, a road was built from Clinton (a town on the Mississippi River, situated within less than three miles of Lyons City), on or near the line established by the survey and map made and filed by the Air Line Company, as aforesaid, to Cedar Rapids, by another company (the Chicago, Iowa and Nebraska), which had no land grant, and was in no manner connected with the Air Line Company, or privy to its contract with the State. By reason of this fact it had become clearly unnecessary to build another road from the Mississippi River, at Lyons City, along the line occupied, substantially, by the road already built, and hence the grant by the State, of March 26, 1860, to the Cedar Rapids Company, required that company to build at once, westwardly from Cedar Rapids to the Missouri River, along the line surveyed and established as aforesaid. Under this arrangement, it appears that the company proceeded with the construction of its road west of Cedar Rapids, on the designated line, until it had completed the same as far as the town of Nevada, a distance of about one hundred miles.

At this stage of the proceedings under the grant of 1856, Congress, by an act amendatory of said grant, approved June 2, 1864 (13 Stat., 95), authorized the Cedar Rapids and Missouri River Railroad Company to "modify or change the location of the uncompleted portion of its line, as shown by the map thereof" (meaning the map filed by the Iowa Central Air Line Company), "so as to secure a better and more expeditious line to the Missouri River, and to a connection with the Iowa branch of the Union Pacific Railroad;" and also "to connect its line by a branch with the line of the Mississippi and Missouri Railroad Company." This amendatory act further provided that "the said Cedar Rapids and Missouri River Railroad Company shall be entitled for such modified line to the same lands and to the same amount of lands per mile, and for such connecting branch, the same amount of land per mile as originally granted to aid in the construction of its main line, subject to the conditions and forfeitures mentioned in the original grant." And further,

That whenever said modified main line shall have been established, or such connecting line located . . . . . the Secretary of the Interior shall reserve and cause to be certified and conveyed to said company, from time to time as the work progresses on the main line, out of any public lands now belonging to the United States, not sold, etc., ... within fifteen miles of the original main line, an amount of land equal to that originally authorized to be granted to aid in the construction of the said road, by the act to which this is an amendment. And if the amount of lands per mile, granted or intended to be granted, by the original act, to aid in the construction of said railroad, shall not be found within the limits of the fifteen miles therein prescribed, then such selections may be made along said modified line and connecting branch, within twenty miles thereof.

The act also required the construction of a branch road from the town of Lyons, the starting point of the main line as provided for in the original act, to some point at or west of Clinton on the road which had been theretofore built by private enterprise, as aforesaid, from Clinton to Cedar Rapids, in order to connect Lyons with the main line of road across the State to the Missouri River, as originally contemplated.

The land in question is situated east of the town of Cedar Rapids, and your office decision states that the same was "selected" by the railroad company, December 21, 1877. This selection was rejected and held for cancellation, on the stated ground that the supreme court had, in the case of the Cedar Rapids Railroad Company v. Herring (110 U. S., 27), "decided that the company was not entitled to any lands east of Cedar Rapids."

The company alleges in its appeal, in effect, (1) that there was no such holding as that stated, by the supreme court, in the case referred to ; (2) error in rejecting its claim to the land and holding its selection thereof for cancellation ; (3) error in not holding that the land was lawfully subject to selection by the company, and that the selection as made was in all respects a valid selection ; and (4) error in not approving the selection.

It is proper further to state that neither the Cedar Rapids, nor the Air Line Company, upon which the grant was first conferred by the State, ever built any part of the main line of road east of Cedar Rapids. The branch connecting Lyons City with the Chicago, Iowa and Nebraska road, at Clinton, was built. The main road west from Cedar Rapids to the Missouri River was built by the Cedar Rapids Company on the modified line adopted under the amendatory act of 1864 ; and thus, by means of said connecting branch from Lyons City to Clinton, and the road built from Clinton to Cedar Rapids by the Chicago, Iowa and Nebraska Company, as aforesaid, and that built from the latter place, west, by the Cedar Rapids Company, was secured the line of road across the State from Lyons City to the Missouri River which was intended to be secured by the original act of 1856. The connecting branch with the line of the Mississippi and Missouri Railroad Company, authorized by the act of 1864, was not built.

The assignments of error in the appeal are so general and indefinite in character, that, considering them alone, it is impossible to determine in what particulars the company claims to be aggrieved by the decision appealed from. Such general allegations can in no reasonable sense be considered specifications of error. An appeal should set forth in brief and clear terms the specific points of exception to the decision, or ruling complained of. (See Rules of Practice.) Such is not the case here, but looking to the brief filed by counsel for the company in support of its appeal, its claim is found to be, in effect, that, under the act of 1864, it is entitled, for the road which it constructed, namely, from Cedar Rapids to the Missouri River, to six sections per mile, as measured by the length of the road thus constructed, and that the unappropriated lands lying along, and within the fifteen mile limits of the *entire* old line of road as located under the act of 1856, constitutes the *source* from which the grant, under the act of 1864, should be satisfied; that the company is not limited under the act of 1864 to lands lying west of Cedar Rapids, but is entitled to take the lands east, as well as west thereof, lying within fifteen miles of the original main line, until the quantum of the grant is satisfied; that *all* the lands which vested in the State by virtue of the original location of the road, should first be taken, and that the company should not take any lands, other than those originally *granted*, except to make up the deficiency; that the selection of the tract in question was made in strict accordance with the act of 1864, as construed by the supreme court in the Herring case, and should therefore be sustained.

It is proper to state in this connection, that the company has furnished no basis for its selection of the tract in controversy, nor is there anything in the record even tending to show that any basis was given when the selection was made. There is no allegation that any particular tract of land was lost in place, by reason of which this tract is selected by the company, as indemnity, nor is there anything to show that the same is claimed as indemnity, aside from the fact that it is situated within the fifteen mile limit of the grant of 1856, and is stated to have been "selected."

The tract is included in a list of twenty-one different tracts, some of which are represented to be in the fifteen mile limits, and others in the six mile limits of the grant, filed by the company in your office, which is denominated a "supplemental list of selections on account of lands claimed by said company as inuring to it, and to which it is entitled, under and by virtue of the grants and provisions" of the "acts of Congress, approved May 15, 1856, and June 2, 1864;" and this is the only showing made by the company, in reference to its selection of this tract.

In the case of the Cedar Rapids Company *v.* Herring, *supra*, the supreme court had said act of 1864 under consideration. In its opinion, speaking with special reference to the fourth section of the act, the court said, "that the purpose of this enactment was—

1. To relieve the company from the obligation to build that part of its line as found in the Land Office, between the Mississippi River and Cedar Rapids, because there already existed a road between those points built by another corporation.

2. To require the company to connect the city of Lyons with that corporation's road, so that it would be, as originally intended, the Mississippi terminus of the land-

grant road across the State. This required the construction of about two and a half miles of road.

3. To authorize the company to change the location of its road yet to be constructed west of Cedar Rapids for its convenience.

*   *   *   *   *   *   *

6. To adjust the amount of lands, to which the company would be entitled under this new order of things, and to enlarge the source from which selections might be · made for the loss of that not found in place.

This latter it accomplished by declaring that *all* the sections within the fifteen-mile limits shall be subject to such selection on the same terms on which only alternate sections could previously be selected; and if this limit, which had exclusive reference to the line first located, did not satisfy the grant, then selection could be made within twenty miles of the new line.

The railroad company claimed in that case that it was entitled under the act of 1864, for the road constructed by it, to six sections per mile, as measured by the length of the road as originally located from Lyons City to the Missouri River, under the act of 1856, notwithstanding the fact that it never built any part of the main line east of Cedar Rapids. The parties interested adversely to the company's claim, asserted that the length of the road, *as actually constructed* by the company, should be taken as determining the quantum of the grant. Upon the question thus raised, the court in adopting the latter view presented, among other things, said:

If Congress simply meant that the company, notwithstanding the change in the line of its road, should have the lands it would have had if it had built the whole of the original line, it would have been easy to express this purpose. In such case no description of the grant, as for such modified line, nor of the same amount of lands per mile, would have been necessary. If such was the purpose, the use of this language was unnecessary and was confusing. If, however, it was the purpose of Congress to measure this grant under the new circumstances by the length of the modified line, and give the same number of sections per mile of the line thus modified, the language is, in our opinion, appropriate and unambiguous. The words "the same lands," which plaintiff's counsel insist mean *all* the lands of the old grant, are intended, we think, to show that the lands are to be taken along the line of the old survey; that the odd sections on each side of that old line, which became vested in the State when it was established, should be a part of the new grant to this company, and that the deficiencies should, in like manner, be made up by sections within the fifteen mile limit of that line.

It is thus seen that what the supreme court really decided in the Herring case, as touching the question involved herein, was simply that the quantity of land to which the company is entitled under the grant of 1864 is to be determined by the length of the road actually constructed by it, and not by the length of the road as originally located under the act of 1856. That for this constructed road, it is entitled to six sections of land per mile, to be taken along the line of the old survey; the odd sections, which originally became vested in the State, constituting a part of its new grant, and the deficiencies to be made up by selections within the fifteen mile limits of the old line, or if necessary to obtain the full quantum of the grant, within twenty miles of the new line.

The court does not say that the company is not entitled to any lands east of Cedar Rapids, nor is there anything in its decision which necessarily implies that such was intended to be the effect thereof. On the contrary, it seems to me that the language used by the court, in speaking of the words "the same lands," quoted in the opinion from the act of 1864, namely, that these words "are intended, we think, to show that the lands are to be taken *along the line of the old survey*," clearly indicates that the court entertained a different view of the matter.

I see nothing, therefore, in the decision of the court in the Herring case to preclude the company from selecting lands lying within the indemnity limits of the old line east of Cedar Rapids, in lieu of lands lost in place west of Cedar Rapids, if found necessary so to do, in order to make up the full quantum, of six sections per mile, to which it is entitled for the road actually constructed by it west from Cedar Rapids to the Missouri River.

As already stated, the tract in question lies in the indemnity belt of the old line east of Cedar Rapids, and, if the selection thereof by the company was on account of lands actually lost in place, which loss could not be supplied from land within the fifteen mile limits of the old line west of Cedar Rapids, I see no reason why such selection may not be sustained, as coming within the provisions of the act of 1864.

But, as we have seen, the company has furnished no basis for its selection of the tract, nor does it appear that the same is in fact claimed as indemnity for lands lost in place; and it is therefore impossible, upon the showing made, to determine whether the selection should, or should not, be approved. Clearly, until a basis for the selection is furnished by the company, it can not be determined whether it is, or is not, entitled to the land selected. The company should, therefore, be called upon to designate the land lost in place for which the tract in question is claimed as indemnity, if so claimed, or if not claimed as indemnity, to state the ground upon which its claim thereto is based, and the papers are returned to your office for that purpose. (See circular of August 4, 1885, 4 L. D., 90). When the company shall have made the showing required, you will proceed to re-adjudicate its claim, in accordance with the principles herein announced.

Your said decision is accordingly modified.

TIMBER CULTURE ENTRY—AMENDMENT—SECOND ENTRY.

ALEXANDER NORRIS.

To authorize the amendment of an entry it must appear that the record fails to express the original intention of the entryman.

A timber culture entry for less than one hundred and sixty acres exhausts the right of entry under the timber culture law, and such an entry can not be enlarged to include a tract which the entryman, at the time of making the original entry, supposed was not subject to such appropriation.

First Assistant Secretary Chandler to the Commissioner of the General Land Office, September 16, 1889.

I have considered the appeal of Alexander Norris from your office decision of February 24, 1888, involving the W. ½ of NW. ¼, and SE. ¼, of NW. ¼, of section 14, T. 3 S., R. 1 W., Bozeman land district, Montana.

Norris made timber culture entry April 13, 1883, for the NE. ¼, SW. ¼, of said section 14. On July 19, 1887, he filed his verified application, bearing date the day aforesaid for an amendment of his said entry "by adding thereto the W. ½ of NW. ¼, and the SE. ¼, of NW. ¼, same section."

These tracts are marked on the township plat of survey as "mineral land."

Norris in his said application deposes that "when he made said entry the land now wanted had been returned as mineral, that it stood then and yet stands upon the official plat as mineral, that he has always supposed he could not secure it for said reason; that now understanding said return as no bar to entry of the desired tract, he now applies therefor." He asserts that he is and has been acting in good faith, and has hitherto complied with the requirements of the timber culture law regarding his entry actually made and "that he will submit to the conditions to be imposed by the department as to compliance with law upon the tract desired." He also deposes that the said tracts are non-mineral in character and that the section of which they form a part is devoid of timber.

By your said office decision Norris' application was refused.

He appealed.

In your said office decision it is stated:

The law provides that "no person shall make more than one entry under the provisions of this act." To grant his request is in substance allowing an additional or supplemental entry. He had the whole domain to select from when he made his former entry. He was in no way restricted or limited to less than one hundred and sixty acres, and he took the forty in satisfaction of his privilege from choice. If he now finds that he erred in so doing and repents his action this office has no discretionary power to aid him as he may see fit to change his mind.

If Norris had included in his application to make his original entry the tracts he now asks for, he would have been afforded an opportunity to show their non-mineral character and succeeding in that would have been allowed to make entry for them. He did not however, so far as the record shows evince any desire to include these tracts in his entry. More than four years after his entry he applies for the privilege to amend the same by adding tracts thereto that he never intended should be included therein. Conceiving the law to be that lands returned as mineral could not be entered under the timber culture law, he limited his application for entry to forty acres. His present application therefore is not asking an amendment of the entry in accordance with the original purpose of the entryman; his entry covered all that he intended should be covered by it; and his application now is an after-thought. It seems to me, therefore, that Norris' application is virtually an application for an additional or second entry. In the case of A. J. Slootskey (6 L. D., 505), the difference between an amended entry and a second or new entry is clearly pointed out. To authorize an entry to be amended the record must fail to express the original intention of the party, and the record is amended to bring it in accord with such intention. If Norris' entry was amended according to his prayer, it would date as of the date of the original entry, April 13, 1883, and it would follow that he has failed to comply with the requirements of the timber culture law for more than six years, for hitherto he limited his cultivation and planting of trees as for an entry of forty acres only.

The timber culture act knows nothing of an additional entry; considering this application then as an application for a second entry we are met by the difficulty that the timber culture law provides, "that no person shall make more than one entry under the provisions of this act," while therefore Norris' entry of April 13, 1883, for forty acres lives, it is beyond the power of this Department to allow him a second entry; surely no person can under the law hold two timber culture entries simultaneously. It follows therefore that your said decision must be affirmed.

PRE-EMPTION PRIVATE ENTRY—PRACTICE.

ULITALO v. KLINE ET AL.

Failure to make final proof and payment for offered land, within twelve months from settlement, renders the land subject to the entry of any other purchaser.

The decision of the Commissioner refusing to order a hearing is appealable, if it amounts to the denial of a right.

First Assistant Secretary Chandler to the Commissioner of the General Land Office, September 17, 1889.

I have considered the appeal of Peter Ulitalo from your office decision of May 9, 1888, affirming the action of the local officers rejecting his application to make homestead entry for the S. ½ of the NW. ¼ and the S. ½ of the NE. ¼ of Sec. 20, T. 139 N., R. 36 W., Crookston, Minnesota land district.

On December 1, 1884 Ulitalo filed pre-emption declaratory statement for said land, it being then offered land. On December 23, 1887, he applied to make homestead entry for said land. This application was rejected for conflict with a private cash entry made September 28, 1887 by Frank J. Kline and Philemon T. Devereaux. Ulitalo appealed from the decision of the local officers, and asked that a hearing be had. Your office affirmed the action of the local officers and refused to order a hearing.

The affidavit accompanying said appeal and which is corroborated, sets forth that Ulitalo who is of foreign birth with but little knowledge of the English language, settled on this land November 26, 1884, and has since that time continuously resided there; that he had built thereon a hewed log house fifteen by fifteen feet, and had cleared and placed under cultivation five acres of the land, said improvements being worth $200; that he had no knowledge of the requirements of the law in respect to making payment within twelve months after filing, but supposed he could hold the land by residence the same as under the homestead law; that as soon as he saved money enough to pay the land office fee, expense of travel and interpreter's fee, he, on December 23, 1887 applied to make homestead entry for said land; that he did not suppose anybody could or would cause him any trouble in regard to this land and the first intimation he had of any other claim to this land was when his homestead application was rejected; that he has every reason to believe that the cash entry by Kline and Devereaux was made for the purposes of acquiring his improvements on said land and for the purpose of extorting money from him; that neither of said parties ever lived on said land or made any improvements there, and asks " that a hearing may be ordered to enable him to prove the allegations set forth in the foregoing affidavit, and that he may be restored to his rights in the premises."

The law provides that proof and payment must be made for offered land within twelve months after settlement and in default thereof the land shall be subject to the entry of any other purchaser.

Ulitalo failed to make his proof and payment within the time specified by law, and said land was, at the date of the cash entry of Kline and Devereaux so far as the record now before me shows, subject to such entry. It appears from Ulitalo's own statement that said land was subject to private cash entry and he does not allege that the law relating to private cash entries was not complied with by said Kline and Devereaux. The law prescribes the manner in which such an entry shall be made and so that said law is strictly complied with this Department has no authority to inquire into the motives of the party in making said entry or the reasons that determined him to select the particular tract applied for.

In this case by Ulitalo's failure to comply with the law (and whether such failure was the result of ignorance or not can make no difference, the rights of other parties having intervened), the land became subject to private cash entry, and in the presence of such an entry he was precluded from asserting further claim thereto.

The question as to whether a hearing should be granted is a matter resting in the sound discretion of the Commissioner, and an appeal will not lie from the decision of your office ordering a hearing. The Commissioner's discretion in such matters will not be disturbed unless there is a clear and satisfactory showing of an abuse of it. Reeves v. Emblen (8 L. D., 444).

The decision of your office refusing to order a hearing is when it amounts to a denial of a right, appealable. James H. Murray (6 L. D., 124). Although it can hardly be said that the refusal of your office in this case amounted to a denial of a right, yet inasmuch as your office accepted the said appeal and transmitted the papers to this Department, I have deemed it best to decide the questions presented.

I do not find any abuse of the discretion vested in your office, and must therefore refuse to disturb the decision complained of. This does not deny to Ulitalo the right of contest as claimed in his appeal. If he shall hereafter file an affidavit in due form alleging a failure on the part of the private cash entrymen to comply with the law, or the existence of any illegality in said entry, it will be the duty of your office to duly consider the same.

Ulitalo complains that your office was inconsistent in denying him a hearing, and in the case of Peter Hyry, similar in all respects, awarding a hearing. If it be true that different action was had in cases entirely alike, that was inconsistent; but that fact would not justify this Department in rendering a decision not in accord with the former rulings on the question involved.

The decision appealed from is affirmed.

DESERT LAND ENTRY-COMPACTNESS.

JOSEPH SHINEBERGER. (ON REVIEW).

The requirement of "compactness" is statutory, and an entry in obvious violation thereof is not protected by the fact that it was made prior to the issuance of departmental instructions with respect to said requirement.

A departmental requirement of further proof, as to the character of the land covered by a desert entry, is within the supervisory authority of the Secretary of the Interior.

Secretary Noble to the Commissioner of the General Land Office, September 17, 1889,

On April 8, 1879, Joseph Shineberger made desert land entry for certain tracts (hereinafter described) in the Helena Montana district. He made final proof and payment on November 14, 1881 upon which final certificate was issued by the local office.

By letter to the local office dated May 13, 1887, your office directed the boundaries of the said entry to be adjusted " so as to make it compact."

By the same letter Shineberger was required to furnish further proof to show the source of his water right and that " he takes the same by prior appropriation," and also the number location and dimension of his lateral ditches, and that there is no adverse claim.

Shineberger appealed and on February 18, 1889 (8 L. D., 231), the Department in view of the " fact that the original entry was allowed at a time when the rules and practice of the Land Department were far less stringent in reference to the requirements of compactness than at present," affirmed the said decision of your office—

With the modification that upon further proofs showing satisfactorily the original desert character of the land, its actual reclamation from desert land to agricultural and such information in respect to compactness as may most fairly meet the law and the necessities of the case, the allowance of the entry may be reconsidered to the extent that justice shall by the facts as presented demand.

A motion to review the said departmental decision has been filed by the attorneys for Shineberger.

Of the three assignments of error upon which the said motion is based, the first and second allege that the Department after finding that the entry was in conformity with the regulations in force at its date, and after citing authorities to show that the departmental instructions now prevailing were applicable only to entries made subsequently thereto, erred in requiring this entry, made prior to such instructions, to be so amended as to conform therewith. The third assignment of error is to the effect that the Department erred in requiring further proof of the desert character of the land after finding by its said decision that the law had been complied with.

By reference to the decision now under consideration it appears that " no instruction defining the word 'compact' or in any way restricting the form of desert land entries was promulgated until September 3, 1880—7 C. L. O., 138, when the rule now in force was adopted."

By the said instructions desert land entries were required to be " by legal subdivisions compact with each other, as nearly in the form of a technical section as the situation of the land and its relation to other lands will admit of" and the side lines of such entries were in no case "permitted to exceed one mile and a quarter when the full quantity of six hundred and forty acres is entered." The limit as to side lines to be proportionately decreased when a less quantity is taken.

The material question that is raised by the first and second assignments of error was disposed of by the Department in the case of J. H. Christensen (9 L. D., 202) whereby the decision under consideration in so far as it conflicted with that cited, was overruled. In that case a desert land entry for two hundred and eighty acres, made as in the case at bar prior to the instructions referred to and completed thereafter had been made to cover a strip of land on both sides of a stream, one and one half miles in length and less than three-eighths of a mile in width.

In the case cited the Department held that the requirement of compactness being statutory an entry in obvious violation thereof is not protected by the fact that it was made prior to the said instructions *supra*.

The records of your office show that the entry of Shineberger embraced the W. ½ SW. ¼ Sec. 3, E. ½ SE. ¼, NE. ¼, N. ½ NW. ¼ Sec. 4, NE. ¼ NE. ¼ Sec. 5 T. 11 S., and E. ½ SW. ¼, E. ½ NW. ¼ NW. ¼ NW. ¼ Sec. 33, SW. ¼ SW. ¼ Sec. 34 T. 10 S., R. 10 W., an aggregate of 635.18 acres in the district named, and that the greater part of said entry is intersected by a stream.

By a straight line from the north-west to the south-east corner of the land, the distance between said points, *i. e.*, the extreme length of the entry is shown to be two and five eighths miles.

A very considerable part of the tract in question is only a quarter of a mile wide while the greatest width at right angles to the line mentioned is about three quarters of a mile. That the entry is in obvious violation of the statutory requirement with regard to compactness (19 Stat. 377), is in my opinion too plain for discussion. Moreover, the land embraced therein is intersected by a stream. The circular instructions of September 3, 1880, *supra*, required the reformation of "entries heretofore made . . . . running along the margins or including both sides of streams and not being compact in any true sense." This ruling is sustained by the Christensen case.

I can, therefore, in the light of the authority cited see no reason why Shineberger should not be required to amend his entry so as to make it a proper one under the law.

With regard to the third allegation of error, it is sufficient to say that the character of the land involved being a matter that affects the legality of the entry, the requirement of further proof in relation thereto was clearly within supervisory authority, which the law vests in the Secretary of the Interior over all proceedings instituted to acquire portions of the public lands.

In accordance with the views expressed herein, you will direct the boundaries of Shineberger's entry to be so reformed with regard to "the situation of the land and its relation to other lands," J. H. Christensen, *supra*, as to meet the statutory requirements of compactness.

The said departmental decision of February 18, 1889, is modified accordingly. The affidavits of Shineberger and others (filed with the motion) to the effect that the land at the date of his entry was desert in character, and that he (Shineberger) has expended large sums thereon, are returned for appropriate action by your office.

HOMESTEAD—SOLDIERS DECLARATORY STATEMENT—ACT OF MARCH
2, 1889.

RICHARD T. HENNING.

Under the act of March 2, 1889, the filing of a soldiers' declaratory statement, previous
thereto, is not held to exhaust the homestead right.

*First Assistant Secretary Chandler to the Commissioner of the General
Land Office, September 17, 1889.*

I have considered the appeal of Richard T. Henning from your office
decision of May 21, 1888, involving his application to be allowed to
make homestead entry for the SE. ¼ Sec. 25 T. 6 S. R. 36 W., Oberlin
land district Kansas.

The records of your office show that Henning October 9, 1879, filed
his soldiers' homestead declaratory statement No. 2851 for the SE. ¼
Sec. 5 T. 6 R. 35 W., Kansas; that on June 21, 1880, he filed his pre-
emption declaratory statement No. 17469 for the same land, and that on
January 13, 1888, he made cash entry No. 5599 thereon.

On February 24, 1888, Henning made application to be allowed to
make homestead entry for the SE. ¼ Sec. 25 T. 6 S., R. 36 W., Oberlin
land district, Kansas.

Attached to the application is Henning's affidavit; in it he states
that he was advised by attorneys-at-law that the filing of his soldiers'
homestead declaratory statement for the SE. ¼ of the said section 5 on
October 9, 1879 "did not exhaust his homestead or any other right;"
that he, acting upon such advice, filed a pre-emption declaratory statement for the said land June 21, 1880, and subsequently made cash entry therefor. He further states that he has resided on the land now
applied for since about September 15, 1885, and made valuable improvements thereon—describing them—at an expense, including costs of litigation, of more than seven hundred dollars.

Your office, holding that "Henning has exhausted his rights under
the homestead law," by your said decision rejected his application.

Applicant appealed. Attached to his appeal is his corroborated affidavit bearing date August 24, 1888. In it he again describes his said
improvements and states " that he is an actual bona fide resident" upon
the said land.

Your said decision was in accord with the law and rulings of this
Department at the time the same was rendered. I refer to circular of
December 15, 1882 (1 L. D., 648), also to Stephens *v.* Ray (5 L. D., 133),
and Maria O. Arter (7 L. D., 136). The case now, however, seems to
come within the provisions of the act of Congress approved March 2,
1889 (25 Stat. 854), entitled " an act to withdraw certain public lands
from private entry and for other purposes," and due opportunity should
be given the applicant for an application thereunder. To this end he
should be notified that if within sixty days after notice hereof, he shall

make such application in accordance with said act and the regulations thereunder, it will receive due consideration, and that in the mean time final action herein will remain suspended, but that if he fails to make such application within the time specified, his claim will be finally rejected. George W. Mason (8 L. D., 457).

Your decision is accordingly modified.

———

SECOND TIMBER CULTURE ENTRY—APPLICATION.

SAMUEL P. KANE.

An application to make a second timber culture entry reserves the land embraced therein.

Failure to exercise the right, once accorded, to make a second entry, will, in the absence of explanation, preclude favorable action on a subsequent application of a similar character.

First Assistant Secretary Chandler to the Commissioner of the General Land Office, September 17, 1889.

I have considered the appeal of Samuel P. Kane from your office decision of March 7, 1887, rejecting his application to make timber culture entry for the SW. ¼ of section 3 T. 15 N., R. 31 W., Wa Keeney land district Kansas.

The records of your office show that Samuel P. Kane made timber culture entry No. 2185 at Neligh, Nebraska, on September 22, 1883 for the SW. ¼ of section 15 T. 24 N., R. 15 W.

On September 29, 1883, the register and receiver of Neligh land district, Nebraska, transmitted to your office Samuel P. Kane's application to amend said entry so as to embrace in lieu thereof the E. ½ NW. ¼ and W. ½ SW. ¼ Sec. 21 same township and range.

This application was supported by an affidavit corroborated by the testimony of the county surveyor as also by a letter from said officers accompanying the case, showing that an error was made in describing the tract which Kane intended to enter, owing to the destruction of many of the marks of government surveys, that after survey to be made of the tract which he supposed he had entered, he found that the greater portion of the land was embraced in section 16, hence his application to amend.

Your office December 8, 1883, held that while the application to amend the entry could not be granted because applicant never intended to enter the land now applied for,—it was competent for your office to authorize Kane to make a new entry for the tract described. Entry No. 2185 was accordingly canceled and Kane informed thereof and of his rights in the premises.

On February 15, 1886, Samuel P. Kane presented to the local officers of the land district Wa Keeney, Kansas, his application to make timber

culture for the SW. ¼ section 3 T. 16 N., R. 31 W., land district aforesaid. The local officers rejected the application "for the reason that
no satisfactory evidence is furnished showing that applicant has been
granted permission by the Honorable Commissioner of the General
Land Office to make a second timber culture entry for any tract of land
he may choose to enter."

Kane appealed to your office.

By your said office decision of March 7, 1887, the action of the local
officers was sustained. Appellant thereupon filed his appeal to this
Department.

Kane's application of September, 1883, was virtually an application
to make a new or second entry for the lands therein described. Because the greater portion of the land he actually intended to enter was
embraced in section 16, reserved to the State "for the purpose of being
applied to schools," he asked to be allowed an entry for different land,
describing it. See case of A. J. Slootskey (6 L. D., 505), where the
distinction between an amendment of an entry and a second entry is
pointed out.

Your office by said letter of December 8, 1883, allowed Kane's application for a second timber culture entry on lands specifically described
by him. Though notified of this he failed to perfect the entry. His
prayer had been granted, but he chose to forego the benefits of your
said office decision. After the expiration of more than two years he
again comes and asks to be permitted to make a new timber culture
entry for other lands without assigning any reason why he failed to
avail himself of the privilege by your office granted to him on his former
application. On such application the lands therein described were reserved for his entry. Florey and Moat (4 L. D., 365); Bracken v.
Mecham (6 L. D., 264); Pfaff v. Williams et al., (4 L. D. 455); Maria C.
Arter (7 L. D., 136).

He had the opportunity to make the entry thereon according to his
expressed purpose and without showing any cause or assigning any
reason he failed to do so; it seems therefore that his present application, apparently without equity, should not be allowed.

Your said office decision is accordingly affirmed.

———

[Circular.]

DEPARTMENT OF THE INTERIOR,
GENERAL LAND OFFICE,
Washington, D. C., September 5, 1889.

To the Registers and Receivers of the United States District Land Offices
in California, Oregon, Nevada, and Washington Territory.

GENTLEMEN: By circular of May 1, 1880 (7 C. L. O., 52; 2 C. L. L.,
1458), under the timber and stone act of June 3, 1878 (20 Stat., 89),
this office instructed the registers and receivers of the proper district

land offices that claimants under said act would be required, after the proper publication for sixty days, as prescribed in the act, to make the necessary proof and payment within ninety days from date of their original applications, and that in default of the proof and payment, at the expiration of the ninety days, the applications would be canceled. It appears that up to that date, there had been no regulation for restricting the claimant as to the time within which he should make proof and payment for the land, and it was deemed proper by said circular to fix a reasonable limit therefor. By subsequent circular of July 16, 1887 (6 L. D., 114), this regulation was renewed, with added regulations, by which the registers and receivers were directed that in the notice to be furnished by the register to the applicant for publication, the time and place for making proof and payment should be specified. The regulations of the latter circular were reproduced in the general circular of this office of January 1, 1889.

Cases having arisen, in the Seattle, Washington Territory, land district, in which it was found impracticable, from the pressure of business, under the various laws for the disposal of the public lands, for the district land officers to properly consider and act upon all the cases arising under the said act within the period of ninety days, as prescribed, the matter was submitted for the consideration of the honorable Secretary of the Interior, and an expression of his views elicited, as per letter from the Acting Secretary to this office of the 22d ultimo. Concurring with the views therein expressed, I am of opinion that the ninety days regulation referred to should not be longer continued, and it is hereby dispensed with. The registers will hereafter fix the date for making proof and payment in the notices furnished by them, in this class of cases, at a reasonable time, after due publication, having due regard to the exigencies of business at their respective offices.

Respectfully,

WM. M. STONE,
Acting Commissioner.

Approved :
GEO. CHANDLER,
Acting Secretary of the Interior.

SWAMP LAND GRANT—FIELD NOTES OF SURVEY.

NITA *v.* STATE OF WISCONSIN.

In adjusting the swamp grant on field notes of survey, where the intersections of the lines of swamp lands with those of the public survey alone are given, such intersections may be connected by straight lines to determine the character of the legal sub-divisions.

The decision of a commission, mutually agreed upon between the government and the State, that a certain tract is swamp land, will not prevent the Department from reviewing such decision, or considering other evidence, in finally determining the true character of said land.

The burden of proof is upon the State when the field notes of survey do not, *prima facie*, show the land to be of the character granted.

To establish the claim of the State, it must show that the greater part of the particular sub-division is subject to the grant.

Secretary Noble to the Commissioner of the General Land Office, September 20, 1889.

I have before me the appeal of the State of Wisconsin from your office decision of November 23, 1886, holding for rejection the said State's claim, under the swamp-land grant of September 28, 1850 (9 Stat., 519) to the SE. ¼ NE. ¼ Sec. 26, T. 29 N., R. 19 E., Menasha district, Wisconsin.

The said SE. ¼ NE. ¼ was, on the 12th of June 1883, included with the SW. ¼ of the same quarter-section in Saimon Nita's homestead entry, No. 2370 (*i. e.*, S. ½ NE. ¼ Sec. 26). This entry was afterwards suspended for conflict with the State's swamp-grant claim, as to the SE. ¼ of the quarter-section.

By the decision appealed from, your predecessor, Commissioner Stockslager, held as follows:

The greater part of the tract in conflict is designated on the plat of survey as swamp land, but from an examination of the field-notes of survey, on file in this office, I am of the opinion that such designation is not warranted by the facts as set forth in said field notes, and that less than one-half of the land is swamp land. In view of the foregoing the claim of the State for the tract in controversy is this day held for rejection.

Upon being notified of this action of your office, the State appealed, accompanying its appeal with a sworn statement by C. F. Fricke, the chief clerk of the State's Commissioners of Public Lands, setting forth as follows the grounds of objection to the decision appealed from:

(1) On the 13th day of August, 1881, by a commission appointed by the Commissioner of the General Land Office of the United States and the Governor of the State of Wisconsin, under an arrangement made by the Secretary of the Interior and the Governor, to make a final settlement and adjustment of the swamp lands under the act of Congress approved September 28, 1850, I find that the south east quarter of the north east quarter of section No. 26, in township No. 29 north of range No. 19 east of the 4th principal meridian, Wisconsin, was decided by said commission to be swamp land within the meaning of said act, the record of which is now on file in Division "K" of the General Land Office at Washington D. C., and that said decision is final.

(2) Upon examination of the field notes and plat of the government survey of said tract I find that on the line between sections No. 25 and 26 at seventeen (17) chains from the section corner they enter a dense uncultivable cedar swamp bearing NW. and SE., and continue sixty-three (63) chains in said swamp to the corner of sections Nos. 23, 24, 25 and 26, and on the line between sections Nos. 23 and 26 they leave the swamp at thirteen and a half (13.50) chains bearing north and south, from the corner of sections Nos. 23, 24, 25 and 26; which according to the rules laid down by the Commissioner of the General Land Office as a guide for the commission appointed by him and the Governor of the State of Wisconsin, to adjust the swamp land grant, and shown by the line of swamp in diagram herewith (proves) that the south east quarter of the north east quarter of section No. 26 ...... is more than half swamp.

The former point—that the report of the special commission is final —was expressly denied by the Department in the case of Wisconsin v. Wolf, (8 L. D., 555).

As to the second point, based on the showing made by the field-notes, I find in the record a copy of said field-notes, together with a plat, furnished by your office, showing " the lines of intersection of the swamps on the east and north lines of Sec. 26, drawn in accordance with the decision of the Secretary of the Interior of April 17, 1880, in reply to Commissioner's letter of April 16, 1880, to wit,—"by straight lines'." In 1 Lester, 543, the rule was laid down as follows:

When the field notes are the basis, and the intersections of the lines of swamp or overflow with those of the public surveys alone are given, those intersections may be connected by straight lines; and all legal subdivisions, the greater part of which are shown by those lines to be within the swamp or overflow, will be certified to the State; the balance will remain the property of the government.

(See also Knudson v. Minnesota, 7 L.D., 424).

The application of this rule to the present case results as the official plat shows, in classifying the tract in question as one, the larger part of which is *not* swamp or overflowed land within the meaning of the grant.

Under date of November 5, 1888, Saimon Nita and Joseph Peck made a joint affidavit, containing the following declarations:

That when said Saimon Nita first saw said land in 1882 and when said Joseph Peck first saw said land in 1880, it was then covered with a growth of small poplars and small second growth of pine; that it was four to six feet above level of adjacent swamps and was all dry land and not swamp land; that the soil was and is sandy and dry; that the affiant Saimon Nita has since 1882, cleared about twenty-five acres of said forty acre tract and cultivated same and that the soil so cleared and cultivated is dry and sandy; that the remaining fifteen acres is the same kind of soil as upon the cleared land; that no part of said forty acre tract now is or ever could have been swamp land, excepting perhaps one-half acre in the south-west corner thereof; that the east part of said forty acre tract is in no wise different from or lower than the west part; that the map representing about two-thirds of said tract as swamp land is incorrect; that said Nita has cleared and improved said tract and built thereon, investing $700, to $800, thereon.

Everything considered, the case is substantially like that of Wisconsin v. Wolf (8 L.D., 555), and, in my opinion should be disposed of in the same way. The State will be allowed sixty days after receipt of notice of this decision, within which to institute the usual proceedings for a hearing herein before the local land officers. The field-notes failing to show *prima facie* the swampy character of said tract, the burden of proof will be on the State to show that the greater part of the forty was of the description of lands granted, to wit: "swamp and overflowed lands, made unfit thereby for cultivation." Should an application for a hearing be made within the time designated, the entryman will be duly notified thereof and afforded full opportunity to be heard in defense; and in default of such application, the claim of the State will stand rejected, and Nita's homestead entry will be passed upon in the regular course of business in your office.

The decision appealed from is modified accordingly.

———

SOLDIERS ADDITIONAL HOMESTEAD—PRACTICE.

JOHN R. NICKEL.

A certificate of additional right will not be issued, where the applicant, by a previous additional entry, exhausted his rights under section 2306 of the Revised Statutes, as then construed by the Department.

An additional entry may be made under the act of March 2, 1889, where the applicant has exhausted his rights under sections 2289, and 2306 R. S., without securing one hundred and sixty acres of land.

An appeal should be from the original decision, and not from the refusal to reconsider such decision.

First Assistant Secretary Chandler to the Commissioner of the General Land Office, September 20, 1889.

I have considered the appeal of John R. Nickel from the decision of your office, dated September 19, 1888, refusing to reconsider your office decision, dated November 21, 1888, rejecting his claim for an additional homestead, filed January 16, 1833.

Said claim was based upon his original entry, of the NW. ¼ of the SW. ¼ of Sec. 4, T. 22 N., R. 15 E., Menasha, Wisconsin, and was rejected because the claimant had exhausted his right to an additional entry, in entering under the homestead laws the S. ½ of the NW. ¼ of Sec. 4, T. 34, R. 2 E., in said State.

On August 30, 1888, counsel for claimant applied for a reconsideration of said decision rejecting said application, and filed the affidavit of the claimant, who swears, among other things, that he made soldier's additional homestead entry at Wausau, Wisconsin, in November, 1874, for eighty acres; that he applied, at that time, to enter one hundred and twenty acres and was refused by the register and receiver, because he had forty acres in addition to his adjoining farm entry of forty acres.

On September 19, 1888, your office considered said application for reconsideration, and refused the same, for the reason, that, prior to February 27, 1875, the ruling of the Department was that a soldier, who entered land under section 2289 of the Revised Statutes as an adjoining farm entry, which with the original farm contained one hundred and sixty acres, could not make an additional entry under section 2306 of the U. S. Revised Statutes; that, subsequently, said ruling was changed, in the case of Eli P. Sweet (2 C. L. O., 18), and the applicant was allowed to make additional entry of enough land to make up one hundred and sixty acres entered under the homestead law, without regard to the quantity owned by him at the time he made homestead entry; that, as the applicant acquiesced in the ruling, rejecting his said application for one hundred and twenty acres, he was not entitled to a certificate of right to a second additional entry, nor could he be permitted to make any entry of that kind.

The appellant insists that said decision is erroneous: 1st, In holding that the claimant acquiesced in the wrongful action of the register and receiver in restricting his entry to eighty acres. 2d, In not deciding the case under second clause of Rule 48, of Rules of Practice, as amended December 8, 1885.

With said appeal is filed the affidavit of the claimant, alleging that he was not notified of his right of appeal, and supposed that the register and receiver were the proper officers to apply to for said land.

The appeal should have been taken from the decision of your office, dated September 19, 1888, and not from the decision refusing the motion for reconsideration. Rule of Practice 81 (4 L. D., 46); amended December 8, 1885.

Section 2306 of the U. S. Revised Statutes provides that:

Every person entitled under the provisions of section 2304, to enter a homestead, who may have heretofore entered, under the homestead laws, a quantity of land less than one hundred and sixty acres, shall be permitted to enter so much land as, when added to the quantity previously entered, shall not exceed one hundred and sixty acres.

The record shows that the claimant made an adjoining farm entry of forty acres under the provisions of section 2289 of the Revised Statutes; that he owned and resided upon a forty acre tract at the time he made said adjoining farm entry, and that on November 17, 1874, he made soldier's additional entry of eighty acres, under the provisions of said section 2306.

It is quite evident from the foregoing, that the contention of appellant can not be maintained. The decision of the local officers, allowing only eighty acres additional, in November 17, 1874, was not "contrary to existing laws and regulations," but was in compliance therewith, as construed by the Department. Moreover, the claimant made said additional entry and thereby exhausted his right under said act, as construed by the Department at that time. While the applicant is not entitled to have a certificate of his right to make a second additional entry, yet, since it appears that he has entered, under the homestead law, only one hundred and twenty acres of land, he may be allowed to make another homestead entry of forty acres, under the provisions of the act of Congress, approved March 2, 1889 (25 Stat., 854).

The decision of your office is modified accordingly.

ACT OF JUNE 15, 1880—PENDING CONTEST.

PIERPOINT *v.* STALDER.   (ON REVIEW.)

A purchase under section 2, act of June 15, 1880, during the pendency of a contest, is good as against the government, and all persons except the contestant; and such purchase may be recognized as valid, if the contestant waives his preference right of entry.

First Assistant Secretary Chandler to the Commissioner of the General Land Office, September 20, 1889.

I am in receipt of your office letter of August 29, 1889, whereby you return a letter, which had been informally referred to you, dated August 14, 1889, from P. C. Hughes, an attorney at Larned, Kansas, to myself, in regard to the case of Pierpoint *v.* Stalder, 8 L. D., 595, involving the SE. ¼ of Sec. 8, T. 18 S., R. 32 W., Wa Keeney land district.

In the decision rendered in said case on June 8, 1889, the Department sustained the contest of Pierpoint against the cash entry made by Stalder, February 26, 1886, under the act of June 15, 1880 (21 Stat., 237). By the same decision your office was directed to cancel both the homestead and cash entries of Stalder, and to allow the application of Pierpoint, made August 6, 1886, to make homestead entry for the land.

Mr. Hughes, as attorney for Stalder, represents in his said letter that Pierpoint can not be found, and suggests that the said decision be so modified as to allow, in the event of Pierpoint's failure to appear, the cash entry of Stalder to remain intact. Mr. Hughes submits, with his said letter, a letter from the register, dated June 28, 1889, who states that no action has been taken in said case, "as we are trying to ascertain the parties' address." Mr. Hughes also submits a postal card, addressed to himself, and which he states is from the postmaster at Scott City, one and a half miles from the tract named. This card, postmarked August 15, 1889, sets out that "Pierpoint's address is unknown to us."

You state that the modification suggested by Mr. Hughes would in your opinion "accord with the general practice in this class of cases," and cite Smith *v.* Ferguson (7 L. D., 195), Smith *et al. v.* Mayland (Id., 381).

In the cases cited the Department held that a purchase under the act of June 15, 1880, while a contest is pending, is good as against the government and all persons, except the contestant, and that such purchase may be recognized as valid, if the contestant waives his preference right of entry.

It appearing that, as stated, the whereabouts of Pierpoint are unknown, and it being therefore possible that he may waive his preference right of entry, I can see no reason why the purchase of Stalder should not be recognized.

The cash entry of Stalder for the tract named will therefore be reinstated, and made subject to the rights of Pierpoint.

The said departmental decision of June 8, 1889, is modified accordingly.

CONTEST—INTEREST OF THE GOVERNMENT—CONTESTANT.

SAUNDERS v. BALDWIN.

The government is a party in interest and entitled to judgment on the facts, however such facts may have been disclosed, and whatever the rights of the private parties to the contest may be as against each other.

Whether the contestant is actually entitled to a preference right is a question that can only arise on his attempt to exercise such right.

First Assistant Secretary Chandler to the Commissioner of the General Land Office, September 19, 1889.

I have before me the appeal of John K. Baldwin from your decision of March 26, 1888, affirming the action of the local officers holding for cancellation his homestead entry, No. 11749, made November 13, 1882, on the SW. ¼ Sec. 8, T. 143 N., R. 54 W., Fargo district, Dakota.

On September 4, 1885, Thomas P. Saunders initiated contest against said entry, on the ground that the entryman had "wholly *abandoned* said tract, and that he (had) changed his residence therefrom for more than six months next preceding date of filing this complaint." Upon this contest trial was had November 17, 1885, both parties being present in person and by attorney.

At the conclusion of the contestant's evidence, the contestee filed a written motion to dismiss the contest, on the ground that the evidence failed to prove the charge. No decision seems to have been made upon this motion; but the contestee proceeded with the evidence for the defense.

The decision of the local officers, rendered January 25, 1886, is to the effect that, while the case made by the contestant's witnesses would, if taken by itself, be wholly insufficient to sustain the contest, yet as the testimony of the entryman and his witnesses clearly proved that Baldwin had all along resided in Chicago and not on the homestead tract, the entry should be canceled.

This decision your office affirmed.

On the appeal now under consideration the entryman insists that it was error to consider the testimony for the defense at all, the testimony for the contestant having been insufficient to sustain the charge, and he, the entryman, having duly moved at the proper time, to dismiss the contest upon that ground.

There can be no question in view of the facts brought out by the entryman and his witnesses, as to the propriety of cancelling the entry, on the ground that the entryman never resided on the tract at all.   These facts having, in a way which conclusively establishes them as against the entryman, come to the knowledge of the Department, the latter can and must, of its own motion if necessary, take appropriate action upon them, wholly without regard to the question whether the contestant's evidence, taken by itself, would have sufficed for cancellation. The government is a party in interest and entitled to judgment according to the facts, however those facts may have been disclosed, and whatever be the rights of the private parties to the contest as against each other. Taylor *v.* Huffman, 5 L. D., 40; Hegranes *v.* Londen, id., 386.

The failure of the contestant to establish his charge has a bearing only on the question whether he should be allowed a preference right of entry as a successful contestant; and that is a question which will arise only when the contestant seeks to exercise his supposed right by actually making an entry of the tract by virtue of that right. Moore *v.* Lyon, 4 L. D., 393; Warn *v.* Field, 6 id., 238; Hemsworth *v.* Holland, 8 id., 400.

Upon these grounds the said decision is affirmed.

INDIAN LANDS—ALLOTMENTS—PATENT—ACT OF FEBRUARY 8, 1887.

LAC DE FLAMBEAU INDIANS.

The treaty of September 30, 1854, is not repealed, changed, or modified by the act of February 8, 1887.

The right of allotment is conferred by the treaty of 1854, and patents for allotments thereunder should be in accordance with the terms of said treaty, whether the selections and allotments were made, or the approvals signed before or after the passage of the act of 1887.

Secretary Noble to the Commissioner of the General Land Office, September 23, 1889.

I acknowledge the receipt of your communication of 20th ultimo, returning to the Department three schedules of selections of allotments made to members of the Lac de Flambeau band of Chippewa Indians, under the provisions of the treaty of September 30, 1854, (10 Stat., 1109), which were transmitted to your office with Department letter of December 12th last, with directions to issue patents in the name of the allottees in the form and the legal effect as required by the 5th section of the general allotment act of February 8, 1887, (24 Stats. 388).

You recommend, in view of the action taken by the Department in the case of the selections made for certain members of the Bad River band, that Department instructions as to the form of patent be modified so as to agree with Department letter of March 2, 1889.

As Department letter of December 12th, 1888, was based upon a decision rendered by the Assistant Attorney General for the Department of the Interior, I deemed it proper to refer the matter to that office for an expression of opinion as to what kind of a patent should issue to the allottees named in the within schedules. I am now in receipt of an opinion dated 18th instant, wherein it is held " that the right of allotment being secured to these Indians under the treaty stipulations of 1854, when said allotments are made, patents thereon should be issued in accordance with the terms of said treaty, whether the selections and allotments were made or the approvals signed before or after the passage of the act of 1887."

Concurring in the opinion of the Honorable Assistant Attorney General, I have to direct that patents issue to the allottees named in the schedules (herewith returned) in accordance therewith.

A copy of the opinion of the Honorable Assistant Attorney General is enclosed for your information.

OPINION OF THE ASSISTANT ATTORNEY GENERAL.

By reference of Acting Secretary Chandler, I am in receipt of a communication, and accompanying papers, from the chief of the Indian division of your office, asking for an opinion as to the proper form in which patents should be issued for lands allotted and to be allotted to the Lac de Flambeau band of Chippewa Indians, in Wisconsin, and I beg leave herewith to submit my views upon the matters involved.

By section three, article two, of the treaty of September 30, 1854, (10 Stat., 1109), with the "Chippewa Indians of Lake Superior and the Mississippi," a tract of land, lying about Lac de Flambeau, equal in extent to three townships, was set aside " for the Wisconsin bands" of said Indians. By article three it was provided that the reservation was to be surveyed at the discretion of the President, who

may assign to each head of a family, or single person, over twenty-one years of age, eighty acres of land for his or their separate use; and he may, at his discretion, as fast as the occupants become capable of transacting their own affairs, issue patents therefor to such occupants, with such restrictions of the power of alienation as he may think fit to impose.

Some allotments have been made of the lands set aside for the Lac de Flambeau Indians, under this treaty, the condition of patents issued on the allotments being, that the patentee and his heirs " shall not sell, lease, or in any manner alienate said tract without the consent of the President of the United States."

On February 8, 1887, (24 Stat., 388), Congress passed " An act to provide for the allotment of lands in severalty to Indians on the various reservations," etc., the first section of which provides:

That in all cases where any tribe or band of Indians has been, or shall hereafter be, located upon any reservation created for their use, either by treaty stipulation or by virtue of an act of Congress or executive order setting apart the same for their use, the President of the United States be, and he hereby is, authorized, whenever in his opinion any reservation or any part thereof of such Indians is advantageous for agricultural and grazing purposes, to cause said reservation, or any part thereof, to be surveyed, or resurveyed if necessary, and to allot the lands in said reservation in severalty to any Indian located thereon in quantities as follows : To each head of a family, one-quarter of a section ; to each single person over eighteen years of age, one-eighth of a section ; to each orphan child under eighteen years of age, one-eighth of a section ; and to each other single person under eighteen years now living, or who may be born prior to the date of the order of the President directing an allotment of the lands embraced in any reservation, one-sixteenth of a section ; *Provided*, That in case there is not sufficient land in any of said reservations to allot lands to each individual of the classes above named in quantities as above provided, the lands embraced in such reservation or reservations shall be allotted to each individual of each of said classes *pro rata* in accordance with the provisions of this act: *And provided further*, That where the treaty or act of Congress setting apart such reservation provides for the allotment of lands in severalty in quantities in excess of those herein provided, the President, in making allotments upon such reservation, shall allot the lands to each individual Indian belonging thereon in quantity as specified in such treaty or act: *And provided further*, That when the lands allotted are only valuable for grazing purposes, an additional allotment of such grazing lands, in quantities as above provided, shall be made to each individual.

Section four provides that any Indian, not residing upon a reservation, who shall make settlement upon the public lands may upon application to the local land officers have the same allotted to him in manner and quantity as provided for the reservation Indians.

Section five then provides :

That upon the approval of the allotments provided for in this act by the Secretary of the Interior, he shall cause patents to issue therefor in the name of the allottees, which patents shall be of the legal effect, and declare that the United States does and will hold the land thus allotted for the period of twenty-five years, in trust for the sole use and benefit of the Indians to whom such allotments have been made, or, in case of his decease, of his heirs, according to the laws of the State or Territory where such land is located, and that at the expiration of said period the United States will convey the same by patent to said Indian or his heirs as aforesaid, in fee, discharged of said trust and free of all charge or incumbrance whatever.

The President is also authorized in his discretion to extend said period ; and any contract or conveyance, touching the allotted lands, made before the expiration of the trust, is declared to be absolutely null and void.

In view of this legislation, the question is now asked : " What kind of patent should issue where allotments were made under the treaty of 1854 and subsequent to the act of 1887 ?"

The question now submitted to me, is not an entirely new one in this Department, but was partially considered by your immediate predecessor, and fully by mine, resulting in views somewhat at variance. In an opinion upon this question, the then Assistant Attorney General, on March 29, 1887, said: (5 L. D. 520–525)

It seems to me that sections one and five of said act, when read together, furnish an unmistakable answer as to what was the Congressional will in the premises. It will be remembered that one of the provisos incorporated in said section one is to the effect—"That where the treaty or act of Congress setting apart a reservation provides also for the allotment of lands in severalty in quantities in excess of those herein provided for, the President, in making allotments upon such reservation shall allot the lands to each individual Indian belonging thereon in quantity as specified in such treaty or act."

Section five provides "That upon the approval of the allotments provided for in this act by the Secretary of the Interior" meaning, of course, all allotments provided for by this act—" He shall cause patents to issue therefor in the name of the allottees, which patents shall be of the legal effect and declare that the United States does and will hold the land thus allotted for the period of twenty-five years in trust for the sole use and benefit of the Indian," etc.

Inasmuch, then, as Congress prescribes but this one kind of patent for all these Indian allotments, and inasmuch as the allotments so provided for embrace the lands held in severalty under previous acts of Congress or treaty stipulation (as well as lands not so held), I can see no escape from the conclusion that Congress intended the one form of patent for both classes of allotments.

On December 5, 1888, Secretary Vilas wrote to the Commissioner of Indian Affairs that the foregoing opinion "relates only to allotments made subsequent to the passage of the act of February 8, 1887, and recognizes expressly the rights of Indians in allotments previously made to be unaffected."

And he directed that as to allotments "made and approved" before the passage of said act, they should be completed by the issue of patents under the treaty. But as to allotments made, under the treaty, since the passage of the act of 1887, the patents thereon should take the form prescribed by that act, as, in accordance with the above opinion of the Assistant Attorney General, "it so far operates as an amendment of the treaty." Following this, on December 11, 1888, a schedule of allotments, made to the La Pointe or Bad River Band of Indians, under the same treaty, approved by the President January 3, 1888, was transmitted to the Commissioner of the General Land Office, with instructions to issue patents thereon under the act of 1887, inasmuch as the approval of the President was after the passage of that act. On the next day three schedules of allotments, under said treaty, to the Lac de Flambeau Indians, approved by the President November 29, 1887, and January 3, 1888, were sent to the Commissioner of the General Land Office, with instructions to issue patents thereon in the form directed in the letter of the previous day. On March 2, 1889, in letters to the Commissioner of Indian Affairs and the Commissioner of the General Land Office the Secretary, in relation to allotments to the La Pointe or Bad River Band of Indians, on further consideration, modified his views, and said, that where allotments are actually made, under the treaty, before the date of the passage of the act of 1887, though not approved until thereafter—

the patent should take the form which had been prescribed previously for allotments, and that the approval of the President has relation to the time of the allotment, and confirms rights created by the allotment, subject only to that approval. . . . . . . I am in doubt, on further reflection, whether, if allotments be made wholly and entirely under the treaty, and not under the act of 1887, patents should not, in that case, also take the same form.

but, inasmuch as the question was not before him then, on the schedules presented, he did not formally decide it. It would seem however from the very plain intimation given that the correctness of the opinion of the Assistant Attorney General was seriously questioned by the Secretary, "on further reflection."

In view of the foregoing, the question which first presents itself is, does the act of 1887 affect the treaty of 1854, and if so, to what extent?

Considering the treaty in this case as of no more dignity than an ordinary statute, the repeal of which involves no question of good faith with another people, it is to be remembered that there is in the statute of 1887 no express reference whatever to the treaty of 1854, and no repeal or change in terms of any of its provisions. Therefore, any contention that the treaty is in any way affected by the subsequent act is based entirely upon an alleged implication.

The rule, that repeals by implication are not favored, is as well settled as any canon of construction known to the books. Such implication to be adopted must be necessary and unavoidable to the extent of otherwise leaving a positive and irreconcilable repugnancy between the two acts; or, as the supreme court said, in State v. Stoll, 17 Wall., 430—

It must appear that the later provision is certainly and clearly in hostility to the former. If by any reasonable construction the two statutes can stand together they must so stand. If harmony is impossible, and only in that event, the former law is repealed in part or wholly as the case may be.

In the light of these considerations I fail to see that the treaty of 1854 is repealed, changed or modified by the act of 1887. I fail to see that, because after provision was made, in the most solemn manner, for the ultimate disposition of the whole title of the government to certain specified lands, Congress passed an act making general and different provisions for the allotment in severalty of the lands within all Indian reservations to all the Indians living thereon, that such subsequent general legislation can, with any propriety, be held to affect the former special legislation. The rule being, in this respect, as I understand it, that a general act is not to be construed as repealing a particular act, without express reference thereto, or a necessary inconsistency between the two. For the supposition is, that the legislature, having had its attention directed to a particular subject, and having made provision in relation thereto, does not intend by a general law afterwards to disturb the former action or detract from the sufficiency of its own work when no such intention is mentioned. And another general rule may be invoked, which is, that all statutes are prospective in their operation; and courts have uniformly refused to give to them a retrospective operation, where vested rights may be affected; unless compelled to do so by language so positive and unequivocal as to leave no room to doubt that such was the intention of the legislature. United States v. Heth, 8 Cranch, 398.

It should be recollected that between the time of the ratification of the treaty and the passage of the act of 1887 thirty-three years had passed away, and the scheme of allotting lands in severalty to the Indians—at first an experiment of doubtful promise, incorporated into few of the earlier treaties—had become part of the settled policy of the government, and was and is now regarded as the most potent instrument in aid of the disruption of the tribal relations and the introduction among th em of the habits and arts of civilized life.   This is part of the history of the times; and to carry out, what from experiments had been shaped into the settled policy, the act of 1887 was passed. The theory on which it was based and the purpose to be accomplished were the same as those of the treaty, but the conditions through which the end was to be attained were somewhat different and more precise. Under the treaty, the time of the issue of the patents, and their conditions and restrictions, are left entirely within the discretion of the President, who established the condition and restriction that the patentee and his heirs " shall not sell, lease or in any manner alienate said' tract without the consent of the President of the United States." Under the act two patents are required and the conditions thereof are clearly prescribed.   The first or preliminary patent is to contain a clause declaring that the title to said lands is to be held in trust by the United States for the fixed period of twenty-five years, unless extended by the President, at the end of which time the second patent is to be issued, conveying an absolute fee simple, free of any trust or charge whatever.

In all this I find nothing conflicting, or which should cause a repeal, modification or change in any of the provisions of the treaty as to the character and mode of issuing the patents to the Indians in question, and no reason why each may not stand side by side and operate independently upon its own subject matter without clashing; the treaty upon the particular lands for the disposition of which it provides; and the act upon other lands of which no such disposition had been theretofore made.

In short, to hold that the act of 1887 is to control or alter the treaty, it seems to me, would be a violation of all the rules or construction herein recited, and an ignoring of all the meritorious considerations presented.

In relation to the second proviso of the first section of the act of 1887, providing for the issue of patents for allotments in excess of the amounts allowed by said act, where a treaty or other act provided for such larger quantity, and which proviso, placed in juxtaposition with the first clause of the fifth section of said act, seems to be the controlling reason for the opinion of my predecessor, I may add that, I do not see in this proviso, either by itself or when placed in juxtaposition—a most unsafe criterion of continuity—anything to cause me to waver in the conclusion arrived at here.   If it can be so construed as to avoid conflict with the former legislation in the shape of the treaty, we are bound so to construe it.   To my mind, it not only can be so construed, but it can not properly be otherwise .construed.   I think the proviso was simply inserted from abundant caution, and means, and was intended to mean, no more nor less than what it plainly says, namely:

that, where allotments for larger amounts were otherwise authorized by law, it should be the duty of the President yet to carry out those provisions, regardless of the later legislation.

This is made the more plain when this proviso is placed in its proper position and construed in connection with the first section of the act of which it is a part, and the otherwise apparently absolute language of which it is intended to qualify. That language is, " That in all cases " where Indians may be located upon a reservation, whether created "by treaty stipulations," or otherwise, the President is authorized, in his discretion, after survey, to allot the lands thereof, in severalty, to said Indians in prescribed quantities. Now, the proviso comes in, qualify-ing the above language, and excepts out of "all cases" those particular cases, where by treaty or former act allotments are authorized to be made " in quantities in excess of those herein provided," and directs, in relation to them that the President shall make the allotments "in quantity as specified in such treaty or act."

Here, then, it will be observed, that this section provides first for allotments, in the discretion of the President, in all Indian reservations ; and, second, recognizes that allotments in some reservations have been provided for in previous treaties and acts of Congress ; and particularly guards the provisions of such treaty or act as to the *quantity* of the allotment therein designated. In other words, it makes general what was before special—*i. e.*, the policy of allotments to individual Indians. It does not enact new methods of allotment in cases already provided for but in cases not provided for.

It is further to be noted that this first section relates entirely to allot-ments of land ; not one word therein referring to the issue of patents or making title thereto. So, in regard to section two, which provides for the selection by the Indians of "all allotments set apart under the pro-visions of this act ; " section three also declares that " the allotments provided for in this act shall be made by special agents," etc., whilst section four authorizes the allotment of public lands to non-reservation Indians settling upon them, and directs that patents issue to them as thereinafter directed. This brings us to section five, where the ques-tion of the title is dealt with and provision made for passing the ulti-mate fee from the United States to the Indians.

This fifth section declares that upon the approval of " the allotments provided for in this act" patents shall issue therefor in the form pre-scribed. Patents are to be issued on allotments provided for in this act alone—not in this act and former acts or treaties. This section, as those preceding it, referring expressly, in unmistakable terms, to " allotments provided for in this act," must beyond question, in my opinion, exclude any contention that the act related to or made provision for any other allotments, or the issue of patents thereon. The proviso before quoted, having no more scope than to say plainly that allotments otherwise authorized were not to be interfered with.

On reflection, it will be seen there was a wise purpose on the part of Congress in thus limiting the trust character of the patents to be thereafter issued, to those allotments " provided for by *this* act; " that is, to reservations in which allotments were for the first time provided. Otherwise we would have two kinds of titles to land in the same reservations, and two kinds of patents held by members of the same tribe, under the same treaty or act of Congress, the result of which would be interminable confusion. If Congress desired to impress the trust for the fixed term of twenty-five years upon all allotments thereafter made to Indians it could easily have so declared. Not having done so, it is fair to assume that its purpose must have been to limit the trust patents to the new class of allotments provided for in that act. This view is strengthened by the language of the fourth section thereof, which declares, in relation to the non-reservation Indians, who shall have lands alloted to them out of unappropriated public lands, " patents shall be issued to them for such lands in the manner and with the restrictions as herein provided." The conclusion is irresistible, to me, that allotments theretofore provided for, by act of Congress, or treaty, shall be patented as prescribed in those acts or treaties.

I am, therefore, of the opinion, that the right of allotment being secured to these Indians under the treaty stipulation of 1854, when said allotments are made, patents thereon should be issued in accordance with the terms of said treaty, whether the selections and allotments were made or the approvals signed before or after the passage of the act of 1887; for the treaty is the source of power, all these acts are performed in pursuance of its authority, and the title when perfected relates back to that source and cuts off any intervening claim.

Very respectfully,

GEO. H. SHIELDS,
Assistant Attorney-General.

DESERT LAND ENTRY—FINAL PROOF.

HUGH CAMERON.*

The circular regulations of June 27, 1887, were not intended to have a retroactive effect; and final proof proceedings begun before said regulations were received at the local office may be properly completed under the previous regulations.

First-Assistant Secretary Chandler to the Commissioner of the General Land Office, May 20, 1889.

I have considered the appeal of Hugh Cameron from your office decision of March 19, 1888, holding for cancellation his desert land entry for W. $\frac{1}{2}$ SW. $\frac{1}{4}$, Sec. 9, and NE. $\frac{1}{4}$ SE. $\frac{1}{4}$ Sec. 8, T. 11 N., R. 21 E., Helena, Montana, land district.

---

* Omitted from Vol. 8.

It appears from the record that Cameron made desert land entry for said land and first payment thereon July 23, 1884, and that just prior to the expiration of three years he sent two witnesses to the local office to testify in his final proof before the local officers, and these witnesses arrived and made oath to proof before the register and receiver on July 22, 1887, but the local officers had, on that morning as claimed by the appellant, or about that time, as stated by themselves, received the circular of June 27, 1887 (5 L. D., 708) requiring that publication of notice be made as in homestead and pre-emption cases.

Claimant was not himself before the register and receiver having made his affidavit before an officer within the county in which the land was situated, to save the expense of going himself to the local office which was at a great distance from the land.

His final proof offered was rejected by the register and receiver because there had been no publication of notice of intention to make the same as required by said circular of June 27, 1887.

Your office in affirming the decision of the local officers, said—

I am now in receipt of your letter of December 19, 1887, stating that said entryman made proof, but not at the same time and place; that he did not advertise; that he was so notified and has taken no further action. Said entry is therefore this day held for cancellation.

The grounds of appeal are substantially, that your said decision is erroneous because his proof was made in accordance with the requirements in force at the date of his entry, and because it is provided in said circular that the same shall not be retroactive in effect, and your requirements and those of the local officers violate the said provision.

Your first ground for cancellation is the fact that entryman did not make his final proof affidavit at the same time and place as his witnesses.

While section 7, of the circular of June 27, 1887, says, "The affidavits of applicants and witnesses must in every instance, either of original application or final proof, be made at the same time and place and before the same officer," section 16, of the same circular provides that "Nothing herein will be construed to have retroactive effect in cases where the official regulations of this Department in force at the date of entry were complied with."

I find from the record that entryman made his final proof before the probate judge of Fergus county, Montana, on July 21, 1887, the day before the evidence shows the said circular to have reached the local office, and as this affidavit and the manner and place of making the same was in accordance with the official regulations of the Department then in force, it would be giving a retroactive effect to said circular to now reject his proofs for said reason.

As he commenced making his proof on July 21, 1887, by making the said affidavit, and as we have seen this was in accordance with the regulations then in force, he would have the right to complete his evidence already commenced under the regulations for the Department.

The claimant shows that his witnesses were required to travel three hundred and twenty miles in going to and returning from the local office, and that he had expended a large sum of money in paying their expenses, and it appears to me that to stop him in the middle of his proof already properly commenced, and to require him to give notice by publication and again transport his witnesses and himself the three hundred and twenty miles, for the purpose of offering the same proof, would be to give to the said circular a retroactive effect contrary to its express terms. Your said decision is accordingly reversed and if proof is otherwise sufficient patent may issue.

HOMESTEAD ENTRY—DEATH OF ENTRYMAN—PATENT.

CLARA HULS.

Where the death of the homesteader is disclosed by the record patent should issue in the name of the heirs generally.

First Assistant Secretary Chandler to the Commissioner of the General Land Office, August 31, 1889.

The homestead entry made January 24, 1879, by Florence J. Miller, for the W. ½ of the SE. ¼ Sec. 28, T. 22 S., R. 12 W., Larned, Kansas, was amended by your office letter of September 10th following, so as to embrace the N. ½ of said quarter section. On July 24, 1881, the homesteader (Miller) was married to James H. Huls. The homesteader died January 24, 1884, leaving an infant child. Her husband made final proof in May, 1885. Final certificate, dated May 8, 1885, was issued to "James H. Huls, husband of Florence J. Huls, *nee* Florence J. Miller, deceased."

By decision of March 14, 1888, your office held that the rights of the infant child, under section 2292 of the Revised Statutes, must be protected. In pursuance of the instructions contained in your said office letter, the register changed the said final certificate and inserted therein the name of the infant child, Job Wilbur Huls, instead of the name of the husband, James H. Huls.

On February 6, 1887, James H. Huls was married to Clara Ring. He died on September 25, 1887. The said Clara Huls, *nee* Ring, to whom no notice of your said decision had been sent, and who swears that she was without knowledge of the same, until August 3, 1888, filed on September 20, 1888, her appeal to the Department.

In said appeal counsel insist that your office erred in directing the said final certificate to be changed, as aforesaid, and in failing to have the same "so corrected that the patent should issue to James H. Huls and Job Wilbur Huls, as heirs of Florence J. Huls."

The homesteader had at the time of her death resided upon and cultivated the land for a period of just five years. Having complied with the homestead law, final proof in support of the entry made by her was properly and legally made, under section 2291, by her husband as one of her heirs. (Compiled laws of Kansas, 1881, Ch. 33, Secs. 8 and 28).

Section 2292 of the Revised Statutes, upon which the decision of your office is based, provides, that the right and fee to land covered by a homestead entry shall inure to the infant child of the homesteader, when both parents of such child die before final proof. Section 2292 does not, therefore, apply to the case at bar, because the entry was completed by the infant's father, before the latter's death. That the homesteader's husband, by making final proof as aforesaid, acquired upon the issue of the final certificate a vested interest in the land, as an heir of his deceased wife, is undoubtedly true. But the record shows that the said husband is dead. No patent therefore can be issued in his name, as the government will not issue its patent to a person not in existence as a matter of course.

A patent in the name of a deceased person conveys no title. Galloway v. Finley, 12 Peters, 264. Matters of inheritance should be determined in the courts, and not by the Department. No decision, therefore, is made with regard to the rights of the parties hereto.

The record showing a compliance with the law in regard to residence, cultivation, proof and payment, you will cause a patent to be issued to the heirs of the homesteader generally, without specifically naming them, i. e., to the heirs of Florence J. Huls, nee Miller, deceased, for the N. ½ of the said quarter-section.

The decision appealed from is modified accordingly.

ADDITIONAL HOMESTEAD—RAILROAD GRANT—ABANDONMENT.

NEILSON v. NORTHERN PAC. R. R. CO. ET AL.

The additional homestead entry provided for in the act of March 3, 1879, is only allowable where the applicant was legally restricted to eighty acres, and the land applied for is subject to entry.

A homestead entry covering part of a previous pre-emption claim of the entryman, is in law an abandonment of that part of said claim not embraced within the entry.

The status of land at the date of definite location determines whether it will pass under the grant.

Secretary Noble to the Commissioner of the General Land Office, September 23, 1889.

The land involved in this case is the E. ½ of NW. ¼ of Sec. 31, T. 136 N., R. 43 W., Fergus Falls district, Minnesota, and is within the ten mile granted limits of the St. Paul, Minneapolis and Manitoba Railroad, and also within the twenty mile granted limits of the Northern Pacific Railroad. The map of definite location of the former road was filed December 19, 1871, and of the latter, November 20, 1871, and said land was embraced within the withdrawal in favor of the latter on filing map of general route, August 13, 1870.

On January 11, 1871, Lars Neilson filed a pre-emption declaratory statement, embracing said E. ½ of the NW. ¼ of Sec. 31, and also lot 1 and SE. ¼ of SW. ¼ of Sec. 30, in said township and range, alleging settlement, July 28, 1870. June 26, 1871, Neilson applied to transmute his pre-emption filing to a homestead entry on all the land embraced in said filing, but the officers denied the application, on the ground, that, said E. ½ of the NW. ¼ being in an odd numbered section, was covered by the withdrawal of August 13, 1870, in favor of the Northern Pacific Railroad Company. and he thereupon, as he states, on the advice of the register, made homestead entry on the SE. ¼ of SW. ¼, and the SW. ¼ of SE. ¼ of said Sec. 30. The first of these forty acre tracts embraced in his homestead entry had formed part of the tract covered by his preemption claim, and his house was located thereon at the time he made the homestead entry and he continued his residence thereon as before. November 21, 1877, he made final proof, in support of his homestead entry, showing compliance with the homestead law, and, June 24, 1878, received a patent.

November 16, 1883, Neilson made the application now under consideration to enter said E. ½ of N.W. ¼ of Sec. 31, as an additional homestead under the act of March 3, 1879 (20 Stat., 472). With this application he filed an affidavit, which sets forth, in substance, that at the time he made his homestead entry (June 26, 1871), he applied to make entry of one hundred and sixty acres, including said E. ½ of NW. ¼ of Sec. 31, which had been embraced in his prior pre-emption filing, but the register refused to allow him to enter any part of said section 31, on the ground that it "belonged to the railroad company;" that he "was unjustly restricted to eighty acres by said register, and could prove that his prior settlement on lot 1 and E. ½ of NW. ¼ of Sec. 31 and SE. ¼ of SW. ¼ of Sec. 30" (the land embraced in his pre-emption filing) "exempted said tract in section 31 from the grant to the railroad company." The local officers· ordered a hearing, which was had, January 17, 1884, and on which it was shown that Neilson settled on the tract covered by his pre-emption claim July 28, 1870, as alleged in his declaratory statement (his dwelling being on the SE. ¼ of SW. ¼ of Sec. 30, which he retained under his homestead entry), and the facts relating to his preemption claim and subsequent homestead application and entry, as hereinbefore set forth and as stated in his affidavit, were established.

The local officers rejected the application of Neilson to enter said tract as an additional homestead, holding: ·

The land applied for is within the granted limits of the St. Paul, Minneapolis and Manitoba Railway Company, whose right attached December 9, 1871 (date of definite location), at which time there was no valid adverse claim to the land, as Neilson abandoned his claim under his filing (pre-emption) by filing a homestead, which he afterwards occupied and proved up in compliance with law.

The act of March 3, 1879, under which Neilson's application is made, provides, that, "any person who had, under existing laws, taken a homestead on any even section within the limits of any railroad . . . . land grant, and who by existing laws shall have been restricted to eighty acres, may enter under the homestead laws an additional eighty acres adjoining the land embraced in his original entry, if such additional land be subject to entry."

There are two objections to the allowance of Neilson's application under said act. First, the act only applies to cases of parties who have been *legally* ("by existing laws") restricted to eighty acres. Neilson alleges that he was "unjustly" so restricted, and in view of the fact, that his settlement on his pre emption claim was shown to have been made July 28, 1870, before the withdrawal (of August 13, 1870,) had been made, this allegation would seem to be true. By section 2281 of the Revised Statutes (act of March 27, 1854, 10 Stat., 269), it is provided that:

All settlers on public lands which have been or may be withdrawn from market in consequence of proposed railroads, and who had settled thereon prior to such withdrawal, shall be entitled to pre-emption at the ordinary minimum to the lands settled on and cultivated by them.

Under this statute, Neilson's pre-emption filing was valid for the one hundred and sixty acres covered by it and on applying to transmute said filing into a homestead entry, he was entitled to enter the land covered by his filing, and was therefore unlawfully restricted to eighty acres.

In the second place, it is essential under the act of March 3, 1879, that the land applied for shall be "subject to entry." If, as found by the local office, Neilson abandoned his pre-emption claim to the land, June 26, 1871, when he made his homestead entry on another tract, and said pre-emption claim ceased to exist by reason of said abandonment, then the land became subject to the railroad grants which subsequently attached on the filing of the maps of definite location, and said grants having so attached, the land would not be "subject to entry." The question then, on this branch of the case, is, whether the claim of Neilson had been abandoned prior to the filing of the maps of definite location, or was at the dates of the filing of said maps a subsisting claim, such as would except the land from the grant. The cases of Ramage *v.* Central Pacific R. R. Co. (5 L. D., 274) and Kansas Pacific Ry. Co. *v.* Dunmeyer (113 U. S., 629), cited in your office decision, hold, that, where a claim is subsisting at the date when the railroad's rights attach under its grant, the subsequent abandonment of the claim does not inure to the benefit of the company or cause the grant to attach to the land which had been covered by the claim. It is nowhere held, that a claim abandoned and ceasing to exist before the grant attaches would except land from the grant. The rights of the road are determined by the status of the land at the point of time when the grant attaches.

I am of the opinion, that Neilson in fact as well as in law abandoned his claim to the land in section 31 at the time (June 26, 1871,) he made his homestead entry.

While, in making homestead entry on the SE. ¼ of SW. ¼ (which had been part of his pre-emption claim on which his dwelling was located) and the SW. ¼ of SE. ¼ of Sec. " 30," Neilson, as he claims, acted upon the advice of the register and apparently acquiesced in the action of that officer in restricting him to eighty acres and the even numbered sections, he yet testified that he continued to claim and use said E. ½ of NW. ¼ of Sec. 31, " ever since he took his homestead," and, in your office decision it is found, that " he has fenced and cultivated the E. ½ of NW. ¼ of Sec. 31 all the time from date of settlement (July 28, 1870), and has never given up his claim to said tract. On cross-examination, however, Neilson testified, not that he had fenced and cultivated the entire eighty acres, as might be inferred from the above quotation from your office decision, but, as follows: " The fence extended about two or three rods on to Sec. 31. I did not know where the lines [between sections 30 and 31] were when I did the breaking. The breaking I have on Sec. 31 was done in 1877, 1878, and 1882, on the NE. ¼ of NW. ¼—I have never done any breaking on the SE. ¼ of NW. ¼." It thus appears, that Neilson's fence extended only from thirty-three to forty-nine and a half feet on to section 31, and, from his statement in that connection, that he did not know where the line between sections 30 and 31 ran, it might be inferred, that his fencing was extended by mistake on to section 31. Said fencing and his breaking were confined to the NE. ¼ of NW. ¼ of said section 31, and he had done nothing on the SE. ¼ of NW. ¼ thereof. As to this last named forty, it is admitted that one Louis Johnson has between twenty and twenty-five acres of breaking and eighty rods of fencing thereon " worth at least $120.00," and the testimony shows, that Johnson commenced breaking and improving said forty acre tract in 1877 and had continued to crop and improve it every year since. No objection to Johnson's claim or improvement of this tract is shown on the part of Neilson ; on the contrary, the weight of the testimony tends to show, that he recognized the title of the railroad company to the land and Johnson's right to acquire it from the company. On this point Johnson testified, in answer to the question, whether he had any conversation with Neilson in 1877 about his (Johnson's) taking said forty,

Yes, I had. I was counselling with Neilson at that time about that land as I lived with him. I asked him, if anybody had written to the company about it, and he told me he thought not, but that he, Neilson, wanted the NE. ¼ of NW. ¼, as it would be handy for him to get to the lake, but he, Neilson (thought) "the balance of the land was clear."

He further testified, that Neilson promised to write for him (Johnson) to the railroad company "for the land ;" that he commenced to improve it in 1877 and had " cropped and improved" it every year since;

that Neilson knew of his improving the tract and never objected, and that he (Johnson) would not "have taken the land and put the improvements on it," if Neilson had told him he claimed it.

Neilson on being asked on cross-examination, whether before Johnson improved said forty acre tract, he (Johnson) had any conversation with him (Neilson) about Neilson's claim thereto and Johnson's taking it, answered, "I can not recollect;" and, being called on to state, whether he wrote the letter to the railroad company, "making application for the forty" for Johnson, said, "I do not recollect and will not say."

The fact that the testimony of Johnson is positive, and that of Neilson, negative, taken in connection with Johnson's improvement and cultivation of the land every year since 1877, without protest or objection on the part of Neilson, tends strongly, if not conclusively, to show that Neilson (in 1877, when the conversation is alleged to have occurred and Johnson's improvements began) recognized the claim of the company to at least forty acres of the tract, the whole of which he testified he had claimed "ever since his homestead entry."

It is clear, that the making homestead entry of another tract was an abandonment in law of his claim to that part of the tract covered by his pre-emption filing which was not embraced in his homestead entry. The initiation and consummation of the homestead entry was necessarily under the law, during the period of such consummation, a relinquishment of the pre-emption claim. Moreover, when a pre-emption filing is transmuted into a homestead entry, the former is merged in the latter and ceases to have an independent existence, even though (as in this case) the homestead entry embraces only a part of the land covered by the filing—as the filing can not be transmuted as to part of the land embraced in it and remain intact as to the remainder. While the action of the local office in restricting his entry to eighty acres and to the even section, appears to have been erroneous, he did not appeal therefrom, but, thereby acquiescing therein, made and perfected his homestead entry, and has never since asserted any rights under his pre-emption filing, to the land in dispute; but at the expiration of more than twelve years from the initiation of his homestead entry and about six years after he had perfected that entry, he makes application under the act of March 3, 1879. His conduct from the time of making his homestead entry to his present application is inconsistent with the idea, that after said entry he continued to assert a claim to the land; but, admitting that he did, such claim, if not positively unlawful, would at least have been without any legal basis to rest upon. (Nix v. Allen, 112 U. S., 129.)

Neilson's claim having, in my opinion, ceased to exist, both in fact and in law, some months *prior* to the filing of the maps of definite location, the land became subject to the grants and the rights of the companies thereunder attached when the said maps were filed. The land was not, therefore, " subject to entry " at the date of Neilson's applica-tion, and said application, if otherwise unobjectionable, was, for that reason, properly denied by the local officers.

Your office decision is reversed.

PATENT: RAILROAD GRANT—ACT OF APRIL 21, 1876.

OFFUTT v. NORTHERN PAC. R. R. Co.

Title is not passed by an instrument in the form of, and purporting to be a patent, where such instrument is neither sealed nor delivered.

A private cash entry of land within the primary limits of a grant, made after the map of general route was filed, but before notice thereof was received at the local office is not protected by the act of April 21, 1876, if the entryman was not an actual settler on the land.

Secretary Noble to the Commissioner of the General Land Office, September 24, 1889.

On January 18, 1888, your office held for cancellation the private cash entry of James W. Offutt, now deceased, for the SE. $\frac{1}{4}$ of SE. $\frac{1}{4}$, Sec. 33, T. 17 N., R. 1 W., Olympia land district, Washington, on the ground that said entry is in conflict with the grant to the Northern Pacific Railroad Company.

March 8, 1888, Milford Offutt, who it appears is a brother of said decedent, appealed from said decision, and service of copy of appeal is acknowledged by the attorney of said company.

The described tract of land is within the granted limits of said com-pany's grant, as shown by its map of general route and definite loca-tion of the line of its road opposite said tract.

The company's said map of general route was filed August 13, 1870, and notice of the same was received at the local land office October 19th following. Between these two dates, to wit, on September 8, 1870, Offutt purchased said tract, paying therefor the sum of fifty dollars, and received from the register of the local land-office a certificate which *prima facie* entitled him to a patent for said tract.

You transmitted with the record herein an instrument in the form of a land-patent, dated May 2, 1872, purporting to grant the title of the United States in and to the described tract of land to James W. Offutt. This instrument, however, has never been sealed or delivered, and therefore did not in fact pass the title of the United States in and to said land. McGarrahan v. Mining Company, 96 U. S., 316; Section 459 Revised Statutes.

Your office correctly held herein that " a statutory withdrawal fol-lowed the filing of the map of general route" (August 13, 1870), and that the tract in controversy "was not subject to private cash entry on September 8, 1870," the date of Offutt's said entry, unless made by an actual settler on the land.   Appellant, as appears from your said office decision, was advised November 22, 1887, "that all entries made in good faith by actual settlers prior to the time notice of the withdrawal was received at the local office were confirmed by the act of April 21, 1876" (19 Stat., 35), and "that if his brother was an actual settler upon said tract, that upon receipt of proof thereof his entry would be passed to patent. December 10, 1887, he replied that such proof can not be made."

In his appeal said Milford Offutt makes the following statement, to-wit:

My brother, the entryman, had constructed upon said tract a cabin, which he let to others as tenants of himself, and the latter, as said tenants, made improvements upon the tract by sowing a part of the soil in hay, and I further desire to state that I deem the entry and the letting by my brother to have been in both cases intended in good faith, and that it was his intention to retain the said tract to his own use.

The facts as stated—presumably as strong as they could be made to appear in proof—do not show that said entryman, James W. Offutt, was, during his lifetime, an actual settler on said tract of land, or bring said entry within the provisions of the act of April 21, 1876.

The decision of your office holding said entry for cancellation is there-fore affirmed.

SCHOOL LAND—MINERAL LAND.

ABRAHAM L. MINER.

The title of the State under the school grant vests, if at all, at the date of survey ; and if the land is in fact mineral, though not then known to be such, the sub-sequent discovery of its mineral character will not devest the title which has already passed.

If a settler on school land prior to survey abandons his claim thereto, a third party can not set up the fact of such settlement to defeat the title of the State.

The case of the "State of Colorado," 7 L. D., 490, overruled.

Secretary Noble to the Commissioner of the General Land Office, September 25, 1889.

September 6, 1887, Abraham L. Miner made application under the homestead law, to enter the NE. ¼ of Sec. 16, T. 16 N., R. 5 E., Mount Diablo meridian, Marysville district, California, and said application was on the same day rejected by the register of said district, on the ground "that the tract applied for was granted to the State of California for school purposes under the act of March 3, 1853." (10 Stat., 244).

On appeal, your office, by decision of February 29, 1888, rejected said application, "for the reason that the records of this (your) office show the land to be mineral land," and said office decision concluded, as fol-lows: " Should an application be made for a hearing to determine as to the character of the land at the date of survey, or at the present time, or both, the matter would be considered."

It is to be observed at the outset, that the proper inquiry in such cases is, not what was the character of the land at date of survey or any particular time, or what it now is, (as seems to be the idea intended to be conveyed in the above quotations from your office decision), but was the land *known* to be mineral at the date when, but for that fact, or the intervention of a valid settlement claim, or other legal bar, the State's title would have vested under the act of 1853. The State's title vests, if at all, at the date of the "completion of the survey," (Cooper *v.* Roberts, 18 How., 173; Virginia Lode, 7 L. D., 459); and, if the land, although in reality mineral, was not then *known* to be mineral, the subsequent discovery of its mineral character would not devest the title which had already passed. State of California *v.* Poley and Thomas, 4 C. L. O., 18; Virginia Lode, 7 L. D., 459; J. Dartt, 5 C. L. O., 178; Townsite of Silver Cliff *v.* Colorado, 6 C. L. O., 152; State of Colorado, 6 L. D., 412; Mining Co. *v.* Consolidated Mining Co., 102 U. S., 175.)

In the case of the State of California *v.* Poley and Thomas, *supra*, this question is considered at some length by Secretary Schurz, and it is held: first, that under the grant by the act of March 3, 1853 (10 Stat., 244), of sections sixteen and thirty-six to California for school purposes, the title to said sections vests in the State upon survey thereof, if their mineral character was unknown at that date; and, second, that having so vested, it is not subject to be devested by the subsequent discovery of the mineral character of the land.

As to said first proposition, Secretary Schurz says, " In compliance with the established doctrine of the courts, it must, I think, be held, that the title vested in the State at the date of survey, when the land was not known to be mineral, or was not treated as such by the government."

The last clause of this quotation, "or was not treated as such by the government," refers to the proviso of section three of said act of 1853, which prohibits the subdivisional survey of mineral land—it being held that by surveying sections sixteen and thirty-six, in the face of said statutory prohibition, the government treats them as non-mineral and subject to the grant. The doctrine, that the " title vests in the State at the date of survey " is properly characterized as " the doctrine established by the courts," and the case of Cooper *v.* Roberts (18 How., 173) is cited, in which the reason of the rule is clearly stated by Justice Campbell; as follows:

Until the survey of the township and the designation of the specific section, the rights of the State rest in compact—binding, it is true, the public faith, and dependent for execution upon the political authorities. Courts of justice have no authority to mark out and define the land which shall be subject to the grant. But when the political authorities have performed this duty, the compact has an object, upon which it can attach.

The act itself contemplates, that the State's title shall attach at the date of survey, as the only express reservations contained in the act of sections sixteen and thirty-six from the operation of the grant are those made by section seven as to settlements on said sections, or where the same " may be reserved for public uses or taken by private claims," and these reservations are limited to such settlements, reservations or private claims as are made prior to the survey.

Having arrived at the conclusion, that the title of the State vested or attached " at the date of survey, when the land was not then known to be mineral," Secretary Schurz next discusses the question (involved in said second proposition), whether having so vested, it can be affected or changed by the subsequent discovery of the mineral character of the land, using the following language:

If, following the doctrine of the courts, the grant of school lands takes effect at the date of survey, can the character of the land, subsequently determined, change or affect said title ? If it can, for how long a period can such change be affected ? If for three years, why not for ten or fifty, or after the title derived from the State has been transmitted through numerous grantees ? For lands confessedly non-mineral at the date of survey, may, many years thereafter, be ascertained, through the improvements in mining operations, to be valuable as mineral lands. To maintain such a doctrine, might result in placing in jeopardy, the title held by grantees to all the school lands in California, and could only be authorized by the most positive and clearly expressed provisions of law. In my opinion there is nothing in the act which can thus be interpreted.

This doctrine is re-affirmed in the other departmental decisions cited *supra*, and seems to be recognized by the supreme court of the United States in the case of Mining Company *v.* Consolidated Mining Company (102 U. S., 175). In that case the plaintiff asserted title to the land in controversy under a patent from the State of California, and the defendant under patent from the United States. The title conveyed by the State of California to the plaintiff rested on the grant of school lands under the act of 1853, and that of defendant on the acts of Congress concerning the possession and sale of mineral lands. The court, after calling attention to the fact, that three several mining claims had been located on said land respectively, in 1851, 1853 and 1863, and " that the original locators of said claims and their grantees had held undisturbed possession thereof ever since" and had worked the same, and, consequently, that the mineral character of said lands was established and well known long before and at the time of the survey, which was approved September 3, 1870, proceeds to state the question involved in the case, as follows:

The question, and the only question, presented for our consideration is very sharply presented by this statement of facts and the acts of Congress pertinent to the subject; and it is, whether under these acts the title of the land in question became fixed and vested absolutely in the State of California, on the ascertainment by the survey of 1870, that it was part of the thirty-sixth section of the township in which it lies.

The court then, after considering the provisions of the act of 1853 pertinent to the question, and the history of the legislation of Congress in reference to mineral lands in general, holds, that although there is no express exception of mineral lands from the operation of the grant of sections sixteen and thirty-six to California for school purposes by the act of 1853, yet "Congress did not intend to depart from its uniform policy in this respect—in the grant of those sections to the State," and consequently that mineral lands were excluded from the grant; and, having so found, decides, in answer to the question above stated, "that the land in controversy being mineral land, and well known to be so when the surveys of it were made, did not pass to the State under the school section grant."

In this case it is to be observed, that the date of survey is made the point of time at which the title either does or does not vest in the State; and, attention having been first called to the facts showing that the mineral character of the land was established and well known before and at the time of the survey, it is then held, that in consequence thereof, the title to the land "did not pass to the State under the school section grant." If this conclusion be correct, the converse of the proposition would seem to follow, namely, that the mineral character of the land not being established and known at the date of survey, the title would pass. ·

The title having once passed to the State, the land is from that time subject to disposal by the State, and to allow the title to be devested by the subsequent discovery of the mineral character of the land, would not only, as shown by Secretary Schurz in the quotation above, work great hardship and injustice to the State's grantees and render insecure titles to school lands in said State, but would also be contrary to the settled policy of the government in this particular. By section 2258 of the Revised Statutes (act of 1841, 5 Stat., 455—Sec. 10), it is provided, that "Lands on which are situated any *known* salines or mines" shall not be subject to pre-emption, and the supreme court of the United States, in commenting on this statute, say :

A change in the conditions occurring subsequently to the sale (pre-emption cash) whereby new discoveries are made, or by means whereof it may become profitable to work the veins or mines, can not affect the title as it passed at the time of the sale. The question must be determined according to the facts in existence at the time of the sale. Colorado Coal Company *v.* United States (123 U. S., 328).

This rule is general and applies to all modes of acquiring title to public lands. In Deffeback *v.* Hawke (115 U. S., 404), the court say :

It is plain from . . . . . the legislation of Congress, that no title from the United States to land known at the time of sale to be valuable for its minerals . . . . . can be obtained under the pre-emption or homestead laws or townsite laws, or in any other way than as prescribed by the laws specially authorizing the sale of such lands . . . . . We say lands *known* at the *time of their sale* to be thus valuable, in order to avoid any possible conclusion against the validity of titles which may be issued for other kinds of land, in which, years afterwards, rich deposits of minerals may be discovered. It is quite possible that lands settled upon as suitable only for agricultural purposes, entered by the settler and patented by the government under the pre-emption laws, may be found, years after patent has been issued, to contain valuable minerals. Indeed, this has often happened. We, therefore, use the term *known* to be valuable for mineral *at the time of the sale,* to prevent any doubt being cast upon titles to land afterwards found to be mineral in their character from what was supposed when the entry of them was made and the patent issued.

In this quotation the doctrine is reiterated and made as emphatic as possible, that the title to mineral land passes unless it is known to be mineral at the date of "*sale*;" and while the word patent occurs, it seems to be used as synonymous in that connection with the word " sale," as it is immediately afterwards held, that although the patent in that case did not issue until January 31, 1882, yet when issued, "it related back to the inception of the right of the patentee" and that " the right of the government passed to him" January 31, 1878 (four years before patent), when he entered the land " by paying the government price therefor." This doctrine of operation of a patent by relation is illustrated in the case of the Pacific Coast Mining and Milling Company *v.* Fick *et al.* (8 Sawyer, 645). In that case, the grantor of the plaintiff entered the land, paid for it, and received his certificate of purchase on December 19, 1874; the mining location of defendants was made, August 14, 1875, and patent was not issued upon the certificate of purchase of the plaintiff's grantor until September 6, 1876, more than a year after the mining location of defendant. But the court says,

This can make no difference in the rights of the parties . . . . . When patent finally issues it attaches itself to the entry and relates to the date of the entry . . . . . The entry and patent are regarded as one title. The title of the plaintiff dates from the date of entry and payment, and not from the date of the patent.

As the title vests at the *date of sale* in pre-emption and private cash entries, and, according to the "established doctrine of the courts," the title of the State vests in school lands at *date of survey*, the principle announced in the foregoing cases is applicable to the case under consideration and those cases are authority for the proposition, that the discovery of the mineral character of school lands after the title has passed to the State on survey thereof will not affect or devest that title. The reasons for the application of the rule to school land grant cases stated by Secretary Schurz, in State of California *v.* Poley and Thomas, *supra,* are as cogent as (and similar to) those laid down by the supreme court of the United States in cases of acquisition of title to public lands by pre-emption, cash entry or otherwise. The decisive question in all these cases is, has the title vested? If it has, not only the policy of the government as indicated by Congressional legislation, but also the wholesome spirit pervading the common law in favor of the quieting of titles, steps in and forbids the setting aside of such title, because of facts subsequently developed and which were unknown when the title passed. It is better, that the lesser evil of lands in fact mineral being acquired in a mode different from that prescribed by law for the acquisition of lands known to be mineral, should be submitted to, than that the title to the State should in cases of subsequent discovery of mineral be devested, thus unsettling all titles to school lands, both to and from the State, lessening the value of such lands in the hands of the State and its grantees in all cases and in some cases depriving innocent purchasers entirely of their vested rights.

There is one decision of this Department, however (State of Colorado, 7 L. D., 490), in conflict with the position herein taken. In that case it is said,

The grant of school lands to the State of Colorado expressly excepts therefrom all mineral lands, and in lieu of such lands, the State is entitled to select other lands as indemnity therefor. The survey of the public lands causes the grant to attach to the sixteenth and thirty-sixth sections of such lands only as were contemplated by the grant, but it does not fix the title of the State to any mineral lands, because such lands are expressly excepted from the operation of the grant, and if the mineral character of the land *is known prior to certification*, other land in lieu of said sixteenth and thirty-sixth sections should be certified to the State.

This, it is manifest, establishes a very uncertain rule. Under it, the State's title attaches to non-mineral lands at the date of survey; to lands in fact mineral, but not known to be such until after certification, it attaches at date of certification; and, if the mineral character of such land be discovered subsequent to the survey and before certification, it does not attach at all. As at the date of the survey, lands *in fact nonmineral* and those *not then known to be mineral*, are apparently equally subject to the grant, and as to mineral character are not then distinguishable, the title under this rule must necessarily remain unsettled for a length of time after survey to the former class of lands held to be subject to the grant, as well as to those held not to be so subject. The evils and injustice resulting from a rule so uncertain in its operation, will be appreciated, when it is considered, that, as is the case in reference to issuance of patents in ordinary cases, certification of school lands may not be made, and generally is not, for years after survey. Uniformity and certainty are essential elements of any just rule of law or system of laws. The necessity for a uniform and certain rule as to the vesting of title under school land grants, is too manifest for argument. The rule laid down by Secretary Schurz in State of California *v.* Poley and Thomas, *supra*, and uniformly maintained by the decisions of the Department until said case of State of Colorado, *supra*, possesses the requisites of uniformity and certainty.

Certification occupies the same relation to school land grants as patent does to ordinary cases of acquisition of title to public lands, and as the latter (as is well settled) relates to the date of sale or entry and becomes operative from that date, so the former should when made relate to and take effect as of the date of the survey. In the case of Samuel W. Spong (5 L. D., 193), the statutory exception of mineral lands from the grant to the Central Pacific Railroad Company is construed to include only lands "*known* to contain valuable minerals prior to the issuance of the patent, and that subsequent discoveries would not affect the title of the company to the lands and mines subsequently discovered." It might at first glance appear, that the use of the words "known to contain valuable minerals prior to issuance of patent was intended to fix the date of the patent and not the date when the company's title attached under the grant, as the point of time when knowledge of the mineral character of the land would prevent the vesting of the title. This will be readily seen, however, not to have been intended, as that case turned upon the clause in the company's patent excluding mineral lands, should any such be subsequently found to exist in the tracts described in the patent, and this Department, after citing a number of decisions of the supreme court of the United States, to the effect that the issue of said patent was a determination by the proper tribunal that the lands covered by it were granted to the company and that the Land Department had no authority to insert such a clause in the patent, held that therefore, notwithstanding said clause in the patent, the subsequent discoveries of minerals would not affect the title of the company. The holding that the discovery of mineral after issue of patent would not affect the title, does not conflict with the doctrine laid down in the present case. If such discovery at any time after survey in case of school land grants or after the company's title attached under a railroad land grant, would not affect the title, a fortiori it would not after patent. This is true of all the cases in which the words "known to be valuable for mineral prior to patent" (or of similar import), are used, and in none of these cases is it held or intimated, that the discovery of the mineral character of the land after the title has vested by survey or otherwise (as the case may be), and before patent, would devest the title which had passed prior to such discovery. This precise question was not involved in said cases.

In said case of State of Colorado, it is said, "The survey of the public lands causes the grant to attach . . . . . to such lands only as were contemplated by the grant," and it is held that lands in fact mineral, though not known or discovered to be such at date of survey, were not "contemplated by the grant."

The better and safer conclusion is, in my opinion, arrived at in the case of Samuel W. Spong, *supra*, namely, that,

While the exception of mineral lands from the grant to the company is clear and explicit, yet it does not appear from a careful consideration of the language of said grant that Congress intended to grant only such lands which may after the lapse of an indefinite number of years prove to be agricultural in character.

In the present case, the fact, that the act of 1853 granting school lands to California, prohibits the survey of mineral lands, tends strongly to show that Congress "contemplated," that the grant should attach to all the sixteenth and thirty-sixth sections which were in fact surveyed and were not then known to be mineral, and the consequences hereinbefore referred to of adopting a different construction, lend great weight to this view.

It is to be noted that in all the cases (including said case of State of Colorado), the test as to whether the grant finally attaches is not the character in fact of the land, but knowledge of that character at some particular point of time. From the statement in "State of Colorado," that "if the mineral character of the land is known prior to certification," lieu land should be certified to the State, the necessary inference is that the date of certification is selected in that case as that point of time; in all the other decisions of this Department, the date of survey is selected. I am of the opinion that the great weight of reason and authority sustain the latter position.

Said case of State of Colorado practically overrules the prior departmental decisions on the question, extending through a long series of years, without reference to said decisions, and without citing any authority, or giving any valid reason for the new rule announced therein, and being in conflict with the view herein expressed, is overruled.

As stated at the outset of this opinion, your office rejected Miner's application "for the reason that the records of this" (your) "office show the land to be mineral," it is also previously stated in said decision, that "it does not appear, whether the land was known to be valuable for the mineral it contained prior to or at the date of the survey of the township in 1867." This being the case, it is impossible to determine from the record, so far as the question is affected by the character of the land, whether or not the land passed to the State for school purposes under the grant of the sixteenth and thirty-sixth sections by the act of March 3, 1853.

By section seven of said act, it is provided,

That where any settlement, by the erection of a dwelling house, or the cultivation of any portion of the land, shall be made on the sixteenth and thirty-sixth sections, before the same shall be surveyed . . . . . . other land shall be selected by the proper authorities of the State, in lieu thereof.

It is contended by Miner, "That by reason of the prior admitted settlement and entry of one Benj. Selling on said tract," the said tract, (irrespective of its character as mineral or non-mineral land) "did not pass to the State of California, under the grant . . . . . for school purposes by the act of March 3, 1853, but was excepted therefrom" under said section seven of said act, and that, therefore the question is between Miner and the government. It appears, however, that Selling abandoned his claim to hold the land by virtue of settlement and improvement as against the State and has acknowledged the State's title by purchase from the State and receiving the State's patent. Miner does not claim under or in any way connect himself with Selling's alleged claim by settlement, but seeks by means of it to defeat the title of the State, and thus leave the land (if not known to be mineral) in a condition to be subject to his entry under the homestead law. Selling, "however, was under no obligation to assert his claim" as against the State, and having abandoned it, a third party can not set it up, and "the title of the State became absolute" as of the date of the completion of the survey in 1867, unless as above shown, the land was known to be mineral at or prior to said date. (Water Mining Company *v.* Bugbey, 96 U. S., 167). The title of the State not being intercepted by any settlement claim under section seven of the act prior to the completion of the survey, the "question" is one between the government, on the one side, and the State of California or those claiming under the State, on the other, and the decision of said question depends on the determination of the fact, whether or not the land was known to be mineral at or before the completion of the survey. If it was not so known to be mineral the title passed to the State, but, if it was so known, the title remained in the government, subject to be devested by entry under the mineral laws. In the former event, the title to the land having passed to the State, it is not subject to Miner's application to enter under the homestead laws of the United States, and, in the latter event, being known to be mineral, it can not be appropriated by such entry. The decision of your office, denying said application, is therefore affirmed.

Should a hearing at any time be ordered in behalf of the government or on the application of those claiming under the State, as to the character of the land, the investigation on such hearing will be directed to ascertaining, 1st, the character of the land, as mineral or non-mineral, and, 2d, if mineral, whether it was known to be such at or before the completion of the survey.

———

RAILROAD GRANT—FINAL PROOF PROCEEDINGS.

RANDOLPH *v.* NORTHERN PAC. R. R. CO.

By the failure of a railroad company to respond to notice of intention to submit final proof it waives all right to deny facts set up in said proof; but if the record shows that the land passed under the grant the award should be in favor of the company notwithstanding its default.

Secretary Noble to the Commissioner of the General Land Office, September 26, 1889.

I have before me the appeal of the Northern Pacific Railroad Company from your decision of May 13, 1887, holding for confirmation Joshua A. Randolph's pre emption cash entry, made December 31, 1886, for the NE. ¼ SW. ¼, NW. ¼ SE. ¼ and lots 3 and 4, section 25, town 43 N., range 6 W., Boise meridian, Lewiston district, Idaho.

The tract in question falls within the primary limits of the grant to the Northern Pacific Railroad Company, for the benefit of which a withdrawal was ordered by your office letter of November 29, 1880, acknowledged by the local office December 15, 1880.

The map of general route, opposite this tract, was filed February 21, 1872 (the map of 1870 never having been accepted for Idaho). The statutory requirements as to the completion of the road (Sec. 8, act of July 2, 1864, 13 Stat., 370; joint resolution May 7, 1866, 14 Stat., 355; joint

resolution, July 1, 1868, 15 Stat., 255) were construed by the departmental decision of June 11, 1879, (Public Domain, p. 877) as providing
that the entire road must be completed by July 4, 1879. The portion
opposite the land in question was not declared completed until November 26, 1881, when it was accepted by the President.

Your letter states that "The records show that Randolph made declaratory statement, No. 3092, for the land in question June 2, 1886,
alleging settlement September 25, 1884;" but that "no other entry or
filing appears to have been made therefor (except the entry now under
consideration) nor does it appear that the same has been selected"—*i. e.*,
listed—"by the railroad company."

You further find that—

Mr. Randolph's final proof was made after due posting and publication of notice,
and shows full compliance with the requirements of the law; and that "no appearance was made in behalf of the railroad company to contest the claim of Randolph,
in response to the published and posted notice of his intention to make final proof,
although said railroad company was specially cited to appear." And thereupon you
hold that by such failure said company waived whatever claim it might otherwise
have asserted in the premises, and is barred from objecting to subsequent action
on the entry by (your) office (Forrester, 1 L. D., 475; St. Paul M. & M. R'y. Co., *v.*
Cowles, 3 L. D., 226; Nor. Pac. R. R. Co. *v.* Buckman, 3 L. D., 276).

There can be no question that the company, by failing to appear in
answer to Randolph's notice, waived all right to deny the facts set up
by Randolph's proof, or to protest against the legal implication of the
record upon which the local office acted, and of which record, of course,
the final proof in question formed a part. Not having appeared to oppose, the company, like any other regularly cited and defaulting party
to a legal proceeding, must unquestionably stand upon the case as
made. But—surely—not upon any other case than that which the
whole record makes; and if that case is one upon which the company
has in law the better right, the judgment should go accordingly, notwithstanding the "default." *Ex facto jus oritur.* Failure to appear
is not a contempt of court, to be punished arbitrarily by forfeiture of
rights which even the record made by the other side shows to exist: it
simply commits the defaulting party to that record, even when in some
(or all) particulars it is one which it (the absent party) might, on the
hearing, have corrected. This view is in no wise inconsistent with the
authorities which you cite, it being the fact in every one of them that
the "case made" at least included an affirmative impeachment of the
company's right.

In the "Forrester" case, for instance (1 L. D., 475), the Secretary's
ruling upon this point was expressed as follows:

I do not think it necessary to discuss the question of practice raised by counsel for
the railroad company, inasmuch as Forrester's final proof shows that he settled upon
the tract subsequently to the date of the definite location of the company's road, but
prior to withdrawal therefor, and has in good faith complied with the legal requirements. His entry undoubtedly is confirmed by the first section of the act of April
21, 1876.

In the case of "Cowles" (3 L. D., 226), the "case made" showed the following facts :

The tract in question is within the twenty-mile (indemnity) limits of said railway, withdrawal for the benefit of which became effective February 15, 1872. One Antonio Dijarley filed declaratory statement covering the tract in question, July 23, 1872, alleging settlement April 15, 1870. On July 9, 1877, said Cowles made homestead entry of the land, and due time applied to make final proof.

In the case of "Buckman" (3 L. D., 276), the decision was, that "as Buckman's proof showed settlement after the company's right had attached, but prior to the receipt of the notice of withdrawal at the local office his entry is confirmed by the first section of the act of April 21, 1876 (19 Stat., 35)."

In other cases, not cited by you, the same thing holds good. Thus, in the Gilbert decision (1 L. D., 466), it is set forth that—

The record shows that Gilbert appeared at the hearing had February 10, 1879, and introduced testimony establishing the validity of John I. Brown's pre-emption claim to the land in question, upon which he resided "until the summer of 1870," which uncontroverted proof rendered it competent for the department to regard Brown's claim as valid on April 15, 1870, the date on which the withdrawal became effective.

In the case of Mathew Sturm (5 L. D., 295), one portion of the opinion seems on its face to ignore the distinction here asserted, and to assume that a default at the final proof must of itself be held to destroy even those rights of the company which the record as a whole shows to belong to it. But, in the first place, the intimation to this effect seems to have been little more than a dictum, it having been made with reference to a tract not then "in question" before the Department, the appeal under consideration being Sturm's and not the company's, and the only formal decision made being an affirmance of the Commissioner's decision in favor of the company; secondly, the intimation in question is made to rest upon the authority of the Forrester case (*supra*), which case I have already shown not to be authority for such a view.

In the more recent case of Brady, on review (5 L. D., 658), the decision went upon the ground that the company, not having "selected" the indemnity land there in question, had "no vested right" thereto, and that therefore the executive withdrawal which formed the only obstacle to Brady's claim might "be revoked at any time and the lands restored to entry at the will of the same official that made it :"

If it is within the power of the Department to revoke the withdrawal as to all the lands, it surely has the power to revoke the withdrawal of a part of said lands, and the decisions of the Department that have crystallized into a general rule may become as effective for that purpose as the order of the Secretary directly withdrawing all the land.

In the case of Vasquez *v.* Richardson (3 L. D., 247), Richardson, after duly published notice, offered proof and payment. Vasquez did not appear at the hearing, but subsequently protested and asked for a re-hearing. This the Department held he could not have ; but it did not hold that in deciding the case upon the proof offered by Richardson, the local officers were at liberty to deny to Vasquez any rights which that proof itself showed him to possess.

In the case of Northern Pacific *v.* Dow (8 L. D., 389), the evidence adduced at the hearing shows that Huss—the original pre-emptor—settled upon the land in the fall of 1870, while the railroad's line was definitely located November 21, 1871. "Upon this testimony and the homestead proof made"—and not simply because the company made no appearance at the hearing—"the local officers rendered an opinion in favor of Dow."

In the present case the record shows nothing whatever tending to except the particular tract involved from the grant to the company, which geographically included it. It was neither proved nor alleged that either Randolph himself or anybody else, had any claim or settlement to or upon the land at the date of definite location (or even between that date and the "receipt of notice of withdrawal at the local office.)" On the contrary, as you expressly find, Randolph's first settlement upon the land took place September 25, 1884, long after the definite location, and "no entry or filing appears to have been made," other than Randolph's own filing of June 2, 1886, and his cash entry founded thereon.

Upon such a record there could be no question that the company's right attached to the tract in question at the date of definite location, and the absence of the company from the hearing of Randolph's final proof in no way alters the case made, or its legal consequences.

The company does not ask to be allowed to disprove, or deny, the facts alleged or proved by the entryman; but those facts—to wit, settlement and inhabitancy years after the company's right attached,—are themselves inherently incapable of altering the result, by revoking or annulling a previously vested right.

DESERT LAND ENTRY—MODE OF IRRIGATION—PRACTICE.

VIBRANS *v.* LANGTREE.

The desert land act does not prescribe a particular mode of irrigation, but under the rulings of the Department it is required to be such as to evince the good faith of the claimant and render the land suitable for agriculture.

The fact of permanent reclamation warrants the acceptance of periodic flooding, accomplished by means of a dam, as a proper mode of irrigation.

It will not be presumed, on motion for review, that papers improperly in the record were considered or acted upon, if the conclusion reached was warranted by competent evidence.

If the evidence is such that fair minds might reasonably differ as to the conclusion that should be drawn therefrom, a motion for review can not be allowed on the ground that the decision is against the weight of evidence.

Secretary Noble to the Commissioner of the General Land Office, September 26, 1889.

This is a motion by William Vibrans for review of the departmental decision of February 18, 1889, in the case of said Vibrans *v.* Thomas

Langtree (unreported), involving the latter's desert land entry for the N. ½ of NW. ¼ of Sec. 8, the NE. ¼ of NE. ¼ of Sec. 7, the SW. ¼, the S. ¼ of NW. ¼, and lots 3 and 4 of Sec. 5, and E. ½ of SE. ¼, the SE. ¼ of NE. ¼ and lot 1, Sec. 6, T. 23 N., R. 119 W., Evanston district, Wyoming Territory.

Vibrans protested against the allowance of Langtree's entry on said land, on two grounds: 1st, That Langtree had "not constructed ditches and conveyed water" on the land as required by law, and, 2d, That Langtree was "not seeking to make entry of said land for his own use and benefit."

As to the first of these grounds of protest, it appears, as stated in said departmental decision, that "the land, with the exception of about twenty-five or thirty acres in the north west corner, was irrigated by flooding the same during about three months in the spring with water from Bear river," which runs through the tract, and the flooding was caused by a dam built across said river, of which Langtree was part proprietor, having bought a one-ninth interest therein for $1000.00. Prior to the entry some grass grew along sloughs comprising about one-eighth or one-tenth of the land, and some hay was cut. During the third year after the entry, Langtree "raised on the land from fifty to a hundred, and, the fourth year, from four hundred to five hundred tons of hay." It further appears from the testimony, that there was "no natural water supply" and that a quantity of water sufficient for raising a crop was conducted on the land, by the flooding resulting from said dam. No effort to distribute the water through canals or ditches was shown to have been made, and it does not appear that such method of distribution was necessary.

In the departmental decision, the conclusion at which both your office and the local officers arrived on the evidence—"that the claimant had reclaimed the land"—is concurred in, and it is held, that, while—

"It is true he" (Langtree) "did not construct a system of ditches or canals, and is without the means of putting water upon the land, except certain periods of the year," yet, "The act of March 3, 1877 . . . . does not prescribe a particular method of irrigation. It simply provides, that the entryman should reclaim the land by conducting water thereon within three years from the date of entry. This the claimant has done, and the fact of reclamation is evidenced by the crops of hay that have been raised upon the land."

The facts are not disputed, but it is contended by counsel for the motion, that the above finding on the facts "is materially inconsistent with the law and the established rulings and requirements of this Department." In support of this contention, he cites the cases of Wallace v. Boyce (1 L. D., 26), George Ramsey (5 L. D., 120), Charles H. Schick (ib., 151), and the letter of instructions issued from your office, September 3, 1880 (7 Copp, 138), and that of Secretary Teller to Commissioner McFarland, of February 9, 1885 (3 L. D., 385). I have examined these cases and letters of instruction, and find nothing therein inconsistent with the departmental ruling in the present case. The substance of these decisions and instructions is, that the proof should show, that water sufficient for purposes of irrigation and permanent reclamation has been brought to the land and properly distributed, so that substantially the entire tract is in fact irrigated in a manner to render it suitable for cultivation and that evinces the good faith of the claimant; and that merely bringing the water on the land without so distributing it, is not sufficient. It is true, the mode mentioned of bringing the water on the land and distributing it is by ditches, and that is the usual and perhaps better mode, when practicable, at an expense not too greatly disproportioned to the value of the land sought to be reclaimed; but, as said in the above quotation from the departmental decision, the desert land act "does not prescribe a particular mode of irrigation," and all that is required by the said decisions and instructions, fairly construed, is, that the mode of irrigation shall be such as "evinces the good faith of the claimant" and renders the land suitable for agriculture. The mode of irrigation is wisely left to be determined by the circumstances of each case. It does not appear in this case, that irrigation by ditches was practicable, or, if so, that it would answer the purpose of reclamation better than the mode adopted. The periodic flooding by means of the dam seems to have carried water upon the land in sufficient quantity, and to have distributed it in a manner to enable the claimant to raise crops, and this in connection with his payment of $1000.00 for an interest in the dam sufficiently evinces his good faith.

It is strenuously insisted, that the departmental decision was erroneous in holding that " the fact of reclamation is evidenced by the crops of hay that have been raised upon the land." In the letter of Secretary Teller to Commissioner McFarland (3 L. D., 385), while it is said, that an agricultural crop raised on the land is not the only proof of reclamation, and not conclusive, as there may be exceptional years in which crops may be raised with little or no artificial irrigation, yet, in the absence of exceptional conditions to which the crop could be attributed, the raising a crop on land artificially irrigated would be the best evidence of " perfect and complete" reclamation. This is nothing more than reasoning *a posteriori*, the inference of cause from effect. It does not appear, that the crops were raised by the claimant in exceptional years and could have been attributed to anything else than his irrigation of the land, and there was, therefore, no error in finding, that the " fact of reclamation was evidenced by the crops raised."

The second ground of protest which is insisted upon in the motion and argument for review, that Langtree was " not seeking to make entry of the land for his own use and benefit," is based upon a bond executed by Langtree in the penalty of $600.00, conditioned for the conveyance on acquiring title thereto of the land entered to the obligee therein, one

Christie.   It is said in the departmental decision, that "The testimony as to the intent of this bond is somewhat uncertain," but I am of opinion, that, as found in said decision, the weight of evidence is in favor of the statement of Langtree, that it was intended as collateral security for the payment of money.   Langtree had his option, either to pay the penalty or convey the land ; a penalty in a sum, so small as compared with the value of the land (as indicated by the amount expended on it), was wholly inadequate to compel or induce a conveyance, and could not have been intended for that purpose.   This, together with the fact that Langtree offered to pay the penalty, and other circumstances in connection with the transaction which is unnecessary to mention, tend strongly to establish the correctness of the decision on this point.   At any rate, there is no " palpable preponderance " of evidence to the contrary, and the most that can be claimed is, that " fair minds might reasonably differ as to the conclusion to be drawn from the evidence," and where this is the case, a motion for review of a departmental decision can not be granted, on the ground that it is against the weight of evidence.   (Mary Campbell, 8 L. D., p. 331).

The conclusion reached in the departmental decision and by your office and local officers, was authorized by the facts regularly established in evidence on the hearing, and the failure alleged in the motion " to expunge from the record certain papers, partly in the nature of evidence, calculated to prejudice the case of contestant, and improperly in the record," is not ground for review of said decision.   No motion was made to " expunge " said papers ; it is neither averred nor shown that they were considered by the Department or in any way influenced said decision ; and it can not be presumed, on motion for review, that papers improperly in the record were considered or acted on, when the conclusion arrived at was warranted by competent evidence, taken in accordance with the rules prescribed for that purpose.

There being circumstances developed on the hearing, which raised a doubt or "suspicion" as to the character of the land—whether it was in fact desert and subject to entry under the act of March 3, 1877—it was the right and duty of this Department by virtue of its general supervisory authority in such matters, to cause an investigation to be made in reference thereto, and there was no error in so doing.   If Vibrans has acquired, as he claims, any preferred rights by bringing on the hearing in which these circumstances were disclosed, those rights will not be prejudiced by the investigation ordered.

The motion for review is denied.

FINAL PROOF–RAILROAD GRANT–ACT OF APRIL 21, 1876.

OATLIN *v.* NORTHERN PAC. R. R. Co.

General notice of intention to submit final proof is legal notice to a railroad company, and if it fails to respond thereto it will be as effectually bound by the record as though present.

Failure of the company however to appear, will not warrant an award to the settler of land shown by the record to have passed under the grant.

The right of a pre-emption settler on lands within the limits of a railroad grant, before notice of the withdrawal of said lands is received at the local office, is protected by the act of April 21, 1876.

The protection extended by said act is equally applicable whether the withdrawal is legislative or executive, on general route or definite location, or within granted or indemnity limits.

A pre-emption settler on lands within the limits of a railroad grant, before notice of withdrawal is received at the local office, is entitled to purchase at the minimum price.

Secretary Noble to the Commissioner of the General Land Office, September 26, 1889.

By the decision of your office, dated May 5, 1888, William E. Catlin is permitted to make pre-emption cash entry—on the payment of two dollars and a half per acre—for the SE. ¼ of NE. ¼, Sec. 14, the W. ½ of NW. ¼ of SW. ¼, Sec. 13, T. 8 N., R. 6 E., Helena land district, Montana. This land is within the granted limits of the Northern Pacific Railroad Company's grant of July 2, 1864 (13 Stat., 365), and said company on being notified of said decision duly appealed to the Department.

The line of the definite location of appellant's road was filed in your office July 6, 1882, and notice of the same was received at the land office of the district in which the tract of land in controversy is situated, June 21, 1883. Catlin filed for the described lands April 13, 1883.

At the time said company's map of definite location was filed, two of the forty acre tracts, above described, in said odd numbered section, were included in pre-emption filings, which appellant admits excepted them from its grant. The tract in controversy is the SW. ¼ of the NW. ¼ of said Sec. 13.

In pursuance of a general notice of his intention so to do—no special notice being given to said company—Catlin, on January 2, 1886, made final pre-emption proof. This proof shows due compliance with law, and is entirely satisfactory.

In the decision appealed from your office held, that as the railroad company did not appear at the time and place mentioned in Catlin's said notice and object to his entry, it " was guilty of laches, by reason of which it is held to have waived its right to assert claim to the land covered by Catlin's filing, or to object to the consummation of the same," citing Forrester *v.* Atlantic and Pacific R. R. Co., 1 L. D., 475.

The said company, by its attorney, assigns error in said decision as follows, to wit:

1st. Error to rule that because the company did not file formal protest when Catlin offered proof, it is estopped from now setting up any right to the land.

2d. Error not to have ruled that the land being vacant and unappropriated at the date when the company filed its map of definite location, its right then vested by law and Catlin could not thereafter acquire a right therein.

3d. Error not to have canceled Catlin's entry for said tract, and not to have awarded the land to the company.

The decision of your office seems to be based solely on the ground that the railroad company, by reason of its *laches* has waived all right to assert claim to the land in dispute. This it has not done, for if the right of the company attached to this particular tract prior to the time it was settled upon and filed for by Catlin, and that fact appears in the record, then, the decision herein must be in favor of the company, not-withstanding the fact that it failed to appear and show cause why the entry should not be allowed. The notice given by Catlin, however, was legal notice to the railroad company of his intention to make final proof. The company has had its day in court, and is bound by the record as effectually as though present. This is as far as the case cited by your office—and numerous cases following it—goes. See Northern Pacific Railroad Company *v.* Joshua A. Randolph (9 L. D., 416), this day decided.

Appellant insists, that even admitting the correctness of the Forrester case, Catlin's entry is still open to the company's objection to the same because it was not allowed by the local officers. Catlin's proof was satisfactory, and his application to make final entry was rejected solely because he insisted that he had a right to purchase the land filed for at one dollar and a quarter per acre, while the local officers insisted that he should pay therefor two dollars and a half per acre. This is a matter which does not concern appellant, and it is difficult to discover how a matter which concerns only the government and the settler, and which is entirely foreign to its interest can affect the question involved herein. But, even if the fact that this entry has not yet been allowed is a material fact, still appellant's claim for the tract in controversy can not be sustained, under the rulings of the Department.

Said tract is outside of the limits of the withdrawal made for the benefit of said company, February 21, 1872, on its map of general route, and notice of the withdrawal made by its map of definite location was not received at the local land-office of the district in which said tract is situated till June 21, 1883. Catlin's settlement was made April 10, and his declaratory statement filed April 13, 1883, each of said acts being performed more than two months before said notice of withdrawal was received at the local land-office.

The proof made by Catlin shows that he has complied with the pre-emption law; that he is a qualified pre-emptor, and actually settled upon and filed for the land in dispute, prior to the time when notice of withdrawal was received at the local office, and that his settlement and filing were made in good faith. It has been repeatedly held by this Department that when the right of such a settler attaches to lands within the limits of a railroad land-grant, " prior to the time when notice of the withdrawal of the lands embraced in such grant was received at the local land-office of the district in which such lands are situated," his filing and entry are confirmed by the act of April 21, 1876 (19 Stat., 35), and that, upon making proper proof, a patent should be issued to such pre-emption or homestead settler. And whether the withdrawal be on map of general route or definite location, or is a legislative or executive withdrawal, or whether the lands may be in the granted or indemnity limits, makes no difference so far as the rights of the settler are concerned. See St. Paul, Minneapolis and Manitoba Ry. Co. v. Evenson, 5 L. D., 144, and cases cited; Northern Pacific R. R. Co. v. Dudden, 6 L. D., 6; Northern Pacific R. R. Co. v. Burns, ib., 21; Jacobs v. Northern Pacific R. R. Co., ib., 223; Kimberland v. Northern Pacific R. R. Co., 8 L. D , 318.

According to the well-settled rulings of the Department, appellant has no valid claim to the tract of land in controversy.

Catlin tendered one dollar and twenty-five cents per acre for the land included in his pre-emption claim. This tender was rejected by the local officers, and two dollars and fifty cents demanded. Catlin declined to accede to this demand, and appealed. On appeal your office sustained the action of the local officers, and in doing so says: " These lands became double minimum, and were to be sold at $2.50 per acre, except where claims were initiated prior to definite location, in which case the price would be $1.25 per acre," and the case of Lawrence W. Peterson (11 O. L. O., 186) is cited as sustaining said ruling. The case cited is not directly in point. Peterson settled in March, 1871. Map of definite location was filed November 21, 1871, and Peterson claimed that the land was not subject to the double-minimum rate, until date of definite location. But there had been in the Peterson case an executive withdrawal, made September 15, 1870, on map of trial line, and the price of the land was then fixed at two dollars and fifty cents per acre. It must be inferred that Peterson, at the time he settled, had notice of the increased price, for otherwise he would not have rested his right to enter at the lower price on the ground he did. Here, Catlin had no such notice. His settlement and filing were made before notice was received at the local land office of the withdrawal on map of definite location, and the land filed for was not within the limits of any former withdrawal. The definite location did not operate, as has been determined herein, as a withdrawal of the lands settled upon by Catlin, until notice of such withdrawal was received at the local office. His case, therefore, comes within section 2281 of the Revised Statutes, which provides as follows:

All settlers on public lands which have been or may be withdrawn from market in consequence of proposed railroads, and who had settled thereon prior to such withdrawal, shall be entitled to pre-emption at the ordinary minimum to the lands settled on and cultivated by them.

Your said office decision is therefore so far modified as to permit Catlin to make pre-emption cash entry at the rate of one dollar and twenty-five cents per acre; and the same as modified is hereby affirmed. See also Northern Pac. R. R. Co. v. Yantis, 8 L. D., 58, as to land in odd numbered section.

HOMESTEAD ENTRY—RESIDENCE—HUS AND AND WIFE.

L. A. TAVENER.

A husband and wife, living as one family, can not maintain separate residences at the same time and in the same house, so that each by virtue of said residence may perfect an entry under the homestead law.

Secretary Noble to the Commissioner of the General Land Office, September 27, 1889.

On November 2, 1881, Lydia A. Tavener made homestead entry, No. 7173, for the E. ½ of the SW. ¼ of Sec. 5, T. 27 N., R. 7 W., Niobrara land district, Nebraska. On the same day J. F. Fanning made homestead entry of the adjoining tract, the SE. ¼ of said Sec. 5. On April 26, 1882, the two parties named were married. Three days later, on April 29, 1882, they claim to have established residence—he upon the tract claimed by him, and she upon the tract claimed by her—in a house built upon the line between the two quarter-sections and partly upon both. On November 8, 1886, husband and wife appeared at the local office at Niobrara, where the husband made proof of having, with his family, resided since November 2, 1881 (four years and one week) upon the SE. ¼ of Sec. 5. Final receipt having been issued to him, his wife applied to make final proof upon the adjoining tract. In said proof she shows specifically that she had been careful to occupy the end of the house which was located on her own claim; and there is corroborative testimony such as that of John M. Rose, who states under oath:

That I have slept at the house over night at different times, and did at one time in the spring of 1884, board at their place for three weeks; and that during my stay there the said Lydia A. Fanning, formerly Lydia A. Tavener, did sleep upon her own claim, viz., the E. ½ of the SW. ¼ of Sec. 5, T. 27 N., R. 7 W.

The register rejected the proof upon the ground that—

J. F. Fanning, husband of claimant, has this day made proof, upon the tract adjoining, which was accepted, and receipt issued; and for the further reason that husband and wife can not hold two different tracts, and comply with the law as to residence upon and cultivation of both at the same time, although the house is built across the line and occupied by both parties.

The receiver endorsed upon the proof the following:

This proof is approved, and I recommend the issuance of final certificate, for the reason that it is shown that at date of entry, November 2, 1881, claimant was duly qualified to make the same, being a single woman over the age of twenty-one years, and a citizen of the United States; that her marriage at a subsequent date did not invalidate her rights by virtue of said entry; and it satisfactorily appears that she has complied with all the legal requirements of the homestead law to date.

In support of this position counsel for appellant cites the case of Maria Good (5 L. D., 196). But the cases are by no means parallel. The Department in the Maria Good case recognized "the right of a married woman to complete a homestead claim initiated by entry before marriage." The obvious meaning being, to complete it by complying with the requirements of law—among others that of actual residence upon the land. This, it is clear the claimant in the case at bar has not done. A husband and wife, living as one family, can not maintain separate residences at the same time, and as the husband has been permitted to prove up on his residence, the wife can not also prove up on account of her residence in the same house with her husband and during the same period. Your office decision is affirmed.

PRACTICE—CONTEST—NOTICE OF FINAL PROOF.

ATLANTIC AND PACIFIC R. R. CO. v. ARMIJO.

An application to contest the validity of an entry may be properly rejected if the affidavit therefor is not corroborated as required by the rules of practice.

A railroad company that fails to respond to the settler's notice of intention to submit final proof is bound by the record in said proceedings.

Secretary Noble to the Commissioner of the General Land Office, September 26, 1889.

September 15, 1885, Jesus M. Armijo made application to enter, under the homestead laws, the N. ½ NE. ¼ and lots one and two, Sec. 15, T. 2 N., R. 5 W., Santa Fe land district, New Mexico, alleging that he commenced his settlement thereon about April 1, 1870.

This land is within the granted limits of the Atlantic and Pacific Railroad Company (act of July 27, 1866, 14 Stat., 292), and the line of its road was definitely located March 12, 1872.

Said company was notified of Armijo's said application, and filed its objection to the allowance of the same. These objections were overruled by the local office and said entry allowed on September 22, 1885. From this action of the local office no appeal was taken.

November 23, 1885, Armijo made final homestead proof and subsequently obtained final certificate No. 1356, entitling him, *prima facie*, to a patent for the land entered. In passing upon this proof, your office, on March 8, 1887, found that Armijo's "claim was initiated prior to the definite location of the road, and that under the established rulings of the Department the land was excepted from the grant."

May 6, 1887, the railroad company, by its attorney, moved for a review of said decision, and asked that a hearing be ordered upon the allegation of certain facts contained in the affidavit of Ignatio Baca Y. Chaves, and which facts, if established by proof, would show that Armijo had not lived on said tract of land as shown in his final homestead proof. This motion was overruled by your office decision of April 11, 1888, on the following grounds:.

1st. The affidavit of Mr. Chaves is not corroborated, and the hearing is not asked on the grounds of newly discovered evidence.

2d. The company's failure to appear and contest Armijo's claim when opportunity was presented was a waiver of its right, and is now estopped from setting up the illegality of Armijo's entry. Citing Brady v. Southern Pacific R. R. Co., 5 L. D., 407 and 658.

From this decision the company appeals, and assigns the following errors therein, to wit:

1. In holding this company concluded by its failure to appear when final proof was made by Armijo; and

2. Denying its right to present hearing to determine the facts alleged as to Armijo's failure to reside upon his alleged homestead, and the falsity of his proof.

Section three of the act (*supra*), under which appellant claims title to the land entered by Armijo, excepts from the grant to said company all lands which were not—

free from pre-emption or other claims or rights, at the time the line of said road is designated by a plat thereof, filed in the office of the commissioner of the general land office; and whenever prior to said time, any of said sections or parts of sections shall have been granted, sold, reserved, occupied by homestead settlers, or pre-empted, or otherwise disposed of, other lands shall be selected by said company in lieu thereof.

Your office found from the evidence submitted by Armijo in support of his claim that it was initiated prior to the definite location of said road, and that the land in dispute was excepted, by the provisions of the act quoted from appellant's grant. This finding is based on the sworn statement of the homestead claimant and two disinterested witnesses in support of the fact disputed by the railroad company, and their statements are only impugned by the sworn statement of one person.

In cases of applications to contest the validity of an entry, which has been allowed and remains of record, the rules of practice (rule 3), adopted after mature consideration, provide that " the affidavit of the contestant must be accompanied by the affidavits of one or more witnesses in support of the allegations made."

Since the appellant's application for a hearing in this case did not come up to the requirements of a rule of the Department believed to be reasonable and just, no error is perceived in your denial of said application. And as appellant had its day in court when the original entry was made in this case, and also failed to appear and object to Armijo's final proof, no error is discovered in the refusal of your office to reconsider the decision of March 8, 1887. See Northern Pacific Railroad Co. v. Joshua M. Randolph, 9 L. D., 416; Northern Pacific Railroad Co. v. William E. Catlin, id., 423.

The decision of your office is accordingly affirmed.

DESERT LAND ENTRY—REPAYMENT.

JOSEPH ADLER.

If at the date of the initial entry, lands are properly held at double minimum, and so entered, but subsequently reduced by statute, repayment of the excess over twenty-five cents per acre can not be allowed but credit therefor may be given on completion of the entry.

Secretary Noble to the Commissioner of the General Land Office, September 26, 1889.

I have considered the appeal of Joseph Adler from the decision of your office, dated June 22, 1888, affirming the action of the local officers at Los Angeles, California, requiring him to pay at the rate of two dollars and fifty cents per acre, for Sec. 25, T. 5 N., R. 6 W., S. B. M., and demanding the sum of fifty cents per acre upon filing of his declaration, under the provisions of the desert land act of Congress, approved March 3, 1877 (19 Stat., 377), upon which certificate No. 749 was issued by the register and receiver on April 19, 1888.   "

The record shows that said section was within the limits of the grant by act of Congress, approved July 27, 1866 (14 Stat., 292), to the Atlantic and Pacific Railroad Company, which was forfeited by act of Congress, approved July 6, 1886 (24 Stat., 123), by which the lands " adjacent to and coterminous with the uncompleted portions of the main line " were restored to the public domain; that the appellant offered his desert land declaration for said section with a tender of twenty-five cents per acre, which was refused by the receiver, who demanded fifty cents per acre, as a first payment; that the appellant paid said last-named sum under protest, and, on appeal to your office, requested that the sum of twenty-five cents per acre so unjustly demanded by and paid to said receiver be refunded, for the reason that said desert land act expressly provides that the first payment shall be twenty-five cents per acre, and that neither said granting act, nor the act of forfeiture, nor any other act of Congress, require that said land shall be sold at a higher rate than one dollar and twenty-five cents per acre.

Your office affirmed the action of the local office, for the reason that " Neither the act of forfeiture nor any subsequent act of Congress has changed the price of land embraced in said section," and that under the circular of instructions, dated June 29, 1887, the local officers were informed that the price for desert lands was the same as those sold to pre emptors, " viz: single minimum lands at $1.25 per acre, and double minimum lands at $2.50 per acre.   (Sec. 2357 U. S. Rev. Stat.)."

The question of the price of said forfeited lands was elaborately considered by my predecessor, Mr. Secretary Lamar, on December 10, 1886, (5 L. D., 269), and your office was directed to "instruct the local officers in New Mexico that the even and odd numbered sections within the forfeited limits will be disposed of at two dollars and fifty cents per acre."

On December 15, 1886, as I am advised, your office gave the instructions to the local officers at Los Angeles, California, to hold all the forfeited lands at double minimum price. In accordance with said instructions, the appellant was required to pay fifty cents per acre as a first payment for the land. Since said decision of your office was rendered, Congress passed the act, approved March 2, 1889 (25 Stat. 854), the fourth section of which reads as follows:

That the price of all sections and parts of sections of the public lands within the limits of the portions of the several grants of lands to aid in the construction of railroads which have been heretofore and which may hereafter be forfeited, which were by the act making such grants or have since been increased to the double minimum price, and, also, of all lands within the limits of any such railroad grant, but not embraced in such grant lying adjacent to and coterminous with the portions of the line of any such railroad which shall not be completed at the date of this act, is hereby fixed at one dollar and twenty-five cents per acre.

In the case of Annie Knaggs (9 L. D., 49), the Department held that: "Repayment can not be allowed for the excess over one dollar and twenty-five cents per acre paid on a desert entry within railroad limits, though the land was held at single minimum at the date of the initial entry."

While I am not disposed to change the ruling of Secretary Lamar, as to the price of said lands at the date of the initial entry of the appellant, and must, therefore, decline to order a repayment of the sum applied for, yet, as the decision in the Knaggs case fixed the price of the land at the date of final entry as the rate at which it must be sold, and since the act of March 2, 1889, has fixed the price of said land at one dollar and twenty-five cents per acre, the appellant, when he makes final entry, will be allowed to purchase said land at one dollar and twenty-five cents per acre, upon showing due compliance with the law, and he may then receive credit for the amount already paid.

The decision of your office is modified accordingly.

———

DESERT LAND ENTRY—FINAL PROOF—NON-IRRIGABLE LAND.

MARTHA W. FISHER.

A desert land entry may be sent to the board of equitable adjudication, where the failure to submit final proof within the statutory period is due to ignorance, accident or mistake.

In the absence of conclusive evidence of negligence, an entryman may be permitted to relinquish the non-irrigable land included within his entry and submit proof for the remainder.

First Assistant Secretary Chandler to the Commissioner of the General Land Office, September 28, 1889.

I have considered the appeal of Martha W. Fisher from the decision of your office, dated June 15, 1888, refusing to modify its decision, dated

November 28, 1887, sustaining the action of the local officers rejecting her final proof in support of her desert land entry, No. 1378, of lots 1 and 2, and the S. ½ of the NE. ¼ of Sec. 2, T. 14, R. 69 W., made March 24, 1884, at the Cheyenne land district, in the Territory of Wyoming.

Said proof was rejected by the local officers, for the reason that only thirty acres of the land were shown to have been reclaimed, and the final proof was not presented within three years from the date of said entry. On appeal, your office found from the proof, that "only ten acres of lot 1, and twenty acres of the SE. ¼ of the NE. ¼ of Sec. 2, have been irrigated," and the one hundred and twenty-eight acres remaining were considered non-irrigable. It was, therefore, held that the final proof was not in compliance with section twelve of the circular of your office of June 27, 1887, (5 L. D., 708).

On December 3, 1887, the local office forwarded the request of the entryman, that said final proof be accepted for the two subdivisions upon which water has been conducted by her, and that she be permitted to make final payment for the same. Your office, on June 15, 1888, refused this request, for the reason that "the claimant should have known prior to making the entry whether the lands embraced therein were susceptible to reclamation, for, if not, such lands were not subject to entry under the desert land act." This action of your office appellant insists was erroneous.

An examination of the final proof fails to disclose any reason for not reclaiming the land and making proof thereof within the time prescribed by law. If, however, the claimant has substantially complied with the requirements of the statute in good faith, and the failure to make due proof was the result of ignorance, accident or mistake, in the absence of an adverse claim, the entry could be allowed and submitted to the board of equitable adjudication for its consideration, in accordance with the appropriate rule (6 L. D., 799).

There can be no fixed rule providing that in every case the entryman must absolutely know that every portion of the land entered can be reclaimed. The main questions to be determined in each case are: (1) Was the land desert in character, and the entry compact in form, and (2) Was the entryman duly qualified, and has he complied in good faith with the requirements of the statute. David Gilchrist (8. L. D., 48).

There is no adverse claimant, so far as the record discloses, and it would seem that, in the absence of conclusive evidence of laches, the claimant should be permitted to relinquish that portion of her entry which she shows to be non-irrigable, and submit new proof, and, if she brings herself within the provision of said rules, her proof may be accepted and submitted to said board. Morris Asher (6 L. D., 801); Adam Schindler (7 L. D., 253); George F. Stearns (8 L. D., 573); W. R. Williams (9 L. D., 137); Andrew Leslie (idem., 204).

The decision of your office is accordingly modified, and the claimant will be allowed to make supplemental proof before the local officers, within a reasonable time (say sixty days from due notice hereof), which should clearly show the non-irrigable character of the lands not reclaimed, the reason why final proof was not duly made, and the extent of the reclamation of the tracts applied for. The local office will pass upon the sufficiency of said proof, and the same will be duly considered by your office in accordance with the views herein expressed.

PRE-EMPTION FINAL PROOF—CULTIVATION.

THOMAS C. BURNS.

In the absence of evidence warranting an imputation of bad faith, breaking may be accepted as sufficient proof of cultivation, where the residence and improvements of the entryman are found satisfactory, and the failure to raise a crop is explained.

First Assistant Secretary Chandler to the Commissioner of the General Land Office, September 28, 1889.

In the matter of the appeal of Thomas C. Burns from the decision of your office, bearing date June 6, 1888, rejecting his proof for lots 1, 2, 3, and 4, of Sec. 19, T. 107 N., R. 64 W., in the district of lands subject to entry at Mitchell, Dakota Territory, and requiring new proof, I find upon examination of the record, that on March 26, 1883, Burns made declaratory statement No. 20641, for said land, alleging settlement on March 25th. That on October 3rd, of same year he made proof and payment.

His residence was established on the land March 25, 1883, and was continuous up to date of proof, more than six months.

His improvements consist of a house and he has broken five acres of land. No crop was raised on the land broken and in a supplemental affidavit, filed in this department since the decision of your office, Burns gives as a reason for not raising a crop that " after the breaking was done, it was too late to plant it to crops."

The length of residence, and improvements made bring the claimant within the rule, as the word cultivate has been heretofore construed. John E. Tyrl, 3 L. D., 49; Clark S. Kathan, 5 L. D., 94; John W. Alderson, 8 L. D., 517; T. H. Quigley, 8 L. D., 551; Caroline Welo, 8 L. D., 612.

Taking into consideration the presumption of good faith, his failure to raise a crop having been explained, and there being no evidence of bad faith, or facts from which bad faith can be inferred, I am of the opinion that the proof should be accepted and the entry stand.

Your decision is, therefore, reversed.

[Circular.]

DEPARTMENT OF THE INTERIOR,
GENERAL LAND OFFICE,
Washington, D. C., September 19, 1889.
Registers and Receivers, United States District Land Offices.

GENTLEMEN: In addition to and explanatory of the circular issued by this office on the 8th of March last (8 L. D., 314), in regard to the act of March 2, 1889 (25 Stat., 854), for your information and the information of settlers who apply for leave of absence from the tracts covered by their several settlements, under the third section of said act, and other parties interested, it is hereby directed that any settler so applying shall submit with his application to the register and receiver of the proper land office his affidavit, corroborated by the affidavits of disinterested witnesses, setting forth the following facts, viz:

1. The character and date of the entry, date of establishing residence upon the land, and what improvements have been made thereon by the applicant.

2. How much of the land has been cultivated by the applicant, and for what period of time.

3. In case of failure or injury to crop, what crops have failed or been injured or destroyed, to what extent, and the cause thereof.

4. In case of sickness, what disease or injury, and to what extent claimant is prevented thereby from continuing upon the land; and, if practicable, a certificate from a reliable physician should be furnished.

5. In case of "other unavoidable casualty," the character, cause, and extent of such casualty, and its effect upon the land or the claimant.

6. In each case full particulars upon which intelligent action may be based by the register and receiver.

7. The dates from which and to which leave of absence is asked.

The foregoing is not to be understood as imposing restrictions upon settlers over and above what the statute contains, or to modify the conditions therein prescribed for the enjoyment of the right, but merely to indicate what facts should be set forth in the required affidavits, leaving with the registers and receivers of the several district offices the duty of making application of the law to the particular cases presented, subject, of course, to the supervisory authority of the Department.

Respectfully,

W. M. STONE,
Acting Commissioner.

Approved:
JOHN W. NOBLE,
Secretary of the Interior.

2816—VOL 9——28

JOHN C. WEBER.

A misdescription of the land in the notice of intention to submit proof calls only for republication, if the proof shows compliance with the law in good faith.

An order for new publication and proof should not be made before the sufficiency of the proof submitted has been, in all respects fully considered and adjudicated.

First Assistant Secretary Chandler to the Commissioner of the General Land Office, September 30, 1889.

On November 22, 1883, John C. Weber, as appears from his application and the receiver's receipt for entry fees, made homestead entry No. 2173 for the NE. ¼ of SE. ¼, the SW. ¼ of NW. ¼, and lot 4 Sec. 5, and the SE. ¼ of the NE. ¼ in Sec. 6, T. 66 N., R. 20 W., Duluth land district, Minnesota.

This entry as apparently made, is not legal in its entirety because the NE. ¼ of the SW. ¼ of Sec. 5 is not contiguous to the other land described therein.

On August 29, 1884, Weber made commutation proof before the register and receiver at Duluth for the land above described except said non-contiguous tract for which, in said proof, he substituted the NW. ¼ of the SW. ¼ of said Sec. 5. The notice of his intention to make proof, however, described said non-contiguous section as embraced in his entry and does not describe the NW. ¼ of the SW. ¼ of said Sec. 5, as being included therein. In an affidavit, made August 30, 1884, for the purpose of having the papers in the case corrected so as to conform to his alleged intention at the time he made his homestead entry, and to secure a final certificate, Weber says that the land he applied to enter was the NW. ¼ of the SW. ¼, the SW. ¼ of the NW. ¼ and lot 4 in Sec. 5, and the SE. ¼ of the NE. ¼ in Sec. 6, T. 66 N., R. 20 W., of the 4th P. M.; that it was then his intention to enter the same, and that the land intended to be entered was marked on the plat book of the local land office as entered by him, and that there was no adverse claim to the same. Upon this affidavit and the proof made, Weber was allowed by the local land officers to commute his said homestead entry to cash entry, No. 7172, for which entry he obtained, August 30, 1884, a final certificate, which *prima facie* entitles him to a patent for the land last above described.

Weber gave notice that he would make proof in support of his claim before the local officers at Duluth on August 27, 1884, and did not make such proof, as stated above, till August 29, 1884. In an affidavit filed with the proof, he gave as the reason for his failure to appear on the day advertised that he could not secure the attendance of one of his witnesses on that day. This reason was accepted as satisfactory by the local office. Prior to February 2, 1886, Weber's said commuted cash entry was suspended by your office and at that date he amended his original homestead application by making the description of the tracts applied for correspond with the description of the land for which he made proof and obtained his final certificate.

By letter of your office, dated August 8, 1888, the following instructions and directions were given to the local office in this case.

It will, however, be necessary to make new publication and proof with correct description of the land as shown by the amended application, ... which proof when made, you will transmit in a special letter to this office, with a reference to this letter, as to initial and date, when the case will have further consideration. The certificate which gives the proper description will remain suspended awaiting such action on the part of the claimant, of which you will inform him and of his rights of appeal.

From this decision Weber has duly appealed, and he complains that the effect of your office decision is to inflict upon him an unreasonable hardship, and that " the ends of justice, and the requirements of the law, would be fully met by requiring, if necessary, new publication; and if, on the day set for hearing, no adverse claimants, or intervening rights appeared, permitting the final proof made August 30, (29), 1884 to stand as the proof in the case."

The record in the case shows the land above described to be situated about one hundred and forty miles from the local office, and appellant's complaint is well founded provided his final proof shows compliance in good faith with the homestead law. If it does this, the aforesaid erroneous description appearing in the notice of his intention to make final proof would not require new proof, but new publication only. The general sufficiency of the proof made by appellant August 29, 1884, does not seem to have been considered by your office. Its sufficiency, irrespective of the objections pointed out by your said office decision, should have been passed upon so that if found insufficient the objection to the same might be pointed out to the entryman to the end that any objection to the same which it was in his power to properly obviate might be met when he made new proof. Otherwise after making new publication and new proof, the entryman might be required to again do the same thing in order to meet some objection to the new proof which existed in his original proof and which objection might have been easily obviated had the entryman's attention been called to it in the first instance. In other words all objections to the final proof offered in a case should be pointed out and the sufficiency of the proof in other respects stated, before the entryman is required to make new publication and new proof.

The proof produced in this case and accepted by the local land officers, has been examined by the Department and found insufficient to satisfactorily show that the entryman established an actual residence on the described land at the time alleged by him, or at any other time, with the intention of making the same his home to the exclusion of a home elsewhere, and for the purpose of cultivating said land.

*   *   *   *   *   *   *

Had this proof been satisfactory, new publication only would have been required, but for the reasons above given the decision of your office, requiring new proof and new publication is affirmed.

———

FINAL PROOF PROCEEDINGS—NEW PROOF.

ARNOLD OERTLI.

The Department will pass on the merits of a case as presented by the whole record, where new final proof is submitted, pending appeal from the Commissioner's rejection of the first.

The good faith of a claimant may be shown by acts performed subsequently to the submission of final proof.

First Assistant Secretary Chandler to the Commissioner of the General Land Office, October 1, 1889.

In the matter of the appeal of Arnold Oertli from your office decision of July 20, 1886, rejecting his proof and holding for cancellation his cash entry on the NW. $\frac{1}{4}$ of section 12, T. 128 N., R. 57 W., in the district of lands subject to entry at Watertown, Dakota, I find that claimant made homestead entry covering this land on April 21, 1883, and offered commutation proof May 20, 1885, proving that he established his actual residence upon the tract April 20, 1883. That he is unmarried. That his residence has been continuous. That he has been absent at intervals from a week to one month engaged in preaching, he being a minister and a "circuit rider." That he had in cultivation twenty-six acres. Built a house twelve by eighteen feet, frame with board roof, tar papered.

The proof was rejected by your said office decision, and he was given the privilege of making new proof during the life-time of his claim.

Pending the appeal he has made new proof which was transmitted to this Department with your office letter of September 12, 1889, and I shall proceed to decide the case upon all the facts before me in accordance with the decision in Pierpoint v. Stadler, (8 L.D., 595).

By the new proof it appears that he is now married, that his improvements are valued at $1,245, including a $700 house, a $400 barn and granary. That he has two horses, one cow, one steer, one calf, poultry in abundance, and every indication that he intends to make this his domicile; that he has continuously resided upon the property except when called away by his pastoral labors. In view of his subsequent residence the value of improvements made and the explanation of absences from the tract, I am satisfied of the good faith of this claimant, and think that he should be allowed to perfect his title to this land and acquire a home.

The proof will be accepted and a patent ordered.

S. N. ORR.

A timber culture entry should not be allowed if the returns show timber in the section, but a hearing may be ordered, if the correctness of the return is questioned, to determine whether in fact the land is subject to timber culture entry.

First Assistant Secretary Chandler to the Commissioner of the General Land Office, October 1, 1889.

I have before me the appeal of S. N. Orr, from your office decision of April 30, 1888, approving the action of the local officers at Oberlin, Kansas, in rejecting his (said Orr's) application, dated February 4, 1888, to make a timber culture entry on the NW. ¼, Sec. 14, T. 4, R. 33 W., Oberlin district, Kansas.

In support of his said application Orr filed his own affidavit, corroborated by that of two other witnesses, making the following statement as to the amount of timber upon said section 14:

There are eight small hackberry trees in said section, all under three inches in diameter. The eight trees mentioned are only brush; none of them would make posts or do for wood. There are thirteen cottonwood trees, all of them under three inches in diameter, and five that are over three inches. There is one cottonwood tree two and one-half feet in diameter but it is not fit for lumber or posts. There is no marketable timber in the whole section. There is not sufficient timber in the section to supply one family in wood. No posts or rails could be made of the timber. It is mostly brush.

The local officers rejected the application, on the ground that "the plats show that there is timber in the section."

Under date of April 30, 1888, your office, by the decision appealed from, affirmed this action "in view of the fact that the plats . . . show timber in the section, and as the evidence presented fails to show the said section to be composed exclusively of prairie lands or other lands wholly naturally devoid of timber."

In the substantially similar case of James Hair (8 L. D., 467), the Department held that "an entry should not be allowed where the returns show timber in the section but a hearing may be ordered, if the correctness of the return is questioned, to determine whether the land is in fact subject to timber culture entry."

In pursuance of the practice thus prescribed, you will order a hearing, under the rules and regulations of your office, and at which a special agent shall represent the government, for the purpose of determining whether or not the section is 'devoid of timber' within the spirit of the act and said decision. In the meantime, Orr's application will stand suspended. If, on the hearing, the testimony discloses the fact that practically the section is prairie land or devoid of timber, Orr's application will be entertained.

Your decision is modified accordingly.

HARRENKAMP *v.* HIVELY.

Ten days additional are allowed for filing appeal when notice of the decision is given
through the mail by the local office.

In the event of disagreeing decisions of the local officers, the Commissioner may
properly dispose of the case on its merits, in the absence of appeal.

*First-Assistant Secretary Chandler to the Commissioner of the General
Land Office, October 3, 1889.*

I have considered the case of Joseph Harrenkamp *v.* Andrew Hively,
involving the SE. ¼, section 14, T. 2 S., R. 67 W., Denver land district,
Colorado.

Andrew Hively filed his pre-emption declaratory statement for the
said land December 14, 1882, and submitted his final proof June 9, 1885;
Joseph Harrenkamp filed his protest against its acceptance and a hearing having been ordered the same was had before the local officers December 9, 1886. At such hearing both parties were present and represented by their respective attorneys.

The local officers having considered the evidence in the case, were
divided in their opinion, the receiver deciding that the said proof be
rejected and the register being of the opinion that claimant "is entitled
to his entry."

Both parties having been notified of such decisions, failed to appeal.

The records and testimony having been properly transmitted to your
office, you after careful examination of the evidence found "that the
opinion of the register is substantially correct," and by your office decision of March 6, 1888, affirmed his decision.

The protestant having filed his appeal to this Department June 19,
1888, the claimant protests against its allowance for the reasons,—
"First, That said appeal was not taken within the time allowed by law.
Second, That no appeal having been taken from the ruling of the reg-
ister and receiver, no appeal can be taken from the decision of the
Commissioner."

The objections to the appeal are not well taken. Regarding the first,
the files in the case show that notice of your said office decision was
given by the register and receiver to the protestant on April 16, 1888,
through the mails. The filing of the appeal on June 19, was, therefore
in time. See Rule 87, of the Rules of Practice. The second objection
to the appeal can not be sustained for in the event of disagreeing decisions by the local officers, their decision will not be considered final
as to the facts in the case. See Rule 48. An appeal is a proper proceeding by a party desirous to be heard in the superior court, when an
order or judgment of the lower tribunal does in any manner affect or
dispose of his rights or interests. On a divided opinion of the local
office no judgment can be rendered nor order made. Your office prop-

erly disposed of the case, without the appeal of either party. See Rule 49.

Having, therefore, carefully considered the evidence in the case, I find that the facts have been set out fully and correctly in your office letter of the said date, March 6, 1888. Since I concur in the conclusion therein stated, your said office decision is affirmed.

———

FINAL PROOF PROCEEDINGS—NEW NOTICE.

WILLIAM M. KEMP.

Final proof submitted under indefinite notice, may be accepted, in the absence of protest, after republication.

First Assistant Secretary Chandler to the Commissioner of the General Land Office, October 3, 1889.

I have considered the appeal of Wm. M. Kemp from your office decision of December 16, 1887, rejecting his proof on his pre-emption filing for the SE. ¼, Sec. 7, T. 113, N., R. 75 W., Huron land district, Dakota.

He filed his pre-emption declaratory statement May 3, 1882, alleging settlement on May 1, same year.

He made his final proof on December 14, 1883, before the clerk of the district court, in and for Sully county, Dakota; the notice of his intention to make proof, as signed by the register and published reads, that his proof would be made on that day " before the clerk of court of record in and for Sully county, Dakota Territory."

His proof was accepted by the local officers and cash certificate issued December 21, 1883.

Your office having examined the proof, by your said decision determined " that the proof is not conclusive as to the entryman's good faith, the same is, therefore, rejected and ninety days allowed the claimant to re-advertise and make new proof."

From this decision the entryman appealed to this Department.

The proof shows that Kemp is a duly qualified pre-emptor he is a native born citizen, single and of the age of twenty-four years. He made his first settlement on the tract May 1, 1883, by erecting a house thereon; he established his residence on his claim May 10, the same year, and claims the same to have been continuous till time of proof. His improvements consist of a house of the size of eight feet by ten feet, shingle roof, six acres of breaking and a well, total value of improvements one hundred dollars. He states that he used the tract " as a home and for farming purposes." He says nothing about crops being raised on the land and it must therefore be presumed that no crops were raised; this neglect or omission, however, I think may be excused, considering that he moved on the land as late in the season as May 10. The proof was duly corroborated by his two witnesses.

Considering the case on the merits the proof should be accepted. It was accepted by the local officers and payment made for the land nearly six years ago. Since no bad faith is apparent, no further question on the proof should be raised at this late day, were it not for the insufficiency in the notice for proof, it being stated therein that claimant's final proof would be made " before the clerk of court of record in and for Sully county, Dakota Territory."

Regarding this point the case is similar to that of Jacob Semer (6 L. D., 345) and Milo Adams (7 idem, 197). In the first cited case it is said—

The notice in this case is not sufficiently definite and explicit and it shows carelessness on the part of the local officers that such notice was allowed to go to publication and that proof made thereunder was received by them . . . . The giving of proper notice is a statutory requirement and can not be waived or excused.

In conformity then with authorities cited, I direct that the claimant be required to give notice anew of his intention to submit final proof and that if, upon the day advertised for final proof, no p rotest or objection is filed then the proof heretofore made may be accepted as final proof.

If protest or objection is filed, then the claimant must make new proof, but under the ruling in the said case of Jacob Semer, referring to the case of Alfred Sherlock (6 L. D., 155), such proof will be sufficient, if it shows compliance with the law up to the date of the final certificate.

Your decision is modified accordingly.

———

TIMBER-CULTURE CONTEST- RELINQUISHMENT—ACT OF MAY 14, 1880.

WEBB v. LOUGHREY ET AL.

A relinquishment filed pending contest does not defeat the right of the contestant to be heard on the charge as laid by him; and while his preference right is dependent upon his ability to establish said charge, the relinquishment is presumptively the result of the contest, though such presumption may be overcome.

If the contestant does not invoke the aid of the relinquishment, but independently thereof proves the facts alleged by him, the relinquishment has no effect on his preference right.

First Assistant Secretary Chandler to the Commissioner of the General Land Office, October 3, 1889.

This record involves the rights of the contestant of a timber culture entry, and of one who files relinquishment of the entry and makes homestead entry of the land, subsequent to the initiation of such contest.

On May 8, 1882, William Loughrey made timber culture entry for the E. ½, SE. ¼, NW. ¼, SE. ¼, and SW. ¼, NE. ¼, Sec. 6, T. 11 S., R. 3. W., S. B. M., Los Angeles, California.

On December 29, 1886, George W. Webb filed affidavit of contest against said entry alleging failure to comply with the law in the matter of planting, and also an application to make homestead entry of the tract. The affidavit of contest is dated on December 27, and indorsed, " Filed December 30, 1886," but it is sufficiently established that it was actually filed on December 29. It was executed before J. O. W. Paine, notary public in San Diego county, California, and transmitted by mail.

On December 27, 1886, the date of the affidavit of contest, Loughrey executed a relinquishment of said entry before Chauncey Hayes, notary public, at Oceanside, San Diego county, California. On December 30, 1886, said relinquishment was filed by one Jose A. Peters, the entry was canceled, and Peters allowed to make entry of the tract. These papers also arrived by mail.

On December 31, notice on Webb's contest issued and was served on Loughrey. Peters was not notified. On March 3, 1887, hearing was had before the local officers when Webb appeared and submitted testimony. Loughrey made default. The local officers held that the testimony showed a failure to comply with the law on the part of Loughrey, as alleged; that the contest was prior to the relinquishment, and the latter inured to contestant's benefit; and recommended the cancellation of Peters' entry, and the allowance of Webb's. Peters was notified of said decision and appealed. Your office on March 15, 1888, held that Peters' rights were subject to those of contestant, and directed the local officers to notify Webb that he would be allowed thirty days to perfect his entry by " showing his qualifications to do so." Pending such action or in default thereof Peters' entry was allowed to stand.

From said decision Peters presents this appeal.

The main question presented by the record is, whether the rights of Peters so initiated as above set forth, are superior to those of the contestant.

The act of May 14, 1880 (21 Stat., 140) provides:

That when a pre-emption homestead or timber culture claimant shall file a written relinquishment of his claim in the local land office, the land covered by such claim shall be held as open to settlement and entry without further action on the part of the Commissioner of the General Land Office.

Sec. 2. In all cases where any person has contested, paid the land office fees, and procured the cancellation of any pre-emption, homestead, or timber culture entry, he shall be notified by the register of the land office of the district in which such land is situated of such cancellation and shall be allowed thirty days from date of such notice to enter said lands.

Both parties claim under this act; Webb as a preferred contestant under section two and Peters, by virtue of the relinquishment and entry, under section one. It does not appear that either is acting in bad faith.

In the case of McClellan v. Biggerstaff (7 L. D., 442), it was said:

While it is true that a relinquishment filed pending a contest is *prima facie* the result of the contest, such presumption is not conclusive, and on proof it may appear that the relinquishment was in fact not the result of the contest, in which event the rights of the contestant must depend upon his ability to sustain the charge as laid by him.

And a hearing was ordered to determine the fact of abandonment, as alleged by the contestant.

If this is the law, Loughrey's relinquishment filed pending the contest and Peters' entry filed at the same time, will not necessarily defeat the contest rights of Webb. His rights will "depend on his ability to sustain the charge as laid by him." He has maintained the charge and therefore, should prevail.

The case of Sorenson v. Becker (8 L. D., 357), looks in the same direction. It is a timber culture contest wherein a relinquishment (dated one day prior to the initiation of contest) was filed, with application to enter, one day after the filing of the contest. It was said that if the alleged failure to comply with the law, as alleged, in fact existed when the contest was filed, then the contestant, "should not be deprived of the legitimate fruits of his diligence in bringing that failure to the notice of the proper authorities by a relinquishment filed subsequently to his application to contest and make entry." A hearing on the merits was also ordered in that case. Becker had contested the entry of one Leonard, and Sorenson filed the said relinquishment. I quote from the case:

> Becker claims that because Leonard's entry was canceled upon relinquishment filed after the filing of his contest affidavit he became entitled to a preference right to enter said land. This does not, however, necessarily follow. The right is extended to one who "has contested, paid the land office fees and procured the cancellation" of an entry by the provisions of the second section of the act of May 14, 1880, (21 Stat., 140). Unless it be found that the filing of this relinquishment was brought about by the filing of the contest affidavit the contestant is not under the decisions of the Department entitled to a preference right of entry.

And it was ordered that the question whether the relinquishment resulted from the attack by Becker, be investigated at said hearing. It will be seen, therefore, that the case is in line with the case of McClellan v. Biggerstaff.

So in Kurtz v. Summers (7 L. D., 46) a hearing was had on the merits after the cancellation of the entry on a *bona fide* relinquishment filed pending contest, and proceeded on the theory that a preference right would be secured by sustaining the allegation of contest, notwithstanding the *bona fides* of the relinquishment. The testimony on the merits was considered by the Department.

In Johnson v. Halvorson decided June 2, 1881, (8 C. L. O., 56), it was held:

> When a relinquishment is filed, as in this case, before the final disposition of a contest regularly commenced, it should be treated as evidence in such contest, and as relieving the contestant of producing any further evidence in support of his case. Upon the filing of such relinquishment while the contest is pending, the entry in contest, should be held as canceled in accordance with the first section of the act of May 14, 1880, and the contestant should be notified of his preferred right of entry under the second section of the act, and your office of the filing of said relinquishment.

This ruling has been modified by subsequent decisions to the extent indicated in the Biggerstaff case, *supra*.

In John Powers (1 L. D., 103), decided September 30, 1881, the preference right was awarded the successful contestant, though the actual cancellation of the entry was effected by a relinquishment filed after the case was closed in the local office.

In Haskins *v.* Nichols, decided August 1, 1882, (1 L. D., 145), it was said:

> As Haskins commenced this contest prior to Nichols's relinquishment of the tract, the relinquishment relieved him from producing evidence in support of his allegation and he had the right to continue the contest to final determination, and thus secure a preference right to enter the tract as held in Johnson *v.* Halvorson.

See also Glaze *v.* Bogardus (2 L. D., 311). Thomas A. Bones, (ibid., 619), Bivins *v.* Shelly, (ib., 282).

In Mitchell *v.* Robinson (3 L. D., 546), the relinquishment of the entryman, Long, together with the declaratory statement of Robinson was filed pending the contest of Mitchell and it was said:

> The relinquishment was accompanied by an adverse claim to file upon the land and before Mitchell could acquire a preferred right of entry, by virtue of his pending contest, it was necessary for him to pursue it to a successful termination and obtain a forfeiture of the entry.
>
> If the contestant obtain a judgment, his preferred right of entry is not to be defeated, because the relinquishment antedates, if presented after, the contest. For it is not to be permitted that the rights of vigilant contestants shall be thus defeated by the execution and retention of relinquishments.

See also Pfaff *v.* Williams (4 L D., 455); Hopkins *v.* Daniels (ibid., 126), and Pickett *v.* Engle (4 L. D., 522).

The case of Croughan *v.* Smith (4 L. D., 413), is not in conflict with this line of decisions, for in that case the contestant failed to appeal from the decision of your office, adverse to her.

See also Hemsworth *v.* Holland (8 L. D., 400).

From a review of these decisions it appears that the constant opinion of the Department on the question at issue is properly represented in said Biggerstaff and Kurtz cases, *supra*, that when relinquishment is filed pending contest the preference right of the contestant will depend on his ability to sustain the charge as laid by him, that such relinquishment is presumed to be the result of the contest, but that such presumption may be rebutted, and that the contestant is entitled to a hearing on his allegation of contest.

But independently of the decisions, I am of opinion that a proper construction of the statute leads to the same result. The question presented is analogous to that in Freise *v.* Hobson (4 L. D., 580) where it was held that pending a contest the right of purchase conferred by section two of the act of June 15, 1880, is suspended. Is not a like solution of this question a proper one? Two parties claiming to be innocent and pursuing the law are in conflict. In such cases the usual solution is found in the maxim *qui prior est tempore potior est jure.* And this maxim has been invoked by the supreme court in the settlement of conflicting claims to public land. In Shepley *v.* Cowen (91 U. S., 330) two patents had been issued under the act of September 4, 1841, one in 1850 on a State selection made in 1849, the other to a pre-emptor in 1866, settlement having been made in 1835. The court said:

The party who takes the initiatory step, in such cases, if followed to patent, is deemed to have acquired the better right as against others to the premises. The patent which is afterwards issued relates back to the date of the initiatory act, and cuts off all intervening claimants . . . But it was not intended by the 8th section of the act of 1841, in authorizing the State to make selections of land, to interfere with the operation of the other provisions of that act regulating the system of settlement and pre-emption. The two modes of acquiring title to land from the United States were not in conflict with each other. Both were to have full operation that one controlling in a particular case under which the first initiatory step was had.

And again :

In all such cases, the first in time in the commencement of proceedings for the acquisition of the title, when the same are regularly followed up, is deemed to be the first in right.

In the case at bar "two modes" of procuring cancellation of the entry and title to the tract were initiated independently of each other, the one by securing and filing a relinquishment and making a new entry, the other by giving proof of a default. Both were legal and in the absence of the other each was competent to accomplish the end proposed. Upon the filing of the relinquishment the land became open to settlement and entry. Upon the successful termination of the contest the contestant was entitled to a preference right of entry. These two separate results of the two modes of procedure are based on separate provisions of the same act, the act of May 14, 1880, and on that alone. And yet a conflict arises on the separate provisions of the same act. It becomes necessary therefore, in executing the act to give such a construction to it, if possible, as will relieve this apparent conflict. Prior to its passage the relinquishment did not take effect upon filing, but only after examination by the Commissioner, and the successful contestant had no preference right. A stranger might intervene after cancellation of an entry on contest and deprive the successful contestant of the reward of his labor. To suppress this abuse the second section of the act was passed. It secured to the successful contestant, for the first time, a right to enter the land in preference to others, as a reward of his labor and expense. The law favors the contest and rewards the contestant. Now while the first section declares that upon relinquishment the land shall be open to entry, it does not provide that a subsequent entry shall be superior to all other claims. Nor did the section contemplate such a provision. The section was passed to avoid abuses that existed under the practice of submitting relinquishments to your office. The work of the Department was unnecessarily increased, claimants suffered from delay and in many cases their rights were jeopardized. The section was passed to remedy these evils.

The construction of this section should be broad enough to suppress the mischief and advance the remedy, but I know of no rule of law that would extend it beyond that point, especially so as to destroy or impair a new right granted by the next section. I, therefore, conclude that the entry here in question was made subject to the contest, "under which the first initiatory step was had."

And this conclusion is equitable. Peters is not equally innocent with Webb. If he chose to purchase a relinquishment at a distance from the local office he took the risk of an adverse claim intervening pending the filing of the relinquishment. The relinquishment in no way affected the status of the land until filed. Wiley v. Raymond (6 L. D., 246). To protect himself fully he should have gone himself or procured the entry-man to go to the local office and file the relinquishment, being prepared to make his own entry at the same time. He would thus have had notice of the adverse claim,—the contest. And this is in analogy with the purchase of an interest in land generally. The purchaser is charged with notice of the record.

It is not now denied that Loughrey failed to comply with the law.

In conclusion, the contestant is entitled to his preference right, when he procures the cancellation of the entry by showing the truth of his allegations of contest; as said in Hoyt v. Sullivan (2 L. D., 283) "generally, where the contest has been properly brought, a relinquishment has been construed as evidence in aid of the suit and not allowed to bar the preference right. But this is presumption merely, and if it be conclusively shown that it was an entirely independent transaction, and not evidence of prior abandonment, it will not so inure to aid the original contestant." It is only then in cases where the contestant relies on the relinquishment as evidence to support his contest that it can be shown to be "an entirely independent transaction," and so rebut the presumption arising on filing a relinquishment that it was the result of a prior contest. If the contestant does not invoke the relinquishment in his aid, but proves the facts alleged by him, independently thereof, the relinquishment can have no effect on his preference right whatever.

For the reasons herein set forth the decision appealed from is affirmed.

———

PURCHASE UNDER SECTION 7, ACT OF JULY 23, 1866.

CADY v. QUEEN ET AL.

The right of purchase conferred by section 7, act of July 23, 1866, is alienable, and descends to heirs upon the death of the purchaser.

An applicant for the right of purchase under said section must show (1) that he has, in good faith, for a valuable consideration, purchased land of Mexican grantees or assigns, which is excluded from the final survey of the grant, and (2) that he has used improved and continued in the actual possession of said land according to the lines of his original purchase.

The effect of the right of purchase under said section, is to withhold the lands covered thereby from the general operation of the pre-emption law.

As between a pre-emptor and one claiming the right of purchase, the question of the
applicant's laches can not arise, for the facts on which said right depend, exclude, if established, the acquisition of a pre-emption right by settlement.
As between the government and a claimant under this section, the Department has
no right, in the absence of statutory authority or general regulations, to fix a
time within which the right of purchase shall be exercised in a particular case.

Secretary Noble to the Commissioner of the General Land Office, October
4, 1889.

I have examined the record in the appeal of M. K. Cady from your
office decision, in the case of Martin K. Cady *v.* Wm. D. Queen and the
University of California, rendered January 8, 1887, involving, as between Cady and Queen, the preference right to enter lot 13, Sec. 26
and lot 1, Sec. 35, and lots 1, and 2, Sec. 36, all in township 6, range 6 W.,
in the district of lands subject to entry at San Francisco, California,
and as between Cady and the University the right to lot 3 and the NE.
¼ of the NW. ¼ of section 36 in the same township, and find—

That on November 12, 1880, Queen filed declaratory statement for
lots 10, 11, 12 and 13 Sec. 26, lot 1 Sec. 35, and lots 1 and 2, Sec. 36,
T. 6 R. 6 W., alleging settlement April 23, 1880.

The University of California made selection January 12, 1882, of lot
3, and the NE. ¼ of the NW. ¼ of Sec. 36 above mentioned. Said lands
were listed in list No. 11—approved June 7, 1883.

June 30, 1884, Cady made application in writing. duly verified, to
purchase all of lot 1 Sec. 35; all of lot 13, Sec. 20; part of lot 3 Sec.
25; part of lots 1, 2 and 3 Sec. 36; part of NE. ¼ NW. ¼ Sec. 36 and a
small portion of lot 4 of Sec. 36; all in T. 8, R. 6 W., and upon this
application this contest arose and summons was issued to Queen and
the University, both of whom appeared before the local officers, and a
hearing was had.

Cady claimed the right to purchase the land he applied for under
the seventh section of the act of July 23, 1866 (14 Stat., 218), entitled
"An act to quiet titles in California."

Queen insisted upon his right to purchase the lands claimed by him
under the pre-emption laws, and the University of California holding
that the lands claimed by it having been listed to it, in list No. 11, approved June 7, 1883, was not subject to sale.

The local officers sustained Cady's application, as to all except the
land claimed by the University, upon authority of the case of Hill *et
al., v.* Wilson *et al.,* 11 C. L. O., 151, and held—as to the lands claimed
by the University, that they having been listed to the State they had
no jurisdiction. Queen appealed. Cady did not appeal.—Your office
decision of January 8, 1887, reversed the decision of the local officers,
except as to the lands listed to the University, and denied Cady's application.

The above lands are within the exterior boundaries of the Rancho

Agua Caliente, the history of which is given in detail in case of Hill et al., v. Wilson et al., (11 C. L. O., 151), to which case I refer.

This grant was for a specified quantity of land (two and one-half leagues in length by one-fourth league in width) within boundaries, embracing a larger amount.

This grant was originally petitioned for and conceded to Lazara Pina, who, before confirmation transferred the land to M. G. Vallijo to whom it was confirmed.

Vallijo by a series of mesne conveyances transferred a portion of the same including the lands in dispute to Cornelius L. Place, who was the owner thereof from, as early as 1879 until his death in December, 1880.

The final survey, the plat of which was filed August 16, 1880, ex-cluded certain lands, including the tracts in dispute from the grant.

The evidence shows that at that time (August 16, 1880) the lands here in dispute, as well as other lands which were surveyed and pat-ented as a part of the grant, all in one compact body, were in the actual possession of Place, by his tenants, and that he and his grantors used and improved them;

That there was a vineyard of about eighty acres on the tract, a por-tion of which was on land excluded from the grant by the final survey, and is on the land in dispute. Much of the land was used for grazing purposes, and there was a two story adobe house, barn and other out-buildings; reservoirs, swimming baths and a fishing pond on the tract in 1880.

After the death of Place, the entire tract was sold by the executors of Place to one Lovegrove, on July 26, 1881, and afterwards on Octo-ber 1, 1881 Lovegrove conveyed the same to Martin K. Cady. After the death of Place his executors went upon the land, and the tenants attorned to them, and after the purchase of Lovegrove the tenants at-torned to him, and when Lovegrove sold to Cady he went into actual possession of the tract and has made improvements of great value thereon, none of which, however, are on the land in dispute.

Queen settled upon the land covered by his declaratory statement in April 1880. He built a house twelve by twelve feet; built some fence; some roads; cleared and grubbed some eight or ten acres; cultivated two or three acres in oats and hay, besides gathering the crop from that portion of the vineyard which was excluded from the grant by the final survey, and which he fenced off from the remainder of the vineyard—the quantity so fenced off is estimated at from one and one-half to three acres. He claims to have resided upon the land continu-ously from the date of his settlement.

The decision of your office, reversing that of the local officers, is based upon the ground that "the purchase of Cady, though direct by mesne conveyance from the Mexican grant and his assign was not made until after the plat embracing the land in contest was filed, and the

Agua Caliente Rancho surveyed and patented" thus holding that the right conferred by section 7, of the act of July 23, 1866, is not assignable.

In this view I cannot concur. It was held in the case of Wilson v. California and Oregon R. R. Co. in 1873, reported in 1 C. L. L., at page 471, upon authority of Myers v. Croft (13 Wallace 291), that this right is alienable, and decends to heirs upon the death of the purchaser.

This case was followed, and the same doctrine reaffirmed in Welch v. Molino et al., (7 L. D. 210) and I think the rule upon which these cases are based, viz:—that it is for Congress, and Congress alone to impose restrictions, limitations or conditions upon the exercise of any right or privilege conferred by its acts, with reference to public lands— is the true one, and should be followed.

Before proceeding to the decision of the other questions presented by this record, it is proper to ascertain what is necessary to be shown by the claimant, Cady, in order that he may be entitled to exercise the right conferred by section 7, of this act.

Said section reads as follows:

And be it further enacted, That where persons in good faith and for a valuable consideration, have purchased lands of Mexican grantees or assigns, which lands have subsequently been rejected, or where the lands so purchased have been excluded from the final survey of any Mexican grant, and have used, improved and continued in the actual possession of the same as according to the lines of their original purchase, and where no valid adverse right or title (except of the United States) exists, such purchasers may purchase the same, after having such lands surveyed under existing laws, at the minimum price established by law, upon first making proof of the facts as required in this section, under regulations to be provided by the Commissioner of the General Land Office, etc.

As applied to purchasers under the Rancho Agua Caliente grant, the claimant must prove—

1st. That he has purchased, in good faith, for a valuable consideration, lands of Mexican grantees or assigns, which have been excluded from the final survey of the grant, and

2nd. That he has used, improved and continued in the actual possession of the same as according to the lines of his original purchase.

The local officers as well as your office find in this case that Place had purchased in good faith and for a valuable consideration a portion of the Rancho Agua Caliente of the Mexican grantee and his assigns, and I think this finding is supported by the evidence: The lands in dispute were within the lines of his purchase, and were excluded from the final survey of the grant:

It is found by the local officers and by your office that Cady is the assignee of Place as to his right in these lands, and I think this finding is supported by the evidence.

It is found by the local officers that Cady and his grantors have "used, improved and continued in the actual possession" of these lands as according to the lines of the original purchase of Place, in which finding your office inferentially concurs, and deferring somewhat to these two concurring decisions, there being some conflict in the evidence, I find that Cady and his grantors have so "used, improved and continued in the actual possession" of said lands.

These facts being found, these lands are strictly within the letter and spirit of the section above cited, and the effect of the act was to withhold them from the general operation of the pre-emption laws. See act of March 3, 1853, Sec. 6 (10 Stat., 244); Hosmer v. Wallace, (97 U. S., 575).

These lands were not then subject to the operation of the pre-emption laws, by force of the statutes under consideration, and by reason of the *use*, and *actual possession* of Place and his assigns, which must be, and is found as a fact, or Cady's claim would have no foundation.

In the case under consideration the alleged settlement of Queen was made in April, 1880, and the township plat was filed the following August.

This act of settlement at that time was undoubtedly that of a trespasser and wrongdoer, as until official segregation was made, Place was entitled to the exclusive possession of his entire purchase, within the exterior limits of the grant, and this regardless of his actual possession. Van Reynegan v. Bolton (95 U. S., 33).

And these lands were, at that time, expressly excepted from the operation of the pre-emption laws. (Sec. 6, 10 Stat., 244.)

After segregation, his use, improvement and *actual possession*, as according to the lines of his original purchase, operate by virtue of said statutes no less to prevent the acquirement of any valid pre-emption right.

The question has been discussed whether Cady, by his laches has not forfeited his right under section 7, of the act of July 23, 1866.

According to my views, above expressed, this question can never arise, as between a settler and the claimant under the Mexican grant, for the reason that before he can make successful claim to purchase under this section, the claimant must prove *use, improvement, and continuous actual possession*, as according to the lines of his original purchase. If he does not prove this his claim must fail. If he does prove this, it makes the attempt to acquire a pre-emptive right by settlement invalid, by reason of the actual occupancy of another.

And as between the government and a claimant under this section, I am of the opinion that this Department has no right, in the absence of action by Congress, or general regulation on the subject to fix any time within which the right conferred by it shall be exercised in any particular case. The right conferred is assignable;—a thing of value—and it would be assuming a responsibility which I deem unauthorized, for this Department to prescribe any conditions, limitations or restrictions upon its exercise, in this particular case, not contained in, or authorized by, the act itself, or a general regulation on the subject. The decisions cited to the contrary are not, in my judgment controlling ones.

The case of Cerro Bonita Quick-silver Mines, decided by this Department in 1877 (4 C. L. O., 3), and the case of Vejar v. The State of California, decided by this Department in 1883 (11 O. L. O., 18), were both decided on different grounds, and the remarks made in those cases upon this question were *dicta*.

For the above reasons the application of Cady will be granted, and that of Queen rejected.

The decision of your office is reversed so far as the rights of Cady and Queen are concerned.

The lands claimed by the University of California having been listed and approved, this Department has no jurisdiction of that controversy, and your office decision as to those lands is affirmed.

***

PRE-EMPTION LAW—RESIDENCE.

JESSE F. WAGNER.

Land may be taken under the pre-emption law, though not habitable during the winter months on account of its altitude.

First Assistant Secretary Chandler to the Commissioner of the General Land Office, October 3, 1889.

I have considered the appeal of Jesse F. Wagner from your office decision of November 6, 1888, rejecting his proof on his pre-emption filing for the NW. ¼, Sec. 20, T. 12 N., R. 14 E., Sacramento land district, California.

Claimant filed his pre-emption declaratory statement for the said land June 8, 1885, alleging settlement May 15, previous. He submitted his final proof, January 11, 1888; the local officers rejected the proof, because the same shows, " that by reason of the depth of snow the land is inhabitable only a portion of the year and is on that account not subject to entry under any law requiring continuous residence."

Upon appeal your office affirmed the action of the local officers.

The claimant, thereupon appealed to this Department, and the case is before me for consideration.

The proof shows, that Wagner is a single man of the age of twenty-seven years, native born and a qualified pre-emptor. He made his first settlement on the land May 15, 1885, by commencing to build a house. He claims to have moved on the land and established his actual residence thereon on the twenty-ninth of said month. The character of the land is described by him and his witnesses as " mountain land" best fitted for grazing purposes, however, cereals, adapted to the altitude of the land can be raised thereon. Claimant's improvements on his claim consist of and are appraised as follows: A dwelling house of the size of fourteen feet by sixteen feet, built of logs with shake roof, board floor, one window and one door, fifty dollars; a second log house, built of hewed logs, sixteen by twenty-four feet, shake roof, board floor, one door and two windows, three hundred and fifty dollars; a log barn sixteen by twenty feet, shake roof, sixty dollars; thirty acres meadow land fenced with a log fence, one hundred dollars; a barb wire fence around the rest of the land, one hundred and seventy-five dollars; two corrals, twenty-five dollars; clearing ten acres, fifty dollars; total valuation of improvements eight hundred and ten dollars.

He had in his house a full set of furniture, including bed and bedding, cooking stove and cooking utensils; he had also on the land one spring wagon, one four-horse wagon, plow, harrow and other agricultural implements. Of domestic animals he kept on his claim, nine horses, one hundred head of horned cattle, fifteen hogs, two dogs, and two cats. He owns no other personal property, all his possessions are on the land. He has raised no crops, aside from crops of natural hay; besides pasturing his cattle on the meadows, he cut about six tons of hay each year. He states that he has cleared ten acres to put in crops of grain, but that the land was not quite ready for it; grain on this tract must be sown in the spring, not in the fall.

Regarding claimants residence on the land he asserts, that he moved on his claim May 29, 1885, that he then commenced to live there permanently; and that the land ever since had been his actual personal residence and home. He was, however, absent from the tract from November 25, 1885, to April 1, 1886, and from Christmas, 1886, to May 20, 1887; he left again soon after Thanksgiving day; it is asserted by him that he was absent at no other time. When going away from his tract, claimant took with him at the commencement of winter, his cattle and the other domestic animals; he and they stayed during the winter months near Lotus in El Dorado county—this land also lies in that county—at his father's place there situated. While there claimant boarded with his father. The reason why he was not on his land during the winter months is given by him in his proof as follows: "The cause of being absent at those times was on account of the snow covering the ground and it was necessary for me to remove my cattle to the valley. I brought them down to my father's place near Lotus, as I could winter them much cheaper there than to keep them in the mountains."

    *   *   *   *   *   *   *

Your office affirmed the decision of the local officers upon the ground that determined them to reject the proof.

In their and your view, I cannot concur.

Admitting the proof to show, that the land on account of its altitude and the severity of the weather, is not habitable during winter, it does not follow, that for this reason it is not open to pre-emption. The contrary view has been held and expressed by this Department in the cases, Rhoda A. McCormick (6 L. D., 811); Daniel Lombardi (7 idem. 57); I still adhere to the same opinion.

Having then concluded upon the good faith of the party and regard ing his absence from the land as sufficiently explained and accounted for, it is my opinion that the proof should be accepted and that patent, upon his further compliance with the law, be issued to him.

Your said office decision is, accordingly, reversed.

———

HOMESTEAD ENTRY—SETTLEMENT BEFORE SURVEY.
INSTRUCTIONS.

The right to make homestead entry under the act of May 14, 1880, acquired by a settler, who dies prior to survey, may be exercised by his devisee.

The case of Buxton v. Traver cited and distinguished.

Secretary Noble to the Commissioner of the General Land Office, October 4, 1889.

I am in receipt of your communication of the 20th ultimo, calling attention to the decision of the supreme court of the United States in the case of Buxton v. Traver (130 U. S., 232), which you say is interpreted by some as announcing a doctrine inconsistent with the practice of your office following the decision of the Department in the case of Tobias Beckner (6 L. D., 134), and other decisions, allowing parties as heirs or devisees of homestead settlers the benefit of Sec. 2269 of the Revised Statutes, and of the act of May 14, 1880 (21 Stat., 140) and requesting "to be instructed (1) as to whether there is any inconsistency between the decisions of the Department in reference to the subject, and said decision of the supreme court; and (2) as to whether there should be any change in the course of this office as above indicated in dealing with this class of cases."

The case of Tobias Beckner recognized the right of a person, as devisee of a settler whose settlement was made and who died prior to survey, to make homestead entry of the tract settled upon by his devisor, and this ruling is not inconsistent with the decision of the supreme court in the case of Buxton v. Traver. The rule in the case of Beckner will be followed by your office.

———

RAILROAD GRANT—INDEMNITY SELECTION.
ALLERS v. NORTHERN PAC. R. R. CO. ET AL.

An expired pre-emption filing, under which no claim is asserted, does not exclude the land covered thereby from indemnity selection.

A tract is not excluded from indemnity selection by reason of its being within the primary limits of another grant, if it is in fact vacant public land at date of selection, and otherwise subject to such appropriation.

Secretary Noble to the Commissioner of the General Land Office, October 4, 1889.

The Northern Pacific Railroad Company has appealed from the decision of your office, dated May 18, 1888, rejecting its claim to the NE.

¼ of the NE. ¼ and lot 1, Sec. 9, T. 134 N., R. 43 W., Fergus Falls land district, Minnesota.

Four different parties, to wit: J. Henry Allers, Peter Benge, the St. Paul, Minneapolis and Manitoba Railway Company and appellant, each have put forward a claim to perfect title to the described tract of land, and the respective claims of all of said parties were considered in the decision appealed from.

The facts materially affecting the claims of the respective parties, as shown by the record, are as follows:

The described land, it appears, is within the granted limits of the St. Paul, Minneapolis and Manitoba Railway Company's line of road, and within the indemnity limits of appellant's line of road.

June 19, 1871, one Herman Brusmitz filed pre-emption declaratory statement No. 734 on said land, alleging settlement thereon June 7, 1871.

December 19, 1871, the map of definite location of the St. Paul, Minneapolis and Manitoba Railway Company's line of road was accepted by the Secretary of the Interior.

Notice of the indemnity withdrawal made for the benefit of appellant's road was received at the local office January 10, 1872.

December 29, 1883, appellant applied to select said tract as indemnity for lands lost in place.

July 31, 1884, the St. Paul, Minneapolis and Manitoba Railway Company applied for same, as inuring to it under its grant.

August 13, 1885, J. Henry Allers applied to enter same under the homestead law.

August 31, 1885, Peter Benge applied to enter same under the homestead law.

Benge also makes affidavit that he had valuable improvements, and was residing on said land before the applications of Allers and the St. Paul, Minneapolis and Manitoba Railway Company were made, and he asks that a hearing be ordered to determine their respective rights.

On the facts stated, your office held that the Brusmitz filing excepted the described land from the grant to the St. Paul, Minneapolis and Manitoba Railway Company, and that as said land was within the granted limits of the last named company's grant, and was covered by said filing, appellant was not entitled to select the same as indemnity for lands lost in place.

It is also stated in the decision appealed from, that in case said decision should become final, or be affirmed on appeal, a hearing will be ordered to determine the respective rights of Allers and Benge.

The Northern Pacific Railroad Company is the only party offering objections to this decision, and it assigns error therein as follows, to wit:

1. Error to rule that the company was not entitled to select said land, because within the granted limits of the St. Paul, Minneapolis and Manitoba Railroad grant.

2. Error to rule that the expired pre-emption filing of Herman Brusmitz was a bar to the selection of the land by the company as indemnity.

3. Error to recognize the claims of either Allers or Benge, neither of which arose until after the application of the Northern Pacific Company to select said land.

4. Error not to have ordered a hearing to determine the status of the land at date of selection by the company.

The St. Paul, Minneapolis and Manitoba Railway Company has not appealed herein, and the decision of your office, which holds that the pre-emption claim of Brusmitz excepted the land in controversy from the grant made for the benefit of said company, is final. Said tract not having been granted to Minnesota for the benefit of said company, and Brusmitz's claim to the same having been abandoned many years prior to the time appellant applied to select the same, the conclusion follows that it was then, December 29, 1883, vacant public land, to which the United States had full title.

A hearing to determine the status or condition of the land at that time is, therefore, unnecessary. The land being vacant public land on December 29, 1883, does the fact that it is within the geographical limits of the grant made for the benefit of the St. Paul, Minneapolis and Manitoba Railway Company reserve it from selection by the Northern Pacific Railroad Company?

My attention has not been called to any decision of the Department, or of the courts, involving the question here presented, nor do I know of a decision which can be regarded as directly in point in this case. In the absence of authority, and availing myself of the light at hand, it seems to me that the objection to your office decision, pointed out by appellant's first assignment of error, is well taken.

It is true that lands within the limits of the grant made to Minnesota for the benefit of the St. Paul, Minneapolis and Manitoba Railroad Company, and which remained to the United States, were reserved from sale at private entry, until they were first offered at public sale to the highest bidder, and also from sale at less than double the minimum price of public lands generally (see Sec. 4, act March 3, 1865, 13 Stat., 526), but the odd numbered sections within the limits of said grant, and also within the indemnity limits of the grant of July 2, 1864, to the Northern Pacific Railroad Company, were not specifically excepted from selection by the latter company. The grant to this company provides, among other things, that for lands lost in place " other lands shall be selected by said company, in lieu thereof, under the direction of the Secretary of the Interior, in alternate sections, and designated by odd numbers, not more than ten miles beyond the limits of said alternate sections." (See Sec. 3, act of July 4, 1864, 13 Stat., 365). The fact that these selections are to be made under the *direction* of the Secretary of the Interior does not, in my opinion, clothe such officer with the arbitrary power of rejecting a selection made by the company, within the indemnity limits of its grant, of a tract of land in an odd numbered section, which, at the time the selection was made, had not been granted, sold, reserved, or otherwise disposed of, and which was then unoccupied and free from pre-emption or other claims or rights.

The bare fact that the land in controversy is within the granted limits of the St. Paul, Minneapolis and Manitoba Railroad Company's grant—since in fact it was not granted land—does not constitute a bar, in my opinion, to its selection as indemnity land by the Northern Pacific Railroad Company; nor does the expired pre-emption filing of said Herman Brusmitz constitute a bar to such selection. Benge alleges settlement on the land in controversy in June, 1884, which was six months after appellant applied to select the same, and his and Allers's application to enter said land were not made till August, 1885. The claim of the Northern Pacific Railroad Company being prior in time is superior in right to that of either of said parties. No good grounds can be discovered for rejecting the application made by said company, December 29, 1883, to select said tract, and the same is therefore allowed.

The decision of your office is accordingly reversed.

PRACTICE—APPEAL—SETTLEMENT RIGHTS—AMENDMENT.

NORTON v. WESTBROOK.

An appeal will not be dismissed on the ground that it was not taken in time, if the record fails to show when notice of the decision was received.

A settlement made without violence within the unlawful enclosure of another is valid, and will not be defeated by such unlawful occupancy.

Priority of right having been determined as between two settlers, the right of the prior settler to amend an irregular entry is an *ex parte* matter so far as the subsequent settler is concerned.

First Assistant Secretary Chandler to the Commissioner of the General Land Office, October 5, 1889.

On May 8, 1885, John Westbrook made homestead entry for the N. ½ SE. ¼ Sec. 11, and N. ½ SW. ¼ Sec. 12, T. 8 N., R. 28 E., Prescott, Arizona.

On February 5, 1886, John A. Norton filed an affidavit of contest alleging that Westbrook "has never acquired a legal residence upon said tract and has not resided thereon as required by law.

The hearing on said contest was ordered, and had in May 1886, before the judge of the county court of Apache county.

Upon the testimony transmitted the local officers sustained the entry.

Norton appealed and your office by decision of June 7, 1888, affirmed the action below. Norton again appeals.

Counsel for Westbrook move to dismiss the appeal for the reason that Norton failed to appeal from the decision of the local office within the time fixed by the rules of practice.

The decision of the local officers is dated June 7, 1886, and the appeal was filed July 17th following. The local officers state that their decision was "held" for forty days after the said decision "was duly filed and all parties notified . . . . which notification was acknowledged by the attorney of the party in interest."

It does not however appear when the notice of such decision was received by either Norton or his attorney. The latter, whose address is at St. Johns, almost one hundred and fifty miles from the local office, states in the appeal to your office that the "conclusions" reached by the local officers had not been properly stated in the letter of notification and that such letter had not been registered. See rule 44 of practice.

As the record fails to affirmatively show a failure to appeal within the proper time after notice of the decision of the local office, the motion to dismiss is denied.

The evidence is somewhat uncertain in character, but shows with substantial accuracy the matters hereinafter set forth.

Norton since 1881, had claimed about one hundred acres of the land which he seems to have "purchased" from his brother, and which was enclosed by about three hundred and fifty rods of fence built by himself and others. A considerable part of the alleged fence was composed of a natural rock bluff and the balance of "some pole . . . . some stakes and riders and some brush fence." The evidence concerning the condition of this fence is conflicting but shows I think by a fair preponderance that it was not in a good condition and that it would "not turn stock." A house fifteen by fifteen feet had been within said enclosure for about ten years, but which prior to May 1885, and during the period of Nortons' claim appears to have been without a roof and in a practically uninhabitable condition.

Norton cultivated fifty of the one hundred acres enclosed as aforesaid, but such cultivation is not specifically described. He admits that his family never resided on the land but explains that in consequence of the death of his wife which seems to have taken place about 1881, that he could not keep his children thereon. He testified that during the five years preceding the hearing he had slept on the land "about two months during the crop time."

In explanation of his statement that he had lived on the land for five years, Norton testified that he understood "residence" to be a "house."

The records of your office show that the township plat was filed in 1876. Norton states that he attempted to file for the land in 1881, but does not explain why his filing was refused. He also states that he applied to make homestead entry for the land on May 9, 1885, and that his application was rejected by reason of the existing entry of Westbrook.

During the latter part of April 1885, Westbrook—a single man who had previously lived at Springerville some three or four miles distant—had the tract surveyed, and ordered a bill of lumber from a neighboring saw mill. He then moved his personal effects (blankets, clothing camping outfit) thereto, and camped thereon outside of said enclosure for one night on or about April 30, 1885, and during the first two days of May following he laid a foundation also outside of said enclosure, consisting of logs eight inches in diameter at the butt and from two to five inches at the top. He then went to St. Johns, the county seat, and made his homestead affidavit before the clerk of the district court on May 4, 1885, which with his application was presumably sent to the local office by mail. He subsequently returned to the land, moved his lumber inside of the enclosure and built therein a frame house with two rooms, which he furnished and occupied between the 20th and 30th of May 1885. He cultivated three or four acres within said enclosure, and resided thereon continuously from the time last mentioned.

At some time between the 7th and 9th of May 1885, during Westbrooks temporary absence from the land, Norton who had re-married in January 1885, went thereon and repaired the old house in the enclosure and occupied the same with his family until the date of hearing.

The material question that is presented by this appeal is whether or not Norton had acquired such a right to the land as to render invalid the settlement and entry of Westbrook.

This question should, I think, be answered in the negative. Aside from the fact that the evidence tends to show that several different parties cultivated the land during the time that Norton claimed the same, it is clear that prior to May 1885, he had never established or maintained a bona fide residence upon the land. Being until then without any right under the settlement laws, his enclosure, if really his, was an unlawful one, and he can only claim the land by virtue of his settlement in May 1885, and his subsequent residence thereon. But this settlement was made several days after that of Westbrook, and is therefore subject to the latter's rights. It is true that Westbrook's first acts of settlement were meagre, but the record shows that they were made in good faith and that he subsequently complied with the law. Moreover, the evidence does not show the residence of Westbrook within the enclosure claimed by Norton to have been acquired through violence, but on the contrary it creates the impression that Norton made no protest against Westbrook's inhabitancy therein. A settlement made without violence within the unlawful and unauthorized enclosure of another is valid and will not be defeated by such unlawful occupancy. Stoddard v. Neigle (7 L. D., 340).

Counsel urge for the first time on appeal to your office that the entry of Westbrook should not be sustained for the reason that his homestead affidavit was improperly made before the clerk of the court under section 2294 Revised Statutes.

As Westbrook had at the date of said affidavit made his settlement with the intention of residing on the land, I am by no means satisfied that such affidavit was improperly made. But waiving this question, and aside from the fact that this matter is not alleged in the affidavit of contest, the contention that the entry of Westbrook, should be canceled for the benefit of Norton by reason of the said defective affidavit is without force.

Both parties claim the land by virtue of settlement, residence and improvement. In this regard the rights of Norton have been found to be inferior to those of Westbrook. So far as the regularity of the latter's entry is concerned the case is *ex parte*. This being so, Westbrook's homestead affidavit was, on May 29, 1888, as shown by the record, properly amended.

The entry of Westbrook must therefore be allowed and the contest of Norton dismissed.

The decision appealed from is affirmed.

SWAMP GRANT—FIELD NOTES OF SURVEY.

STATE OF ALABAMA.

The correctness of an official report as to what is shown by the field notes of survey will be presumed, in the absence of competent evidence to the contrary.

In the adjustment of the swamp grant on field notes of survey made before the date of said grant, the State is not entitled to lands returned as swamp and overflowed without all the descriptive words in the grant, or words clearly of like import.

Secretary Noble to the Commissioner of the General Land Office, October 5, 1889.

I have before me the appeal of the State of Alabama from your office decision of May 25, 1888, holding for rejection its claim to indemnity, under the acts of March 2, 1855, (10 Stat., 634) and March 3, 1857, (11 Stat., 251) for certain lands described in said decision; and suspending its claim to indemnity (under the said acts) for certain other lands likewise described in said decision, "for the purpose of allowing the State authorities to file additional proof as to the swampy or overflowed character of said lands, as contemplated by the swamp grant of September 28, 1850."

As to the lands of the first class, you reject the claim for indemnity on the ground that such lands "are (according to the field notes of survey on file in your office) dry and fit for cultivation and (accordingly) not of the character contemplated by the act of September 28, 1850."

As to lands of the second class, you ordered the suspension of the claim on the ground that the "field notes are not clear as to the character of said lands." The field-notes here in question were made before the passage of the granting act, and do not describe the lands as having been "made unfit for cultivation" by their being "swamp and overflowed." Neither these words of the grant, nor words "clearly of a like import," appearing in the notes, you held, on the authority (it would seem) of the decision in the case of the State of Louisiana (5 L.

D., 515), that " the State must show by other satisfactory evidence that the lands claimed are of the class contemplated by the grant."

I.

As to the first-named class of lands, a supplemental brief recently filed by the counsel for the State, objects to your said office decision upon the ground that, as was said in the case of Poweshiek county (9 L. D., 124), " it is clear that the act intended to grant not solely such lands as might strictly come under the description, 'swamp lands,' but such as are so ' wet' as to be rendered thereby unfit for cultivation."

This argument wholly ignores the fact that the lands referred to are sufficiently certified by your said office decision to be lands which are " shown by the field notes on file in this (your) office " to be "dry and fit for cultivation," instead of " so ' wet' as to be rendered thereby unfit for cultivation "—as they must be in order to fall within the ruling cited.

Against this official report as to what the field-notes show concerning the land in question, this Department can hardly be expected to take the mere statement of counsel, made *arguendo*, that " as to the lands in question in Alabama the field-notes clearly state that they are ' wet lands.'" The correctness of the official statement must be presumed by this Department, upon the fact of this record, in the absence of any sworn declarations, by one or more witnesses who shall have personally examined the field-notes in question, showing incorrectness of such official statement as to specified tracts of land.

Furthermore, even if we waive the informality of the contradiction, and assume that as the counsel state, the field-notes show these lands to be " wet lands; " even then, the argument is inconclusive, since (as the language quoted itself shows) the ruling is not that " wet" lands passed under the grant, but only that lands " so wet as to be thereby rendered unfit for cultivation," were covered by the act. And the Department can hardly assume " that where the surveyors reported lands as ' wet', they were thereby rendered unfit for cultivation," simply on the strength of counsel's opinion that " the experience of the Department for thirty years proved the fact" (that the surveyor's report of " wet," always implied the requisite degree of wetness).

II.

As to the second, or suspended group of lands, counsel insist that the failure of the field-notes to describe the tracts as " unfit for cultivation," (by reason of their swampy character), does not justify your office's demand for more evidence. The argument is that the word " swamp" is sufficient, without more, and the decision already cited (State of Louisiana, 5 L. D., 414) is sought to be distinguished on the ground that the field-notes there in question seem not to have described the lands as "swamp." But the rule laid down in that case is entirely unambiguous, and leaves no room for this alleged distinction. " Where the field-notes of survey," the opinion says, " have been made since the passage of the act . . . . and with reference thereto, they will be held to entitle the State *prima facie* to the lands returned as swamp and overflowed, without the additional words ' made unfit thereby for cultivation ;' but where made before the passage of that act,"—which is the case here—"all the descriptive words in the grant, or words clearly of a like import, must appear ; and where they do not so appear the State must show by other satisfactory evidence that the lands claimed are of the class contemplated by the grant." This distinctly holds that, where the field-notes ante-dated the act, " they will (not) be held to entitle the State (even) *prima facie* to the lands returned as swamp and overflowed, without all the descriptive words in the grant or words clearly of a like import."

Besides, there is nothing in the record to show that the only respect in which the field-notes are insufficient, is the absence of the phrase to which the argument refers. All that the record shows is the finding of your office that " said field-notes are not clear as to the character of said lands."

For the foregoing reasons your said office decision is affirmed.

MINING CLAIM—MILL SITE.

LE NEVE MILL SITE.

A quartz mill, or reduction works, are the only improvements on which a mill site entry may be based under the last clause of section 2337, of the Revised Statutes.

Secretary Noble to the Commissioner of the General Land Office, October 5, 1889.

June 12, 1886, Ernest Le Neve Foster made mineral entry, No. 3047, at the Central City land office, Colorado, for a mill-site claim of 2.55 acres, described by metes and bounds, and known as the Le Neve Mill-site.

August 14, 1888, your office directed the register and receiver of said land office to notify claimant that there was no evidence on file in the case, " showing that there is a quartz mill or reduction works on said claim," and that he would be allowed sixty days from notice " to furnish satisfactory evidence in accordance with the last clause of section 2337," Revised Statutes. Said officers were also directed to call Mr. Foster's attention to " paragraph 74 of circular approved October 31, 1881," which paragraph prescribes the manner of proceeding in order to obtain a patent for a mill-site, in cases where " the owner of a quartz-mill or reduction works is not the owner or claimant of a (mineral) vein or lode "

In response to the foregoing, Mr. Foster, on August 23, 1888, filed in the local land office his affidavit, in which he deposes and says:

That said mill-site is used for mining purposes, there being upon the same a dam, pen-stock and pipe, which is used for driving a water wheel to compress air for the engine and drills used in mining upon the adjacent lodes, and that said machinery has been erected at a cost of not less than $20,000.

Your office, by decision of September 4, 1888, found that the improvements described were not "the kind of improvements contemplated in the last clause of section 2337 of the U. S. Revised Statutes, under which the entry is made," and directed the local officers to notify claimant, "that satisfactory evidence on this point must be furnished within the sixty days allowed by said office letter (of August 14, 1888), in default of which said entry will be held for cancellation."

From this action Foster has appealed, on the ground that your office erred in holding said improvements not to be ." the kind of improvements contemplated in the last clause of section 2337 of the U. S. Revised Statutes."

That a quartz-mill, or reduction works, are the only kinds of improvements contemplated by the last clause of said section, is clearly manifested by these improvements being distinctly named, and there being no mention of any other kinds of improvements whatever in said clause. The language of the statute is too plain to admit of a construction which would authorize the Land Department to issue a patent on the proof made in this case, and as it is quite evident that the improvements contemplated by the statute in mineral mill-site claims have never been made on the said "Le Neve Mill-site claim," no error can be discovered in your said office decision.

From anything appearing in the record to the contrary appellant may be able to obtain a patent, by making proper application and proof, under the provisions of the first clause of said section 2337.

On the proof made herein, the decision of your office holding said entry for cancellation is affirmed.

TIMBER CULTURE CONTEST—RELINQUISHMENT.

BRAKKEN v. DUNN ET AL.

A relinquishment made and filed pending a contest is presumed, in the absence of evidence to the contrary, to have been the result of the contest, and therefore inuring to the benefit of the contestant.

The rights of the contestant are determined by the status of the land when contest is instituted, and his right to proceed against the entry can not be defeated by a subsequent relinquishment.

First Assistant Secretary Chandler to the Commissioner of the General Land Office, October 5, 1889.

I have examined the record in the appeal of William Rand from your decision in Wm. Rand v. Torger R. Brakken, dated May 21, 1888, rejecting the application of Rand to make a timber culture entry of the SW. ¼ Sec. 26 T. 150 N., R. 60 W., Grand Forks, Dakota, and awarding the right of entry of said land to Brakken, and find :

First. That on March 31, 1882, one Arthur W. Dunn, made timber-culture entry No. 1899, covering said tract.

Second. On July 12, 1886, Torger R. Brakken filed affidavit of contest against said entry, and at the same time his application to enter said land.

In this affidavit Brakken alleged as ground of contest that said Arthur W. Dunn had "failed to cultivate or cause to be cultivated, or to plant to timber seeds or cuttings any part of said tract after the third year after said entry, and that said failure then existed."

At the same time Brakken filed an application for notice by publication as required by the rules of practice, but it does not appear whether a day of hearing was set, or notice ordered.

Third. On July 16, 1886, William M. Rand presented a relinquishment of said entry, executed and acknowledged by Arthur W. Dunn on July 15, 1886, and applied to enter the tract under the timber culture act.

Fourth. The original entry was then canceled, but Rand's application to enter was denied, and he appealed, and with the appeal filed Dunn's affidavit stating that at the time of the relinquishment he (Dunn), had no knowledge of the contest.

Fifth. A hearing was ordered as to the preference right of entry, and was had before the register and receiver on December 1, 1887, at which Brakken and another witness testified to facts tending to show the truth of the allegations in his affidavit of contest and that the contest was made in good faith for his own use.

Rand submitted no testimony, but relied entirely upon the fact shown by the affidavit of Dunn that he (Dunn) knew nothing of the contest at the date of his relinquishment, and though personally present he (Rand) was suggestively silent as to his own knowledge of that fact.

Sixth. The register and receiver held that Brakken had failed to show that the relinquishment was the result of the contest, and hence he had not "procured the cancellation of the entry," within the meaning of section 2, of the act of May 14, 1880.

Seventh. From this decision Brakken appealed to your office.

Eighth. By your decision herein referred to, you reversed the decision of the local officers, rejected Rand's application, and awarded to Brakken the right of entry upon the tract.

It is the holding of this Department, that a relinquishment, made and filed pending a contest will be presumed, in the absence of evidence to the contrary, to have been the result of such contest, and have the legal effect to dispose of the contest in favor of the contestant. See McCall v. Molnar, 2 L. D., 256; Hoyt v. Sullivan id., 283; Hemsworth v. Holland 8 id., 400.

In the recent case of Webb v. Loughrey *et al.*, 9 L. D., 440, this question is very fully considered and therein in construing the act of May 14, 1880 (21 Stat., 140), it is in substance held that upon the written relinquishment of the entryman's claim, the land covered thereby shall be held open to entry to the next applicant, and where a contestant files his affidavit for contest, accompanied with application to enter, and thereafter the claimant relinquishes his entry, the contestant is to be considered first in the race and shall be awarded the preference right to the land if he sustains his contest, notwithstanding the good faith of one who seeks to make entry upon the faith of the relinquishment, and this on the theory that a relinquishment filed after the initiation of contest ought not to be permitted to defeat the acquired right of the contestant to proceed against the entry.

The contestant's rights are determined by the status of the land at the time of the instituting of the contest and his rights can not be defeated by the subsequent act of the entryman relinquishing his claim. The filing of the affidavit and the application to enter is of record in the local office and the entryman, and those seeking to avail themselves of the benefit of his act are bound to take notice thereof and can not acquire a preference right over the same on the ground that they did not know thereof and acted in good faith in making the relinquishment. This must be the true rule. The adoption of any other is to open the door to fraud and collusion between the entryman and any other person whom he desires to favor, and that too, to the defeat of the rights of the contestant who has in good faith instituted proceedings which, if he is permitted to carry out, may ripen into an entry of the tract in controversy. Entertaining these views, your decision is affirmed, and the right of entry awarded to Brakken, the entry of Rand being rejected.

PRACTICE—REVIEW; PRE-EMPTION—SECTION 2260 R. S.

CROGHAN GRAVES.

A motion for review, on the ground that the decision is not supported by the evidence, will not be granted unless it is made to affirmatively appear that said decision is clearly wrong, and against the palpable preponderance of the evidence.

A pretended transfer of land from husband to wife will not defeat the inhibitory provisions contained in the second clause of section 2260 of the Revised Statutes.

The case of David Lee cited and distinguished.

Secretary Noble to the Commissioner of the General Land Office, October 5, 1889.

I have considered the motion filed in behalf of Croghan Graves for review of departmental decision of December 19, 1888 (unreported), adverse to him in the matter of his pre-emption claim for the NW. ¼ of NE. ¼, E. ½ of NW. ¼ and NW. ¼ of NW. ¼, Sec. 12, T. 26 S., R. 9 E., San Francisco, California, land district.

Graves filed declaratory statement, No. 17,129, for said tract April 3, 1883. September 2, 1885, he gave notice of his intention to offer final proof on the 20th of October, 1885.

The final proof disclosed the fact that Graves had previously made homestead entry for another tract of land, and that he had received patent for said homestead tract; that in October, 1882, he, by deed, duly executed and recorded, conveyed to his wife the tract covered by said homestead entry and patent, and soon thereafter moved to the land which he now claims under the pre-emption law.

On these facts, the local officers following, as they said, a previous decision of your office in another case, refused to allow cash entry on the proofs offered. On appeal, your office affirmed that action, and held the pre-emption filing of Graves for cancellation.

Graves appealed to this Department, which by the decision, a review of which is now asked, affirmed your said office decision, for the reason, "that the alleged conveyance to Mrs. Graves was simply a pretended transfer, by which it was attempted to evade the law."

Counsel for the applicant has assigned seven specifications of error, the first of which is, that the conclusion of the local office and of your office, affirmed by the Department, holding "that the conveyance by Graves to Mrs. Graves of the land patented to him under the homestead law, was simply a *pretended* transfer, for the purpose of evading the law and not a *bona fide* conveyance, is not fully and clearly justified by the proof, beyond a reasonable doubt." The other allegations of error are to the effect, that said departmental decision is "a harsh construction of the law," not warranted by the record in the case; that said transfer was authorized by the laws of California and was made in good faith, and when so made the grantor was qualified to make settlement under the pre-emption laws, and was not within the inhibition of section 2260 of the Revised Statutes.

It will be quite unnecessary to enter into an extended argument to show that said motion must be overruled. It is not necessary that the concurrent decisions of the local office, your office and the Department must be "fully and clearly justified by the proof beyond a reasonable doubt." On the contrary, the rule is, that a review of a decision will not be granted, unless it affirmatively appear that is clearly wrong and "against the palpable preponderance of the evidence." Mary Campbell (8 L. D., 331).

The applicant has submitted no new evidence, and due weight must be given to the concurring decisions of the local office, your office and the Department.

The decision of this Department in case of David Lee, 8. L. D., 502, is not inconsistent with the above conclusion. In that case it was held:

The validity of a deed made in good faith from husband to wife is recognized by this Department, where such deed is valid under the laws of the State or Territory in which the land conveyed is located. Hatch v. Van Doren, 4 L. D., 358. . . . . .
If, therefore, said conveyance by Lee was *bona fide* and not resorted to as a mere expedient for evading the law, it was effective to divest him of his title to the land embraced therein.

The Department found that Lee's deed was in "good faith" for a valuable consideration, to wit, $850, actually paid by the wife for the property. Not so in the case at bar. Here the deed was a voluntary one, made only about ten days prior to the alleged settlement, and the finding of the register and receiver, the Commissioner, and Secretary Vilas is to the effect that the conveyance was " simply a pretended transfer, by which it was attempted to evade the law." For the reasons above stated the motion must be denied.

RAILROAD GRANT—INDEMNITY SELECTIONS—ACT OF MARCH 3, 1873.

CHICAGO, ST. PAUL, MINNEAPOLIS AND OMAHA RY. CO.

Under the act of March 3, 1873, the company is entitled to make indemnity selections in lieu of lands settled upon within the indemnity limits of its road between Tomah and Hudson, and which might have been selected if the order of withdrawal had been made on definite location.

Secretary Noble to the Commissioner of the General Land Office, October 7, 1889.

The matters submitted for direction by your office letter of April 30, 1888, growing out of the claim of the Chicago St. Paul, Minneapolis and Omaha Railway Company, successor to the West Wisconsin, to indemnity lands under the act of March 3, 1873 (17 Stat., 634), have been carefully considered.

It appears that by act of June 3, 1856 (11 Stat., 20), Congress granted to the State of Wisconsin, for the purpose of aiding in the construction of a continuous line of railroad from Columbus or Madison, by the way of Portage City, to the St. Croix river, thence to Lake Superior, six odd numbered sections of land per mile on each side of said road, with the right to take indemnity for lost lands within fifteen miles from the line of road. The benefits of this grant in its entirety were conferred by the State upon the La Crosse and Milwaukee Railroad Company.

The map of definite location of the said road, between Tomah and the St. Croix river, the part we are now to deal with, was filed September 7, 1857, a previous withdrawal of the odd sections within the fifteen miles limits having been made on May 29, 1856. The line of road as above located went from Tomah northwesterly to Prescott on the St.

Croix river.   No portion of the road between these points, however, was constructed at this time.   This was the condition of things when the act of Congress of May 5, 1864 (13 Stat., 66), was passed.   By that act the continuity of the original road was destroyed, and provision made for a road from the St. Croix river to Lake Superior, and for another from Tomah to the St. Croix river.   In aid of each road were granted the odd numbered sections to the extent of ten sections per mile on each side thereof, "deducting any and all lands that may have been granted for the same purpose by act of Congress of June 3, 1856, upon the same terms and conditions as in said act," and the indemnity limits were increased to twenty miles.   The benefits of the grant between Tomah and the St. Croix river thereafter became vested in the West Wisconsin Company, and ultimately in the Chicago, St. Paul, Minneapolis and Omaha Company.

A relocation of the line of the road between Tomah and the St. Croix river was made and the map thereof filed June 9, 1865.   This new location followed the old one for some distance, then went further to the north, and by a direct line to Hudson on the St. Croix river, instead of Prescott, the former terminus.   No withdrawal along the line of the road from Tomah to Hudson was made until February 5, 1866, when all the odd numbered sections within the granted and indemnity limits were ordered to be withdrawn.   No reason is assigned for this delay, but it is stated that during the interval between the filing of the new map of definite location on June 9, 1865, and the time of the withdrawal as aforesaid, settlers occupied the designated sections in both the granted and indemnity limits along the new line of road to a very great extent.

This condition of affairs attracted the attention of Congress, and on March 3, 1873 (17 Stat., 634), it passed "An act to quiet the title of settlers on land claimed by the West Wisconsin Railway Company;" the preamble and enacting portion of which are as follows:

Whereas, by the neglect of the Commissioner of the General Land Office to have the lands withdrawn from market embraced in the grant of lands from the town of Tomah to the city of Hudson, in the State of Wisconsin, as soon as the West Wisconsin Railway Company (to which company the said grant belongs) had finally located its road and filed the map of such location, a large amount of lands—about twenty thousand acres—were taken up under the homestead laws and otherwise entered: Therefore,

Be it enacted, etc., That provided said West Wisconsin Railway Company shall waive and release all claims to any lands taken up under the homestead laws or otherwise entered after the final location of their road, as aforesaid, it shall be lawful for said company to make up any such deficiency in the grant, not however to exceed twenty thousand acres, from the vacant odd-numbered sections from the southeastern part or portion of the indemnity limits of the former grant for the branch roads from the said city of Hudson to Lake Superior.

On January 7, 1888, Messrs. Britton and Gray, counsel for the Omaha Company, in a communication to your office, stated that the adjustment of the grants to the road from Hudson to Lake Superior left available sufficient odd numbered sections within the southeastern portion of the indemnity limits of that grant, wherefrom the deficiency in the West Wisconsin grant, as recited in said act, might be satisfied; and, in behalf of the Omaha Company, successor of the West Wisconsin, an offer was made to execute the waiver and release required by said act, provided the officers at Eau Claire, in which district the lands lay, were instructed to accept said release and permit the company to make its selection within the prescribed indemnity limits. With this communication was inclosed a list, aggregating 16,291.89 acres of land, proposed to be released, and for which indemnity under the act of 1873, *supra*, was claimed. Of the lands described in said list, 6,455.24 acres are within the ten miles or granted limits, and 9,132.09 acres within the twenty miles or indemnity limits of the road between Tomah and Hudson.

The right of the company to indemnity, under the act of 1873, for lands within its granted limits, is conceded in your office letter of April 30, 1888. But the right to make other selections, under said act, for lands settled upon within its indemnity limits, is denied, and this is the question presented for determination.

No question can now be raised as to the right of the company to have made its new location, since the act recognizes the legality of that location. Nor can any question be here raised as to whether or not it was the duty of the Commissioner of the General Land Office, upon the filing of the map of the new location, to make a withdrawal.

But the question arises as to what lands were "embraced" in the said grant.

By the act of 1864, under which this company by its new location elected to take, a present grant was made of ten odd numbered sections per mile on each side of the road, with the right to take indemnity, for lost lands in place, in another limit of ten miles. The supreme court, in the case of Winona and St. Peter R. R. Co. *v.* Barney, 113 U. S., 626, construing a similar grant, declared that by these grants Congress in effect said :

We give to the State certain lands to aid in the construction of railways, lying along their respective routes, provided they are not already disposed of, or the rights of settlers under the laws of the United States have not already attached to them, or they may not be disposed of, or such rights may not have attached when the routes are finally determined. If at that time it be found that of the lands designated any have been disposed of, or rights of settlers have attached to them, then other equivalent lands may be selected in their place within certain prescribed limits.

In the Kansas Pacific case (112 U. S., 421), it is said, that by the indemnity clause " a right to select" was given, and in the Cedar Rapids case (110 U. S., 39), it is said that this "right" accrues, as against the United States, when the map of the entire line is filed. Now, then, on June 9, 1865, when the map was filed, we have the company entitled to its place lands, and the "right" to select lieu lands, as against the United States, fixed or vested, and, if the land officers had made withdrawal, as Congress says they ought to have done, also with the "right" to select as against all subsequent settlers. This, then, was the grant conferred by Congress, and of which it intended the company should have the benefit . . . ten sections of land per mile on each side of the road, to be obtained either within the primary or secondary limits, but ten sections the company was to have. On this plain statement it ought to be clear that the right to both place and lieu lands was conferred by the grant, and therefore, necessarily, they were, in the language of the act of 1873, "embraced in the grant of lands" made to aid in the construction of this road. Certainly, if the right to the lieu lands is not conferred by the grant, it is difficult to discern whence that right is derived, or how the company can by any possibility acquire any title thereto. It can not be obtained by selection alone, or possession, or arise out of the exigencies of the case.

But it is urged that by the use of the expression "grant of lands" Congress meant really granted lands, or lands within the primary limits of the grant. I can not concur in this view. The history of the legislation of Congress will doubtless show many instances wherein indemnity and lands other than place lands are referred to as granted lands. One or two instances suggest themselves to me, and may be briefly referred to.

By the ninth section of the Texas Pacific act (16 Stat., 576), it is provided that if, in the too near approach of said railroad to the Mexican border, the number of sections to which the company is entitled cannot be selected, on the line of the road, then a like quantity of land may be selected elsewhere:

Provided, that no public lands are hereby granted within the State of California further than twenty miles on each side of said road, except to make up deficiencies as aforesaid.

Here indemnity lands to be selected for other lost indemnity lands are included in the category of lands "hereby granted." Also, in the case of the Burlington and Missouri River grant, the only one of quantity without lateral limits now recalled, and where the land is to be obtained by selection anywhere along the line of the road, the language of the act is that (sec. 19, act July 2, 1864—13 Stat., 356), "there be and hereby is granted," provided the company accept "this grant" within one year, when the Secretary "shall withdraw the lands embraced in this grant from market." And the supreme court in 98 U. S., 334, construing the act, speak of it all the way through as a "grant," and of the lands, as granted lands, and uphold the right of the company to select them anywhere along the general direction of the road within lines perpendicular to it at each end.

Nor are we without judicial construction in this respect. In the case of the Chicago, Milwaukee and St. Paul Railway v. Sioux City Railroad, in 3rd McCrary's Repts., p. 300, the court said, on this point:

The lands in place and the indemnity lands were granted by Congress for the same purposes. The intention of the grantor with respect to them was exactly the same. Both were subject to the same trusts. The mode of making the title of the trustee

specific was different, but when that title became certain in the trustee by the location of a definite line in the one case, and by selection in the other, it was the duty of
the trustee to apply the two kinds of land to precisely the same trusts.

So in 24 Federal Reporter, p. 892, Barney *v.* Winona, it was held that
the expression, "Lands which may have been granted to the Territory
or State of Minnesota,"

includes all lands the title to which had passed to the Territory or State of Minnesota; whether these lands were lands in place or indemnity lands, and the word
'granted' has the broad, rather than the narrow signification.

So in the St. Paul *v.* Winona Railroad, 112 U. S., 730, referring to the
significant fact that both acts there quoted speak of additional sections
"to be selected, a word wholly inapplicable to lands in place," the
court says, "we think therefore that these additional lands granted to
the appellant . . . . . are lands to be selected," etc.

These citations doubtless might be multiplied largely, but they are
sufficient, inasmuch as they show that the expressions "lands granted,"
"granted lands," "lands within the grant," and similar expressions
have not such narrow and technical meaning as to restrict the use of
them to lands in place or within the primary limits of a grant.   On the
contrary, such expressions are to be construed liberally and broadly,
not standing alone, but in connection with the whole context of the act,
and its true meaning gathered therefrom.   Therefore, on a full consideration of the subject, I am of the opinion that when Congress spoke
of the failure of the Commissioner of the General Land Office to "have
the lands withdrawn from market embraced in the grant of lands,"
etc., it meant the lands in both the primary and indemnity limits.   If,
then, the failure to withdraw the indemnity lands was a wrong in the
eyes of Congress, one of the purposes of the act of 1873 undoubtedly
was to right that wrong by allowing indemnity for such losses as might
be caused by the neglect of the government officer in the premises.

But the act in question was not passed for the sole purpose of bene-
fiting the railroad company.   Studying that act its primary purpose,
the motive for the legislation, is apparent, and was the protection of
settlers who had gone upon land supposed by them to be public, but
which in reality had been granted to the railroad.   According to your
office letter 6,455.24 acres of lands had thus been taken up by settlers
within the primary or granted limits of said road, after its map of definite location was filed.   The grant to the company being *in præsenti*, the
title to every acre of those sixty-four hundred and fifty acres passed to
the company when its map was filed.   There can be no doubt about
this.   The settlers not having the usual notice given by the land officers,
in such cases, went upon these lands and expended their time and
means, in entire ignorance of the rightful claim of the company; and
this unfortunate condition of affairs was brought about by the neglect
of the land officers.   Congress felt under an imperative obligation to
protect these citizens.   Every word and sentence used is formed and

shaped to accomplish this end.   It is entitled " An act to quiet the title
to lands of settlers," etc., not an act to secure the company other lands
in lieu of those lost.   Its preamble recites that, in consequence of the
neglect of the Commissioner to withdraw the lands, that a large amount
have been—not lost by the railroad company—but taken up by settlers.
So, too the enacting clause does not provide for the absolute and un-
conditional indemnification of the company for the lands so appropriated, but such indemnity is granted solely on condition that the settlers may be fully protected, and in default of such protection, the company takes nothing whatever under the act, so that the protection of the
settler is the primary motive and purpose of the act, the indemnification
being concomitant and incidental thereto.

This being so, it must be apparent that to accomplish the great object
in view, Congress was holding out to the company an inducement or
consideration to secure all the settlers in the quiet possession of the
land occupied by them.   The settlers upon the lands within the indemnity limits were safe enough ; they could not be disturbed, because
the company could acquire no right to any such tract until actual selection.   But not so with those in the primary limits.   So the proposition
was plainly put, that, if the company would release all claim against
the settlers, the government would allow indemnity for not only such
lands, as were thus released, in the primary limits, but also for such
lands in the indemnity limits as were vacant at the date of definite location, and might have been selected by it in lieu of lands lost elsewhere along its line, if the withdrawal had been made; the total grant
being largely deficient to an amount estimated at 140,000 acres.   A
mere right to take indemnity for the lands in place would have been
no inducement to the company.   The place lands along and nearest to
the line of its road, improved by settlement and cultivation, already belonged to it, and why should it surrender these lands for others more
remote and therefore probably less valuable ?   But when the government proposed to give the right to select lieu lands for those in the indemnity limits, absolutely lost to and gone forever from the company, a
sufficient consideration to induce it to consent to the proposition of Congress was presented and accepted.

Other reasons might be added, but these are sufficient to bring me to
the conclusion that your office erred in denying to the company the
right to select other lands for those settled upon within the indemnity
limits of their road between Tomah and Hudson, as prescribed in the
act of 1873.

I therefore direct that such allowance be m ade, and a proper list be
sent to me for approval.

RAILROAD GRANT—PRIVATE CLAIM—RESERVATION.

CHILDS v. SOUTHERN PACIFIC R. R. CO.

In the case of a private claim of quantity within larger out boundaries, only so much of said larger tract is reserved for the adjustment of said claim as may be required for the satisfaction thereof.

Lands within the larger out boundaries of an unlocated claim of this class, are subject to the operation of a railroad grant at the date when it becomes effective, except as to the quantity actually required to satisfy said claim.

Secretary Noble to the Commissioner of the General Land Office, October 8, 1889.

The land involved herein is the NW. ¼ of Sec. 31, T. 4 S., R. 3 W., Los Angeles land district, California.

The record shows, that on December 10, 1887, Samuel R. Childs applied to make homestead entry for the tract, tendering the usual fees therefor, and that on the same day his application was rejected by the local officers, for the reason that "the land is within the primary limits of the grant to the Southern Pacific Railroad Company, act, July 27, 1866."

An appeal was taken by Childs from this finding, but on April 17, 1888, the same was affirmed by your office. The case is now before me on appeal by Childs from your said decision.

The records of your office show, and it is expressly admitted in the arguments of counsel for the appellant, that the tract in question lies within the twenty mile, or primary, limits of the grant to said company, made March 3, 1871 (16 Stat., 579), to aid in the construction of its branch line of road, as shown by the map of designated route thereof, filed April 3, 1871. An order of withdrawal, embracing the land in dispute, was made for the benefit of said company April 21, 1871, and notice thereof was received at the local office May 10, following. The records of your office further show, that no entry or filing has ever been made for the tract.

The errors assigned by appellant are substantially the same in both the appeal to your office and that which brings the case here, and they amount, in effect, to a contention that the land in question was excepted from the operation of the grant to the railroad company, because embraced, at the date when the company's rights attached under its grant, within the exterior boundaries, or claimed limits of certain Mexican private land grants, known as the San Jacinto Viejo, and San Jacinto Nuevo; and being upon final survey and definite location of said grants, subsequently made, excluded from the limits thereof, and thereby restored to the public domain, was subject to homestead entry, at the date when appellant's application to enter the same was made.

The grant to the railroad company is of every alternate odd num-

bered section of public land, not mineral, situated within certain prescribed limits, to which the United States have full title, " not reserved,
sold, granted, or otherwise appropriated, and free from pre-emption, or
other claims or rights, at the time the line of said road is designated
by a plat thereof, filed in the office of the Commissioner of the General
Land Office." (14 Stat., 292; 16 Stat., 579.)

By the decision of your office, it is simply held that the land in controversy was not embraced within the exterior limits of the Rancho San
Jacinto (meaning the place or country known as "San Jacinto," out of
which the aforesaid Mexican grants were to be satisfied), as surveyed
by O'Farrell in the year 1845, and was not claimed as being a portion
thereof at the date when the railroad company's said map of designated
route was filed; and that, so far as the records showed, the tract was,
at that date, vacant public land, and, therefore, inured to the company
under its grant.

The first question presented by the appeal from this decision, is,
whether the land in controversy, though lying without the limits of the
O'Farrell survey of 1845, is in fact within the exterior boundaries or
claimed limits of the original tract called "San Jacinto." If it be found
that the land does fall within the boundaries of said San Jacinto tract,
then the further question will arise, as to whether the same was, at the
date when the railroad company's rights attached under its grant, in
such a state of reservation as to bring it within the excepting clause of
said grant.

The case has been elaborately and earnestly argued by counsel, both
for the homestead applicant and the railroad company; and. in view
of the fact that there are now pending before the Department a large
number of cases involving the same questions as here presented, and
the consequent magnitude of the interests at stake, the greatest care
has been taken in their consideration.

There were three several private grants made by the Mexican government, of lands lying in southern California, within the limits of the
tract or area of country known as "San Jacinto." The first of these
grants is called the "San Jacinto Viejo," or Old San Jacinto, and was
made December 21, 1842, to Jose Antonio Estudillo, for four square
leagues " of the land known by the name of San Jacinto." (See Record
of Evidence, Land Commission, California, Vol. 17, 31.) The second,
known as the "San Jacinto Nuevo," or New San Jacinto, was made
January 14, 1846, to Miguel Pedrorena, and describes the land granted,
as " the land named ' San Jacinto,' including the ' Potrero' of the same
name." (Id., Vol. 10, 258–758.) This grant was finally confirmed by
the United States district court, as shown by a copy of the decree of
confirmation, on file in your office, for " the sobrante, or surplus remaining within the boundaries of the tract called San Jacinto . . . . .
over and above certain lands granted to Jose Antonio Estudillo, within
the same boundaries, to the extent of eleven square leagues."

The third grant is known as the "Sobrante de San Jacinto Viejo y Nuevo," and was made May 9, 1846, to Maria del Rosario Estudillo de Aguirre. The original petition filed in February, 1846, set forth that there was remaining a "sobrante," or surplus, "the extent of which is about five leagues, more or less, within the limits of the known rancho of San Jacinto, the general plat of which is in the office of the Secretary of State, and shows in its total extent that it is bounded thus : north by the ranchos of Jurupa and San Barnardino, south by Temecula, west by Huapa, and east by Gorgonio," and asked for a grant of such "sobrante," or surplus. The sub-prefect reported the land as "that remaining vacant from the lands of Old and New San Jacinto, and which is bounded by the lands mentioned in the petition ; and the copy of the plat which I have under my eyes proves to be correct with the original which exists in this government." Upon this report, the Governor of the Department of California, made concession to the petitioner of "the property in fee of the land remaining in Old and New San Jacinto, conformably as shows the general map which agrees with all the antecedents." And in the final grant the land is described as "that which remains as overplus in the ranchos of Old and New San Jacinto, as will appear by the general map of both ranchos, and which corresponds with their expedientes." (Id. Vol. 10–318, and Vol. 13–602.) This overplus was afterwards found to amount to very much more than five leagues, the quantity it was originally supposed to contain, but, in view of the limitation imposed by the Mexican colonization law of 1824, the grant as confirmed by the United States district court (whose decree, a copy of which is filed in your office, was, on appeal, affirmed by the supreme court, 1 Wall., 311), is to the extent only of eleven square leagues of land, described in the decree of confirmation as "the 'sobrante,' or surplus, remaining within the boundaries of the tract of land called San Jacinto," over and above the lands conveyed by the former grants, hereinbefore mentioned, and to the extent aforesaid. (See also United States v. San Jacinto Tin Co., 10 Sawyer, 645).

The reasonable and natural conclusion to be drawn from the foregoing is, that the exterior boundaries of the original tract called "San Jacinto," were formed by, and consisted of the surrounding ranchos of Jurupa and San Barnardino on the north, Temecula on the south, Huapa on the west, and Gorgonio on the east; and that in its total extension, said original tract was coterminous with the surrounding ranchos named. These are the boundaries of "the known rancho of San Jacinto," given in the petition for the last named, or "sobrante" grant, which refers to "the general plat," or map, on file with the Secretary of State; and they are expressly recognized as such by the sub-prefect in his report, who also states that the copy of the plat thereof, then before him, was "correct with the original, which exists in this government ;" evidently meaning the plat referred to in the petition as on file with the Secretary of State. The concession and final grant refer expressly to the petition and sub-prefect's report, and they both describe the land as that shown by " the general map," which it is stated " agrees with all the antecedents."

But by the O'Farrell survey of 1845, referred to in your office decision, which purports to be "a survey and diagram of the Rancho of San Jacinto," it is attempted to be shown that the original place or country called " San Jacinto," embraced a much smaller territory than that lying within the boundaries of the surrounding ranchos above named. This survey was made prior to the date of the grant, " San Jacinto Nuevo," and appears to have been made at the instance of Miguel de Pedrorena, the grantee therein, and with special reference to the petition for that grant. It is described by the United States district court, in United States v. San Jacinto Tin Company, *supra*, as "a rough proximate sketch, made . . . . . without an instrumental survey," and as being "indefinite" in character. In that case, both the district court and the supreme Court, on appeal (125 U. S., 273), sustained the survey and location of the grant known as the " Sobrante de San Jacinto Viejo y Nuevo," although made entirely outside the limits of the O'Farrall survey, and from four and one-half to nineteen miles beyond the boundaries indicated thereby ; and the patent for the same as thus located was upheld.

As finally surveyed and located, a considerable portion of each of the two other grants above named falls outside the limits of said O'Farrell survey, and as thus located patents have issued for said grants. There also remains a large quantity of land within the limits of the O'Farrell survey, which is not included in either of said grants as patented.

In view of all the foregoing, it seems to me there can be little or no doubt, that the place, or tract of land, known as " San Jacinto," out of which the aforesaid three grants, Old San Jacinto, New San Jacinto, and El Sobrante San Jacinto, were to be satisfied, included all the land, be it more or less, lying within the boundaries of the surrounding ranchos above named; and that the O'Farrell survey of 1845 does not truly represent the total extent and exterior boundaries thereof; and I must, therefore, so hold in this case. The land here in question lies· within the boundaries thus determined.

It further appears, that patent was not issued for the first of the aforesaid grants until January 17, 1880, and not for the second until January 9, 1883, although for the third (Sobrante) patent was issued October 26, 1867. The records of your office also show that the first was not finally surveyed until November, 1876, and the second, not until April, 1882, both, years after the railroad company's map of designated route was filed. There appears to have been some sort of survey of these two grants made in the year 1867, but such survey was never accepted or approved by your office or the Department.

It follows, therefore, (1) that the land in question is a portion of what constituted the original tract called "San Jacinto," out of which the aforesaid three Mexican grants were to be severally satisfied, and (2) that at the date when the company's rights attached under its grant, two of these Mexican grants had not been satisfied, and were yet to be finally surveyed and located.

It also appears from an estimate furnished by your office, based upon a sketch, or diagram, of the place or country called "San Jacinto," giving the boundaries thereof approximately, as above described, that the same originally contained about 690,000 acres of land. All but about 160,000 acres of this area is included within the primary limits of the grant to the railroad company. Of this residue something over 16,000 acres are included in private grants other than those here in question; thus leaving of the original tract, outside of the said railroad limits, about 135,000 acres. The aggregate area of the three aforesaid Mexican grants, as patented, is 133,211.41 acres—each, as finally located, is situated entirely within the primary limits of the railroad grant.

It is proper to state in this connection, that the sketch or diagram referred to is not pretended to be an accurate description of the original San Jacinto tract, nor is it intended to show the exact boundaries thereof. It was made to furnish a basis for the estimate aforesaid, and only purports to give the boundaries of the tract approximately as near as can now be done.

The foregoing conclusions give rise to the further question, which will now be considered, viz: whether, by reason of the facts stated, the land in question was excepted from the operation of the grant to the railroad company?

This question may better be stated thus: was all the land lying within the outside boundaries of the large tract or place called "San Jacinto," as herein determined, of which the tract in question formed a part, reserved for the benefit of the aforesaid Mexican private grants, until they were all three finally surveyed and such surveys approved; or was only so much of said large tract as was necessary to satisfy said grants, in fact and in law, so reserved?

It is most earnestly insisted by counsel for the appellant, that the first part of this question must be answered in the affirmative, and numerous authorities are cited with a view to sustaining such contention; while, on the other hand, it is contended with equal earnestness by counsel for the company that the opposite, or latter view, suggested by the question, is the true one and must prevail. To rightly determine this matter, it is proper that we first consider what is the character of the three grants referred to.

Grants made by the Mexican government were of three kinds: (1) grants by specific boundaries, where the donee is entitled to the entire tract, whether it be more or less; (2) grants of quantity, as of one or more leagues, within a larger tract described by what are called out-boundaries, where the donee is entitled to the quantity specified, and no more; (3) grants of a certain place or rancho by name, where the donee is entitled to the whole tract according to the boundaries given, or if not given, according to its extent as shown by previous possession. Higueras *v.* United States (5 Wall., 827); United States *v.* McLaughlin (127 U. S., 428). In the latter case, the supreme court held, that "in the first and third kinds, the claim of the grantee extends to the full limits of the boundaries designated in the grant, or defined by occupation; but in the second kind, a grant of quantity only, within a larger tract, the grant is really a float, to be located by the consent of the government before it can attach to any specific land, like the land warrants of the United States." Now, to which of these classes did the three private land grants in question belong?

The first, or "San Jacinto Viejo," was a grant of quantity (four leagues), within a larger tract, and was, therefore, unquestionably a float, and belonged to the second class named. The other two, though each originally made for the supposed surplus (sobrante) of the tract called "San Jacinto," existing at the respective dates thereof, became by reason of the limitation of the Mexican colonization laws, also grants of quantity (eleven leagues each), within a tract of larger area, and were finally confirmed as such, as has been already shown.

The second or "San Jacinto Nuevo" grant, when made, was for the then supposed surplus (sobrante) remaining over and above the quantity previously granted. It being subsequently ascertained, however, that such surplus contained a much larger quantity than eleven leagues, the maximum amount which could be claimed under said grant, a further or second sobrante grant was made of the same tract called "San Jacinto," known as "El Sobrante de San Jacinto Viejo y Nuevo," which proved to be, in effect, also, a grant of eleven leagues of land, to be located in a much larger tract. I do not think there can be any question, therefore, that these two grants properly belonged also to the second class mentioned, and were mere floats, that is, grants of a certain quantity of land to be located within the limits of a larger area; and I must so hold.

The case of United States *v.* McLaughlin, cited above, was a suit brought by the Attorney-General, on behalf of the United States, against the Central Pacific Railroad Company and others, to cancel and annul a certain patent of the United States, issued November 23, 1875, to said company for certain sections and fractional sections of land in the counties of San Joaquin and Calaveras, California, on the ground that the patent was issued without authority of law, for the reason that all of said lands were within the boundaries of a certain Mexican grant claim, called the Moquelamos grant, and were therefore held reserved for the adjustment and satisfaction of such grant, at the date when the line of said company's road was definitely fixed, by virtue of which the rights of the company attached. The court held in that case that the Moquelamos grant (or rather, the pretended grant of that name) was a grant of the second class above mentioned, namely, a float; and upon the question of the effect of such grants upon the land of the larger area within which they were allowed to be located, the court, after a full consideration of the matter, further held, that it was only the quantity actually granted which was reserved during the examination of the validity of the grant, and that the surplus or remainder of such larger area, over and above the quantity actually granted, was at the disposal of the government as part of the public domain; that if such larger area lies within the limits of a land-grant made in aid of a railroad, such land-grant would take effect, except as to the quantity of land, or float, actually granted in the Mexican grant; and if that quantity lying together was left to satisfy the Mexican grant, the railroad company would be entitled to patents for the odd sections of the remainder. That in all cases of floating Mexican grants, the government retained the right of locating the quantity granted in such part of the larger tract described as it saw fit, and the Government of the United States succeeded to the same right; wherefore the latter Government may dispose of any specific tracts within the exterior limits of the grant, if a sufficient quantity be left to satisfy the float.

Relative to the question now under consideration, the facts in this case are, in all material respects, similar to those in the McLaughlin case, and it seems to me that the court's opinion in that case is decisive of, and must control, the issues here presented.

That opinion, it is asserted by counsel, is in conflict with previous rulings of the supreme court (Van Reynegan v. Bolton, 95 U. S., 33; Leavenworth, Lawrence and Galveston R. R. Co. v. United States, 92 U. S., 733; Frasher v. O'Conner, 115 U. S., 102; Huff v. Doyle, 93 U. S., 558; and other cases of similar import), and is not in accord with the views theretofore entertained by this Department (Sansom v. Southern Pacific R. R. Co., 4 L. D., 357; Rees v. Central Pacific R. R. Co., 5 L. D., 62; Gordon v. Southern Pacific R. R. Co., id., 691). It is enough, however, to know that it is an authoritative declaration of the principles therein enunciated, and is, therefore, the law on this subject, which must be followed. The case was not decided until May 14, 1888, about the date when the appeal herein from the decision of your office was filed. The counsel for appellant seek to escape the force and effect of the court's opinion therein by arguing and claiming that the three several Mexican grants here in question were not floats, but were in fact grants of specific tracts. This claim, as already shown, is utterly untenable and can not be sustained. There is no kind of doubt that the "San Jacinto Viejo" was a floating grant as originally made, and there can be no reasonable question that the "San Jacinto Nuevo" was also, in effect, a float, or, at least, became such upon its confirmation. These two grants were yet to be finally surveyed and located when the grant to the railroad company took effect. Until thus finally located, by the authority of the government, they did not attach to any specific ands within the larger area out of which they were to be satisfied, and therefore, under the authority of the McLaughlin case, only the quantity of land actually necessary to their satisfaction was reserved for that purpose.

Attention is also called to the case of Doolan v. Carr (125 U. S., 618), wherein the supreme court, having under consideration the question as to whether land covered by a Mexican claim was public land within the meaning of the acts of Congress making grants to railroads, in their opinion (page 632), used the following language :

> Those Mexican claims were often described, or attempted to be described, by specific boundaries; they were often claims for a definite quantity of land within much larger out-boundaries, and they were frequently described by the name of a place or rancho. To the extent of the claim when the grant was for land with specific boundaries, or known by a particular name, and to the extent of the quantity claimed within out-boundaries containing a greater area, they are excluded from the grant to the railroad company.

It is contended that Doolan v. Carr, upon this question, and the McLaughlin case, can not be reconciled with previous decisions of the supreme court (the cases above specially mentioned and the additional cases of Durand v. Martin, 120 U. S., 367, and McCreary v. Kaskell, 119 U. S., 327, referred to in the supplemental brief filed by counsel for appellant), but this contention is out of place here, inasmuch as the later cases are authoritative on the question, and must be considered as decisive thereof.

The Viejo and Nuevo, though as finally surveyed and patented are severally situated entirely within the primary limits of the grant to the railroad company, do not embrace any part of the land in question; and in view of all the foregoing, I am constrained to concur in the rejection by your office of the appellant's application to enter the land, and your said decision to that effect is hereby affirmed.

CONTEST—PREFERENCE RIGHT OF ENTRY—NOTICE.

COCHRAN v. DWYER.

Notice of cancellation to contestant's attorney, is, under the rules of practice, notice to the contestant.

During the thirty days accorded the successful contestant, an entry made by another is subject to the preference right of the contestant, but if such right is not asserted within said period, it is defeated by an intervening entry.

First Assistant Secretary Chandler to the Commissioner of the General Land Office, October 7, 1889.

I have considered the case of Charles E. Cochran on his appeal from your office decision of December 29, 1887, holding for cancellation his timber culture entry for NE. ¼ Sec. 28, T. 23 S., R. 32 W., Garden City, Kansas, land district, and awarding to Thomas Dwyer a preference right to enter said tract.

March 24, 1883, one Chas. E. Brooks made timber culture entry for said tract, and said entry was contested by the said Dwyer. The entry of Brooks was canceled upon termination of this contest and the preference right of entry awarded to said Dwyer by your office letter of July 8th, 1885, received at the local office July 14, of the same year.

On August 15th, 1885, Dwyer not having appeared to exercise his preference right, the said Cochran made timber culture entry of said tract in due form and paid the fees and commissions therefor.

On September 4th, Dwyer made entry of the same land as successful contestant, and in the decision appealed from your office sustains his said entry.

When the case was before your office the only evidence of the time when notice was given Dwyer of the cancellation of Brooks' entry and of his preference right, was the *ex parte* affidavit of Dwyer filed with his entry papers on August 29, 1885, and which stated that he had received the said notice August 26, 1885, but with the appeal to this office Dwyer has filed affidavits from which it appears that his attorneys in the contest case received such notice by registered letter not later than July 24, 1885. Notice to counsel was notice to Dwyer; see Rule of Practice 106; George Premo (9 L. D., 70); Clark *v.* Shuff, (7 L. D., 252), and it follows that his thirty days' preference right expired August 23, 1885, several days before he made any attempt to make entry.

An *ex parte* affidavit of Mrs. Foy, a sister of Dwyer, is attached to argument of appellee, alleging that about the first of August, 1885, she tendered the fees and commissions at the local office for her brother and informed the register that Dwyer was sick at Kansas City, and could not attend to the matter in person, and she says the register then and there informed her that Dwyer must be personally present at the local office to make his affidavit and application, and upon this counsel for appellee argue that but for this statement of the register, affidavit might have been sent to Dwyer for his signature and returned within the thirty days. If Dwyer's attorneys had procured from him such an affidavit and presented it at the local office and were now here on appeal from a refusal of the local officers to accept the same, such an argument might be now considered, but what might or might not have been done had such a statement not been made by the register (admitting for the sake of the argument only the *ex parte* affidavit of Mrs. Foy as evidence that the register made such statements,) such contingencies are too remote to raise as issues at this time.

Cochran is now a party in interest and his rights must be considered under the law.

On August 15th, his entry was made and while it may be conceded that it gave him no right at that time as against Dwyer, it was good subject to Dwyer's preference right and when the thirty days had expired Cochran's entry became superior to that of Dwyer and should be sustained. Welsh *v.* Duncan et al. (7 L. D., 186).

Your said decision is accordingly reversed; Dywer's entry or application will be rejected because not made in time, Cochran's right having intervened.

PRACTICE—NOTICE—TRANSFEREE—PURCHASE BEFORE PATENT.

POWERS v. COURTNEY ET AL.

One known to the contestant and local office as an actual party in interest is entitled to notice of a contest, and to be heard therein.

A purchaser of land prior to the issuance of patent therefor takes but an equity, and subject to any infirmities that may exist in the title of his vendor.

First Assistant Secretary Chandler to the Commissioner of the General Land Office, October 10, 1889.

In the matter of the appeal of A. A. Carpenter, from your office decision of July 16, 1888, in the case of Michael Powers v. Joseph Courtney, involving cash entry No. 1328, of the NW. ¼, of Sec. 14, T. 14 N., R. 13 E., in the district of lands subject to entry at Helena, Montana, Courtney was the entryman and when he made his proof, he failed to furnish proof of citizenship. This was not noticed in the local office, but when the case reached your office action was suspended for that reason, and the local officers were requested by your letter of February 26, 1885, to furnish a certified copy of his papers of citizenship.

To this request the local officers replied on December 18, 1885, that Courtney had been duly notified, but had not furnished the required papers, and they were informed that he refused to do so for the reason that he "was induced to file upon the land through the procurement of parties who now (then) hold the title, and which he claims was procured from him by unfair means."

On the same day Powers initiated a contest, alleging that Courtney's entry was fraudulent, and stating under oath facts tending to show that it was so, and that Courtney had not complied with the pre-emption law and that his proof was false.

A hearing was ordered by your office by letter of January 12, 1886. Hearing was set for March 13, 1886, and notice thereof was served on Courtney, the original entryman.

Courtney made default, but Powers the contestant appeared and submitted testimony sustaining his charges.

The local officers recommended the cancellation of the entry, due notice of which was given to Courtney, and he did not appeal.

March 23, 1886, A. A. Carpenter, a citizen of Chicago, Ill., filed a petition as an intervenor, supported by affidavit, setting forth that he had purchased said land from Wm. Wallace for a valuable consideration in 1884. Wm. Wallace having theretofore purchased the same in a like manner from Courtney.

That his deed from Wallace had been of record in the proper office since August, 1884. That he had no notice or knowledge of the contest or of any question as to the acceptance of the proof of Courtney upon said land. That the entry and proof of Courtney were made in good faith, and prayed that the testimony taken at said hearing, be disregarded and that he be allowed after due notice to appear and defend his right to said land.

This petition was overruled by the local officers and Carpenter appealed to your office and by your office decision herein referred to, the decision of the local officers was affirmed and Carpenter's appeal dismissed.

From this decision Carpenter appeals to this Department.

It appears from the letter of the local officers dated December 18, 1885, the day this contest was initiated, that those officers knew that Courtney had disposed of his interest in the land to Wallace and that he (Courtney) made no further claim to it. It appears from the affidavit of contest as well as the deposition of the contestant in support thereof, that he knew that Courtney had conveyed his interest in the land by deed to Wallace, and that he, Courtney, had no further interest in the land, and claimed none.

Under these circumstances the real party (or parties) in interest, as known to the contestant and the local officers, should have notice of the contest, and have an opportunity to be heard in defence of his (or their) equitable right.

In view of all the facts disclosed in this case, I am of the opinion that the petition of the intervenor should be granted and if it appear that he bought from Wallace, that he should have the opportunity to cross-examine contestant's witnesses, and to prove in rebuttal, if he can, the good faith of Courtney, and his compliance with the law, in like manner as Courtney might, had he not transferred his right.

It is claimed by counsel for Carpenter that he, being "an innocent purchaser for valuable consideration without notice," cannot be affected by the alleged fraud of the original entryman. This contention cannot be allowed. It is not only contrary to the rules and practice of this Department but is in conflict with that well settled rule that he who buys an equity, takes subject to existing equities, and subject to any infirmities that may exist in the title of his vendor. Travelers' Insurance Company, 9 L. D.. 316.

Holding these views this case will be returned to the local officers, with directions to proceed with the contest, after due notice to appellant and Wallace, according to law, disregarding the evidence heretofore taken.

Your decision is reversed.

ELMER E. BUSH.

The appeal of a stranger to the record should be disposed of under rule 82 of practice, where such appellant fails to show his right to be heard as an intervenor.

First Assistant Secretary Chandler to the Commissioner of the General Land Office, October 10, 1889.

On July 12, 1883, Elmer E. Bush, filed pre-emption declaratory statement for the W. $\frac{1}{2}$, SE. $\frac{1}{4}$, and NE. $\frac{1}{4}$, SW. $\frac{1}{4}$, and SE. $\frac{1}{4}$, NW. $\frac{1}{4}$, section 27, T. 2 N., R. 38 W., McCook land district, Nebraska.

On January 21, 1884, in accordance with published notice, he made final proof and payment before the clerk of the district court at Culbertson, Nebraska, and the same was approved by the local officers and final cash certificate was issued thereon.

In his final proof Bush stated that he was twenty-two years of age, a native born citizen, and a single man : that he made settlement on the tract, March 27, 1883, and commenced to reside thereon in May of that year, and his residence was continuous. That he used the land for " grazing stock and making hay " having " put up about twenty-five tons."

His improvements consisted of a house, a well, and about two acres of breaking, he also stated that he raised some millet. He did not give the value of his said improvements, but his two witnesses estimated them as being worth, seventy-five dollars.

On June 4, 1888, your office rejected the final proof for the reason that the improvements and cultivation shown, are not conclusive of good faith, and that " the land was erroneously described in the published notice, and the description corrected with a pen," and directed the local officers to require claimant " to give new notice, and to make new proof, showing full compliance with law and the requirements of this office as to improvements and cultivation, within ninety days from the receipt of . . . . notice," and that " in default of compliance herewith, said entry will be canceled."

On August 28, 1888, the Northwestern Cattle Company as grantee of Elmer E. Bush, filed an appeal from your said office decision.

This appeal is not sworn to, and there is nothing in the record in this case to show that said company is a party in interest or entitled to the right of appeal.

This case is similar to that of John Ralls (7 L. D., 454), and in accordance with the rule there announced it is returned to your office for disposition under rule 82 of Rules of Practice.

RAILROAD GRANT—PLAN OF ADJUSTMENT.

CHICAGO, ST. PAUL, MINNEAPOLIS & OMAHA RY. CO.

A claim for indemnity based upon a loss of lands in place taken under the swamp grant, can only be allowed so far as the claim by the State under said grant has been recognized by the government.

On relinquishment indemnity may be allowed for lands improperly patented as within the granted limits, where in fact such lands were excepted from the grant by a prior adverse claim.

The company is entitled to indemnity for losses sustained through the overlapping of the six and ten mile granted limits at the junction of the main and branch lines of the road.

Secretary Noble to the Commissioner of the General Land Office, October 11, 1889.

On January 21, 1888, your office transmitted to this Department a statement showing a further adjustment of the land grants made to the State of Wisconsin by the acts of June 3, 1856 (11 Stat., 20), and of May 5, 1864 (13 Stat., 66), and of which grants the Chicago, St. Paul, Minneapolis and Omaha Railway Company is the present beneficiary.

When the matter of the adjustment of these grants was being considered by this Department in October 1887, my predecessor, Mr. Secretary Lamar, in the decision then rendered and to be found in 6 L. D., 195, suggested that certain errors, which had theretofore been committed in improperly approving lands for the benefit of the road, could be rectified, if the company would relinquish and quit-claim to the United States all title which it might have acquired to said lands. In this suggestion the company has acquiesced, and, having executed and filed in your office proper deeds transferring and making quit-claim of all title to the lands in question, the present re-adjustment is made to correct the former errors.

Having stated an account showing the amount now due the company, four lists, numbered 8, 9, 10 and 11, aggregating 31,596.33 acres of land, are sent me for approval.

It is stated in your letter of transmittal that, in 1864, 7,244.91 acres of land were approved, as indemnity lands, to the main and branch lines of said road jointly; that subsequently, it was ascertained that under the act of May 5, 1864, *supra*, increasing by four sections the grant to said road, 3,454.40 acres of said lands were within the now enlarged primary limits of the Bayfield or branch line thereof, and that the residue, that is 3,790.51 acres of said lands, were likewise within the granted limits of the Superior or main line of the road. In attempting to correct these improper approvals, it is further stated, the error was committed of charging the branch and main line each with one-half of said amounts, thus making a double charge as to the one-half of said lands, or 3,622.45 acres.

In order to correct these errors, the company has reconveyed to the United States the 7,244.91 acres within the granted limits; and list 10 certifies over for the company, as of its granted lands, the 3,790.51 acres, the part thereof which are within its primary limits, as aforesaid. This list is approved.

List 11 certifies over for the company, in the same way, 2,767.60 acres, instead of the full amount of 3,454.40, the residue of the said granted lands reconveyed to the United States. Your letter does not explain the deficiency in this list, but, upon inquiry, it is learned that 686.80 acres, the amount of said deficiency, are claimed by the State as swamp lands, and presumably that amount has been withheld at present for investigation. I have, therefore, approved list 11.

It also appears that 295.88 acres, heretofore approved to the company, had been, prior to the attachment of the company's rights, sold by the United States; and also that 965.17 acres, also approved to the company, were found to have been patented to the State under the swamp land grant. In order to remove any cloud from the title to these lands, the company has executed a reconveyance of the same to the government, and it is proposed to allow indemnity lands to the extent of 1,261.05 acres therefor.

It also appears that among other lands approved to the company heretofore were 20,264.89 acres, which are claimed by the State of Wisconsin under the swamp land grant of 1850. In order to avoid any controversy in relation to these lands, a reconveyance of them was tendered to the government; the deed of conveyance, however, included tracts which, in the aggregate, amounted to 20,304.89 acres.

The aforegoing 20,264.89 acres constituted the amount of swamp lands claimed by the State of Wisconsin, and of which its agent has made selection and duly filed a list. But it appears by an adjustment of said swamp grant, made June 30, 1888, that the claim of the State to those lands has been recognized by your office, for the present, to the extent only of 17,995.41. As these lands are all within the granted limits of said railroad, such of them as do not pass to the State under its prior grant will inure to the railroad grant. Therefore, the said company is only entitled to indemnity to the extent of the said 17,995.41 acres, the amount of its present loss. The adjustment as to the residue of the State's claim, and the company's rights in those lands, being necessarily left to the future.

Since the above ascertainment and allowance of the swamp land claim of the State, by your office, for the reduced amount the Omaha Company, by its counsel, Messrs. Britton and Gray, have filed in this Department a new deed, conveying to the United States the title to the 17,995.41 acres thus ascertained to belong to the State; and they ask its substitution in favor of the deed before tendered for 20,304.89 acres, which they wish to have returned to the company. As the former deed was never accepted as correct by the government, I think it right this should be done, and so direct, inclosing to you for record the deed for the 17,995.41 acres if examination proves it to be correct.

To meet the aforegoing just claims for indemnity, list 8, for 10,888.08 acres, and list 9, for 14,150.14 acres, have been sent me for approval. These two lists aggregate 25,038.22 acres, or 2,159.31 acres more than appears to be due the company on the aforegoing accounts. This excess arises from the fact that indemnity was proposed to be allowed to the company in said lists to the full extent of the State's claim for swamp lands, instead of the amount, which thus far has been ascertained that the State is entitled to as against the company.

The counsel for the company, in the communication above referred to, call attention to said excess in the lists, and request that certain specified tracts, aggregating 2,237.18 acres, be eliminated from said lists, and that they be approved as to the other lands described therein. I regard the proposition favorably. The elimination would destroy the excess and balance the lists to within 77.87 acres of the amount it is now proposed to convey to the company ; the adjustment of the account would thus be expedited, and the delay incident to the remanding of the lists to your office avoided. I think the request of counsel a reasonable one and should be granted. I have therefore drawn a red line through the tracts specified ; that is to say, in list 8 all of Sec. 5, T. 47 N., R. 15 W., 637.18 acres; all of Sec. 17, T. 47 N., R. 15 W., 640 acres; the W. ½ and SW. ¼ of SE. ¼ Sec. 27, T. 47 N., R. 15 W., 360 acres ; in list 9 the E. ½ of Sec. 15, T. 42 N., R. 5 W., 32 acres; and the NW. ¼ of NE. ¼, SW. ¼ and W. ½ of SE. ¼, Sec. 23, T. 42 N., R. 5 W., 280 acres ; and deducted the amounts thereof from the respective lists and approved them as to the residue of the lands therein described. List 8 being thus approved for 9,250.90 acres, and list 9 for 13,550.14 acres, aggregating 22,801.04 acres.

According to the foregoing, the amounts growing out of these transactions would stand, as follows;

Lands ascertained to have been erroneously approved to the company.

	Acres.
Of granted lands within branch line	3,454.40
Of granted lands within main line	3,790.51
Total granted	7,244.91
Of lands sold by U. S. prior	295.88
Of patented swamp lands	965.17
Of unpatented swamp lands	17,995.41
Total ascertained to have been approved in error	26,501.37

Amounts reconveyed to the United States.

Of granted lands	7,244.91
Lands sold by U. S	295.88
Patented swamp lands	965.17
Unpatented swamp lands by corrected deed	17,995.37
Total reconveyed	26,501.37

Amounts now proposed to be returned to the company.

Of granted lands:

Per list 10, main line	3,790.51
Per list 11, branch line	2,767.60
Total granted	6,558.11

Of indemnity lands:

For lands sold by U. S		295.88
For patented swamp lands		965.17
For unpatented swamp lands		17,995.41
For ¼ of lands within extended grant and erroneously charged to the company		3,622.45
Making total now allowed		22,878.91
Deduct excess over approvals		77.87
Now approved net amount:		
Of list 8	9,250.90	
Of list 9	13,550.14	
		22,801.04

In addition to the above lists, on May 16, 1888, your predecessor also reported that, in the former adjustment of said grants, two sections outside of the limits of the same, but within the granted limits of the Northern Pacific Railroad were improperly patented to the Chicago, St. Paul, Minneapolis and Omaha Railway Company; that the rights of the Northern Pacfic Railroad Company being superior, the former company has reconveyed the lands in question to the United States. In lieu of the lands thus relinquished, the Omaha Company is entitled to other lands to an equal amount. I have, therefore, approved list 12 for 1,278.11 acres, transmitted with said letter, it being the amount of the relinquished sections.

There is yet another matter relating to the adjustment of said grants, and to which your attention is now directed, in connection with what has been hereinbefore said.

By letter of December 12, 1887, addressed to this Department, the counsel of the railroad company call attention to another alleged error made by your office in the process of adjusting said grants, whereby, it is asserted, the company has been deprived of 37,496.67 acres of indemnity land, which is justly due to it.

It is stated that within the angle formed by the overlapping six and ten miles granted limits, at the junction of the main and branch lines of said road, where the additional four sections, under the grant of 1864, on the east side of the main line, fall within the six miles granted limits of the branch line, under the act of 1856, indemnity has been withheld for the lands so lost. And, it is asserted, that the same thing has been done as to the four additional granted sections to the branch line, under the act of 1864, where, within the same angle, those sections, on the northwest, fall within the six miles granted limits of the act of 1856 to the main line. A diagram is attached to the communication of counsel, which clearly illustrates their claim.

There is nothing in the report on the adjustment of the grants, now or heretofore made by your office, or the papers therewith, from which it can be learned whether this statement of the attorneys is correct or not. Personal inquiry at the railroad division of your office leads to the belief that said statement is probably correct. I have, therefore, concluded to act upon the matter at this time, rather than further delay it by reference to your office for report upon the facts, before expressing an opinion upon the law.

When the prior adjustment of these grants was under consideration by this Department before, the principles upon which that adjustment should be made were fully dicussed and plainly stated, 6 L. D., *supra*. I think the rules there laid down show that an error has been committed by your office in denying the indemnity now claimed, if there has been such denial, which I here assume, for the purposes of this communication, to be a fact.

When Congress passed the act of 1864, *supra*, it undoubtedly conferred upon the State of Wisconsin four sections of land per mile, on each side of the road, additional to the six sections given by the act of 1859 to aid in the construction of both the main and branch line of this road. In making the grant, it is not to be supposed that Congress did a vain thing; but, on the contrary, having made the grant, it was intended it should be enjoyed; and no technical rules of law or adroit schemes of adjustment should be permitted to calculate the beneficiaries of Congress out of the bounty intended for them. Four additional sections per mile on each side is what Congress gave; is what the company is entitled to, and that amount it is the duty of your office to allow. If the four additional sections, purported to be granted, are upon the surface of the earth, but for some of the causes, enumerated as sufficient, can not be taken by the company, then it is entitled to other equivalent lands within the indemnity limits, if such can be found. Among the causes sufficient to except land out of such a grant, is its previous appropriation under a prior grant and, in the absence of an express congressional declaration to that effect, it is not seen how the appropriation of the land under a prior grant to the same company should alter either the principle upon which this rule is founded, or the practice which gives efficacy to the statutory mandate.

This company is entitled to six sections on each side under the senior grant, and to four under the junior, along both the main and branch lines. Where these granted limits, or either of them, overlap the limits of a congressional grant of the same date, and therefore of equal dignity, whether for the same or another road, the well settled rule is, that each line of road has the same rights within the lapping limits as the other; and, as there is not land enough to satisfy both grants in full, each can only obtain a moiety of said land. But if within the overlapping limits one grant is older than the other, the older grant takes all the free land within its limits, to the absolute exclusion of the younger, which thereby becomes entitled to indemnity lands to the extent of such loss, if there be the usual indemnity clause in its grant; otherwise, it would get nothing.

By applying this system to the overlapping limits of the branch and main line at the junction, the Omaha Company would get the amount of land which Congress intended it to have along each mile of its constructed road—six sections per mile on each side, under the senior grant, and four under the junior—no more, no less.

I do not think that the proviso in the first section of the act of 1864, *supra*, in any wise affects the conclusion arrived at. In reference to indemnity selections, it is there said that none shall be made "in lieu of lands received under the said grant of June 3, 1856." The lieu lands here claimed are not on account of lands "received" under the grant of 1856, but the claim is made because of the loss of place lands which the company was entitled to receive under the act of 1864, but which it could not get under that act, because they had been appropriated under the prior act of 1856. This same proviso was invoked in a similar manner, on the former consideration of these grants, and it will be seen (6 L. D., 208) that the Department then put the construction upon that I now adopt.

In view of the aforegoing, upon receipt hereof, you will forthwith cause the adjustment of these grants to be re-examined, and, if it appears that the company has been deprived of indemnity as charged by counsel, you will cause a proper list to be prepared, in the usual way, allowing indemnity to the extent that losses have been sustained within said angle, as before stated. Upon the completion of said list, if one be made, it will be transmitted to me; or, upon ascertainment that no such denial of indemnity has been made, you will inform me. And to the end that this grant may be speedily adjusted and closed, in order that the large body of land, withdrawn for the indemnity purposes of this road, may be restored to the public domain and made subject to settlement and entry at as early a day as possible, you are directed to make this matter special, and report to this Department as soon as a proper ascertainment has been reached.

Herewith are returned, with my approval, lists Nos. 8, 9, 10, 11, and 12, and I also transmit for record the papers relating to the matters herein considered.

RAILROAD GRANT—PRE-EMPTION CLAIM.

MISSOURI KANSAS & TEXAS RY. CO. *v.* LYNN.

A withdrawal does not take effect upon land covered by the settlement and filing of a pre-emptor, temporarily absent in the military service of the United States.

Secretary Noble to the Commissioner of the General Land Office, October 11, 1889.

I have before me the appeal of the Missouri, Kansas and Texas Railway Company from your office decision of June 14 1888, holding for cancellation its "selection" of the E. ½, SE. ¼, Sec. 27, T. 23 S., R. 17 E., Independence district, Kansas.

December 3, 1860, the said land was "offered." December 17, 1860, one Harry Evans filed pre-emption declaratory statement No. 565, for the tract in question (together with the W. ½, SW. ¼, Sec. 26) alleging settlement the same day.

During 1861, said Evans, who had then on the tract a house, and ten acres of the land broken and fenced, enlisted in Co. D, 9th Kansas Vol., Cavalry.

On May 5, 1863, a withdrawal for the benefit of the Leavenworth and Galveston Railroad Company, the ten mile ("granted") limits of which geographically included the tract in question, became effective.

On March 6, 1865, the said Harry Evans, who had returned to his claim after the mustering out of his regiment on December 19, 1864, transmuted his filing to a homestead entry for the same tract.

November 28, 1866, the line of the Leavenworth, Lawrence and Galveston road opposite said tract was definitely located.

February 19, 1867, the line of the Missouri, Kansas, and Texas road opposite said tract was definitely located, geographically including said tract within the ten mile granted limits of the grant to said road.

February 12, 1870, Evans' homestead entry was canceled as to the tract in question (E. ½, SW. ¼, Sec. 27) on the theory that the above-mentioned withdrawal of May 5, 1863, operated upon said tract, and prevented the homestead entry (made March 6, 1865) from attaching thereto.

February 14, 1872, final homestead certificate issued to Evans for the tract in section 26 (the portion of his entry remaining after the order of 1870).

June 27, 1879, the two companies made a joint "selection" (listing) of the tract in dispute (E. ½, SW. ¼, Sec. 27), but patent was not issued. During 1879, George H. Lynn, the appellee herein, purchased the supposed title of the Southern Kansas Company (formerly the Leavenworth, Lawrence, and Galveston); and, in 1886, he having in the meantime made all the required payments (aggregating $405.05) he, Lynn, received from said company a warranty deed, purporting to convey to him title to the tract.

October 15, 1887, said Lynn applied to file a pre-emption declaratory statement for the land in question and, on October 31, 1887, the Missouri, Kansas and Texas Company, the appellant here, filed a protest against the application.

February 13, 1888, a hearing was had at the local office, at which Mr. Lynn appeared with his witnesses and submitted proof in support of his pre-emption claim, the company's attorney being present and cross-examining Lynn.

February 28, 1888, the local officers rendered a decision in favor of Lynn, but based their conclusion upon the mistaken assumption that the order made by your office August 25, 1887, (which order in fact applied only to lands within the indemnity belt) had "canceled the selection" of the tract in dispute.

On June 14, 1888, by the decision now under review, your office made the following ruling:

He (Evans) initiated a claim to the land, that was capable of being completed, prior to the date of the grant to either company; and the withdrawal of lands for railroad purposes during his temporary absence in the army could not take effect as to this tract since his filing did not expire during his term of enlistment, and his immediate return to the land, upon muster out of service, is conclusive evidence that he did not intend to abandon his claim when he enlisted. At the time of the definite location of the roads of these companies he was domiciled on the land with his family. The land was evidently excepted from the grants to the company and their selections of the same are accordingly held for cancellation.

This decision is hereby affirmed.

———

[Review.]

JASMER ET AL. *v.* MOLKA.

Motion for review of departmental decision rendered in the above entitled case, February 21, 1889, 8 L. D., 241, denied by Secretary Noble, October 12, 1889.

———

PRACTICE—SECOND CONTEST PREFERENCE RIGHT.

CONLY *v.* PRICE.

An application to contest an entry filed pending government proceedings against said entry, in the absence of some good reason for suspending such proceedings in favor of said applicant, should be received and held subject to the final determination of said proceedings.

A second contest, filed during the pendency of a prior suit, should be received and held in abeyance subject to the final disposition of the pending case.

Notice of cancellation, given through the mail, should be in strict conformity with rules 17 and 18 of practice.

A successful contestant should not be permitted to exercise his preference right in the presence of an intervening entry, until after due action had on notice to the intervening entryman to show cause why his entry should not be canceled.

A preference right of entry can not be secured through a speculative contest.

Concurring decisions of the local and general land offices as to questions of fact are generally accepted as conclusive by the Department, where the evidence is conflicting.

Secretary Noble to the Commissioner of the General Land Office, October 17, 1889.

April 8, 1880, J. W. Perry made homestead entry, No. 2183, for the NE.¼ of NE.¼ of Sec. 21, and N.½ of NW.¼ of Sec. 22, T. 15 N., R. 22 W., North Platte district, Nebraska. In August, 1884, proceedings against said entry were instituted in behalf of the government by Inspector F. D. Hobbs. Conly, the contestant herein, having learned of the proceedings by the government against Perry's entry, and knowing (as he states) "that said entry was fraudulent and had been abandoned" for more than two years by Perry, began improvements on the land August 22, 1884, and having built a frame house thereon, fourteen by sixteen feet, moved his family, consisting of a wife and children, into said house, September 7, 1884, where he and they have since continuously resided. After this action on the part of Conly, which was known to Price, the contestee herein, the said proceedings by the government against the entry of Perry were suspended, "and Price was permitted to contest said entry for abandonment, which he did October 17, 1884. In the meantime, September 23, 1884, Conly made application to file a pre-emption declaratory statement for the land, which was rejected by the local officers, November 14, 1884, because of Perry's entry existing of record. Conly thereupon made application to contest Perry's entry, which was rejected by the local officers on account of the pending contest of Price. At the date set for the hearing of Price's contest, he failed to appear, and it was dismissed, December 8, 1884. Price, however, applied, January 8, 1885, to make a second contest of the entry, and his application was allowed, and Conly, having learned of the dismissal of Price's first contest, on January 22, 1885, renewed his application to contest, which was again rejected, because of the pendency of Price's second contest. Perry having made default at the hearing ordered on Price's second contest, his entry was canceled by your office by letter of June 2, 1885. It appears from the records of the local office, that a letter was mailed June 6, 1885, advising Price of the cancellation of the entry but he claims that the letter was post-marked, July 10, 1885, and that he did not receive it until July 15, 1885. He applied and was allowed by the local officers to make homestead entry of the land, July 27, 1885. Prior thereto, however, on June 9, 1885, the local officers had also allowed Conly to enter the tract under the homestead law.

August 13, 1885, Conly initiated a contest against the entry of Price, alleging, substantially, that Price's contest was fraudulent and speculative, that he had failed to make entry within thirty days from service of notice of the cancellation of the entry of Perry, and had not settled or resided on the land in good faith or improved it in accordance with the law. On hearing ordered and commenced on this contest, September 29, 1885, the local officers, found in favor of the contestant and recommended the cancellation of Price's entry, and your office by decision of September 11, 1888, sustained their action. Price now appeals from said decision.

Several irregularities intervened in the proceedings before the local officers. In the first place, the proceedings by the government against Perry's entry and the subsequent contest of Price being upon the same ground—abandonment, unless the facts, upon which the government proceedings were based, were brought to the knowledge of the inspector by the instrumentality of Price, or he had in some way rendered valuable assistance to the government in the matter, or some other valid reason existed for such action, those proceedings should not have been suspended and Price allowed to contest. One of the leading, if not the main, objects of the act of May 14, 1880 (21 Stat., 140), in giving successful contestants the preference right of entry for thirty days, was to encourage parties to bring to the notice of the authorities frauds and violations of the law by entrymen. In this case the land had been abandoned by Perry for more than two years, this was well known and it would seem there was no difficulty in procuring the cancellation of the entry without the assistance of Price, and it does not appear that Price was instrumental in bringing the abandonment to the knowledge of those representing the government or had in any way assisted them. The suspension of proceedings on the part of the government and allowance of Price's application to contest, gave him an advantage over Conly to which, so far as the record discloses, he was not entitled by any action of his part. (Joseph A. Bullen, 8 L. D., 301.) The application of Price to contest should, in the absence of some valid reason for suspending the government proceedings in his favor, have been received and held subject to the final determination of such proceedings. (United States v. Scott Rhea, 8 L. D., 578.)

In the second place. as stated by your office, Conly's first application to contest should not have been rejected because of the pendency of the contest of Price, but received and held in abeyance subject to the final disposition of said contest. (Churchill v. Seeley et al., 4 L. D., 589.) If this course had been pursued, or Conly had duly appealed from the rejection of his said application, his right to proceed with his contest would have attached on the dismissal of that of Price, December 8, 1884. He did not appeal, however, but on January 22, 1885, renewed his application to contest, which was rejected because of the pendency of a second contest by Price initiated January 8, 1885. By this course, he waived or lost his rights under his first application (Churchill v. Seeley et al., supra), and while his second application should have been received and held subject to the determination of Price's second contest, its rejection was at most error without injury, as the entry was canceled on said second contest of Price. By this cancellation, Price (if his contest was valid) secured the preference right of entry to be exercised within thirty days from the service of legal notice thereof.

This brings us to the consideration in the third place, of an error committed by the local officers as against Price. The entry of Perry was canceled, as before stated, June 2, 1885. The only notice of the cancellation was by letter, mailed June 6, 1885. This letter is not claimed to have been registered as required by Rule of Practice 17, and there is no proof of receipt of the letter by Price as required by Rule of Practice 18, which provides, that "Proof of service by mail shall be the affidavit of the person who mailed the notice, attached to the post-office receipt for the registered letter." Price admits the receipt of the letter, but not until July 15, 1885. Notice not having been given as required by Rule 17, and consequently, it being impossible to prove service thereof as required by Rule 18, the application of Price to enter the land, made July 27, 1885, must be held to have been in time, and the local officers were in error in not so holding. (Churchill *v.* Seeley *et al.*, *supra.*) The necessity for and importance of strict conformity to Rules 17 and 18 are illustrated in this case.

In the fourth place, the entry of Conly having been made, June 9, 1885, when the period within which it was incumbent on Price to exercise his preference right (if he had any) had not expired, was subject to such preference right. As, however, "two entries should not be placed of record for the same tract of land at the same time," the local officers, when Price subsequently (July 27, 1885,) made application to enter, should have received the same, but, before allowing it, should have given Conly due notice thereof and opportunity to show cause why his entry should not be canceled and Price, as successful contestant, allowed to perfect his entry. (Boorey *v.* Lee, 6 L. D., 643.) The local officers did not pursue this course, but allowed the entry of Price, and thereupon Conly, as before stated, contested said entry and hearing was had thereon. This contest and hearing, however, subserved the purpose and will be considered as a response by Conly (and hearing thereon) to a notice to show cause why his entry should not be canceled and that of Price allowed.

The testimony on the hearing shows, that Conly went upon the land, August 22, 1884, and having built a framed dwelling thereon, moved his family and effects thereto, September 7, 1884, and has since continuously resided on the tract as a home to the exclusion of one elsewhere; and that his improvements consisted of said dwelling, fourteen by sixteen feet, and a sod addition thereto, twelve by sixteen feet, a stable and corral, a shed—twenty by twenty-five feet—, pig-pen, cellar, well, twelve or fifteen acres broken and fenced, and over thirty acres surrounded by posts for fencing—all of the value of from $250.00 to $300.00.

His entry is, therefore, not subject to cancellation on the ground of failure to comply with the requirements of the homestead law, but, if so subject at all, it is only because of the assertion by Price of a valid preference right of entry as successful contestant of the entry of Perry. Price's right of entry is predicated upon his claim of a preference right as a successful contestant. If his contest was invalid because fraudulent or speculative, or for any other reason not in good faith, then he acquired thereby no preference right of entry, and his entry (or application to enter, as it is herein considered) was without any basis upon which to rest, and is therefore no ground for cancelling the entry of Conly. (Dayton v. Dayton, 8 L. D., 248.) In Conly's affidavit on which the hearing was ordered, it is charged "that Price had been in the habit of contesting entries and withdrawing the same for a money consideration, and had offered to withdraw" his contest in this case "for $100.00, and that his said contest was for speculative purposes and not in good faith." In the notice of the hearing served on Price, these and the other charges stated at the outset of this decision, were set forth, and he should have been prepared to meet them. The testimony on the part of Conly tends to show, that Price had made and abandoned three other contests for a moneyed consideration and had, in like manner, proposed to abandon his claim now in question. Although the testimony introduced by Conly is specific as to contests abandoned and amounts received for such abandonment, Price on being afterwards put upon the stand, is only asked by his counsel the general question, whether he had ever made any speculative contests, and he answers, simply that he never had. The testimony as to his offer to abandon "for pay" his present claim, is also specific, but there is no specific denial by him, that he made such offer. He only states on this point, that he made the contest "for his own benefit." This might be true, and the contest might still have been made with a view of abandonment for a consideration. The local officers found that "Price had instituted other contests and abandoned them for pay and had offered to abandon this one in question for pay." The testimony as to this matter, taken in connection with his meagre improvements and inhabitancy of the land, in my opinion, sustains the conclusion of the local officers, that Price's contest of Perry's entry was "speculative" or made with a view of "selling out" or being "bought off." If made for such a purpose, it was not in contemplation of law a *bona fide* contest, upon which a preference right of entry can be based.

Part of Conly's testimony was taken before a notary public, C. W. Root, at Arnold, Nebraska, on a day subsequent to the taking of the other testimony in the case. Price was neither present in person nor represented at the taking of said testimony, and claims that neither he nor his attorneys had notice thereof. He made a motion to strike out said testimony and for a rehearing, on the ground of said alleged want of notice. A notice of the hearing before Root was issued by the local officers and is in the record, with the affidavit of Conly attached show-ing personal service by him of a copy thereof on Price, March 31, 1886, more than thirty days before the day, May 4, 1886, set for said hear-ing. Price in support of his motion filed his own affidavit, that said notice was not served on him on said day or at any time, and that he had no notice whatever of said hearing, and, also, affidavits of two other parties and his attorney, tending to corroborate his own. Conly filed the affidavits of himself and wife (who claimed to have been pres-ent at the service of the notice) to the contrary. The local officers found, that Price was duly served with said notice and overruled his motion, and were sustained by your office in said finding. The refusal to grant said motion is one of the grounds of appeal in the present case. As a general rule, concurring decisions of the local and general land offices as to questions of fact are accepted as conclusive by this Department, where the evidence is conflicting. (Chichester v. Allen, 9 L. D., 300.) I find no sufficient ground for making the present case an exception to that rule.

The conclusion attained by the local officers and your office, that the entry of Price should be canceled and that of Conly allowed to remain intact, is concurred in. Your office decision is, therefore, affirmed.

FINAL PROOF PROCEEDINGS—NOTICE—PROTEST.

TUTTLE v. PARKIN.

A protest serves to call attention to irregularities in final proof, and for such purpose a formal contest is not necessary.

Special notice of intention to submit final proof should be given adverse claimants of record.

First Assistant Secretary Chandler to the Commissioner of the General Land Office, October 17, 1889.

From the record in the matter of the appeal of A. H. Tuttle, from your office decision of March 31, 1888, in the case of A. H. Tuttle v. J. C. Parkin, involving a conflict between homestead entry of said Tuttle, No. 218, upon the S. ½, SE. ¼, Sec. 1, and the N. ½, NE. ¼, Sec. 12, T. 25, R. 50 W., Chadron land district, Nebraska, and cash entry No. 942, of John C. Parkin, as heir of John A. Parkin, based upon declaratory statement No. 5199, for same land, it appears:—

1st. That on August 3, 1885, John A. Parkin made declaratory state-ment No. 5199, for said land alleging settlement June 24, 1885;

2nd. That said John A. Parkin died April 11, 1887;

3rd. That on September 12, 1887, Alvin H. Tuttle made homestead entry No. 218, for the same land.

4th. On December 22, 1887, John C. Parkin one of the heirs of John A. Parkin gave notice of his intention to make final proof to establish the claim of said heirs on February 7, 1888.

5th. Publication of said notice was duly made and the same was duly posted in the land office.

6th. On February 7, said John C. Parkin made proof corroborated by two witnesses which tended to show that settlement was made as alleged. That John A. Parkin resided on this land, from June 24, 1885, till his death in April, 1887, except that he was absent in the fall of 1885, two weeks, and from January till April, 1887, which last absence is satisfactorily explained, and that his family never did reside there, but lived in Iowa. His improvements consisted of a house fourteen by sixteen feet. Board and sod cellar eight by ten feet, a sod stable, ten acres of breaking, developing a spring, shrubbery, plants etc., the total value being estimated from one hundred and seventy-five to three hundred dollars.

7th. Tuttle, who had in the mean time made a homestead entry covering the same land, was not cited at the time proof was made by John C. Parkin, and in his affidavit subsequently filed, he swears that he had no knowledge that such proof was to be made.

8th. On March 19th, 1888, said Tuttle filed a motion in the form of a protest, supported by affidavit, stating among other things, that the proof made by John C. Parkin was false and fraudulent. That no such improvements existed as therein stated and asking that the proceedings be set aside that he might have an opportunity to show these facts.

This motion, or protest, was treated by your office as an affidavit of contest, and the entry having been allowed, and remaining of record, your office held that the motion should be denied because the affidavit was not corroborated as required by Rule 3, and because if all the allegations were true the facts stated would not invalidate said entry.

In my judgment the decision of your office is erroneous. In the first place the motion or protest filed is not an affidavit of contest, and should not have been so treated. It was its object not to initiate a formal contest, for no formal contest was under the circumstances necessary, but was a paper filed in your office by Tuttle for the purpose of calling its attention to an irregularity in the proceedings of the local officers, affecting his rights, and asking that, on account of such irregularity, those proceedings be set aside and he be permitted to establish his right.

In case of conflicting pre-emption claims, " no formal contest is necessary, but when either party offers to make proof, the other, who should always be specially cited, may appear at the time and place fixed and proceedings should thereupon be had in the same manner as in contest cases." Instructions, September 17, 1884, 3 L. D., 112. And it is required by the instructions of the Land Office that adverse claimants of record should always be specially cited, both in homestead and pre-emption notices of intention to make proof. See Instructions, November 25, 1884, 3 L. D., 196.

In this case no citation was issued to the homesteader, whose entry was of record in the same local office, and if the averments in his affidavit be true, the proof should never have been accepted.

This case will, therefore, be remanded with instructions to direct the local officers to require the heirs of John A. Parkin, to make new proof, after new notice, and that the appellant Tuttle be specially cited to appear at the time and place fixed, and then that proceedings be had in the same manner as in contest cases.

The decision of your office is reversed.

———

PRACTICE—MOTION FOR REVIEW.

PRESTINA B. HOWARD. (ON REVIEW.)

On motion for review the facts and issues in another and independent case, pending in the General Land Office, can not be considered by the Department.

Secretary Noble to the Commissioner of the General Land Office, October 19, 1889.

In the matter of the motion for review of the decision of the Department rendered February 23, 1889, in the case of Prestina B. Howard (8 L. D., 286), modifying your office decision of January 7, 1888, and allowing Mrs. Howard to amend her application to make homestead entry of SW. ¼, section 33, T. 32 S., R. 63 W., Pueblo district, Colorado, so as to show that said application is made as heir of one B. Benivetes, instead of being made in her own right, which motion is made by Adam W. Forbes, who claims a pre-emption right in the same property.

I find that claimant first presented her application to enter said land under the homestead law, November 23, 1886. This was rejected by the local officers on the ground that the land was embraced in the derivative claim of Thos. Leitensdorfer under the Vigil and St. Vrain grant.

On appeal, your office reversed the action of the local officers holding that the claimant was protected by the act of February 25, 1869.

Thereupon the claimant duly renewed her application, which was rejected a second time by the local officers, because it appeared she was a married woman, and she appealed.

This decision was affirmed by your office January 7, 1888, and the decision of this Department here sought to be reviewed, held that such decision was correct as the application then stood, but held that Mrs. Howard was entitled to make entry of this land under the homestead law, as heir of her father under the provisions of the act of May 14, 1880 (21, Stat., 140), and so modified your decision as to permit her to amend her application by showing that she made it, as heir of said Benivetes, instead of in her own right.

Forbes appears and asks a reconsideration of this decision, alleging in himself a pre-emption right, and that when he applied to make cash entry of a portion of the land, Mrs. Howard appeared and filed affidavit of contest, and a hearing was had—in which one of the issues made was as to the settlement and rights of Benivetes, which were assumed as existing, in the decision of this case, and that, that case is now pending in your office, and asking that this case be reconsidered in connection with that contest.

When this case was decided, no such issue or question was presented.

The case was correctly decided upon the issues and facts then before the department, and, on review, I can not consider the facts and issues in another and independent case, pending in your office. The motion is denied.

PRIVATE CLAIM—ACT OF JUNE 2, 1858.

CALEB BIGGS.

Scrip under the third section of the act of June 2, 1858, cannot be issued, where it is apparent that the original settlement claim, set up as the basis therefor, has already been satisfied.

Secretary Noble to the Commissioner of the General Land Office, October 19, 1889.

On June 17, 1872, D. C. Hardee, made application to the United States surveyor general of Louisiana, for the issuance to him of eight certificates of location of eighty acres each under section 3, act of June 2, 1858. (11 Stat., 294).

Hardee bases his claim to said certificates of location or scrip on the following statements, to wit:

The private land claim of Caleb Biggs for six hundred and forty acres of land situated in the parish of Feliciana, as reported by the Commissioners, Cosby and Skipwith, in their report of July 24, 1821, and numbered 155 in their list of actual settlers (see American State Papers Green's Edition public lands, Vol. 3, page 447), was confirmed to the said Caleb Biggs, his heirs and legal representatives, by act of Congress approved August 6, 1846 (9 Stat., 66) and remains wholly unlocated and unsatisfied.

At a succession sale of the estate of the deceased confirmee had, on the 21st day of March 1872, in the parish of East Feliciana, this claim was sold at public auction and was purchased by D. C. Hardee of the parish of East Feliciana.

No further steps were taken in this matter, so far as shown by the record, for more than fourteen years after said application was filed.

December 4, 1886, Hardee's attorney, referring to this application says, " under the decision of the Secretary of the Interior known as the ' Garrett case' the claim has been suspended." He also at that time filed with the surveyor general of Louisiana a duly certified copy of the record of the proceedings had in 1872 in the matter of the Bigg's succession, and—in view of departmental decision of September 17, 1886, (Lettrieus Alrio 5 L. D., 158)—asked that the case be then considered and that " the relief so long denied" be granted.

After considering the evidence before him the surveyor general found that Biggs had sold in 1811, his settlement claim to a tract of land in Feliciana to one Samuel Davis; that the settlement claim of Samuel Davis, reported in the list of Cosby 1813 under No. 15, and the settlement claim of Caleb Biggs, reported in the list of register and receiver 1821 under No. 155, is one and the same claim, and that the claim of Samuel Davis was surveyed and located as Sec. 62, T. 1 S., R. 4 W., in the Greensburg land district Louisiana.

The surveyor general therefore rejected Hardee's application for scrip and so notified his attorney, April 16, 1883.

From the decision of your office dated, October 9, 1888, affirming said decision, Hardee has appealed to the Department, and his attorney contends that your office erred in holding said claims No. 15 and No. 155 to be identical and based on one and the same settlement. The fact that in 1811, Caleb Biggs surrendered and deeded to Samuel Davis all his right, title and claim to a tract of land situated in said parish of Feliciana, and to which he had at the time a settlement claim, is not disputed by appellant. Nor is the fact that the Davis claim has been fully satisfied disputed by him. He insists, however, that your office—

erred in presuming that Cosby and Skipwith, sworn and commissioned public officers, who issued in 1820 their certificate of confirmation, No. 780, on the claim of Samuel Davis, as purchasers under C. Biggs violated their duty in the following year by reporting the same Biggs as entitled to a donation for the same land by reason of the same settlement.

From the facts disclosed by the record in this case, the inference is clear that the certificate and report, issued and made as stated, did in fact relate to one and the same settlement claim.

Finding the fact as stated, however, imputes no willful violation of duty to said officers. Public officers do not enjoy total exemption from mistakes by any means, and that there was a mistake in this matter admits of but little doubt. The deed from Biggs to Davis is dated February 26, 1811, and each of the parties are described therein as then being residents of Wilkinson county, Mississippi. By this deed Caleb Biggs, in consideration of one thousand dollars, grants and surrenders to Samuel Davis, his heirs and assigns (I quote the description given in said deed)—

all that tract of land which I settled, improved and kept in cultivation from year to year since the year seventeen hundred and ninety, lying and being in west Florida on the waters of Bayon Tunica, bounded by the Bayon Tunica creek and Stewart's line on the south; on the east by Col. F. Kimball's line; on the north by the line of demarcation, and on the west by the lands of Christian Nelson . . . containing at least four hundred and forty acres.

Below Biggs' signature appears the following note, to wit—"The above date of seventeen hundred and ninety is left blank for want of knowing the exact date at this time. Done before signing."

The deed contains full warranty of title except as against the government.

Cosby and Skipwith in said certificate No. 780, dated June 27, 1820, say—

We certify that Samuel Davis is entitled to a section of land situated in the parish of Feliciana on which he now resides as an actual settler by purchase from C. Biggs, and so reported by the Commissioner in his report of actual settlement claims.

The order for the survey and location of this claim is dated June 24, 1825, and the description of the land is therein described as follows, to wit:

To begin on the line of demarcation at the line of C. Nelson, leaving to him his improvements, and run thence with the line of demarcation to F. Kimballs line, thence with his line to the line of Ann Kerr, thence with her line to Bayou Tunica, thence with said Bayou to Nelson's line and with it to the beginning, so as to include six hundred and forty acres, or as nearly as may be found within those bounds.

The tract of land thus surveyed and located is said Sec. 62 above described, and is situated in the parish of Feliciana.

The report of Cosby and Skipwith, referred to in appellant's application as the basis of his claim, shows the tract of land reported in Biggs' name to be in the parish of Feliciana, and to be for an original settlement made by Biggs in 1797.

The Davis claim reported by Commissioner Cosby in 1813, was not for a tract of land originally settled upon and improved by Davis, but for a tract settled upon by some one else in 1797, the right to which he had acquired by purchase. (See American State papers—Green's Ed., Vol. 3, p. 63). Before said survey and location of the Davis claim was ordered, proof was made that Biggs originally settled on the land described therein some time in 1797 or 1799. The surveyor general of Louisiana in passing on this case says—"After an exhaustive search through all the records in this, and in the register's office, no evidence of any other tract of land claimed by C. Biggs could be found." He also says that the location of the Davis claim (said Sec. 62) "corresponds exactly with the description made by Biggs in his act of sale to Davis; also with the calls of the order of survey issued in 1825 and all other papers."

The conclusion reached by the surveyor general that the settlement claim to the tract of land settled upon by Biggs, and which he sold in 1811, is the same settlement claim reported by Cosby and Skipwith, as aforesaid, seems to me to be fully warranted by the facts above stated.

The third section of the act of March 3, 1819 (3 Stat., 528), grants but one tract of land to the actual settler, or his legal representatives, and there is no evidence whatever that Biggs ever claimed or pretended to have settled upon or cultivated two distinct tracts of land in the parish of Feliciana or any place in the State of Louisiana, or that since his sale to Davis either he or his heirs ever pretended to have a possessory right, or any claim whatever to any tract of land so situated, by virtue of having settled upon and cultivated the same prior to April 15, 1813. The fact that no claim of a right to a donation grant from the government for six hundred and forty acres of public land was ever asserted by Biggs in his lifetime, or by his heirs since his death—the time of his death no where appears in this record—of itself raises a strong presumption that at the time of his death he did not own the claim now put forward and asserted—for the first time—more than sixty years after Biggs deeded the possessory right above mentioned to Davis.

The conclusion reached by the Department in this case makes it unnecessary to go into the question of the sufficiency or insufficiency of the record in said succession proceedings to show appellant to be the legal representative of Biggs.

The decision of your office herein is affirmed.

PRE-EMPTION FINAL PROOF—ADVERSE CLAIM.

COBBY v. FOX.

A failure to show compliance with the law, in any essential particular, by one tendering pre-emption final proof in the presence of an adverse claim of record, subjects his claim to the right of the adverse party.

First Assistant Secretary Chandler to the Commissioner of the General Land Office, October 22, 1889.

The case of Thomas H. Cobby v. Leland W. Fox is before me on appeal by Fox from the decision of your office, dated June 28, 1888.

The parties hereto are adverse pre-emption claimants for the SE. ¼ of Sec. 2, T. 12 S., R. 19 E., Stockton land district, California. The official plat of said township was filed August 1, 1874, and the tract in contest is unoffered land.

March 26, 1884, Cobby filed declaratory statement, No. 12361, for the described tract, alleging settlement thereon March 20, 1884.

April 28, 1886, Fox filed declaratory statement, No. 13456, for the same tract, alleging settlement thereon April 20, 1886.

Cobby gave due notice that he would make final proof before the register and receiver of the local land office on September 28, 1886, and therein specially notified Fox to appear and show cause, if there were any, why he (Cobby) should not be allowed to enter said land.

In pursuance of said notice the parties herein submitted testimony in support of their respective claims on September 28 and 29, 1886.

October 12th following, the local officers decided that (I quote): "The testimony submitted by claimant (Cobby) does not show a satisfactory or sufficient compliance with the requirements of the law as to the matter of residence, and his proofs are therefore rejected. The land should not be awarded to either party." No appeal was taken from this decision.

On January 14, 1887, your office concurred in the rejection of Cobby's proof, but so far modified said decision as to allow him " to give new notice and make new proof at any time within the lifetime of his filing." The record does not show that Fox had notice of this modification of said decision.

In February following, Cobby gave notice that he would, on March

15, 1887, make final proof before the local officers, and again notified Fox as before of his intention so to do. On the day set, each of the parties appeared in person and by counsel.

After considering the evidence, the register and receiver found as follows: "The claimant Cobby has made his actual and continuous residence on the land in contest since April 25, 1886, being absent prior to that time." And Cobby's cultivation and improvement of the land, at the time of said second hearing, appearing satisfactory, the local officers held that he "should be allowed to complete his entry and pay for the land in contest."   •

Fox appealed from this decision, and in passing on the case the then (June 28, 1888) Acting Commissioner, addressing the local officers, said: "I do not consider comment upon the case, or upon Fox's appeal and argument, necessary under the circumstances. Your decision is affirmed, and you will so notify the parties in interest." From this decision Fox prosecutes his present appeal to the Department, and the case presented by the record has been fully considered.

The modification of the decision of the register and receiver, made by your office as above stated on January 14, 1887, was erroneous. Cobby having elected to make final proof, in the face of the duly recorded adverse settlement claim of Fox, must stand or fall by the record then made in the case. Wade v. Meier (6 L. D., 308); Jacobs v. Cannon (ib., 623); Wright v. Brabander (ib., 760); Hults v. Leppin (7 L. D., 483).

A failure to show compliance with law in any essential particular by a party tendering pre-emption proof in the face of a recorded adverse claim subordinates, at least, the claim of such party to the claim of the adverse party. *Prima facie* the recorded adverse claim is a valid claim and its invalidity should in some manner be made to appear before the party, who once makes proof and fails to show a substantial compliance with the pre-emption law, can be permitted to make new proof in support of his claim.

Above and beyond this, it seems to me quite clear that Fox's claim to the land in controversy is superior to that of Cobby's. The evidence taken at the two hearings had in this case satisfactorily shows, that Fox settled upon this land on April 20, 1886, and that Cobby, though he built a house thereon before filing, never in fact established an actual residence on said land prior to April 25, 1886; that at the time of Fox's settlement the only improvements found on the land was the cheap board house built by Cobby more than two years before, a small quantity of plowed ground, a partially sunk well, and some thirty or forty small fig trees unprotected by any kind of a fence. It is satisfactorily shown that Cobby's house had no chimney or stove in it prior to the time of Fox's settlement, and that, at that time, grass was growing up to the door-way, unmarked by any indications of a path through it; that there was, in short, nothing whatever about the house at that time to indicate that it had ever been used as a human habitation, except a bunk and the torn pieces of a bed-quilt or comfort. That this house had not in fact been used as a residence by Cobby for more than two years before Fox's settlement, the evidence, when taken altogether, leaves but little doubt.

Cobby's said entry will be canceled, and Fox will be allowed ninety days from the time he receives notice of this decision within which to make final proof and payment for said tract of land.

The decision of your office is accordingly reversed.

___

MINING CLAIM—POSTING—PRACTICE—REVIEW.

BRIGHT ET AL. *v.* ELKHORN MINING CO.

It is not sufficient in a motion for review to allege generally that the decision is contrary to the law and evidence. The motion should specify the errors of law, and point out the particular evidence relied upon to secure a change of ruling.

It is too late to raise a technical objection to the affidavit of posting, after action on said affidavit and the allowance of the entry.

The affidavit of posting may be properly made by a claimant whose knowledge of the fact is derived from personal observation at various times of the plat and notice as posted, and from such information with respect thereto as could be accepted by a reasonably cautious man.

Neither the evidence, nor the finding thereon, should be considered on the final adjudication of another and independent case, where such evidence was not offered at the hearing in the latter case.

Secretary Noble to the Commissioner of the General Land Office, October 26, 1889.

This is a motion by A. F. Bright and T. T. Nicholson for review and reconsideration of departmental decision of March 15, 1889, in the case of said Bright and Nicholson *v.* The Elkhorn Mining Company, involving mineral entry, No. 1099, made by said company, May 14, 1884, at Helena, Montana, for the A. M. Holter lode claim.

Said departmental decision is a simple affirmance of your office decision of July 13, 1888, adverse to said Bright and Nicholson, in the matter of their protest against the issuance of patent to the Elkhorn Mining Company for the claim in question.

It was alleged by these protestants, among other things, substantially, (1) that said A. M. Holter lode claim was never properly located, or its boundaries sufficiently marked, and (2) that plat and notice of intention to apply for patent were never posted on the claim during the statutory period of publication. This protest was carried to a hearing, and by direction of your office the inquiry was confined to the two allegations above set forth. Upon the testimony submitted the local officers found against the protestants, and in favor of the validity of the entry in question, and their finding was sustained by your office in the decision, the formal affirmance of which by this Department is now complained of.

The alleged grounds upon which the motion for review is based are:

1. That said decision is contrary to the weight of the evidence in the case, and is unsupported by the testimony.

2. It is not made out fairly by a preponderance of evidence in the case that a copy of the plat of survey, together with a notice of application for patent, was posted on said claim, as required by law.

3. The decision is contrary to the law of the case.

4. The affidavit of posting copy of plat of survey, with notice of application for patent, required by law to be made by the claimant, was not made by a claimant who had any personal knowledge of the fact of such posting, but was made by a person who derived his information by hearsay only, and was therefore not in compliance with law.

5. The said decision is in other respects irregular and contrary to law.

The motion has been elaborately argued by counsel for all the parties both orally and by brief, and the same has been carefully considered.

The first, third and fifth of the alleged grounds of review are very general in character and do not set out with any degree of clearness, in what particulars the decision of which a review is sought, is claimed to be erroneous. The mere allegations that the decision "is contrary to the law," and "to the weight of evidence," and "is unsupported by the testimony," and "is in other respects irregular and contrary to law," do not in themselves indicate or point out any particular matter, or ground of error, and are not sufficiently specific to warrant or justify a re-examination of the case. They can in no reasonable sense be considered specifications of error. Motions for review should clearly and specifically set forth the grounds of error complained of. (George W. Macey et al., 6 L. D., 781). It is not sufficient to merely allege that the decision complained of is contrary to the weight of evidence, but the particular evidence on which the change of ruling is claimed, should be specifically set forth (Long v. Knotts, 5 L. D., 150); and this principle applies with equal force to the allegations that the decision "is unsupported by the testimony," "is contrary to the law," and "in other respects irregular," and to all general terms of like nature. If the rule were otherwise, the Department would be compelled to twice examine every case wherein the defeated party or his attorney might see fit to allege simply that the decision was against the weight of evidence, or was contrary to the law; a practice, which, for obvious reasons, can not be allowed to prevail. (Albert H. Cornwell, 9 L. D., 340.)

Now, if the three "grounds" mentioned were the only grounds of error, so-called, alleged in this motion for review and reconsideration, the same, for the reasons stated, might properly be dismissed without further saying. But the second and fourth allegations of the motion are sufficiently specific in character to meet all reasonable requirements in this respect, and inasmuch as an intelligent consideration of the questions thereby presented has necessitated a re-examination of the whole record in the case, the same has been reviewed on its merits, notwithstanding the defects in the motion, as above pointed out.

The evidence in the case, which is very voluminous, and in some respects conflicting, has, therefore, all been re-examined and again carefully considered. The facts disclosed by the record are found to be set forth with substantial accuracy and sufficient fullness in the original decision of your office, and it is not deemed necessary that the same shall be here restated in detail.

Upon the question as to whether the law was complied with in the matter of the original location and marking of the claim in controversy, there is some degree of conflict in the evidence, but the weight thereof is very decidedly in favor of the view that the requirements of the statute in this respect have been, in all particulars, substantially met. The decision complained of is, with reference to this question, therefore, not only not "contrary to the weight of evidence in the case," but is fully sustained thereby.

With respect to the question of posting of plat and notice, presented by the second alleged ground of error in this motion for review, there is very little conflict in the testimony, and that is rather apparent than real. Conceding such conflict, however, to be decided and positive, to the full extent thereof, it is nevertheless shown by an overwhelming preponderance of the evidence, that the plat of survey and notice of intention to apply for patent were duly and regularly posted in a conspicuous place on the claim during the entire statutory period of publication. The evidence in behalf of the Elkhorn Mining Company on this point, independently of that of A. M. Holter, the president of said company, is by seventeen witnesses, and is in most part direct, positive and convincing in character, while that of the protestants is by a less number of witnesses, and is vague, indefinite and unsatisfactory, and would scarcely warrant a conclusion against the fact of such posting, and the regularity and continuance thereof during the statutory period mentioned, even if it stood alone, and was left to its contest with the legal presumptions arising from the *prima facie* showing, based on the formal entry papers of said company. Upon the whole testimony there is, therefore, no room for any reasonable doubt that such plat and notice were in fact posted on the claim in the manner prescribed by the statute.

Thus, it is seen that in respect of the defaults charged in the affidavit of protest, the evidence clearly and satisfactorily establishes, as matters of fact, that the claim was properly located and marked on the ground, and that the plat and notice were actually posted thereon as the law requires. Unless, therefore, there is something in the technical objections, made by counsel, to the formal proof of the posting of the plat and notice, which will now be considered, to warrant the vacation of the departmental decision complained of, the same must be sustained.

It is claimed by counsel for the protestants in their brief, that the affidavit of A. F. Bright and J. L. Smith, as to the posting of such plat and notice filed in the local office in obedience to the requirement of section 2325 of the Revised Statutes, was void and without legal effect, because made before a notary public (one John H. Shober), who, it is alleged, was at the time of taking the same attorney for the company, and also interested pecuniarily in the claim.

It is not shown, however, by anything in the record, what pecuniary interest, if any, Shober had in the claim at the time mentioned (October 10, 1883), or has since had, nor does it appear what was the extent of his relations with the company as its attorney, if, indeed, he was in fact its attorney at that date. But, conceding that at the date of said affidavit Shober was interested pecuniarily in the claim in controversy, and was the general attorney for the Elkhorn Mining Company in all matters relative to its interests in respect of said claim, can it be reasonably contended that these facts, presented at this late day, should avail the protestants to secure the cancellation of the entry in question? I think not. It seems to me that if said affidavit were technically defective, for the reasons stated, admitting them to be founded on fact, the proper time to have taken advantage of such defect was when the affidavit was presented and filed for action thereon by the local officers, and before the entry was made. It is too late, in my judgment, to raise the question of such supposed defect, which, if indeed a defect at all, is purely technical in its nature, after the affidavit has been acted upon by the local office and the entry allowed. It should be borne in mind that it is *the fact of posting* the plat and notice on the claim, that forms in part the basis of the applicants' claim for patent. The affidavit is, more properly speaking, the means prescribed by which the *fact* of such posting is to be shown. The provision of the statute, in respect to such affidavit, is, that after the applicant for patent shall have posted the plat of his claim and notice of his application, as required, he " shall file an affidavit of at least two persons that such notice has been duly posted." It was evidently the intention of Congress, by this provision, to prescribe what should be offered by the applicant, and accepted by the government, as *ex parte* proof of the act of posting, and also the manner in which such proof should be presented. In this case the directions of the statute in this respect were strictly followed. The affidavit filed, being in all respects, therefore, in due form, was accepted by the officers of the government and the entry allowed without objection being made. On the protest, subsequently presented, alleging, among other things, that the plat and notice mentioned in the affidavit had not been in fact posted on the claim as therein stated, or during the period of publication as required, a hearing has been had, and by the testimony submitted thereat, it is abundantly established, not only that said plat and notice were posted on the claim, as stated in said affidavit, but, also, that they remained continuously so posted, until long after the expiration of the time prescribed. Upon the state of facts thus revealed at the hearing, whereat all the parties interested were either present in person, or represented by counsel, there can be no question, in my judgment, even admitting the affidavit to have been originally defective in respect of the points named, that the entry attacked must be sustained. At most the defects charged could have rendered the affidavit voidable only, and not void absolutely, and it is too late, after the purposes of the affidavit have been fully accomplished, as in this case, to raise with avail the question of the defects claimed, conceding them to be such.

In this view of the matter it is not deemed necessary, for the purposes of this decision, to pass upon the question as to whether said affidavit was or was not, for the reasons alleged, originally defective; or to consider the authorities cited by counsel on this point. This question can more properly be determined when it shall be presented in due time, in a case where it fairly arises on the face of the record.

It may be also said that the foregoing considerations apply as well, and with equal force, to the objections raised in the fourth alleged ground of error in the motion for review, against the final *ex parte* affidavit of A. M. Holter, the president of the company, filed with the entry papers, showing that the plat and notice, above mentioned, had been posted in a conspicuous place on the claim during the sixty days period of publication. Said affidavit is in all respects in due form, and it is not denied that the same was regularly made and duly filed, but it is claimed that the affiant (and such claim is based on his testimony taken at the hearing) did not know by means of personal observation of the fact of such continous posting during the entire time required, and that, therefore, his affidavit was not made in compliance with the law. The requirement of the statute in this regard is that, "at the expiration of the sixty days of publication the claimant shall file his affidavit, showing that the plat and notice have been posted in a conspicuous place on the claim during such period of publication." Now, the affidavit thus required was made and filed, and the testimony in the case abundantly demonstrates the truth of the statements thereof, as to the fact of such continuous posting. The affidavit was accepted for the purposes of the entry, without question or objection, as proof of the matters therein stated, and, if there ever could have been any point in the objection now urged, which it is by no means intended here to concede, it certainly can not avail the protestants at this late day.

True, the testimony of said Holter shows that he did not have, when he made said affidavit, a personal knowledge of the fact of such posting, based solely and entirely on a continuous personal observation of the plat and notice as posted, but it is wholly unreasonable to suppose that any person could have a continuous personal observation of a continuous posting of sixty days duration, or that the statute requires it. There is no direction given in the stature as to the manner in which the information or knowledge, upon which the affidavit is to be based, shall be obtained; and, inasmuch as Holter's testimony shows that he had sufficient knowledge of the matters sworn to by him, obtained both from personal observation at various times of the plat and notice as posted, and from information in respect thereto received through others upon whom he could rely, to enable any reasonably cautious man to make the affidavit required, I can see no merit whatever in the objection made thereto.

Lastly, it is urged by counsel for the protestants that the record in the case of A. F. Bright *et al. v.* The Elkhorn Mining Company, which came up from the same local land office, wherein the case at bar originated, and was finally decided by this Department, December 19, 1888, should have been considered along with the record in this case in determining the issues here presented.

The case referred to arose on the protest of Bright and others against the issuance of patent to the Elkhorn Mining Company under its placer mineral entry No. 1085, made January 7, 1884, alleging substantially, (1) that the land covered by the entry was not valuable for placer minerals; (2) that no labor had been performed or improvements made thereon by the claimant, or its grantors, for placer mining purposes, and (3) that claimant sought title to the tract for townsite purposes; and several of the prominent witnesses who testified at the hearing had in that case are also witnesses in the case at bar. The decision of the Department in the former case, after discussing the testimony at considerable length, affirmed the decision of your office, holding the entry in question for cancellation, and it is with a view to impeaching the credibility of some of the witnesses who testified in this case, in behalf of the Elkhorn Mining Company, that counsel sought, and now insist upon, a consideration of the record referred to. It is claimed that the final decision in that case, in effect, found the witnesses, whose evidence is attacked in this case, to be "liars and defrauders;" that they were guilty of "fraud which involved false swearing and deliberate deception, trickery, and villainous proceeding." The request of counsel in respect thereto was first made on the original appeal herein to this Department, and the question thereby presented was then considered, although no specific mention is made thereof in the decision of which reconsideration is now sought.

It is not seen by what authority said record, or any part thereof, could have been considered on the appeal, or can now be considered, as evidence in the case at bar. This case arose on a protest alleging an interest adverse to the mineral claimant, and was brought here originally because of the adverse interest alleged. (See departmental decision awarding the appeal, 8 L. D., 122.) While, therefore, apparently *ex parte* in nature, it is in fact a contest so far as the questions before the Department are concerned, and must be determined, with reference to all matters touching the introduction of testimony by either party, upon principles applicable to contests. There was no attempt made at the hearing herein to introduce, as evidence, any part of the record referred to, although the hearing in that case had taken place months before; and it would be contrary, in my judgment, to well established rules governing the introduction of testimony, to allow, as a matter of legal right, such record to be brought into the case, after the hearing is regularly closed, as evidence to be considered upon the final hearing thereof.

In view, however, of the grave and sweeping assertions made by counsel, with respect to the effect of the final decision in that case, the record therein has been examined and informally considered, and it may be said that the same furnishes no reasonable grounds for such assertions. There was no affirmative finding of fraud in that case. The entry was canceled, because the evidence fell short of establishing the mineral character of the land embraced therein, as an affirmative and present fact, and on the ground that the proof did not show the improvements to have been made for the purpose of developing the claim as a placer mine; and it was further said that the location of a townsite on the claim under the particular circumstances of the case was " strongly persuasive " that the application was not made in good faith. There is nothing whatever in the record to justify the claim of counsel for the protestants here, in reference thereto.

Upon careful review of the whole record herein, I must decline to interrupt the decision complained of, and the motion to reconsider the same is denied.

———

RAILROAD GRANT—ACT OF STATE LEGISLATURE.

St. Paul, Minneapolis & Manitoba Ry. Co. v. Fogelberg.

Lands to which full and legal title was perfected in the St. Paul and Pacific R. R. Co. prior to the act of the State legislature of March 1, 1877, were expressly excepted from the operation of said act, and a subsequent deed of reconveyance from the State would not invest the Department with jurisdiction over such land.

Secretary Noble to the Commissioner of the General Land Office, October 26, 1889.

I am in receipt of your office letter of May 4, 1889, transmitting a letter from the attorneys for the St. Paul, Minneapolis and Manitoba Railway company, calling attention to an alleged oversight in the consideration of the case of the Northern Pacific Railroad Company and the St. Paul, Minneapolis and Manitoba Railroad Company v. Carl Fogelberg, involving the E. ½ of the NW. ¼ and the E. ½ of the SW. ¼ of Sec. 11, T. 135 N. R. 43 W., 5th P. M. Fergus Falls, Minnesota land district.

On December 19, 1888, this Department rendered a decision in said case affirming the decision of your office dated June 21, 1887, allowing Fogelberg's homestead application for this land.

The facts in said case as presented to the Department by said company on appeal are as follows :

The land involved is within the indemnity limits of the St. Paul, Minneapolis and Manitoba Railway (St. Vincent extension) and was patented on account of the grant in aid of said road on June 14, 1875. In accordance with the provisions of the act of the Minnesota legislature approved March 1, 1877, (Laws of Minn. 19 Session Special, 257), the governor of said State by deed dated June 23, 1880 reconveyed these tracts with other lands to the United States for the benefit of Carl Fogelberg, a settler on said lands prior to the passage of said act of March 1, 1877.

These being the facts then before this Department, it was said

The claim made by the St. Paul company is in all respects similar to that made by the same company in the case of the St. Paul, Minneapolis and Manitoba Railway Co. *v.* Morrison (4 L. D., 300) and of the same company *v.* Chadwick (6 L. D., 128). On the authority of these cases your decision adverse to said company is affirmed.

It is now said by the attorneys for said company that the governor of Minnesota by deed executed February 23, 1877, conveyed to the St. Paul and Pacific Railroad Company, the predecessor of the St. Paul, Minneapolis and Manitoba Company, among other lands, all of said Sec. 11 T. 135 N., R. 43 W., 5th P. M., and that said deed was filed in your office prior to the decision of your office of June 21, 1887, and of this Department of December 19, 1888. It is claimed that by this deed the legal and full title to the land involved had been perfected in said company prior to the passage of the act of March 1, 1877, and that therefore the governor of said State had no authority for his act in executing the deed of June 23, 1880, and that said deed is void and of no effect. It is contended that the error in said decision caused by the failure to consider said deed from the governor of Minnesota to the railroad company is one which the Department should *sua sponte* correct. In your office letter of May 4, 1889, in regard to this deed of 1877 being on file in your office it is said—

In relation to this point I desire to state that the certified copy of the deed was filed in this office as a part of the case of Charles W. Hazen, in 1886, and at the date of the decision of June 21, 1887, was before the Secretary of the Interior. The company did not mention said deed in connection with the proceedings in the case of Fogelberg nor in its appeal from the decision in said case.

It may be stated here that the papers in the case of Charles W. Hazen were returned to your office March 8, 1888, for further consideration in view of the fact that additional evidence had been filed with or after the appeal from your office.

A re-examination of the papers in the case shows that said deed from the governor of Minnesota to the railroad company was not offered in evidence at the hearing had in this case, and that it has never been mentioned in any of the appeals or arguments filed by the attorneys for said company until this letter of April 12, 1889. If the interests of said company alone were at stake or to be affected no good reason has been presented for interfering to change the former decision. Inasmuch, however, as other interests are involved, and in view of the fact that if this Department had no jurisdiction to dispose of the land involved, the decision in favor of the homestead applicant could avail him nothing in the end, I have deemed it best to reconsider this case.

An examination of the records of your office discloses the fact that, with their letter of July 19, 1886, transmitting an appeal in the Hazen case, heretofore referred to, the attorneys for the St. Paul, Minneapolis and Manitoba Railway Company transmitted to your office a certified copy of a deed executed February 23, 1877, by the governor of Minnesota and purporting to convey the tract here in question, together with other lands, to the St. Paul and Pacific Railroad Company. If this deed was duly and regularly executed under proper authority it operated to pass to the grantee therein, legal and full title to the land described therein, and such land was not affected by the act of the State legislature of March 1, 1877, being expressly excepted from the operation thereof by the phrase limiting said act to those tracts "to which legal and full title has not been perfected in said St. Paul and Pacific Railroad Company, or their successors or assigns."

If the title to said land passed to the company February 3, 1877, the State had no further control over it and the attempted reconveyance by the governor to the United States of June 23, 1880, was of no effect, and could not operate to reinvest the United States with title to said land or to authorize the interference by the government in any manner with its control or disposition. This being true, it follows that this Department had no jurisdiction over this land on December 19, 1888, and that the decision of that date assuming as it did a right in the Department to dispose of said tract was in error. Said decision must be, and is hereby revoked and set aside.

Inasmuch, however, as Fogelberg, has not had an opportunity of contradicting the allegation that the land applied for by him had passed from the jurisdiction of this Department prior to the date of his application, such opportunity should now be afforded him. The case will therefore be returned to your office, and you will immediately give Fogelberg notice that he will be allowed ninety days, from receipt of such notice, within which to show cause why his homestead entry, made January 15, 1889, should not be canceled. If Fogelberg shall not, with the period specified, submit some valid objection to said deed his entry should be canceled. If he shall make objection to the same, you will consider such objection, and, after a hearing—if one shall be deemed by you necessary—adjudicate the case upon all the facts then before you, and in accordance with the views herein expressed. If such adjudication shall finally result in the cancellation of Fogelberg's entry, it should be without prejudice to his right to make entry under the homestead law for other lands.

The decision of your office of June 21, 1887 is accordingly modified.

FLORENCE BREY.

In determining whether a pre-emption settlement is in violation of the second inhibition of section 2260 R. S., the character of the land from which removal is made,
and the purposes for which said land was used may be taken into consideration.

*First Assistant Secretary Chandler to the Commissioner of the General
Land Office, October 26, 1889.*

I have considered the appeal of Florence Brey from your office decision of July 7, 1888, rejecting her proof for her pre-emption filing on
the S. ½ of SW. ¼, section 14, and W. ½ of NW. ¼, section 23, T. 3 S., R.
19 E., Stockton land district, California.

Brey filed her pre-emption declaratory statement for the said land
October 28, 1887, alleging settlement on the eighteenth previous.

Claimant made her final proof June 5, 1888, before the local officers.
Rejecting the proof they said,

Her proof appears sufficient as to residence and improvements and her acts show
good faith; but from her testimony it appears that she owned one-third interest in a
tract of agricultural land of seven acres in Santa Clara county in this State, whereon
she had resided for about five years prior to her settlement on said pre-emption and
which she left for the purpose of settling on her pre-emption claim. In our opinion
this disqualifies her from acquiring a right of pre-emption under the prohibitive clause
of sub-division two, Sec. 2260, Revised Statutes.

You say:

He (she) could not reside upon and make his (her) living by agriculture upon such
an interest. The prohibition of the statutes has uniformly been held to settlers upon
agricultural lands only. The case in question is held as coming within the spirit of
the decision in Sturgeon *v.* Ruiz (1 D. L., 490).

Your office, however, rejected the proof, because "unsatisfactory in
the matter of residence and improvements."

Again claimant appealed and the case is now before this Department
for consideration.

The proof shows that Florence Brey is of the age of thirty-eight
years, native born and unmarried; she made her first settlement on
the land October 18, 1887, by hauling lumber to the claim to be used
for building a house. She did move actually on the land and commenced living there permanently about November 20, 1887. By that
time her house was built and she moved into it. She says that this
tract has been her actual residence and home ever since. Being
questioned whether her residence on the land had been actual and
continuous or at intervals, she states "Actual and continuous. I have
lived there all the time and had no other home." She was absent once
in February about three weeks, while "attending to some business" in
Santa Clara.

Her improvements are stated in the proof as follows: a "pine lumber
house, shake roof," of the size of twelve by twelve feet; house has a floor,

is battened outside and lined and papered inside, value about seventy-five dollars. A chicken house eight feet by ten, value eight or ten dollars; between four and five acres plowed, cost about six dollars; about half an acre with fruit trees, vines, etc., spring, brush fence and three acres of clearing; total value of improvements about one hundred and fifty dollars. She kept on the land from the time she moved on it, necessary household and kitchen furniture and garden tools and implements. Domestic animals she had none, except two dozen chickens. While on the land she raised a crop of vegetables, no other crop. She states "I did not sow the other land because the season was too dry and I could not get it plowed in time any way;" she used the land "for a home and farming purposes."

To the question "Did you leave other land of your own to settle on your present claim? she answered, "I owned one-third interest with my brother and sister in a tract of about seven acres in Santa Clara, where I lived for five years and which I left to go and reside on this land."

Claimant's testimony was duly corroborated by her witnesses.

Claimant's proof regarding residence, improvements and cultivation seems unobjectionable; her residence comprised, counting from time of her settlement a period of seven months and a half, her house was well supplied with furniture and her improvements, though not large, indicate her good faith. She raised vegetables sufficient for her own use on an acre of ground and gives, it seems, a good excuse for not having sown crops on the rest of her breaking. No fact in the case tends to show bad faith on her part.

The question whether the claimant had quitted or abandoned her residence on her land to reside on the public land in the same State in violation of the second inhibitive clause of said section 2260, of the Revised Statutes must be determined by the following rules. In the case of Austrian v. Hogan (6 C. L. O., page 172), it was held that the inhibition extends only to agricultural lands. In Sturgeon v. Ruiz (1 L. D., 490), it was determined that a pre-emptor who moves from his own home in a city, town or village upon a pre-emption claim, is not debarred. (See also 6 C. L. O., 172.) In the case of Payne v. Campbell (8 L. D., 267), it was held that joint ownership in lands clearly brings the claimant within the inhibition. Of course if the land is not agricultural the rule in Payne v. Campbell does not apply. The record fails to disclose the nature and character of the land removed from sufficiently to enable me to say whether it was agricultural land or not within the scope of the above cited cases. You will, therefore, require supplementary proof as to the location and character of the land removed from and the uses to which it was put by the claimant and if within the requirement herein, the proof of claimant will be accepted and upon her further compliance with the requirements of the pre-emption law, patent be issued.

Your said office decision is accordingly modified.

PRIVATE CLAIM—ACTS OF MARCH 8, 1819, AND JUNE 2, 1858.

JAMES BARBUT.

A claim founded upon a British grant is not confirmed by section one, act of March 3, 1819, if it had not been sold and conveyed, or settled upon and cultivated prior to the treaty of 1783, nor by section two of said act, as that is only applicable to claims derived from Spanish authority, and covered by commissioner's list " B," nor by the third section of said act as that embraces only claims of actual settlers prior to April 15, 1813, who had no written evidence of title.

Scrip can not issue under section 3, act of June 2, 1858, if the claim, alleged as a basis therefor, has not been confirmed by some act of Congress.

Secretary Noble to the Commissioner of the General Land Office, October 26, 1889.

I have considered the case of David C. Hardee on his appeal from your office decision of May 8, 1888, refusing to grant him certificates under the act of June 2, 1858, for the alleged claim of James Barbut to whose rights under a British patent appellant claims to have succeeded.

Barbut's claim was for two thousand acres in that part of Louisiana lying west of Pearl river and east of the Mississippi.

By treaty of 1783 between Great Britain and Spain the ownership of the territory in which the land is situated, which had been claimed by both of said governments, was conceded to Spain it being only stipulated that British subjects residing therein should be allowed a certain time to sell their lands and the Spanish government agreed to hold such sales good.

This land subsequently passed to the United States by the Louisiana purchase, and by act of April 25, 1812 (2 Stats., 713) Congress provided for the appointment of a commissioner in each of several districts to receive proof from parties who claimed lands under any alleged right whatever, derived under the French, British or Spanish governments, and report a list of such claims and the alleged right on which the claim was based etc., with recommendations for the guidance of Congress in action thereon.

One James O. Cosby was the commissioner for the district in which the patent in the case under consideration was to be located.

To his report he attaches four lists of claimants, viz., A, B, C and D. List A, " Register of claims to land in the district west of Pearl river, in Louisiana, founded on complete grants derived from either the French, British or Spanish government, which in the opinion of the undersigned commissioner, are valid agreeable to the laws, usages, or customs of such government." In his report upon the said list "A" said Commissioner states that not one out of fifty of the British claimants availed themselves of the privilege of selling their lands within a certain time, and thereafter the Spanish government treated all such claims as had not been confirmed by it, as vacant and indiscriminately re-granted the lands to any person who applied therefor under the law.

List B is entitled—" Register of claims to land . . . . founded
on orders of survey, (requettes,) permission to settle or other written
evidence of claims derived from either the French, British, or Spanish
authorities, which in the opinion of the commissioner, ought to be confirmed." Of this list he says they were claims to land originated by the
Spanish authorities prior to the purchase of Louisiana by the United
States, and agreeably to the laws, usages, and customs, of the then existing government would have been completed by the same power which
granted them.

The other lists need not be further mentioned herein.

The claim of James Barbut was given in said list "A," being numbered 361 under a British patent, dated October 17, 1774, for two thousand acres in Feliciana parish, not surveyed but inhabited from 1809
to 1814.

The claims in list "B" all originated under the Spanish government,
none being under British patents or grants. For said Commissioner's
report see American State Papers—Public Lands, Vol. 3, Green's Edition, pages 35 to 72.

By the act of March 3, 1819, (3 Stat., 528), Congress, acting on the
report of the said commissioners, undertook to adjust said claims. The
first three sections of said act, which are all it will be necessary to now
consider, are as follows:

Be it enacted by the Senate and House of Representatives of the United States of
America, in Congress assembled, That all the claims to land, founded on complete
grants from the Spanish government, reported to the Secretary of the Treasury, by
the commissioners from the districts east and west of Pearl river, appointed under
the authority of an act, entitled "An act for ascertaining the titles and claims to lauds
in that part of Louisiana which lies east of the river Mississippi and island of New
Orleans," which are contained in the several reports of the commissioners, and which
are, in the opinion of the commissioners, valid, agreeably to the laws, usages, and
customs of the said government, be and the same are hereby, recognized as valid and
complete titles against any claim on the part of the United States, or right derived
from the United States. And that all claims founded on British grants, contained in
the said reports, which have been sold and conveyed, according to the provisions of
the treaty of peace, between Great Britain and Spain, of the third of September, one
thousand seven hundred and eighty-three, by which that part of Louisiana,
lying east of the island of Orleans, was ceded to Spain, under the denomination of
West Florida, or which were settled and cultivated by the person having the legal
title therein, at the date of said treaty, are recognized as valid and complete titles,
against any claim on the part of the United States, or right derived from the United
States.

2. And be it further enacted, That all claims reported as aforesaid, and contained
in the several reports of the said commissioners, founded on any order of survey, requette, permission to settle, or any written evidence of claim, derived from the Spanish authorities, which ought, in the opinion of the commissioners, to be confirmed,
and which by the said reports appear to be derived from the Spanish government,
before the twentieth day of December, one thousand eight hundred and three, and
the land claimed to have been cultivated and inhabited, on or before that day, shall
be confirmed in the same manner as if the title had been completed: Provided, That
in all such claims, where the plat and certificate of survey made prior to the fifteenth
day of April, one thousand eight hundred and thirteen, under the authority of the

Spanish government, in pursuance of such claim, has not been filed with the said commissioners, such claim shall not be confirmed to any one person for more than twelve hundred and eighty acres: and that for all the other claims to land comprised in the reports aforesaid, and which ought, in the opinion of the commissioners, to be confirmed ; the claimant to such lands shall be entitled to a grant therefor as a donation : *Provided*, That such grant, as a donation, shall not be made to any one person for more than twelve hundred and eighty acres; which confirmation of the said incomplete titles and grants of donations, hereby provided to be made, shall amount only to a relinquishment forever, on the part of the United States, of any claim whatever to the tract of land so confirmed or granted : *And provided, also*, That no such claim shall be confirmed to any person to whom the title to any tract of land shall have been recognized under the preceding provisions.

Sec. 3. And be it further enacted, That every person or his or her legal representative, whose claim is comprised in the lists, or register of claims, reported by the said commissioners, and the persons embraced in the list of actual settlers, or their legal representatives, not having any written evidence of claim reported as aforesaid, shall, where it appears, by the said reports, or by the said lists, that the land claimed or settled on had been actually inhabited or cultivated, by such person or persons in whose right he claims, on or before the fifteenth day of April, one thousand eight hundred and thirteen, be entitled to a grant for the land so claimed, or settled on, as a donation : *Provided*, That not more than one tract shall be thus granted to any one person, and the same shall not contain more than six hundred and forty acres; and that no lands shall be thus granted which are claimed or recognized by the preceding sections of this act.

On January 8, 1830, the local officers at St. Helena, issued to James Barbut a certificate of confirmation, but this the Land Department declared null and void by a letter to the local officers dated July 20, 1830 (2 Public Lands, Laws, Inst., & Ops., 742), notice of which was given Barbut July 26, 1830.

No appeal was taken by Barbut from this ruling and no further effort seems to have been made by him to procure any land under said patent.

On March 8, 1872, the public administrator of the parish of East Feliciana filed a petition in the court of probate, alleging that James Barbut had died intestate in said parish many years before leaving some property consisting of an old deferred land claim against the United States which should be inventoried and sold according to law, and asking for an order of sale.

The appraisement was made as two thousand "arpents" instead of acres, and was valued at $50.00, and was sold to said Hardee for that sum which was exactly the court costs in said case.

Hardee, on June 14, 1887, applied to the surveyor general of Louisiana for certificates of location under section 3 of the act of June 2, 1858 (11 Stats., 294), claiming that the issuance of such certificates was authorized by the following portion of section 3, of said act, viz :

that in all cases of confirmation by this act or where any private land claim has been confirmed by Congress, and the same, in whole or in part, has not been located or satisfied, either for want of a specific location prior to such confirmation, or for any reason whatsoever other than a discovery of fraud in such claim, subsequent to such confirmation, it shall be the duty of the surveyor-general of the district, in which such claim was situated, upon satisfactory proof that such claim has been so confirmed, and that the same, in whole or in part, remains unsatisfied, to issue to the claimant, or his legal representatives a certificate of location for a quantity of land equal to that so confirmed and unsatisfied, which certificate may be located upon any public lands of the United States subject to sale at private entry at a price not exceeding one dollar and twenty-five cents per acre.

This application was refused by the surveyor-general of Louisiana in a letter to the attorneys for Hardee dated August 26, 1887, but said decision was subsequently reconsidered by him, and allowed in part, and with letter of December 21, 1887, he transmitted certificates to the amount of 1280 acres with his reasons for issuing the same, to your office for approval.

Your said decision of May 8, 1888, held said certificates for cancellation, and said,

As there is nothing in said report (Report of J. O. Cosby hereinbefore explained) to indicate that said claim had ever been sold or conveyed, nor inhabited or cultivated at the date of the treaty of 1783, it cannot be held that it is recognized by the first section of said act of 1819.

This identical claim having been declared void and of no effect by this office, and the Secretary of the Treasury, I must decline to authenticate said certificates.

Within the prescribed time counsel filed in your office a motion for review in which they say that in their original application to the surveyor general they admitted that as Barbut had neither sold his claim nor resided thereon at the date of said treaty of 1783, his right to two thousand acres had not been recognized as valid against the United States by section 1, of the act of 1819, but claimed that " his claim being in a category of claims recommended for confirmation by the commissioner (Cosby) and founded on written evidence of title, with settlement and cultivation from 1809 to 1814, was valid as a donation for 1280 acres of land as a donation, under the second proviso of section 2 of the act (of 1819).

And counsel further claimed that if not entitled under section 2 aforesaid to 1280 acres that the claimant is entitled to six hundred and forty acres as a donation under the third section of said act.

Counsel claimed also that "had the certificates been issued for 1280 acres under the act generally, or under section 2, and such certificates had been held void such ruling would be involved in the case and its correctness would be vital to the rights now claimed by the legal representatives of Barbut."

Your office by decision of September 20, 1888, denied said motion for review and adhered to the former decision, and held that the action of July 20, 1830, rendered the matter *res adjudicata* and said,

It has been the uniform ruling of this department that one Commissioner of the General Land Office has no authority to review a decision of his predecessor that has become final. (6 L. D., 4, and cases therein cited.)

Aside from this and considering the question of recognition and confirmation as if they were original ones, it is plain to me after a careful examination of the act, that claims founded upon British grants were recognized as valid and complete titles against any claim on the part of the United States by section one of the aforesaid act of 1819, under the conditions therein set forth, only.

They were either valid and fully recognized as a whole or void *in toto*: that the provisions for confirmation in the succeeding sections of the act apply to claims and headrights embraced in Commissioner Cosby's reports, registers and lists, entirely separate and distinct from "Register "A" and that Barbut's claim does not stand confirmed as a donation for either 1280 or six hundred and forty acres.

Upon his appeal to this office the claimant alleges error on the part of your office in holding,

1st. That the right of Barbut, being based on written evidence of title derived from a foreign government, supported by proof of settlement and cultivation thereunder from 1809 to 1814, and being in a category of claims recommended for recognition and confirmation by the Commissioner was not valid as a donation for twelve hundred and eighty acres under the 2nd provision of section 2, of the act of March 3, 1819.

2nd. In holding that said right supported by proof of actual settlement and cultivation by Barbut prior to the 15th of April, 1813, and being in a category of claims recommended for recognition and confirmation by the commissioner, was not granted as a donation for six hundred and forty acres by section 3 of said act of March 3, 1819:

3rd. In holding that the letter from the bureau to the local office at St. Helena of July 20, 1830, and the subsequent notice from the bureau to claimants of July 26, 1830, constituted decisions on the question now before the bureau controlling your judgment and discretion as matters *res adjudicata*.

Prior to the act of April 25, 1812, under which Cosby was appointed commissioner much land in Mississippi Territory had been claimed under British patents, and in a letter dated August 13, 1823, sent by the Land Department to the register and receiver of the land district in which Barbut's claim was to have been located, instructions were given them construing the said act of 1819, and in said instructions they were directed that,

The principles recognized in this act in confirming private claims founded on written evidence are in conformity to the principles on which similar claims in the other land districts within the States of Louisiana and Mississippi have been confirmed, and the distinguishing character of which is, that *no* claim founded on any order of survey, requette, permission to settle, *or any written evidence*, should be confirmed as a complete title, unless it was derived from the Spanish, British and French governments, previous to the day on which their respective authorities over the domain was considered to have ceased, *and unless actual settlement was made on the land previous to that period*; but in all *other* cases, when the written evidence appears to have been fairly obtained, the lands have been confirmed as donations, to an extent not exceeding twelve hundred and eighty acres; and in exercising your power of supervision over the cases confirmed by the act of the 8th of May, 1822, you should keep these principles constantly in view.

(2 Public Lands, Laws, Inst., and Ops., 717; 3 Stats., 707.)

Upon examination of rulings in regard to "similar claims" above referred to I find in a letter to the register and receiver for the district west of Pearl river, in Mississippi, dated November 5, 1805, this language (2 id., 671):

It was not the intention either of the commissioners who concluded the agreement between the United States and Georgia, or, so far as I have understood it, of the legislature, to extend donations to any but actual settlers. The holders of British or Spanish complete grants, who were not settlers, will be left to their remedy by law, if they think that their claim can be be supported.

By letter to register and receiver of the land office at St. Helena, La., dated August 13, 1823 (Id., 717), they were instructed that,

The 1st section of the act of the 3rd of March, 1819, confirms all the claims reported by J. O. Cosby in his report marked "A" dated ——, as complete grants derived from the French, British, and Spanish governments;

*　　*　　*　　*　　*　　*　　*

The second section confirms first, all claims in the report of Mr. C. (J.) O. Cosby, marked "B" which appear from that report to have been cultivated and inhabited on or before the 20th day of December, 1803, for the full amount of the claim provided the plat and certificate of survey, made prior to the 15th day of April 1813, had been filed with the commissioner previous to the date of his report; if such survey has not been filed, the confirmation is limited to twelve hundred and eighty acres.

2nd. All claims stated in said report, marked "B," which were not inhabited and cultivated on the 20th day of December, 1813, to their full extent, provided they do not exceed twelve hundred and eighty acres; and provided, also, that no claim shall be granted as a donation to any person claiming under a complete patent, or a confirmed survey with settlement.

It will be noticed that the above states that section 2 of the act of 1819 applies only to Cosby's list marked "B," and I think this ruling correct because, upon examination of said list I find that each claim was "derived from the Spanish authorities," and all were dated subsequent to said treaty of 1783, and upon examination of said section 2 of the act of 1819, I find that it only applies to claims which upon said reports appear to be derived from the Spanish government.

Section 3 of the act of 1819, under which counsel for Hardee claim that he is entitled to at least six hundred and forty acres as a donation, just as clearly applies only to claims of which there is no written evidence, but where the land had been actually inhabited or cultivated either by the original claimant or his grantees on or before April 15, 1813.

It appears to me that Barbut's claim was not confirmed by the first section of the act of March 3, 1819, because it had neither been sold and conveyed nor settled upon and cultivated at the time of the treaty of 1783. It is not confirmed by the second section because that section applied only to titles derived from Spanish authorities and enumerated in list "B" of J. O. Cosby, Commissioner.

It is not confirmed by section 3, of said act because that applies only to actual settlers prior to April 15, 1813, who had no written evidence of title.

There is no claim of confirmation by any other law than the act of 1819, and as it has not been confirmed by any law of Congress, claimant has no right to certificates under said act of 1858.

It will not be necessary to consider the question of *res judicata*.

Your said decision is affirmed and said certificates will be canceled.

PRACTICE–ATTORNEY–APPEAL ; TIMBER CULTURE CONTEST.

TUCKER v. NELSON.

Proceedings for the disbarment of an attorney, to be recognized by the Department, should be reported as required by circular of March 19, 1887.

An appeal will not be dismissed on the ground that appellant's attorney has been disbarred, where there is no official record of disbarment.

A timber culture entry must be canceled if made within a section that is not devoid of timber.

First Assistant Secretary Chandler to the Commissioner of the General Land Office, October 26, 1889.

I have considered the case of W. H. Tucker *v.* Peter B. Nelson on appeal of the former from your office decision of June 1888, dismissing his contest against Nelson's timber culture entry for NW. ¼ Sec. 14 T. 33, R. 48 W., Valentine, Nebraska land district.

Entry was made January 30, 1885, and contest was initiated February 8, 1886, upon the allegation that the " section had growing upon it a thrifty growth of ash, elm, and box-elder trees, amounting to ten acres."

Upon the evidence taken at the hearing, the local officers decided against the entryman, and on appeal your office by the decision complained of, reversed their decision.

Appeal from your said office decision was filed in the local office August 8, 1888, and on August 14, a motion was filed by counsel for contestee, to dismiss the appeal upon the ground that Samuel A. Ballard who files the appeal as attorney for contestant " is not an attorney who can practice before the Land Office, having been debarred from practice." Upon the back of the motion is endorsed—

We certify that Saml. A. Ballard, the attorney who takes the within appeal was suspended from practice as an attorney and has not been restored.

This was signed by the local officers. Nothing else in regard to such suspension or disbarment appears in the record, nor can I find anything further on file or of record in the Department in regard thereto. No briefs or arguments are filed by either party.

In the absence of any further showing in regard to such alleged disbarment or suspension of said attorney, I do not think the contestant should lose his right of appeal. No date is given for such suspension, and it does not appear that contestant had knowledge thereof. It seems to me that proceedings for disbarment of an attorney to be recognized by this Department should be reported at once to the Department as required by circular of March 19, 1837. (5 L. D., 508.)

I will therefore proceed to consider the appeal as though no such question was raised, and the motion to dismiss is hereby overruled.

Your said office decision is stated to be based upon the ruling in case of James Spencer (6 L. D., 217) that the ruling decision at the date of the application to enter governs, which in this case is Box r. Ulstein (3 L. D., 143) in which it was held that

The question as to whether a section is devoid of timber is to be determined by ascertaining whether nature has provided, what in time will become an adequate supply (of timber) for the wants of the people likely to reside in that section.

In your said office letter it is also said :

The preponderance of the evidence shows that very few of said trees are fit for timber, those of any size being snarly and decayed.

While the number of large trees is not given by any witness, most of them say the large trees are part of them sound and that a great many stumps are visible, showing where the larger growth has been in part cut down and taken away, but it is clear that there is a tract containing not less than sixteen acres, extending for more than a mile on both sides of Big Bordeaux Creek, which flows for more than a mile through said section, and which for the width of from fifty to a hundred steps is covered more or less thickly with elm, ash, box-elder and cottonwood; that acount of an average acre showed more than a thousand trees of these kind, most of them being young and thrifty; that timber had been cut from said section to make rails, build a stable, and other outbuildings and a dam, besides considerable taken away for firewood; and that many stumps showed that trees had been cut prior to the acquaintance of the witnesses with the land in question. The surrounding country is not shown to be prairie, as stated in your said letter, but on the contrary it appears from the testimony that for miles along said creek the timber is about the same as in section 14, and that about eight or ten miles up the stream it is large enough for saw timber. It also appears that within a few miles is a body of timber known as Pine Ridge.

While the rule in Box r. Ulstein, *supra*, is properly stated in your said decision, yet an examination of said case will show that it was held therein that—

Sixty-seven hundred and fifty trees on a section, or the probability that from the existing natural supply there will be that number in the future, is clear proof that the land is not devoid of timber.

I am convinced that in the case at bar, there are many more than that number of trees and saplings now growing, which will, as said in Box v. Ulstein "make timber trees."

Your said office decision is accordingly reversed.

PRACTICE—NOTICE—CANCELLATION.

NEAL v. McMULLEN.

An *ex parte* showing, made without notice to the entryman, will not warrant an order of cancellation.

First Assistant Secretary Chandler to the Commissioner of the General Land Office, October 28, 1889.

May 31, 1887, John McMullen made homestead entry, No. 9342, on the SE. ¼ of SW. ¼ of Sec. 1 and NE. ¼ of NW. ¼ of Sec. 12, T. 22 N., R. 3 E., Ironton district, Missouri. Your office by letter of February 19, 1889, held said entry for cancellation, because of the claim of one George A. Neal to said land.

It appears that, September 24, 1857, Calvin Dickey located military bounty land warrant, No. 44,341 (War of 1812, Act of 1855), on the " SE. ¼ of SE. ¼ " of Sec. 1, the NE. ¼ of NW. ¼ and NW. ¼ of NE. ¼ of Sec. 12, in said township and range. It is claimed, that the location was intended to be made on the " SE. ¼ of SW. ¼ " of Sec. 1, instead of " SE. ¼ of SE. ¼ " of that section. The location as made being on land not contiguous, it was for that reason canceled by your office, August 28, 1860. On July 31, 1861, your office directed the local officers to re-locate said warrant on the land claimed to have been originally intended, namely, the " SE. ¼ of SW. ¼ " of Sec. 1, the NE. ¼ of NW. ¼ and NW. ¼ of NE. ¼ of Sec. 12, of said township and range. There is nothing in the record showing that the local officers took any notice whatever of the said direction of your office. Nearly sixteen years thereafter, March 29 1887, the local officers transmitted to your office the application of said George A. Neal to have the said SE. ¼ of SW. ¼ restored to market for cash entry. Your office, by letter of May 13, 1887, instructed the local office to allow said John McMullen, the appellant, to make homestead entry on said quarter-quarter section, and that in section 12, embraced in said entry, which was accordingly done May 31, 1887, as stated at the outset.

It further appears that J. C. Tully had purchased the tracts in section 12 from the original locator Dickey, and George A. Neal had purchased them from Tully. Both Neal and McMullen claim to have re-sided on and improved the land. Your office, by letter of June 18, 1888, instructed the local officers, as follows :

You will notify Mr. Neal that if he will make an application for the cancellation of McMullen's homestead entry, and transmit to this office certified copies of deeds from Dickey to Tully and Tully to Neal—also an abstract of title duly certified by the proper county officer, and an affidavit that he (Neal) has never conveyed said lands, prompt action will be taken looking to the cancellation of the homestead entry and to the re-instatement of Dickey's location upon the SE. ¼ of SW. ¼ of Sec. 1, the NE. ¼ of NW. ¼ and NW. ¼ of NE. ¼ of Sec. 12, T. 22 N., R. 3 E.

Neal having complied with the conditions laid down in said letter of June 28, 1888, your office by letter of February 19, 1889, held McMullen's entry for cancellation, and allowed him sixty days after notice within which to appeal. McMullen duly appealed to this Department, assigning as one ground of appeal (and the only one necessary to notice herein), "That the defendant" (McMullen) " has never had his day in court . . . . . by notice as required by law."

This point is well taken, as the entry of McMullen appears to have been held for cancellation on the *ex parte* application and showing of Neal, without any notice to McMullen or any opportunity being given him to show cause why his entry should not be canceled. It is a fundamental principle in our system of jurisprudence, applicable as well to proceedings before tribunals created under the land laws as to courts in general, that the personal or property rights of a party can not be passed upon or taken from him without " due process of law," of which notice and an opportunity to be heard (" day in court ") are essential elements.

You are accordingly instructed to direct the local officers to order a hearing to be had, after due notice of time and place to all parties in interest, for the determination of the question as to the superiority of right to the land in dispute.

———

PRACTICE—CONTINUANCE—HOMESTEAD CONTEST—RESIDENCE.

REDDING *v.* RILEY.

A continuance can not be demanded as a matter of right on the ground that the applicant's attorney is engaged in a trial in another court.

The failure of a homesteader to establish residence within six months from entry warrants cancellation, if such default is not cured prior to the initiation of contest.

Official duty can not be accepted as an excuse for absence from the land, if residence in good faith was not acquired prior thereto.

First Assistant Secretary Chandler to the Commissioner of the General Land Office, October 30, 1889.

I have considered the case of John B. Redding *v.* Francis C. Riley, upon the appeal of the latter from your office decision of July 31, 1888, holding for cancellation his homestead entry for the SE. ¼, of section 18, T. 114 N., R. 53 E., Watertown land district, Dakota.

Riley made homestead entry for the said land June 26, 1885, and on April 12, 1886, John Redding instituted contest against the said entry, charging in his affidavit that the said Riley " has wholly abandoned and changed his residence for more than six months since making said entry and next prior to the date herein, that said tract is not settled upon and cultivated by said party as required by law. "

Hearing on the contest was appointed for June 7, 1886; on that day both parties appeared and were represented by their respective attorneys. Claimant's attorney moved that a continuance of the trial be ordered; he based his motion upon his affidavit which showed that he could not then attend the hearing being obliged forthwith to leave, in order that he might attend as attorney to the trials of two jury cases then pending and about to be tried in the district court of Lyon county, Minnesota.

The local officers denied the motion; the trial during which defendant was assisted by other counsel proceeded.

The local officers after considering the evidence rendered a decision in favor of the contestant and were, of the opinion that claimant's entry should be canceled. Upon appeal your office affirmed the ruling of the local officers, upholding their action in refusing the said continuance as also their opinion in reference to the merits of the case.

The claimant thereupon filed a further appeal in which he claims error on account of the said refusal of his motion for a continuance, as well as in the decision upon the merits. The case, therefore, is now before this Department for consideration.

The continuance was properly denied; Rule 20 of the Rules of Practice states when a postponement of a hearing can be demanded as of right. The engagement of counsel of a party in a trial in another court is not a ground peremptorily demanding a continuance. Besides, the party after the refusal of his motion went to trial and had the assistance of counsel; he has therefore not been injured by the denial of his said motion.

Regarding the merits of the case the testimony shows that when claimant, on June 26, 1885, made entry for the lands he was the sheriff of the county of Hamlin, Dakota; his term of office was to expire January, 1887. At the time of his entry he was a single man, but married February 4, 1886 He never built a house on the lands until after the institution of the contest. He broke from twelve to fifteen acres during June and July, 1885; no crops were raised on the land. Witnesses on the part of contestant assert that claimant's home during the period covered by his entry was part of the time at his brother's, two or three miles away from the land, and part of the time at Castlewood, the county seat of Hamlin county. The land in question lies within the said county and is about ten miles distant from its said county seat. From claimant's own testimony it appears that he sojourned on the land for about a week during the months of August, September and October, 1885, living in a wagon. He does not pretend to have lived on the land at any other time previous to contest, nor had he a house there until thereafter. These occasional visits, for his presence on the land for a week, distributed over three months could not have been more than visits, did not constitute a residence, and in fact claimant does not seriously assert that he ever prior to contest established a residence upon the land, but seeks to excuse this failure to comply with the law, by claiming that his business as sheriff and the law required him " to be at the county seat all the time." The Revised Codes of Dakota, page 368,

Sec. 66, requiie that a sheriff "shall keep his office at the county seat." This comprises the material part of the evidence.

The failure of a settler to establish his residence within six months from entry upon lands entered by him as a homestead, will cause the forfeiture of the entry in presence of a contest if such default at the time of its initiation has not been cured. And it is only when the settler has established his residence on his homestead in good faith and is afterwards called away by official duty, that such absence will not work a forfeiture. He can not successfully plead an office as an excuse for a continued absence from his claim when he never before the initiation of the contest, made the land his residence. Harris v. Radcliffe (2 L. D., 147); A. E. Flint (6 L. D., 668); James A. Jenks (8 L. D., 85).

I am therefore of the opinion that your said decision is fully supported by the law governing the case and the same is, therefore, affirmed.

PRACTICE—ATTORNEY—RESIDENCE—COUNTY OFFICIAL.

REEVE r. BURTIS.

A motion to dismiss an appeal, on the ground that the attorney taking the same is not acting under authority, must be dismissed, if, in response thereto due showing of authority is made by said attorney.

When a *bona fide* settler has established a residence and is afterwards called away by official duty, such absence will not work a forfeiture of his rights.

First Assistant Secretary Chandler to the Commissioner of the General Land Office, October 31, 1889.

I have considered the case of Geo. H. Reeve v. A. H. Burtis, upon appeal of the former from your office decision of August 15, 1888, dismissing his contest against the latter's homestead entry for SE. ¼, Sec. 4, T. 24, R. 33, Garden City, Kansas, land district.

Burtis made entry September 17, 1883, and on February 6, 1886, Reeve initiated his contest upon the charge of abandonment.

At hearing duly had the local officers found that,

The evidence shows beyond doubt that the defendant maintained his residence in good faith on the tract in dispute until a short time prior to his election to the office of county clerk of Finney county, Kansas, November 3, 1884, after which he ceased to reside thereon, for the reason that his official duties demanded his presence at the county seat (Garden City).

The local officers in their decision also say, substantially, that under former rulings of the Department such conduct would not constitute abandonment, but they say,—

This ruling, however, has been recently changed by Hon. Commissioner Sparks, who now holds that when the duties of a public officer demand his continued absence from his homestead, he must either surrender the office or homestead, and the law must be as strictly construed with reference to public officers as with private individuals. . . . . . We cannot stop to consider the justness or unjustness of Comr. Sparks decision on this point, but it is clear in our own minds that we cannot run counter to that opinion, hence we must hold in the case at bar, that Deft. Burtis did abandon his homestead on or about November 5, 1884, and has not since had actual residence thereon which now defeats his claim.

From this decision an appeal was taken to your office and this appeal contestant moved to dismiss upon the ground that Messrs. Lauck and Orner who filed said contest were not the authorized attorneys for contestee, and upon said motion being overruled his counsel attempted to appeal from such ruling but the appeal was denied by your office upon the ground that your said ruling was an interlocutory order and could not be appealed. This question of the right of appeal from such ruling is waived by counsel for contestant in their brief and they ask that the action of your office upon said motion to dismiss entryman's appeal be considered on its merits in the final disposition of the case by the Department.

Upon the filing of said motion to dismiss, your office called upon said Lauck and Orner to make a showing of their authority to represent Burtis, and in response thereto they filed an authorization by said Burtis dated October 14, 1887, in due form together with the affidavit of said Burtis and one of said Lauck, to the effect that said firm had been duly employed after hearing below to prosecute an appeal to your office.

These affidavits fully explained all the matters alleged in contestant's motion to dismiss the appeal, and a hearing was unnecessary to determine their status as attorneys in the case; and it follows your office properly overruled said motion.

In passing upon entryman's appeal your office found that the defendant had established residence on the land and removed from the same about the time he was elected clerk, and in your decision it is said,

This under the rulings of the Department does not work a forfeiture of his entry; under such conditions the entryman is supposed to maintain a constructive residence on the land. A. E. Flint (6 L. D., 668). For this reason your decision is reversed, and the said contest dismissed.

The testimony though conflicting, shows by a fair preponderance, that entryman established his residence upon said land in good faith about the last of February, 1884, that he repaired and enlarged his house thereon at that time; that he had several acres of land broken and cultivated to crops and set out trees thereon during the spring and summer of 1884; that he had in said house his bed, a stove, cooking utensils and sufficient household and kitchen furniture and made the same his home and residence continuously; that about the last of July or first of August, 1884, a cyclone or tornado entirely destroyed said house and scattered the material of which it was built, and its contents over the prairie; that within thirty days claimant began the erection of another house but before the same was fully completed he was elected county clerk of the county and to properly discharge his duties was compelled to reside in the county seat. That he qualified as clerk about November 5, 1884, and since that time he has not actually resided upon the land in controversy, but has completed the house and has continued to improve the land reducing several acres to cultivation each year and has caused lateral ditches to be made from an irrigating ditch to said land for purposes of irrigation.

It further appears that soon after his election to said office, claimant addressed a letter to the Commissioner of the General Land Office to which he received a reply as follows:

GENERAL LAND OFFICE,
Washington, D. C., Nov. 22, 1884.

A. H. BURTIS,
  County Clerk, Garden City, Kansas.

SIR: In reply to your letter of the 13th instant, I have to state that it is held that, when a party to a homestead or pre-emption claim who has established residence thereon is elected or appointed to an office the duties of which require his presence at some place other than on his claim, he forfeits none of his rights while holding such office, provided he keeps up the improvements and cultivation and otherwise acts in good faith. Such rule does not apply where residence has not been established on the land.

Very respectfully,

L. HARRISON,
Ass't. Commissioner.

It has been the rule of the department that "When a *bona fide* settler has established a residence and is afterwards called away by official duty, such absence will not work a forfeiture of his rights." James A. Jenks, 8 L. D., 85; Cassius C. Hammond, 7 L. D., 88; A. E. Flint, 6 L. D., 668; Harris *v.* Radcliffe, 2 L. D., 147.

Following this rule, your decision is correct and is hereby affirmed.

HOMESTEAD ENTRY—RESIDENCE.

ALONZO W. LAIRD.

One who enters a tract with no intention of establishing residence in good faith and subsequently submits fraudulent final proof, can not cure the wrong, and acquire title to the land by returning to the same after said proof has been rejected, and his entry held for cancellation.

First Assistant Secretary Chandler to the Commissioner of the General Land Office, October 31, 1889.

I have examined the record in the matter of the appeal of Alonzo W. Laird, from your office decision of February 6, 1886, holding for cancellation his homestead entry No. 12, and his commuted cash entry No. 237, upon NW. ¼, Sec. 12, T. 6 N., R. 36 W., McCook land district, Nebraska.

On June 15, 1883, Laird made his homestead entry upon said land numbered 12, and on February 6, 1884, commuted the same to cash making proof which was approved by the local officers. Payment was made, and final certificate issued on the same day.

The final proof showed continuous residence except for a few weeks at a time from June 20, 1883, to date of proof, and improvements consisting of a house and twelve acres of breaking.

On October 13, 1884, special agent George B. Coburn, reported that the residence of claimant, was never established on the land and that the improvements were not such as to suggest good faith, and upon this report a hearing was ordered by your office November 18, 1884.

Notice was duly given and said hearing had before the local officers on June 9, 1885. Both parties appeared at the hearing. The United States was represented by Special Agent Coburn and defendant by counsel. The United States introduced four witnesses including the special agent, and claimant introduced three. The testimony tended to show that about the time of the opening of the Land Office at Mc-Cook, Nebraska, the claimant went there and made homestead entry of the land, he never having seen it. That shortly after this he procured a dug-out to be built, and about five acres to be broken by one Bingham, who performed similar services for several entrymen in that neighborhood about that time. That he, claimant, between the date of his entry, June 15, 1883, and the date of his proof February 6, 1884, was at the land four times staying a week the first time, and the other times, less than a week.

The house was not habitable, and up to June, 1885, the portion of land broken had not been cultivated.

The claimant had no stock, household furniture, or farming tools, upon the claim. And throughout he seems to have had in mind a compliance with the letter of the law with a view to acquire title to this land, rather than an intention to make this his home. In short, I am thoroughly satisfied that the claimant never established a *bona fide* residence upon this land.

His original proof shows, that he had resided continuously upon the land, that he had been absent three or four times for a period of about two weeks each time, and that ten acres were broken.

This proof was evidently wrong and claimant must have known this. The local officers held that the cash entry should be canceled but that the homestead entry should be allowed to stand, subject to new proof. Upon appeal your office held that the evidence showed that the original homestead entry had not been made in good faith, and were it otherwise the homestead entry would fall with the failure of the cash entry, upon authority of Greenwood v. Peters (4 L. D., 237).

In this decision I concur. After your said decision claimant makes new proof (*ex parte* and without notice), showing residence on this claim from July 10, 1885, to February 13, 1886.

This subsequent going upon and living upon the land can not aid the claimant. It is true, we have, in many instances, considered evidence of the acts of claimants subsequent to final proof, in *continuing* to reside upon and improve their claims, as tending to show good faith *ab initio*, but we have never held, nor is it the law, that one who enters upon land in the first place with no intention of residing there, and attempts to colorably comply with what he understands to be the letter of the law, ignoring its spirit and true intent, and then makes fraudulent proof can, after his entry has been reported and held for cancellation, cure the wrong, and acquire title to the land he had originally attempted to acquire illegally, by merely moving on the land without raising a crop, though nearly three years had elapsed from his original entry.

The homestead entry was evidently fraudulent in its inception, and its illegal character has at no time been changed. The entries will both be canceled. Your office decision is affirmed.

SURVEY OF ISLAND—SECTION 2455 R. S.—IMPROVEMENTS.

CATHERINE MILNE.

An island surveyed on the petition of a settler should be offered at public sale as an isolated tract.

The right of a settler prior to survey, to remove such improvements as can be severed from the realty, may be properly conceded where the land is sold under section 2455 R. S., as an isolated tract.

Acting Secretary Chandler to the Commissioner of the General Land Office, November 2, 1889.

I am in receipt of your letter of the 29th ultimo, transmitting the application of Catherine Milne, dated May 20, 1889, with affidavits, plats, and other accompanying documents, relating to the survey of an island in Lake Pistakee (or Pistaqua), situated in Sec. 4, T. 45 N., R. 9 E., of the 3d Principal Meridian, Illinois.

The application and the accompanying affidavits show that the island contains about four acres; that the width between the island and the nearest main land is about fifty feet, and the depth of the water about eight feet; that the island extends about twenty-five feet above high-water mark; that the land contained therein is fit for agricultural purposes, and has already been improved, said Catherine Milne having built a house thereon and broken three acres thereof—the value of said improvements being about eight hundred dollars.

Notice of the application for survey has been served upon the proprietors of the land upon the main shore adjacent to the island, and they have filed no protest against it.

Charles H. Tryon, county surveyor of McHenry county, Illinois (in which the island is situated), files with the application an offer to survey said island for the sum of twenty dollars.

In my opinion the facts set forth warrant the allowance of the application; and you are hereby authorized to contract for the survey of the same in accordance with your recommendation.

Should such survey be made, I would suggest that the island be of-fered at public sale as an isolated tract, under Sec. 2455 R. S.—such sale being made subject to the right of Catherine Milne to remove such improvements made by her as can be severed from the realty, and to any other rights on her part that upon further investigation by your office it appears should be protected by the government.

PRACTICE—APPEAL—CERTIORARI.

FRANK QUINN.

An appeal will not lie from the refusal of the General Land Office to take up a case until reached in the regular order of business.

The Commissioner's discretion as to the advancement of cases will not be interfered with, in the absence of a gross abuse thereof, and when that is alleged, the supervisory action of the Department should be invoked by certiorari.

Acting Secretary Chandler to the Commissioner of the General Land Office, November 2, 1889.

I have considered the appeal of Frank Quinn from the decision of your office of October 19, 1889, declining to grant the application of Quinn to have his entry for the SE. ¼ of the SW. ¼, the W. ½ of the SE. ¼ of Sec. 22, and the NE. ¼ of the NW. ¼ of Sec. 27, T. 63 N., R. 11 W., Duluth, Minnesota, now pending in Division "G" of your office, taken up for immediate action and approved for patent.

You decline to grant said application upon the ground that there are many entries of this class awaiting examination by your office, no one of which can be taken up and acted upon in preference to others, without special reason therefor appearing, but that justice requires they be dealt with in this respect according to some rule equitable to all.

An appeal will not lie from the action of your office in refusing to advance cases, and the appeal in this case is hereby dismissed. Your discretion as to the advancement of cases will not be interfered with, except where there is a gross abuse of it, and when that is alleged, the supervisory action of the Department should be invoked by certiorari.

HOMESTEAD CONTEST—SUFFICIENCY OF CHARGE.

DAVIS v. FAIRBANKS.

A homestead contest filed five years after date of the entry is not sufficient if confined to the words of section 2297 R. S., but should set forth specifically, and in what particulars, the entryman in said period, and prior to initiation of contest, failed to comply with the law.

First Assistant Secretary Chandler to the Commissioner of the General Land Office, November 2, 1889.

I have considered the case of Franklin J. Davis, v. Cornelius M. Fair-banks, upon the appeal of the former from your office decision of July

24, 1888. The land involved in the said contest is the NE. ¼, NW. ¼, N. ¼, NE. ¼, and SW. ¼, NE. ¼, of section 33, T. 23 S., R. 2 W., Salt Lake City land district, Utah.

Fairbanks made homestead entry for the said land August 2, 1882. On November 5, 1887, Davis filed in the local office a contest affidavit against the said entry, executed October 31, charging therein

that the said Cornelius M. Fairbanks, has wholly abandoned his said homestead entry for a period of more than six months at one time since making the said entry, and is not now residing upon and cultivating said tract as required by law.

On the day appointed for the hearing, January 4, 1888, both parties appeared. The claimant moved to dismiss the contest upon the grounds that the allegations in the contest affidavit were insufficient and indefinite and did not charge a continuation of an abandonment to the date of contest. Davis, after a suggestion by the local officers to amend his said affidavit, refused to change the same, whereupon the local officers granted the motion and dismissed the contest.

Contestant appealed to your office.

In this appeal he asserts, that the local officers, construing section 2297, of the Revised Statutes, erred by holding that an abandonment of a homestead to effect a cancellation of the entry on a contest, must have existed at the time of the initiation of such contest and for six months next prior thereto. He also requested to be allowed to amend his contest affidavit, if his appeal should not be sustained by your office.

Your office affirmed the action of the local officers, and allowed the plaintiff to amend his affidavit. In your said decision it is said, "The construction of section 2297, Revised Statutes, recognized by this office, requires that the abandonment charged against the homestead claimant must exist at the date the charge is made."

Contestant appealed to this Department from your said decision.

By the contest affidavit, two charges are preferred against the claimant. First, that he abandoned his said homestead for a period of more than six months at one time since making the said entry. Second, that he was not at the time of making the affidavit residing on and cultivating said tract as required by law.

If the facts charged do not necessarily authorize a judgment of cancellation of the entry, the contest affidavit must be deemed insufficient.

In considering this question, it should be remembered that the contest was begun three months after the expiration of five years from entry. This is important.

By the law and departmental regulations the settler is required to establish his residence on his homestead within six months from entry and to reside thereon and cultivate the same for the term of five years from the time of such entry.

If he establishes his residence after the expiration of six months, but before contest, provided he otherwise complies with the law his default is cured and his entry stands. Stayton v. Carroll (7 L. D., 198); and Hall v. Fox (9 L. D., 153).

After the expiration of five years from entry, the presumption is that claimant has complied with the law and the departmental requirements. It is then, I think, not sufficient to charge a default in the words of the statute, for section 2297 of the Revised Statutes, which states what the charge against the entry shall be also requires such charge to be made within the term of five years. I think that after the expiration of such term, it should unequivocally appear from the charge that, if the same was true, the claimant had not earned his claim by a compliance with the law within the term of five years from entry or before the initiation of the contest. As the charge stands its truth may be consistent with the fact of claimant's full compliance with the law by a five years' continuous residence and cultivation at the time the contest was begun. Claimant might have commenced his residence one or two days after the expiration of the first six months from entry, and might have complied afterwards with the law; while the charge under those circumstances would be literally true, the claimant, upon due proof of the facts would be entitled to patent. I must, therefore, hold the first charge deficient. If contestant therefore persists in his contest, he must state the time of abandonment more specifically in the charge; it should clearly appear that claimant's term of five years' residence has not wholly expired and that, therefore, the entry is still open to contest

The same reason holds good against the second charge. At the time it was made the claimant was, according to the homestead law, presumably no longer required to reside upon and cultivate his claim. The charge is, therefore, also deficient.

The claimant in his answer to contestant's appeal urges that the part of your office decision allowing the contestant the privilege to amend his said contest affidavit be not sustained by this Department. Claimant's argument on this part of the decision, in absence of an appeal by him therefrom can not be considered.

Your office decision is affirmed.

HOMESTEAD ENTRY—TOWNSITE SETTLEMENT.

DOUD ET AL. *v.* SLOCOMB.

A homestead entry for lands originally settled upon by the claimant and others as a townsite, and actually occupied for the purposes of trade and business, is illegal and must be canceled.

First Assistant Secretary Chandler to the Commissioner of the General Land Office, November 2, 1889.

The case of Theron A. Doud, *et al. v.* Silas A. Slocomb is before me on appeal by Slocomb from the decision of your office, dated May 31, 1888, holding for cancellation his homestead entry on lot 7, the W. ½ of SE. ¼ and the NE. ¼ of SW. ¼ of Sec. 36, T. 49 N., R. 1 E., Coeur d'Alene land district, Idaho.

The official plat of survey of said township was filed November 15, 1886, and a part of the above described tract is marked thereon as the town of Kingston.

On May 31, 1887—six months and a half after said plat was filed—Slocomb entered the described tract as a homestead. Subsequently, Doud and five other parties, representing themselves to be residents and property owners of said town, asked for a hearing to determine their rights to the occupancy of lands included in the site of said town. In their petition asking for this hearing they represented, among other things, that in December, 1883, one W. R. Wallace and others located and platted said town, and that the plat was filed with the recorder of Kootenai county, Idaho, in 1884; that streets were laid out, a large number of lots sold and deeds made, and that over thirty buildings were erected; that said town of Kingston had at one time three hundred inhabitants and then had over sixty; that Kingston was a place of trade for the surrounding country, with a railroad running through it, and containing a United States post office, a school, and numerous places of business, hotels, stores, shops, feed stables, saloons, etc., and that a homestead had " been filed on over one-half of the town contrary to law."

The only entry or filing of record affecting the land occupied by said parties is that of Mr. Slocomb, and the hearing asked for was, on October 1, 1887, ordered by your office and duly had before the local land officers on December 28, 1887.

The register and receiver disagreed in opinion in this case, and your office held— " Aside from the question as to the existence of a town on the tract covered by Slocomb's entry "—that said entry must be canceled, " for the reason that the principal use he (Slocomb) made of the land was the running of a hotel, bringing the land within the limitation of section 2258, Revised Statutes."

The testimony taken at said hearing satisfactorily shows that Slocomb went to the said town of Kingston in April, 1884, and has since resided there; that he or his wife bought a lot and a half in Kingston of two of the original projectors of the town, and that he has since bought eleven or twelve lots in said town; that his chief business since he came to Kingston has been keeping a lunch house, hotel and store, though in 1887 he had on some of these town lots about one and a half acres in garden; that his hotel, stable, outbuildings, and other improvements, all situated within the limits of said town as platted, are valued at from two thousand to three thousand dollars.

It is also satisfactorily shown, that in addition to Slocomb's hotel and other improvements, there is situated in that part of the town of Kingston, covered by said entry, a part of the house of one Hening; the general merchandise store of one Herrington, in which the United States post-office is located; the carpenter shop and family residence of petitioner, Doud; the family residence of petitioner A. M. Van

Cleave; and a number of vacant buildings; and that Herrington and Van Cleave, at least, have resided in said town since 1884.

It is also shown that the railroad runs through said town, and has there a kind of depot, and that there are divers business places and a school in that part of the said town not included in Slocomb's entry.

That said homestead entry is illegal, and that it should be canceled, is clearly shown by the evidence herein. Lands subject to entry under the homestead law are described as unappropriated, public lands, subject to pre emption (Sec. 2289, R. S.), and section 2258 of the Revised Statutes, cited by your office, provides, among other things, that lands "selected as the site of a city or town," and "lands actually settled and occupied for purposes of trade and business, and not for agriculture" shall not—unless otherwise specially provided for by law—be subject to the right of pre-emption.

That the land upon which appellant's residence and improvements are situated was originally settled upon and occupied as a townsite by him and others, and that it was "actually settled and occupied for purposes of trade and business," rather than for agricultural purposes, I think there can be no reasonable doubt. See also Fonts v. Thompson (6 L. D., 332), and Lyons et al. v. Ivers (ib., 746).

It will be noticed that the land in controversy is part of a school-section. No decision is made herein as to the rights of the townsite claimants, or as to the right of the territorial authorities to show that the land in question is subject to the grant for school purposes.

The decision of your office is affirmed.

PRIVATE CASH ENRTY—EQUITABLE ADJUDICATION.

St. Paul, Minneapolis & Manitoba Ry. Co. v. Listoe.

A private cash entry of land, once offered, and thereafter excepted from an indemnity withdrawal by a homestead entry which is subsequently canceled, may be referred to the board of equitable adjudication.

A private entry should not be allowed of land once included within a withdrawal, or covered by a pre-emption filing, until after re-offering or restoration notice.

No presumption as against the good faith of an entry can arise from the mere fact that the entryman was formerly the register of the land office in the district where said entry is made.

Acting Secretary Chandler to the Commissioner of the General Land Office, November 2, 1889.

I am in receipt of your communication, dated October 2, 1889, relative to departmental decision of August 16, 1889, in the case of the St. Paul, Minneapolis and Manitoba Railway Company v. Loren Listoe, involving private cash entry, No. 2,927, of lots 8 and 9, of Sec. 27, T. 132 N., R. 45 W., 5th P. M., and the application of said Listoe to purchase at private cash entry lots 3, 4, 5, 6 and 7, of Sec. 27, and lots 1, 2, 5 and 6, of Sec. 35, same township and range.

Your office, on January 23, 1888, found that:

Sections 27 and 35, Twp. 132 N., R. 45 W., are within the twenty mile indemnity limits common to the main line and St. Vincent extension of the St. Paul and Pacific, now St. Paul, Minneapolis and Manitoba Railroad ; _

that the lands covered by said cash entry, and some of the tracts embraced in said applications were excepted from the withdrawal made for the benefit of said company by reason of certain filings; that

It has been uniformly held that offered lands withdrawn from market for any purpose are not subject to private entry after such withdrawal, until they have been again offered, or restored to market in accordance with legal requirements; . . . . It has been also held that a withdrawal for railroad purposes, or a filing or entry of record, without regard to the validity thereof, operates as a bar to private entry, until the conditions of the previous paragraph are complied with. (See John C. Turpen, 5 L. D., 25.)

Your office affirmed the action of the local office, in rejecting the applications of Listoe to purchase said tracts, because within the limits of the withdrawal for idemnity purposes, and held for cancellation his said cash entry. Said decision of your office also states, that " The attorneys of the railroad company will be notified by this office." The local officers were directed to advise all other parties in interest, allowing the usual right of appeal. Listoe appealed, and the Department modified your said office decision, stating that:

The lands in said township were offered at public sale, on October 28, 1861. The local officers accepted payment for the land included in said cash entry more than five years ago, and there does not seem to be any good reason why the entry should not be submitted to the Board of Equitable Adjudication for its consideration under the appropriate rule. Let such action be taken.

The Department further called attention to the fact, that an inspection of the records of your office showed that said lots 1, 5 and 6 were not only within the limits of said withdrawal but were also embraced in pre-emption declaratory statements, made in 1866 and 1869, that there had been no selections of said lands by the railroad company, and that, under the ruling in the Turpen case (*supra*), the applications were properly rejected by the local officers.

In said communication of your office it is stated that: " This case appears to be precisely like that of John H. Allen, decided by this office, October 17, 1885, and by the Department December 8, 1888, adversely to the entryman." It is further stated, that your office has no information respecting the grounds upon which said departmental decision is based, extending Listoe equitable consideration, except the period of time which has elapsed since the allowance of the entry by the local officers, referred to in said decision.

My attention is also called to " a fact" not referred to in your office decision, and probably not known to the Department, which in your judgment "detracts materially from Listoe's equitable standing," namely: that he was register at the Fergus Falls local land office from September 22, 1875, until June 1, 1883, and presumably knew that the land covered by his said entry was not subject to entry; that the fact that both he and said Allen, the receiver at said office, presented applications, and were allowed to make private cash entries of numerous tracts " situated as this is, indicates that they were endeavoring to secure, by reason of their superior knowledge—acquired while public officers—advantage over the rest of the world, in the matter of the acquirement of title to lands of this class, and that they were not innocent purchasers in good faith."

It is further stated, that the railway company is not a party in interest, because the land was excepted from the withdrawal, and the company had not made any selection thereof; that the question is one in which the entryman and the United States are the only interested parties, and should have been entitled, " Listoe v. The United States."

You ask an early consideration of the matter, and to be advised whether any change in " your decision will be made."

The decision in the Allen case was a formal affirmance by my predecessor, Mr. Secretary Vilas, of the decision of your office, dated October 17, 1885. The departmental decision in the Listoe case might seem, at first blush, to be inconsistent with the Allen case. But a careful examination of the two cases shows, that they are not precisely alike, and not necessarily in conflict. It is true that the lands covered by both entries are within the indemnity limits of the withdrawal for said company. But in the Listoe case it clearly appeared, and was so stated, that the land was excepted from the withdrawal, while in the Allen case the land was not so excepted. Besides, if there were an apparent inconsistency, there can be hardly any question but that the latest decision must be regarded as the correct exposition of the law.

Upon the record presented, there can be no doubt but that the decision of Acting Secretary Chandler, in the Listoe case, was correct and fully warranted by the decision of this Department.

It is not apparent why the name of the company should not appear in the case, as your office gave it notice of its decision and right of appeal. But the railroad question being eliminated, the case stands precisely like any other cash entry made of lands upon which a homestead application had been filed and canceled, prior to the cash entry. That such cash entry may be confirmed by the board of equitable adjudication has been repeatedly decided by this Department. Rule 13th, established by said board October 3, 1846, provides for the confirmation of " all bona fide entries on lands which had once been offered, but afterward temporarily withdrawn from market, and then released from reservation, where such lands are not rightfully claimed by others." (General Circular, 1884, p. 76.)

In the case of Pecard v. Camens et al. (4 L. D., 152), my predecessor,

Secretary Lamar, adopted the views of Assistant Secretary Jenks, holding that private entries could be submitted to said board, where the land had once been offered, then increased in price, and again offered, and while in that condition declared by Congress to be subject to sale at the first price, although no restoration notice had been given.

The Pecard-Oamens case was cited with approval by Acting Secretary Muldrow, in the case of Wilhelm Boeing (6 L. D , 262), and also in the case of Frank V. Holston (7 L. D., 218). The same case was cited by Mr. Secretary Vilas in the case of Irwin Eveleth (8 L. D., 87), where the question was carefully considered in an elaborate opinion, in which numerous authorities are cited. See also Secretary Vilas' decision in the case of George M. Wakefield (idem., 189), and the decision of the Department in the case of Delbridge v. Florida Railway and Navigation Company (idem., 410), where it was expressly held that, "A private cash entry, made in good faith, of land included within an indemnity withdrawal, may be referred to the board of equitable adjudication, where the withdrawal is subsequently revoked and no adverse claim exists."

It is, therefore, quite evident that said decision, directing that said entry of Listoe should be submitted to the board of equitable adjudication, upon the record as then presented, was correct and in accordance with the great weight of authority, as shown by said departmental decisions. Nor am I persuaded that the fact, that Listoe was the register of said land office from September 22, 1875, until June 1, 1883, warrants the conclusion indicated by you, that, in making said entry on March 22, 1884, he was getting any "advantage over the rest of the world" by reason of the knowledge that he acquired while holding said office. This land was offered at public sale twenty years ago, and was excepted from the railroad withdrawal, by a homestead entry which had been canceled nearly five years before Listoe made his cash entry.

It may be conceded that Listoe must be presumed to know the law, but that presumption must attach also to the local officers, who permitted him to make said entry and accepted payment for the land. He had been out of office more than nine months before making said entry, and there was no law or regulation prohibiting him from making the entry that did not apply equally to all other persons.

There is no good reason, in my judgment, for changing said decision, and you are so advised.

MINING CLAIM—PROTEST—PROOF OF POSTING.

TANGERMAN ET AL. *v* AURORA HILL MINING CO.

In a hearing ordered to test the validity or regularity of a mineral entry it rests with the protestant to overcome the legal presumption that the entry is regular and valid, and establish by a preponderance of the evidence the charge as alleged.

The value of testimony as to compliance with law in the matter of posting, is not diminished by the fact that the witness was occasionally absent from the mine.

Secretary Noble to the Commissioner of the General Land Office, November 4, 1889.

On August 14, 1888, your office declined to allo v an appeal from the decision thereof dismissing the protest of H. W. Tangerman and others against the issue of patent to the Aurora Hill Mining Company, successor to J. L. Greeley, claimant of the Prospectus lode claim, being mineral entry 244, made November 20, 1880, at Carson City, Nevada. On application made by the protestants to that effect, you were directed to certify the papers in the case up to this Department for such action as might be deemed appropriate, and in pursuance of that direction, the case is now before me.

As stated, the entry was made August 19, 1880; and on October 21, 1886, the protest of Tangerman and others was transmitted to your office, the substantial allegation therein being that plat and notice were not posted on the claim during the period of publication as required by section 2325 of the Revised Statutes. This allegation being supported by affidavits a hearing was ordered and had, at which both sides submitted testimony and argument; on consideration of which, the local officers were of the opinion that—

The applicant has failed to produce sufficient evidence to warrant us in finding that the plat and notice of application for patent for the Prospectus Lode remained posted on said claim continuously during the sixty days period of publication.

There was manifest error in this finding of the local officers, because they seem to have utterly ignored all presumptions in favor of the regularity and legality of the previous entry and to have assumed that, in the hearing ordered, the entryman, or those claiming under him, were called upon, in the first instance, to prove that everything had been done which was proper to be done before entry could be made, and to explain irregularities alleged to have existed prior to that time. These officers do not find that protestants rebutted the force of the legal presumption in favor of the regularity of the entry; nor that they sustained the allegations by sufficient evidence, or a mere preponderance of testimony, but the finding was that the *applicant* "failed to produce sufficient evidence" to show a former compliance with the law. The error here is so manifest as to require no further comment.

Your office decision finds from the evidence, that notice was posted upon the claim, but that it does not appear satisfactorily that the plat was posted or that the notice remained continuously posted during the period of publication. However, it was held that inasmuch as a *prima facie* showing on this point had been made when entry was allowed, the burden of the proof was on the protestants to show that the plat and notice were not posted as required by law; and this they had failed to do.

The specifications of error, on appeal, are, in substance: finding, from the testimony adduced, (1) that notice remained continuously posted during the period of advertisement; (2) that the plat was ever posted; (3) that an application to enter under such circumstances could be confirmed, by the board of equitable adjudication; and (4) error in considering the *ex-parte* proof presented with the application for patent instead of deciding the case exclusively upon the testimony taken at the hearing.

Inasmuch as your office did not refer the case to the board of equitable adjudication for confirmation, but merely expressed an opinion that such reference might have been made the third specification of error is at least premature and need not be discussed.

In relation to the fourth specification of error, I do not understand, from the decision of your office, as a matter of fact, that the testimony submitted with the application for patent was considered in arriving at the conclusion expressed. But I do understand that you felt it your duty to consider the full force and effect in law and fact of the previous entry, and to regard it as creating a presumption that all the legal prerequisites had been complied with, including, of course, the submission of competent and proper proof of the continuous posting of plat and notice during the prescribed period. In giving this weight and consideration to the previous entry it is insisted very earnestly that your action is in conflict with the case of James Copeland, 4 L. D., 275, and that of Etienne Martel, 6 L. D., 285, which are cited as being conclusive of the question. I do not so understand their rulings.

Without, however, entering into a discussion on this point, or admitting the correctness of the legal propositions as laid down by counsel for the protestants, it is not clearly seen how, if their contentions as to the law were correct, it would benefit their side of the case, in view of the testimony submitted at the hearing.

*   *   *   *   *   *   *

Edward T. Greeley, a mining engineer, formerly interested in the Prospectus mine, testified, that he saw the official survey thereof made, and identifies Exhibit No. 1 as a correct copy of that survey. He swears positively, that both notice and plat of the mine were posted, about August 18, or 19, 1880, in an open box, nailed to the lode-line post, and remained there about ninety days, he thinks; knows it was notice of the Prospectus, because he read a portion of it. He saw it in August, September, October and November.

H. G. Blasdel, a director and the manager of the company, after testifying to the purchase of the property from James L. Greeley, now deceased, states that he was present at the official survey and knows of his own knowledge that both plat and notice were posted in a box on the lode line stake of the Prospectus about the middle of August, 1880. He compared the plat and notice with those the surveyor had and believes the copy here filed is correct. Witness was absent during the months of August, September and October for several days at a time, but otherwise was almost daily at the mine, and passed by and repeatedly saw the plat and notice, and finally took them down and removed them after the period of publication expired, about the last of October, or first of November, 1880.

In my opinion, the testimony of Blasdel and Edward T. Greeley conclusively refutes any showing whatever made by the protestants, and also successfully shows—more than claimants were bound to do here—that both plat and notice were duly posted and so remained during the prescribed time. Both of these witnesses swear positively, directly and unequivocally to the facts. Applying the rule, as given before, in relation to the weight to be given to the testimony of a witness to an affirmative fact as against one who testified to a mere negative, and who may have forgotten, the testimony of Blasdel and Greeley must be accepted as against that of Williams.

One of the counsel who argued this case in behalf of the protestants seems to think that the testimony of Edward Greeley should be looked upon with suspicion, because he was a cousin of James Greeley, the original locator of the Prospectus. The facts show, that James Greeley disposed of all interest in the claim and was paid therefor in October, 1880, and died shortly thereafter. Evidently the witness Greeley had no interest, direct or indirect, in the case at the time of the hearing, and his testimony should not be subject to suspicion on that score. The same counsel deprecates the according of undue weight to the testimony of the witness Blasdel, because he had been governor of the State of Nevada. This has not been done, for there was no occasion to weigh his character. Had there been, the fact that he was twice selected by the people of that State as their chief executive would probably have weight as showing that he was regarded at home as a reputable man. Nor is it thought that the fact that he was occasionally absent for days from the mine militates against the force of his testimony as to the continued posting of plat and notice, as insisted by counsel. The Department never has required, and it would be most unreasonable for it to require, proof that the notice and plat remained posted each hour of each day of twenty-four hours during the prescribed period of sixty days. The law is based upon reason, and a reasonable showing that its requirements have been performed is all that is asked. I think that has been done in this case.

I therefore affirm your judgment.

HOMESTEAD—PREFERRED RIGHT OF ENTRY.

EUGENE G. F. MORATH.

The failure of a homestead applicant to exercise, within a reasonable time, a preferred right of entry, warrants the presumption that said applicant has abandoned his claim.

First Assistant Secretary Chandler to the Commissioner of the General Land Office, November 4, 1889.

I have considered the case of Eugene G. F. Morath on his appeal from your office decision of August 4, 1888, rejecting his pre emption declaratory statement for SE. ¼, NW. ¼, and S. ½, NE. ¼, Sec. 8, T. 33 S., R. 63 W., Pueblo, Colorado, land district.

The record shows that on September 20, 1887, Morath presented his declaratory statement for said land and offered and tendered to the local officers the proper fees therefor, and that said application was by them rejected because it appeared from the record of the local office that said land was "within the limits of the derivative claim of Thomas Leitensdorfer under the St. Vrain and Vigil grant."

Upon appeal your office by the decision complained of rejected his application but for the reason that on May 19, 1888, the application of Ma. Dolores Alerez for said land had been allowed, and the alleged settlement of Morath was subsequent to the filing of said homestead application.

With his appeal Morath files his affidavit alleging that he made settlement on said land September 17, 1887, and established his home thereon, and that he is still in actual occupancy and possession of the same in good faith under the pre-emption law.

No appeal seems to have been taken from your office decision of May 19, 1888, which was based upon the ruling of the Department in Rafael Chacon *et al.* (2 L. D., 590).

By said decision the land in controversy was restored to the public domain and as the homestead applicant was a party to the case decided by your office letter of May 19, 1888, her rights were adjudicated and as it was adjudged that the Vigil and St. Vrain grant did not include the land in controversy it followed that the rights of Mrs. Alerez might be allowed to attach as first legal applicant, and it was ordered that her entry be allowed "upon payment of the proper fee and commissions, and evidence of present qualifications." In other words a preference right of entry was awarded to her, but as appears from the record and from an examination of the plats and files in your office, she has neglected to exercise her privilege. More than a year has elapsed since such preference right was awarded and it must be presumed that she has abandoned her claim thereunder and Morath being an actual settler and the next applicant in point of time, is entitled to file declaratory statement.

Your said decision is modified accordingly.

RAILROAD LANDS—TIMBER TRESPASS.

Thomas Nestor.

Cutting timber, for the purpose of speculation, from land included within the forfeited limits of the Marquette, Houghton and Ontonagon Railroad Company, and
in controversy between cash purchasers and actual settlers, should not be permitted pending the determination of the legal status of said land.

Acting Secretary Chandler to the Attorney General, November 5, 1889.

I have the honor to transmit herewith copy of a letter, dated the 2d
instant, from the Commissioner of the General Land Office, enclosing
copy of a report from F. W. Worden, a special agent of this office, with
accompanying letters and telegrams, relative to timber trespass alleged
to have been committed by one Thomas Nestor upon lands within the
grant to the Marquette, Houghton and Ontonagon Railroad Company,
which were forfeited by act of Congress approved March 2, 1889. Since
said act of forfeiture a large number of settlers have located on said
lands, apparently in good faith, and have improved the same with the
expressed intention of making homes thereon ; but, for reasons not necessary to enter into in detail, the local office rejected their applications
to enter; thereupon the applicants appealed to the General Land Office,
where the cases are now pending.

It appears that said Nestor asserts title to the timber in question by
purchase from the Michigan Land and Iron Company, which claims to
have bought the land from the railroad company.

Special Agent Worden reports that at the date of his investigation
Nestor had already cut and put on skids one million feet of pine lumber, and had a large force at work cutting and skidding at the rate of a
thousand feet a day.

Said act of March 2, 1889 (25 Stat., 1008), provides—

That where the original cash purchasers are the present owners this act shall be
operative to confirm the title *only* of such cash purchasers as the Secretary of the Interior shall be satisfied have purchased without fraud, and in the belief that they
were thereby obtaining valid title from the United States.

And no sales or entries are thereby confirmed, "or any tract in such
State selection, upon which there were *bona fide* pre-emption or homestead claims on the 1st day of May, 1888, arising" (from) " or asserted
by actual occupation of the land under color of the laws of the United
States."

I concur in the opinion expressed by the Commissioner that,

Until the titles to the cash entries within the limits of this forfeited railroad grant
have been passed upon by the proper officers, and confirmed in accordance with the
provisions and restrictions of the act of Congress declaring the forfeiture, and the
Secretary of the Interior is satisfied that such purchase was "without fraud," etc., all
persons should be enjoined from cutting the timber solely for speculative purposes
from such lands as are known to be in controversy between cash entrymen and actual
settlers under the homestead or pre-emption laws.

I therefore have the honor to request that proper action be taken, without delay, to prevent the wholesale destruction of timber, by said Nestor and all other parties, upon the lands in question, pending decision by the proper authorities as to the rights and titles therein involved.

———

SECOND HOMESTEAD ENTRY—ACT OF MARCH 2, 1889.

JOHN J. STEWART.

The right to make a second homestead entry conferred by the act of March 2, 1889, validates such an entry, made prior thereto though not authorized by the law when made.

An additional homestead entry, made prior to the passage of said act, may, under the provisions of section six thereof, be permitted to stand though unauthorized by law when made.

First Assistant Secretary Chandler to the Commissioner of the General Land Office, August 12, 1889.

John J. Stewart, on December 5, 1868, made homestead entry No. 1720, for the W. ½ of the NW. ¼ of Sec. 21, T. 25 N., R. 6 E., Ironton land district, Missouri. Upon this tract (according to his affidavit, accompanying his appeal), he continued to reside for about a year, during the greater portion of which time he or his family were sick—the location being near the Black River and the low-lands adjoining. By advice of friends and his family physician, he removed to a higher and healthier location—also relinquishing his former homestead entry.

On November 19, 1872, he made homestead entry No. 4261 for lot 1 of the NW. ¼ of Sec. 30, T. 25 N., R. 6 E., same land district (containing 82¼ acres). In an affidavit accompanying this entry he stated that he had never "perfected or abandoned" a homestead entry.

On August 30, 1879, he made final proof on said last-named entry (No. 4261).

On July 15, 1879, he made additional homestead entry No. 5532, for the N. ½ of lot 2 of the NW. ¼ of Sec. 30, same township and range (containing 44 acres), under the act of March 3, 1879. Upon this he made final proof June 27, and final certificate was issued December 10, 1885.

Claimant stated, by letter of December 5, 1884, that he had served in the United States army during the late war. In his affidavit accompanying his appeal he explains that he "was not in the regular army of the United States, but was in the State service at the time of Morgan's raid, and being an illiterate man" he at first supposed this was equivalent to being in the United States army.

Claimant offers a corroborated affidavit, showing that he has resided on the land embraced in his second homestead entry (No. 4261) continuously since February, 1873; that he has cleared and cultivated between fifty and sixty acres thereof, has planted between twelve and fifteen hundred fruit trees now in bearing; has built upon it, first a log house, and afterwards a frame house, both now used as one dwelling; has a large barn and other buildings—said improvements being worth from fifteen hundred to two thousand dollars, and constituting his entire property.

Your office, by decision of July 9, 1886, held Stewart's second homestead entry (No. 4261) and his additional homestead entry (No. 5532) based thereon, for cancellation, on the ground that he had exhausted his homestead right by his first homestead entry (No. 1720).

Whether or not, under the circumstances of this case, the objection raised would be sufficient to defeat Stewart's right to make a second homestead entry under the law in force at the date of his entry, the second section of the act of Congress approved March 2, 1889 (25 Stat., 854), allowing—

Any person who has not heretofore *perfected title* to a tract of land of which he has made entry under the homestead law, to make homestead entry of not exceeding one quarter-section of public land subject to such entry, etc.—

authorizes his entry of lot 1 of the NW.¼ of said section 30. And although I am of the opinion that he was not entitled to make additional homestead entry of the N.½ of lot 2 of the NW.¼ of said Sec. 30, under the laws then in force, the sixth section of said act of March 2, 1889, secured to him the right to make entry of additional land to an amount which, added to his original entry, shall not exceed one hundred and sixty acres,

Provided that in no case shall patent issue for the land covered by such additional entry until the person making such additional entry shall have actually and in conformity with the homestead laws resided upon and cultivated the lands so additionally entered, and otherwise fully complied with said laws.

Under this provision of said act, I think it clear that the claimant is entitled to have his original entry approved for patent; and that if he has not complied with the provisions of said statute as to actual residence upon and cultivation of said additional entry, action as to this part of the entry should be suspended until he is able to show that he has fully complied with the terms of the statute.

Your decision of July 9, 1886, is modified as above indicated.

PRACTICE—APPEAL—CONTEST—APPLICATION.

HUROT *v.* MINEHAN.

A mistake in the appellant's name will not defeat the appeal where the matter appealed from is otherwise clearly identified.

A general charge of "fraud" against an entry will not warrant an order for a hearing.

A legal application to make homestead entry, is, while pending, a segregation of the land covered thereby.

First Assistant Secretary Chandler to the Commissioner of the General Land Office, November 14, 1889.

December 17, 1886 Denis Minehan applied to make homestead entry on the SE. ¼ of SW. ¼ of Sec. 3, T. 114, R. 28, Redwood Falls District, Minnesota. His application was on the same day rejected by the local officers on the ground, that the land "appeared to be railroad land." Fourteen days thereafter, on December 31, 1886, an appeal was filed by the attorney of Minehan in the name of Denis "Hinehan." The appeal however, identified the matter appealed from as the rejection by the local officers of the said application of Minehan, by giving the date of said rejection and the numbers of the land involved, and attached to it was the said application itself, signed "Denis Minehan." The ground of appeal was, "that said tract was vacant land and subject to entry under the homestead law."

January 4, 1887, four days after said appeal had been taken, the local officers allowed Adam Hurot to make adjoining farm homestead entry (No. 3776) on said land. Your office by letter of September 23, 1887, called the attention of the local officers to Minehan's appeal, and in reply the register wrote, September 27, 1887,—

I will say in answer, that the entry of Adam Hurot was a mistake, the fact that Mr. Minehan had appealed on December 31, 1886, from a rejection of this office being over-looked, as there was no note of the same made on the tract book. Mr. Hurot at the time he made application for the tract produced a letter from Geo. E. Skinner, agent of the H. & D. R. R. Co., stating that said tract did not belong to said company and on the strength of that the entry was allowed by the former register.

Your office thereupon, by decision of December 3, 1887, sustained the appeal taken by Minehan as above stated and held the entry of Hurot for cancellation. Hurot now appeals from said decision.

In said appeal he alleges, that "the filing" (application to make homestead entry) "of Denis "Hinehan" is fraudulent and made for the purpose of covering up; that he (Hurot) "has valuable improvements on said tract of land and is the only person who has," and that his entry "was the first *legal* entry made or applied for on said tract."

These allegations, if properly verified by affidavit and made sufficiently *specific*, would be ground for an application for a hearing. They are not so verified, however, and, as they now stand, are too general

2816—VOL 9——35

and indefinite to authorize the ordering of a hearing thereon. The charge of fraud, if intended to apply to the application of " Minehan," should specify wherein the fraud consists. If it is intended by the remainder of said allegations to claim, that Hurot had the prior right to enter the land, under section three of the act of May 14, 1880 (21 Stat., 140), then it should have been averred, that he had settled upon the land with the intention of claiming it under the homestead law before Minehan's rights attached and had after such settlement made his homestead entry within the time " allowed settlers under the pre-emption laws to put their claim on record."

The fifth and sixth assignments of error are based upon the theory, that because of the mistake made by the attorneys in taking out the appeal in the name of " Hinehan," there was no appeal taken by " Minehan." This position is untenable, in view of the fact, as above shown, that it clearly appeared from the appeal itself and the papers accompanying it, that it was taken from the rejection of " Minehan's," application.

The application of Minehan to enter the land, being in all respects regular and having been kept alive by his appealing from its rejection within the prescribed time, segregated the land from the public domain, and the land was not open to the entry of Hurot January 4, 1887, as claimed by him in his fourth assignment of error. As these facts were of record and the allowance of Hurot's entry was " by inadvertence," said entry was properly held for cancellation by your office. It further appearing, that there was in fact no railroad claim to the land and that Minehan's application was improperly rejected, there was no error in sustaining his appeal from said rejection.

The decision of your office is affirmed without prejudice to the right of Hurot to a hearing on sufficient application properly verified.

HOMESTEAD CONTEST—RESIDENCE—ABANDONMENT.

BATES v. BISSELL.

The Land Department is not bound by an opinion of the Commissioner expressed on a partial and *ex parte* statement of the facts.

The residence of a married man is presumptively where his family resides.

In the presence of a valid adverse settlement right, the effect of abandonment can not be obviated by returning to the land and again establishing residence.

If the duties of an office are not inconsistent with the maintenance of residence on the land, they can not be accepted as an excuse for absence therefrom.

First Assistant Secretary Chandler to the Commissioner of the General Land Office, November 15, 1889.

The case of Augustus E. Bates v. Oliver C. Bissell is before me on appeal by Bates from the decision of your office, dated June 7, 1888.

The tract of land in controversy herein is the NW. ¼ of Sec. 8, T. 139 N., R. 94 W., Bismarck land district, Dakota.

The official plat of said township was filed September 14, 1882, and on the day following Bissell entered the described tract as a homestead.

On October 24, following, appellant made homestead entry for the same land.

These conflicting entries caused your office to order a hearing in the matter, which hearing accordingly was had before the local office · on August 17, 1883.

It appears that the register and receiver sustained the Bates' entry. On appeal to your office, the decision of the local office was reversed, and Bates' entry was directed to be canceled.

On appeal by Bates from this decision, it was affirmed by departmental decision, dated January 9, 1886 (unreported). Notice was issued by the local officers to the parties on February 2, following, and ten days thereafter, February 12, 1886, Bates instituted the present contest. In his corroborated affidavit of contest he charges, among other things, that Bissell had changed his residence from said tract of land for more than six months since making his said entry; that since August 17, 1883, neither he nor any of his family had lived thereon, and that said land was not settled upon and cultivated by Bissell as required by law.

A hearing was duly had herein before the register and receiver, at Bismarck, on March 29, 1886, which resulted in disagreeing opinions— the register holding that Bissell's entry should be canceled, and the receiver that Bates' contest should be dismissed. On appeal, your office affirmed the decision of the receiver, and Bates appealed.

The case is now before the Department for consideration on this appeal.

After a full and careful consideration of the evidence produced at the hearing had herein, the following are found to be the material facts as shown by the preponderance of said evidence:

On May 2, 1882, Bissell and his wife, with others, calling themselves a colony, reached the near neighborhood of the land in question. Soon afterwards, he commenced the erection of a dwelling house, at what is now the village of Gladstone, Dakota, and finished it about the last of May. Bissell was chosen postmaster at said village, and says he built his house for a post-office and for a home for his wife. The house was sixteen by twenty six feet, and is valued at four hundred dollars. It was comfortably furnished, and up to a date subsequent to the institution of this contest (February 12, 1886,) his wife made it her home, and the post-office was kept in one room. He also had a stable near this house, where he kept his team of horses and other domestic animals. His personal property kept at the house at Gladstone was worth about five hundred dollars. Bissell testifies, that he made his homestead (settlement) in the spring of 1882. This presumably was by breaking land, for he afterwards says, on cross-examination, that he took his bed on to the land some time in the summer—the time in the summer he could not state. The cheap house, or shack, as he and the witnesses call it, was built on the land before he assumed the duties of post-master, which was on July 12, 1882.

Prior to August 17, 1883, Bissell had broken two disconnected pieces of the land in controversy, one containing about ten and the other about eleven acres. The larger piece he cultivated to crop in 1884 and 1885.

The date of the first hearing between these parties was August 17, 1883. At this time Bissell had on said tract a building eight by ten, which he claimed to be his residence. This building was boarded up and down and battened, was covered with a board roof, and its only floor was the ground on which it was built, covered by a single strip of carpet. This building was not inhabited, nor was it habitable, in the winter time. During the summers of 1882 and 1883, Bissell lodged therein, as testi-fied to by him, from one hundred and fifty to two hundred nights. He had it furnished with a cast iron stove with two openings, a small kettle, a frying pan, a water bucket, a board used for a table, some table ware, a rough bedstead and a few bed clothes. There were no chairs in the house, and the estimated value (by Bissell) of his entire household goods was from fifteen to twenty dollars. The house Bissell thinks cost him about thirty dollars, as lumber was very high. During all the time Bissell slept in this house and claimed it as his residence, his wife was living in the Gladstone house, which was only about half a mile distant. Bissell says he continued to occupy the building for ten days or two weeks after the hearing of August 17, 1883, and that thereafter he lived at his house in Gladstone, until the 4th or 5th of February, 1886. The house on the claim was destroyed by a prairie fire about September 25, 1885. From September 25, 1885, to February 5, 1886, there was no house on the claim and at about the date last given, Bis-sell again commenced sleeping in another shanty, which he moved on the ground and fixed up after receiving notice of the aforesaid depart-mental decision of January 9, 1886, and that he continued to live there up to the date of hearing in this case, March 29, 1886. He started to move the Gladstone house to the land in controversy on March 15—three days after the initiation of the present contest—and got it placed on the land on the 24th of the same month. On March 15 Bissell put the post-office in charge of a deputy postmaster. Mrs. Bissell continued to live at Gladstone up to March 15th or 20th, and was living, presum-ably, with her husband on said tract at the date of hearing, March 29th. As an excuse for not living on the land in controversy from the latter part of August, 1883, up to February 4th or 5th, 1886—a period of nearly two years and a half—Bissell says, that it was very inconvenient for him, under the circumstances, to live on the land, and that he had been told it was not necessary for him to do so; that to satisfy himself on this point, and as to whether he could be excused from living on the land, he wrote to the Land Office at Washington and got a letter from the Commissioner in regard to the matter.   The said letter is made an exhibit in the case by Bissell, and is dated January 5, 1883, more than seven months anterior to the date of said first hearing between these parties (August 17, 1883,) and to the time he entirely abandoned his habit of sleeping on the land in controversy.   Said letter is as follows:

SIR:—In reply to your letter of the (no date) relative to your homestead entry upon the "partially" surveyed public lands in Dakota, and the conflicting claim of Mrs. Bates, you are advised, that no entry or filing of a married woman, who still claims and holds the relationship of wife to a husband in health and sound mind, and who continues to provide and care for her, would be valid or recognized by this office, either as acting for herself or (as) her husband's agent.

In making a statement of your case for the consideration of this office, you should make it in form of an affidavit, corroborated by two or more credible witnesses, and forward the same through the register and receiver of the District in which the land in question is embraced.

Your appointment to the position of postmaster, and your absence from your claim consequent upon the duties of said office will not jeopardize your land, *provided* you received your appointment subsequent to your settlement and residence upon your claim, and that you keep up your improvements thereon.

And at this time Bates was claiming adversely to Bissell and had improvements upon the land consisting of about ten acres of breaking, a comfortable dwelling house twenty by thirty, with wing fourteen by sixteen, and an additional room eight by eight.   The house had a cellar, two chimneys, was ceiled inside and out, the rooms were ten feet between joists, and most of them papered; for out-buildings he had a barn, carriage shed, coal shed and a chicken house.   The value of these improvements at that time was about $1,000.

This letter shows upon its face that the Commissioner had no correct or reliable information in regard to the nature of the conflicting claims to the land in dispute, or the improvements thereon, and he informed Mr. Bissell therein that his case should have been stated " in the form of a corroborated affidavit," thus giving him to understand that any opinions he gave could not be relied upon any further than they were borne out by the facts and circumstances of the case.   But if Bissell had in fact relied implicitly on the opinion expressed by the Commissioner in said letter from the date of its receipt, and if he had in fact brought himself strictly within the " conditions prescribed"—which in my opinion he has not—still neither your office nor the department, would be bound by an opinion expressed on an *ex parte* statement of the alleged facts made by a claimant in his own behalf in the presence of an adverse claim to secure a prejudgment of his case before it was presented for decision in the regular course of business.

It is my impression from the record now before me, that Bissell at no time established a residence upon this tract, although on the facts before the Department when the case was formerly here, it was held that he had so established a residence.   Bissell's wife never lived on the tract, and the greater part of his household goods were at Glad-

stone, where he had a comfortable home and where he resided from
about August 17, 1883, to February 5, 1886.

It has repeatedly been he'd by this Department that the residence of
a married man is held to be where his family resides. Spalding v. Colfer, 8 L. D., 615; Stroud v. De Wolf, 4 L. D., 394. But granting that
Bissell at one time established a residence on said tract, the testimony
clearly shows a practical abandonment thereof when he left the tract
in August, 1883.

But your decision, after finding that Bissell established his residence
on the land in dispute about May, 1882, proceeds:

He (Bissell) continued to reside on the claim until about August 17, 1883, since
which time he has resided at Gladstone with his wife performing his official duties,
until about the 4th or 5th of February, 1886, when he again established residence on
the claim. . . . Filed with the record is an official letter from this office of date
of January 5, 1883, containing the following statement: "Your appointment to the
position of postmaster, and your absence from your claim consequent upon the duties
of said office, will not jeopardize your title to your land, *provided*, you received your
appointment subsequent to your settlement and residence thereon." Claimant swears
that he left his claim to reside at the post-office, solely on the strength of said letter.

The evidence shows that he continued to cultivate and improve the claim, hence
it must be construed that he is within the condition prescribed by said letter (letter
above quoted), and even granting that claimant had abandoned his claim by changing his residence therefrom to the post-office at Gladstone the defect had been cured
prior to the initiation of contest.

In view of the foregoing, the decision of the register is reversed and that of the receiver dismissing the contest is affirmed.

The exceptions taken to this decision and the errors assigned by appellant's attorney are:

1st. In holding that his (Commissioner's) letter to Bissell of January 5, 1883, affords
a legal excuse for non-residence.

2d. In holding that Bissell's failure of residence, if such there was, was cured prior
to this contest;

which, in my opinion, are well taken.

It can not be contended with any show of reason that the Commissioner intended, or could, on an *ex-parte* presentation of this adverse
claim, by this letter, furnish any justification for Bissell's abandoning
this tract of land for a more comfortable residence in the town of Gladstone, and certainly the circumstances surrounding the case are not in
keeping with good faith to hold that there was any excuse for his failure to reside upon or cultivate the tract until after the decision was in
his favor, and then individually set himself down in this building, moved
upon this tract to keep up a colorable compliance with the provisions
of law. It does not appear that a proper discharge of his duties as
postmaster would cause an enforced absence from his claim, or, in the
language of the Commissioner, that his absence therefrom was "consequent upon the duties of said office."

The evidence shows that the village of Gladstone contained only about
fifty inhabitants, and that the surrounding country is sparsely settled;
that a book-case, or something like it, with pigeon-holes, served for all

the mail matter at said office, and that the number of letters received daily did not exceed from twenty-five to fifty. The duties of such an office could not have been very onerous, and though it may have been somewhat more convenient for Mr. Bissell to reside in the town of Gladstone than on its outskirts, the necessity for so doing is not apparent. The law does not require a postmaster to reside in the building in which the office is kept, but only "within the delivery of the office to which he is appointed" (section 3831 R. S.), and the presumption is that the house in which appellant and his wife are now living, and which is situated on said tract of land, is within the delivery of said office. Nor was the abandonment of "his claim by changing his residence therefrom to the post-office at Gladstone" cured by the act of again establishing a residence thereon prior to the initiation of the present contest.

In the absence of an adverse claim, appellant's entry might be permitted to stand, but, in the face of a claim asserted in good faith for over three years by a party residing on the land during all of that time, and having improvements thereon reasonably valued at a thousand dollars, this can not be permitted.

On the facts shown herein, I am clearly of the opinion that Bissell's entry should be canceled, and hereby direct the cancellation of the same. The decision of your office is accordingly reversed.

PRACTICE—RES JUDICATA.

JAMES A. SKINNER.

On a proper case shown, and in the absence of an adverse claim, a decision of the Department rendered upon an incomplete record may be set aside and the case considered upon its merits.

First Assistant Secretary Chandler to the Commissioner of the General Land Office, November 16, 1889.

On July 8, 1882, James A. Skinner filed Osage declaratory statement for the N. ¼ SE. ¼, NE. ¼ SW. ¼ and SE. ¼ SE. ¼ Sec. 5 T. 31 S., R. 15 W., Independence, Kansas, alleging settlement July 1, 1882, said land being part of the Osage Indian trust and diminished reserve land, subject to disposal under the act of May 28, 1880 (21 Stat., 143).

On April 3, 1883, Henry M. Morton filed Osage declaratory statement for said N. ¼ of the SE. ¼ and NE. ¼ of SW. ¼ of said Sec. 5, alleging settlement same date.

On August 5, 1884, Skinner offered final proof, which was rejected by the local officers on account of a pending contest filed by Morton, upon which a hearing was had November 18, 1884, at which both parties submitted proof. The local officers decided in favor of Morton, and your office upon appeal rejected the proof submitted by Skinner and held his filing for cancellation upon the ground that he was not an actual settler upon the tract within the meaning of that term as employed in the act of May 28, 1880, and that an actual settler under said act, as ruled in the case of Morgan v. Craig (10 C. L. O., 234), "is one who goes upon the land *animo manendi*, or as the court remarks in Lytle v. State of Arkansas (22 How., 193), for the purpose of seeking a home." Your office further held that Morton's rights will be considered when he shall offer proof in due form. From this action Skinner appealed, and while his appeal was pending before the Department Morton relinquished his claim to the tract, and on August 5, 1886, the local officers allowed Skinner to make entry of said tract upon the proof submitted August 5, 1884, and a new pre-emption affidavit was made of that date.

It appears that filing of the relinquishment by Morton and the action of the local officers in allowing the entry of Skinner was not reported to your office or the Department and on May 11, 1888,—nearly two years after the allowance of said cash entry—the decision of your office in the case of Morton v. Skinner, holding the filing of Skinner for cancellation, was affirmed by the Department upon the ground that Skinner had not made a *bona fide* settlement upon the tract prior to Morton's settlement.

On May 31, 1888, the local officers transmitted the entry papers of Skinner and reported that a compromise was effected between Morton and Skinner on August 5, 1886, by which Morton relinquished his claim to the tract filed for by him, and on the same date Skinner made Osage entry of said tract and the SE. ¼ of SE. ¼ of said Sec. 3, being the same land embraced in his filing made July 8, 1882, no new proof being submitted but only a new pre-emption affidavit. You held said entry for cancellation upon the ground that it was erroneously allowed for the reason that Skinner's claim in the case of Morton v. Skinner was rejected—not on account of conflict with Morton, but because the testimony showed that he was not an actual settler, and that the decision of the Department cancelling the filing upon which his entry is based, has never been set aside.

Upon these facts the question now presented is, whether upon this appeal the claimant has such a standing before the Department as to authorize the Department in a proper case made to revoke its decision of May 31, 1888, cancelling the filing of Skinner and to now pass upon the merits of his entry, there being no adverse claim to the tract.

While the judgment of the Department cancelling the filing of Skinner remained unrevoked no legal entry could be made of the tract under said filing, and there was no error in the decision of your office holding said entry for cancellation. Nor could the Department grant relief if adverse right would be affected thereby, but as the entry has been allowed by the local office upon the original filing—although improperly allowed—and the case being before the Department from the decision of your office, holding said entry for cancellation, I can see no reason why the Department may not upon a proper case made, revoke its decision of May 31, 1888, cancelling the filing upon which the entry was made, and pass upon the merits of the entry, especially in view of the fact when such decision was rendered it was not known that Morton had relinquished his claim and that Skinner had been allowed to make entry of the tract.

The decision of the Department was based upon the supposition that there was an adverse claim existing at the date of said decision, which was adverse to Skinner for the reason that it did not appear that he had made a *bona fide* settlement prior to the settlement of Morton.

I have carefully examined the testimony submitted by Skinner, and also the testimony offered at the hearing upon the contest of Morton, and from this it appears that he was an actual settler upon the land, and was residing thereon at the date of entry, and that he has the qualifications of a pre-emptor. With this appeal he has also filed his affidavit corroborated by two witnesses, showing that he settled upon and improved said land in July 1882, and in the fall of said year built a house thereon; that in 1883 he built an addition to said house; that he has cultivated a portion of the land each year since 1882, has fenced about one hundred and fifty acres of said land and that his residence upon said land was continuous up to date of entry, and that he has continued to occupy and improve it to the present time for his own use and benefit.

From a full consideration of this case I am satisfied that the entry of Skinner should be approved for patent.

The decision of your office is reversed.

SCHOOL LAND—PRIVATE CLAIMS.

ISHAM M. BARNARD.

That a school section was embraced within a private claim will not exclude it from the school grant, if in fact the section was not "sold or otherwise disposed of by any act of Congress."

A pending unapproved indemnity selection will not bar the State from the assertion of its right under the grant to the section in place.

First Assistant Secretary Chandler to the Commissioner of the General Land Office, November 16, 1889.

I have before me the appeal of Isham M. Barnard from your office decision of October 25, 1888, rejecting his application to make pre-emption filing for lot 1, of SE. ¼, Sec. 9 and lot 1 of NE. ¼, and NE. ¼, SE. ¼, Sec. 16, T. 22 S., R. 59 W., Pueblo district, Colorado.

The ground of your said decision is, that the tract in section sixteen, which is covered by the application, passed to the State as school land under the (seventh section of the) act of March 3, 1875 (18 Stat., 474).

This ruling I approve, the "section sixteen" in question having been public land of the United States not "sold or otherwise disposed of by any act of Congress." The circumstance that the land was embraced in the derivative claim of Fosdick and Hollis under the Mexican grant to Vigil and St. Vrain, does not militate against this view, inasmuch as the derivative claim in question was rejected by the Commissioners under the act of February 25, 1869 (15 Stats., 275), and that rejection is held to have been final, so far as the executive is concerned. (Order of the President, March 2, 1877, *in re* claim of Craig; Rafael Chacon, 2 L. D. 590; 3 L. D. 110).

The fact insisted on in the assignment of errors, that the State, by list No. 2, selected indemnity for said section sixteen, on the supposition that the section was not available, can not change the result, the selection not having been approved, but, on the contrary, suspended by your office letter of June 21, 1888, in the matter of the application of Abigail L. Fowler to enter the N. ¾ SW. ¼, of said section sixteen.

The decision appealed from is accordingly affirmed.

SCHOOL LANDS—SETTLEMENT BEFORE SURVEY.

ODILLON MARCEAU.

The protection extended by the act of February 26, 1859, is limited to those who have, prior to the survey in the field, made a settlement with a view to pre-emption.

A purchase after survey of the possessory right and improvements of one who settles on school land prior to survey, does not carry with it any right to the land as against the school grant.

Secretary Noble to the Commissioner of the General Land Office, November 18, 1889.

The land involved in this case is the NE. ¼ of Sec. 36, T. 14 N., R. 21 W., Helena district, Montana. Said land is in a section reserved for school purposes, under section 1946 of the Revised Statutes, which is as follows:

Sections numbered sixteen and thirty-six in each township of the territories of New Mexico, Utah, Colorado, Dakota, Arizona, Idaho, Montana, and Wyoming, shall be reserved for the purpose of being applied to schools in the several territories herein named, and in the States and Territories hereafter to be erected out of the same.

The act of February 26, 1859 (11 Stat., 385—now Sec. 2275 R. S.), provides:

That where settlements with a view to pre emption have been made before the survey of the lands in the field, which shall be found to have been made on sections sixteen or thirty-six, said sections shall be subject to the pre-emption claim of *such settlers;* and if they, or either of them, shall have been or shall be reserved or pledged for the use of schools or colleges in the State or Territory in which the lands lie, other lands of like quantity are hereby appropriated in lieu of such as may be patented by pre-emptors.

The land in the present case was surveyed "*in the field*" September 29, and 30, 1870, and plat thereof was filed in the local office, November

1, 1870. It appears from affidavits on file in the record, that one, Frederick Bucier, settled on the land in 1867 and improved and cultivated it until October 10, 1870, when Odillon Marceau purchased from him his improvements and went into possession of the land and has since, with his family, resided upon it as a home, cultivating it each year, and that he has improvements thereon to the value of $1,000.00. Said Marceau after so settling upon the land made application to file a pre-emption declaratory statement therefor, which was denied by the local officers on the ground that the tract was in a section reserved for schools and that his (Marceau's) settlement was made subsequent to survey. On appeal by Marceau, your office sustained the action of the local officers, holding that:—

The only person who could successfully contest the reservation in favor of the Territory would be Bucier, who settled upon the tract prior to survey, providing he had maintained his residence since such settlement, but Marceau settling subsequently to the subdivisional survey could not defeat the claim of the Territory.

Marceau now appeals to this Department, claiming that, as he " bought out Bucier on the 10th of October, 1870, and then settled on the land," and the plat of survey was not filed until November 1, 1870, he was " as a matter of law a settler on the land before survey," and therefore " entitled to file on the tract " under said act of February 26, 1859 (Sec. 2275, Rev. Stat.).

This contention can not be maintained. The act only protects settlements " with a view to pre-emption made *before* the survey of the land *in the field.*" The " field " survey of the land was made, as before stated, September 29, and 30, 1870, before Marceau's settlement, and it is well settled by the decisions of this Department, that " a purchase after survey of the possessory right and improvements of one who settled on school land prior to survey, does not carry with it any right to the land as against the grant." (Thomas F. Talbot, 8 L. D., 495; Thomas E. Watson, 6 L. D., 73; John Johansen, 5 L. D., 408; Thomas E. Watson, 4 L. D., 169.) The statute (act of February 26, 1859—Sec. 2275, Rev. Stat., *supra*) expressly limits the right given therein to " such settler " as shall have *before* the " survey in the field " made a settlement with a view to pre-emption—the object being "to protect the inchoate right of a settler who went upon the land prior to survey *without notice* that the land settled upon was school land." (Thomas F. Talbot, *supra*.) As the survey in the field determines the character of the land, as being or not being school land, a settler thereafter on school land was, in the judgment of Congress, chargeable with *notice* of the character of the land, and the act therefore only protects settlers prior to such survey.

The decision of your office is affirmed.

PRE-EMPTION—TRANSMUTATION—ACT OF MARCH 2, 1889.

JOHN P. NEWCOMB.

Under the act of March 2, 1889, a pre-emptor is entitled to the right of transmutation, even though he may have had the benefit of the homestead law.

First Assistant Secretary Chandler to the Commissioner of the General Land Office, November 18, 1889.

I have considered the case of John P. Newcomb on his appeal from your office decision of September 7, 1888, refusing to permit him to transmute his pre emption filing for N. ½, SW. ¼, and SW. ¼, NW. ¼, Sec. 5, T. 14 S., R. 78 W., Leadville, Colorado, land district, to a homestead entry.

Your said decision says,—

Newcomb admits having made a former entry in Louisiana (New Orleans homestead entry 112), February 6, 1867, for eighty acres, but swears in an affidavit submitted that soon after said entry he went upon the land, but the people were so hostile towards a northern man that he was afraid to locate and therefore was compelled to abandon said entry. He also swears he desires to transmute said filing because he has not the money to complete the filing under the pre-emption law; and that he has improvements on the land, consisting of a house of three rooms, corral, stable, well and fence, and nearly six miles of irrigating ditch; and that he will be compelled to lose said improvements unless this application is granted.

Your said decision is based upon the ground that the law restricts parties to one homestead entry, and that the showing did not warrant an exception being made to the rule in this case.

Without stopping to discuss the merits of the excuse offered by claimant for his failure to complete his former entry it will be sufficient for the determination of the case at bar to say that since your said decision, Congress by the act of March 2, 1889, provided for the change of pre-emption filings to homesteads even though the applicant therefor may have had the benefit of the homestead law. (25 Stat., 854).

Your decision is accordingly reversed, and transmutation may be allowed under the said act of March 2, 1889.

PRIVATE CLAIM—STATUTORY LIMITATION.

HEIRS OF JOHN INNERARITY.

Under the act of June 22, 1860, and the acts amendatory thereof, a claimant that did not present his claim, or bring suit thereupon, prior to June 10, 1875, is barred both as to his right and to his remedy under said statute.

The judgment rendered on the remittitur annulled the former decree of the court *pro tanto,* and the amount of land so deducted reverted to the public domain, leaving the claimants interested therein to assert their right in the manner provided by said acts.

Secretary Noble to the Commissioner of the General Land Office, November 16, 1889.

I have examined the appeal of the heirs of John Innerarity from your office decision of June 28, 1888, denying their petition for land scrip under the act of June 22, 1860, entitled "An act for the final adjustment of private land claims in the States of Florida, Louisiana and Missouri, and for other purposes," and subsequent acts on the same subject.

The claim of the petitioners is founded upón a grant made to one John Lynde on July 12, 1806, by Juan Ventura Morales, Spanish Intendant of West Florida.

The lands included in this grant were situated east of the Mississippi River and south of the 31st parallel of latitude, and were a part of the disputed territory, which, after the cession of Louisiana to the United States in 1803, was claimed by them as a part of Louisiana, and by Spain as a part of West Florida.

For a portion of the period during which this dispute existed, viz., from 1803 to 1810, this territory remained in the possession of Spain, and it made numerous grants therein.

After the treaty of 1819, when as between the two nations the status of this territory was settled, the question of the validity of these grants was frequently before the courts, and they were uniformly held invalid, the court holding: That the stipulation of the treaty of 1819, that all the grants made by Spain before January 24, 1818, or by its authority " in the said territories ceded, etc., should be ratified and confirmed," only covered grants within the territory ceded by that treaty; that lands in that portion of West Florida, having been ceded by the treaty of 1803 were not included in the expression "in the said territories ceded " and hence such grants were, not within the protection of said stipulation.

Foster and Elam v. Neilson (2 Peters, 253); Garcia v. Lee (12 Peters, 511).

Again these claimants sought to establish their titles under the act of May 26, 1824, as applied to this territory by the act of June 17, 1844, and were again unsuccessful the court holding that those acts related to inchoate and incomplete titles, and were intended to provide a means for completing them, and did not relate to grants made by a nation which, at the date of the grant, had no title. United States v. Reynes (9 Howard, 127).

This was the status of the claims of those who had grants of land within this territory, from the Spanish authorities, bearing date from 1803, to 1810 (the time that Spain held possession of the disputed territory), until the passage of the act of June 22, 1860 (12 Stat., 85).

This act was evidently intended to provide a means for the equitable settlement of the claims of those who, relying upon the justness of the claim of Spain to this territory while she was admittedly in possession and exercising prerogatives of sovereignty therein, had purchased or otherwise secured grants to the recognition of which Spain had always considered us pledged, notwithstanding our construction of the treaty of 1819.

This act provided for two courses of procedure; one, the presentation of a petition accompanied by certain plats, surveys and other formalities, to a commission consisting of the local land officers, whose duty it was to receive the same, and hear the evidence and after passing upon the matter, forward the whole with their decision to the Commissioner of the General Land Office, whose duty it was to pass upon the matter and under certain circumstances to report the same to Congress for its action, and the other course being for the claimant to present a petition to the United States district court, where the district attorney was required to appear and defend, and the cause proceeded as in ordinary chancery cases, and the final decision in such case was binding both on the government and the claimant.

The twelfth section of that act is as follows, viz:

Sec. 12. And be it further enacted, That this act shall be and remain in force during the term of five years, unless sooner repealed by Congress; and all claims presented or sued upon, according to the provisions of this act, within said term of five years, may be prosecuted to final determination and decision notwithstanding the said term of five years may have expired before such final determination and decision.

By an act of Congress passed March 2, 1867, (14 Stat., 544) the provisions of said act were continued in force for three years longer and by an act passed June 10, 1872 (17 Stat., 378), the same were continued in force for three years from said last named date.

It will be noted, that except for these acts grantees holding under Spanish grants, of land within this disputed territory after 1803, derived no title from their grant, but were by the act of June 22, 1860, granted a privilege given as a matter of grace, rather than of right, and when Congress granted that privilege it was unquestionably within its province to prescribe the conditions under which and the time within which, that privilege should be exercised.

Congress, recognizing that these grants are based upon ancient transactions which the interests of the government as well as the claimants make it desirable to bring to a conclusion, fixed a time within which the privilege it granted should be exercised, and has twice extended that time.

This legislation is conclusively binding on this Department, and on claimants and any claimant not having presented or sued upon his claim prior to June 10, 1875, is barred of both his right and his remedy under this statute. Heirs of John Wren Scott (3 L. D., 72); United States v. Innerarity (19 Wall., 595).

The history of the title to this particular grant is, that there was granted to one John Lynde, by Morales, Intendant etc., under authority of the Spanish government 32,025 arpens (27,253 acres) of land within the above designated disputed territory, on July 12, 1806.

That on the 11th day of August, 1808, the said John Lynde by an act passed before B. Pedesclaux, notary public, at the city of New Orleans, La., sold and conveyed to John Forbes and Co., 15,134 arpens (12,863.90 acres) of said land.

On January 15, 1861, the heirs of said John Lynde, commenced a suit in the United States district court for the (then) eastern district of Louisiana, for the whole of this land, ignoring the sale and conveyance to John Forbes and Co., above referred to.

Upon final decision of said case the supreme court of the United States, at its December term, 1870, adjudged to the said heirs of said John Lynde the entire quantity of land included in said grant. United States v. John Lynde (11 Wallace, 632).

On December 20, 1872, counsel for the Lynde heirs having learned of said sale and transfer to Forbes and Co., as well as of another sale made by Lynde in his lifetime, amounting to 5470 arpens, entered a remittitur of the aggregate quantity of land described in these two conveyances, viz., 20,604 arpens (17,513.40 acres). Thereupon scrip issued for the remainder—9740.35 acres.

On August 6, 1887, the petitioners filed their petition to this Department, alleging, and showing that the firm of John Forbes and Co., consisted of John Forbes, John Innerarity and James Innerarity, and that they were equal partners in the property of said firm, and that the petitioners are heirs of John Innerarity, and asking that one-third of the 15,134 arpens (12,863.90 acres) of said grant sold as above stated, by Lynde to Forbes and Co., be allotted to them as heirs of John Innerarity.

The share of James Innerarity in this grant was allotted and adjudged to his heirs by decree of the supreme court of the United States, rendered at the October term, 1878.

Upon this state of facts the petitioners are barred both of their right and their remedy as has heretofore been shown no claim having been presented or suit brought until after the expiration of the act of June 22, 1860, and said subsequent acts, by limitation.

But it is contended that the judgment in the case of United States v. John Lynde, *supra*, stands for the full amount and that it has only been partially satisfied, and that the petitioners, upon showing themselves to be the heirs of John Innerarity, are entitled to so much scrip awarded by that judgment as equals one-third of the amount of land sold by Lynde to Forbes & Co., to be applied in satisfaction of said judgment, *pro tanto*. In other words, that the judgment in favor of John Lynde being confessedly for his own land as also what he had sold, will be held to be a judgment in his favor as trustee for those who are shown to be actually entitled to the land, and, alleging that the remittitur above referred to was "in favor of the heirs of John Forbes & Co.," that the same should be construed as an equitable assignment to them of their respective shares.

The record in the Lynde case will not bear such a construction. It appears that on December 20, 1872, at the suggestion of Louis Janin, of counsel for plaintiffs, and upon suggestion that the attorney-general of the United States had instructed the district attorney to file a bill of review based upon the fact that the plaintiffs in that case had recovered land to which, by reason of said conveyances, they were not entitled, it was ordered by the said United States district court for the said district of Louisiana "that said plaintiffs by their counsel be now allowed to enter a remittitur of scrip for 17,513.40 acres of land and that said decree in their favor be accordingly amended by making a deduction therefrom of the quantity of land so sold by the said John Lynde, to wit, 17,513.40 acres *thus reducing the same to a decree for* 9,740.35 *acres in scrip.*" The entry was accordingly made as appears by a certified copy of the minutes of said court for the 20th of December, 1872, on file in your office.

This record is susceptible of but one construction, and that is that it annulled said decree *pro tanto* and the amount of lands so deducted, again reverted to the public domain and the representatives of the firm of Forbes & Co., were left to their remedy under the said act of Congress, and having, by their own laches, failed to avail themselves of that remedy, the petitioners have lost whatever of right they ever had.

The petition is denied and your said office decision is affirmed.

PRACTICE—APPEAL—SPECIFICATIONS OF ERROR.

HORTON *v.* WILSON.

On appeal to the Department the appellant must file specifications of error clearly and concisely designating the errors of which he complains.

First Assistant Secretary Chandler to the Commissioner of the General Land Office, November 20, 1889.

In the case of Hiram Horton *v.* Albert Wilson, involving the latter's timber culture entry for the NE. ¼ of Sec. 23, T. 116, R. 58, Watertown District, Dakota, said Horton appeals from your office decision of July 30, 1888, sustaining the action of the local officers in dismissing his contest of said entry.

The appellant's assignments of error are as follows :

1. The Commissioner erred in dismissing the contest.
2. The Commissioner erred in sustaining the decision of the local office.

These allegations are insufficient under Rule of Practice 88, which requires, that on appeal to this Department the appellant shall file specifications of error "clearly and concisely designating the errors of which he complains." Pederson *v.* Johannesson (4 L. D., 343).

Apart from this, however, I am of the opinion, after a careful examination of the voluminous testimony adduced at the hearing, that said testimony fully sustains the conclusion reached by both your office and the local officers, to the effect that claimant had in good faith complied with the requirements of the timber culture law, and said contest was unfounded.

Said appeal is dismissed and the decision of your office affirmed.

PRACTICE—NOTICE—TRANSFEREE.

VAN BRUNT v. HAMMON ET AL.

A transferee, holding under a final certificate, is entitled to be heard in defense of the entry, but if he fails to file a statement in the local office showing his interest under said entry, he can not plead want of notice as against the contest proceedings of another.

The question of notice is jurisdictional and may be raised at any time, and when raised, or apparent on the face of the record, the Department is bound to take cognizance thereof.

In service of notice by publication posting a copy in the office of the register, during the period of publication, is an essential without which notice is incomplete.

First Assistant Secretary Chandler to the Commissioner of the General Land Office, November 21, 1889.

Charles S. Allyn appeals from your office decision of November 18, 1887, rejecting his application to have the case of Rulif P. Van Brunt *v.* Andrew J. Hammon, involving the latter's homestead entry, made November 27, 1883, for the E. ½ of the NW. ¼ and the NW. ¼ of the NW. ¼, Sec. 12, and the NE. ¼ of the NE. ¼ Sec. 11 T. 15 N. R. 22 W., North Platte, Nebraska—commuted to cash entry February 13, 1885—reopened, and a rehearing ordered with permission to him to interplead and protect his rights in the premises.

It appears from the record in the case referred to, that a hearing was ordered therein by your office October 24, 1885, upon the complaint of Van Brunt, under oath, charging in substance, that Hammon, the entryman, had not complied with the law in the matter of settlement, residence and improvement and that the entry was made in the interest of the Brighton Ranch Company, and was therefore fraudulent.

The hearing took place in March 1886, upon notice by publication, the contestant alone appearing. Testimony was introduced in support of the charges laid, and thereupon the local officers found in favor of the contestant. From this finding no appeal was taken.

Allyn alleges in his application, which is sworn to by himself, supported by the corroborating affidavit of another, and purports to have been filed July 19, 1887, that on April 14, 1885, Hammon sold the land in question to him for the sum of $500, and executed a warranty deed therefor; that he was not advised of the pendency of the contest by Van Brunt until long after the time had elapsed within which he could have interposed a defense thereto; that he is a *bona fide* purchaser of the land, and that if allowed a hearing, he can prove that Hammon complied with the law in all respects and that the entry was made by him in good faith.

In denying the application, your office held in effect, that while it is true purchasers from an entryman, after final certificate, have such a standing before the Land Department as entitles them to be heard in defense of their interests, if the entry should be attacked, yet the government deals only with its own grantees and cannot undertake to follow subsequent transfers, to settle questions which may arise upon such transfers, or attempt to adjust the character of alleged *bona fide* purchases from its grantees, (citing R. M. Sherman *et al.*, 4 L. D., 544; John C. Featherspil, Id., 570; C. P. Cogswell, 3 L. D., 23; R. M. Chrisinger, 4 L. D., 347). That inasmuch as Allyn, after his purchase from Hammon, failed to file in the local office a sworn statement setting forth the character of his interest in the land, which would have entitled him to notice of any proceedings against the entry of Hammon (citing American Investment Company 5 L. D., 603), he is bound by the notice given to the entryman Hammon by publication, and is concluded by the result of the trial had upon such notice.

This holding is undoubtedly in accord with the settled practice of the Department, as shown by the authorities cited in support thereof, and the more recent case of William W. Waterhouse (9 L. D., 131). The doctrine thus enunciated would be conclusive against the application of Allyn in this case but for the fact that an examination of the record shows the notice by publication not to have been given in accordance with the rules prescribed for the giving of such notice. The question of notice is jurisdictional and may be raised at any time, and when raised, or if appearing on the face of the record, the Department is bound to take cognizance thereof. Watson *v.* Morgan (9 L. D., 75).

In this case there is no proof in the record that a copy of the notice was posted in the register's office during the period of publication, as required by rule 14 of practice. This is an essential part of a notice by publication, and without it the notice is incomplete.

In the case of Parker *v.* Castle (4 L. D., 84) it was held that the sending of a copy of the notice by registered letter and the posting of a copy on the land are essential parts of a notice by publication.

In Kelly *v.* Grameng (5 L. D., 611) it was held that notice by publication includes the posting of a copy of the notice on the land in controversy and that if such posting is omitted the notice is incomplete and jurisdiction is not acquired; and further that the record must show affirmatively all matters of notice requisite to confer jurisdiction.

It is equally true that notice by publication includes the posting of a copy in the register's office during the period of publication, for this is as distinctly and plainly required as either the posting on the land, or the sending by registered letter. See also Watson *v.* Morgan, *supra.*

These are all constituent and essential parts of notice by publication, and the absence of any one of such essential parts, is fatal to the notice, and renders it inoperative for the purposes designed. Kelly *v.* Grameng, *supra.*

In this view of the matter, it is clear that both the local office and your office were without jurisdiction to hear and determine the issues presented by Van Brunt's contest.

It has been repeatedly held by this Department that in contest cases jurisdiction is acquired by due service of notice upon the claimant, and if there has been no legal notice to the claimant, then there is no authority in the local office or your office to adjudicate his rights.

Stayton v. Carroll (7 L.D., 198) and cases there cited.

It is apparent that the publication of notice in this case was irregular and was not sufficient to confer jurisdiction upon the Land Department to hear and decide the same.

You will, therefore, direct that a rehearing be had in the case upon proper notice under the rules, both to the claimant and to Allyn, his transferee. When such rehearing shall have been had you will readjudicate the case upon the testimony submitted thereat, and your said office decision is modified accordingly.

Inasmuch as but for the defect in the notice herein, the application of Allyn must have been denied, the case furnishes an opportune occasion for a reiteration of the principle announced in the case of the American Investment Company (5 L. D., 603). In that case it was held that an assignee or mortgagee may file in the local office, under oath, a statement showing his interest in any pending entry, and have the same noted on the records of the office; and thereafter he will be entitled to notice of any adverse action in reference to such entry.

If this rule were strictly followed in every case of sale and transfer before patent issues, the transferee would always be in a position to require service of notice whenever the entry of the claimant from whom he purchased is attacked and thus secure to himself the right to be heard in defense of his interests. It is a wise provision, intended for the protection of purchasers prior to patent, by securing to them notice of any proceedings affecting their interests, and it would be well if all such purchasers would take advantage of it. Otherwise they must take the risk of having cases in which they are interested, heard and finally determined without their knowledge.

MINERAL ENTRY—ADVERSE CLAIM.

PETIT v. BUFFALO GOLD AND SILVER MG. CO.

All rights or interests adverse to the applicant will be held as adjudicated in his favor if not asserted in the manner and within the period provided by the statute.

First Assistant Secretary Chandler to the Commissioner of the General Land Office, November 21, 1889.

On July 17, 1888, your office declined to allow appeal from decision thereof, dismissing the protest of Caroline S. Petit against the issue of patent to the Buffalo and Idaho Gold and Silver Mining Company, for the Silver Tide lode and mill-site claim, being mineral entry No. 71, made October 14, 1884, at the Hailey, Idaho, land office. Application was then made by Petit to this Department for certiorari, which was granted, and in pursuance thereof the papers in the case are now before me.

An examination of the record discloses that on November 1, 1883, application for patent for the lode claim and mill-site was filed by the company in the local office, setting forth the discovery and location of the Silver Tide lode by the grantors of the company on April 1, 1877. Due publication and posting were made from November 3, 1883, to January 5, 1884. During this period, and on December 31, 1883, Mrs. Petit, claiming to be " the lawful owner and entitled to the possession of about three-fourths acres of said Silver Tide lode and mill-site," as described in the application, filed in the local office a " protest against the issuing of a patent thereon," declaring that she " does dispute and contest the right of said applicant therefor," and asked that " all further proceedings in the matter be stayed until a final settlement and adjudication of the rights of the contestant can be heard in a court of competent jurisdiction."

On April 24, 1884, the Buffalo Gold and Mining Company moved to dismiss the adverse claim of Mrs. Petit, and that said company be allowed to proceed with its application for patent. No action appears to have been taken on this last motion, but, on October 14, 1884, proofs, showing full compliance with the prerequisites of the law having been filed, and also the certificate of the clerk of the proper court that no suit involving the right of possession to any portion of the Silver Tide Lode or Mill-site was then pending, or had been pending during the five years previous, the company was permitted to make payment and entry in accordance with the application; and on October 17, 1884, the papers in the matter were transmitted to your office. Four days thereafter protest was again filed by Mrs. Petit in the local office against the issue of patent, the substantial allegation being that the land embraced in the application is not the same as was included in the Silver Tide lode as originally located; that by the survey filed said location has been deflected from its true course so as to overlap and include land in which protestant has an interest, and which was not within the lines of the proper location of said lode. The detailed allegations, as set forth in the other papers filed with this protest, are the same as those in the adverse claim or first protest—in fact, they seem to have been copied therefrom. These papers were duly forwarded to your office.

On June 2, 1885, the attorney of Mrs. Petit called your attention to this protest, and asked that you reject the survey of the Silver Tide claim and mill-site, and cause another to be made to conform to the alleged original location of the lode, or that a hearing be ordered to ascertain whether or not the survey conforms to the location.

On April 1, 1887, Commissioner Sparks wrote to the register and receiver, that " the original and amended location certificates on file do not describe the ground with sufficient definiteness to enable me to establish the locus of the claim," and a hearing was ordered, " for the purpose of determining whether the said Silver Tide lode claim, as surveyed, applied for and entered, follows the course of the vein and falls within the limits of the claim as located." In accordance with these in-structions, a hearing was had, after due notice; testimony and argu-ments were submitted by both sides. On October 11, 1887, the register and receiver decided in favor of claimants, and recommended that the protest be dismissed. November 10, 1887, a rehearing was asked for, which was denied, and an appeal taken to your office, where, on May 3, 1888, the decision of the register and receiver was affirmed.

Mrs. Petit, having due notice of the application of the company, filed an adverse claim, which not being duly prosecuted, as required by law, was properly disregarded by the local officers, who allowed the entry to be made.

Section 2326 of the Revised Statutes provides that:

It shall be the duty of the adverse claimant, within thirty days after filing his claim, to commence proceedings in a court of competent jurisdiction to determine the question of the right of the possession, and prosecute the same with reasonable dili-gence to final judgment; and a failure so to do shall be a waiver of his adverse claim.

In relation to this subject, it was said by this Department, in the case of the Snow Flake Lode, 4 L. D., 30:

All the prerequisites of the law were complied with; due publication was made whereby adverse claimants were notified to come in: failing to do so within proper time the entry was made as a matter of course. Thereafter other parties were pre-cluded from setting up adverse claim in their own behalf for the premises, for it is considered that, where notice was properly given, all matters which might have been tried under the adverse proceedings are treated as adjudicated in favor of the appli-cants; and all controversies touching the same are to be held as fully settled and disposed of, as though judgment had been regularly entered in their favor.

Under the statute and its construction by this Department, as above, if Mrs. Petit claimed any rights or interests in the premises adverse to those of the company, they must be treated as having been "adjudi-cated in favor of the applicant," and can not and will not be considered in the determination of this case. Her claims and pretensions being thus eliminated, the case becomes one between the United States and the applicants for patent only, the question being as to compliance on their part with the prerequisite conditions of the law.

*   *   *   *   *   *

TIMBER CULTURE—SALE AND RELINQUISHMENT.

WILLIAMSON v. WEIMER.

The sale and relinquishment of a timber culture claim afford proper grounds for a contest, and if proved call for cancellation of the entry.

First Assistant Secretary Chandler to the Commissioner of the General Land Office, November 21, 1889.

I have considered the case of Benjamin F. Williamson v. William B. Weimer upon the appeal of the latter from your office decision of August

7, 1888, holding for cancellation his timber culture entry for the SE. ¼, of section 12, T. 28 N., R. 14 W., Niabrara land district, Nebraska.

Weimer made timber culture entry for the said land July 6, 1883, and on June 27, 1885, Williamson initiated contest against it, charging that " Weimer has for a valuable consideration sold said claim and relinquished the same in writing and that the entry thereof was fraudulent from its first inception and that one J. M. Rosebury is holding said relinquishment and is holding a bond for a deed to said tract of land given by said William B. Weimer."

Hearing was set for August 24, 1885. At the time appointed both parties appeared and were represented by their respective attorneys. The contestant presented his testimony, the claimant cross examined contestant's witnesses but failed to introduce any testimony. When the evidence was closed, claimant filed a motion for the dismissal of the contest for the reason that the evidence in the case did not support the charges made and because there was no legal evidence before the local officers. No direct order seems to have been rendered upon this motion, but the local officers having considered the evidence in the case rendered dissenting decisions, the receiver deciding in favor of the claimant, the register for the contestant.

Each party filed an appeal in the case. Your office by your said decision affirmed the action of the register and held claimant's entry for cancellation.

Claimant thereupon presented his appeal from your said decision and the case is before this Department for consideration.

It is shown by the evidence in the case, that claimant had, prior to contest, parted with his interest in the claim by a sale of it to one Roseberry for the consideration of two hundred and seventy-five dollars. The sale had been fully consummated; the papers by which the land was conveyed, including a relinquishment had been executed by claimant and delivered to the said Roseberry, and the consideration at least a large part of it had been paid to claimant and by him used to assist his father. These facts were proven by legitimate testimony. In a conversation which the claimant held with the contestant and in a letter written by the former to a relative all the facts above set out were admitted by the claimant. The letter was properly admitted in evidence. The declarations of Roseberry which he made, the claimant not being present, are not competent testimony and have not been considered. The papers executed and passed to Roseberry on the sale were not produced in evidence; Roseberry himself was not a witness in the case, but claimant's attorney in the cross-examination of contestant, who had been shown these papers by Roseberry proved their character and substantially their contents. It is wholly immaterial whether the papers for the sale were properly executed and acknowledged; if the claimant for a valuable consideration received, sold the claim and his improvements thereon, no matter how the papers are made out, his interest in the claim is at an end; thereafter he holds it not for his own use and benefit and the entry, upon the facts being shown, will be canceled. See Lilly *v.* Thom (4 L. D., 245); Pickett *v.* Engle (4 L. D., 522);

On the day of trial, after its close, claimant filed with the local officers his affidavit and the affidavit of the said Roseberry. These affidavits are not evidence and their contents can not be considered.

Your said office decision is affirmed.

TIMBER CULTURE CONTEST—PLANTING—CULTIVATION.

MALE *v.* HEIRS OF QUACKENBUSH.

A slight deficiency in the acreage planted will not justify cancellation where a greater number of trees are growing on the land than is required on the statutory ten acres at date of final proof.

That the land is in a weedy condition will not warrant a finding of bad faith in cultivation if the requisite number of trees are in a healthy growing condition.

First Assistant Secretary Chandler to the Commissioner of the General Land Office, November 21, 1889.

I have considered the case of Charles Male *v.* The Heirs of John Quackenbush upon the appeal of the former from your office decision of July 16, 1888, dismissing his contest against the entry of John Quackenbush for the NE. ¼ of Sec. 18, T. 132 N., R. 48 W., Fargo land district, Dakota.

On March 21, 1878, John Quackenbush made timber culture entry. He died February 20, 1883, leaving surviving him a widow and three children, respectively of the ages of twenty-one, seventeen and thirteen years. On January 4, 1886, Charles Male filed his affidavit of contest, alleging,

That the said Quackenbush in his life-time and his heirs and representatives since his death, have wholly failed to cultivate ten acres to seeds, trees or cuttings upon said tract and have failed to plant trees, seeds or cuttings on the ten acres required by law to be planted on said land within the time required by law.

Hearing was set for February 17, 1886. The parties by their respective attorneys stipulated that the hearing be continued to March 17, 1886, and that the testimony be taken in the case on that day and succeeding days before Charles E. Wolfe, notary public.

The testimony was accordingly so taken. The local officers having considered the same rendered a decision as follows:

The plaintiff contends that the requisite amount of breaking was not done within the two years next following the date of entry, but we attach no importance to this point, for it lacked at most, but a portion of an acre, and no bad faith on the part of the entryman is shown. Then again, there had been twenty-seven acres or thereabouts, of the tract broken before the commencement of the contest. The contestant has also failed to show, we think, that the requisite area was not planted to tree seeds or that the land planted did not receive the proper cultivation during the life-time of the entryman and up to the time of his death. But since that time, what little cultivation or attention it has received seems to have been entirely inadequate to answer the requirement of the timber-culture laws, as we understand them ; and we are of the opinion that upon this branch of the case the plaintiff has substantially established the truth of the complaint. We, therefore, find as conclusion of law that the entry should be canceled, and it is so adjudged and determined.

The heirs of the entryman having appealed to your office, you, in your said office decision, hold with the local officers " that no ground for cancellation is shown to exist on the score of failure to plant the area required by law to be planted."

Upon the question of the cultivation of the trees your office concluded that sufficient cultivation under the circumstances of the case, has been shown by the testimony, you therefore reversed the decision of the local officers and dismissed the contest.

The contestant appealed from this decision of your office and the case is now before this department for consideration.

Upon the charge of the contestant, that ten acres had not been planted to trees, your office and the local officers concur in the opinion that the same is not sustained by the evidence.

In your said decision, it is stated,

By the testimony of one surveyor who measured the land in this tract, planted to trees, seeds and cuttings, there are 9.56 acres. Other evidence corroborated by measurement places the area so planted at 9.77 acres. Either measurement tends to show that a *bona fide* effort to plant the area required by law was made and that the shortage if any really exists, is to be excused as the consequence of a mistake.

On this part of the case the proof shows that the entryman caused to be broken what was supposed to be ten acres in the spring of 1878; eighty rods east and west and twenty rods north and south. The area actually broken was in fact ten acres or very little short of it. This area with the exception of small strips on the east and west ends of it was planted to trees; the western part, approximately six acres, to white willow cuttings in the spring of 1880, the eastern part, approximately four acres, to box elder seeds in the spring of 1884. The said eastern portion was replanted with cuttings or tree seeds twice, because of failure of growth of the trees; the last time in the fall of 1883. The area so planted to trees contained according to one measurement nine acres and fifty-six one hundredths, according to another survey made in the interest of the defendant, nine acres and seventy-seven one hundredths.

The number of trees growing on this area was shown by the evidence on the part of the contestant to be seven thousand five hundred and twenty-six. Admitting this number to be correct, though defendant's witnesses make the number of trees upon an actual count much larger, it appears that there were more trees growing on this land than the law requires at the time of final proof; under these circumstances it seems to me that the slight deficiency in the area planted to trees should

not cause the cancellation of the entry. Most assuredly I can not conclude that the good faith of the entryman or his heirs is thereby impugned.

Regarding the question whether the trees planted were cultivated
and properly cared for the testimony is very conflicting. The condition
of the land planted to trees has been shown to have been weedy and
grassy for years. Witnesses that lived in the neighborhood of the land
testify that they saw little or no cultivation during the later years of
the entry. On the part of the defence the condition of the land is
hardly denied. Wells Quackenbush, the son of the entryman, testifies
that there has been cultivation of the land planted to trees more or less
every year since the trees were planted up to 1885. He is supported
by other testimony in this statement. In the year 1885 the western
part planted to trees in 1880 was left uncultivated, the trees growing
on the eastern part were cultivated by hoeing; it appears that a man
was engaged in that year about two weeks, in clearing the trees of
weeds. It seems that aside from the weeds the trees are in a healthy
condition. I think that good faith may well be found from the exer-
tions made by the defendants and their ancestor regarding the planting of trees and their culture. At any rate a large number of trees
more than are ultimately required at time of final proof, are growing on
the land. I do not think the entry should be canceled. Your decision
is therefore affirmed.

TIMBER CULTURE CONTEST—PRIORITY OF RIGHT.

ARTHUR B. CORNISH.

A contest, filed during the pendency of proceedings by the government against the
entry, confers no preference right on the cancellation of the entry under said
proceedings.

Failure to appeal from the refusal of an application to contest an entry is a waiver of
any precedence that might have been asserted under the contest.

The rejection of a timber culture contest necessarily carries with it the accompanying
application to enter.

*First Assistant Secretary Chandler to the Commissioner of the General
Land Office November* 21, 1889.

I have considered the case of Arthur B. Cornish on his appeal from
your office decision of September 11, 1888, rejecting his application to
make timber culture entry for W. ½, SW. ¼, and W. ½, NW. ¼, Sec. 29
in T. 15 N., R. 22 W., North Platte, Nebraska, land district.

It appears from the record that on September 19, 1887, Watson R.
Savidge filed affidavit of contest against the timber culture entry of
Samuel L. Savidge for said land made December 9, 1882, and notice
issued citing said parties to appear on November 17, 1887.

On November 16, 1887, Cornish presented an affidavit of contest against said claim, subject to that of Savidge. With his affidavit of contest Cornish presented an application to make timber culture entry for said land.

It appears however, that by letter "P" of November 11, 1887, your office had instructed the local officers to call upon the original entry-man to show cause why his entry should not be canceled as recommended by the report of a special agent of the Land Department, and the local officers informed the said Watson R. Savidge of this fact and told him that no testimony could be taken upon his contest, and he, therefore, did not attend upon the day set for the hearing and his contest was dismissed.

On November 21, 1887, said Cornish by his attorney asked that notice issue on his contest, but this was refused by the local officers for the reason that the said proceeding was pending on the part of the government looking to the cancellation of said entry. From this decision of the local officers Cornish took no appeal.

On March 19, 1888, your office canceled the said entry upon testimony procured by the special agent, and on March 30, Watson R. Savidge was allowed to make homestead entry for the tract.

On March 31, 1888, Cornish appeared at the local office and claimed that he was the first legal applicant for said land because of his application filed November 16, 1887, and that he should have a preference right of entry by reason of his having presented said contest affidavit.

Upon refusal of the local officers to allow Cornish to make entry on March 31, 1888, he appealed to your office, which by the decision complained of, affirmed that of the local office.

Pending this appeal said W. R. Savidge on August 17, 1888, relinquished his homestead entry for said land and on the same day timber culture entry was made therefor by James A. Davis.

This entry of Davis was in turn canceled April 23, 1889, and timber culture entry therefor was made by one Levi Stevens on the same day.

As the government had instituted proceedings looking toward the cancellation of the original entry, and upon which it was subsequently canceled, and which proceedings were pending when both the contest of W. R. Savidge and that of Cornish were filed, neither of them acquired any preference right of entry by reason of such contests. Drury v. Shetterly (9 L. D., 211).

Had Cornish appealed from the refusal of the local officers of November 21, 1887, to issue notice upon his affidavit of contest, he might have maintained his application to contest as pending under the rule in Conly v. Price (9 L. D., 490), but by failure to appeal from their said decision he lost or waived whatever precedence he might have had by reason of such contest affidavit and application to enter.

By the cancellation of the original entry March 19, 1888, said land became part of the public domain and the local officers very properly permitted W. R. Savidge to make entry for said land, not under any preference right but as the first legal applicant, and when Cornish ap plied on March 31, 1888, claiming to be first legal applicant, and desiring to proceed and prove the allegations of his contest affidavit he had no other or different rights at that time than a stranger to the record, and he can only be considered as a person who on March 31, 1888, applied to contest a timber culture entry which had been canceled on March 19, 1888, and homestead entry for the same land made by another party. No contest would of course lie against an entry which did not exist at the time it was offered, and his application on March 31, 1888, was, therefore, properly rejected.

Such rejection necessarily carried with it his application to enter. Drury *v.* Shetterly (9 L. D., 211).

Your said decision is accordingly affirmed.

MINING CLAIM—LOCATION—EXCLUDED GROUND.

INDEPENDENCE LODE.

A location, under which the land containing the improvements has been excluded in favor of a subsequent locator, will not support a mineral entry under section 2325.

Secretary Noble to the Commissioner of the General Land Office, November 22, 1889.

I have considered the case of mineral entry No. 1734, Independence Lode, Leadville, Colorado, land district, on appeal of Samuel Selden *et al.*, owners of said claim from your decision of February 26, 1888, holding for cancellation said entry.

The ground of your said decision is,—

satisfactory evidence of the existence of mineral within claimed ground, and of the statutory expenditure upon the claim as entered, required by office letter of May 26, 1884, not having been filed within the time allowed, nor since.

Said letter of May 26, 1884, directed to the local officers, is as follows,

Gentlemen ;

I have examined the papers in the matter of mineral entry No. 1734 made June 9, 1883, by S. Selden, *et al.*, upon the Independence lode claim, and find that the location thereof is based on a discovery in ground excluded from the application and entry, and included in the "Winnie" lode claim, survey No. 2305.

The Independence claim was located August 30, 1881, *prior* to the location of the Winnie which is of date October 26, 1881.

The location of the Independence appears to have been regular in all respects, and is, as far as disclosed by the record, a valid location. The case is thus brought within the ruling of the Hon. Secretary of the Interior in the matter of the Kangaroo Tunnel Lode Number Two *v.* the Metropolitan Number Two Lode * (9 C. L. O., 55).

The claimants will, therefore, be allowed sixty days from date of notice, in which

---

* This case is reported under the title of "Gustavus Hagland."

to show by clear and satisfactory proof, that at the date of application for patent for the Independence lode claim, the existence and continuation of the lode within the *claimed* ground was well known and determined; and that the $500 in labor and improvements, certified to by the surveyor-general, were expended for the purposes of developing a vein or lode *therein*.

On March 17, 1886, your office directed a letter to the local officers concerning said mineral entry No. 1734, in which it was said,—

I am now in receipt of your letter of February 8, last, transmitting additional evidence, consisting of an affidavit by S. Selden and a deed purporting to convey to the Independence lode owners the ground in conflict with the Winnie lode claim on which the discovery shaft of the Independence claim is situated.

The records of this office show that said conflicting area is embraced in the prior application and entry of the Winnie lode claim, survey No. 2306, mineral entry No. 1512, your series. Therefore the deed submitted cannot be considered. The said conflicting area being embraced in a prior subsisting application for patent can not be patented to another and later applicant, and the Independence lode entry can only be considered with reference to the area actually applied for, and embraced therein, which excludes said conflict.

It appears from the record that the Independence lode was regularly located upon the ground and within the lines now asked to be patented, but subsequent to the location of said lode the Winnie lode was located crossing the Independence lode nearly at right angles at the point where the discovery shaft of said Independence lode is situated and embracing said shaft within its said lines. The owners of the Winnie subsequently applied for a patent and the owners of the Independence, in pursuance of an agreement to that effect, made no protest as adverse claimants, and the owners of the Winnie made a deed to them for the conflicting portions of the claim.

The evidence shows that the discovery shaft upon the Independence has been sunk to the depth of sixty-nine feet and according to the surveyor-general's certificate this discovery shaft constitutes the whole of the improvements upon the Independence claim, and while he certifies that its value is not less than five hundred dollars, it appears to be entirely within the boundaries of another claim.

In Gustavus Hagland (1 L. D., 591), it was held that if no adverse claim is filed during the required period of publication, it is assumed that the applicant is entitled to patent, and no agreement of parties can control this statutory provision.

In Antediluvian Lode and Mill Site (8. L. D., 602), it was held that patent will not issue on an application wherein the land upon which are situated the discovery shaft, and improvements is expressly excepted therefrom, and the proof fails to show the discovery or existence of mineral on the claim as entered, or the requisite expenditure for the benefit thereof.

The owners of the Independence claim having waved all right to the portion of their original location covered by the subsequent location of the Winnie, have thereby expressly excluded the conflicting territory from the Independence, and as all their improvement is within such territory, it follows that there has not been the necessary improvement made *within* the boundaries of said Independence claim, as required by section 2325, Revised Statutes.

Your said decision is accordingly affirmed.

TIMBER AND STONE LANDS—SETTLEMENT RIGHTS.

JOHN W. SETCHEL.

The Department has full jurisdiction over a timber land entry, and may for proper reasons cancel the same at any time before patent, and this jurisdiction is not affected by the claim of a transferee.

While the timber land act does not exclude from the operation of the pre-emption law lands chiefly valuable for timber and stone, yet settlement claims on such land should be carefully scrutinized.

A pretended or colorable settlement, made for the purpose of securing the timber on the land, will not support a pre-emption entry for said land.

First Assistant Secretary Chandler to the Commissioner of the General Land Office, November 23, 1889.

I have considered the case of John W. Setchel on his appeal from your office decision of September 12, 1888, holding for cancellation his pre-emption cash entry for W. ½, SE. ¼ and E. ½, SW. ¼, Sec. 14, T. 1 N., R. 2 E., H. M., Humboldt, California land district.

On March 3, 1883, Setchel filed his declaratory statement for said land alleging settlement December 15, 1882, and on December 22, 1883, he presented his final proof and after making payment received cash certificate.

On July 5, 1886, Special Agent B. F. Bergen reported that he had made personal examination of said tract and found that the improvements consisted of a small cabin worth about $15, with no land fenced or cultivated; and he further reported that the land was timber land and wholly unfit for cultivation if cleared.

Upon this report, a hearing was ordered and upon the evidence introduced by both parties the local office found against the entryman and your office on appeal reached the same conclusion.

After making cash entry Setchel sold the undivided one-half of the land to George M. Connick, the consideration being $150. Said Connick had made the first improvement on the land and Setchel had purchased his improvements before filing his declaratory statement.

The grounds of appeal from your decision are substantially; error in holding that the land was of such character that it could only be disposed of under the timber land act; in holding that the government had jurisdiction to cancel a cash entry after a purchase in good faith by one who has no notice of any deficiency in the proof; and lastly, that the said decision is not sustained by the evidence.

It appears from the evidence taken at said hearing that said land is high and mountainous, very badly cut up by ravines and gulches, very steep and quite rocky. The whole tract is very heavily timbered with redwood and with some pine and fir; most of the witnesses estimating that not less than ten million feet of lumber was growing thereon. They also testify that it would cost $500 to $600 per acre to properly clear the land and that there was no sawmill within reach for the purpose of manufacturing the timber into lumber.

The majority of the witnesses who had made personal examination of the tract testified that but little of the land could be plowed if cleared, and that only in patches so small as to be practically useless for farming purposes. That when cleared the land could only be used for raising grass and perhaps fruit, and would not be worth more than from $10 to $15 per acre.

It further appears that with the exception of two abandoned cabins, situated on opposite corners, there is not the least improvement on the tract, no ground cleared, fenced or cultivated. The entryman however introduced evidence showing that he had built a shanty on adjoining land through mistake and had cut the small timber and part of the large timber from about three acres, and had put a rail fence around the same, and that he had dug up with a grubbing hoe or spade about three-fourths of an acre on which he had planted a few beans and potatoes and sowed a little oats. The cabin on this land had been crushed by a falling tree after final proof and never rebuilt.

The claimant testified that part of the land might be cultivated if cleared but he could not estimate the amount which could be cultivated, he said, however, he did not think there was as much as forty acres.

The claimant in reply to a question regarding his object in making the entry said,

I thought I would go out there and clear up a piece and set out a few fruit trees, and the time would soon come when it would be logged off, and then it would be a small job to clear it.

Q. Did you expect to clear it off and put it under cultivation when you applied to enter it?

A. No, sir; not at once.

The claimant also further replied to cross interrogatories as follows;

Q. Would you consider the land involved in your pre-emption entry susceptible of cultivation were the timber cleared off?

A. Yes, sir; for fruit raising and pasture land.

Q. Could any of it be plowed?

A. Well, yes; some of it could be plowed.

Q. Can you ride over it in its present condition on horseback?

A. Yes sir; quite a good part of it.

Upon the second ground of appeal it is sufficient to say that the line of departmental decisions holding that the government has jurisdiction of an entry and may for proper reasons cancel the same at any time before patent and this regardless of the claims of any transferee, and that a transferee before patent takes it subject to any infirmities which may appear against the entry, is unbroken.

Upon the issue raised by the first ground of appeal there are several decisions.

In Hughes *v.* Tipton (2 L. D., 334), it was held that lands "unfit for ordinary agricultural purposes," when heavily timbered were those meant by the words of the timber land act of June 3, 1878 (20 Stats., 89), "valuable chiefly for timber, but unfit for cultivation."

It is also held in said case that if the land covered with timber had a surface so precipitous, rocky, or broken, as to unfit it for raising crops in the "ordinary manner and quantity," it would be chiefly valuable for timber. Or if the patches of arable land scattered here and there aggregated a less quantity than those parts unfit for cultivation the same rule would obtain.

In Wright *v.* Larson (7 L. D., 555), it is said that while lands chiefly valuable for timber and stone, and unfit for ordinary agricultural purposes, are not excluded from settlement by the act of June 3, 1878, yet settlement on such lands

should be closely scrutinized, and the fact that the land is of such a character, might be a circumstance, taken in connection with the other facts in the case, shedding light upon the question of the *bona fides* of the settler.

It was further said in Wright *v.* Larson:

It appears from the evidence, that the tract in dispute was six or seven miles from any other settlement in a dense forest of fir timber, and accessible only by a foot path, that it had been returned by the surveyor-general as timber land, and had on it (according to the estimate of the witness) 4,000,000 feet of merchantable timber; and, ... it appeared from the testimony incidentally that the soil was poor, broken and gravelly, and that it would require the expenditure of an amount wholly disproportionate to any possible returns which could be expected from such land to clear and prepare it for cultivation.

In the case at bar, the evidence shows that claimant was an unmarried man and after making the improvement above mentioned upon the land adjoining, he remained most of the time at a place forty or fifty miles distant from the land where he was at work, making infrequent visits to said claim, and that soon after final proof he had entirely abandoned the tract not even rebuilding the house after it was crushed by the falling tree, although as he testified he had no suspicion that it was not upon the land entered until he had heard the testimony at the hearing.

The large amount of merchantable timber on the land, and its worthlessness for ordinary agricultural purposes taken in consideration with the amount and character of the improvements, the slight duration of actual residence shown and the claimant's statement that he had not intended to prepare the land for cultivation, until such time as it should be "logged off" and thereby rendered easy to clear, together with the whole record, convinces me, that his was not a *bona fide* settlement for the purpose of establishing a home on the land, but that it was a pretended or at most a colorable settlement, made with a view to securing the benefit of the timber thereon, and that Mr. Connick can not stand in the position of a *bona fide* purchaser of this tract so as to prevent the government from inquiring into the facts surrounding this entry has been too often decided by the department to merit further discussion. Traveler's Insurance Co., 9 L. D., 316.

Your said office decision is accordingly affirmed.

PROCEEDINGS ON SPECIAL AGENTS' REPORT—TRANSFEREE.

UNITED STATES *v.* THOMAS ET AL.

Under any proceedings that may involve the cancellation of an entry, a transferee has the right to be heard on the question of the entryman's compliance with law.

A transferee may file with the local officers a statement, under oath, disclosing his interest in any entry, and thereafter be entitled to notice of any proceedings against said entry.

The local officers are under no obligation to search the county records, before giving notice of a hearing or contest, to ascertain whether the land has been transferred or encumbered.

If a special agent in his investigation of an entry is informed of a transfer he should search the records for evidence thereof.

A transferee whose interest is duly shown on the county records, may be allowed a hearing, where the entry, without notice to him, is canceled under proceedings based upon the report of a special agent.

First Assistant Secretary Chandler to the Commissioner of the General Land Office, November 23, 1889.

I have considered the appeal of Nicholas Petcovich, transferee of Rush Thomas, from your office decision of October 4, 1888, refusing to re-open the case of the United States *v.* Rush Thomas, decided by your office August 4, 1888, involving the title to NE. ¼, Sec. 12, T. 12 S., R. 19 E., M. D. M., Stockton, California.

It appears from the record that Rush Thomas made homestead entry for said land June 5, 1886, and in August, 1887, he presented final commutation proof which showed that he had established residence on said land with his family November 24, 1886, and that he had occupied the same continuously thereafter, not having been absent more than a few days at a time and his family were not absent at all. His house was a double plank house with two rooms and a hall and contained household and kitchen furniture in sufficient quantities. He had also out buildings and had cultivated to crop about forty acres. No apparent defect existed in said proof and final certificate was issued and payment for the land was made.

On February 18, 1888, R. W. Anderson, a special agent of the general land office reported that on January 27, 1888, he had made personal examination of the land and that he did not find the entryman on the land and that he had not been there since making final proof; that said land was reported sold but he had not been able to find any deed on record. He reported the existence of improvements upon the land and cultivation of the same about as shown in final proof, and stated that entryman with his wife and children had resided upon the land for the time required by law, but upon the affidavit of one Dan McGraw, he recommended the entry for cancellation as fraudulent because made for the use and benefit of one J. N. Walker.

Upon this report your office held said entry for cancellation by letter of April 10, 1888; personal service of notice was given entryman, but there being no appeal, on August 4, 1888, your office canceled said entry.

On September 15, 1888, one Nicholas Petcovich filed in the local office an application asking that said case be re-opened and alleging under oath that he was a transferee, in good faith after final proof, by deed made and recorded September 27, 1887, and had not been notified of any objection to the entry and asking that he be allowed to show that said entryman had fully complied with the law in good faith.

Upon this application your office by letter of October 4, 1888, said,

There was nothing in the record before this office to show that the land had been sold to Petcovich, and it is not shown that your office (the local office) had knowledge that such was the case, and he was therefore not entitled to notice. See case of Cyrus H. Hill, 5 L. D., 276.

The application for a hearing presented by said transferee alleged under oath that said Petcovich and one Mahoney had purchased said land from said entryman on September 27, 1887, and that on the same day they had filed their deed therefor in the office of the recorder of deeds for the county in which the land is situated and that the same was duly recorded long before the said special agent made his alleged search of the records, and that on December 1, 1887, said Petcovich had purchased from said Mahoney his interest in said land and that on the same day the deed from said Mahoney was filed for record and duly recorded. He further states that on the 6th day of December, 1887, he started to Europe on a business trip, from which he did not return until July 10, 1888, when he returned to the county in which said land is situated but that he received no notice of proceedings to cancel said entry and had no knowledge thereof until the 9th day of September, 1888. He presented also the affidavit of Rush Thomas contradicting all the allegations of the special agent upon which cancellation was made and also presented certified copies of the two deeds hereinbefore mentioned showing the date of filing for record in each.

In your said decision reference is made to the case of Cyrus H. Hill (5 L. D., 276), as authority therefor.

Upon inspection of said case I find the facts therein differ materially from those in the case at bar. It appears also that when served with notice entryman appealed; and it further appears that the special affidavit of entryman filed as part of his final proof admitted such a state of facts in regard to residence as precluded the theory of any showing that he had complied with the law, and the mortgagee does not appear to have alleged any new facts tending to show compliance with the law, or to have alleged that compliance with the law could be shown. It will be observed too, that the said Hill decision was upon a motion for review, and would require a much stronger showing than if made upon an appeal.

That a transferee of land after final proof but before patent, has the right to be heard upon the question whether the entryman has complied with the law, in any proceedings looking toward the cancellation of the entry, has been the uniform ruling of this Department. See R. M. Sherman (4 L. D., 544), and Windsor v. Sage (6 L. D., 440), and authorities cited. And while the transferee may be allowed to show that the entryman had complied with the law, the local officers are under no obligation to make a search of county records for the purpose of ascertaining whether or not the land has been transferred or encumbered before giving notice of hearing or contest. (Wm. W. Waterhouse, 9 L. D., 131). Especially where vendees of entrymen may file statement under oath of their interest with the register and receiver and be entitled to notice of all subsequent proceedings. American Investment Co. (5 L. D., 603).

There is nothing in said Waterhouse decision which should be construed to bar a hearing in this case, as, if the special agent had done his full duty after being informed that the land had been sold as stated in his report, by searching the records, the deeds to Petcovich would have been discovered and notice given him by the local officers.

Your decision is accordingly reversed, the entry will be re-instated, and a hearing will be ordered after due notice to all parties in interest.

TIMBER CULTURE APPLICATION—RULE 53 OF PRACTICE.

SABEN v. AMUNDSON.

An application to make timber culture entry, while pending, segregates the land covered thereby.

During the pendency of a case on appeal, the local office is prohibited from taking any action that will affect the disposal of the land involved.

The right of a third party to enter land involved in a pending contest must remain in abeyance until final disposition of the contest.

First Assistant Secretary Chandler to the Commissioner of the General Land Office, November 25, 1889.

July 11, 1882, Jeff. Amundson made application to enter under the timber culture law the S. ½ of NW. ¼ and N. ½ of SW. ¼, Sec. 29, T. 102 N., R. 25 W., Worthington district, Minnesota. The application was rejected by the local officers, because of conflict with the claim of the Chicago, Milwaukee and St. Paul Railway Company to said land. Amundson having appealed from the ruling of the local officers, your office, by letter of November 18, 1888, decided the case adversely to the railway company, holding its selections of the land for cancellation. The company thereupon appealed, and, by decision of February 25, 1889, this Department modified your office decision by directing a hearing to be had "to determine the status of the tract at date of selection, and whether it was occupied by a qualified pre-emptor." (8 L. D., 291).

On September 13, 1887, while Amundson's appeal from the ruling of the local officers was pending before your office, they allowed Andrew O. Saben to make timber culture entry for a part of the land, namely, the N. ½ of SW. ¼ of said section, and about the same time allowed such entries on the remainder of the tract to be made by Albert Johnson and George Hendrickson. By your office decision of May 26, 1888, the entries of said Saben and said other entrymen were held for cancellation, because of the pendency at the date of their allowance of the prior application of Amundson. Saben now appeals to this Department, alleging, in substance, as ground of appeal, 1st, that the land was public land open to his entry notwithstanding the pendency of Amundson's application, and, 2d, that Amundson had "forfeited by laches all his rights to said land if any he ever had."

The application of Amundson while pending segregated the land from the public domain. This being so, it was not subject to the entries of Saben *et al.* Moreover, after a case has been sent up on appeal, the local officers are expressly forbidden by Rule of Practice 53 from taking any "further action affecting the disposal of the land" involved. The entry of Saben having been allowed without authority was properly held for cancellation by your office.

If, as alleged by appellant, Amundson has by his laches forfeited whatever rights he may have had, this would be ground of contest. So long as Amundson's application remains pending, the only mode open to Saben of acquiring a right to enter the land, is by contest initiated and prosecuted to a successful issue, according to the rules and regulations prescribed therefor. If he file an affidavit of contest pending the disposition of the case between Amundson and the railway company, it should be received and held without further action until the final adjudication of said case. (Eddy *v.* England, 6 L. D., 530.)

The decision of your office is affirmed.

PRACTICE—REVIEW—TRANSFEREE.

CHAS. W. MCKALLOR.

That a transferee is injured by the decision is no ground for review, as his rights are
    in no sense other or different from those of the entryman.

Review will not be allowed on the proposition that a re-examination of the evidence
    may bring about a different result.

If fair minds might reasonably differ as to the conclusion to be drawn from the evi-
    dence, a review will not be granted on the ground that the decision is not sup-
    ported by the evidence.

If no new question is presented, or evidence offered, a motion for review must be de-
    nied.

*Secretary Noble to the Commissioner of the General Land Office, Novem-
    ber 27, 1889.*

I have before me a motion for review of the departmental decision
dated November 27, 1888, in case of Charles W. McKallor, involving
his pre-emption cash entry for E. ½, SE. ¼, Sec. 21 and S. ½, SW. ¼, Sec.
22, T. 153 N., R. 68, Grand Forks, Dakota, land district.

The motion for review is made in behalf of F. I. Kane, transferee of
McKallor's interest, and Joseph C. Hilliard, mortgagee of the land.

Said motion is based upon substantially the following grounds:

1. Because said decision works irreparable injury to said transferee.

2. Because such transferee believes that upon a more careful and considerate examination of the evidence the Department will reverse its said decision.

3. Because said decision is a rigid and strict construction of the provisions of the
law and in opposition to the settled and uniform liberal and beneficial construction
adhered to in most cases.

4. Because the record shows the entryman to have acted in entire good faith and
did the best he could, under the circumstances, to comply with the law.

5. Because said decision fails to apply and give effect to the rulings of the Department in force at the time of entry, under which rulings the compliance shown is
ample to protect a purchaser after final proof and before patent.

Hillard the mortgagee, in his motion to intervene, simply alleges that
he loaned money to entryman in good faith, and took a mortgage on
said land to secure the same relying upon the final receipt of the local
officers as showing that the law had been fully complied with.

Neither Kane nor Hilliard allege an ability to show any different
facts in regard to residence and good faith of entryman.

There is no claim of any newly discovered evidence, and no suggestion of any material fact or point of law not discussed or involved in the
original decision is contained in the motion, nor does it suggest any reason why the supervisory jurisdiction of the Department should be
invoked.

That the transferee may sustain injury by the decision is no ground
for review as his rights are in no sense other or different from those of
the entryman, and the same may be said of the claim of the mortgagee.
A. A. Joline (5 L. D., 589).

The second ground of the motion is substantially upon the theory that the Department did not give careful and considerate examination of the testimony presented by the record before rendering the decision. No such charge can be given any weight whatever.

Review will not be allowed when the motion rests upon the proposition that a re-examination of the evidence before presented may bring about a different result.

Nor will such motion be granted upon the ground that the decision is not supported by the evidence, if fair minds might reasonably differ as to the conclusion to be drawn from the evidence.   Mary Campbell (8 L. D., 331).

As the questions raised by the motion for review are the same as those adjudicated in the decision and no additional evidence is offered the motion should not be allowed.   Fort Brooke Military Reservation (on review) 3 L. D., 556.

The motion is denied.

———

PRACTICE—REVIEW—REHEARING.

KELLEY v. MORAN.

Errors not alleged on appeal can not be set up as ground for review.

An allegation of newly discovered evidence, as a basis for a rehearing, should specifically set forth when the alleged discovery was made.

A rehearing will not be awarded on the ground of newly discovered testimony where it appears that said testimony was, or ought to have been, known before trial and no sufficient excuse is shown for not procuring it.

Newly discovered evidence, merely cumulative in character, will not authorize a rehearing.

Secretary Noble to the Commissioner of the General Land Office, November 27, 1889.

In the case of Milton H. Kelley v. James H. Moran, involving the latter's homestead entry, No. 3434, on the SW. ¼ of Sec. 34, T. 14 N., R. 29 W.; North Platte district, Nebraska, said Moran filed, January 21, 1889, a motion for a rehearing and review of the departmental decision in said case, rendered October 9, 1888.

This motion came up for consideration July 2, 1889, and this Department then addressed your office the following letter, stating the case as presented on said motion and the answer thereto, and calling for the transmittal of the record therein :

Said entry (Moran's) was made February 12, 1883.   Milton H. Kelly initiated contest against the same November 21, 1884, charging abandonment and failure to establish residence.

Hearing was had before the local office January 21, 1885, and on the evidence adduced that office found against the entryman, and recommended the cancellation of his entry.   Your office sustained that finding and held the entry for cancellation.

On appeal, this Department found that the entryman had failed to comply with the law in the matter of residence, and therefore affirmed your said office decision.

Now comes Moran, by his attorney, and moves a review of said departmental decision, and assigns as reasons therefor the following :

1st. That he did not have a fair trial on the hearing in said case.

2d. That he was not permitted to have all of his witnesses sworn.

3d. Because of newly discovered evidence.

Accompanying said motion is an affidavit of claimant, setting out that certain of his witnesses (three of whom he names) did not appear at the trial until the case had so far progressed that his other witnesses had been sworn and had testified, and contestant was offering evidence in rebuttal. That, though he asked at this stage of the proceedings to have one of said tardy witnesses put on the stand and sworn, the register refused to allow said witness, or any of the three whom he names, to be sworn and to testify, ruling that taking of testimony in rebuttal having been entered upon, no further testimony should be introduced by claimant. Claimant further avers that had said witnesses been permitted to go on the stand, they would have testified that affiant had actually and continuously resided on the tract in question for more than nine months preceding the commencement of the contest; that he had eaten, slept and cooked in the house on said land, and that he had ten acres cultivated to crop each year thereon.

As to the newly discovered evidence, he avers that one Purdy would, if present and permitted to testify, swear that he saw affiant at his house nearly every day for six months preceding contest, he (the witness) having passed affiant's house driving cattle to graze; that said witness would also testify that affiant had over ten acres of said tract in an excellent state of cultivation.

Contestant, by his attorney, opposes said motion for review and rehearing, on the ground that the reasons advanced in support of said motion are clearly insufficient, because :

1st. Moran, by electing to appeal from the action of the local office, waived his right to a new trial, if any such existed.

2d. The alleged newly discovered evidence would be merely cumulative.

3d. It does not appear that Moran could not have taken advantage of all the reasons set out in the motion by moving for a new trial before the register and receiver before appealing from their decision.

4th. Said motion is not accompanied with any affidavit that it is not made for the purpose of delay, but is made in good faith.

5th. Said contest has proceeded to a successful issue, Moran's entry having been canceled, and Kelly, the contestant, having been allowed under his preference right to enter the land.

The above objections on their face seem to be pertinent and not without force, but as notice thereof does not appear to have been served upon the claimant, and as their verity can probably be tested by an examination of the record in the case, you will please transmit, at as early a day as practicable, the same, with the return of this letter, to the Department for further examination.

The record has been transmitted, as requested, and carefully examined. The charge by Moran that he "did not have a fair trial on the hearing" before the local officers appears to be based on his allegation, "that he was not permitted to have all his witnesses sworn" and examined. If the local officers erred in not permitting him to introduce said witnesses, this was matter which he could and should have set up on his appeal from their decision. He did not do so, however, but both on his appeal to your office and to this Department chose to stand upon the evidence admitted, claiming that it showed compliance with the law on his part, and that, therefore, the decisions of the local and our office against him were erroneous. To allow him to now set up the alleged erroneous action of the local officers in not permitting him to examine said witnesses, would be to authorize the presentation of his case piecemeal, and this would result in the indefinite prolongation of the litigation.   In case of appeal the general rule is, that " a party is not at liberty to rely upon one set of objections before the court below, and then seek to reverse their judgment upon grounds which had not been distinctly presented for their adjudication." (Hilliard on New Trials, 2d Ed., p. 722.) This rule applies with fully as much, if not greater, force to motions for rehearing or review, and, being necessary to secure to litigant parties the termination of their legal controversies, is of great practical importance and, at least in cases *inter partes*, should be binding on the courts.   Kelley having, at considerable outlay of time, labor and expense, successfully contested the issues, presented by Moran on his appeal to your office and this Department and upon which he elected to rely, has a right to claim that Moran should be held . to his election, and that the case should not now be re-opened at his in- stance on account of an alleged error of which he was cognizant from the outset, but failed to set up.

The allegation by Moran of newly discovered evidence is wholly in- sufficient to authorize the granting of a rehearing. Such allegation should set forth when the alleged discovery was made, in order that it may be determined whether it was acted upon without unnecessary de- lay.   Moreover, as it is claimed that the witness passed Moran's claim and saw him there nearly every day for six months before the contest, it would appear that Moran ought to have known this fact, and he should therefore have averred facts showing a sufficient excuse for his failure to procure the testimony at the hearing.   A rehearing " will not be awarded on the ground of newly discovered testimony, when it ap- pears that the testimony was or ought to have been known to the party before trial and no sufficient excuse is shown for not procuring it. There must have been no delay; and the proof of diligence must be clear." (Hilliard. *supra*, 495; Weldon *v.* McLean, 6 L. D., 9).

Even if due diligence had been shown, however, the said evidence is only "additional evidence, of the same kind and to the same point," as that of Moran and his witnesses at the hearing. It is therefore " merely cumulative (Hilliard *supra* 499), and as it would not, in my opinion, when taken in connection with the evidence introduced, authorize a different conclusion from that arrived at, is no ground for a new trial. "Every one," says Livingston, J., in the case of Steinbach *v.* The Co- lumbian (2 Caines, 129), "must perceive the inconvenience and delay which will arise from granting new trials upon the discovery of new testimony or other witnesses, to the same fact. It often happens that neither party knows all the persons who may be acquainted with some of the circumstances relating to the point in controversy. If a sugges- tion then, of the present kind be listened to, a second, if not a third and fourth trial may always be had. There may be many persons yet unknown to the defendant, who may be material witnesses in this cause, and this may continue to be the case after a dozen trials." (Weldon *v.* McLean, *supra;* Davis & Pennington *v.* Drake 6 L. D., 243).

Motions for rehearings, or for review of a departmental decision, are only allowed " in accordance with legal principles applicable to motions for new trials at law." (Rule of Practice, 76.) The present motion, as shown above, is not in conformity with those principles, and is, moreover, unaccompanied by the affidavit of either Moran or his attorney, that it "is made in good faith and not for the purpose of delay." (Rule of Practice, 78). The motion is denied.

While Moran does not in said motion raise any question as to the correctness of the departmental decision and the decisions of your office and the local officers on the evidence taken .at the hearing, I have duly considered said evidence, and am of the opinion that it fully sustains the conclusions arrived at in said decisions.

PRACTICE—SECOND CONTEST—HEARING.

REEVES *v.* EMBLEN.

While as a rule an entryman should not be called upon to defend against issues already litigated, the Department will not interfere with the discretion of the Commissioner in the matter of ordering hearings, unless a clear abuse of such discretion is shown.

Secretary Noble to the Commissioner of the General Land Office, November 27, 1889.

By letters dated May 15, and May 28, 1889, your office transmitted respectively the papers in the case of David W. Reeves *v.* George F. Emblen, and also the papers in the case of Frank McCue *versus* the same, both involving the NW ¼ Sec. 23 T. 2 N., R. 48 W., Denver, Colorado.

These papers are forwarded for consideration by the Department in pursuance of my letter of April 27, 1889 (8 L. D. 444), upon Emblen's application for certiorari under rules 83 and 84 of practice.

On November 1, 1888, the local officers at Denver, Colorado transmitted the application of Reeves to contest commuted homestead entry No. 11,579, by George F. Emblen, based upon his homestead entry made November 5, 1885 for said tract. Emblen filed a motion to dismiss the said application for the reason that the matters (fraud and failure to comply with the law) upon which it is based were fully gone over in the said case of McCue *v.* Emblen in which, after a hearing on McCue's protest to Emblen's commutation proof the claim of Emblen had been successively sustained by the local officers, by your office and by the Department. This motion was denied, and a hearing ordered on Reeves contest by your office letter of January 17, 1889.

Upon Emblen's motion for review, your office on February 20, 1889, adhered to its former ruling. From the foregoing decisions Emblen appealed to the Department. His appeal was refused by your office, whereupon, as aforesaid, he applied for certiorari.

The said application is based upon the allegation that in the prior contest of McCue v. Emblen, "Emblen met and overcame each and every charge that is now made by Reeves."

Counsel insist that the charges made in the case of McCue v. Emblen as shown by the specifications of error in McCue's appeal to your office from the action of the local office, are substantially the same as those contained in Reeves' application to contest the cash entry of Emblen.

The matters charged by Reeves are stated generally by your office in said letter of January 17, 1889, as follows:

That claimant (Emblen) made said entry for the purpose of speculating in the same as a townsite; that he conspired with one Will A. Clute and caused himself to be driven off said tract so that he might by fraudulent means obtain title to the same; that the homestead proof offered by George F. Emblen upon said tract May 4, 1886, was false and fraudulent and he never was a settler in good faith on said tract.

The matters contained in McCue's said specifications of error and "in substance" in the application of Reeves to contest, as stated by counsel in connection with the application for certiorari, are set out in my said letter of April 27, 1889.

By this letter it was held that the claimant, Emblen, should not be required to defend against charges that had previously been in issue and passed upon by the Department. Parker v. Gamble (3 L. D., 390).

The said application of Reeves to contest the entry of Emblen was by your said office letter of January 17, 1889, returned to the local office as a basis for the hearing therein ordered, and there is no copy of the same among the papers now before me. But the charges, therein contained have, as aforesaid, been generally stated. Upon the application of Emblen for this writ, I deemed it but proper from the showing therein made to grant his prayer, and if from an examination of the record, it was just to the parties, to put an end to his being harassed by further contests upon issues already litigated. With that end in view, I have carefully examined the record in this case and find nothing that indicates an abuse of the discretion of the Commissioner herein, nor such a state of facts as will justify me in interfering with your order directing a hearing as heretofore made, hence the appeal of the defendant is dismissed and you will proceed in the case in the manner originally designed by you and as though this writ had not been granted.

ANDERSON v. BAILEY.

The motion for review of the departmental decision rendered December 13, 1888 (7 L. D., 513) denied by Secretary Noble November 29, 1889.

FINAL PROOF—COUNTY JUDGE.

INSTRUCTIONS.

Under the departmental circular of March 30, 1886, a county judge in the State of
Nebraska, is not authorized to take pre-emption or commuted homestead final
proof.

*Secretary Noble to the Commissioner of the General Land Office, November
30, 1889.*

I am in receipt of your letter of the 21st inst., requesting instructions
as to whether the county judge of Sheridan county, Nebraska, is authorized "to administer oaths in pre-emption and commuted homestead
final proofs under departmental circular of March 30, 1886 (4 L. D.,
473)."

Said circular provides:

Hereafter the following rules will be observed in making final proof in pre-emption
and commuted homestead cases:

1. The entire final proof, including the final affidavit of the claimant, his testimony,
and the testimony of his witnesses shall be taken before the officer designated in the
published notice of intention to make final proof, and at the time therein named.

2. Such final proof shall be taken only before the following officers: the register or
receiver of the proper land district or the clerk of the county court, or of any court
of record, of the county and State, or district and Territory, in which the land is situated, or before such clerk in some adjacent county, in case the land lies in an unorganized county.

Section 2262 Revised Statutes, requires, in pre-emption cases, that
the claimant shall make such final affidavit "before the register or receiver:" section 2301 provides that in case of a commuted homestead,
proof of settlement and cultivation shall be made "as provided by law
granting pre-emption rights."

The act of June 9, 1880 (21 Stats., 169), provides that the affidavit required by sections 2262 and 2301 "may be made before the clerk of the
county court or of any court of record, of the county and State or district and Territory in which the lands are situated; and if said lands
are situated in any unorganized county, such affidavit may be made in
a similar manner in any adjacent county in said State or Territory, and
the affidavit so made and duly subscribed shall have the same force and
effect as if made before the register or receiver of the proper land district; and the same shall be transmitted by such clerk of the court to
the register and receiver with the fee and charges allowed by law."

It will be observed that said circular, in so far as the question here
is involved, closely follows the words of the statute.

The question was presented to your office by the protest, in form of
an appeal, of the county judge of said Sheridan county, who alleges
that said county court is a court of record having a seal; that such

county judges have authority to administer oaths and affirmations; that under the laws of Nebraska a county judge is *ex officio* clerk of the county court.

It may be conceded that these courts are courts of record and have a seal. Schell *v.* Husenstine (15 Neb., 9); State *ex rel.* Fossler *v.* Webster (7 ib., 469); and that such judges may administer certain oaths and affirmations. The statute and regulations above quoted, however, do not authorize the judge, in that capacity, to administer the oaths in question. That is a function of the clerk only.

The only question that remains is, whether such a judge is *ex officio* clerk of his court.

The protestant furnishes no authorities in support of his position on this question.

In the Fossler case, *supra*, the supreme court of the State held that the county court has no jurisdiction over applications for naturalization of aliens under section 2165 Revised Statutes, which provides that an alien who desires to become a citizen of the United States " shall declare on oath before . . . . a court of record of any of the States, having common law jurisdiction and a seal and a clerk," etc. The judgment was based on the ground that no authority is given for the appointment of a clerk for the county judge, by the laws of the State. An examination of the statutes of said State shows that the office of clerk of the county court is unknown to the law.

I therefore conclude that said judge is not authorized to administer the final oaths in question.

I am aware that in the case of John Skelton (4 L. D., 107), it was held that the judge of a county court of Colorado was authorized by virtue of section 2165 R. S., to admit an alien to citizenship. But that ruling rests on the ground that the laws of that State provided for the office of such clerk, its duties and compensation, and, further that the judge, if he prefer, " may elect to perform the duties of clerk and receive the compensation and fees therefor." That case is, therefore, distinguishable from the one at bar. If a practice existed of allowing the judge in question to administer such final affidavits, it must be considered as abolished by said circular of March 30, 1886.

It does not appear that any hardship is worked by the circular in question, or by the law. The statutes of the State provide for the election of a clerk of the district court, in each county having a population of 8,000 inhabitants, and in counties having a population of less than that number the county clerk is *ex officio* clerk of the district court. (Compiled Stat., Neb., p. 258.)

That court is a court of record and the clerk thereof is qualified to administer the oaths in question.

PRACTICE—SECOND REVIEW—RES JUDICATA.

FROST ET AL. *v.* WENIE.

A second motion for review will not be entertained except upon the suggestion of some new fact or question not previously presented or considered.

The decision of an Assistant Secretary of the Interior is in contemplation of law the act of the Secretary, and of the same legal effect.

The Secretary of the Interior, acting through an Assistant, may re-open and reverse his own decision, rendered by another Assistant, without violating the doctrine of *res judicata* as applied to the decisions of the head of a Department.

Secretary Noble to the Commissioner of the General Land Office, November 30, 1889.

This is a motion for review of the departmental decision of April 4, 1889, in the case of Thomas F. Everett *v.* Frederick T. M. Wenie. Most of the matters involved in the present motion have been before this Department and passed upon at least once, if not oftener, in the four decisions rendered in the controversy. Yet all of them have been as fully argued, orally and on brief, in the present application as though none of them had ever before been presented or considered. The effort will be to make the conclusion arrived at so plain there can be no further misapprehension or controversy in regard to it.

The facts, arising out of the controversy over these lots, have been so often recited in the numerous decisions made therein, three of which are published in the "Land Decisions," that the statement now will be confined to such matters as bear more directly upon the disposition of the present motion.

By the second article of the treaty, with the Great and Little Osage tribes of Indians, of June 2, 1825 (7 Stat., 240), a reservation was established in what is now the southern portion of the State of Kansas, for the use of said tribe or nation, " so long as they may choose to occupy the same." By the second article, as amended, of the treaty of September 29, 1865 (14 Stat., 687), with the same Indians, they ceded to the United States a portion of their reservation, extending its entire length, from east to west, and twenty miles wide from north to south ; which lands were to be held in trust for said Indians, to be surveyed and sold for their benefit, " at a price not less than one dollar and twenty-five cents per acre, as other lands are surveyed and sold," and the net proceeds of such sales were to be placed in the Treasury of the United States to the credit of said tribe of Indians.

Fort Dodge military reservation was established June 22, 1868, by, and defined in, general orders No. 17 from Headquarters, Department of Missouri, issued May 29, 1868. The southern boundary of the military reservation as thus defined overlaps the northern boundary of that portion of the Indian reservation, ceded by the second article of said treaty, for about eight miles in length from east to west, with an average width of about two miles from north to south; and these conflicting limits are traversed, for a greater portion, in an easterly and westerly direction by the line of the Atchison, Topeka and Santa Fe Railroad, which has a right of way through the same.

A reference to the legislation of Congress, affecting these lands, seems appropriate, at this point, before entering upon a consideration of the motion for review. The act of January 9, 1837 (5 Stat., 135), provided in substance, that all moneys, received from the sale of lands, theretofore or thereafter ceded by Indians, under treaties, directing either the payment to them of the proceeds of the sale of the same, or the investment thereof, should be paid into the United States Treasury, and the amounts required be withdrawn therefrom, as other moneys are paid in and withdrawn, under the direction of the President; and that special accounts of the funds under the treaties should be kept and reported to Congress. Subsequently, the act of July 22, 1854 (10 Stat., 308), was passed, by section twelve of which it was declared, that all lands to which the Indian title has been or shall be extinguished in the Territories of Nebraska and Kansas shall be subject to the operations of the pre-emption act of September 4, 1841 (5 Stat., 453). This act was supplemented by the act of June 2, 1862 (12 Stat., 62), which made *all* land belonging to the United States, to which the Indian title has been or shall be extinguished, subject to the provisions of the pre-emption act. Inasmuch as the homestead act of May 20, 1862 (12 Stat., 392), provided that entries under that act could be made upon all lands subject to pre-emption, Congress found itself, at the ratification of the treaty of 1865, in the position of, probably, being unable to carry out the trust, on which the Osage lands were ceded, under existing general laws. It, therefore, had recourse to special legislation, whereby the proper mode of disposing of these lands was pointed out, and from time to time quite a number of acts were passed with this object in view. This legislation will be found in the joint resolution of April 10, 1869 (16 Stat., 55), the acts of July 15, 1870 (16 Stat., 362), of May 9, 1872 (17 Stat., 90), of June 23, 1874 (18 Stat., 283), of May 28, 1880 (21 Stat., 143), and of June 16, 1880 (21 Stat., 291). The general purpose of all these acts appears to have been to promote the sale of the lands, ceded by the Indians, to actual settlers having the qualifications of pre-emptors, at the stipulated price; and to secure to the Indians the proceeds of said sales; and, by the last act, where some of said proceeds had not been paid over or where some of the lands had been donated to Kansas for school purposes, reimbursement to the Indian fund was provided for.

Such was the condition of legislation when, on December 15, 1880 (21 Stat., 311), Congress passed, "an act to authorize the Secretary of the Interior to dispose of a part of the Fort Dodge military reservation," etc. It was recited that, whereas a "portion of the Fort Dodge

military reservation " was no longer needed for military purposes, therefore, it was enacted that the Secretary of the Interior shall cause—

all that portion of the Fort Dodge military reservation, in the State of Kansas, being and lying north of land owned and occupied by the Atchison, Topeka and Santa
Fe Railroad Company, for right of way for its railroad, ... to be surveyed,
sectionized and subdivided as other public lands, and after said survey to offer said
lands to actual settlers only under and in accordance with the homestead laws of the
United States. *Provided* said Atchison, Topeka and Santa Fe R. R. Company shall
have the right to purchase such portion of said reservation as it may need for its use,
adjoining that now owned by it, not exceeding one hundred and sixty acres, by paying therefor the price at which the same may be appraised, under the direction of
the Secretary of the Interior.

On October 1, 1881, Daniel M. Frost made homestead entry at Garden City, land office, in Kansas, for lots 9, 10, 11 and 12, Sec. 25, T. 26
S., R. 25 W., and lots 14 and 15, Sec. 30, T. 26 S., R. 24 W., containing
88.65 acres. These lots are within the lapping limits of the two reservations, and north of the Atchison, Topeka, and Santa Fe Railroad.
On October 25, 1881, Frederick W. Boyd, claiming settlement October
22, presented at the local land office his pre-emption declaratory statement for the lots in question, and also for two other lots, which are not
involved in this controversy; and November 5, 1881, Frederick T. M.
Wenie, claiming settlement November 2, presented pre-emption declaratory statement for the same lots applied for by Boyd. Both of these
applications were rejected, because of conflict with the prior entry of
Frost; whereupon appeals were taken to the Commissioner of the General Land Office, who, on April 17, 1882, affirmed the action of the
local officers, and the case was brought here. Pending said appeals, on
August 9, 1882, Wenie filed an application to contest the entry of Frost
on the ground that the lands included therein were Osage trust lands,
and not subject to such entry; and, on August 18, 1882, Frost gave
notice of his intention to commute his entry to cash and make final proof
in support thereof on September 20 following. These papers were forwarded to your office for instructions. On September 6, 1882, the local
officers were advised that in view of the fact that Frost's entry was
regarded as a valid appropriation of the land, and in view of the pendency of the appeals, the hearing on Wenie's contest would not be
ordered, and Frost's application to commute would be suspended. Following this action on his application to contest the legality of Frost's
entry, on March 5, 1884, Wenie filed in the local office an application to
the Secretary to have said case remanded for trial on questions of fact
not appearing in the record before the Department; it being alleged in
said application, (1) that Frost did not apply to make his homestead
entry at the local office, but that the same was presented to and accepted by Morris, the register, while the latter was at Dodge City, sixty
miles from the district land office; (2) and that Frost had theretofore
exercised his right of purchase of Osage lands, and can not acquire title
to another tract of said lands. This application was mislaid in your

office, and was not before this Department when said appeals were considered.

On September 7, 1885, Acting Secretary Jenks affirmed the judgment below, as Frost appeared " to be an actual *bona fide* settler;" and authorized the commutation of said entry to cash upon the submission of satisfactory proof of compliance with the requirements of the law. (4 L. D., 145.) Under this decision, on December 9, 1885, Frost proceeded to submit final proof to the register and receiver, whereat Boyd and Wenie filed protest, and the latter also a motion for review of the decision of Acting Secretary Jenks; said motion being filed within proper time after notice. Hearing was had, testimony submitted, and on July 24, 1886, the register and receiver dismissed the protest of Wenie and Boyd and accepted proof of Frost. This decision was affirmed by your office June 17, 1887. Boyd having relinquished all claim to the lots in question, the case was brought here on the appeal of Wenie, the record containing also his motion for review of the former departmental decision.

On consideration of the record then presented, Acting Secretary Muldrow, on October 4, 1887, held, in effect, that the act of December 15, 1880, before cited, did not apply to the lots in question, which could only be entered as Osage lands, under the provisions of the act of May 28, 1880, before cited, and, it being admitted by Frost that he had theretofore availed himself of the right of pre-emption in the purchase of other Osage lands, he was not qualified to make a second entry therefor; that the former decision of Acting Secretary Jenks, affirming the validity of Frost's said entry of the lots in controversy, could not avail him, because it was made upon an incomplete record. Therefore, Mr. Muldrow revoked the former decision, ordered the cancellation of Frost's entry, and directed that the filing of Wenie for the lots in question be received. (6 L. D., 175.) On November 14, 1887, Frost filed an application for the review and reversal of said decision, which review was had and the reversal denied by my predecessor, Secretary Vilas, on February 15, 1888, who said:

> I am satisfied that Congress, by the act of December 15, 1880, had no intention of repealing the act of May 28, 1880, or any portion thereof, since such repeal would work an impairment of the rights guaranteed to the Indians by the treaty of 1865 . . . . Manifestly, the intention of Congress can be ascertained only by consideration of the treaty of 1865 and the two acts above mentioned *in pari materia*, and so considering them, I have no difficulty in arriving at the conclusion, that the tract in question cannot legally be entered by Frost for the reason that having made one Osage entry he is not a qualified pre-emptor. (6 L. D. 539.)

It would seem that the claim of Frost to these lots, under his homestead entry had thus been finally decided and settled, so far as this Department was concerned. The case had been heard here, and decided against him; heard again on review and the former judgment adhered to. And now an elaborate argument is made to show, and the Department is asked to declare, that these judgments were all wrong.

There are circumstances under which a re-review would be proper. Such occasions, however, are rare and most exceptional. To say nothing of those on which the Secretary, in the exercise of what the supreme court in Lee v. Johnson (116 U. S., 48) calls, "that just supervision which the law vests in him over all proceedings instituted to acquire portions of the public lands," might think proper, of his own motion, to re-open a cause, the circumstances under which an application for re-review may be made by a defeated party were clearly stated and the rules of procedure, in relation thereto, plainly set forth by my predecessor Secretary Vilas in the case of Neff v. Cowhick (8 L. D., 111). There it was said :

> Hereafter let the rule be that no motion for a review shall be filed. If the defeated party is able to present any suggestions of facts or points of law not previously discussed or involved in the case, it may be done by petition which shall contain all the facts and arguments . . . . . Such petition should not reargue points already twice passed upon, but should be limited to the office indicated of suggesting new facts or considerations not *presented before*.

This rule was promulgated January 22, 1889, and the present motion for review by Frost was filed on May 2, 1889.

To obviate the charge of violating this rule, in behalf of Frost, it is asserted, that his is but a motion for the review and reversal of the decision in Everett v. Wenie, decided by this Department April 4, 1889 (unreported), and of which decision there has been no review heretofore asked or had. This is literally true, but only to the extent that the motion is filed in the Wenie-Everett case, and asks a reversal of that decision. But, in point of fact, under color of a motion to review that case, to which Frost was no proper party, he in reality asks a reversal of the judgment rendered in the former case of Wenie v. Frost. There can be no doubt about this. An examination of the specification of errors, of the elaborate brief of counsel, all show beyond any question that this is so. And were this Department to grant the application of Frost it would necessarily reverse the decisions of Secretaries Vilas and Muldrow, and re-instate the canceled homestead entry of Frost. This would be doing by indirection that which the Department would not do directly. That this is so, an examination of the circumstances under which Frost presents himself before this Department in this proceeding, and his contentions therein will abundantly substantiate.

When, in pursuance of the decision of Acting Secretary Muldrow, Wenie after filing declaratory statement for said lots, offered, on February 13, 1888, to make final proof for the same at the local office, a protest against the allowance thereof was filed by Thos. F. Everett, and also by said Frost. The first point of Frost's protest is that the final proof should not then be proceded with because he, Frost, had a motion for review of the decision in Wenie v. Frost pending undetermined before the Department. This application for review it will be recollected was denied on February 16, 1888, or three days after the protest was filed. The second point is,

Protestant alleges that said land is not subject to entry under the provisions of the act in reference to Osage Indian trust lands for the reason that the said act, in so far as it applies to this land was repealed by the act of December 15, 1880.

A reference to the decision of either Secretary Vilas or Muldrow will show it was therein held that said land was subject to entry *only* " under the provisions of the act in reference to Osage Indian trust lands," and that said act was *not* repealed by the act of December 15, 1880.

The third point of the protest is that he, Frost, " having complied with the provisions of the act of December 15, 1880 . . . . has a prior right to said land both in law and equity, as against any other person or persons." This "prior right" is exactly what the Department had decided he did not have against Wenie, and could not get under the act of December 15, 1880.

The reception of the protest of Frost was objected to by Wenie on the ground that Frost's claim in the premises had been finally and adversely determined by the Department. With the filing of the protest, Frost was, at that time, content, offered no evidence at the hearing ordered on said protests, and does not appear to have been present thereat in person or by attorney. The register and receiver, in their decision of September 12, 1888, approving the final proof of Wenie and dismissing protest of Everett, make not the slightest reference to that of Frost in any way, and he alleges that he was not notified of their said decision. On December 8, 1888, your office affirmed the action of the local officers, accepted the final proof of Wenie and dismissed the protests of Everett and Frost, stating as to the latter that—

The question raised therein is *res judicata*, having been decided against him by said departmental decision of October 5, 1887, and again on motion for review, by departmental decision February 15, 1888.

From the rejection of his protest and the acceptance of Wenie's final proof, Everett, on February 4, 1889, appealed and on April 4, 1889 the said judgment was affirmed here. May 2, 1889, Frost appears and alleges that his appeal from the action of the Commissioner, though taken in time after notice thereof, was not duly transmitted, and therefore was not in the record before the Secretary on April 4, 1889, when the last decision was made; and he now moves that said decision be reopened, re-considered and reversed because (1) contrary to law and evidence; (2) because it does not pass upon his interest which he has a right to have adjudicated under his appeal from the Commissioner's decision dismissing his protest; (3) and because of error in accepting Wenie's final proof in view of his, Frost's, former homestead entry.

The recital of these facts points to but one conclusion, and shows beyond even plausible contention that Frost seeks by this motion to have the decisions of Secretaries Muldrow and Vilas re-opened and reversed, the pre-emption claim of Wenie rejected, the homestead entry of him, Frost, re-instated and the land awarded to him thereunder.

In order to meet the rule of *res judicata* as applicable to such a condition, and also the well settled principle that one Secretary will not disturb the final decision of his predecessor, it is insisted that the judgment of Mr. Jenks, awarding the land to Frost was final, and that it was beyond the power of Mr. Muldrow to re-open it, and therefore this Department should recognize the first decision as binding, and utterly disregard those of Mr. Muldrow and of Secretary Vilas.

The first decision was made upon an incomplete record; it was so made by Mr. Jenks on September 7, 1885, and that of Mr. Muldrow on October 4, 1887, during the incumbency of my predecessor, Secretary Lamar, which commenced in March, 1885, and terminated in January, 1888. Messrs. Jenks and Muldrow were assistants to the Secretary, and on proper occasions acted in his stead. The decision of each was, in contemplation of law, the act of the Secretary and had the same legal efficacy and no more. The right of a Secretary for so satisfactory a reason, to re-open and reverse his own decision, can not be denied. There is, therefore no force in a contention which virtually insists that Secretary Lamar, acting through Mr. Muldrow, violated the rule of *res judicata* in re-opening and reversing his own decision announced through Mr. Jenks; the fact being beyond dispute that an important part of the record had been mislaid and was not before or considered by Mr. Jenks.

Considering the motion for review by Frost, in every aspect in which it has been presented, in my opinion, the matters heretofore stated demand that it should be denied, which is accordingly done. His appeal in said case having no more merit than the motion for review, it is dismissed.

Disposing of Frost's motion and appeal thus, it is not necessary to a determination of his rights that I should express my views upon the other questions so exhaustively argued by his counsel.

Having thus relieved the cause of the claims and contentions of Frost, it remains to dispose of the motion, in behalf of Everett, for a review and reversal of my decision of April last, dismissing his protest and accepting the final proof of Wenie for the tracts in question under his declaratory statement.

The motion for review charges, in substance, error of fact in finding, from the evidence that Wenie settled actually and in good faith upon the lots in controversy, prior to the summer of 1887, when Everett made settlement and established his residence thereon; and error of law in holding that Wenie could acquire any right by settlement prior to the cancellation of Frost's homestead entry on October 4, 1887, at which time both Wenie and Everett were living on the tract and therefore have equal right to the same; and further that the failure of Wenie to protest the final proof of him, Everett, on March 14, 1887, legally concluded the former from the assertion of an adverse right as against the latter.

None of the matters set forth in the present motion are new. But they were presented to, and considered by the register and receiver in the matter of Everett's protest against Wenie's final proof. The ruling then was adverse to the former upon each point specified in the motion here, as will be seen by reference to the decision of the local officers in the record before me. The same points were again presented, argued before and specifically passed upon adversely to Everett, in your office decision of December 6, 1888. Again the same matters were presented to me, and fully argued, considered and decided adversely to him in my decision of April 4, 1889.

Notwithstanding the careful examination which these points have all heretofore received, the clear and uniform decisions, as recited, adverse to Everett, the record of the cause has been again faithfully examined, on this motion, the testimony weighed, the arguments of counsel patiently considered, and I have no difficulty whatever in arriving at the conclusion that the motion for review should be dismissed.

The reasons, which bring me to this conclusion now, were heretofore set out fully and in detail, in my former decision. and need not now be repeated.

RAILROAD GRANT PRE-EMPTION CLAIM.

UNION PACIFIC RY. CO. v. HAINES.

An unexpired pre-emption filing of record at date of definite location, raises a *prima facie* presumption of the existence, at that time, of a pre-emption claim, sufficient to except the land covered thereby from the operation of the grant.

A hearing to determine the validity of such a filing at date of definite location will not be ordered, in the absence of any allegation that said claim had then ceased to exist by abandonment or otherwise.

Secretary Noble to the Commissioner of the General Land Office, November 30, 1889.

The Union Pacific Railway Company appeals from the decision of your office of August 10, 1888, rejecting its claim, under the grant of July 1, 1862 (12 Stat., 489), to the NW. ¼ of SE. ¼ Sec. 3., T. 3 S. R. 70 W., Denver district, Colorado.

Said land is within the granted or primary limits of the applicant's road, the right of which attached to granted lands on date of definite location, August 20, 1869. Lands to which a "pre-emption or homestead claim may have attached at the time the line of the road was definitely fixed," are excepted from the grant. (Sec. 3, act of July 1, 1862, *supra*.)

Your office rejected the claim of appellant, because it appeared from the records that one Fred. Shumph on March 7, 1867, about two years and five months before the definite location of appellant's road, had filed a pre-emption declaratory statement embracing said land, alleging settlement, December 24, 1866,

In your office decision it is said:

The original declaratory statement claimant having asserted his claim to the land prior to the definite location of the company's road, and the time for the completion of such claims having been extended to July 14, 1872, by the acts of July 14, 1870, and March 3, 1871, (16 Stat., pp. 279, 601), the land was thereby excepted from the grant.

The appellant contends that your office erred—

In holding that said tract was excepted from the grant to the company by the mere pre-emption filing of Shumph on the records, and in the absence of any proof whatever that said pre-emption claimant ever made actual settlement on the land or in any manner complied with the requirements of the pre-emption laws;" that "without such settlement and compliance with law, a pre-emption claim is a nullity," and "that the acts of July 14, 1870, and March 3, 1871, cited by the Commissioner, did not and could not in any manner extend or affect the filing of Shumph unless he had made actual settlement," etc., and that such compliance with law cannot be presumed.

The appeal concludes with a prayer,—

That the decision of your office be reversed, or that a hearing be ordered with notice to all parties in interest, to determine the facts in the case and the status of the tract at the date of the definite location of the road.

It is true, settlement and improvement of the land are essential to the validity of a pre-emption claim, but it is a principle of law that men are presumed to act in accordance therewith, and, while this presumption is not conclusive, the burden is upon him who would rebut it, to make a *prima facie* showing of illegality by proper allegations and proof.

Conceding for argument's sake, that the *validity* of a pre-emption claim as dependent on the claimant's compliance with the law, can be inquired into by a railroad company in a case like the present, there is nothing in the record in this case and nothing *alleged* by the appellant, showing or tending to show, that Shumph had not complied with the law up to the date of the definite location of the road, and was not then complying therewith.

In the case of Neilson *v.* Northern Pac. R. R. *et al.*, (9 L. D., 402), this Department held, that a claim which had been abandoned and ceased to exist *before* the definite location of the road, did not except the land from the grant. It is neither averred nor does it in any way appear, that the claim of Shumph had ceased to exist by abandonment or otherwise when the line of definite location of appellant's road "was fixed."

The land in this case appears to have never been "offered," and, under the act of March 3, 1843 (5 Stat., 619), which was the law in force as to "unoffered" filings at the date of Shumph's filing and of the definite location of the road, he had three months from date of settlement (December 24, 1866) within which to file his declaratory statement, and might make proof and payment for the land at any time before the commencement of a public sale in which it might be embraced. (1 Lester, 374; 2 id., 24). As the land has never been proclaimed for sale or embraced in any public sale, Shumph's filing was an " *unexpired* " filing at the date of the definite location of appellant's road, (August 20, 1869) under said act of 1843, without reference to the acts of July 14, 1870 and March 3, 1871 cited by your office.

An "unexpired" pre-emption filing of record at the date of definite location of a road raises at least a *prima facie* presumption of the existence at that time of a "pre-emption claim." Northern Pacific R. R. Co. *v.* Gjuve (8 L. D., 380).

The application of the appellant for a hearing must be denied in the absence of the allegation (and existence, so far as the record discloses) of any facts authorizing such hearing.

The decision of your office is affirmed.

———

PATENT—CERTIFICATION—LAND DEPARTMENT.

IOWA RAILROAD LAND CO. *v.* SLOAN.

After patent, or certification where patent is not expressly required, the Land Department has no authority to entertain proceedings for the disposal of the lands involved, or to annul or cancel such patent or certification.

A patent, or certification, can not be vacated or limited in proceedings where it comes collaterally in question.

Secretary Noble to the Commissioner of the General Land Office, November 30, 1889.

October 1, 1874, the SE.¼ of Sec. 33, T. 90 N., R. 47 W., Des Moines district, Iowa, was certified or "listed" to the State of Iowa, under the grant for the purpose of aiding in the construction of certain railroads, contained in the act of May 15, 1856 (11 Stat., 9), and, on January 15, 1875, said land was patented by the State to the Iowa Falls and Sioux City Railroad Company.

On May 3, 1888, nearly fourteen years after the list embracing the land had been certified to the State, the local officers permitted George N. Sloan to make timber culture entry of the tract. The attention of your office having been called by the attorney for the railroad company to the status of said land at the time of the allowance of Sloan's entry, your office, by letter of June 29, 1888, instructed the local officers, as follows:

As the land at that time (May 3, 1888—date of allowance of Sloan's entry) had already been disposed of by the railroad certification, it was not subject to further disposal by this Department. The entry of Sloan was clearly illegal, and is held for cancellation, subject to appeal within sixty days.

Subsequently, August 1, 1888, your office wrote the local officers:

I have now to direct that you will advise Mr. Sloan, that his entry will be allowed to stand, if he desires, awaiting the adjustment of the railroad grant, or, as the entry was illegal, it will be canceled.

From this action of your office the Iowa Railroad Land Company, as "successor in interest" of the Iowa Falls and Sioux City Railroad Company (the State's patentee), appeals to this Department, claiming that being admitted by your office to be "illegal", the entry should have been canceled, and not allowed to remain upon the record as a cloud upon its title.

So far as the record transmitted to this Department discloses, the action of your office in said second letter was *mero motu* and no distinct reason is assigned therefor. "Legal title passes as completely by certification, if patent is not expressly required by law, as though patent had issued," and when the legal title has so "passed from the government, this Department is without authority over the lands to which such title relates." (Garriques *v.* Atchison, Topeka & Santa Fé R. R. Co., 6 L. D., 543; Frasher *v.* O'Connor, 115 U. S., 102; 10 Stat., 346.) When patent (or certification, in cases where patent is not expressly required) has issued for land, although "a void instrument issued without authority, it *prima facie* passes the title," and "precludes the further exercise of departmental jurisdiction over the land until such patent is vacated by judicial action." (John P. S. Voght, 9 L. D., 114, and cases therein cited.) The act of May 15, 1856, does not require patents to be issued for the land granted therein, and, therefore, the certification in this case passed the legal title as effectually as patent would have done. (Southern Minn. Ry. Co. *v.* Kufner, 2 L. D., 492.) This being the case, Sloan, "if he possess such an equitable right to the premises as would give him the title if the" certification "were out of the way," must seek his remedy in a court of equity; but, "if he occupy with respect to the land no such position as this, he can only apply to the officers of the government to take measures" (if any ground therefor be shown) "in its name to vacate the" certification "or limit its operation. It can not be vacated or limited in proceedings where it comes *collaterally* in question." (Steel *v.* Smelting Works, 106 U. S., 447.)

By the act of March 3, 1887, (24 Stat., 556), providing for the adjustment by the Secretary of the Interior of "railroad land grants" not theretofore adjusted, it is made the duty of the Secretary of the Interior where it shall appear pending or on the completion of such adjustment, that lands have been, from any cause, prior to said act "erroneously certified or patented," to demand from the railroad company a relinquishment or reconveyance to the United States of all such lands, "and on the failure of the railroad company to comply within ninety days after such demand, the Attorney-General is required" to commence and prosecute in the proper courts the necessary proceedings to cancel such patents or certifications and "restore the title to the land covered thereby to the United States." There is nothing in the act, however, which authorizes the allowance of entries on the lands embraced in the erroneous patents or certifications pending the adjustment of the grant and before they have been restored to the public domain by cancellation of such patents or certifications. On the contrary by providing for the restoration of the title to these lands to the United States by cancellation of the patents or certifications on direct proceedings by the Attorney-General in the " proper courts," Congress recognized the doctrine laid down by this Department and the supreme court in the cases above cited, namely, that after patent or certification has issued and while they remain uncanceled, this Department has no *jurisdiction*, either to annul or cancel such patent or certification, or to take any steps or entertain any proceedings for the disposal of the lands involved therein. (In this case it does not even appear, that the certification could be canceled on proceedings by the Attorney-General under said act of 1887, as it is not alleged and there is nothing in the record showing or tending to show, that said certification has been found, or is, from any cause, erroneous.)

The allowance of the entry in this case being not only "illegal," but, it appearing from matter of record that it is *void* for want of jurisdiction, the entry should be canceled, and I so direct.

The decision of your office is modified accordingly.

RAILROAD GRANT—HOMESTEAD ENTRY—EXECUTOR.

STINSON *v.* SOUTH & NORTH ALABAMA R. R. Co.

There is no authority in the land laws for an executor to consummate the inchoate claim of a deceased homesteader.

Secretary Noble to the Commissioner of the General Land Office, November 30, 1889.

This is an appeal by S. S. Stinson, as executor of the will of Jedediah Stinson, deceased, from the decision of your office of April 2, 1888, rejecting the application of said S. S. Stinson, as such executor, to perfect the claim of said decedent to the NE. ¼ of NE. ¼ of Sec. 3, T. 8 S., R. 3 W., Huntsville district, Alabama, as an adjoining farm.

The action of your office was upon the ground that "the land in question is within the six mile primary limits of the grant of June 3, 1856 (11 Stat., 18), as revived and renewed by the act of March 3, 1870 (16 Stat., 580), for the South and North Alabama Railroad Company, as shown by said company's map of definite location, filed May 30, 1866," and that, "the records of your office do not show, nor is it alleged that any claim had attached to said land at the date of definite location, which would have operated to except the same from the railroad grant."

The appellant not having filed a sufficient specification of errors, " clearly and concisely designating the errors" complained of, as required by Rule of Practice 88, and there being no evidence of service on the opposite party of a copy of the notice as required by Rule 93, your office, under Rule 82, notified him to amend his appeal and show compliance with Rule 93 within fifteen days from service of such notification. He failed to amend his appeal, and simply filed an affidavit, that he had "given notice," without stating of what. His application to be allowed to perfect the claim of his testator is upon the ground "that to the best of his knowledge and belief, Jedediah Stinson, in his lifetime, did deposit it in the United States land office at Huntsville, Ala., the entry money for said land under the act allowing settlers to enter for the use of an adjoining farm." There appears to be no record evidence that the decedent ever entered the land, and the allegations of the appellant's application, if true, do not show an entry.

Without reference to the defective character of the appeal above referred to, and the meagre showing as to the decedent's ever having initiated a claim to the land under the law, and without passing upon the status of the land as affected by the railroad grant, the application of the appellant must be rejected on the ground, that there is no authority in the land laws for an executor to consummate the inchoate claim of a deceased homesteader. (Rev. Stat. 2291; H. A. Gale, 6 L. D., 573; Richard Clump, 3 L. D., 384; John Kavanaugh, 9 L. D., 268.) If land acquired under the homestead law could in any event " become liable to the satisfaction of debts contracted prior to the issuance of patent therefor," (Rev. Stat., 2296,) there is no showing of facts in this case which would warrant the intervention of an executor under the general law for the protection of creditors. (John Kavanaugh, *supra*, p. 269.)

The action of your office in rejecting the application is affirmed.

EXECUTIVE RESERVATION–FORT MISSOULA.

JAMES H. T. RYMAN.

An entry will not be allowed of land over which the War Department assumes and exercises full control for military purposes, and which is actually held and possessed by the military acting under direction of said Department.

Secretary Noble to the Commissioner of the General Land Office, December 2, 1889.

On July 25, 1887, James H. T. Ryman, made application to enter under the desert land act the S. ½ of the NE. ¼ of section 30, T. 13 N., R. 19 W., Helena land district, Montana. The local officers rejected said application because the same was " for land embraced in Fort Missoula military reservation."

Ryman appealed. In your office decision of October 10, 1887, approving the action of the local officers, you state—" The record of this (your) office shows that by executive order dated February 19, 1877, the President set apart as a military reservation for the use of the military of Fort Missoula, Sec. 31, T. 13 N., R. 19 W., six hundred and forty acres and on the 5th day of August, 1878, the President by executive order enlarged the original Fort Missoula reservation by adding thereto portions of Sec. 30, 13 N., 19 W., including the tract Mr. Ryman desires to enter."

From your said office decision Ryman appealed to this Department stating as his grounds of appeal and specifications of errors—

The Honorable Commissioner of the General Land Office erred in rejecting said application on the grounds that said land was included in the Fort Missoula reservation.

The Honorable Commissioner erred in holding that said land was included in and comprised a portion of said Fort Missoula military reservation.

The Honorable Commissioner erred in holding that said land was not public land of the United States subject to entry under public land laws of the United States.

The Honorable Commissioner erred in not allowing said application to file on said land, because the executive order setting said land apart as an addition to the military reservation was null and void and of no effect.

That at the time said executive order was made setting said land apart as an additional reservation for the use of the military of Fort Missoula, Montana Territory, a former executive order had been made and there had been set aside for military reservation at said Fort Missoula, a tract of land consisting of six hundred and forty acres; the limit allowed by law for military purposes at one place, and that said tract of land was so occupied as a military reservation at the time said additional reservation was made, and both of said reservations were so occupied as military reservations at said Fort Missoula at the time the said James H. T. Ryman made application to file on said tract under the said desert law.

It is claimed on behalf of Ryman that the reservations of Fort Missoula laid within the original Territory of Oregon as established by act of Congress, August 14, 1848, and that by act approved February 14, 1853, military reservations within the said Territory should not exceed in area six hundred and forty acres at any one point.

He urges that six hundred and forty acres having been set apart as a military reservation for Fort Missoula, by executive order of February 19, 1877, the enlargement of the same, by order of August 5, 1878, was illegal and such latter order void and of no effect.

The records show that on February 19, 1877, by executive order bearing date on that day, section 31, in said township and range, containing six hundred and forty acres of land was set apart for a military reservation for the use of the military at Fort Missoula, Montana Territory. That afterward, August 5, 1878, by a further executive order the following tracts of land containing five hundred and sixty acres were set apart for military purposes as an addition to the original reservation, to wit: The SE.¼, of the SE. ¼, the SW. ¼, of the SW. ¼, the N. ½ of the SW. ¼, the S. ½, of the NW. ¼, and the S. ½, of the NE. ¼, of section 30, T. 13 N., R. 19 W., and the S. ½, of the NE. ¼, and the SE. ¼, of section 25, T. 13 N., R. 20 W.   The land covered by Ryman's application is a part of the said additional reservation.

It further appears after a careful investigation, that these reservations are situated west of the summit of the Rocky mountains and were within the limits of the Territory of Oregon, as originally established by the act of Congress of August 14, 1848 (9 Stat., 323).   They were situated within the Territory of Washington when the same was organized by act of March 2, 1853 (10 Stat., 172).

The Territory of Montana was formed by act of Congress of May 26, 1864 (13 Stats., 85) of land the western portion of which was within the Territories of Oregon and Washington. The land covered by these reservations then became a part of the Territory of Montana.

The act of Congress of September 27, 1850, (9 Stat., 496) provides among other matters for the survey and the making of donations to settlers of the public lands in Oregon.

Section 14 of the said statute enacts

that such portions of the public lands as may be designated under the authority of the President of the United States, for forts, magazines, arsenals, dockyards, and other needful public uses, shall be reserved and excepted from the operation of this act.

The act of Congress of February 14, 1853, (10 Stats., 158) is amendatory of the act of September 27, 1850. The ninth section of it enacts

That all reservations heretofore as well as hereafter made in pursuance of the fourteenth section of the act to which this is an amendment, shall for magazines arsenals, dockyards, and other needed public uses except for forts, be limited to an amount not exceeding twenty acres for each and every of said objects at any one point or place and for forts to an amount not exceeding six hundred and forty acres at any point or place.

In a letter of this Department addressed to your office bearing date February 27, 1889, regarding the case at bar this Department referred to section 6 of the act of Congress of July 17, 1854, (10 Stats., 305) by which the provisions of the act of February 14, 1853, above referred to, were extended to the Territory of Washington; also reference was had to section 13 of the act of May 26, 1864, (13 Stats., 91) it sets out that all laws of the United States "which are not locally inapplicable" have force and effect within the Territory of Montana. Construing said section nine of the act of February 14, 1853, herein mentioned, it was said in said letter that the restrictions therein enacted became the rules for a large extent of country, politically organized as the Territory of Oregon. That the rule established by said section was in force irrespective of its political organization and that a change of the latter by dividing the said Territory into two or more Territories would not affect the rule or abrogate it in any part of the locality for which it was enacted. Regarding the construction of the said section heretofore made by this Department, the letter cited the case of Fort Boise Hay Reservation (6 L. D., 16); also Fort Ellis (idem., 46).

The conclusion was therefore expressed in the said letter that the said executive order of August 5, 1878, was in contravention of the provisions of an act of Congress and therefore necessarily unauthorized and of no force and effect.

Since it, however, appeared that the War Department assumed for military purposes, full control over the land covered by the said executive order and that the military in fact held possession of the same, and in order that applicants for this land might not be placed in the position of contending with that branch of the government now in the actual occupation thereof; it was thought best to suspend further action upon the application to enter said lands, until communication might be had with the War Department with a view to obtaining a relinquishment of said reservation, held as it was considered in contravention of the provisions of law.

You were therefore advised by said letter to transmit to the Secretary of War a letter setting forth the facts in connection with said reservation and to ask that such action might be taken as would relieve said land from the existing order of reservation of August 5, 1878, if such action should be deemed by the said Secretary appropriate and in accordance with law.

You were further asked upon a receipt of a reply to such communication to transmit the same to this Department for further directions in the case.

Your office having in compliance with said directions transmitted to the Secretary of War a letter as required, the reply by the War Department dated October 1, 1889, and signed by the Secretary of War is now before me for consideration.

From this reply it appears that the War Department for guidance in its action in this matter, is controlled by the opinion of the Attorney General whose advice therein had been sought. In this opinion as is set out in said reply, the Attorney General holds,

that the President was fully empowered to make said order (meaning the order of August 5, 1878, extending the limits of the said reservation); that while it remains unrevoked the land covered by it is not open for entry or settlement and that the restrictive act of February 14, 1853, providing that military reservations in Oregon Territory should not exceed in area six hundred and forty acres at any one point, is wholly inapplicable to these lands in Montana.

While the War Department assumes and exercises for military purposes full control over the land in question and the military, under order of the said department, holds actual possession of it, this Department will not interfere, and Ryman's application must therefore, be denied.

Your said decision is affirmed. Together with the papers in this case, your office transmitted, accompanying your letter of January 12, 1888, the papers appertaining to James H. T. Ryman's application to make timber culture entry for lot 4, of said section 30, also papers appertaining to Gust. Moser's application to make timber culture entry for the SE. ¼, of the SE. ¼, of the said section. These applications are pending before your office; they are returned to you for appropriate action.

HOMESTEAD LAWS—JOINT RESOLUTION OF MAY 14, 1888.

MARTHA A. CARTER.

The joint resolution of May 14, 1888, did not repeal section two, act of June 15, 1880. Section two of said act is a part of the homestead system, to the whole of which the name "homestead laws" is generically applied in the provision of said resolution that only under said "laws" should lands in said State be disposed of during the period specified.

Secretary Noble to the Commissioner of the General Land Office, December 2, 1889.

I have before me the appeal of Martha A. Carter, from your office decision of October 18, 1888, holding for cancellation the cash entry (No. 37521) made by her May 23, 1888, under the second section of the act of June 15, 1880 (21 Stat., 237), for the W. ½, NW. ¼, Sec. 7, T. 7 S., R. 2 E., Huntsville district, Alabama.

The tract in question was covered by homestead entry No. 2698, made March 9, 1869, by Charles Carter. Said entry was canceled August 29, 1879, for failure to make final proof.

On May 23, 1888, the appellant, Martha A. Carter, as the widow of said Charles Carter, purchased the tract under the second section of the act of June 15, 1880.

On October 18, 1888, by the decision appealed from, your office held the cash entry so made, for cancellation, upon the ground that said entry was illegal as not constituting a disposal of the land "under and according to the provisions of the homestead laws," whereas the joint resolution of May 14, 1888 (25 Stats., 622), provided that (during a period which included the date of Mrs. Carter's purchase) "offered" lands in Alabama should be disposed of "*only*" "under and according to the provisions of the homestead laws."

This conclusion I do not approve.

In my opinion, the joint resolution referred to was not intended to repeal, as to the public lands in Alabama, the second section of the act of June 15, 1880. While an entry under that section is, no doubt, a "cash entry," in one sense and not merely the consummation of the homestead entry on the previous existence of which the right to purchase is based, it still remains true that such a "cash entry" is by the statute allowed only in view of the prior homestead entry, and stands in much the same relation to the latter as would a cash entry made under the "commutation clause" of the homestead act. The making of such entries is not what is technically meant, in public-land law, by "private sale," against which it is that the prohibition in the resolution was really directed. In my opinion, the act of June 15, 1880, is in fact a part of the "homestead" system, to the whole of which the name "homestead laws" is generically applied in the provision of the resolution that only under those "laws," should lands in Alabama be disposed of during the period mentioned.

That the widow of an entryman may purchase under the act of June 15, 1880, notwithstanding that the entry has been canceled for failure to make final proof within the time prescribed, has been determined by this Department (and is not disputed here). Northern Pacific R. R. v. Burt, 3 L. D., 490; Northern Pacific R. R. v. McLean, 5 L. D., 529.

Your said office decision is accordingly reversed.

RE-EMPTION—SECTION 2260 R. S.

RICHARDS v. WARD.

One who quits or abandons his residence on lands in which he holds and owns an undivided interest, to settle on public land in the same State or Territory is within the second inhibition of section 2260 of the Revised Statutes.

Secretary Noble to the Commissioner of the General Land Office, December 2, 1889.

I have considered the motion for review, filed by Wm. H. Richards in the above entitled cause, and find that the only question presented in the motion is, whether a person who quits and abandons his residence, on land in which he owns an undivided interest, to reside on the public land in the same State or Territory, is within the inhibition contained in the second clause of section 2260, of the Revised Statutes.

Said inhibition is as follows: "No person who quits or abandons his residence on his own land to reside on the public lands in the same State or Territory" shall acquire any right of pre-emption under the provisions of section 2259, R. S.

This inhibition has been the subject of construction by this Department in numerous cases, and it may be considered as well settled,—

1st. That one who quits or abandons his residence even upon his own property, within a town or city, said property not being agricultural lands, does not come within the inhibition. Instructions of Commissioner Thos. A. Hendricks to register and receiver, January 12, 1857, 6 C. L. O., 1872. Sturgeon v. Ruiz (1 L. D., 490 and 2 C. L. L., 534)

2nd. That one who quits or abandons his residence on lands of which he is the equitable, but not the legal owner, to reside on public lands within the same State or Territory, is within the inhibition. Ware v. Bishop (2 L. D., 616); Frank H. Sellmeyer (6 L. D., 792); Ole K. Bergan (7 L. D., 472).

3rd. That the fact that the land so quit, or abandoned is under mortgage for less than its value, will not take it out of the prohibitory provision. Frank E. Crozier (7 L. D., 195).

4th. Following these cases, and as it seems to me, a corollary to them, this Department held expressly in the case of Payne v. Campbell (8 L. D., 367), that joint ownership in land clearly brings a claimant within this inhibition.

I adhere to this decision and am satisfied that the conclusion therein reached is the only correct one to be reached in this case. Each owner has in respect to his share, all the rights which a tenant in severalty has, except only that of sole possession. 1 Washburne on Real Property, (4 Ed) 652, and 416.

If he wishes to convey this interest, even to his co-tenant, he must do so by the same kind of a deed that would be necessary to convey the entire title.

It is urged that ownership is a right by which a thing belongs to some one in particular to the exclusion of all others. This may be adopted as a correct definition and a man to whom an undivided share of a farm belongs, is the absolute owner of that share, and has in it the largest estate known to the law. Tenants in common are frequently referred to in the law books as " owners." See 1 Washburne on Real Property, (4 Ed.) 652.

And each tenant in common is considered to be solely and severally seized of his share, and may convey his estate. 24 N. Y., 505; Gerards' Titles to Real Estate, 91.

In my opinion one who quits or abandons his residence on lands in which he holds and owns an undivided interest to settle on public land in the same State or Territory, is within the inhibition of this section. It is true that this Department has held that an undivided interest in land will not sustain an adjoining farm entry, under Sec. 2289, Revised Statutes, but the principal reason given for that decision is that in cases of undivided ownership, it cannot be known whether the portion of the common estate which will be allotted to the applicant, will when partitioned, adjoin the land he applies to enter, and that *contiguity* of the original farm to that entered is an essential under this section.

I do not consider this decision as questioning the force of that reasoning or the authority of that case.

The motion for review is denied.

NANNEY *v.* WEASA.

Service by publication is not authorized in the absence of an affidavit, and such other evidence as may be required by the local office, showing that due diligence has been used, and that personal service can not be made.

In such a case the contestant must state specifically what efforts have been made to secure personal service.

In publication of notice rules 13 and 14 of practice must be strictly followed both in the period of publication and mailing notice to the entryman.

First Assistant Secretary Chandler to the Commissioner of the General Land Office, December 3, 1889.

This case comes up on the appeal of Wm. N. Nanney from your office decision allowing Henry Weasa a re-hearing upon the contest of the former against him,

On April 1, 1884, Henry Weasa made timber culture entry for the SE. ¼, section 9, T. 31 N., R. 44 W., Valentine land district, Nebraska.

On May 15, 1885, Wm. N. Nanney instituted contest against said entry charging "that the said Henry Weasa has failed to break or caused to be broken five acres of said tract, during the first year after entry and has failed to cure the defect at date of filing this affidavit and that he has wholly failed to comply with the timber culture laws in regard to breaking said tract." In his said contest affidavit contestant further states "after using due diligence affiant swears, that he is unable to know the whereabouts of the claimant and asks that notice may be had by publication."

Hearing was set for July 22, 1885. The claimant was not personally served with notice of contest and an attempt was made to obtain service upon him by publication. The notice was advertised in a newspaper, as appears from the affidavit of the publisher, for four consecutive weeks, first publication on July 4, 1885, the last on July 25, 1885. It also appears that a copy of the notice was mailed June 24, 1885, by registered letter to the claimant at Gordon, Nebraska, that being considered his last known post-office address. In other respects rules 13 and 14 of the Rules of Practice were complied with.

On the day appointed for the hearing, July 22, 1885, certain proceedings were had in the said case. Regarding the same the local officers under date of October 14, 1885, reported to your office as follows:

On the 22nd day of July, 1885, this case was called for trial. Contestant appeared with his witnesses whose testimony was duly taken. Claimant made special appearance by his attorney, O. P. Warner, who filed an affidavit, asking that the case be continued, for the reason that the claimant alleged having had no notice, which motion was allowed and the case continued to October 13, 1885, on which day the case was kept open until 4 p. m. Claimant failed to appear either in person or by attorney. After an examination of the case we are of the opinion that the allegations made by contestant are sustained and recommend that the entry be canceled. Parties in interest were notified this day and thirty days allowed for appeal.

The recitals in the said report are not borne out by other records and files in the case. It appears from the record that the *ex parte* testimony of Nanney and two corroborating witnesses was taken July 22, 1885, it is in the form of two affidavits. The proof is endorsed on the back "cause continued for further proof for October 13, 1885, at 10 o'clock a. m. Regr. & Rec'r. Attys., contestant D. Daly, claimant Sheffer." There is further on file a written motion by O. P. Warner, defendant's attorney, in which he asks for the dismissal of the contest on account of "the insufficiency" of the service of notice of contest and because claimant had fully complied with the law regarding the breaking of five acres during the first year of his entry. It does not appear when this motion was filed; in it however the attorney refers to affidavits filed in support of it. These affidavits made by Weasa and two other persons bear date August, 1885. It seems, therefore, that the motion could not have been filed in the local office before that month. In the said affidavits it is shown, that Weasa broke five acres on the land in July, 1884, and that he resided then and had resided for the past five years in the city of Blair, Nebraska. In none of the affidavits a continuance is asked. No other motion or affidavits made on behalf of the claimant before the local officers are on file in the case; and the record fails to show the order for a continuance, or the authority of an attorney Sheffer to appear for the claimant, aside from the said endorsement on contestant's proof.

Upon the report your office canceled Weasa's entry, September 28, 1886.

On May 11, 1888, Weasa made application for a re-hearing upon the said contest. His application is in form of an affidavit duly corroborated, bearing date May 8, 1888. He therein sets out that about a week before the date of his affidavit he learned of the cancellation of his said entry, that he has complied with the requirements of the law, that he was not personally served with notice of the contest; that his residence was at Blair, Washington Co., Nebraska, which was well known among the neighbors to his claim and that he had no knowledge of the said contest. He asks a re-hearing upon the grounds, that he was not legally served with notice of the contest, and that he performed all the requirements of the timber culture law.

Nothing in the record, aside from the statement of the local officers, shows that Weasa was notified of their decision in favor of contestant

Your office, by your said decision of June 18, 1888, granted Weasa's application and ordered a re-hearing in the said contest.

From this decision contestant appealed.

The claimant in this case was never legally served with notice of the contest. Before service by publication can be resorted to, it must be shown by the affidavit of the contestant, and such other evidence as the register and receiver may require that due diligence has been used and that personal service can not be made. The party is required to state what effort has been made to get personal service. See Rule 11, of the Rules of Practice. In this case no foundation was laid for a service by publication; the loose statement in the affidavit of contest, that contestant after using due diligence, swears that he is unable to know the whereabouts of the claimant is not a compliance with the rule. It is not shown what efforts, if any, were made to get personal service.

But aside from this, claimant was never served even by publication of notice. To make such a service legal Rules 13 and 14 of the Rules of Practice must be strictly complied with. In this instance the first insertion of the publication of the notice was not thirty days prior to the day fixed for the hearing but only eighteen days; and the notice was published only three weeks before hearing, the fourth publication being on July 25, three days after the day of trial. Again, the registered letter, containing copy of notice, was mailed June 24, twenty-eight days before day of hearing, not thirty as required by said Rule 14.

It is clear that the defendant was not properly served with notice of contest in this case. On account of the contradiction in the papers sent up from the local office it is impossible to determine whether the appearance for the defendant was such as could properly be called general and sufficient to confer upon the local officers jurisdiction to adjudicate the case upon its merits.

In view of the allegations of the defendant and contradictory character of the record as made in the local office it seems to me the ends of justice will be best subserved by returning this case for a rehearing before the local officers after due and legal service of notice thereof on the defendant.

The decision appealed from is, therefore affirmed.

———

TIMBER CULTURE CONTEST—SALE AND RELINQUISHMENT.

VANDIVERT v. JOHNS.

Proof of an offer to sell and conditional acceptance of such offer will not warrant cancellation of a timber culture entry.

No legal effect can be attributed to a relinquishment executed for use only in the event of certain contingencies, and left in the possession of the entryman's agent.

Secretary Noble to the Commissioner of the General Land Office, December 3, 1889.

The case of Samuel W. Vandivert v. Thomas S. Johns is before me on appeal by Vandivert from the decision of your office, dated May 12, 1888.

September 20, 1882, said Johns entered, under the timber culture law, the NE. ¼ of Sec. 8, T. 25 S., R. 19 W., Larned land district, Kansas.

Contest proceedings were initiated against said entry June 29, 1885, by appellant, but, on account of a recent fire in the local land office, no further steps were taken in the matter, till October 26, following, and on account of two subsequent continuances, each granted on appellant's application, the hearing herein was not had till April 6, 1886. Said hearing was had before the register and receiver on the following charges, or allegations, made by appellant at the initiation of the contest, to wit:

Thomas S. Johns has relinquished his said entry and abandoned the same, having sold all his right, title and interest to the same contrary to the provisions of the timber-culture law, and to his affidavit made at time of entry, wherein he swore that he did not take said land for speculative purposes.

Thomas Doak was the only witness offered in support of these allegations, and the sum and substance of his testimony is as follows:

On June 18, 1885, the witness and the entryman came to a mutual understanding that the latter would sell his said claim and the improvements thereon to the former, provided said witness could make a good, or perfect, timber-culture entry for said land. Witness valued the entryman's improvements at $600.00, and he was to have given him for the claim a house and lot in Kinsley, Kansas, valued by witness at $1500.00, and about $450.00 in cash. In pursuance of this understanding, witness and the entryman, and one Bartholomew—who was acting for each of the parties and who was to receive from each two and a half per cent on the value of their respective properties—went to the land office at Larned, Kansas, for the purpose of securing witness' entry on the described land. On account of the suspension of business at the land office at that time this entry could not be made, and witness then, June 19, 1885, made out a contest affidavit against said entry, charging that claimant had sold the land, and left said affidavit with his attorneys, in Larned, with instruction to file the same when business in the land office should be resumed. Witness also made out a deed to said house and lot, and a note for the money, which was to be given for said claim, and the entryman made out a relinquishment of his entry, and these instruments were placed in the hands of said Bartholomew, who was to hold them till the land office was again open for business, and after witness' entry was made said deed and note were to be delivered to the former entryman. Just when this was done does not appear in evidence. Some time in September, or October, 1885, witness concluded that he would not contest said entry, and went to the entryman and told him to consider the trade off.

The local officers rendered dissenting opinions—the receiver holding that contestant's allegation, "that this entry was sold for a valuable consideration, is not proven—there was at most only an attempt to sell;" and the register holding, "that the entry of defendant was made with 'speculative intent,'" and "held for purposes of sale."

In passing on the case on appeal, the Assistant Commissioner in delivering the opinion, says:

After a careful examination of the testimony, in connection with the circumstances attendant upon the initiation and prosecution of the suit, I am of opinion that the receiver held with good reason that the allegation of sale remained unproved, and that the complaint should be dismissed.

After fully considering the evidence and argument of counsel herein, the Department concurs with your office in holding that this contest should be dismissed.

It is clear that the proof does not show a sale by the entryman. There was an offer to sell and a conditional acceptance of the offer, but no sale. The entryman and the witness Doak came to an understanding as to the terms on which the former would part with his claim, but the trade was declared off by Doak and acquiesced in by the entryman, and that was the end of the matter. The entryman's offer to sell his improvement and all interest in and claim to said land does not of itself warrant the cancellation of his entry and the forfeiture of his claim. White v. McGurk et al., 6 L. D., 268. Nor did the entryman in fact relinquish his claim and authorize the cancellation of his entry. The papers which were prepared and placed in the hands of Bartholomew were to be delivered and become effective and binding on the parties only in the event that Doak could safely secure a valid entry on the described tract of land. Under the state of facts shown, the several instruments, called a relinquishment, a deed, and a note, were not in legal contemplation such instruments, so long as they remained in Bartholomew's hands, and the contemplated entry had not been made. They proved utterly ineffectual as legal or binding instruments, and were presumably returned to the respective parties and destroyed as so much waste paper.

Nor do the facts in this case show, in my opinion, that said entry was made with speculative intent and has since been held for speculative purposes. For anything appearing to the contrary, the entryman may have in the best of faith made said entry, and the affidavit which accompanies all such entries, to wit: that it was made for the cultivation of timber, "and not for the purpose of speculation."

In the case cited by appellant's attorney (Picket v. Engle, 4 L. D., 522), as supporting the contention that Johns's entry should be canceled, the recital of facts shows that the sale in that case had been fully consummated and the relinquishment filed in the local land office. That case is therefore not in point here.

The decision of your office dismissing this contest and leaving said entry intact is affirmed.

TIMBER LAND ENTRY—REPAYMENT.

F. E. HABERSHAM.

A timber land entry made on proof prematurely submitted is an entry "erroneously allowed" for which repayment may be accorded.

Under an entry thus allowed the applicant should not be required to test his right to enter the tract as against an intervening adverse claim.

Secretary Noble to the Commissioner of the General Land Office, December 3, 1889.

I have before me the appeal of F. E. Habersham from your office decision of September 8, 1888, rejecting his application for repayment of the purchase money paid by him on timber-land entry of the W. $\frac{1}{2}$, SW. $\frac{1}{4}$, Sec. 8, T. 35 S., R. 6 W., Roseburg district, Oregon.

On September 6, 1883, Habersham filed in the local land office the usual sworn statement under the timber-land act of June 3, 1878, (20 Stat., 89), and on the same day posted and published notice of his application as required by law.

On October 9, 1883, before the expiration of the period of sixty days prescribed by the statute—the testimony of witnesses as to the character of the land and improvements, was taken before a notary public, but the record does not show when this testimony was presented to the local officers.

November 2, 1883, Habersham conveyed his interest to H. B. Miller.

On December 11, 1883, one Charles Ladd filed a declaratory statement for the same tract, alleging settlement December 5, 1883; but no protest was filed against Habersham's application, nor was any contest ordered or initiated, when Ladd filed his declaratory statement.

Under date of January 2, 1884 receipt and certificate issued to Habersham; but in a letter of December 30, 1884, the register said:

Proof of Habersham was received in due time after publication, and was suspended to give ample time for Ladd's protest, if he should make one, and in that way entry was omitted till January 2, 1884, by neglect on account of other business demanding attention at the time.

June 3, 1884, Ladd transmuted his pre-emption filing to a homestead entry, and thereupon your office held Habersham's cash entry for cancellation, as being in conflict with Ladd's said homestead entry.

December 16, 1885, this Department, on the appeal of Habersham, overruled the action of your office, and directed that the case be remanded to the local office, with instructions to require Habersham to submit proof *de novo;* notice to be given to Ladd of the time and place of receiving such proof, and he (Ladd) to be allowed opportunity to file protest but the testimony to be confined to the *bona fides* of Habersham's application and the character of the land (4 L. D., 282).

Under date of June 16, 1888, the local officers transmitted to your office separate relinquishments by Habersham and Miller, his grantee, together with an application by Habersham for the return of the purchase money paid by him.

September 1, 1888, your office announced the cancellation of Habersham's cash entry, in view of the relinquishments so filed.

September 8, 1888, your office denied the application for repayment, on the ground that Habersham's deed to Miller, having been "prior to his making final proof and payment," proved the falsity of the applicant's sworn statement as to his desiring the land for himself exclusively.

On appeal, Habersham points out that (as is above recited) the "final proof and payment" were in fact made before the date of the deed to Miller, though for reasons of their own the local officers did not issue the certificate until January 2, 1884. I am not prepared to find that the sworn statement of September 6, 1883, was affirmatively shown to be false by the one circumstance that on November 2, thereafter the applicant made a conveyance of his interest to Miller.

The Department decision already mentioned (4 L. D., 282), in effect held that the entry for which Habersham paid his money was "erroneously allowed," as having been made on testimony prematurely taken; for which reason the Department declined to confirm said entry, though it allowed the applicant an opportunity to make due proof thereafter. This in my opinion fairly brings the case within one of the classes in which repayment is allowed by the second section of the act of June

16, 1880 (21 Stats., 287),—to wit, cases in which the entry "was erroneously allowed and cannot be confirmed." (See Naphtali Inglet, 8 L. D., 491; D. D. Wintamute, 8 L. D., 636; Oscar T. Roberts, 8 L. D., 423; E. L. Choate, 8 L. D., 162). I do not think that Habersham should be required to proceed with his application, against the protest and opposition of the intervening adverse claimant, Ladd.

The decision of your office is accordingly reversed.

PRACTICE—MOTION TO DISMISS—INTERVENOR.

VERONICA SIEGEL.

A motion, made by a stranger to the record, to dismiss a proceeding pending before the Department will not be entertained, but such an applicant may be heard as an intervenor when the case comes up for final action.

First Assistant Secretary Chandler to the Commissioner of the General Land Office, December 4, 1889.

I am in receipt of an application filed by Veronica Siegel, asking that the appeal of Christ Gilbertson from the rejection of your office of his application to file pre-emption declaratory statement for the SW. ¼ of Sec. 15, T. 48 N., R. 50 W., Marquette, Michigan, be dismissed.

Said application was refused by the local officers and by your office, upon the ground that the land was covered by the prior homestead entry of Veronica Siegel, made January 25, 1889.

A motion to dismiss a proceeding pending before the Department will not be entertained where said motion is made by one not a party to the record, but the applicant may ask to intervene and may set up any ground of defence tending to show that the claim of Gilbertson should be rejected as being in conflict with Siegel's right to the land, which will be considered when the case comes up in its order.

You will notify the applicant of this action.

RAILROAD GRANT—MINERAL LANDS.

CENTRAL PACIFIC R. R. Co.

A hearing to determine the character of land claimed under the grant, but returned as mineral, is not authorized in the absence of an application to select and due notice thereof.

Secretary Noble to the Commissioner of the General Land Office, December 4, 1889.

I have considered the case of the Central Pacific Railroad Company on appeal from your office decisions of October 12, 1887, and March 14, 1888, the latter being a refusal to reconsider the former which refused to consider the testimony taken at a hearing ordered by the local officers to determine the question of the mineral or non-mineral character of the odd sections in T. 17 N., R. 9 E., M. D. M., Sacramento, California, land district.

The whole township was reported as mineral by the surveyor general.

It appears from the record that the hearing upon which testimony in the case at bar was taken, was initiated by W. H. Mills, land agent of said railroad company, making application at the local office for such hearing, whereupon the local officers fixed a time and place for the hearing, and the register of the local office states that the docket entries in the local office do not show the fact of any notice either personal or by publication, but that he is informed that publication was had.

If any written application was presented by said Mills it does not appear in the record.

At the hearing ordered as above evidence was submitted upon which the local officers decided some of the lands to be agricultural or non-mineral in character and transmitted the testimony with the record to your office.

Upon inspection of the record your said office decision of October 12, 1887, was rendered in which it is said

> I do not find that any application for the hearing was made in writing or formally in any manner.
>
> Neither the record in the case nor the records of this office disclose that any application to select any of said lands by the company was ever made.

Your said decision further states that the proper practice to obtain a hearing should be first an application to select; second, publication and posting of notice; third return of testimony taken at a regular hearing; and you held that in this case the evidence taken at the hearing held by order of the local officers could not be considered by you, and you ordered that the record and testimony be returned to the local officers with instructions to them to notify the said railroad company " that when an application to select any of the lands is made to you, you will proceed upon the application as indicated, considering the record and testimony in this case.

On November 9, 1887 the attorney of said company filed in your office a motion to reconsider said decision, which motion was overruled and denied by your said office decision of May 14, 1888, and quoted therein is a considerable part of your former decision and in reply to the argument of counsel to the effect that certain cases which he claimed were similar to the one at bar had been decided upon testimony taken at a hearing initiated in a similar manner, you say,

> The question as to the proper order of proceedings was fully considered in said decision of October 12, 1887 and the conclusion therein reached I believe to be, not only necessary for the proper protection of the interest of the government, but, the contest practice under the laws and regulations. That there have been instances where it has not been followed is no good reason why the practice should not be adhered to in the future or govern in this case.

In your said decision I fully concur. In the circular of September 23, 1880, it is provided that in case of an application " to enter or select, as agricultural land under any act of Congress other than the pre-emption or homestead acts, lands returned as mineral by the surveyor general " the applicant will be required to publish for thirty days a notice of intention to so enter or select.

I know of no law or regulation of the Department providing for a hearing as to the non-mineral character of land returned as mineral upon the mere suggestion of a party that he would like to have the same done, and notice is certainly necessary to protect both the government and possible mineral claimants.

Your requirement that the company first make selection is not unreasonable or contrary to law and your said decision is accordingly affirmed.

PRE-EMPTION FINAL PROOF–PAYMENT–CERTIFICATE.

R. M. BARBOUR.

Failure to make payment at the time of submitting final proof will not defeat an entry, made prior to the adoption of the regulations which require proof and payment to be made at the same time.

If the final certificate bears a later date than the proof, the entryman may show by his own affidavit, that at the date of the certificate he had not transferred the land.

First Assistant Secretary Chandler to the Commissioner of the General Land Office, December 3, 1889.

I have considered the case of R. M. Barbour on appeal from your office decision of October 5, 1888, holding for cancellation his pre-emption cash entry for SW. ¼, NE. ¼, and NW. ¼, SE. ¼, Sec. 36, T. 2 N., R. 6 W., Santa Fé, New Mexico, land district.

Claimant made final proof before a clerk of the court in the county where said land is situated on August 14, 1884, after notice duly published, and the same was filed in the local office August 15, but suspended by the local officers for want of non-mineral affidavit, and because claimant had not signed his first name in full, and because the purchase money did not accompany such proof.

On August 16, 1884, such corrections were made and the proof was returned to the local office with two hundred dollars to pay for said land.

The land was found by the local officers to be double minimum and claimant was notified that two hundred dollars more would be required ; and in the meantime the local officers held the proof without formal action thereon until September 17, 1884, when the remainder of the purchase price having been paid in, cash certificate issued.

Subsequently a special agent of the land office reported said entry as fraudulent, and a hearing was had at which the local office decided in favor of the entryman and your office in the decision complained of does not dissent from their opinion except upon one point, viz: It appears from the record that Barbour made a conveyance of the land to Reed and Burton, and his deed to them is dated August 30, 1884, something over two weeks before the date of his final certificate and in your decision it is held that in the face of his deed made to Reed and Burton seventeen days before the date of his final certificate claimant could not make affidavit as required by the rules showing continued residence and non-alienation of the land between final proof and date of certificate, and for that reason you held the entry for cancellation.

The evidence submitted at said hearing upon this point shows that shortly after claimant had submitted final proof, he was harrassed by debts and threats of his creditors to proceed against him by suits and consulted his attorney in regard to selling the land, and that said attorney suggested to him the possibility of making a sale to Reed and Burton, a cattle firm who had recently purchased land for a cattle range in the vicinity of the tract in controversy. Whereupon entryman authorized said attorney to make a sale to Reed and Burton if the same could be done, and as he was himself contemplating an immediate journey he made a deed to said Reed and Burton and placed the same in the hands of his said attorney to be used in case of a sale in his absence, but at this time he had made no agreement or contract whatever. After this deed was executed and so left in the hands of said attorney, notice was received by entryman from the local officers to the effect that said land upon inspection of the record proved to be double minimum. Upon this entryman borrowed two hundred dollars and sent the same to the local officers about September 10, or 12, 1884. When the certificate was issued September 17, 1884, the deed was still in the hands of said attorney and no bargain or other agreement to sell said land had yet been made.

That subsequently and about September 25 to 28, claimant being unable to raise the money to pay his debts or buy stock for his farm, which was grazing rather than agricultural land, sold the same to Reed and Burton and notified his said attorney to deliver to them the deed which was done, but by oversight or neglect said attorney failed to properly change the date to correspond to the time of actual sale.

At the time entryman presented final proof there was no prohibition either in law or by the rules and regulations, against the making of proof and payment at different times; and it was usual to accept such proofs when otherwise satisfactory, if the dilatory action was shown not to have been caused by bad faith or other impropriety on the part of the entryman. Ida May Taylor (6 L. D., 107). No change was made in this practice until November 18, 1884, when instructions were issued requiring proof and payment to be made at the same time (3 L. D., 188).

On February 19, 1887, departmental instructions were issued (5 L. D., 426), section 8 thereof being as follows:

When proof is made before register and receiver and certificate does not bear the date of said proof, require of register and receiver explanation thereof, and if the delay was caused by failure to tender the money at date of making said proof require final affidavit, with corroborating proof to cover date certificate was issued.

This rule was modified January 2, 1889 (8 L. D., 3) so that upon a corroborated affidavit of entryman that he still continued to reside upon and had not transferred the land at the date of the certificate, in cases similar to the one at bar, would be sufficient to correct such irregularity, and by instructions of July 17, 1889 (9 L. D., 123), this rule was again modified so that claimant is only required to show by his own affidavit that at the date of the certificate he had not transferred the land.

This fact the evidence fully shows in the case at bar, the erroneous date of the deed being fully explained by his own testimony and that of the attorney in whose hands the deed was left.

Your said decision is accordingly reversed and patent will issue.

DESERT ENTRY—FINAL PROOF EQUITABLE ADJUDICATION.

EDWARD C. SIMPSON.

The law does not authorize an extension of the time within which to make proof upon a desert entry, but proof submitted after the expiration of the statutory period may be equitably considered if a sufficient explanation is furnished.

In such a case the explanation should be clear and explicit and show that the entryman did not fail through want of diligence on his own part, but was prevented from effecting reclamation by obstacles that could not be foreseen or overcome.

Secretary Noble to the Commissioner of the General Land Office, December 3, 1889.

February 10, 1885, Edward C. Simpson made desert land entry, No. 2312, for the SE. ¼ of SE. ¼ of Sec. 3, S. ½ of S. ½ of Sec. 2, N. ¼ of Sec. 11 and E. ½ of NE. ¼ of Sec. 10—all in T. 50 N., R. 81 W., Buffalo district, Wyoming Territory, making the first payment thereon (twenty-five cents per acre) as required by the statute.

The three years from the date of the entry, within which proof of reclamation and final payment are required to be made expired February 10, 1888, and the claimant having failed to make such proof and payment, the register (pursuant to circular of August 28, 1880, 7 C. L. O., 106), by letter of March 10, 1888, notified the claimant of his default and required him within ninety days from service of said notice, "to show cause why his claim should not be declared forfeited and his entry canceled for non-compliance with the requirements of the law," In response to this notice, the claimant (jointly with fourteen other entrymen, who had made desert land entries in the same locality about the same time, the status of whose entries was the same as that of claimant and who had received the same notice to show cause, and are now prosecuting appeals to this Department involving the same questions as are involved in this case,) filed a statement, verified by affidavit, June 11, 1888, setting forth, substantially, that,

The lands included in said entries are situated about nine miles east of the military post of Fort McKinney; that the entrymen, at the time said entries were made, "associated themselves together for the object of constructing an irrigating ditch from Clear Creek to said lands for the purpose of conveying water thereto and making reclamation thereof; that a line of ditch was surveyed, beginning at a point on Clear Creek near said military post and crossing a portion of the military reservation upon which the same is situated; that early in the year, 1885, an application was presented to the proper military authorities for permission to construct said ditch from the point where it is taken out of Clear Creek to the point where the same crosses the line of said reservation; that they (the entrymen) had reason to believe and did believe, that no objections would be raised thereto, as other parties had been given permission to construct ditches across said reservation, but to their great surprise, their request was denied; that soon thereafter, a second application was made to said authorities for said permit, which was allowed, September 16, 1886; that the line of ditch mentioned in said permit is the only one that can be used to convey water to said lands and Clear Creek is the only stream from which water can be conveyed thereto, and said ditch will be fully fifteen miles long from the head thereof to the point where it will enter said lands, and from that point, the number of miles of ditch and lateral ditches necessary to the reclamation of said lands, will aggregate fully eighty-five miles, making a total of one hundred miles, of main and lateral ditches, which will cost $40,000.00; that by reason of the delay encountered in obtaining the permit to construct the ditch across the reservation, they were unable to perform "any work of any amount during the season of 1886," and "were delayed hindered and obstructed in perfecting and completing their arrangements for the work of the season of 1887, and that owing to the enormous amount of labor required to construct the main and lateral ditches, the same could not be performed during one season; that said lands were entered in good faith, that they have paid the government twenty-five cents per acre thereon and are ready and willing to pay the additional one dollar per acre as soon as said reclamation can be completed, and that they do not constitute a corporation or members thereof engaged in controlling, dealing in or handling, large tracts of land, but their association is for the purpose of enabling them to construct the ditch and thus, by their joint efforts in that direction, be enabled to reclaim their several and individual tracts of land," to which no one or two settlers can afford the enormous expense of constructing a ditch.

This response to the notice to show cause concludes with the prayer, that further and additional time be granted them " to complete the reclamation of said lands." Your office by decision of July 26, 1888 (from which the claimant in this case and said other entrymen severally appeal), held, that the law did not authorize the granting of the request for further time, " but in the event they " (the entrymen) " are prepared, they will be allowed sixty days, wherein to make final proof, under the decision of the Secretary of the Interior, June 16, 1888, in case of Morris Asher." (6 L. D., 801.)

Attached as exhibit "A" to the said statement submitted by the claimant and said other entrymen, is a letter from the Assistant Adjutant General, dated May 15, 1885, notifying them that their application for permission to construct the ditch across the said reservation had been disapproved by the Secretary of War, and, also, as exhibit "B", the permit finally granted, bearing date September 16, 1886, and signed by General R. C. Drum, as acting Secretary of War.

It thus appears the claimant obtained the permit about a year and a half after entry. It is not shown what efforts he put forth, beyond making the two applications, to obtain the permit, and it does not appear that he might not have sooner obtained it. If, as he states, he had reason to believe there would be no objection, why did he not begin work on that part of the ditch outside the reservation? He had notice before entry of a possible delay or obstruction, as he knew the main irrigating ditch had to be cut through the reservation; the exercise of due diligence, therefore, required him to ascertain before making entry, that there would be no difficulty or delay in obtaining the necessary permit. The statement submitted is, moreover, defective in not showing what, if anything, had been done toward reclaiming the land at the date of said showing, June 11, 1888, nearly two years after the permit had been granted by the military authorities. The permit, as above stated, was granted September 16, 1886, and under your office decision which was rendered July 26, 1888, sixty days after notice thereof was granted for making final proof. This gave the claimant the two seasons of 1887 and 1888, after granting of the permit in which to make reclamation. The claimant states that it would require more than one season to complete the work of reclamation. If we are to infer from this that two seasons would be sufficient, then he should have been prepared to make proof within the time prescribed in your office decision.

The decision of your office is affirmed.

PRACTICE—MOTION TO DISMISS—PRE-EMPTION—SECTION 2260.

KIMBREL v. HENRY.

A motion to dismiss an appeal will not be entertained if due notice thereof has not been served upon the appellant.

The inhibition of the second clause of section 2260 R. S., extends as well to one who holds under an equitable title as to one who holds under a legal title.

Removal from a homestead claim after submission of final proof therefor, is covered by said inhibition, though final certificate had not issued at the date of said removal.

First-Assistant Secretary Chandler to the Commissioner of the General Land Office, December 5, 1889.

I have considered the case of Martin M. Kimbrel, protestant, v. Edwin R. Henry, involving the SW. ¼, section 35, T. 28 S., R. 26 W., Garden City land district, Kansas.

Henry filed his pre-emption declaratory statement for the said land November 22, 1886, alleging settlement on the eighteenth of said month.

Martin M. Kimbrel made homestead entry for the said land December 31, 1886.

On November 7, 1887, Henry made his final proof on his said pre-emption before the clerk of the district court of Ford county, Kansas, he omitted to file or introduce proof of publication of notice to make final proof as required.

On the same day Kimbrel filed his protest against the acceptance of the proof for the following reasons:

1st. That he the said Kimbrel, in good faith is a settler upon and desires to prove up the said land under the laws in reference thereto.

2nd. That the said Edwin R. Henry, is the owner of one hundred and sixty acres of land in Ford county, Kansas, and moved from the same upon the land herein described, for the purpose of entering said land.

3rd. That said Henry has not settled upon and improved the said described land as the law requires.

By agreement of the parties the taking of testimony was set for December 15, 1887, before the said clerk and on this day by mutual consent continued to December 22, 1887.

Protestant appeared at place and time as stipulated; claimant did not appear. His default was caused by an unavoidable accident, as is shown by his affidavit and parties thereupon came to the understanding, "that the question involved in said case was a question of law and that the determination of said question of law should rest upon the testimony of this affiant (the said claimant) as his testimony on his own behalf in answer to question forty-five, in this affiant's final proof." The question referred to is: "Did you leave other land of your own to settle on your present claim?" Claimant answered "I moved from tract embraced in my homestead H. E. 34–28–26–to settle on this tract on December 6, 1886, final receiver's receipt for my homestead was issued and dated December 23, 1886."

On March 15, 1888, Kimbrel on due notice to claimant, moved the local officers, because of the said answer, to reject claimant's final proof. This motion was granted and Henry appealed.

As the ground for appeal, he alleges, that he did not own the NE. ¼, Sec. 34, township and range, aforesaid, the land from which, as it is claimed, he removed, because "no patent or certificate of purchase or receipt for money paid or other papers purporting to convey title" of such land had been issued to him.

The records of your office show, that Henry made homestead entry for the said NE. ¼, section 34, March 28, 1885, and that final certificate issued thereon December 23, 1886. You, therefore, by your office decision of April 20, 1888, rejected his proof and held his filing for cancellation as illegal "under section 2260, Revised Statutes."

The claimant, thereupon, August 8, 1888, filed his appeal to this Department. The same is in form of an affidavit and shows among other matters, that Henry made proof on his homestead November 15, 1886; that on November 18, he filed his declaratory statement for the tract in question; that on December 6, 1886, he moved from his homestead to his said pre-emption claim, fifteen-days before the final receipt for the former was issued to him. He claims as a consequence that he did not remove from land belonging to him, to reside on his preemption claim.

On August 28, 1888, Kimbrel by his attorneys filed a motion for the dismissal of the appeal of Henry "for the reason that no notice of appeal, specification of error or copy of brief was served upon Martin M. Kimbrel, or his attorneys, as required by the rules of practice."

This motion, because it does not appear that claimant was served with notice of it cannot be entertained. In the absence of notice to Kimbrel no action could be taken in the case injuriously affecting his interests. Henry has, however, submitted his claims to the Department and an inspection of the record shows that upon his own statement those claims cannot be sustained. At the time he removed from the land covered by his homestead entry, he had submitted final proof showing, as is evidenced by the acceptance thereof, compliance with the requirements of the homestead law, and he therefore held the equitable title to that land. The inhibition of the second section 2260 R. S., extends as well to one who holds under an equitable title as to one who holds the legal title. Frank H. Sellmeyer (6 L. D., 792); Ole K. Bergan (7 L. D., 472).

Henry's filing was therefore invalid and the decision of your office rejecting his final proof and holding his filing for cancellation must be and is hereby affirmed.

PRE-EMPTION ENTRY—RESIDENCE.

ESTEY *v.* WALLACE.

The law contemplates that the residence of the pre-emptor must be upon the tract claimed at the date when he submits final proof and makes payment therefor.

Acting Secretary Chandler to the Commissioner of the General Land Office, December 5, 1889.

James H. Wallace has filed a motion for review of departmental decision of June 11, 1888, in the case of Hiram S. Estey *v.* said Wallace, involving the claim of the latter, under the pre-emption law, to the SE. ¼ of Sec. 1, T. 117, R. 69, Huron land district, Dakota.

Wallace filed pre-emption declaratory statement for said tract December 8, 1883, alleging settlement June 4, 1883. He offered final proof February 19, 1886, when he was met by the protest of said Estey, who had made homestead entry of the tract January 27, 1886. A hearing followed, and from the evidence adduced the local office, your office, and the Department, decided that, if Wallace ever resided upon the tract, he had abandoned such residence—his actual residence for more than two years prior to offering final proof having been in the village of

Faulkton, where he was partner in a " store," and his family never having been in the Territory to exceed thirty days. These facts as to residence are in effect conceded by appellant, who bases his motion for review substantially upon the ground that, having at one time resided upon the tract for six months, he was not compelled to continue such residence until he made cash entry.

In regard to this contention it would seem that nothing further need be said than again to concur in the conclusion of your office, that " the law undoubtedly contemplates that the residence of the pre-emptor must be upon the tract pre-empted, at the date when he offers proof and payment for the land ; argument or citation of authorities in support of this view of the matter is unnecessary, for any other construction would be in marked conflict with the spirit of the . . . . pre-emption law." The motion is denied.

TIMBER CULTURE ENTRY—" DEVOID OF TIMBER. "

MALOCH v. GILCHRIST.

A timber culture entry allowed in accordance with departmental rulings, under the statutory limitation of such entries to lands "devoid of timber," should not be canceled under a later and more rigid construction of the statute.

First Assistant Secretary Chandler to the Commissioner of the General Land Office, December 9, 1889.

I have considered the case of Samuel T. Maloch v. Howard H. Gilchrist upon appeal of the former from your office decision of August 20, 1888, dismissing his contest against the timber culture entry of said Gilchrist for S. ½, NE. ¼, and N. ½, SE. ¼, Sec. 4, T. 30 S., R. 7 W., Garden City, Kansas, land district.

Gilchrist's entry was made September 5, 1878, and no charge is made that he has not fully complied with the law in regard to planting and cultivation and his testimony to the effect that he had fully complied with the law in these matters it was not attempted to contradict.

Affidavit of contest was filed May 22, 1885, and the charge therein was,

That at the time of making said entry said section of land specified in his application was not composed exclusively of prairie lands, or other lands devoid of timber but was composed of lands, and a tract of land containing an adequate supply of timber of mature growth for the inhabitants of one section of the public lands, and more, namely ; at least ten thousand thrifty and growing timber trees, and that said entry made as aforesaid was improperly and illegally made in this that: said land was not subject to entry under the timber culture laws.

A hearing was had August 28, 1885, and upon the evidence the local officers decided against the contestant and recommended that said contest be dismissed.

Your office upon appeal affirmed their decision.

It appears from the evidence taken at the hearing that before claimant made his entry he visited the tract and noticed that there were a
few cottonwoods, willows and hackberry trees and considerable small
brush growing on the section and when he went to make entry he
stated fully such fact to the receiver of the local office and was by him
advised that such trees and growth were not recognized by the government as timber and if the whole of such growth upon the section was
upon the land he desired to enter, it would still be considered "devoid
of timber," under the rulings and he might lawfully enter the same
under the timber culture law.   Upon this advice claimant made entry
and proceeded to plant and cultivate, and he testifies that but for said
advice he would not have entered the land.

The evidence is to the effect that a stream called Crooked Creek
crosses the section and that only in high water does the stream reach
what the witness calls its banks which are sixty or more feet apart, and
during most of the year the water is confined to a small part of this
space; that nearly all of the trees and brush upon the section are confined to the space between said banks and below high water mark.
Claimant testifies that the trees on said section at the time of entry did
not exceed two hundred and were of scrubby growth and comparatively
worthless.   Claimant admits that there are now trees of natural growth
upon the section, amounting to two hundred of six inches or more in
diameter and that counting brush of all kinds there are probably ten
thousand.

Claimant's statements are corroborated by six witnesses who have
known the land, some from 1877, and the latest from 1880, and all agree
that the increase in the amount of timber on the section is due to the fact
that almost ever since claimant's entry the fires and the cattle have been
kept out of the creek bottom.

Contestant's witnesses claimed that much of the natural timber on the
section is elm and walnut, one of them stating that the elm and walnut
together amount to one-fourth of the whole, but this is entirely refuted
by the unanimous testimony of claimant and all his witnesses to the effect that there is not a walnut or elm of *any* size upon the said section or
any where along the creek.

Contestant first saw the land in April, 1885, two of his witnesses saw
it first in August of that year and one had seen it in 1883.

The question to be decided is, was the section "devoid of timber" in
September, 1878, so that claimant could lawfully make timber culture
entry thereon ?

Evidence of the trees and brush now growing thereon tends by the
way of inference to prove the condition of the land in 1878 but such evidence is inferential merely and when numerous witnesses who saw and
examined the land at or about the date of entry testify positively to its
condition at that time, such inferential evidence cannot be allowed to
prevail over said direct testimony.   The rapid increase in the growth

of timber is accounted for by its protection from fire and cattle and its growth within the banks of a stream which kept the roots plentifully supplied with moisture thereby promoting rapid growth.

The question then is whether two hundred scrubby cottonwoods, willows, and hackberries, and patches of brush, growing upon the section as shown by the evidence, rendered claimants entry under the timber culture law illegal and void.

It appears from the evidence that nearly all the trees growing upon the section at the date of the entry were cottonwood trees and as cottonwood was not regarded as timber by the Department when claimant's entry was made (See Cudney v. Flannery, 1 L. D. 165), they may be eliminated from consideration, and this would leave only the large willows to be considered for claimant swears that the hackberries were so small he would call them only brush and this is corroborated by one of contestant's witnesses, who in 1885, cut down a hackberry, presumably one of the largest, for it was cut with a view of ascertaining its age for the purpose of testifying in this case, and it measured one and a half inches in diameter and showed but nine rings of growth. There is no definite testimony as to the number of willows but the contestant only shows that about three-fourths of the growth was hackberry and the remainder elm and cottonwood so there could have been but few willows.

I do not think the evidence shows the section to have had thereon at the date of entry timber of such kind and quantity as to require the cancellation of the entry.

The entry was made when the departmental rulings in force permitted timber culture entries even when there was a considerable growth of scrubby timber along a stream within the section, and it has been held that in such cases entries should not be canceled upon the ground that the section is not "devoid of timber." Candido v. Fargo (7 L. D., 75).

Your said decision is accordingly affirmed.

———

TIMBER CULTURE ENTRY—FINAL PROOF.

CHRISTIAN ISAAK.

Under timber culture entries made prior to the regulations of June 27, 1887, the time occupied in the preparation of the soil and planting the trees may be computed on final proof as forming a part of the statutory period of cultivation.

First Assistant Secretary Chandler to the Commissioner of the General Land Office, December 9, 1889.

Christian Isaak has appealed to the Department from your office decision September 17, 1888, rejecting the final proof offered in support of his timber culture claim, made May 3, 1879, embracing the NW. ¼ of Sec. 34, T. 99 R. 61, Yankton land district, Dakota.

The ground of said rejection was that the proof failed to show cultivation for a period of eight years from the completion of planting the entire acreage of trees. The Department has decided (see John M. Lindback, 9 L. D., 284), that in cases of timber-culture entry made prior to the regulations of June 27, 1887, the time occupied in the preparation of the soil and planting the trees may be computed on final proof, as forming a part of the statutory period of cultivation.

The papers in the case of said Isaak are therefore returned herewith for the action of your office in accordance with the ruling in the case above cited.

APPLICATION FOR SURVEY—RES JUDICATA.

TIMOTHY B. CASE.

The denial of an application for the survey of an island will not preclude favorable action upon the subsequent application of the same or another party, if a proper showing is made thereunder.

Acting Secretary Chandler to the Commissioner of the General Land Office, December 9, 1889.

On October 6, 1888, the Department concurred in the recommendation of your office that the application of Timothy B. Case, for the survey of an island, situated in Long Lake, sections 11 and 14, township 5 N., range 6 E., Michigan, should not be allowed, for the reason that objections to said survey had been filed by E. W. Craine and J. D. Craine, who claimed to be the owners of parts of the island in question.

By letter of July 23, 1889, you transmitted a communication from Clarence Tinker, Esq., attorney at law, calling attention to said case, and enclosing copies of deeds of certain parties to Jesse D. and Elam W. Craine, of Michigan, with affidavit, signed by David Handy, praying for the re-opening of the rejected application of Timothy B. Case for the survey of said island. He states in said letter that Case had no notice of the filing of said affidavits "and was never informed of it or given an opportunity to refute them until it was too late to have a re-hearing under the rules."

The departmental decision upon the former application will not prevent this party, or any other party, from making another application at any time for the survey of this island, and if it is shown that said island is public land of the United States, and that no claim or riparian right exists, the survey of the island may be ordered upon an application hereafter, if all the essential facts be shown. There is not sufficient evidence of the character of this island or of the claims of the adjacent proprietors to enable the Department to pass upon this application, and the papers are therefore returned to your office with directions to notify the parties of this action.

PRACTICE—CERTIORARI—RULE 72.

GIBSON *v.* VAN GILDER.

The discretionary authority vested in the Commissioner of the General Land Office, by Rule 72 of Practice, to order a further hearing or investigation in a case, will not be controlled by the Department in the absence of an apparent abuse thereunder.

Acting Secretary Chandler to the Commissioner of the General Land Office, December 10, 1889.

This is an application filed by Henry C. Gibson contestant praying that an order may issue directing that the record in said case be certified to the Department under Rules 83, and 84, Rules of Practice. From said application and the accompanying exhibit it appears that contest was filed against the homestead entry of Henry Van Gilder, alleging:

That said proof was made with intent to defraud the United States of title to said lands, and was fraudulent in this that the said Henry Van Gilder never established a *bona fide* residence on said tract; that he only lived himself on said land a part of the time, and that his family resided in Persyville, Ohio, where he was engaged in business, and that his family never resided on said land or in Meade county, Kansas, and that the said entry was made in bad faith and not for the purpose of a home, but for speculation, and that said Henry Van Gilder left for his home in Ohio, immediately on making proof on said land and has never returned to said land since.

Upon this contest a hearing was had September 6, 1888, to which date the case had been continued by stipulation of parties, and at said hearing the plaintiff offered evidence in support of his contest, the defendant failing to appear.

The local officers rendered a decision September 11, 1888, and found that the testimony fully sustained the plaintiffs allegations and recommended the cancellation of the entry. From this decision no appeal was taken, and on October 23, 1888, they transmitted the case to your office.

By letter of April 30, 1889, defendant transmitted to your office a motion for a re-hearing upon the ground of newly discovered evidence. You denied this motion upon the ground that under the rules, motion for re-hearing except when based on newly discovered evidence must be filed within thirty days from notice of the decision, and that a re-hearing will not be granted on the ground of newly discovered evidence, where such evidence tends simply to discredit or impeach a witness, nor unless it is of such character as to necessarily cause the trial court to arrive at a different conclusion. But while your office in terms rejected this motion it held that "as the record does not contain sufficient evidence to enable me to render an intelligent decision, I hereby remand the case for further hearing under Rule of Practice 72." Whereupon the petitioner files this application praying that the ruling of the Commissioner be reversed upon review by virtue of a writ of certiorari for the reason—

First: That said decision in remanding said case, a copy of which is above set out, is interlocutory and no appeal lies therefrom.

Second: That said plaintiff is injured thereby, without remedy other than this writ, in this: That witnesses resided near and were well acquainted with the facts in this case at the time defendant made default as above set out, have removed from the vicinity of said tract and beyond the reach of plaintiff. That the evidence submitted upon the part of plaintiff in the face of the default made by the defendant is sufficient to warrant the cancellation of defendant's entry.

Third: That the Hon. Commissioner has no authority to disturb the findings of fact by the register and receiver, when no appeal from their action is taken, except in the following cases to wit,

1. (Rule 48.) Where fraud or gross irregularity is suggested on the face of the papers.

2. Where the decision is contrary to existing laws or regulations.

3. In the event of disagreeing decisions by the local officers.

4. Where it is not shown that the party against whom the decision was rendered was duly notified of the decision and of his right of appeal.

The petitioner further alleges that none of the above reasons exist to authorize the Commissioner to disturb the ruling of the local officers, and that this case does not come within Rule 72, as the discretion of the Commissioner will not be exercised upon a finding of fact by the local officers when no appeal is taken from their decision.

Rule 72 is as follows:

When a contest has been closed before the local land officers, and their report forwarded to the General Land Office, no additional evidence will be admitted in the case unless offered under stipulation of the parties to the record, except where such evidence is presented as the basis of a motion for a new trial or in support of a mineral application or protest; but this rule will not prevent the Commissioner, in the exercise of his discretion, from ordering further investigation when necessary.

Under this rule the Commissioner may grant a re-hearing before the local officers upon a motion for review, although filed after the expiration of the time allowed for appeal from the decision of the local officers, or of a motion for review of their decision, and after the case has been transmitted to the General Land Office; and he may also, in the exercise of his discretion, order a further investigation or hearing when necessary to enable him to render an intelligent decision in the case, although no motion for re-hearing is filed, and the Department will not control the Commissioner in the exercise of this discretion unless there is an apparent abuse of it.

The defendant in his motion for review showed no sufficient ground which would as a matter of right entitle him to a re-hearing; but the Commissioner granted a re-hearing upon the ground that the record does not contain sufficient evidence to enable him to render an intelligent decision, and the petitioner fails to show in his application anything to the contrary further than that the local officers found that the plaintiff had sustained his allegations.

The remanding of this case for further hearing does not violate Rule 48 because that rule must be considered in connection with Rule 72, which allows the Commissioner in his discretion to make further investigation, and to have additional testimony before him before passing upon the merits of the case, or passing upon the decision of the local officers.

The application is refused.

—

PRACTICE—INTERVENOR—RULE 102.

ELMER E. BUSH.

A general statement under oath, by the intervenor's attorney, that said intervenor is the present owner of the land can not be accepted as a satisfactory compliance with rule 102 of practice.

First Assistant Secretary Chandler to the Commissioner of the General Land Office, December 12, 1889.

On July 12, 1883, Elmer E. Bush filed pre-emption declaratory statement for the W. ½ of the SE. ¼ and NE. ¼ of the SW. ¼ and the SE. ¼ of the NW. ¼ of Sec. 27 T. 2 N., R. 38 W., McCook land district, Nebraska.

In your office his final proof under said statement was rejected, and he was required to make new proof. On August 28, 1888, the North-western Cattle Company filed an appeal from that decision. Because there was nothing in the record to show that said company had any interest in the land involved, or had any right of appeal, the case was returned to your office for disposition under Rule 82. By letter of November 16, 1889, you returned the papers. An examination shows that the original appeal, with the addition of an oath by the attorney of said company as follows: " O. H. Herring on oath says he is attorney for the Northwestern Cattle Co.; that said company is the present owner of the land entered by Elmer E. Bush as described in the foregoing appeal as he verily believes," has been refiled.

Rule 102 of rules of practice provides that " No person not a party to the record shall intervene in a case without first disclosing on oath the nature of his interest." There has not been a compliance with the requirements of this rule. The wording of the rule would seem to require that the affidavit should be made by the party in interest in person, or in the case of corporations by the proper officer. If an oath made by an attorney could be accepted in any case as a compliance with that rule, it could only be after a full statement of his means of knowledge and of such facts as would show affirmatively and positively that the party seeking to intervene had at that time a present interest in the subject-matter involved. This has not been done in this case. For failure to comply with the requirements in such cases, the appeal herein must be and is hereby dismissed.

FINAL PROOF—EQUITABLE ADJUDICATION.

SIVERT OLSON.

Under rule 9, of the rules observed in passing upon final proof, the failure of the entryman to submit his own proof on the day advertised may be cured by equitable action, if the proof was accepted by the local office prior to the regulations of February 19, 1887.

The case of Martin Gleeson cited and distinguished.

First Assistant Secretary Chandler to the Commissioner of the General Land Office, December 12, 1889.

On November 2, 1883, Sivert Olson filed his pre-emption declaratory statement for the SE. ¼, Sec. 23, T. 130 N., R. 58 W., Fargo land district, Dakota, alleging settlement July 1, 1883.

In the published notice of his intention to make final proof it is stated that the proof in support of his claim would be made November 7, 1884 and that the testimony of the witnesses was to be taken November 5, 1884, before a notary public, giving his name and place of office.

The testimony of the witnesses was taken as advertised. The claimant gave his testimony at the local office on January 13, 1885; no notice of postponement appears to have been given. The final proof was approved by the local officers and entry made the same day by warrant location No. 114,766.

Your office having examined the proof by decision of August 10, 1887, required the claimant, on account of the said irregularity, to re-advertise and make new proof as to himself and allowed him ninety days to comply with such order.

The local officers reported November 18, 1887, that claimant's attorney was duly notified by registered letter August 16, 1887, of your said office decision and that no action had been taken in response thereto.

Your office, thereupon, by letter of January 21, 1888, instructed the local officers to notify the claimant or parties in interest of the decision of August 10, 1887.

On June 9, 1888, the local officers by letter informed your office that the claimant and Mrs. Emma Sproat, mortgagee, were notified by registered letter on February 24, 1888, and that no action was taken by them. It appears from the proof of service inclosed that the registered letter addressed to the claimant at Straubville, D. T., never reached him; the letter was returned to the local officers endorsed " the person addressed not in Straubville."

On August 22, 1888, your office by decision of that date held the entry for cancellation under Rule two of circular of February [19] 21, 1887 (5 L. D., 426).

Of this decision the claimant, his attorney and the said mortgagee were notified by registered letter, September 24, 1888. Registered letter addressed to claimant was returned to local office November 7, 1888, as uncalled for.

On November 1, 1888, one Knudt A. Nipstad filed his appeal from your said office decision. His appeal is accompanied by his affidavit bearing date October 29, 1888, from which it appears that he purchased the said land from the claimant on or about April 1, 1885; that since the purchase he has made valuable improvements on the land. That he has erected a frame dwelling house of the value of eight hundred dollars, a barn worth about seven hundred dollars and has broken one hundred and fifteen acres. He states, that after diligent search and inquiry he is unable to find Olson or discover his residence, and that it is therefore impossible to procure the required new proof by Olson.

It appears that the proof of the claimant was not taken within ten days following the time advertised for the submission of it. Section 7 of the act of Congress approved March 2, 1889 (25 Stat., 854) has therefore no applicability to this case and the same is, for that reason, not controlled by Martin Gleeson (9 L. D., 283).

It seems that the case at bar, provided the proof is otherwise satisfactory, must be governed by Rule 9 of the "Rules to be observed in passing on final proofs" (9 L. D., 123). This rule reads "Where final proof has been accepted by the local officers prior to the promulgation of said circular of February 19, 1887, except that it was not taken as advertised the cases may be submitted to the Board of Equitable Adjudication for its consideration." See James H. Robertson *et al.* (9 L. D., 297).

I have therefore examined claimant's proof upon its merit.

It shows that Sivert Olson was a duly qualified pre-emptor. His family consisted of a wife. He first made settlement on the said land July 1, 1883, building a sod house. His improvements on the land are described as follows: A frame dwelling house, fourteen by eighteen feet, with shingle roof, lumber floor, two windows and two doors; a sod stable, sixteen by thirty feet with lumber roof, a sod storehouse twelve by twelve feet with lumber roof, and a well thirty feet deep, walled up, holding eight feet of water. The improvements are appraised at the value of three hundred dollars. He cropped four acres to oats.

Claimant established his actual residence on the land April 15, 1884. He and his witnesses state that his residence on the claim was from that day till time of proof continuous.

I am of the opinion that the proof is satisfactory, and that the only objection which can be urged against its acceptance is the irregularity noticed in your said office decision. In accordance therefore with Rule 9, hereinbefore cited I direct that the case be submitted to the Board of Equitable Adjudication.

Your said office decision is accordingly modified.

DESERT LAND ENTRY—FINAL PROOF—EQUITABLE ADJUDICATION.

GEORGE W. MAPES.

On failure to submit final proof within the statutory period, the claimant should be
allowed ninety days within which to show cause why his entry should not be
canceled.

Equitable consideration may be given final proof submitted after the expiration of
the statutory period, if the delay is satisfactorily explained.

*First Assistant Secretary Chandler to the Commissioner of the General
Land Office, December 12, 1889.*

On June 4, 1885, George W. Mapes made desert land entry for the
W. ½, SW. ¼, section 26, SE. ¼, S. ½, NE. ¼, NE. ¼, SW. ¼, SE. ¼, NW. ¼
section 27, NE. ¼, and SE. ¼, NW. ¼, section 24, T. 24 N., R. 13 E., containing six hundred acres, Susanville land district, California.

On October 7, 1885, Mapes was called upon by your office to re-adjust
said entry, it being non-compact. On January 29, 1886, he asked to ·
change his entry to the W. ½ SW. ¼, SW. ¼ NW. ¼, Sec. 26, E. ½ NW. ¼,
E. ½ SW. ¼, and E. ½, Sec. 27, T. 24 R. 13 E., containing six hundred
acres.

By your office letter of March 31, 1886, the said entry as amended
was allowed.

According to the report of the local officers the said Mapes was notified by them about June 30, 1888, by registered mail, that the statutory
period within which he was required to make proof had expired and
was asked to show cause why his said entry should not be canceled.
It seems the notice did not mention the period within which such cause,
if any existed, should be shown by the entryman.

On August 23, 1888, more than forty days having elapsed and the
entryman having failed to show any cause why his said entry should
not be canceled, the local officers reported the said entry to your office
for consideration.

Your office by letter of September 21, 1888, canceled the said entry.

In the meantime and within ninety days from June 30, 1888, to wit:
on September 13, 1888, the said Mapes filed his application, praying that
the time within which to make his final proof and payment for the
land covered by his entry may be extended to May 1, 1889. The application is in form of an affidavit; in it Mapes deposes among other matters, that he, ever since the amendment of his entry supposed that the
latter would be dated from the time of its acceptation by your office
March 31, 1886, and that the period in which final proof had to be made
would not expire until three years thereafter. That during those portions of the seasons of 1886 and 1887 "when it was practical to plow
and scrape out ditches for the conducting of water to the said lands and
distributing the same over the land" sickness of members of his family,

who had to be kept by him away from home in San Francisco and in
Reno, Nevada, where he was obliged to attend them personally, "prevented him from personally attending to the difficult task of getting
water onto his said land, or commencing the excavation of ditches for
that purpose until during the year 1888."

The applicant further deposes—

That for the proper reclamation of the said lands, affiant is compelled to construct
a ditch four and one-half miles in length, on which said ditch he has already caused
much work to be done and affiant at this time has five men and four horses with plows
and scrapers diligently at work on the said four and one-half miles of ditch and on
the lateral ditches for the proper distribution of the water over said land after it had
been conducted to the same.

Applicant further states that he entered the land in good faith always endeavored to accomplish the reclamation as early as possible
and now intends to prosecute the work until the lands are fully reclaimed; that "at this season of the year," the ground is extremely
dry and the work can not be done as rapidly as in the early part of the
year, when the ground "is more easily plowed and handled." The affidavit was duly corroborated by two witnesses.

Your office by your decision of October 15, 1888, denied the said application. On December 1, 1888, applicant appealed to this Department from your decision cancelling the entry. By the instruction of
your predecessor to the local officers of the said land district of Susanville, dated August 28, 1880, (see 2 C. L. L., 1384) it was required that
claimants, under the desert land law, who had allowed the limitation
provided by the statute to expire, without making the final proof and
payment for the land, should be notified of their non-compliance with
the law and that ninety days would be allowed to each of them within
which to show cause why their entries should not be canceled. The
same regulation is embodied in the circular from the General Land Office issued January 1, 1889. See circular, page 38. This provision was
not observed in the case at bar. Before ninety days from notice to
claimant had expired your office canceled the entry and within the said
period he made his application for the extension of time to make his
proof.

It seems therefore that your office decision of cancellation was rendered prematurely. It is true that there is no authority for granting
an extension of time in making final proof in desert land entries.
Richard A. Ballantyne (3 L. D., 8), but the Department will, in absence
of an adverse claim, give an equitable consideration to final proof submitted after the expiration of the statutory period, if the delay is satisfactorily explained. Oscar Cromwell (8 L. D., 432). The rules 29 and
30 of the "additional rules" of equitable adjudication of April 28, 1888
(6 L. D., 799), provide for the submission of the final proof to the board
of equitable adjudication after the expiration of the statutory limit.
Rule 30 enacts that if claimants failure to reclaim the land and make

proof and payment within the statutory period " was the result of ignorance, accident or mistake or of obstacles which he could not control
and there is no adverse claim," the proof when made should be so submitted.

It seems to me that the facts set out in Mapes' affidavit duly corroborated, show that he made his entry in good faith, that he meant to
comply with the law, but was prevented from diligently prosecuting
the work of cultivation by sickness in his family and that at the time of
cancellation of his entry and the filing of his application much work had
been done by him in that manner and money expended. I think, therefore, that the said entry, there being no adverse claim, should be re-
instated, and that the local officers be directed by your office to allow
the claimant, within ninety days after notice hereof, to make payment
for the land and proof of reclamation of the lands covered by his entry
and also proof bringing said entry within the purview of Rule 30 aforesaid, when the same will be submitted for confirmation to the Board of
Equitable Adjudication. See case of Joseph Himmelsbach (7 L. D.,
247).

The decision of your office is modified accordingly.

PRACTICE- APPEAL—CERTIORARI.

OLNEY *v.* SHYROCK.

An appeal will not lie from an interlocutory order of the Commissioner.

The Department will not review, on certiorari, an interlocutory order of the Commissioner, in the absence of due cause shown for such action.

A decision of the Commissioner sustaining a motion to dismiss an appeal is interlocutory, and does not affirm the decision of the local office, or dispense with the necessity of a final decision upon the merits of the case.

Acting Secretary Chandler to the Commissioner of the General Land Office,
December 13, 1889.

This is an application filed by James Olney, praying that an order
may issue requiring you to certify to the Department the record in said
case.

From said application and exhibits filed therewith it appears that
Shryock made final proof upon his pre-emption claim for the NW. ¼ NE. ¼
Sec. 18, T. 33 S., R. 63 W., Pueblo, Colorado, April 17, 1888, and in said
notice specially cited Olney to appear and show cause why his homestead entry for the E. ½ SE. ¼ SW. ¼ SE. ¼ Sec. 18, and "NW. ¼ NE. ¼"
same township and range should not be canceled so far as it conflicted
with the said pre-emption filing; that upon said hearing the local officers decided that said entry should be canceled so far as it conflicted
with the declaratory statement of Shryock ; that within thirty days from

said decision petitioner filed an appeal from the decision of the local officers which was dismissed by your office on motion of Shryock and upon the ground that plaintiff Olney failed to serve upon defendant or his attorney notice of appeal and specifications of error as required by Rule 43 [46] of Rules of Practice.   Petitioner alleges that he is *informed and believes* that Shryock and his attorney had full knowledge of the filing of said appeal before the expiration of the thirty days allowed by the rules; "that he believes that he has a good, meritorious and equitable claim to the land in controversy, and that the same is disclosed in his appeal and in the record of the case, and in the evidence taken at the time of said final proof and protest." These are substantially the sole grounds upon which this application is based.

It therefore appears from the foregoing that the record does not disclose any proof of service upon the defendant, nor is it even alleged that service of the appeal was made upon either the defendant or his attorney, but simply that the defendant and his attorney had knowledge of the fact that an appeal had been filed within the thirty days allowed for appeal.

Without passing upon the question whether the Commissioner erred in dismissing this appeal, this application should be refused for the reason that no final decision of the Commissioner has been rendered from which an appeal will lie, and no ground is shown why the issues presented in this application should now be brought before the Department upon writ of *certiorari* for the reason that all these questions may be considered by the Department upon the appeal of either party from the final decision of the Commissioner upon the merits of the case.   The decision of the Commissioner dismissing this appeal was a mere interlocutory proceeding, and did not affirm the finding of the local officers or dispense with the necessity of the final decision of the Commissioner upon the merits of the case.   Whether the appeal had been dismissed or not, he would still have been required to pass upon the question as to whether the decision of the local officers was final as to the facts under Rule 48, and this question can in like manner be determined by the Department should the case come before it on appeal from the final decision of the Commissioner.   The petitioner may also file any papers tending to show that service of said notice of appeal was perfected within the time allowed, all of which may be considered by the Department as part of the record in the case, in the event of appeal by either party from the final decision of your office.

I see no ground for granting this application, and it is therefore refused.

ALABAMA LANDS—ACT OF MARCH 3, 1883.

LORENZO D. EVINS.

The act of March 3, 1883, protects only such homestead entries as had been theretofore made.

Lands reported as valuable for coal prior to the passage of said act are not subject to entry until after public offering.

An entry of such land made without the prerequisite offering, may be suspended until after offering, and if the land is not then sold, be re-instated as of the date originally made.

An *ex parte* showing as to the character of the land is not sufficient to overcome the correctness of the mineral list in which the land is described as "valuable for coal."

Secretary Noble to the Commissioner of the General Land Office, December 14, 1889.

This case involves the adjoining farm homestead entry, No. 15,120, of Lorenzo D. Evins, for the SW. ¼ of NE. ¼, Sec. 2, T. 4 S., R. 5 E., Huntsville district, Alabama. The entry was made August 21, 1885, and, about two years thereafter, August 19, 1887, was held for cancellation by your office, on the ground that said land was "described in the mineral list on file in" your "office as containing coal."

By act of March 3, 1883 (22 Stat., 487), entitled "An act to exclude the public lands in Alabama from the operation of the laws relating to mineral lands," it is provided:

That within the State of Alabama all public lands, whether mineral or otherwise, shall be subject to disposal only as agricultural lands: *Provided, however,* That all lands which have heretofore been reported to the General Land Office as containing coal and iron shall be first offered at public sale: *And provided further,* That any *bona fide* entry under the provisions of the homestead law of lands within said State heretofore made may be patented without reference to an act approved May 10, 1872, entitled "An act to promote the development of the mining resources of the United States," in cases where the persons making application for such patents have in all other respects complied with the homestead law relating thereto.

The entry of Evins having been made after this act became a law, does not come within the purview of its second proviso, which protects only such homestead entries as had been theretofore made. The land had been reported as valuable for coal in 1879, prior to the passage of the act, and had not been "offered at public sale," as lands so reported were by the first proviso required to be before becoming subject under the act "to disposal as agricultural lands."

Evins, December 11, 1888, appeals from your said office decision, alleging, under oath, that he had, from the date of his entry, complied in all respects with the law as to said entry, and also setting forth facts, tending to show that the land did not in fact contain coal or mineral of any kind. His statements as to compliance with the law and the character of the land are corroborated by three affidavits of parties living near and who claim to know the land.

Conceding for argument's sake that a hearing might be ordered to determine the character of the land, Evins does not make application therefor, and his showing being *ex parte* and based on the opinion of himself and others, who do not appear to be experts, can not be held sufficient in itself to rebut the presumption of the correctness of the mineral list in which the land is "described as containing coal."

The entry of Evins may, however, be held suspended pending the offering of the land at public sale, and, if the same be not sold upon such offer, then said entry may be proceeded with as of the date when originally made. (Nathaniel Banks, 8 L. D., 532). It is directed that this course be taken, and the decision of your office is modified accordingly.

———

SCHOOL INDEMNITY—CERTIFICATION.

STATE OF CALIFORNIA *v.* BODDY.

By certification title to an indemnity selection passes to the State for the land covered thereby as completely as though patent had issued, and precludes the exercise of further departmental jurisdiction over the land until such certification is vacated by judicial proceedings.

Secretary Noble to the Commissioner of the General Land Office, December 14, 1889.

The land involved in this case is the fractional E. ½ of NE. ¼ of Sec. 31, T. 47 N., R. 7 E., Mount Diablo meridian, Susanville district, California.

This tract having been subdivided into lots 1 and 2, was under that description, May 5, and June 29, 1883, selected by the State of California "through its proper officer as school land in lieu of deficits in certain fractional townships," and said selections were "approved" or certified to the State April 19, 1884. About two years thereafter, April 15, 1886, Louisa Boddy was allowed to make timber culture entry on a tract of land embracing said lots 1 and 2, and your office by decision of September 25, 1888, held the entry for cancellation as to said lots 1 and 2, because as to them it was in conflict with said State selections.

Louisa Boddy now appeals to this Department, alleging that said State selections were on May 25, 1885, prior to the date of her timber culture entry, "duly canceled on the plats and records of the land office by authority of the Hon. Commissioner's letter ‘C’ of that date, and the proper State authorities duly notified thereof," and that, no appeal having been taken by the State, "said cancellation thereby became final."

It appears from a letter of the register of October 2, 1888, addressed to Mrs. Boddy and by her made a part of the record in the case, that the cancellation directed by said letter "C" referred to in her appeal was of a prior selection by the State and did not affect the said selections made, as above stated, May 5, and June 29, 1883, under which the land was certified to the State, April 19, 1884.

As patent is not required to be issued by the government to the State of California for lands embraced in indemnity school land selections, "the legal title passes to the State for such lands as completely by certification, as though patent had issued," and thereafter this Department is precluded from the further exercise of jurisdiction over land so certified, until such certification is vacated by appropriate proceedings in the proper forum. Frasher *et al. v.* O'Connor, 115 U. S., 116; 10 Stat., 346; John P. S. Voght, 9 L. D., 114; Steel *v.* Smelting Co., 106 U. S., 447.

The decision of your office is affirmed.

DES MOINES RIVER LANDS ERRONEOUS CERTIFICATION.

FAIRCHILD v. DES MOINES VALLEY R. R. CO.

Proceedings are authorized under the act of March 3, 1887, to set aside an erroneous certification where, at the date of said certification, the land was covered by a settlement claim which was maintained and asserted at the date of the confirmatory act of March 3, 1871, and hence excepted therefrom.

Secretary Noble to the Commissioner of the General Land Office, December 16, 1889.

The land involved herein is the N. ½ of the NE. ¼ and lot 3 of Sec. 26, T. 99 N., R. 37 W., in the State of Iowa.

These tracts were, on October 21, 1863, selected by the State as indemnity, under the act of July 12, 1862 (12 Stat., 543). This act extended the grant of August 8, 1846 (9 Stat., 77), made to the State for the improvement of the Des Moines river, so as to include certain lands within five miles of said river, between the Raccoon Fork and the northern boundary of the State (Homestead Company *v.* Valley Railroad, 17 Wall., 153), and provided for indemnity to the State for all lands within the limits of such extension, which had been previously sold or otherwise disposed of by the United States, with certain exceptions therein specified. It also authorized the State to apply a portion of the lands thereby granted to aid in the construction of the Keokuk, Fort Des Moines, and Minnesota Railroad, now known as the Des Moines Valley Railroad. The selection aforesaid was based on losses supposed to have been sustained by the State under its said grant of 1846, extended as aforesaid by the act of July 12, 1862, by reason of a previous grant of May 15, 1856 (11 Stat., 9), made to the State to aid in the construction of certain railroads therein.

The tracts in question were certified to the State June 14, 1866, as indemnity lands, under said act of July 12, 1862, for the benefit of the Des Moines Valley Railroad Company, and have been since conveyed by the State to said company.

The records of your office show, that on August 24, 1865, S. M. Fairchild filed his pre-emption declaratory statement for these tracts, together with lot 6 of Sec. 23, same township and range, alleging settlement July 26th of the same year; that, subsequently, to wit, on October 3, 1866, he relinquished his filing and made entry for the lands embraced therein under the homestead laws. He made final proof under his homestead entry October 20, 1871, and final certificate was duly issued thereon.

It further appears that your office canceled his entry on April 9, 1872, to the extent that it covered the tracts in section 26, and approved the same July 27, 1876, as to the tract in section 23.

A patent was issued to Fairchild, apparently through a misapprehension, for all the land covered by his final certificate, but this patent was subsequently recalled and canceled, and on March 1, 1878, a new patent was issued to him embracing the tract in section 23 only.

It now appears, however, that the supposed losses, which furnished the basis for the selections made by the State in 1863, and for which these indemnity lands were certified June 14, 1866, as aforesaid, did not in fact exist.

By the act of May 15, 1856, *supra*, there was granted to the State of Iowa, to aid in the construction of certain railroads therein specified, every alternate section of land, designated by odd numbers, for six sections in width on each side of said roads, with the proviso—

That any and all lands heretofore reserved to the United States by any act of Congress or in any other manner by competent authority, for the purpose of aiding in any object of internal improvement, or for any other purpose whatsoever, be, and the same are hereby, reserved to the United States from the operation of this act, except so far as it may be found necessary to locate the routes of said railroads through such reserved lands, in which case the right of way shall be granted, subject to the approval of the President.

The lands, the supposed loss of which to the State (under the act of 1846, as extended by the act of 1862, and known as the "river grant") furnished the basis for the indemnity selection and certification aforesaid, being situated above the Raccoon Fork of the Des Moines river, were originally considered as having passed to the State under the act of May, 1856, and as therefore constituting a proper basis for indemnity under the act of July, 1862. But in the case of Wolcott *v.* Des Moines Navigation Company (5 Wall., 681), in which these several acts of Congress were fully considered by the supreme court, it was held that the proviso in the act of May, 1856, above referred to, covered all the lands above the Raccoon Fork, which had been theretofore reserved from sale by the Commissioner of the General Land Office by withdrawal under the original grant of 1846, then supposed by some to be a grant of lands above, as well as below the Raccoon Fork, and that none of the lands so reserved had passed to the State under the railroad grant of 1856, but were expressly excepted therefrom by said proviso. It thus appears that there was in fact no basis for the indemnity selections made by the State under the river grant, as extended by the act of July, 1862; and, in the case of the Homestead Company v. Valley Railroad (17 Wall., 153), it was further held by the supreme court, that certification to the State of indemnity lands under the act of July, 1862, selected on the aforesaid basis, was erroneously made, and that neither the State nor the railroad company took anything thereunder.

The title to the lands so erroneously certified was, however, confirmed to the State and its grantees by special act of Congress, approved March 3, 1871 (16 Stat., 582); but with the proviso—

That nothing in this act shall be so construed as to affect adversely any existing legal rights or the rights of any party claiming title, or right to acquire title to any part of said lands under the provisions of the so-called homestead or pre-emption laws of the United States, or claiming any part thereof as swamp lands.

By your office letter of January 27, 1888, the papers in the case were transmitted to the Secretary of the Interior, for consideration and action under the provisions of the act of March 3, 1887 (24 Stat., 556), accompanied by the statement that the parties in interest had been notified thereof, and that the case would be held up by the Department for thirty days before final action, in order that they might make such showing in the premises as might be desired. The papers thus transmitted are now before me, and, though the time limited has long since elapsed, no appearance has been entered or showing made in the case, either by the State of Iowa or its grantee—the Valley Railroad Company.

The selection of the tracts in question by the State in October, 1863, having been made without any basis therefor, as shown, was undoubtedly an invalid selection, and the certification to the State which followed in June, 1866, was, consequently, an erroneous certification. The claim of Fairchild, which was initiated in 1865, was *prima facie* a valid one in its inception, subject only to the invalid selection of the State, and it being shown by the record that he was still persisting in the assertion of title, or right to acquire title to the land covered thereby, at the date of the passage of the act of March 3, 1871, *supra*, his claim was expressly protected by the proviso of said act, under which alone the State, or the Valley Railroad Company can assert any legal right to the land.

The second section of the act of March 3, 1887, *supra*, entitled "An act to provide for the adjustment of land grants made by Congress to aid in the construction of railroads and for the forfeiture of unearned lands, and for other purposes," declares—

That if it shall appear, upon the completion of such adjustments respectfully (respectively), or sooner, that lands have been, from any cause, heretofore erroneously certified or patented, by the United States, to or for the use or benefit of any company claiming by, through, or under grant from the United States, to aid in the construction of a railroad, it shall be the duty of the Secretary of the Interior to thereupon demand from such company a relinquishment or reconveyance to the

United States of all such lands, whether within granted or indemnity limits; and if such company shall neglect or fail to so reconvey such lands to the United States within ninety days after the aforesaid demand shall have been made, it shall thereupon be the duty of the Attorney-General to commence and prosecute in the proper courts the necessary proceedings to cancel all patents, certification, or other evidence of title heretofore issued for such lands, and to restore the title thereof to the United States.

It being clearly shown by the foregoing that the tracts in question, were erroneously certified to the State, under the act of July 12, 1862, for the use and benefit of the Des Moines Valley Railroad Company, and that they were expressly excepted from the confirming act of March, 1871, above referred to, by the then existing settlement claim of Fairchild, under the homestead law; and neither the State nor said railroad company having appeared, in pursuance of the notice given by your office, to show cause why proceedings should not be taken in accordance with the provisions of said act of March 3, 1887, to secure the restoration of said lands to the government, you will proceed at once, under the second section of said act, to make demand upon said company for a relinquishment or reconveyance to the United States of such lands. When ninety days from the date of such demand shall have elapsed, you will report the result thereof to this Department, for such further proceedings under said act as may be found necessary.

SWAMP LANDS–CONSTRUCTION OF THE GRANT.

STATE OF IOWA (STORY COUNTY).

The third section of the act of September 28, 1850, enlarged the provision of the act of March 2, 1849, by including not only such lands as might strictly come under the description "swamp-lands," but also such as were so "wet" as to be rendered thereby unfit for cultivation.

Secretary Noble to the Commissioner of the General Land Office, December 17, 1889.

Certain lands in Story county, Iowa, alleged to be swamp land, and if such granted to said State of Iowa by the swamp-land acts of September 28, 1850 (9 Stat., 519), March 2, 1855 (10 Stat., 634), and March 3, 1857 (11 Stat., 251), have since the first-named date been disposed of by the United States, and the State of Iowa claims indemnity for the same.

In the fall of 1885 and winter of 1885–6, special agent A. B. Evans, in pursuance of instructions from your office, made an investigation of said lands in Story county (among others), for which indemnity was claimed. He took the testimony of persons who had long been residents in the vicinity, and some of whom had known the tracts in question at and before the passage of the swamp-land act. All were certified by notaries public or officials of the county to be "respectable and credible citizens." The testimony was taken in accordance with regulations issued by your office; and an examination thereof shows it to have been apparently careful, thorough, and satisfactory. Agent Evans, in his report, dated April 2, 1886, says of the four hundred and fifty-nine tracts of alleged swamp land examined by him:

The selections seem to have been made with more than ordinary care; and from their locations, topography, and general surroundings, I am free to believe the State's claim for indemnity is a good one, *on every tract of land on which proof was filed.*

In the spring of 1887 your office—upon what ground or for what reason does not clearly appear from the record transmitted—directed Special Agent Albert Akers to re-examine said four hundred and fifty-nine tracts in Story county. Agent Akers made his report October 6, 1887, the substance of it being that no one of said four hundred and fifty-nine tracts was in fact swamp land.

Your office, by decision of November 1, 1887, rejected the claim of the State for indemnity, "for the reason that evidence on file in" your "office shows that said lands are not of the character contemplated by the act of September 28, 1850." Application for review and reconsideration of said decision was denied, and the decision re-affirmed by your office, August 7, 1888.

The "evidence on file" is not specified in your said office decision; but it is safe to conclude that reference is had to the report of Special Agent Akers and the accompanying testimony.

Much of the testimony taken before the two agents respectively appears difficult to reconcile; but the difference can mainly be accounted for by the fact that the investigation by the last agent (Akers) was made upon the basis of a stricter and narrower construction of the swamp-land act than that held by Agent Evans, or by this Department.

It will be seen that the principal question at issue in this appeal is similar to that argued before the Department with the appeal in the case of the State of Iowa in the matter of the claim of Poweshiek county for indemnity on account of certain alleged swamp and overflowed lands in said county, decision in which case was rendered by the Department July 19, 1889 (9 L. D., 124). Said decision held that the third section of the swamp-land act of September 28, 1850, enlarged the provisions of the act of March 2, 1849 (9 Stat., 352), by including "not solely such lands as might strictly come under the description, 'swamp-lands,' but such as were so 'wet' as to be rendered thereby unfit for cultivation."

From an examination of the record in the case of Story county, Iowa, now before me, it appears that the principal ground of error alleged is the refusal of the special agent (Albert Akers), acting under the direction of the General Land Office, to allow witnesses to testify as to the character of the land. The State agent, Isaac R. Hitt, states under oath that said agent declared that by "swamp lands" were meant

" land that would not grow anything but bullrushes ; " land that "would swamp a horse or a man ; " that " wild grass lands were not considered swamp lands, no matter how wet they were ; " that "the word 'wet' was not in his instructions." The State agent adds :

While I was present during his examination of witnesses, he frequently declined to allow me to cross-examine them unless I did it in a way to suit him. . . . .
Said that he represented the United States government, and had a good notion to arrest some of the State's witnesses and send them to the penitentiary. Said Akers did as a matter of fact go to some of the State's witnesses and tried to make them believe they did not understand the questions to which they had given answers ; and when he failed to convince them did actually threaten them with arrest. . . .
Akers and I agreed that he would return on the 15th of November to complete the investigation in Story and Boone counties, and *take additional testimony*. . . .
If he could get them (*i. e.*, witnesses,) sooner he was to advise me. He left Nevada, Story county, the next day, as I supposed for Jefferson county, Illinois, and never put in any appearance. . . . But on the contrary forwarded his report on Story and Boone counties to the General Land Office before the 1st November.

The preceding statements appear to be in substance corroborated by affidavits on file in the case.

The same question being involved in the case at bar that was in issue in the Powesheik case, a similar disposition should be made of both. The Department will not undertake to decide the character of the specific tracts here in controversy, nor of any of them. The record is returned to your office with direction that you proceed to examine the same in accordance with the instructions contained in said departmental decision of July 19, 1889, in the case of Powesheik county. If you find the testimony taken by Special Agent Evans sufficient to satisfactorily show whether or not the lands in questions, or any of them, are, by reason of being overflowed, rendered so swampy *or wet* as to be unfit for cultivation, you will decide accordingly, unless the facts reported by said Special Agent Akers are such as to cast serious doubt upon the correctness of said testimony. But should you find, from an examination of the record, in the case of any tract or tracts, that the testimony already taken is insufficient to enable you to arrive at a satisfactory conclusion as to the true character of said tracts, a re-examination thereof may still be ordered (see case of Hardin County, Iowa, 5. L. D., 236), the special agent who may make such examination being instructed to allow the State Agent to show whether the land, at the date of the swamp-land act (September 28, 1850,) was by reason of its "swamp" or "wet" condition unfit for cultivation without artificial drainage.

APPEAL—REPAYMENT—ALABAMA LANDS.

MICHAEL SHANNON.

An application for repayment is, in effect, an abandonment or waiver of a pending appeal that involves the entry for which repayment is asked.

An entry of land reported valuable for coal prior to act of March 3, 1883, and not subsequently offered, is an entry "erroneously allowed," for which repayment may be accorded in the absence of bad faith on the part of the entryman.

Secretary Noble to the Commissioner of the General Land Office, December 19, 1889.

Michael Shannon, May 31, 1888, made homestead entry, for the SE. ¼ of Sec. 27, T. 18 S., R. 8 W., Montgomery district, Alabama. By letter of July 17, 1888, your office held said entry for cancellation, because the land had been reported as valuable for coal before the passage of the act of March 3, 1883 (22 Stat., 487), and had not been offered at public sale as required by the first proviso to said act before lands so reported become subject thereunder to disposal as agricultural lands.

December 18, 1888, Shannon appealed from said action of your office. After taking said appeal, however, May 24, 1889, he filed an application for repayment of the fees of the local officers paid by him on making said entry. With said application he surrenders the duplicate receipt given him by the receiver, and endorsed on said receipt is his relinquishment to the United States of all claim to said land.

Said application and relinquishment of all claim under the entry must be held to be a waiver or abandonment of the appeal, and the same is accordingly dismissed.

The land having been reported as valuable for coal before the act of March 3, 1883, and not having been offered as required by the first proviso thereto, the entry was "erroneously allowed," and there being nothing to indicate that Shannon acted in bad faith in making the entry it is directed that his application for repayment be allowed. (Act of June 16, 1880.)

———

PRACTICE—NOTICE—GENERAL APPEARANCE.

GUMAER v. CARINE.

General appearance by the defendant, without objection to the service of notice, waives all defects therein.

First Assistant Secretary Chandler to the Commissioner of the General Land Office, December 19, 1889.

The case of Henry P. Gumaer v. Luke Carine, or Luke Cairns, is before me on appeal by the latter from your office decision of September 1, 1888, holding for cancellation his homestead entry on the S. ½ of the NE. ¼ and the N. ½ of the SE. ¼ of Sec. 8, T. 5 N., R. 66 W., Denver land district, Colorado

Appellant insists that your office erred in holding that all defects in service of notice were waived by the authorized appearance of defendant without objection to the service of notice; and, also, in holding that defendant had abandoned said tract and failed to comply with the law as to residence thereon.

That a full appearance in a case by a defendant, without objection to the service of process, waives all defects therein is too well settled to require the citation of authorities.

The evidence produced at the hearing had herein fully sustains the decision of your office holding said entry for cancellation, and the same is affirmed.

TIMBER CULTURE CONTEST—SUFFICIENCY OF CHARGE.

STANTON v. HOWELL.

An allegation that no part of the first five acres was cultivated during the fourth year, and that there has been no cultivation of any portion of the tract since, is equivalent to an allegation that the default continues at the date of the affidavit of contest.

Commencement in good faith to cure a default prior to the initiation of contest, justifies the dismissal thereof.

First Assistant Secretary Chandler to the Commissioner of the General Land Office December 20, 1889.

I have considered the case of S. C. Stanton *v.* Jane Howell on the appeal of the former from your office decision of May 24, 1888, dismissing his contest against the latter's timber culture entry for SE. ¼, Sec. 20, T. 3 N., R. 33 E., La Grande, Oregon, land district.

This entry was made October 11, 1880, and on June 8, 1885, contest was initiated, the allegations being that defendant did not during the fourth year of said entry, to wit, the year ending October 11, 1884, and commencing October 11, 1883, cultivate and protect the five acres planted in trees the third year of said entry and did not during said fourth year cultivate the second five acres for the purpose of growing trees thereon, and has not since said fourth year properly cultivated and protected any portion of said land for the purpose of cultivating timber thereon.

A hearing before the local office was had at which both parties were represented and the local officers decided against the entry and recommended its cancellation. Your office on appeal reversed their said decision and the contestant appeals.

It appears from the record that claimant in 1880 purchased a relinquishment of a former claimant to said land for $400; that in 1881 she caused nearly all of said land to be broken and sowed to wheat, and in the spring of 1882 the remainder of the quarter section was broken; that in 1882 all the quarter section except six or seven acres was again sown to wheat; in the spring of 1883 six acres of the land were replowed thoroughly harrowed and planted to cuttings of balm trees (one witness calls them cottonwood). These trees were cultivated by hoeing twice during the summer of 1883 and made an excellent growth.

During the year 1884 the second five acres which had formerly been in wheat was allowed to grow up to volunteer wheat and about the first of October 1884, it was cultivated by being thoroughly plowed and harrowed and was then planted in box elder seeds and again harrowed.

The winter and spring following the planting of these seeds was dry and unfavorable to their germination and but few of them came up.

February 9, 1885, claimant made application for an extension of time based upon her affidavit corroborated by those of two others to the effect that by reason of drouth in the summer of 1884, most of the cuttings planted on the first five acres in the spring of 1883 had died and it would be necessary to replant the same, and this application was held by the local officers without action until June 11, 1885, when said application and affidavits were forwarded to your office with two affidavits of contest against said entry for special instructions, and your office ordered a hearing upon the contest of Stanton.

In a brief filed August 15, 1885, counsel for contestant concede as follows: " The Hon. Commissioner's findings concerning the second five acres are doubtless correct and we do not claim anything from our exceptions thereto."

This leaves for consideration only the question of the first five acres.

In your said decision you say—the first charge " is insufficient as it is not alleged that the said default continued at the time of contest, and the same should have been amended, on objection, or the said charge dismissed."

I do not think this objection well taken.

It will be observed that the first of the allegations in the contest affidavit attacks the entry as to the first five acres for failure to cultivate the same during the fourth year, the next clause refers to the alleged default in regard to the second five acres, while the third clause is, " and has not *since* said fourth year properly cultivated and protected *any portion* of said land."

It seems to me that an allegation that no part of the first five acres was cultivated during the fourth year and that there has been no cultivation of *any portion of the tract* since, is equivalent to an allegation that the default continues at the date of the affidavit of contest.

But conceding that the continuance of said default is properly alleged the next question is whether or not the evidence shows such a state of facts as to require the cancellation of the entry or any part of it.

The witness Elgin who was doing the work for the claimant testified that in the year 1884 the cuttings planted in 1883 were nearly all dead and in November of that year he plowed them all under, and the contestant on cross-examination stated that they were plowed under at that time.

It also appears from the evidence that the spring of 1885 was extremely dry until after the season of planting trees was past.

The evidence fairly sustains your suggestions that the selection of balm as the kind of timber to be grown upon the land was an error of judgment, as it was shown that balm only grew naturally close to the streams and not on high dry and sandy soil like the land in controversy. It may also be conceded that under the evidence it was a mistake in judgment not to cultivate the first five acres during the summer of 1884, and that had they been cultivated many if not all the trees, might have been saved; but there is nothing in the evidence tending to show that either of these delinquencies was the result of bad faith or that the claimant was in any manner endeavoring to evade complying with the law; on the contrary the whole record indicates the utmost good faith upon her part.

It is unnecessary to discuss the question of her failure to cultivate the trees during the season of 1884 for the reason that as soon as she discovered that the trees were dead in November, 1884, she at once began to cure said default by plowing up the ground preparatory to replanting, and in February, 1885, she took another step in that direction by applying for an extension of time.

A commencement in good faith to cure a default prior to initiation of contest, has been held to justify its dismissal. Boulware v. Scott (2 L. D., 263).

The evidence shows that replanting was fully and thoroughly done after initiation of contest but before the hearing and the delay is explained by the fact of drouth during the spring months. Conrad v. Emick (7 L. D., 331).

The record showing good faith on the part of claimant and that she had commenced to cure her default long prior to the initiation of the contest, your decision is affirmed.

FINAL PROOF—NEW PUBLICATION.

HERBERT HIGGINS.

Proof taken at a later day than first named therefor is not open to objection, if due publication of a notice including the change of date is subsequently made.

A defect in final proof, caused by the substitution of a witness, may be cured by a new publication containing the names of the witnesses who testified, and such proof may be then accepted in the absence of protest.

First Assistant Secretary Chandler to the Commissioner of the General Land Office, December 23, 1889.

I have considered the appeal of Herbert Higgins from your office decision of July 19, 1888, involving the NE. ¼ of Sec. 35, T. 153 N., R. 58 W., Grand Forks land district, Dakota.

Higgins filed his pre-emption declaratory statement for the said land February 9, 1883, alleging settlement November 17, 1882. He made his final proof before H. D. Fruit, a notary public, at Michigan City, on November 19, 1883. The proof was accepted by the local officers and cash certificate issued.

Your office by said decision of July 18, 1888, on account of irregularities in the making of the final proof, required "new proof after due publication." Claimant appealed.

It appears that a witness not named in the notice for proof was substituted for one of the witnesses advertised; the testimony of two witnesses only was taken.

Besides this irregularity apparent on the record, it is stated in the letter of your office of said date, that the proof of Higgins was not made on the day designated in the published notice. The proof, I think is not open to this charge. Underneath the regular notice as published, stating that proof would be made before Walter H. Griffin, notary public at Michigan City, Dakota on October 18, 1883, is this additional notice—"The above proof will be taken before H. D. Fruit, notary public at Michigan City on November 19, 1883."

This notice, together with the said addendum was duly published for the period required by the regulations of this Department, I therefore conclude that the proof was taken at the time advertised and that the only irregularity in this case is the substitution of a witness not designated in the notice for one named therein.

Rule 4 of the "rules to be observed in passing on final proofs" approved July 17, 1889 (9 L. D., 123), reads—

When a witness not named in the advertisement is substituted for an advertised witness, unless two of the advertised witnesses testify, require new advertisement of the names of the witnesses who do testify at such time and place as you may direct; and if no protest or objection is then filed, the proof theretofore submitted, if satisfactory in all other respects, may be accepted.

This rule is the declaration of a principle established by decisions of the Department before the adoption of the said rule. See Wenzel Paours (8 L. D., 475); also Amos E. Smith—idem, 204.

I have therefore considered the case on the merits. The proof shows, that Higgins, a qualified pre emptor, is a married man, his family consisting of a wife and four children. He made his first settlement on the land November 17, 1882, by building a house and established his residence therein May 17, 1883. It is claimed by himself and his witnesses that claimant's residence on the land was continuous from that day till time of proof. He was absent from the land while on a visit elsewhere for about six weeks during parts of the months of September and October. This was his only absence.

His improvements consisted of a dwelling house of the size of twelve by fourteen feet with an addition six by eight feet, a well, and five acres of breaking. His house had floors, doors, and windows. The total value of the improvements as given by claimant is two hundred and thirty-five dollars; his witnesses respectively appraise them at two hundred and fifty and two hundred and twenty-five dollars. Claimant used the land for agricultural purposes, and raised potatoes on part of his five acres of breaking.

The proof seems to be satisfactory and unobjectionable except for the irregularity of the substitution of a witness, not named in the notice for one named therein; this being the case it seems that in accordance with rule 4 above set out and cases cited, the irregularity can be cured, in the absence of protest or objection, by a new publication, giving in the notice the names of the witnesses that testified at the submission of the proof. It is therefore directed, that such new publication be made; that should no protest or objection be filed in the case, the proof already made be accepted, and that there being no other legal objection, the entry be passed to patent. See case of George F. Lutz (9 L. D., 266).

Your said decision is accordingly modified.

——

PRATICE—CERTIORARI—APPLICATION.

SMITH v. HOWE.

An application for certiorari will be denied if a copy of the decision complained of is not furnished.

Secretary Noble to the Commissioner of the General Land Office, December 23, 1889.

In the case of Sherman W. Smith v. Jacob W. Howe, involving Howe's mineral entry No. 24, Cheyenne land district, Wyoming, Wm. M. Slaughter, attorney for said Smith has filed application for certiorari.

Whether said application should be granted or not is a question which the Department cannot decide intelligently without a copy of the decision complained of—which applicant has failed to furnish. The application is therefore denied, and herewith transmitted to your office.

(Johnson v. Bishop, 2 L. D., 67; John Waldock, 4, L. D., 31; L. W. Bunnell, 5 L. D., 588; P. O. Satrum, 8 L. D., 485.)

RAILROAD GRANT—ACT OF MARCH 3, 1887.

WINONA AND ST. PETER R. R. CO.

Under the act of March 3, 1887, it is mandatory upon the Secretary of the Interior to demand a recouveyance of title, if the grant is unadjusted, and lands have been erroneously certified or patented to or for the benefit of the company.

The certification of lands covered by homestead entries at date of definite location is erroneous and without authority of law.

The existence of settlement claims at date of definite location excepts the land covered thereby from the operation of the grant; and lands thus excepted afford no basis for indemnity under the act of June 22, 1874.

The said act requires the adjustment of the grant "in accordance with the decisions of the Supreme Court," and it is no defense to action thereunder that the certification in question followed existing departmental rulings, if in fact such rulings are in conflict with the decisions of said court.

Secretary Noble to the Commissioner of the General Land Office, December 26, 1889.

On January 10, 1888, your office transmitted to this Department a petition, numerously signed by parties claiming to be settlers on certain tracts of land in the State of Minnesota, which they state had been improperly certified or patented to said State for the benefit of the Winona and St. Peter, and the St. Paul and Sioux City railroads, under the act of March 3, 1857 (11 Stat., 195), and supplements, making a grant to aid in the construction of said roads. The petition asked that the government cause suit to be instituted to restore the title of said lands to the United States so that the claims of the settlers thereon might be recognized. With said petition your office sent two lists, in which the status of each tract was fully set forth : list A, described the lands within the odd sections, which had been approved to the State, and list B, lands in the even sections, which had been certified to the State for the benefit of the Winona and St. Peter Railroad, in lieu of lands relinquished under the act of June 22, 1874 (18 Stat., 194).

On February 21, 1888, said lists were returned by Secretary Vilas, with instructions to call upon the Winona and St. Peter and St. Paul and Sioux City Railroad companies to show cause before your office, within thirty days, why proceedings should not be taken in accordance with the provisions of the act of March 3, 1887 (24 Stat., 556), to secure the restoration of said lands to the United States.

On June 22, 1888, your office transmitted, separately, the answer of each company, with the views of your predecessor upon the showings made. The answer of the Winona and St. Peter Railroad Company is accompanied by an application of the Winona and St. Peter Land Company, which as assignee of the railroad company, asks to be allowed to intervene, and as such intervenor files an answer to the rule. I will first consider the case as it affects the claims of these two companies in the premises.

According to the statements of your office, list A comprises a number of tracts, parts of odd-numbered sections, within the granted limits of said road; all of them, except a portion of one tract, appear to have been covered by homestead entries at the date when the rights of the road are stated to have attached.   Said entries were subsequently canceled, and the tracts covered thereby were certified to the State of Minnesota, and by it transferred to the Winona and St. Peter Company as of its granted lands.   The excepted tract, referred to above, was covered by a pre-emption declaratory statement, filed June, 1861, and which is yet uncanceled on the records of your office.   This tract was certified over in the same way and passed to the company.

List B comprises a number of other tracts of land, being parts of odd-numbered sections within the granted limits of said road, which are stated by your office to have been covered, at the date when the company's rights attached, by homestead entries and pre-emption claims or rights.   These tracts were accepted as bases for the selection of lieu lands by said company, under the provisions of the act of June 22, 1874 (18 Stat., 194), and the selected lands in the even numbered sections, described in list B, were certified over to the State for the benefit of said road.

It is asserted in behalf of the settlers that the certification of the tracts in the odd-numbered sections, as described in A, and of those in the even numbered sections, as described in B, under the circumstances, was erroneous, and that it is the duty of this Department to demand from said company a reconveyance of said lands, in compliance with the provisions of the first and second sections of the act of March 3, 1887 (24 Stat., 556), and in this view your office concurs.

The sections referred to are as follows:

That the Secretary of the Interior be, and is hereby authorized and directed to immediately adjust, in accordance with the decisions of the Supreme Court, each of the railroad grants made by Congress to aid in the construction of railroads and heretofore unadjusted.

Sec. 2. That if it shall appear, upon the completion of such adjustments respectively, or sooner, that lands have been, from any cause, heretofore erroneously certified or patented, by the United States, to or for the use or benefit of any company claiming by, through, or under grant from the United States, to aid in the construction of a railroad, it shall be the duty of the Secretary of the Interior to thereupon demand from such company a relinquishment or reconveyance to the United States of all such lands, whether within granted or indemnity limits; and if such company shall neglect or fail to so reconvey such lands to the United States within ninety days after the aforesaid demand shall have been made, it shall thereupon be the duty of the Attorney-General to commence and prosecute in the proper courts the necessary proceedings to cancel all patents, certification, or other evidence of title heretofore issued for such lands, and to restore the title thereof to the United States.

Many grave questions, supposed to be involved in a consideration of this matter, have been presented to the Department and argued with much zeal and ability by the counsel for the company, but, in view of the conclusion arrived at, it is not deemed necessary to refer to or discuss them.

The adjustment act of March 3, 1887, would seem to be mandatory in respect to the duty imposed upon the Secretary by the first and second sections thereof. If the two prescribed conditions are found to exist, it becomes his plain duty to obey the mandate of the law. These two conditions are, (1) that the grant in aid of the road is "unadjusted," and (2) that lands have been "erroneously certified or patented by the United States" to or for the benefit of the company. Do these conditions exist in the present case?

Is the grant in question unadjusted? It is argued, in behalf of the company, that its grant has been practically adjusted some time past, that no further claims for lands have been asserted or prosecuted by the company for many years, and that such acquiescence and silence for so long a period is an admission that its claims have been fully satisfied, and would fairly justify a conclusion that its grant should not be classed as "unadjusted."

It may perhaps be difficult to determine, in some cases when a land grant has reached that point when it can properly be held to be finally adjusted.   Certainly Congress does not seem to consider the certification or patenting of land for the benefit of a grantee to be, of itself, a technical or final adjustment of the grant, even to the extent to which the patenting has been completed. Because in the adjustment act it is directed that suit be brought to set aside such certification or patent in case of error, if discovered "upon completion" of the adjustment, or "sooner." But in relation to the grant now under consideration, it is not necessary to discuss any of these questions, inasmuch as an inspection of the records of your office shows that as late as July, 1887, said company filed two lists of lands claimed by it, which lists, though rejected by the local officers, are yet pending before you for further action. It must be held, therefore, that the first condition exists and the grant is "unadjusted."

I pass to the second question: Have lands been erroneously certified or patented by the United States to this company?

It is admitted by the company that the tracts described in the two lists were certified, as stated, for its benefit, but it is denied that such certification was erroneous, either in law or fact.

It is denied that the tracts in "A" were covered by settlement claims at the time the rights of the company attached to the granted sections, because, it is asserted, that up to 1882 when the decision of the supreme court in the case of Van Wyck v. Knevals, 106 U. S., 360, was made to the contrary, it was held by the Land Department that the rights of such grantee companies to the coterminous lands, within the primary limits, attached at the dates of the surveys in the field of the line of road. That acting under this construction of long standing, the land officers adjusted the grant and certified over many of the described lands, inasmuch as the alleged settlement claims thereon were initiated subsequent to the surveys in the field, though prior to the filing of the map of definite location. Other tracts, it is said, were covered by fraudulent and invalid claims, so proven by the respondent, on contest, to the satisfaction of the land officers, which tracts were thereupon also certified over for the benefit of said company, and it is claimed that these matters which happened so long ago are based upon executive action, duly considered and regularly had in accordance with the then established construction of the law in that behalf, that after so considerable a lapse of time the company ought not now to be compelled to defend its title so vested against the government, whose proper officers, with a full knowledge of the law and the facts, determined that respondent was legally and justly entitled to the lands in question.

Inasmuch as the first section of the adjustment act directs the Secretary to adjust such grants " in accordance with the decisions of the supreme court," and it is conceded that the court, in the case referred to, decided that the route was not definitely fixed, in contemplation of law, until a map of the line thereof was filed with and approved by the Secretary of the Interior, it is not seen how this Department can now say, under the rule established by Congress, that the route was fixed prior to filing of the prescribed map, because such erroneous view of the law had theretofore prevailed.

As to those entries admittedly in existence at the time of the attachment of the company's rights, but which were subsequently canceled, it may be true, as asserted, that the Department then held that the company took whatever right the government had to lands within the granted limits, and that a record of adverse claim could be rebutted either by proof of illegality or of abandonment, whereupon the grant by its inherent force would re-assert itself and take the tract in question as though it had never been within the exception. Yet, inasmuch as the supreme court decided, in the case of Kansas Pacific Railway Company v. Dunmeyer (113 U. S., 629–641) and other cases, that lands within the exceptions of a grant at the dates of definite location did not, upon their subsequent reversion to the government by abandonment or otherwise, pass to the company, it would seem that these last rulings may not be disregarded under the mandate of Congress to adjust the grant " in accordance with the decisions of the supreme court."

It is further insisted in behalf of said companies, that the pre-emption and homestead rights set up did not except the lands in question from the grant. The exception in the grant of 1857 is of " lands sold or otherwise appropriated, or to which the rights of pre-emption have attached ; " and it is said that such pre-emption " right" could only attach " by executed compliance with all the requisites of the pre-emption law ; " that no such compliance is shown or asserted, but that the recorded evidence of an asserted claim is improperly accepted as establishing the pre-emption " right" referred to in the act. It is strenuously asserted also that the right to make an homestead entry on the public lands, not having been established until 1862, five years after the grant was made for the benefit of the company, it is not possible that such entries should, in the contemplation of Congress, have been intended to form one of the exceptions to the grant to the State. And the grant being a present grant, it can not be reasonably held that Congress, after specifying exceptions, retained the right to continue to carve out of the grant further exceptions by subsequent legislation. Anticipating the answer that Congress did reserve such right, by excepting from this grant, at the date of definite location, "lands otherwise appropriated," an excerpt is given from the Dunmeyer case, last cited, as being conclusive upon that point.

As I read that portion of the opinion in the case, its quotation is not very apposite to the point. The sole question then being discussed in that branch of the case was, whether a statutory mandate that lands "shall be reserved from sale" also reserved them from pre-emption or homestead claim; and the court said, that "in the terminology of the laws concerning the disposition of the public lands, each of these words has a distinct and well known meaning in regard to the mode of acquiring rights in these lands." But the court did not say that, in order to except from the operation of a present grant, which became effective only on definite location thereafter, lands which might in the meantime be disposed of or appropriated by authority of law, it was necessary for Congress to enumerate the particular manner in which the excepted lands were to be taken, and that general and comprehensive terms would not effectuate a reservation or exception from the grant.

Without entering upon a full discussion of this question, it may be said, in a general way, that this Department is unwilling to assume that, when the grant was made for the road in question, Congress intended to restrict the disposal of public land between its termini, prior to the definite location of the road, to the specific methods enumerated in the grant. Such an assumption could only be based upon the presumption that when Congress, by the act of May 20, 1862, invited citizens to enter homesteads upon unappropriated public land, it was with the proviso that those homesteads, with their improvements, were liable to be appropriated by others through the subsequent location of a line of railroad, opposite to them, under a grant made prior to the passage of the homestead act. It is inconceivable that such consequences were overlooked or that such wrong and injustice was contemplated with complacency, or proposed to be tolerated.

I think it was the manifest purpose of Congress, in relation to the grant we are now considering, to except from its operation, at the time of the definite location of the road, any land which had been appropriated or disposed of in accordance with law. This conclusion in no way deprives the company of anything to which it was entitled. For, as was said by the supreme court, in the case of the Kansas Pacific Railway Company v. Atchison Railroad (112 U. S., 414–422), until the definite location of the road, "the appropriation of lands even within the limits of the grant, much less so of lands without them, was in no respect an impairment" of the rights of a company claiming under a prior grant.

To the same effect is the ruling of the United States supreme court in the case of the Hastings and Dakota Railroad Company v. Julia D. Whitney and John Whitney, decided December 9, 1889 (not yet reported), wherein the court, speaking of the effect of a homestead entry of land in an odd numbered section within the primary limits of a grant for the benefit of said company, at the date of definite location of its line of road, said: " So long as it remains a subsisting entry of record, whose legality has been passed upon by the land authorities and their action remains unreversed, it is such an appropriation of the tract as segregates it from the public domain, and therefore precludes it from subsequent grants."

I therefore hold that homestead entries of record at the date when the line of the company's road was definitely fixed according to law constituted such an appropriation, under the laws of Congress, of the lands thereby covered, as to except the same from said grant, and the subsequent certification of the same lands to the State was erroneously made, being without authority of law. As to the single tract covered by a pre-emption filing, as stated herein, demand will not now be made, the question involved being reserved for future action by this Department.

In regard to the lands in list B, it is contended that the act of June 22, 1874, under which the selections were made, intended that in the administration of the same " the decision of the Land Office," as to the time when the rights of the road attached, should be conclusive; and that, in this case, the land office held, under the then construction of the law, that the right of the company to the relinquished lands attached at the time of the survey in the field, which was prior to the date of the settlement claims; and that, therefore, the lieu lands were properly allowed and certified under said act.

The conclusion heretofore arrived at, that the right of the road did not attach to the granted sections until the filing and approval of the map of definite location, precludes the necessity for answering the point suggested, inasmuch as the tracts, made the bases for the selections in list B, were covered at the date of definite location with settlement claims, consequently were excepted from the grant, and do not come within the purview of the act of June 22, 1874, which made provision only for the case where the settlement claims were recognized and allowed " subsequent" to the company's rights.

Having thus come to the conclusion that the two conditions required by the adjustment act of 1887 exist, the law seems to impose upon me the duty of making a demand, in accordance with the provision of the act of 1887, for the reconveyance to the United States of the lands found, under the views herein expressed, to have been erroneously certified. You are, therefore, directed to demand from the Winona and St. Peter Railroad Company a reconveyance of the lands described in said lists, except the tract herein referred to as covered by a pre-emption filing. And, if the company neglect or fail to make said reconveyance within ninety days, after demand, you will prepare and transmit to this Department a report of the fact and a record of all the proceedings in relation to the matter, to be forwarded to the Attorney-General, that he may take proper action in the premises, in accordance with the provisions of the last cited act of Congress.

CIRCULAR—ACCOUNTS.

DEPARTMENT OF THE INTERIOR,
GENERAL LAND OFFICE,
Washington, D. C., December 4, 1889.
Registers, receivers, and disbursing agents.

GENTLEMEN: With a view to uniformity in the manner of making up the monthly and quarterly returns required from the United States district land officers, it is expected that in future, when preparing returns that may become due from your respective offices, you will be governed by the following rules:

1. In filling up the register's certificates of purchase, and receiver's receipts for ordinary cash entries, homestead affidavits, and the final certificates, the Christian name of the purchaser or entryman, as the case may be, should be written out in full in every instance, special care being taken with respect to the correct orthography of the name, as well as in the discrimination between male and female names where they nearly resemble each other in sound or spelling, and the name of the county and State in which the party resides should invariably be inserted in the respective documents, as should his or her post-office address. When there are two or more purchasers of the same surname in a certificate of purchase the surname is to be repeated in each case, thus: John Brown, James Brown, and William Brown; not John, James, and William Brown. To avoid ambiguity in the description of lands, where two or more subdivisions of the same quarter section are embraced in one entry, they should be described in the certificate, receipt, etc., thus: Northeast quarter of the northeast quarter and southwest quarter of the northeast quarter of section ——; the west half of the northeast quarter and the southeast quarter of the northeast quarter of section ——; and not the northeast and southwest quarters of northeast quarter of section ——; or west half and southeast quarter of northeast quarter of section ——. The register should observe the greatest particularity in regard to the manner in which the application of a purchaser or entryman is made out. Where the tracts are bounded by a river they are to be designated with reference to the bank of the

river upon which they are situated; thus, on the right or left bank of
the river in descending, and *not* north, south, east, or west of the same.
This rule for describing the land being equally applicable in the case of
the certificate of purchase, receiver's receipt, etc. In the case of cash
entries the application should be retained upon the files of the register's
office, while in homestead cases they should be sent up to this office,
accompanied by the settler's affidavit and the receiver's receipt.

2. In every instance the certificate of purchase, the receiver's cash
receipt, the homestead application, affidavit, and receipt should be
neatly trimmed and folded over a tin folder, corresponding in size with
the pattern herewith inclosed; the edges should be turned under on
each side, and the number of the entry, name of land district and State,
together with the character of the entry, should be plainly written on
the back of each case. In the case of a cash entry the register's certificate of purchase should be folded on the outside of the receiver's
receipt, and, in the event of there being an assignment or pre-emption
proof connected with the case, they should be, if practicable, placed on
the inside of the receipt. But if the proof is too voluminous to permit
of its being filed in this manner, it is then to be folded as nearly as
possible to the size of the other papers and bound to them with a tape
or paper band. The proof should have indorsed upon it the number of
the entry to which it pertains and the name of the pre-emptor. The
number of the declaration and description of the tract for which the
same is filed in every instance should be indorsed in red ink upon the
back of the certificate of purchase. In homestead entries the application, properly indorsed, with the number of the entry and name of the
settler, should be folded upon the outside of the affidavit and receipt.
The homestead certificate issued upon the filing of the final proof,
should be folded a trifle larger than the papers alluded to, so as to
permit of their being placed within it, upon the case being finally disposed of. Agricultural college scrip should be folded with the application on the outside, with the register's and receiver's number and the
number of the scrip indorsed upon it; the register's and receiver's number in *red ink*.

3. The practice of using half or fractional numbers for the receiver's
receipt must be discontinued. In future the receipt issued for payments on account of excesses in warrant and homestead cases, additional payments on graduated entries, payments on account of double
minimum lands located with military warrants, and agricultural college
scrip, must be numbered consecutively, with full numbers, in accordance with the regular cash entries, and should have indorsed upon them
in *red ink* the number and description of the case with which they are
respectively connected. No certificates of purchase are required in
these cases, nor is it necessary to send up separate or special abstracts
in cases of payment on account of homestead excesses, such payments
being reported in the regular cash returns.

4. The registers of homestead and timber-culture entries and receipts must exhibit the true areas embraced by the respective entries; the several columns of said returns must be properly added up and the footings stated; and from the footing of the column appropriated to the area of the lands entered there must be deducted the aggregate area of the excesses over the 160 acres, etc., specified in the homestead and timber-culture laws, the remainder, after making said deduction, being the proper area to be inserted in the fee statement. In the case of locations with college scrip, where the area is less than that shown by the face thereof, the former must be inserted in the fee statement under the heading "Quantity actually located," etc., but you are *not* in any case to insert under that heading an area greater than that embraced on the face of the scrip, inasmuch as the excess will have been reported in the regular cash returns. The same rule is equally applicable in the case of locations made with military bounty-land warrants.

5. The number of the excess receipt, if any, *must be* indorsed, in red ink, on the back of the case with which it is connected. All excess receipts should be sent up with your *cash returns.*

6. In the case of additional payments on account of graduated entries, payments on homestead entries commuted to cash, and entries allowed under the second section of the act of June 15, 1880, also on account of double minimum lands located with military bounty-land warrants or agricultural college scrip, and where cash is substituted for a warrant or scrip location that has been adjudged invalid, the area of the tracts embraced thereby should be stated in your cash returns, in *red ink*, and must be deducted from the footings of your abstracts thereof, the remainder being the proper area to be inserted in your monthly account current, for the reason that the area of said homestead entries and invalid warrant and scrip locations will have been already accounted for in the returns in which the original entries and locations were reported, and the area of the double minimum lands, located with warrants or scrip, will be embraced in the abstract thereof for the month in which the locations were made.

7. Where payment for land is made with Revolutionary bounty-land scrip, by law receivable in the form of money in satisfaction of lands subject to sale at private entry, and also in payment for unoffered lands which are embraced in pre-emption entries, a regular cash certificate of purchase and receiver's receipt should be issued and numbered in accordance with the regular current cash series; the receiver indorsing upon his receipt the amount paid in scrip and stating the number of the latter. The United States should be credited in the cash column of the monthly and quarterly returns with the entire amount of purchase money of the land described in the certificate and receipt, the amount received in scrip to be specified in the column of the returns appropriated to that purpose, and the government is to be debited in the

receiver's monthly and quarterly accounts with the amount of scrip actually applied in payment or part payment for such land, the scrip to be sent up, as vouchers, with the monthly accounts.

Under existing regulations, assignments of scrip must be attested by two witnesses and should be written out in full, with the name and residence of the assignee properly inserted in the body of the assignment; and when surrendered in payment for lands it is to be properly relinquished to the United States attested by two witnesses. Where practicable, both the assignment and relinquishment are to be written out upon the back of the scrip. With respect to the form of the relinquishment, and instructions in regard to the manner of operating with this character of scrip, you are referred to the circular of November 16, 1830, part 2, Laws, Instructions, and Opinions, p. 436, No. 370.

8. Pre-emption declarations filed under the act of September 4, 1841, should be kept on the files of the register's office. Homestead declarations filed under the act of June 8, 1872, should also be retained on said files, and sent to this office with other necessary papers when the entry is completed.

9. The fees collected upon original and re-locations made with military bounty-land warrants and agricultural college scrip, are to be computed at the rate of 2 per cent. upon the area expressed upon the face thereof. A separate, distinct, and consecutive series of register's and receiver's numbers is required to be kept and reported of locations issued under the several acts, and returns thereof made upon abstracts provided therefor.

10. Private land scrip locations will be reported in the receiver's monthly fee statement, under the heading indicated therein, giving the date of the act under which the scrip was issued, the register's and receiver's numbers of the locations, and the total number of acres actually located during the month, less excess of area, re-locations, and commuted homestead entries. No fees are to be charged for such locations unless authorized by act of Congress.

11. At the end of each month, whether any business has been done during the same or not, you are to send up to *this office* a monthly account current, fee statement, and detailed account of fees collected for taking testimony. If no business has been transacted during the month, that fact is to be stated upon the face of the account, in which the United States is to be credited with any balance that may have been standing against the receiver at the termination of the month immediately preceding. In the fee statement, the fact of there having been no business transacted, is to be noted by inserting under its several headings the words "no business."

12. In preparing your monthly abstracts you will select the number of sheets required and place them together in *book form* in order that they may be properly bound. Previous to transmitting the same, the register and receiver are required to carefully examine the certificates

of purchase, receiver's receipts, etc., and compare the respective returns, the one with the other, and each with the applications, plats, and tract books, with a view to detecting any errors or discrepancies that may exist therein. (See 33d clause of circular of May 25, 1831, the circulars of September 29, 1831, January 5, 1849, etc.)* The fact of such examination and comparison having been made, is to be certified to by the register and receiver, or one of them, upon the monthly abstracts of sales, etc. The respective abstracts should be folded separately, and have indorsed upon them the name of the land office, the character of the entries embraced by them, the name of the month and year in which such entries are made, and the lowest and highest register's and receiver's numbers that appear on the same.

13. *Receiver's accounts.* In addition to the monthly abstracts or registers of receipts, the receiver is required to render to this office, at the end of every month, a monthly account current, in which the United States is to be credited with the aggregate amount received during the month, from the sales of the public lands, specifying the area thus disposed of; the amount received as additional payments on graduated entries, on homestead entries commuted to cash; the amount received in cash on account of double minimum land located with military bounty-land warrants or with agricultural college scrip; the amount received as register's and receiver's fees for filing pre-emption declarations for locating military warrants and agricultural college scrip, together with any other fees they may be legally authorized to collect; also, the $10 and $5 payments on homestead entries, commissions on the value of the lands embraced thereby, and the commissions payable at the time of filing the final homestead proof. In the same account, the United States is to be debited with such sums as the receiver may deposit during the month to the credit of the United States Treasurer, the amount which may be paid out on Treasury drafts, and the amount received in Revolutionary scrip, the numbers of which must be specified. By a regulation of the Department the register is required, at the end of every month, to examine the public moneys in the possession of the receiver, and report the result of such examination, by indorsing upon the monthly account a certificate, in the following form, viz:

This is to certify that I have, on this date, examined the public moneys in the hands of the receiver, and find that the same amount to the sum of $——, and consist of the following funds, viz: (Here describe the character of the funds.) $——.
Witness my hand this —— day of ——.

A. B., *Register.*

14. QUARTERLY ACCOUNTS.—*Detailed quarterly cash account to be prepared on form No.* 4–106. At the termination of each quarter of the calendar year, the receiver is to forward to *this office* a quarterly account current, in which he is to credit the United States, in detail, with the amount received for each particular entry—giving the area—of lands actually sold during the quarter; each additional payment made on

—————
* 2 Pub. Lands, Laws and Inst., 444 and 457, and 1 Lester, 322.

account of graduation entries, and payments to complete the purchase money of lands previously sold; the amount received in payment
of commuted homestead entries; the sums of cash received on account
of double minimum lands located with military bounty-land warrants
or agricultural college scrip; and amounts received as fees for locating
military warrants; agricultural scrip; pre-emption fees, fees for filing
pre-emption declarations and adjudicating claims, together with any
other fees legally accruing to the register and receiver; the $10 and $5
fees for homestead entries with the commissions on the value of the land
embraced thereby, and the commissions payable on filing the final proof,
debiting the United States in said account with such deposits as may
be made during the quarter, payments made on Treasury drafts, and
the amount of Revolutionary scrip applied in payment of lands entered
during the quarter, specifying in the account the numbers of the pieces
of scrip surrendered. Any balance due to the United States at the
end of the quarter must appear upon the debit side of the last sheet of
the account, and should be credited in the account for the quarter next
succeeding.

The columns in this account respectively appropriated to the area and
purchase-money of lands sold, are each to be carefully added up, and
have the footings stated on each page, the last page of the account to
show, by a recapitulation of the sales, the aggregate area and amount
of purchase money of land sold at $1.25 per acre, or more, provided
there is any disposed of at prices greater than the minimum rate.

The areas of homestead entries commuted to cash under section 2301,
R. S., the areas of entries allowed under the second section of the act
of June 15, 1880, and the areas of final desert-land entries are to be
stated in red ink and are *not* to be included in the footings of this
account.

15. *Condensed quarterly account to be prepared on form No. 4–104.*
The receiver is required to send up, in addition to the account alluded
to, a condensed quarterly report, which differs from the former only in
the fact that the lands disposed of and purchase-money received therefor are to be reported in gross instead of detail. The balances, as
shown by these accounts, must correspond with that exhibited by the
monthly account current for the last month in the quarter (provided
the balances accruing at the termination of the months preceding shall
have been correctly brought forward).

16. *Quarterly recapitulation of cash receipts to be prepared on form No.*
4–157. This recapitulation being a very important paper, particular
care will be had in giving the number of entries and acres, opposite
each class, as indicated therein. Observe particularly that you are required to give the acres of homestead entries commuted to cash under
section 2301, R. S., entries allowed under the second section of the act
of June 15, 1880, and final desert entries in red ink, and not include the
same in the total.

17. *Detailed quarterly statements of original and final homestead and original and final timber-culture receipts.* These returns are to be made on the respective monthly abstracts of such receipts, with the necessary corrections, in writing, in the headings thereof, as indicated in the sample forms.

These abstracts are to exhibit the true areas embraced by the respective entries, and the amount of fees and commissions paid thereon, the commissions on homestead entries to be accurately computed on the rated value of the land. The columns must be properly added up and footings stated on each page, and from the footings of the area columns there is to be deducted the aggregate areas of excesses over the 160 acres specified in the homestead and timber-culture laws.

The last page of abstracts of each character of land entries must show by a recapitulation the number of entries made on which $5 and $10 fees were paid separately, together with the aggregate areas thereof and the commissions paid thereon, also the number of entries, the aggregate area of final entries and the commissions paid. Supplemental or additional payments on account of such lands made during the quarter will be reported as an addendum. The returns must be certified to, folded and briefed in the usual manner.

APPROPRIATION CIRCULAR.

[1872. Department No. 57. Warrant Division No. 2.]

TREASURY DEPARTMENT,
Washington, D. C., June 1, 1872.

The attention of disbursing officers and others having public moneys or accounts under their control, is particularly directed to the following provisions of "An act making appropriations for the legislative, executive, and judicial expenses of the Government for the year ending the thirtieth of June, eighteen hundred and seventy one," approved July 12, 1870, and the regulations for carrying the same into effect.

"SEC. 5. *And be it further enacted*, That all balances of appropriations contained in the annual appropriation bills and made specifically for the service of any fiscal year shall only be applied to the payment of expenses properly incurred during that year, or to the fulfillment of contracts properly made within that year; and such balances not needed for the said purposes shall be carried to the surplus fund: *Provided*, That this section shall not apply to appropriations known as permanent or indefinite appropriations. * * *

"SEC. 7. *And be it further enacted*, That it shall not be lawful for any Department of the Government to expend in any one fiscal year any sum in excess of appropriations made by Congress for that fiscal year, or to involve the Government in any contract for the future payment of money in excess of such appropriations." (16 Statutes, 251.)

To comply properly with these provisions of law, it is necessary that moneys and accounts pertaining to one fiscal year shall not be blended with those belonging to another.

Accounts for the quarter ending June 30, must embrace all compensation earned and all expenses incurred up to and including that date, so that no charges for services performed or articles purchased prior to the first of July, shall appear in subsequent accounts.

Where an officer is unable to close his account for the 30th of June promptly, and at the same time meet all outstanding expenses properly chargeable to the appropriations for the preceding year, he will make regular supplemental accounts under the old appropriation and will not carry the unexpended balance into his account with the new.

Where a contract has been legally made requiring payment out of any appropriation of the preceding year, officers are authorized to retain to their credit a sufficient amount of the old appropriation to meet the expenditure when it shall become due under the contract. In all such cases a supplemental account must be made as provided in the previous paragraph.

As soon after the 1st of July as possible, and after having paid all liabilities incurred on behalf of the Government during the previous year, or having made suitable provisions for their payment by retaining a sufficient amount on hand or on deposit to their credit, officers should deposit to the credit of the Treasurer of the United States the balance remaining in their hands or to their credit, either with the Treasurer of the United States himself, some one of the assistant treasurers or designated or National bank depositaries, who will issue certificates of deposit in duplicate therefor, the original of which should be forwarded to the Secretary of the Treasury. *This certificate should always specifically state the appropriation to be credited and the fiscal year for which the appropriation was made.*

In making this deposit care should be taken to provide, in the manner hereinbefore directed, for any outstanding checks which may be unpaid at the time.

Supplemental accounts for expenditures under expired appropriations must be rendered either monthly or quarterly as the rules of the office may require.

Officers stationed at places remote from means of rapid communication, and holding public moneys in their personal possession (which can only legally be done by permission of the Secretary of the Treasury), are directed to report to the proper controlling officer the amount of this money belonging to the prior fiscal year, and the Comptroller will direct what disposition shall be made of it and notify the officer accordingly.

R. W. TAYLER,
First Comptroller.
J. M. BRODHEAD,
Second Comptroller.
W. T. HAINES,
Commissioner of Customs.

Approved:
    GEO. S. BOUTWELL,
        Secretary.

CIRCULAR INSTRUCTIONS CONCERNING THE PAYMENT OF TREASURY DRAFTS AND OFFICIAL CHECKS OF PUBLIC DISBURSING OFFICERS.

[1877. Department No. 27.   Ind Treasury Division No. 28.]

TREASURY DEPARTMENT,
Washington, D. C., February 13, 1877.

The following sections of the Revised Statutes of the United States and the subsequent regulations are published for the information and guidance of all concerned:

"SEC. 306. At the termination of each fiscal year all amounts of moneys that are represented by certificates, drafts, or checks, issued by the Treasurer, or by any disbursing officer of any department of the government, upon the Treasurer or any assistant treasurer, or designated depositary of the United States, or upon any National bank designated as a depository of the United States, and which shall be represented on the books of either of such offices as standing to the credit of any disbursing officer, and which were issued to facilitate the payment of warrants, or for any other purpose in liquidation of a debt due from the United States, and which have for three years or more remained outstanding, unsatisfied, and unpaid, shall be deposited by the Treasurer, to be covered into the Treasury by warrant, and to be carried to the credit of the parties in whose favor such certificates, drafts, or checks were respectively issued, or to the persons who are entitled to receive pay therefor, and into an appropriation account to be denominated 'outstanding liabilities.'

" SEC. 308. The payee or the bona-fide holder of any draft or check the amount of which has been deposited and covered into the Treasury pursuant to the preceding sections, shall, on presenting the same to the proper officer of the Treasury, be entitled to have it paid by the settlement of an account and the issuing of a warrant in his favor, according to the practice in other cases of authorized and liquidated claims against the United States.

" SEC. 309. The amounts, except such as are provided for in section three hundred and six, of the accounts of every kind of disbursing officer, which shall have remained unchanged, or which shall not have been increased by any new deposit thereto, nor decreased by drafts drawn thereon, for the space of three years, shall in like manner be covered into the Treasury, to the proper appropriation to which they belong ; and the amounts thereof shall, on the certificate of the Treasurer that such amount has been deposited in the Treasury, be credited by the proper accounting officer of the Department of the Treasury on the books of the Department, to the officer in whose name it had stood on the books of any agency of the Treasury, if it appears that he is entitled to such credit.

" SEC. 310. The Treasurer, each assistant treasurer, and each designated depositary of the United States, and the cashier of each of the National banks designated as such depositories, shall, at the close of business on every thirtieth day of June, report to the Secretary of the Treasury the condition of every account standing, as in the preceding section specified, on the books of their respective offices, stating the name of each depositor, with his official designation, the total amount remaining on deposit to his credit, and the dates, respectively, of the last credit and the last debit made to each account. And each disbursing officer shall make a like return of all checks issued by him, and which may then have been outstanding and unpaid for three years and more, stating fully in such report the name of the payee, for what purpose each check was given, the office on which drawn, the number of the voucher received therefor, the date, number, and amount for which it was drawn, and, when known, the residence of the payee."

REGULATIONS.

1. Hereafter any Treasury draft or any check drawn by a public disbursing officer still in service which shall be presented for payment before it shall have been issued three full fiscal years, will be paid in the usual manner by the office or bank on which it is drawn and from funds to the credit of the drawer. Thus, any such draft or check issued on or after July 1, 1873, will be paid as above stated until June 30, 1877, and the same rule will apply for subsequent years.

Any such draft or check which has been issued for a longer period than three full fiscal years will be paid only by the settlement of an account in this Department, as provided in section 308 above published ; and for this purpose the draft or check will be transmitted to the Secretary of the Treasury for the necessary action.

2. The reports of independent Treasury officers, National bank depositories, and public disbursing officers, required by section 310 above published, will be rendered promptly to the Secretary of the Treasury at the close of each fiscal year.

3. Whenever any disbursing officer of the United States shall cease to act in that capacity, he will at once inform the Secretary of the Treasury whether he has any public funds to his credit in any office or bank, and, if so what checks, if any, he has drawn against the same which are still outstanding and unpaid. Until satisfactory information of this character shall have been furnished, the whole amount of such moneys will be held to meet the payment of his checks properly payable therefrom.

4. Hereafter, at the close of each fiscal year, the Treasurer, the several assistant treasurers, and designated and National bank depositories, will also render to the Secretary of the Treasury a list of all disbursing officers' accounts still unclosed which have been opened on the books of their respective offices or banks more than three fiscal years, giving in each case the name and official designation of the officer, the date when the account with him was opened, and the balance remaining to his credit.

5. In case of the death, resignation, or removal of a public disbursing officer, any check previously drawn by him and not presented for payment within four months of its date will not be paid until its correctness shall have been attested by the Secretary or Assistant Secretary of the Treasury.

6. If the object or purpose for which any check of a public disbursing officer is drawn is not stated thereon as required by departmental regulations, or if any reason exists for suspecting fraud, the office or bank on which such check is drawn will refuse its payment.

CHAS. F. CONANT,
Acting Secretary.

The Commissioner of the General Land Office is made by law (section 456, R. S.) the auditing officer of all accounts relative to the public lands, and receivers of public moneys and other officers acting as disbursing agents will be held to the strictest accountability for all expenditures pertaining thereto, and no expenses incurred by them will be passed to their credit unless in accordance with the provisions of this circular.

The following sections of the Revised Statutes govern these disbursements:

SEC. 3623. All officers, agents, or other persons receiving public moneys shall render distinct accounts of the application thereof according to the appropriation under which the same may have been advanced to them.

SEC. 3678. All sums appropriated for the various branches of expenditure in the public service shall be applied solely to the objects for which they are respectively made and for no others.

SEC. 3683. No part of the contingent fund appropriated to any Department, bureau, or office, shall be applied to the purchase of any articles except such as the head of the Department shall deem necessary and proper to carry on the business of the Department, bureau, or office, and shall, by written order, direct to be procured.

Under existing laws appropriations are made for the use of district land offices under the following head: Salaries and commissions of registers and receivers, expenses of depositing public moneys, contingent expenses of land offices, expenses of hearings in land entries, and depredations on public timber.

From and after July 1, 1882, receivers of public moneys acting as disbursing agents *will render separate and distinct accounts of expenditures under each appropriation, and the sums advanced them for disbursement will be applied solely to the objects for which they are made.*

In order that this regulation may be strictly complied with notice will be sent from this office, immediately upon the requisition being drawn of the appropriation or appropriations from which the amounts are taken, and to the credit of which they are to be placed.

The account under appropriation for salaries and commissions of registers and receivers will include all earnings of the local land officers not exceeding $750 each per quarter. Register's receipt for salary, etc., must accompany this account.

The account for expenses of depositing moneys will include express charges, or, where the deposits are made in person (as may be directed by the Treasury Department), actual traveling expenses to and from the designated depository. Receipts from express company, or, where deposits are made in person, an itemized account of all expenses incurred, with receipts for all sums expended exceeding $1 (with exception of sums paid as fares on railroads or other modes of public conveyance) together with a certificate under oath that the route traveled is the usual and most direct one must accompany this account.

The account for contingent expenses will include all the authorized expenses (as per section 3683, R. S.) of district land offices not embraced in the two first-named accounts, but no credits will be allowed disbursing agents on this account unless the expenses charged have been first authorized specifically by this office. Receipts are required for all items of expense, and the date of authorization is to be invariably noted.

All disbursing accounts will be rendered quarterly and promptly within three days from the expiration of the period for which they may be due, except as hereinafter provided.

In these accounts the disbursing agent will credit the United States with the amounts of such Treasury drafts as may be issued in his favor under each appropriation, debiting the United States with the legally authorized expenses thereunder. The balances, if any, will be carried forward to the succeeding quarter until the end of the fiscal year.

At the discretion of this office, receivers of public moneys may be authorized to make disbursements out of the appropriation "for depredations on public timber." Disbursements under this head will be rendered in a separate account having no connection whatever with their regular accounts as disbursing agents.

Surveyors general will render quarterly disbursing accounts under the several annual appropriations as communicated to them in the annual instructions from this office, in accordance with the general provisions of this circular.

Other officers (special agents, etc.), in the absence of special instructions, will be governed by the general provisions of this circular.

Receivers of public moneys are particularly cautioned against confounding their duties as receivers with those as disbursing agents. Under section 3617, R. S., all moneys coming into their possession from the disposition of public lands must be covered "into the Treasury without abatement or deduction on account of salary, fees, costs, charges, expenses, or claim of any description whatever." Hence they can not legally appropriate or pay over any portion of such on account of salary, commissions, etc., until the amount necessary for those purposes shall have been placed in their hands as disbursing agents by Treasury drafts.

This provision of law does not, of course, interfere with Treasury regulations authorizing receivers to pay Treasury drafts in their own favor out of public funds.

It is essential for the proper apportionment of expenses that registers and receivers shall transmit to this office by June 1, each year, estimates of the amount required to defray all the necessary expenses of their offices during the ensuing fiscal year, with request that the necessary authority be given them to incur such expenses. Without such authority being first obtained, no advance will be made for incidental expenses under any circumstances whatever, and all charges of that character will be disallowed in adjustment of accounts.

Quarterly estimates for funds to meet the authorized expenses of local offices will be made by the disbursing agent within the first ten days of the quarter for which such funds are required; but no advances will be made where the local officers are in arrears for any returns required by law or existing regulations, or where the instructions relating to the deposit of public moneys have not been complied with.

Receivers of public moneys will be careful not to estimate in excess of the probable expenses of their offices. A very slight degree of care and discretion will enable them to closely approximate their quarterly expenses, and carelessness in this matter, as evidenced by considerable balances in their hands at end of quarter, will necessitate the assumption by this office of an average, which may at times work inconvenience.

Estimates for advances must in every case be made the subject of a special communication.

EXPENSE OF HEARINGS IN LAND OFFICES.

In hearings ordered upon reports of special agents, you are advised that the rates of compensation to witnesses summoned on behalf of the Government have been fixed as follows:

The actual necessary fare or transportation of each witness will be paid, and in addition thereto one dollar and fifty cents ($1.50) per day in lieu of living expenses and one dollar and fifty cents ($1.50) per day in compensation for the time devoted to the case.

The per diem allowances will be held to cover the time necessarily employed both in going to and returning from the place of hearing, as well as the necessary time in attendance at said hearing; *provided*, the shortest or cheapest practicable route is taken in going and returning, etc.

Special agents will certify to the transportation expenses of each witness, and to the time necessarily employed.

Estimates of expenses of hearings will be made on this basis, on blank form 4-638, after the time has been fixed for holding the hearings.

The disbursing account for expenses of hearings in land entries will be rendered upon the final hearings of the cases named in each estimate of expenses (form 4–638) except in change of bond or retirement from office, in which event, you will render an account and deposit balance as required in accounts under other appropriations.

By the instructions of the Treasury Department, as contained in the circular of June 1, 1872, herein embodied, disbursing agents will deposit all balances remaining in their hands at the expiration of the fiscal year or as soon thereafter as possible. These balances must be deposited to the credit of the Treasurer of the United States on account of the appropriations to which they may belong, which appropriations must be named in the certificates of deposit. If balances exist on account of salaries and commissions, expenses of depositing, and contingent expenses each, three deposits must be made covering the amount under the respective heads.

Should a balance be found due the disbursing agent at the end of the fiscal year, the same will be liquidated by Treasury draft.

Under no circumstances will such balances, either of debit or credit, be brought from the accounts of *one fiscal year into those of another*, except under the appropriation of hearings in land entries.

In cases of change of bond or retirement from office, accounts will be rendered and balances deposited as at the end of a fiscal year. Care will be taken that no balances under an old bond shall be carried into the accounts pertaining to a new one. Accounts under an old bond will be made to include the day immediately preceding the date of the new bond.

In transmitting disbursing accounts the appropriations under which they are rendered will be specified, and those under which no business has been transacted will also be specified.

In cases of differences between the accounts as rendered by disbursing officers and as audited by this office, a statement of such differences will be furnished the officer by the First Comptroller of the Treasury.

Promptness and accuracy in rendering estimates and accounts will greatly facilitate the public business, particularly with reference to making proper allowances for clerk hire and other incidental expenses.

19. It is expected that, from day to day, you will keep the preparation of your respective returns in such a state of forwardness as to enable you to complete and transmit them to this office within three days from the termination of the month or quarter for which they may be due. Forms for the preparation of the several returns required, properly trimmed, folded, and indorsed, will be forwarded to you. By carefully conforming thereto, and strictly observing the rules suggested in the foregoing instructions, you will obviate the necessity of an extensive special correspondence, and thereby greatly facilitate the business operations of this office.

20. In view of the inconvenience attendant upon the rapid accumulation of letters upon the files of this office, it becomes necessary to modify

the requirements of our circular of July 20, 1853, *so far as it relates to the manner of transmitting your respective monthly returns*. Hence, in future, instead of sending a special letter with each description of returns, you will advise us by a *single*.*letter*, stating the *number of packages transmitted and the contents of each package*. Be particular to see that they are all forwarded in the *same mail*, and that *no portion* of them are sent up until the *close of the month*.

21. The receiver's regular quarterly returns, also any *Indian* accounts that may be due from his office, should *all* be inclosed in one package and sent up by *special* letter. For further instructions in regard thereto he will be governed by *rule eleven* of this circular, which is *applicable to quarterly as well as to monthly accounts*.

Be pleased to acknowledge the receipt of this circular.

Very respectfully,

LEWIS A. GROFF,
Commissioner.

Approved December 4, 1889:
JOHN W. NOBLE,
Secretary of the Interior.

———

SWANSON *v.* ANDERSON.

Motion for review of the decision rendered in the above entitled case February 27, 1888, 6 L. D., 550, denied by Secretary Noble, December 27, 1889.

———

PRACTICE—REVIEW—APPEAL—CERTIORARI.

SHELDON *v.* WARREN.

Except when based upon newly discovered evidence, motions for rehearing must be filed within thirty days from notice of the decision.

The rules of practice limiting the time within which appeals may be taken, and motions for review made, will, in all contest cases, be strictly enforced, in the absence of valid excuse, or circumstances calling for the exercise of supervisory authority.

Matter which might, and should have been, set up on appeal, but was not within the prescribed time, does not furnish sufficient ground for certiorari.

Acting Secretary Chandler to the Commissioner of the General Land Office, December 28, 1889.

This is an application by Freeland S. Warren under Rule of Practice 83 "for an order directing the Commissioner to certify" to this Department the proceedings in the case of Harry F. Sheldon, contestant, against said Warren, involving the latter's homestead entry, No. 5407, for the SE. ¼ of Sec. 22, T. 120, R. 66, Huron district, Dakota Territory.

It appears from a letter of the register of October 4, 1889, addressed to Warren and attached as an exhibit to his present application and made a part thereof, that his entry was held for cancellation February 9, 1887, on the hearing of said Sheldon's contest; that notice of said action was duly given Warren's attorney, and an appeal was filed by him July 18, 1887, which your office November 21, 1887, refused to en-'tertain, because not filed in time, and thereupon action was suspended as required by Rule of Practice 83; that Warren filed an application for certiorari under Rule 83, which was denied by this Department June 15, 1888 (6 L. D., 800), and June 23, 1888 (not reported), the entry was canceled and case closed; that Warren then waited until May 9, 1889, nearly eleven months after his entry had been canceled and the case closed and after Sheldon, the contestant, had made homestead entry on the land, and then made application for re-instatement of his entry "with a view to a rehearing;" that, having been advised of the said entry of Sheldon, your office, June 14, 1889, denied said application of Warren for a re-instatement of his entry, "with a view to" a rehearing, and Warren, August 5, 1889, filed an appeal to this Department, which your office refused to transmit, and because of said refusal, he now applies to this Department a second time for a certiorari.

The ground upon which Warren makes his present application, is that he was not allowed a "full and fair hearing on the contest." This alleged error might and should have been taken advantage of on appeal, and is, substantially, what he sets up in his appeal to this Department, the refusal to transmit which is the basis of said application, and was, doubtless, the ground of his original appeal from the action of the local officers on the hearing recommending his entry for cancellation. He was in default in the *first* place, in not appealing in time from the adverse action of the local officers at the hearing, and no excuse whatever is given therefor; and, when your office refused to entertain his appeal from the action of the local officers, because not taken in time, he applied for a certiorari, which was denied by this Department. Thereupon, your office canceled the entry and marked the case closed. He did not appeal from this action of your office, but about eleven months thereafter and after the contestant had entered the land, applied for a re-instatement of his entry with a view to a rehearing of his case. Except when based on newly discovered evidence, motions for rehearing must be filed within thirty days from notice of the decision (Rule of Practice 77). There is no claim of newly discovered evidence, or that his application for rehearing was made in time, or that there was any excuse for his delay. His application for a rehearing having been denied by your office, he files an appeal from that ruling, and, on the refusal of your office to transmit said appeal to this Department, he again applies for a certiorari. If this appeal had been transmitted, it would not have been sustained by this Department. By his gross laches (which appear to be wholly without excuse), Warren has forfeited any right he may have had to have the case re-opened for the correction of the errors alleged to have been committed by the local officers on the hearing. The Rules of Practice limiting the time in which appeals may be taken and motions for rehearing made are obviously of the greatest practical importance, being necessary to put a period to vexatious litigation and to secure to parties litigant the termination of their legal controversies, and, at least, in cases *inter partes* will be strictly enforced in the absence of valid excuse or of circumstances strongly calling for the exercise by this Department of the directory and supervisory powers conferred upon it by law. (Rules of Practice, bot. p. 17). Such excuse not being shown, or such circumstances not appearing, matter which might and should have been set up on appeal, but was not within the prescribed time, is not sufficient ground for a certiorari under Rule of Practice 83.

The application is denied.

REPAYMENT—DESERT LAND ENTRY.

ALBERT S. HOVEY.

Repayment of the first instalment of the purchase money, paid under a desert entry, can not be allowed in the absence of evidence showing that the failure to perfect the entry was not due to the negligence of the entryman.

First Assistant Secretary Chandler to the Commissioner of the General Land Office, December 28, 1889.

I have considered the appeal of Albert S. Hovey, from the decision of your office dated August 22, 1888, rejecting his application for repayment of the first installment of the purchase money paid by him on his canceled desert land entry for the NE. ¼, the SE.¼, the N. ½ of the NW. ¼ and the SE. ¼ of NW. ¼ Sec. 22, and the W. ½ of NW. ¼ and W. ½ of SW. ¼ Sec. 23, and NW. ¼ of NW. ¼ Sec. 26, T. 20, N, R. 5 W, containing six hundred and forty acres of land in the Helena land district, Montana.

On October 27, 1884, Hovey made entry for said tract under the provision of the act of March 3, 1877 (19 Stat., 377), and at the same time he paid to the receiver twenty-five cents per acre for said land which amounted to the sum of $160.

On November 9, 1887, notice was served upon Hovey to show cause why his said entry should not be canceled for failure to make proof and payment within the time required by law from date of entry.

On February 3, 1887, he appeared in person at the local land office, and then and there surrendered his original duplicate certificate for said land, with the following relinquishment written across the back of said certificate, and duly acknowledged—

I hereby relinquish all my right, title and claim to the within described tract to the United States, this 3rd day of February 1888.

ALBERT S. HOVEY.

The local officers thereupon filed said reliuquishment and canceled said entry that same day.

On August 14, 1888, claimant filed an application for the re payment of the purchase money paid by him upon said land, and in his affidavit alleges as follows:

That he made said entry in entire good faith and with the *bona fide* intention of reclaiming said land, and upon the promise, contract and agreement of a certain company and organization known as the Florence Canal Company, which was organized for the purpose of constructing a canal about ten miles in length to bring water to said land; that said company commenced said canal and constructed the same a distance of about four miles towards said land, at an expense of several thousand dollars; that said ditch or canal if completed would have furnished an ample supply of water to fully and perpetually irrigate and reclaim said land; but on account of the fact that said company became insolvent and unable to proceed further with the construction of said canal the same was abandoned, so that not being able to procure water to reclaim said land, he was compelled to, and did relinquish said entry and all his interest in said land.

On August 22, 1888, Assistant Commissioner Anderson in denying said application, says:

At the date of said entry there was no adverse right to the lands embraced in said entry, nor was the entry erroneously allowed; but the fault was on the part of the purchaser in not complying with the law under which said entry was made. No reason appears why said entry could not have been confirmed and in my opinion the case shows a voluntary abandonment.

On September 29, 1888, claimant appealed to this Department.

Subdivision 10 of circular of June 27, 1887 (5 L. D., 708), declares that

Persons making desert land entries must acquire a clear right to the use of sufficient water for the purpose of irrigating the whole of the land, and of keeping it permanently irrigated. A person who makes a desert land entry before he has secured a water right does so at his own risk.

(General Circular, January 1, 1889, p. 37.)

Claimant's uncorroborated affidavit accompanying his application for repayment fails to show whether he purchased and paid for any shares of the stock of the Florence Canal Company, or in any manner expended any money or labor or assisted said company in its endeavor to construct said canal so as to obtain water for irrigating said tract. And as there is no evidence in the case tending to show that claimant made any effort to comply with the law, he has thereby failed to bring himself within the provisions of the second section of the act of June 16 1880 (21 Stat., 287).

For the reasons herein stated the decision of your office rejecting his application for repayment is affirmed.

CIRCULAR—TIMBER CULTURE FINAL PROOF.

Commissioner Groff to registers and receivers, December 3, 1889.

The requirement of circular of June 27, approved July 12, 1887 (6 L. D., 280), as to publication of notice of intention to make final proof on timber-culture entries, will not be insisted on, in cases where the original entry was made prior to September 15, 1887. All entries made prior to this date will be adjudicated in accordance with instructions in force prior to the promulgation of said circular approved July 12, 1887.

Approved,

GEO. CHANDLER
        Acting Secretary.

———

CIRCULAR—FINAL PROOF—DESERT ENTRY.

Commissioner Groff to registers and receivers, December 3, 1889.

The requirement of circular approved June 27, 1887 (5 L. D., 708), as to publication of notice of intention to make final proof in desert land entries, will not be insisted on in cases where the original entry was made prior to August 1, 1887. All entries made prior to that date will be adjudicated in accordance with instructions in force prior to the promulgation of said circular approved June 27, 1887.

Approved:

GEO. CHANDLER
        Acting Secretary.

INDEX.

Equitable Adjudication.

Evidence.

Fees.

Filing.

Pre-emption.

See *Alienation, Entry, Filing, Final Proof, Residence, Settlement.*

Preference Right.

See *Contestant.*

Private Claim.

Lightning Source UK Ltd.
Milton Keynes UK
UKHW020625120219
337137UK00005B/525/P